Radix Naturalis

Radix Naturalis

Liberation Semiology as Philosophy of Environment

CRAIG CRAMM

☙PICKWICK *Publications* · Eugene, Oregon

RADIX NATURALIS
Liberation Semiology as Philosophy of Environment

Copyright © 2020 Craig Cramm. All rights reserved. Except for brief quotations in critical publications or reviews, no part of this book may be reproduced in any manner without prior written permission from the publisher. Write: Permissions, Wipf and Stock Publishers, 199 W. 8th Ave., Suite 3, Eugene, OR 97401.

Pickwick Publications
An Imprint of Wipf and Stock Publishers
199 W. 8th Ave., Suite 3
Eugene, OR 97401

www.wipfandstock.com

PAPERBACK ISBN: 978-1-4982-9114-9
HARDCOVER ISBN: 978-1-4982-9116-3
EBOOK ISBN: 978-1-4982-9115-6

Cataloguing-in-Publication data:

Names: Cramm, Craig, author.

Title: Radix naturalis : liberation semiology as philosophy of environment / Craig Cramm.

Description: Eugene, OR : Pickwick Publications, 2020 | Includes bibliographical references and index.

Identifiers: ISBN 978-1-4982-9114-9 (paperback) | ISBN 978-1-4982-9116-3 (hardcover) | ISBN 978-1-4982-9115-6 (ebook)

Subjects: LCSH: Human ecology—Religious aspects—Christianity—History of doctrines. | Creation—History of doctrines. | Salvation—Christianity—History of doctrines. | Christian ethics. | Environmental ethics

Classification: BT695.5 C73 2020 (print) | BT695.5 C73 (ebook)

Manufactured in the U.S.A. OCTOBER 29, 2020

In Memoriam:

James Bradley, Leslie Armour, Peter Harris

Fr. Lawrence Dewan, OP

& Rosie

Teachers, Colleagues, Friends

&

For Nicole, Oliver, and Nellie

(Amor omnibus idem)

Ruinosa est: refice eam.
—A*ugustine*

Contents

Introduction: The Outside—Exchanging Atmospheres | ix

ONE: Categories for Philosophy of Environment | 1

TWO: Metaphysics and Preliminary Statement of the Problem | 46

THREE: Pelagianism, Nature, Politics | 94

FOUR: The Ontology of Mastery | 125

FIVE: From Mastery to Stewardship | 161

SIX: Stewardship of Sign | 200

SEVEN: The Language of the Real—Classical and Christian | 232

EIGHT: Augustine on Symbols, Signs, and Things | 261

NINE: Aquinas and Poinsot—Semiotics of Being | 281

TEN: Potentiality and Boehme—Semiotics of Becoming | 312

SUPPLEMENT: *On Beloved Community*
    —Collingwood, Cochrane, and Ecological Civilization | 342

Bibliography | 379
Index | 407

INTRODUCTION

The Outside
Exchanging Atmospheres

WE ARE EXPERIENCING THE death of nature and the birth of environment. *Philosophy of environment* examines this new order of things outside our settled ways of thinking, feeling, and living. The alarming scientific evidence should, by now, be familiar and accepted. What remains contentious is how we make sense of ourselves as a colossal planetary power. Interpretations of this event are often marked by contradictions. The contemporary Green movement, for example, emerges from the collapse of certain streams of European radical politics in the 1970s. A hybrid rises from the wreckage of progressive and reactionary factions: An uneasy marriage is proposed between adherents of social improvement and conservationists. How do you affirm material progress, but deny its traditional environmental effects? The riddle of sustainable development is put forward as one we have to solve for our common future. Outside the West, however, the proposed transition is often viewed as nothing more than logic of the same: Sustainable development is the residual voice of colonization. First world domination of land, labor, and capital continues on with only a change of metaphors. Philosophy of environment, then, must continue to dismantle this regime's operational ideas of nature and politics, allowing room for alternative political ecologies to take their ground.[1]

---

1. On the historical development of environmentalism as a political ideology, see Judt, *Postwar*, 484–503. For its central presupposition, see WCED, *Our Common Future*, 43–49. Concerning the latter's interpretation outside industrialized states, see Escobar, *Encountering Development*, 191–93; Argyrou, *Logic of Environmentalism*, 159.

Orientation to environment means relational being. There is always directedness towards others. Our projects and institutions are situated within what Charles Norris Cochrane (†1945) calls the shared unrest of circumstances or *atmosphere*: "This environment is partly physical, partly psychical and moral. It thus includes geographical elements such as land and sea, the varied possibilities of which he must learn to exploit. But it is also customary and institutional, the 'atmosphere,' e.g., of Athens or Sparta created and maintained by their respective ways of life; the 'conditions' produced whether by peace or war."[2] Communication is sign activity (*semiosis*), occurring as relationships arise and subsist. If relationships are the basic stuff of the universe, communication is a phenomenon coextensive with environment. The things that appear reveal their own language. Across all registers of being there is symbolic exchange of meaning. The occurrence of environmental crisis is a peculiar kind of mistranslation, a dramatic failure of interpretation, characterizing specific Western atmospheres of thought and action. Our ways of dealing with reality have turned rigid and violent—theoretically, practically, and morally—signifying loss of awareness of the accepted harmful relationship. Our strength to break through to other fundamental principles remains an untested potential. We are adrift and exposed to the outside, to being's radical root, to *radix naturalis*.

The present work consists of an overview of philosophy of environment, and an examination of *liberation semiology*. The former introduces the discipline, establishes the problem, and gives a prescriptive direction. The latter follows the circuitous philosophical history of the *semiotic worldview*.[3] Being, communication, and liberation are convertible relationships: This principle offers a chart for philosophy of environment. To pursue such an inquiry is not to retreat to the past. Rather, reassuming this view, scarcely known at all, is an experimental departure from ruinous political ecologies. The world has been sold into bondage. There is no sheltering place: The power of total commodification eclipses all, blinds all. Reawakening the symbolic community's conceptual ground means simultaneous appropriation, displacement, and redistribution. Is it a way, still open, but untaken? I cannot answer with much certainty, but I do know that to not risk, as we are able, in time, is something far worse than failure, insignificance, and the accusation of vain insight. The measure of its faithful deployment will

---

On the role of philosophy within the ecological turn, see Latour, *Politics of Nature*, 10–15; Connelly et al., *Politics and the Environment*, 1–53.

2. Cochrane, *Christianity and Classical Culture*, 519.

3. On worldviews in general and the semiotic version, see Naugle, *Worldview*, 202–96. For the initial claim of a semiotic worldview, see Eco, *Theory of Semiotics*, 22–23. On the Patristic version, see Sayers, "Toward a Christian Esthetic," 84–87.

be determined by affects in the immediate lived order and atmospheres to come.

Chapter 1 presents three categories for philosophy of environment: Ecopolitics, ethics, and environmental cosmology. Each disciplinary division maintains its own way of conceiving the predicament. The first concedes the need for the second. Scientific, political, and economic diagnostics lead to ethics as the dominant prescriptive approach. Ethics is eventually called into question: Can it sufficiently deal with the novel scale and structure of the crisis? Many thinkers turn to environmental cosmology as offering a better perspective on diagnoses and prescriptions. Chapter 2 accepts the latter as the most promising of the categories. It is, however, the least explored and most conceptually problematic. What is the best account of this orientation? The key work is R. G. Collingwood's (†1943) *An Essay on Metaphysics*. Metaphysics is historical thinking on worldviews, identifying, critiquing, and proposing absolute presuppositions; in this work, it provides a coherent framework for understanding the many theorists who take this approach, and their unique kind of analysis. The two founding philosophers of historical metaphysics of environment are Lynn White Jr. (†1987) and John Passmore (†2004). They converge on the same presupposition of our environmental crisis: Anthropocentric salvation through domination of nature. Anthropocentrism presents an elect category of human beings as the self-emancipating center of total value; typically predicated on domination of condemned categories of humanity and, principally and most profoundly, what is external to humanity within the natural environment.

Chapter 3 traces the anthropocentric presupposition of liberation by domination to the early Christian thought of Pelagius (†c. 420/440 CE). *Pelagianism* names the Occidental strain of mastery and self-assertion by the select few of our species, grounding the atmosphere of modern political economy. This chapter identifies the historically situated philosophical figures and ideas that transmit and transform this way of being. Chapter 4 extends the analysis of Pelagianism into the formation of modern science. The synthesis of modern politics and science, i.e., ends and means, forms a *science of order* dedicated to mastery. Chapter 5 first examines some representational criticisms of the modern science of order; then, a reconsideration and defense of historical metaphysics in light of the preceding chapters. A transitional section exposes the paradox of anthropocentrism; it reveals more and more relationships all the way down: Attachments, interconnections, and mutually fragile dependencies. Bruno Latour puts forward the surprising idea that we need to reconsider the doctrine of creation developed by the Church Fathers, to grasp environment otherwise than modern scientific nature or the biblical literalism of creationism. This waypoint leads to symbolic ecology within the Trinity's economy—stewardship. Finally, contemporary environmental stewardship is critiqued and, feasibly, properly *reconverted*.

Chapter 6 develops the idea of stewardship as *liberation semiology*, a view of reality as mutually elevating communication. If the world's own principle is love (*agape*), our fellow creatures are co-subjects of emancipation from human violence. Creation is not, as influential modern thinkers envision, mere material, mere nature, to dominate for the freedom of an exclusive constituency of our species. Reclaiming, reaffirming, and reframing this tradition is the task of the concluding chapters: A speculative prolegomena on *agapeic* theories of the symbol.

Chapter 7 is a gloss of classical antecedents, quickly moving to the early Christian milieu and the formation of the Trinity. The Trinity's priority of relationship occasions a communicative doctrine of images, similitudes, and traces: The symbolist worldview. The source of cosmic semiosis is *vestigia trinitatis*. Creation is the trinitarian economy's vital tissue of profane signs and sacred signatures. As the *codex Dei*, all entities in the universe possess spiritual meaning and value. As the *speculum Dei*, the whole of the universe is divine iconography. Chapter 8 briefly charts the demise of the sacramental interpretation of creation and the rise of modern nature. Between the former and the latter stands Saint Augustine's (†430 CE) alternative of triadic semiotics. Augustine distinguishes between things, symbols, and signs. Thing mentality is rejected: The world is not an aggregate of self-sufficient substances. Signs are primary reality, and they are given a secular domain of operation apart from sacramental symbols. The interpreter is the third term in a communicative relationship, marking the site where the profane and unlimited polysemic drift of signs receives the supplement of its divine referent: The Trinity.

Chapter 9 is the semiotic worldview with a priority of actuality. The trinitarian ontology of Saint Thomas Aquinas (†1274) is developed by John Poinsot (†1644). Both are committed to the reality of essential relationships, and Poinsot demonstrates how, within such a reality, signs communicate substantial forms to interpretative powers. We get to know and love things through their signs. Chapter 10 introduces semiotics as a principle of process. Aristotle's (†322 BCE) *other metaphysics* of potentiality is examined, followed by an introduction to Jacob Boehme's (†1624) alchemical Trinity. God is vital progression, an eternal triumph of love over its own afflicted ground. Boehme's ideas are often heterodox, unsettling, and obscure, but he appears to point to a remarkably original and prescient project, a path not taken, entwining creation and humanity in a common historical process of liberation. Becoming in the symbol of the Trinity reverses the modern drive of anthropocentric domination. Only when all of creation is set free will we earn true emancipation from the primal darkness of our nature.

The work of symbolic mapping is incomplete. The partial reclamation of the semiotic worldview is the basis for future inquiry on modern and contemporary sign theory. To splice together the hanging threads of *Radix Naturalis*, this work will conclude with a *supplement on beloved community*. Through the political theology of ecological civilization offered by R. G. Collingwood and Charles Norris Cochrane, we will briefly sketch the *agapeic* elements capable of addressing our ecological discord through an alternative idea of politics.

The *Anthropocene epoch* challenges us to reopen the concept of nature. Certain emergent trends in science, speculative philosophy, and theology have engaged the endeavor and, unexpectedly, there appears to be a tentative convergence of ideas, if not implicit integration. An increasing number of life scientists, for example, take the position that the study of nature must include the model of language. The communicative autonomy of nature must be assumed to make sense of their findings. In a recent work, we read the following declaration:

> Our path in this search to understand life processes has led us, as biologists, to a semiotic view. Life processes are not only significant for the organisms they involve. Signification, meaning, interpretation and information are not just concepts used and constructed by humans for describing such processes. We conclude that life processes, by their very nature, are meaning-making, informational processes, that is, sign processes (semiosis), and thus can be fruitfully understood within a semiotic perspective.[4]

On the same track, Terrence Deacon's work offers a profound and ongoing synthesis of current science and philosophies of nature; his architectonic presents information as having an "irreducible 'aboutness' relationship that is 'always already there,'" admitting degrees of intentional activity back into nature, "to make sense of the implicit representational function that distinguishes information from other merely physical relationships."[5] More directly, and controversially, Frederik Stjernfelt claims propositions "do not depend upon human language nor upon human consciousness or intentionality, contrary to most standard assumptions. Signs carry truth values, encompassing a much wider array of phenomena."[6] Other creatures,

---

4. Emmeche and Kull, *Towards a Semiotic Biology*, ix.
5. Deacon, "What Is Missing," 190–91.
6. Stjernfelt, *Natural Propositions*, 1.

too, have significant relationships, and Donna J. Haraway pushes past the species barrier on the basis of communication that is "about relationship and the material-semiotic meaning of relating."[7] Relationships express the reality of shared incompleteness. Communication is incomplete activity by incomplete creatures: We need each other to be. That absence, that lack, calls forth its own actualization as symbol. What does not yet exist makes a difference to what is because we are partial, an open wound towards the world. We seek completion, to be, to be made whole in the lost Word of each other.

There are also moral, political, and spiritual perfections in the view that the natural world, like ours, is symbolic. *Radix Naturalis* centers its attention on creation and its signs: The original subject of liberation in Christian thought. I have long held insecurities on the viability of this project—just another marginal voice from, in my case, the literal wilderness, another recourse to religiosity in a dark time, of a life and thought overdue, lacking in confident direction. Recently, however, to my joy and continued astonishment, attending innovative science, many prominent spiritual and intellectual figures, supported by a radical new wave of political theology, are unapologetic and insurgent in their views. They are firm and public in their commitment (the former), flourishing in the work of genealogical analysis and recovery (the latter): A *renaissance* of relational thought and a reconsideration of its trinitarian structure.

Pope Francis, of course, has recently reenergized the neglected environmental aspect of Christian tradition. In his justifiably famous *Encyclical*, Francis reminds us of the primacy of relationships and symbols: "The universe as a whole, in all its manifold relationships, shows forth the inexhaustible riches of God" and, citing John Paul II (†2005), he reaffirms that "God has written a precious book, 'whose letters are the multitude of created things present in the universe.'"[8] To release the sacramental signatures of the world is to realize our own. The beloved community to come belongs to all creation, not just some of us. Bruno Latour takes a more militant stance: "The fusion of eschatology and ecology is not a fall into irrationality, a loss of nerve or some mystical adherence to an out dated religious myth; rather it is a necessity if we want to cope with the threat and stop playing the appeasers who always delay, once again, putting themselves on a war footing in time."[9]

---

7. Haraway, *When Species Meet*, 26.
8. Francis, *Encyclical on Climate Change and Inequality*, 53–54.
9. Latour, *Facing Gaia*, 111.

In the narrow frames of inquiry, the procreant gap between *theologia* and *oikonomia* shines a light in a dark place until day breaks. Giorgio Agamben, for instance, seeks to unlock the mysteries and miseries of contemporary economic governmentality, accepting that "its origin and archetype is the Trinitarian economy."[10] In the diagnosis may be the prescription, and Adrian Pabst sets forth a generation defining reconstruction of politics on "sheer and unreserved relationality," which finds its ground within "the triune structure of the whole of reality, divine and natural."[11] The present work seeks, what can only be, a modest contribution to this intensifying movement of thought.

It could be coincidence, wishful thinking, but the natural language turn in science appears to intersect worldviews, including but certainly not exclusive to Christianity, that express strong commitments to communication and relationships with the natural world. Put another way, what nature may be literally in science does not (at least) contradict what many ancient traditions say it is (or should be) morally and spiritually. In a still to be determined integral fashion, science and strong relationship worldviews may even belong to each other as the idea of nature that we need: A novel fusion of communication and emancipation. In Christian metaphysics, specifically, Saint Augustine first raises the decisive question, but then bypasses it for other more pressing concerns on human community, deferring it forward, perhaps to our time: "Other animals, too, have shared signs, communicating their desires. Now, whether these signs are merely motions apart from any purpose, or whether they are truly intentional, is another question."[12] I think we must answer yes to intentionality, to signification, to sacramental value; something Peter Sloterdijk describes as "the surpluses of first love, once it breaks away from its origins to make its own fresh starts elsewhere," freeing "creative processes that inspire the exodus of humans into the open."[13] On the way to the new spatiality, conceptual waypoints from "Trinitarian theology are indispensable."[14] Being is the place of relationships, signs, and communication. The open—the outside—demands emancipation, a *radix* exchange of atmospheres, not deferral and endless description; it is time to fight for the Earth.

It lies in ruin: Rebuild it. Let us rebegin the truth of trinitarian existence.

10. Agamben, *Kingdom and the Glory*, 153.
11. Pabst, *Metaphysics*, 439.
12. Augustine, *De doctrina christiana* II.2 (my translation).
13. Sloterdijk, *Bubbles*, 12.
14. Sloterdijk, *Bubbles*, 585.

ONE

Categories for Philosophy of Environment

THERE IS STILL WIDESPREAD confusion on the environmental question in general and how to organize this area of thought in particular. *Philosophy of environment* has developed over the past four decades as a response to this cultural and conceptual vagueness: It is, therefore, in philosophical terms, a newborn discipline. How is it best to examine this subject matter? Principles of division generate categories. *Good categorical principles* accurately separate areas of difference, while providing unifying connections. Shared dependencies provide the conditions for specific independencies: The place of departure for one thing is also the place of arrival for another. Distinctions can be made on the kinds of problems that are defined and the questions pursued to face them. Ties to other categories express the mixture of limitations and transitions, where one thing clearly ends and another begins. In unfamiliar spaces, especially, categories are best viewed as heuristic guides for exploring a subject; they are inter-relational, fallible, and revisable—dependent on the findings of an investigation. In the present work, philosophy of environment is divided into three provisional categories: ecopolitics, ethics, and environmental cosmology.

ECOPOLITICS

The ecopolitical environmental crisis is primarily defined by the mounting side-effects of modern industrial civilization. How do we go about minimizing their present and future impact on ourselves and the planet? What are the political and economic entities that determine our environmental practices? On what assumptions do they operate? How can they be transformed? Localized problems concerning land, sea, and air, e.g., over-fishing, have changed into an orthodox metanarrative of total ecological catastrophe. If global warming is not halted, imminent planetary collapse is predicted. If we do not enact a paradigm shift away from fossil fuels, the many-headed hydra of production, consumption, pollution, and population will bring Doomsday. What is the ecopolitical environmental crisis? George Monbiot well summarizes the situation:

> If in the year 2030, carbon dioxide concentrations in the atmosphere remain as high as they are today, the likely result is two degrees centigrade of warming (above pre-industrial levels). Two degrees is the point beyond which certain major ecosystems begin collapsing. Having, until then, absorbed carbon dioxide, they begin to release it. Beyond this point, in other words, climate change is out of our hands: it will accelerate without our help.[1]

Two degrees is the critical threshold: "It is the point at which some of the larger human impacts and the critical positive feedbacks are expected to begin."[2] Ecosystems begin emitting what is poisonous to life instead of absorbing it. The Earth begins to die, perhaps slowly, perhaps rapidly, and we go down with it. For a leading scientific voice, James Hansen: "We are on the precipice of climate system tipping points beyond which there is no redemption."[3] Others claim it is already too late to curb the relentless and inevitable process of global collapse.[4] Monbiot, though, is cautiously optimistic: "There is perhaps a 30 percent chance that we have already blown it," but we can probably turn the apocalyptic tide if we act with a radical agenda to reduce greenhouse gas emissions by 90 percent by 2030.[5] In this short period: "Our aim must be to stop global average temperatures from rising to more than 2 degrees above pre-industrial levels, which means more than 1.4 degrees above the current point."[6] This transition must be enacted without collapsing civilization as we understand and enjoy it. Navigating between the Scylla of global social transformation and the whirling Charybdis of

---

1. Monbiot, *Heat*, xvii.
2. Monbiot, *Heat*, 5.
3. Hansen quoted in Pearce, *With Speed and Violence*, v.
4. See Aitkenhead, "James Lovelock."
5. Monbiot, *Heat*, xviii.
6. Monbiot, *Heat*, 15.

"climate change must, in other words, become the project we put before all others. If we fail in this task, we fail in everything else. But is it possible?"[7]

Given such limited time, coupled with the sheer intractable scale of the problem and what is needed to make any difference (if it's not already too late), and the social risk associated with significantly deviating from business as usual, the whole problem appears paralyzing, if not an invitation to denial, nihilism, and further orgies of excess. But hope springs eternal: Ecopolitical activity has increased dramatically over the past decade. Environment has definitely entered our politics. If we wager that it is not too late, what is to be done to weather the gathering storm? An ecological nexus on a planetary scale must be found between science, technology, economics, and politics. At least in theory, the greening of everything and everyone is both familiar and well underway.[8] The "how to?" question, however, quickly leads to the question, "Why bother?" Monbiot calls for a revolution of morals:

> This must, in other words, be a moral decision, not an economic one. Either we decide that it is right to spend a lot of money seeking to prevent catastrophic climate change or we decide that it isn't, but we must make that decision on the grounds of how we value people and places as people and places, rather than as figures in a ledger.[9]

ETHICS

The ecopolitical crisis, then, is at root a moral problem. The second category of philosophy of environment is ethics. What is ethics? What is environmental ethics? *Ethics* is moral philosophy. Morality refers to commitments concerning right and wrong, good and evil. Moral fidelities encompass judgments, principles, and theories; they guide our actions, define our values, and give us reasons for being the persons we are. Ethics concerns the celebrated question posed by Socrates (†399 BCE): "How ought *we* to live?"

Ethics maintains a twofold distinction: Prescriptive and descriptive. *Prescriptive* ethics tells us what we should believe, how we should act, and why. Prescriptive ethics is a system of allowances and prohibitions. Moral

---

7. Monbiot, *Heat*, 15.

8. This category has turned into a rapidly growing industry of experts, commentators, texts, and their ecopolitical translation (or lack thereof). The best overview of this phenomenon remains Connelly et al., *Politics and the Environment*. Other entry points include Dryzek and Schlosberg, *Debating the Earth*; Stavins, *Economics and the Environment*; Eckersley, *Green State*; NSTI, *Clean Technology*.

9. Monbiot, *Heat*, 51.

commitments are usually grounded on immovable foundations. Prescriptive foundations are Archimedean moral points unaffected by the world of change. Absolute prescriptions are valid for all times, individuals, and situations, without exception. Judgment of right and wrong in this world is only possible from a view that transcends it. We need timeless truths and values in order to know how to act during changing states of affairs. On its own, the contingent world offers little clue as to what is right. We need perennial truths to guide our moral commitments because without them we are lost on an open sea without map or rudder. There is no point of transcendent value by which we can judge or be judged. *Is* cannot give us *ought*. All is permitted: One moral commitment is just as good as any other. Choices of value, and the actions that instance them, become arbitrary impositions of individual lifestyle and, most threatening, the raw will of the victor in the collective clash of competing powers. Good is what prevails, evil is what does not—*Vae victis*.

Practitioners of *descriptivist* ethics deny a timeless moral ground. Morals are historically situated and socially embedded. Prescriptive presuppositions are not provable; they are a view from nowhere. Claims to absolute truth are unjustifiable. Morals are social and personal events of adaptation to novel contexts. There is no absolute right, no absolute wrong. Judgments of good and evil are relative to time, community, individual, and circumstance. Moral pluralism denies absolutism. Defenders of this position often portray adherents to prescriptive ethics as essentially intolerant. If one prescription is right, the others must be wrong. If other claims are wrong or evil, then these errors must be corrected; correction can come in many ways, some of them extremely violent. Relativism means openness to difference. The equivocal is the good; it is not an invitation to closure by a univocal prescription. The engine of prescriptive force runs on a tragic misreading of reality, an inability to deal with change, diversity, and the indeterminate nature of things. The world must fit the prescriptions, not they to the world.

Besides prescriptive and descriptive ethics, there are two other disciplines of ethics: Meta-ethics and applied ethics. *Meta-ethics* concerns the logical, semantic, metaphysical, and epistemological presuppositions of moral thought, language, and action. In short, meta-ethics is *philosophy of* ethics, where followers of prescriptive and descriptive ethics encounter each other and, hopefully, present viable alternatives through reasoned arguments. Many philosophers walk a middle path between prescriptive and descriptive positions. *That* there are objective values can be credibly justified. However, to presuppose that there are perennial moral truths does not deny significant change in *what* they are.[10] Existence and value are related. John Leslie, for example, affirms "some set of needs is creatively powerful," seeking its expression in existence.[11] The content of this set inhabits the world of multiplicity. Finding the good we need *should* be an open, evolving, and consensual project. This approach attempts to avoid the moral disasters of extreme positions.

Prescriptive absolutism signifies complete values, knowing exactly *what* they are for all time, without exception or adjustment to changing circumstances. There will be perpetual war with the world until its contradictions are eliminated. Advocates of unlimited difference respond by denying universals. There is no possibility of guiding values beyond their embedded particularity. Universalizability is the mentality of imperialism. The immoral many must be constrained and saved by the good of the one. Descriptive relativism implies the equilibrium of all morals. Hierarchy is denied. The implausible ethic of embracing all differences equally, though, can quickly degenerate into skeptical suspension of commitment, indifference posing as tolerance, or arbitrariness of commitment without any preferential ground.

Applied ethics is presented as another way between extreme views. Prescriptive principles are mapped onto practical situations. The pluralistic view that results is then the subject of moral debate over which principle or blend of principles best mediates the ethical problem under consideration. The applied ethics approach is popular among professional groups, e.g., business ethics, legal ethics, medical ethics, and defense ethics. Practical dilemmas arise in professional work. These problems often make the right thing to do unclear. Applied ethics addresses the conflict between competing values, authorities, laws, and policies in professional contexts. Applying prescriptive moral theories to the same situation gives a map of alternative courses of action. These courses of action are then debated until agreement on the right thing to do is achieved.

Environmental ethics is a novel form of applied ethics, emerging from professional concerns about the environment, e.g., from foresters, biologists, and ecologists.[12] Environmental applied ethics is unique because it links traditional prescriptive positions to ethical situations outside relations between human beings: The moral status of fauna, flora, and inanimate physical systems. The most developed and influential traditions of applied environmental ethics are consequentialism, deontology, virtue, and holism.

---

10. See Armour, "Values, God, and the Problem," 148.
11. Leslie, *Value and Existence*, 6.
12. See Callicott, "Environmental Ethics," 5–15.

Consequentialism

Consequentialism is a moral philosophy that emphasizes the effects of action. Intentions are not judged good until they translate into good *consequences*. The inherent rightness of the means is not as important as the result it achieves. What occurs before can only be judged on what occurs after. The morality of the antecedent (means) depends on the achievement of its consequent (end): If the former accomplishes the latter, it is good; if not, it is immoral. Preferred outcomes include happiness, pleasure (or reduced suffering), or simply the everyday feeling of satisfaction from getting what you want. An important consequentialist theory for environmental philosophy is *utilitarianism*. Jeremy Bentham's (†1832) version of utilitarian ethics presents the moral goal of a society as *the greatest happiness for the greatest number*; this principle allows the calculation of activities that lead to maximal aggregate benefit. The increased welfare of a society means promoting actions that result in the most happiness, reducing actions that cause discontent.

Bentham's utilitarianism continues to be an influential modus operandi for animal rights activists. In a now famous footnote, he grounds morality on shared feeling, crossing the boundaries of our species: "The question is not, Can they reason? nor, Can they talk? but, Can they suffer."[13] All creatures that can suffer are subject to moral consideration. The limits of feeling mark the limits of moral consideration. Put otherwise: The differences of external identity, now including species along with reason, race, gender, and so on, are annulled of all essence; they are merely accidental expressions of essential feeling. The most influential utilitarian thinker within environmental applied ethics is Peter Singer. First published in 1975, Singer's *Animal Liberation* characterizes our treatment of *other animals* as an urgent moral (and legal) concern. Animals warrant equal rights based on cross-species feelings of pleasure and pain:

> My aim is to advocate that we make this mental switch in respect of our attitudes and practices towards a very large group of beings: members of species other than our own—or, as we popularly though misleadingly call them, animals. In other words, I am urging that we extend to other species the basic principle of equality that most of us recognize should be extended to all members of our own species.[14]

---

13. Bentham, *Introduction to the Principles*, XVII.
14. Singer, "All Animals Are Equal," 26.

Equality is a moral idea of how we should treat others to meet their *interests*. Different interests give rise to different rights, entitlements, and services. All animals are due equal consideration because *sentience* is the shared basis of different interests. Sentience is the "capacity for suffering and enjoying things" and, Singer claims, it "is a prerequisite for having interests at all."[15] If sentience, interests; if interests, moral consideration. If sentience is not present, "there is nothing to be taken into account."[16] Sentience is self-awareness, which is composed of specific powers and their operations, differing from individual to individual and species to species. The Latin *sentire* (feeling) encompasses the embodied dynamics of sensation, perception, and communication. If sentience is the basis for moral consideration, all creatures expressing this property (in various ways and degrees) are equal ethical subjects. Each sentient being must, following Bentham's dictum, *count for one and none more than one*. In Singer's terms, the "interests of every being affected by an action are to be taken into account and given the same weight as the like interests of any other being."[17] Just as the equal consideration of interests is a principle capable of embracing the differences of all human beings, ameliorating oppressions by erasing non-essential distinctions, so with all sentient creatures. To fail to do so means you are guilty of *speciesism*: "The speciesist," Singer tells us, "allows the interests of his own species to override the greater interests of members of other species."[18] Animal liberation joins the struggles of what once was a purely intra-human affair. Other animals are not merely means to our ends, principally their reduction to commodities for eating, wearing, testing, research, companionship, entertainment, and seemingly endless exploitation. Our fellow sentient creatures have interests, pursue the good of their own lives, and they are entitled to the shelter of our laws, resources, and care.

Singer's shifting continuum of moral value makes harming and destroying all sentient animals immoral. His achievement must be recognized as a powerful interruption of business as usual. The very idea of moral solidarity with all feeling creatures is still, for many of us, an astonishing thing to contemplate, let alone change our lives because of its truth. In our time, nonetheless, thanks to Singer and other activists, the previously accepted is becoming increasingly unacceptable. By any estimation, the calculus of everyday suffering that we inflict on other animals is a staggering horror. Continued justification is a potent and regulative blend of interlocking

---

15. Singer, *Practical Ethics*, 57.
16. Singer, *Practical Ethics*, 58.
17. Singer, "All Animals Are Equal," 29.
18. Singer, "All Animals Are Equal," 30.

elements: Selective ignorance, the force of traditional habits and livelihoods, constructed appetites, rigid and outdated science and, most problematic, the global propagation of anthropocentric ideology by the massive vested *interests* of capital and labor. The latter factor signifies planetary homogenization, destroying other ancient ways of life that are less exploitive.

Singer's radical ideas, though, like his utilitarian predecessors, finds its political expression in far more conventional commitments to gradualism and reformism. Progress takes the form of cross-species liberalism. Like past and present (intra-human) corrections of structural exploitation, e.g., racism and sexism, the cultural shock of speciesism will involve a reactionary process of trauma. The long nightmare of normal continues, but if we really wake up to what we are doing, and have done, as a merciless evil, the assuagement of damage and guilt is best approached carefully and inter-generationally. There will be waxing and waning successes and failures, confusion and conflict, as our fellow sentient creatures win their legal rights, protections, and fair distribution of shared wealth. It is best to start with those closest to us in evolutionary terms, the great apes, but the end is full emancipation for all creatures that can feel.

Why should this program be prescriptive, not simply an idiosyncratic, however brilliant, preference? More clearly, what makes this preference preferable for all of us, the collective *we*? Singer's ethics carries implicit metaphysical loyalties of a stronger kind: Animal liberation should and will happen because history favors liberty, breaking beyond the master/slave relationship, evolution runs on symbiotic cooperation and, at root, elevation of the vulnerable is the practical aspect of ultimate goodness.[19] Thoughtful criticism of Singer's position, however, does not center on its lack of metaphysics, professed intentions, or laudable achievements for other creatures thus far. Misgivings arise from the logic of utilitarianism that is further amplified by its cross-species extension. Critique, roughly, focuses on three areas of concern: The calculus of aggregate welfare, its subsequent pluralistic turn, and the ecological limitations of an ethics based on feeling.

Maximizing aggregate welfare (as end) does not absolutely prohibit any act (as means). The suffering of each creature counts as only one unit in the overall total, providing little to no protection for individual interests.

---

19. Singer's connection to aspects of German Idealism—from Hegel to Marx—is not well known or sufficiently investigated, but it appears to be a distinct influence; see his *Marx*, 11–15. Singer shares with the Germans an affinity for radical ideas and their emancipatory presuppositions, but he opts for liberal utility and reform as the latter's political translation. On the rich and varied concept of freedom Singer draws from, different than individual negative freedom, see Schindler, *Perfection of Freedom*, esp. 238–300.

This idea of the right and good requires everyone to produce optimal outcomes or utility. The real is the ledger's abstract aggregate of satisfaction, not the concrete lives. Singer claims all animals are equal. We equally count as one in the overall calculus that optimizes utility. But are we all equally vulnerable as means? Many critics detect structural inequality, targeting the most marginal, as an inherent feature of the logic of utility. Samuel Scheffler, for instance, claims, "this objection can be directed at all consequentialist theories."[20] Aggregate value "demands that we channel resources to the relatively well-off whenever that will lead to the required maximization," and it will "frequently require us to ignore the misery of a few people and concentrate instead on increasing the pleasures of the many."[21] Utilitarianism is a sacrificial ethical system.

Michel Foucault (†1984) exposes Benthamism as a total cultural program. Instrumental rationalization is best described as *panopticism*: The apparatus of surveillance, discipline, and correction functions mechanically across various institutions and the subject-bodies that inhabit them.[22] The force of standardization creates subject-bodies, individuates them as means, serving the end of maximizing aggregate utility. Some participants differ from their predesigned role as means and they are exposed to intensive institutional intervention. Deviant subject-bodies are either corrected, properly individuated, or, if not, disposed of as inoperable collateral damage. *Useless* is the new term for evil. Unorthodoxy is a variable, depending on the system's ideal subject-model. Foucault's disturbing conclusion is that the power of utility is mostly concentrated within the technological means of a society's institutions. A useful subject-body is made "mechanically from a fictitious relation," internalizing external coercion until she "becomes the principle" of her own domination.[23] The force of commodification, for example, becomes celebratory self-commodification, e.g., selfie. Institutions are "laboratories of power," creating a society modelled on the penal colony.[24] The professed ends of a system are, for the most part, incidental; it is the "homogeneous effects of power" that are decisive.[25] The sheer capacity to create and mobilize subject-bodies for any end makes "who exercises

---

20. Scheffler, *Rejection of Consequentialism*, 10.
21. Scheffler, *Rejection of Consequentialism*, 10.
22. See Foucault, *Discipline and Punish*, 195–227.
23. Foucault, *Discipline and Punish*, 202–3.
24. Foucault, *Discipline and Punish*, 204.
25. Foucault, *Discipline and Punish*, 202.

power," and their ideas of the good end, equally suspect.[26] The domination of the means is required by all utilitarian systems.

The logic of collective utility, then, should give us considerable unease. The presentation of individuals as means appears to violate humanistic values, targeting the marginal. There is no concept of inherent value that limits utilization. Singer's inclusion of all sentient creatures compounds utilitarianism's problematic tendencies. By denying the inherent worth of all human beings, regardless of where we place on the sentience scale, his calculus may diminish the rights of vulnerable people.[27] Rights are conditional on present sentient capacities. This calculus will impel us to make moral choices to prefer the interests of greater over lesser sentient individuals. The species of the greater sentient interest cannot be considered. Singer concedes this position in *Animal Liberation*:

> Whatever the criteria we choose, however, we will have to admit that they do not follow precisely the boundary of our own species. We may legitimately hold that there are features of certain beings that make their lives more valuable than those of other beings; but there will surely be non-human animals whose lives, by any standards, are more valuable than the lives of some humans. A chimpanzee, dog, or pig, for instance, will have a higher degree of self-awareness and a greater capacity for meaningful relations with others than a severely retarded infant or someone in a state of advanced senility.[28]

Singer elsewhere attempts to clarify his view, "for me, to compare a human being to a nonhuman animal was not to say that the human being should be treated with less consideration, but that the animal should be treated with more."[29] There is, however, more at issue here than simply a misunderstanding of Singer's intentions.

R. G. Frey presents the problem with cross-species utility in terms of the "comparative value of lives."[30] He uses a thought experiment, where we have to choose between saving a man or a dog: In cross-species terms, who do we save? Being human will offer no intrinsic guarantee. There will be no "winning on hidden grounds" other than sentiency: "We could in theory assign a lower moral status to the dog whatever its condition and whatever

---

26. Foucault, *Discipline and Punish*, 202.

27. See Singer's version of his problems in Germany during the 1990s in Singer, *Practical Ethics*, 337–59.

28. Singer, *Animal Liberation*, 19.

29. Singer, *Practical Ethics*, 347.

30. Frey, "Utilitarianism and Animals," 177.

the condition of the man, but utilitarianism as a general theory did not seem to do so or to provide premises that allow one to do so."[31] If equal moral status is granted, strictly speaking, "the equality could be broken only as we learn more about the nature and condition of the dog, and therefore saving the one became dubious and the other obligatory."[32] Sentience will decide the matter. Which creature, at this present time, expresses this property the most? Following the logic of utility, if the man is sick, near death, or impaired in some sense, and the dog is young, healthy, and flourishing, the dog should be saved. Hypotheticals, false binaries, can be unfair, scaremongering, reinforcing the status quo, but, at the very least, life and relationships will be very different after the collapse of human exceptionalism. The just allocation of limited resources will involve a set of mentalities and practices that many of us, right now, find not so much immoral as surreal, beyond the ethical fields we know. It is certainly beyond my limited imagination to envision the full *panoptic* implementation of Singer's sentience society.

The utopian impulse is directed to making a new *we*. The sacrificial logic of utility erases the present reality of individuals. Bare lives are not recognized as singular and incalculably unique in any meaningful sense. What is real is the measurable aggregate. Individuals only count as means, as represented objects, subject to the metrics of various systems and their predesigned outcomes. Given the horror of history that follows this moral atmosphere in the first half of the twentieth century, especially, it is not surprising that the ascendant political culture of the second half runs counter to utilitarianism. The pluralistic turn that rejects utilitarianism is best articulated by John Rawls (†2002): If we accept the premise that "the plurality of distinct persons with separate systems of ends is an essential feature of human societies, we should not expect the principles of social choice to be utilitarian."[33] A truly just society leaves individuals alone to pursue their own worldviews. Any collective project, any discourse on a common good, *for us*, is automatically suspect; it is marked as a threat to the liberty of ultimate individuals, *for me*.

Despite its dubious ground of non-relational individuals, Jürgen Habermas concedes the political necessity of Rawls's era defining break with the unending clash between systems of collective utility: "Surveying the rubble of philosophical attempts to designate *particular* ways of life as exemplary or universally obligatory, Rawls draws the proper conclusion."[34]

31. Frey, "Utilitarianism and Animals," 177.
32. Frey, "Utilitarianism and Animals," 177.
33. Rawls, *Theory of Justice*, 29.
34. Habermas, *Future of Human Nature*, 2.

Within the current pluralistic milieu, Singer's cross-species project can only (safely) be a singular perspective, confined to likeminded individuals, involving respectful distance from those who do not share its idea of the right and good. Although his ideas suggest that something more is needed to transform society, there is little evidence that Singer promotes the violation of Rawls's political principle of mutual toleration of individual worldviews within the rational and liberal commerce of persuasion.

Another persistent criticism of Singer's cross-species utilitarianism centers on its limitations as an applied environmental ethic. Based on sentience, the circle of moral inclusion grows wider. We move beyond our own species, but the good and right cannot extend to flora and the physical systems upon which all sentient creatures depend. The latter can only be an indirect or derivative ethical consideration. This criticism, as we shall see, follows the next tradition, which professes to incorporate the integral significance of individuals into its environmental ethics framework.

Deontology

Deontology is duty-based ethics. We have an unqualified responsibility to act on certain principles. Our acting as duty requires is independent of all other considerations. We do what is right and good because it is the right and good thing to do. Duty compels us because of the presence of another's inherent value, not for any variable or instrumental property, e.g., expected result and self-interest. Acting on behalf of future outcomes, especially, is ethically questionable because good results are not legitimate measures by which to judge prior activity. The *moral fallacy of affirming the consequent* entails that from the moral truth of the consequent we can infer the moral truth of the antecedent. Evil antecedents can be redeemed if the consequent is *affirmed* as an aggregate good. Retroactive morality, however, is notoriously selective and arbitrary, driven by the force of perspective. The biased omniscience of hindsight, with its capacity to magically rewrite the horrors of the past, cannot be trusted as the ground of morality.

Deontology rejects the ethical fallacy of affirming the consequent. The end does not determine the value of the antecedent means, but from the moral truth of the antecedent we can affirm the moral truth of the consequent. The end and the means form a self-diffusing unity. There is a moral inference from antecedent to consequent that differentiates and communicates to others. The end is the means, the means is the end and, when directed towards a future goal, the means must be just as good as the end it seeks. The latter will be different than the initial antecedent. We do our duty, now, always in a different antecedent state, because it is our duty, and we can only judge a person's actions on the presence or absence of a good will when doing it. Intentions count. Ethical intentionality is the form of the right and good directed to others. Morality based on egoistic self-interest is an immoral contradiction. Reflexivity is the repetition of a self's intentional relation to itself. Self-constitution makes a relation to another a means of a self's relating itself to itself. More simply, I am the only true end; all else is means. Deontological morality, however, abides in our intentional relation to others and, through that relationship of good or ill will, we constitute our relation to ourselves. Our goodness or evil depends on how we relate to others.

A person of good will acts on principle; her intentions towards others are said to be sincere or in good faith. Immanuel Kant (†1804), for instance, claims a good will is the only thing "which can be regarded as good without qualification."[35] A will is good "not because of what it effects or accomplishes, nor because of its fitness to attain some proposed end," but because, "it is good in itself."[36] The goodness of the will is determined by an inviolable law to treat others as ends-in-themselves, never merely as means. In Kant's case, it is found in the various formulations of the *categorical imperative*: "A categorical imperative would be one which represented an action as objectively necessary in itself apart from its relation to a further end."[37] To make an exception of yourself or the collective you represent, as the only end, treating all others as means, violates the moral principle of universalizability. As a precaution against doing wrong, we must abide by the first formulation of the categorical imperative, the Formula of Universal Law: "I ought never to act except in such a way that I can also will that my maxim should become a universal law."[38] If I am unable to universalize the exception, it is wrong; if all others aspire to do what I do, it will destroy the rule, thereby destroying the right and good.

Deontological environmental ethicists continue the tradition of inherent value. Duty based ethics counters the sacrificial logic of utilitarian calculus: In both its collective and egoistic modes, there is an *ontological fallacy*, a way of thinking and being that can easily lead to the moral obscenity of denying the worth of others. Moral value is built-into individual existence. It is not conferred by others because individuals are ends-in-themselves. This equally distributed natural right cannot be overridden by a cross-species

---

35. Kant, *Groundwork of the Metaphysic of Morals*, 61–62.
36. Kant, *Groundwork of the Metaphysic of Morals*, 61–62.
37. Kant, *Groundwork of the Metaphysic of Morals*, 82.
38. Kant, *Groundwork of the Metaphysic of Morals*, 70.

sentient calculus. Present sentient capacities are accidental. They are not essential to the being of an individual. All individual lives are equally as valuable and worth living; they never cease being ends-in-themselves. Therefore, sentience is not a legitimate ground for moral consideration. Being moral is treating other individuals as unique and sacrosanct ends-in-themselves. Other lives have a logically independent value all their own. The proper protection of individuals—especially those who have diminished physical and intellectual abilities or find themselves in social and political danger—is a basic test of this moral duty. Individual humans, *specifically*, are not to be treated as instrumental means. We have unassailable human rights that transcend the contingencies of physical and social life. But can the inherent value of individuals extend beyond human beings?

Kant denies this moral extension but, characteristically, the depth and originality of his analysis opens room for further amendments. Humanity, for Kant, is the only rational animal. Being an end-in-itself is contingent upon the possession of reason. Natural rights are conditional upon being an end-in-itself. Consequently, our moral community is limited to human beings. Only human beings are inherently valuable. We have the capacity to recognize this fact or natural right in other human beings and we are compelled to treat them appropriately. Only rational beings impose on themselves the moral law. Individuals are autonomous only if they demonstrate the ability to act reasonably. An individual can be held morally accountable for the acts she performs or fails to perform on this basis. The test of reasonableness is universalizability, acting on principles we can require other compatibly positioned individuals to act on similarly.

Moral creatures are defined by the presence of reason's lawgiving. The autonomy of reason determines the laws of free choice through its own self-legislation, independently of any influence. The principle of autonomy is thus the legislation of choice by reason. The ground of self-determination lies in reason, in the human subject herself, and not in external causes. Moral self-activity is the ability to freely determine ourselves through reason. We can be reasonable or not. Accept heteronomous external force or not. Free moral activity takes its ground, its motivating cause, from the spontaneity of human willing, which freely unites itself to rational conceptions, quite independently of all external determining causes, acting solely by the universal moral law. Freedom without its reasonable restriction falls into a lawless inclination that is absent from the natural world. This contrary, this evil, contravenes the right and good order of our nature and, presently, the whole of nature. Kant, with typical foresight, warns against the idolatry and hubris occasioned by our species-power. Our sheer will, its unrestricted capacity for violence, poses a question, the planetary scale of which is only now coming into full view: "For it is uncertain whether man will not use his powers to destroy himself, and the whole of nature."[39]

The freedom to be rational is a *sui generis* feature of human beings and, to Kant, it marks the specific difference that makes all the difference for our species. To be ethical is to freely accept the limits of reason's universal moral law. If we make the turn to moral rationality, our obligations to other human beings are direct and unequivocal. We are to act in a way, as rational beings, we would wish all rational beings to act. Duty requires rational beings to treat other rational beings as ends-in-themselves. The rest of nature does not have this reasoning capacity. Whatever lacks reason is not an end-in-itself. Natural rights are denied because there is an absence of inherent value. Therefore, it follows that we have no direct moral obligations to anything that is not an end-in-itself, which is everything outside our own species. What is beyond our species maintains an instrumental value; it is there as means for a human creature that is an end-in-itself. Moral concern for environment, then, can only be indirect. Such things as ecosystems have no moral standing. Our environmental practices are of moral consequence only insofar as they adversely affect human beings. For example, if water is made undrinkable by pollution and people are getting sick, then the moral law requires its correction because human beings are being harmed. The water by itself has no inherent value. Since the environmental crisis is threatening us, it is a moral issue.

Kant does, however, warn against our lawless, thus irrational, inclination for sheer destruction (*spiritus destructionis*) of the contents of the natural world.[40] On the exclusive basis of instrumental use value, we erase nature's aesthetic value, which is "pleasure in loving something without any intention of using it."[41] The instrumental view of nature, although legitimate, must be supplemented by appreciation of nature's beauty. A purely instrumental view of life weakens our moral duty to ourselves and others because we cannot relate to the world in any other way. We are more prone to mistreat human beings, to see each other only as means, if we cannot experience the beauty of nature. Despite our rightful use, serving rational ends, nature has an aesthetic value all its own that our utilization should not eclipse. Without beauty, use turns to abuse.

The ethical standing of animals is akin to nature, generally considered, with additional adjustments. Kant's position is most explicit in a peculiar

---

39. Kant, *Lectures on Ethics*, 125.
40. See Kant, *Metaphysical Principles of Virtue*, 106.
41. Kant, *Metaphysical Principles of Virtue*, 106.

lecture entitled "Of Duties to Animals and Spirits."[42] Animals are included within a category that covers disembodied good and evil spirits and inanimate objects. The lecture explores our "duties to beings that are above us and beneath us."[43] Indirect duties to other animals find their true significance as analogical duties to human beings:

> But since all animals exist only as means, and not for their own sakes, in that they have no self-consciousness, whereas as man is the end, such that I can no longer ask: Why does he exist?, as can be done with animals, it follows we have no immediate duties to animals; our duties towards them are indirect duties to humanity. Since animals are an analogue of humanity, we observe duties to mankind when we observe them as analogues to this, and thus cultivate our duties to humanity.[44]

Our instrumental treatment of animals has a supervening moral rider. We can use animals as a means, providing that usage is not cruel. Again, like ecosystems, animals have no inherent moral value. The prohibition against cruelty does not center on what is done to animals, but on the conscious intention of the person doing the action. Causing pain in and of itself is not an argument for cruelty. For example, surgeons and dentists cause pain as a means to future health. Cruelty means taking pleasure in making another suffer. In John Locke's (†1704) phrase, it is to take "a seeming kind of Pleasure" in causing pain.[45] Cruelty to animals cannot be judged by its effects, but by a person's state of mind. It is not our sadistic treatment of other animals that is morally wrong. What is wrong is the bad moral character it produces, which may lead to the maltreatment of other human beings.

Cruelty to animals is contrary to duty to oneself because it deadens in us the feeling of empathy. Accordingly, for Kant, "a natural predisposition very serviceable to morality in one's relations with other men is gradually weakened and obliterated."[46] In his *Lectures on Ethics*, we read:

> Yet it cannot be denied that a hardheartedness towards animals is not in accordance with the law of reason, and it is at least an unsuitable use of means. Any action whereby we may torment animals, or let them suffer distress, or otherwise treat them without love, is demeaning to ourselves. It is inhuman, and contains an analogy of violation of the duty to ourselves, since

---

42. Kant, *Lectures on Ethics*, 212–13.
43. Kant, *Lectures on Ethics*, 212.
44. Kant, *Lectures on Ethics*, 212.
45. Locke, *Educational Writings*, 225.
46. Kant, *Metaphysical Principles of Virtue*, 106.

we would not, after all, treat ourselves with cruelty; we stifle the instinct of humaneness within us and make ourselves devoid of feeling; it is thus an indirect violation of humanity in our own person.[47]

Kant draws attention to the pedagogical importance of correcting children's cruel behavior. If left to develop, "the progress of cruelty" may culminate in murder and other crimes.[48] Cruelty stains the human character with the propensity for radical evil. The earlier we effectively root it out of a child's intentions and behavior, the better will be the child, the adult the child becomes, and society.

When it comes to our relations with animals, especially in the wilderness, Kant recognizes our traditional frailty and dependency. If our struggle for existence requires the rational utilization of animals, this situation demands that we respect animals, even if they threaten our lives with their uncontrolled presence and absence. To treat them otherwise than with veneration, particularly the vulnerable domesticated animals under our care, undermines our duties to ourselves and others. To engage in the irrational utility of torture or other horrors as a sign of domination, the wanton revel of the triumph of the strong over the weak, is to unleash the abyss of our irrational nature. If we freely follow our inclination and unbounded capacity for inflicting pain and destruction, this "places us lower even than the animals, for in that case there arises in him a lawlessness that does not exist among them."[49] Only human beings can be cruel. The creatures of nature can only be said to be that way in a metaphorical sense. What we usually mean is that we fall victim to their needful actions. If, for example, the starving polar bear attacks and eats my dog, the spectacle may seem unbelievably cruel to me, and my dog, but there is no excessive irrationality present. The cure for our cruelty is love. Love comes from getting to know the lives of other animals, including polar bears. This kind of love, to Kant, seems to be much more affecting than indirect analogical duties or mere aesthetic pleasure of nature: "The more we devote ourselves to observing animals and their behavior, the more we love them, on seeing how greatly they care for their young; in such a context, we cannot contemplate cruelty to a wolf."[50]

There is an important distinction, then, between causing pain to animals on behalf of research, food, income, or some other legitimate human end, and taking pleasure in inflicting pain for its own sake. The former is

---

47. Kant, *Lectures on Ethics*, 434.
48. Kant, *Lectures on Ethics*, 212.
49. Kant, *Lectures on Ethics*, 126.
50. Kant, *Lectures on Ethics*, 212.

rational utility that must be justified as necessary for the preservation and improvement of human life. The latter is gratuitous pain caused for sport or no reason at all. Irrational utility is an indication of moral evil within a person's character that may lead to the harm of other human beings. We judge the heart of a person by her treatment of animals. As with our relations with other creatures, so with our relations with other human beings. To treat other animals *as if* they were ends-in-themselves improves moral character and, consequently, our relations with human beings, who are ends-in-themselves. Good will towards animals is an analogue of good will towards human beings.

Kant's idea of rational morality restricts our use of animals. Cruelty arises from a mentality of irrational utility, realizing itself in wanton domination and destruction (*spiritus destructionis*). When we deal sadistically with other animals, we fail to analogically unite with the universal moral law. Kant's position limits itself to examples of human individuals, where that failure is most apparent but, regarding the origination of cruelty, we need not be methodologically individualistic. The actions of cruel individuals flow from perverse states of mind, but these thoughts and actions may only be effects of a much more concealed and structural cruelty. Tendencies for brutality manifest in an individual, certainly, but they also exist and operate as regulative ideas of culture. Irrational utility is propagated as rational and necessary. To eat meat, for example, when other identically nutritious flora food is readily available cannot be justified. To repeat experiments on animals with the foreknowledge that no new knowledge will be revealed is also immoral. Factory farms, fishing trawlers and, now, the biogenic revolution of commodified and engineered life intimate a moral abyss of freedom unbound. Regulative institutional evil means our society is overflowing with cruelty, serving the irrational ends of appetite, money, and power.

Human individuals who take pleasure in the suffering of animals are thankfully rare. Perpetrators are justifiably condemned, but they are often victims of cruel and traumatic acts themselves. Individualistic spectacles also serve to distract from the immense, directive, and malefic culture of irrational utilization. Collective evil constitutes the normal forms of everyday life. Our acceptance and performance of cruelty is usually not accompanied with perverse pleasure, but something far more troubling—ignorance and indifference. The corruption of the right and good by the accumulating effects of our failed analogical duties to other animals signifies, in Kant's terms, a colossal threat to ourselves and the planet. Instead of reason, we accept mere lawless rationalization as its hollow simulacrum. We worship at the idol of our power: Nature, forgive us, for we know not what we do.

Deontological ethicist Tom Regan claims animals have much more than indirect or analogical moral worth. The cruelty prohibition is problematic and ineffective because it has to do with the intractable problem of mental intentions over actions: "Cruelty has to do with a person's state of mind."[51] Evil resides in the motive, not in the activity. Proof of cruelty will have to focus on the mind of the agent, not on the action, diverting from, amongst other things, a proper assessment of rational or irrational utility that the agent is engaged in, which may be the source of an individual's cruel mind. If a factory farm worker, for example, is caught on video performing brutal abuse to cows, the methodological individualism implicit in the cruelty prohibition singles out the worker's mental state. The factory itself is discounted as a source of irrational utility. Other workers, owners, and complicit consumers, not having the perverse mentality, are outside moral responsibility. Susceptible individuals are scapegoated, portrayed as essentially evil, sidestepping their actions' origin in structural cruelty.

Regan uses the moral example of vivisectors. To call them cruel is to make the essentialist claim that they are evil people, which is, for the most part, wrong, distracting us from the morality of "*what they do.*"[52] There are legitimate moral questions on vivisection as an action: Is *this* act of vivisection a rational utilization of *this* living creature's life? Or is it irrational? Thus, cruel and immoral, likely to produce damaged practitioners? Is institutionalized vivisection ever justifiable? Or is this phenomenon structural cruelty personified? Regan, however, concludes that the cruelty discourse is more hindrance than help: "The more we are able to keep in view how the morality of what a person does is distinct from his/her state of mind, distinct from the presence or absence of taking pleasure in pain, the better the chances for significant dialogue between vivisectors and anti-vivisectors."[53] He argues elsewhere that to lodge the protection of animals on the foundation of cruelty is a categorical "failure to provide an adequate basis for our duties to animals."[54]

Regan maintains that inherent value is present in individuals beyond human beings. Other animals "have a distinctive kind of value in their own right, if we do."[55] Further, "If humans have rights, so do many animals."[56] Regan reforms Kant's position from within. He draws the circle of moral

51. Regan, "Animal Rights, Human Wrongs," 41.
52. Regan, "Animal Rights, Human Wrongs," 41.
53. Regan, "Animal Rights, Human Wrongs," 41.
54. Regan, *Case for Animal Rights*, 199.
55. Regan, "Animal Rights, Human Wrongs," 48.
56. Regan, "Animal Rights, Human Wrongs," 49.

inclusion a little wider. Our inherent value and natural rights are based on having the monopoly on reason. Reason is a certain set of cognitive abilities. These powers are also possessed by some non-human animals.[57] Like marginal case humans, e.g., infants, children, and the physically/intellectually impeded, animals demonstrate varying degrees of reason-having autonomy. Rational activity is shared across species; it is a modal distinction, not a substantial difference exclusive to our species. Therefore, if marginal case humans are considered ends-in-themselves and are due natural rights, so are other animals of comparable capacities. Animals, then, have inherent value, *if we do*.

Regan develops his ideas by identifying one of Kant's moral blind spots. Kant draws the distinction between non-autonomous and autonomous animals. The former can choose, but the latter are free. "All animals," Kant explains, "have their capacity to use their powers according to choice. Yet this choice is not free, but necessitated by incentives and *stimuli*. Their actions contain *bruta necessitas*. If all creatures had such a choice, tied to sensory drives, the world would have no value. But the inner worth of the world, the *summon bonum*, is freedom according to choice that is not necessitated to act."[58] If direct duties to others are only for autonomous agents, then non-autonomous humans fall from the category of inherent value. Only humans that can freely choose the universal moral law without instinctual compulsion or necessity are ends-in-themselves. The actions of non-autonomous humans are *bruta necessitas*. We, the autonomous agents, therefore, only have indirect or analogous duties to non-autonomous humans; that is, we may use them as means, like animals, providing our usage is not cruel. Other humans, the most helpless, can be utilized rationally, e.g., vivisection. Given this troubling inconsistency, we are faced with a moral dilemma: Do we accept the animalization of the most vulnerable humans by their reduction to means? Or do we humanize other animals by including them as individuals with inherent value? There is an opening that requires considerable reconceptualization. Regan achieves a resolution by drawing a careful set of distinctions. Deontological morality now encompasses agents, patients, and their common genus of inherent worth: Subject-of-a-life.

Although only fully rational humans act as *moral agents*, both marginal-case humans and at least some animals can claim the status of *moral patients*. Moral agents are free in Kant's sense. Agents can do right or wrong

---

57. See Regan, *Case for Animal Rights*, 1–81. Since Regan was writing in 1982, there is a rapidly growing body of evidence within the field of ethology, especially of animal intelligence, communication, emotion, and so on. It seems the more we bother to look, the more we find.

58. Kant, *Lectures on Ethics*, 125.

and be on the receiving end of right and wrong activity by other moral agents. Moral patients are unable to formulate moral principles. "Unlike human moral agents," Regan claims, "*they cannot be anything but innocent.*"[59] Moral patients are not free; they have choices within their limited domain of function. Patients are unable to do right or wrong, but what they do may be beneficial or harmful to moral agents. My dog (moral patient), for example, may bite the mailman (moral agent). Moral patients, however, can be on the receiving end of the right and wrong acts of moral agents. For example, the beating of my dog (moral patient) by the mailman (moral agent) is an immoral act even though the dog itself can do no wrong. Unlike the relationship between moral agents, the relationship between moral agents and moral patients is not reciprocal. Moral agents can do what is right or wrong in relation to moral patients, but the actions of moral patients cannot be right or wrong in relation to moral agents.

Regan calls for a new cross-species category of inherent value. Moral agents and moral patients are ends-in-themselves; they are all subjects-of-a-life. These moral entities cannot be regarded as means to an end; they should not be subjects for rational utilization. Subjects-of-a-life maintain value "logically independently of their utility for others and logically independently of their being the object of anyone else's interests."[60] It is, of course, the idea of moral patients that crosses the species boundary. Just like human moral patients, non-human moral patients should be recognized as having inherent individual value and granted their due rights and protections. Human moral agents have direct duties to human and non-human moral patients. The subject-of-a-life category, perhaps surprisingly, has a limited extension. Regan argues that all normal mammals "aged one or more" would qualify in this regard because, along with "the capacity to experience pleasure and pain," they demonstrate "perception, memory, desire, self-consciousness, intention, and a sense of the future."[61] He believes we should treat the members of this set as individuals with inherent value: They should not be sacrificed as means to an end, and must be treated as ends-in-themselves. Seals, to Regan, are an example of subjects-of-a-life:

> Underlying the call for an end to commercial sealing is a growing change in the perception of what seals are. So long as there was no serious challenge to viewing these animals as a renewable natural resource, whose place in the scheme of things was to serve human interests, there could be no serious ethical

---

59. Regan, *Case for Animal Rights*, 295.
60. Regan, *Case for Animal Rights*, 243.
61. Regan, *Case for Animal Rights*, 81.

> challenge to commercial sealing. The serious ethical challenge now being raised is symptomatic of a fundamental change in our perception of these animals.
>
> This change has come about in response to a range of questions, including the following: Are seals aware of anything? Are they capable of experiencing pain or enjoying themselves? Do they have biological and social needs which they take pleasure in satisfying? Do individual animals have an identity over time, so that it makes sense to think of them as faring well or faring ill as their life goes on? . . . In these respects—but not, of course, in all—these animals are like humans.
>
> Against this backdrop, the larger structure of the debate over the ethics of commercial sealing can be seen more clearly. Whereas some people see seals as stocks or herds, with quotas to be harvested or populations to be cropped, others (myself included) see them as individuals, each one of which has a life of its own to live—a life of importance to the individual whose life it is, quite independently of how useful that individual is to others.[62]

Regan is a deontological pioneer within applied environmental ethics. Like his contemporary, Peter Singer, Regan's achievement lies in the profoundly difficult (and dangerous) task of interrupting our regulative evil. The very idea that total anthropocentric entitlement may be wrong in certain cases is still, to many, a reaction generating proposition, especially for powerful interests. Regan is also, perhaps unlike Singer, particularly effective by inscribing the cross-species disruption in terms of individualistic rights, which is the predominant ethical-legal system in the post-war period: If human rights, then some non-human rights follow. Regan's position, though, like that of Singer and deontology's great figure, Kant, has certain problems all its own that we need to take into consideration: Primarily, the justification for violating inherent value and the limits of the subject-of-a-life category.

The great attraction of deontological ethics over utilitarianism is that individuals count. The presence of inherent value severely restricts what we can do to ourselves and others because "inherent value is conceived to be categorical value, admitting no degrees."[63] Collective interests cannot cancel the value of individuals and remain moral. But Regan qualifies the absolute nature of individuals with some, admittedly, very open-ended (non-categorical) hypothetical exemptions. Collective interests can overtake

---

62. Regan, "Ethical Considerations," 1–2.
63. Regan, *Case for Animal Rights*, 244.

the inherent value of individual subjects-of-a-life, e.g., "greater harm" to others.[64] Just as there are justified exceptions that entail individual human rights can be superseded on behalf of collective interests, it follows that the rights of individual animals can also be sacrificed. From a deontological perspective, however, other animals are not merely dispensable commodities or experimental subjects. Subjects-of-a-life are ends-in-themselves; their inherent value must be taken into consideration when decisions are made that affect them. Any proposed activity, rescinding the rights of any and all subjects-of-a-life (human and non-human), must be justified by reason and circumstances. Under what circumstances can collective utility be strong enough, as a rational justification, to sacrifice creatures with inherent value on behalf of other creatures with inherent value? Whether the livelihood of sealers, or any interest that kills or harms mammals of one year or older, can be reasonably justified is an ongoing moral question for deontological environmental ethicists.

Regan admits very flexible provisos for powerful collective interests, allowing them to override the inherent value of individual subjects-of-a-life. When we combine this concession with his *capabilities limit* on the extension of inherent value, the argument can be made that, in practical terms, his deontology is a distinction without much of a difference from Singer's utilitarianism. Inherent value is just as endangered by powerful collective ends as sentience. Clare Palmer, for example, while recognizing the importance of capabilities for the two dominant streams of animal ethics, has turned to human "*relations* with animals" as an alternative; the context of our relations changes "what is owed them."[65] The relational turn signifies that the capabilities approach remains very much in Kant's analogical duties tradition. There is a definite scale of humanistic, if not anthropocentric, value. Based on shared capacities, we have direct analogical duties. Certain other individual mammals have inherent value because they are most like us. All else seems to fall into the domain of means for the elect category of subject-of-a-life.

The genius of Regan's category of moral patients, nevertheless, appears to resist his own restriction on inherent value. If demonstration of reason means finding evidence for distinct types of inferential and communicative activity, all forms of life, including elemental systems, can be considered moral patients. Just as there is nothing so exclusive about human reason that prevents all capable mammals of one year or older from having inherent value, so from mammals to the rest of life and, from life, to existence

---

64. Regan, "Animal Rights, Human Wrongs," 46.
65. Palmer, "Moral Relevance of the Distinction," 701.

as such. Why should the subject-of-a-life category *not* extend *all the way down*? Is not hierarchy by select capacities arbitrary and thus misleading? If we accept a pluralistic continuum instead, there is univocal inherent value. Human moral agents can still be viewed as a uniquely intensive and free kind of creature with inherent value. We are the most dangerous, but we are also the *inner worth of the world*, making us the most capable of taking responsibility for other creatures, systems, and places. Even if we follow the reductionist-materialist view, eliminating free reason from nature, including ourselves, we can still act *as if* nature has inherent value because we still should act *as if* we do. Evolutionary survival, especially in the Anthropocene era, may be directly correlated to the heuristic fiction of universal inherent value.

Regan's ethics leads to complex ontological questions and he well recognizes the "incompleteness" of his work.[66] When taken into the domain of environmental applied ethics, the logical subtleties of sets and individuals, wholes and parts, quickly dilutes the social impact of individual inherent value beyond our species. We end up debating whether we have "direct duties to, say, individual blades of grass, potatoes, or cancer cells."[67] Regan is clear: "Not all living things are subjects-of-a-life."[68] But is this tactical restriction a regress or progress stopper? Is the equality of inherent value the truth of being? The issue is a perennial and knotty one. Regan tends to emphasize the current importance of breaking the species ethics barrier, at least with other mammals of one year or older. He does, however, explore the idea of there being a further distinction within inherent value that, besides subject-of-a-life, can encompass other living individuals, their collections, and physical systems. There are subjects-of-a-life (moral agents and patients) with inherent value and there is another, unnamed, vague category of inherent value that can extend to fish, birds, poultry, plants, insects, microorganisms, elemental processes, ecosystems, and so on. "The very possibility of developing a genuine ethic *of* the environment," Regan admits, "as distinct from an ethic *for its use*, turns on the possibility of making the case that natural objects, though they do not meet the subject-of-a-life criterion, can nonetheless have inherent value."[69] The things of existence reveal their own inherent value.

Nature, as total and all therein, is a subject of some kind, having inherently valuable *subjects-of-existence* of all kinds. Hierarchies of inherent

---

66. Regan, *Case for Animal Rights*, 246.
67. Regan, *Case for Animal Rights*, 242.
68. Regan, *Case for Animal Rights*, 245.
69. Regan, *Case for Animal Rights*, 245.

value are relative to subjects-of-existence. We and other mammals inhabit one such circuit—*subjects-of-a-life*—but to think this is *the* significant moral limit is to deny the distribution of hierarchies of inherent value given equally to all subjects-of-existence, including this *blade of grass*. The struggle for co-existence means being simultaneous co-means and co-ends for each other. We must be very careful how we go about conferring inherent value outside our species. Regan's new moral order encounters immediate ecological concerns. If he and the similar minded are successful, individuals within the new mammalian hierarchy of subject-of-a-life will gain their rights. Hierarchy, however, presents an ecological model of subjugation. Protecting the individuals of one species, e.g., seals, taking them out of the traditional space of human rational utilization, may mean that other non-subject-of-a-life species, e.g., cod and capelin, are utilized more intensively by the seals and other mammals with less inherent individual value. The result may be disastrous for the seals, other mammals, i.e., starvation, and their ecosystem.

Deontology is about human good intentions towards individuals that manifest inherent value; its contribution to applied environmental ethics is substantial and, on the humanistic prohibition of cruelty, operational in most legal frameworks. Deontology, for most of us, defines our current system, but ecological ethics seems to demand a different kind of thinking and relating to the natural world, other than that premised on the immorality of cruelty or on chosen cross-species individuals with certain capacities.

Virtue

Virtue ethics is character-based ethics. Virtuous individuals act for the common good. Aristotle's *Nicomachean Ethics* provides its principal foundations. There is a purpose to human life: Self-realization or happiness. A fulfilled life means having a good character. In order to develop good character, there must be cultivation of emotional, intellectual, and practical virtues. Happiness is activity that conforms to virtue. A virtue occupies the mean of feeling, thought, and action. Vices are excesses and deficiencies, too much or too little. For example, self-respect is a virtue. Vanity is a vice of excess. Humility is a vice of deficiency. Some emotions, ideas, and activities do not admit of a mean, do not participate in degrees of more and less because they are immoral in themselves, e.g., murder, theft, and envy. It is not their excess or deficiency that is bad. There is an indwelling baseness that makes it impossible to ever do right in performing them.

Virtues are operative habits that enact a good character; they develop in the practical trials of time and situation. Persons of good character tend towards happiness. In Aristotle's text, we read: "Thus, the virtues are implanted in us neither by nature nor contrary to nature; we are by nature equipped with the ability to receive them, and habit brings this ability to completion and fulfillment."[70] Virtue individuates a good or excellent human being; it is our self-work of practical reason, constantly seeking the determinate "median relative to us" within the variable or indeterminate situations of our lives.[71] To develop virtue we must completely avoid inherently wrong activity, even if it results in our suffering and death. We must learn to successfully navigate the vices of excess and defect by choosing, relative to us, "a mean which is defined by a rational principle."[72] There are multiple ways of going wrong but, for the practically wise individual, only one way that is right and good. The mean is the proper limitation that can be found within changing situations, a variable invariant, that virtuous people can locate and enact. The good in a situation belongs to the determinate, the balanced limit; evil to the unlimited of excess and the scarcity of privation.

Aristotle's ethics navigates the impasse between individual as individual and individual as a member of a community. He initially sides with the former. There is a clear refusal to diminish the primacy of individuals. The good is embodied within a thing's nature: An end-directed activity to be achieved. Human virtue facilitates an individual's drive for self-perfection. Virtue clears the way for the successful actualization of capacities. But individual self-perfection is not antagonistic to community. Self-interest is neither reasonable nor virtuous; rather, individuals find their true end only in service to their community. Within the social milieu of happiness, virtue is the self-work of practical habit, but individual happiness is incomplete, leading to justice in relation to others as its end. Justice requires action by a virtuous individual on behalf of something-other-than-herself. Justice is the end of ethics; it is the common or communal realization of an individual's self-development of virtue. The logic of the common good is twofold: Ethics is temporally prior to justice because it is developed in the experience of physically embodied and socially embedded individuals, but justice is that for the sake of which individual ethics exists. Virtue finds its perfection of being in justice. Aristotle describes justice as "complete virtue," "the highest of all virtues," whereby "every virtue is summed up," but "not in an

---

70. Aristotle, *Nicomachean Ethics*, 17 (1103a20–25).
71. Aristotle, *Nicomachean Ethics*, 42 (1106b5).
72. Aristotle, *Nicomachean Ethics*, 43 (1107a1).

unqualified sense but in relation to others."⁷³ He draws, I think, the distinction between the individualism of virtue and the communitarianism of justice quite plainly:

> Justice is complete because he who possesses it can make use of his virtue not only for himself but also in relations with others; for there are many people who can make use of virtue in their own affairs, but who are incapable of using it in their relations with others. . . . Justice alone of all the virtues is thought to be the good of another, because it is a relation to our fellow men in that it does what is of advantage to others. . . . The best man is not one who practices virtue towards himself, but who practices it toward others, for that is a hard thing to achieve. . . . The difference between virtue and justice in this sense is clear from what we have said. They are the same thing, but what they are (in terms of definition) is not the same: insofar as it is exhibited in relations to others it is justice, but insofar as it is simply a characteristic of this kind it is virtue.⁷⁴

The transition from a virtuous life to a just life marks the perfection of an individual human being. We change from acting on behalf of ourselves to acting on behalf of others. The rare achievement of the latter becomes, for Aristotle, the defining feature of those fit to participate in political power.

How does Aristotle's abiding framework help us with our current ecological situation? Certain contents of character will constitute environmental virtues and vices. Perfected individuals are required to serve the justice of the common ecological community. What are environmental virtues? How can we develop them? Are traditional virtues amenable to the environmental situation? Are new virtues required? How do we envision the ecologically just community? This aspect of applied environmental ethics is new, but individual practical reason seems indispensable for ecological morality. "Good environmental character," Ronald L. Sandler claims, "leads to proper action."⁷⁵ An environmentally virtuous person accommodates within her character "the richness and complexity of human relationships and interactions with the natural environment and provides guidance on concrete environmental issues."⁷⁶ In other words, she is more likely to do the right thing. Like traditional virtues, environmental virtues adjust themselves to the measured habits of feeling, thought, and action. Environmental virtues,

---

73. Aristotle, *Nicomachean Ethics*, 114 (1129b30).
74. Aristotle, *Nicomachean Ethics*, 114–15 (1130a1–12).
75. Sandler, *Character and Environment*, 2.
76. Sandler, *Character and Environment*, 5.

then, are responsive, justified, and productive. For example, a responsive virtue would be attention or attunement to the immediate ecological surroundings. Vices would include the remoteness of self-interest (a lack) and overwhelming involvement (an excess).

Virtue ethics has well-known problems with adaptability. Lisa H. Newton points out: "It is unable to give concrete advice to a neophyte in a novel situation."[77] Virtue is always understood as part of a tradition, a continuity of similarly arising circumstances.[78] When novel situations arise, traditions undergo radical change, making it difficult to identify what counts as virtue and vice. The environmental crisis may be discontinuous with human-centric traditions of virtue ethics. Who really knows how to be good in this context? But, perhaps, it is enough, for now, to know we still should be. Finding the environmental good is the great political project of our time. There is a strong indication that a new tradition of individualistic virtue ethics is emerging concurrently with the search for an ecologically just common good. Mark Sagoff aptly summarizes our current movement to environmental virtue:

> Our environmental goals—cleaner air and water, the preservation of the wilderness and wildlife, and the like—are not to be construed, then, simply as personal wants or preferences; they are not interests to be "priced" by markets or by cost-benefit analysis, but are views or beliefs that may find their way, as public values, into legislation. These goals stem from our character as a people, which is not something we choose, as we might choose a necktie or a cigarette, but something we recognize, something we are. These goals presuppose the reality of public or shared values that we recognize together, values that are discussed and criticized on their merits and are not to be confused with preferences that are appropriately priced in markets. Our democratic political processes allow us to argue our beliefs on their merits.[79]

There is a significant question on the viability of our current political forms of life. The ecologically just community may require a radical alteration, not just of individual habits, but the entire edifice of global political economy.[80] Without justice, virtue is impossible. The absence of an ecologically just community means individual virtues become *priced* lifestyle preferences in a competitive market of worldviews. Virtue without its just end becomes

---

77. Newton, *Ethics and Sustainability*, 34.
78. See MacIntyre, *After Virtue*, 204–26.
79. Sagoff, *Economy of the Earth*, 28–29.
80. See Connelly et al., *Politics and the Environment*, 54–93.

hollow and elusive. The true specter that haunts us all now is ecology: Can our existing institutions, our centuries-old traditions of the good and just life, really cope and sufficiently change? Or is the dangerous process of collapse and experimentation with reconstruction inevitable?

Given the dependency of virtue on collective justice, Aristotle may again be worth listening to on political economy; not, of course, in all the details of his conclusions for a properly ordered society, which are often neither morally justifiable nor practically retrievable in any significant sense. In our space of crisis, however, perhaps it is best to begin examining perspectives crucially otherwise than our own, especially those that situate the place of nature within human political economy very differently than we currently do. If we must achieve successful changes, it is prudent to start gathering our diverse material as soon as possible. It is beyond the scope of this work to give a full examination of Aristotle's political economy of nature, but I will sketch a few of his pertinent, fertile and, given the presuppositions of our political economy, disruptive ideas.

Aristotle occupies a time of great turmoil in the social order of traditional Greece. One of the crucial deviations is the birth and eventual dominance of exchange value. Greece, as Paul Millet observes, is encountering the full and unprecedented force of at-interest "professional money lending."[81] In this economic light, then, Aristotle is working out his moral and political ideas within and, principally, against this radical process of change: The unlimited acquisition of money dissolves the idea of limit as the good, produces the illusion of human self-generation, independent of the natural world, and reverses the true order of being's value. Economic historians are still divided on the meaning of this Janus-faced era. Greece, in Aristotle's time, is suspended between its indigenous gift economy and the rise of a nascent market economy. As Scott Meikle points out, although Aristotle's response to this rapidly decentering "co-presence" begins "with the Charities, he ends with exchange value."[82] Free marketers cheerlead the latter as the embryonic creation of the modern world; its discovery marks the final order of things. Many others lament for the loss of the former's potentialities. Ecologically aware political economists, specifically, are warning us that, by reform or collapse, any serious confrontation with the ecological crisis will *begin with exchange value and end with the Charities.*[83]

In Aristotle's Greece, the great revolutionary infection of money undermines the embedded good of self-sufficiency or *autarky* provided by

---

81. Millett, *Lending and Borrowing in Ancient Athens*, 189.
82. Meikle, *Aristotle's Economic Thought*, 156.
83. See Klein, *This Changes Everything*, 64–161.

agriculture and other productive human arts. Instead of heterogeneous activity from qualitatively different abilities to qualitatively different needs, we get a conversion to homogeneous production, favoring the quantitative surplus of a few kinds of exchange objects or commodities for trade. Trade brings back money and foreign commodities to offset severely restricted and uniform local production. Dependency on foreign markets signals a new structure based on money and its representatives—traders, lenders, and their increasingly influential social-legal apologists, the sophists. The latter are propagating the philosophical creed that justifies the new system—relativism (individual and cultural) and the maximal utility of self-interested accumulation as the good life.

The culture and power of the Greek port of Piraeus, epicenter of commerce, threatens to dissolve the traditional social-ecological order aligned with Athens.[84] The engine of the cultural trauma is the novel power of the commodity. Useful goods are not commodities because they are quantitatively limited and comprehensive in quality, driven by the needful ends of a community. Commodities are presented as disconnected from their origin in the fragile limitations of nature; they generate the deception that they can be unlimited in quantity. Exchange objects are like the money they embody, seeking to corrupt with unlimited desires those that consume them. The desire for the unlimited is generated in the circular, repeating, and self-amplifying relation between commodity and money. "Since their desire for that is unlimited," Aristotle says of commodities, the corresponding "desire for the thing that produces it is equally unlimited."[85] The desire for more commodities generates the desire for more money.

There is a crisis of value. Acquisitive desire is confused with legitimate need. The great inversion means excess is praised, not condemned, vice is virtue; practical reason no longer serves as an individual's measure of necessary or good limits. Rather, Aristotle witnesses this system turn "all such capacities into the forms of art of acquisition, as though to make money were the one aim and everything else must contribute to that aim."[86] Profit, money, especially money made from the commodity of money itself, is the unlimited good. Limits on production, consumption, and appetites are vices. An excessive individual serves the justice of her community, which is dedicated to the good of unlimited money: The cult of *growth*. The consequences of this novel system include social inequality, debt slavery and dispossession of goods, competitive elimination of ancient solidarities,

---

84. See Garland, *Piraeus*, 58–68.
85. Aristotle, *Politics*, 26 (1258a1).
86. Aristotle, *Politics*, 29 (1258b5).

criminality and, most edifying, environmental degradation from imposing ever higher levels of production, of ever decreasing kinds of commodities, on natural capacities. As it turned out "among the Greeks," according to an always historically perceptive Karl Marx (†1883), "the full development of money appears only in the period of their dissolution."[87]

Aristotle's reception of the Greek transformation offers us a series of challenges and insights that may be relevant to our ecological situation. If we understand our current globalized political economy as a colossal analogue of the ancient Greek crisis and reject it as unsustainable, we must engage the adventure of seeking an ecologically just "political association" that secures virtuous "material conditions of life" for its individual members.[88] Aristotle, with some astonishment, becomes our contemporary. For virtuous individuals to flourish, society must be "instituted for the purpose of attaining some good."[89] For an alternative to what we now call market society or globalization, then, we must reexamine, counter Rawls, its accompanying idea of absolute individuals. Plurality without any constitutive common good means each individual embodies her own version, not just of virtue, but the just social end or worldview that makes an individual's virtue meaningful and operational. But the ecological renewal of the common good should not erase the value of individuals. Aristotle provides adequate (if not excessive) ontological safeguards in this direction.[90]

What the ecological good certainly means, though, is a reversal of the acceptance of the unlimited as the good. Virtue and justice, in its ecological sense, reaffirms the practical reason of limitation for individuals and communities. Vice for individuals and injustice for communities are properly repositioned: "True wealth," Aristotle claims, which "suffices for a good life is not unlimited."[91] Ecologically sustainable communities cannot be dedicated to the unlimited end of money, which Aristotle calls perverse *chrematistic*. The good form of human life is corrupted by a false valuation of its truly useful relationships. Éric Alliez deepens this insight by defining the contagion of the unlimited as a crisis of reference and time. In order for commodification to work as a conventional program, the temporal

87. Marx, *Grundrisse*, 103.
88. Aristotle, *Politics*, 39 (1260b27).
89. Aristotle, *Politics*, 1 (1252a).

90. Some thinkers position, with strong historical justification, Aristotle as the perennial ground for the Rawlsian kind of extreme political nominalism, individualism; see Pabst, *Metaphysics*, 1–53. I tend to follow the more aporetic reading of Aristotle, where the difficulty is the mutual preservation of the commons and the individual; see Booth, *Aristotelian Aporetic Ontology*, 2.

91. Aristotle, *Politics*, 21 (1256b35).

limitations of natural things must be erased by, first, eliminating the idea that "reference governs sense and things govern words."[92] Or, as Deborah K. W. Modrak succinctly phrases it, Aristotle assumes that "the conceptual structure of language mirrors the structure of reality."[93] If this assumption of origination is denied, we have no natural ties to things, only conventional impositions. *Physis* becomes a category of *nomos*.

The power of our conventional signification, through money as the master-signifier, becomes an unlimited and uniform horizon of time that binds all things and blinds us to any outside alternative. There are only temporary monetary-technical restrictions on the drive to create equally as unlimited and uniform commodities. Money is the constitutive mediator between humans and between humans and nature. Money is value; it has, in Antonio Negri's striking phrase, not just "*demiurgic power* which through a sign modifies reality," but "general dominion over realization."[94] Money is the visible god of all potentialities, their profane principle of actualization. The limitations of the natural world signify complex, integral, and multiple time-space relations—their rhythms and folds. But they cannot, as a rule, be recognized as communicating their own meaningful and finite being to test our conventional use-truth value.

Alliez contends that Aristotle constructs his idea of time "on the basis of the denunciative determination of the empire of signs that is common to sophistics and to chrematistics in their work to subvert the order of things."[95] There is also good preliminary evidence to say that, along with his physics and metaphysics, he continues on with this program in his ethics and politics. Modrak makes a convincing argument that even the Law of Non-Contradiction, grounding Aristotle's logic, finds its impetus as a confrontation with "Protagorean relativism."[96] Protagoras (†c. 415 BCE) is the arch-sophist, representing the new power of exchange value and its accompanying philosophy that determines the true value or *measure* of all useful things (*chremata*) in relation to money and its individuating affects. For S. Todd Lowry, the "marketplace" ideas of Protagoras are "an embryonic expression of the utilitarian calculus upon which modern economic theory is based."[97] Being is that which can be priced—bought and sold. All else

---

92. Alliez, *Capital Times*, 18. On the re-emergence of the key concept of *chresis*, see Agamben, *Use of Bodies*, 24–30.
93. Modrak, *Aristotle's Theory of Language and Meaning*, 33.
94. Negri, *Marx Beyond Marx*, 35.
95. Alliez, *Capital Times*, 20.
96. Modrak, *Aristotle's Theory of Language and Meaning*, 60.
97. Lowry, *Archaeology of Economic Ideas*, 131.

is nothing of any significance or it is an incomplete resource, needing an appropriate monetary-technical process to make it into a commodity. Truth itself is relative to perspective but, as is usually lost in a culture so saturated with this presupposition that it automatically signifies liberation, the perspectives of individuals with money are really those that count; only they have the unlimited means to create, sustain, and destroy realities.

If Aristotle is, in any way, a helpful guide, then the ecologically just society must first somehow de-commodify. We must *get real* about value, limits, and the presence of nature's self-communication as the locus of our meaning and truth. Aristotle's naturalized economy remains an intriguing intimation of what is needed to establish environmental virtue ethics for individuals. A much more recent correspondent, perhaps, is found in Karl Polanyi's (†1964) economic ideas. Polanyi, like Aristotle, is convinced that commodification is a disastrous and conventional fiction, obscuring the reality of things—there is an outside, an alternative, a common good for us and nature that can and should be aligned with. Writing near the end of World War Two, he ascribes the catastrophe experienced in the first half of the twentieth century to a series of increasingly extreme protectionist reactions against "the utopian principle of a self-regulating market."[98] On behalf of "man, nature, and productive organization," Polanyi envisions post-war progress as "the shifting of industrial civilization onto a new nonmarketing basis"; it is an unprecedented opportunity to institute a new system by de-commodifying human beings and nature.[99] "To take labor out of the market," for example, "means a transformation as radical as was the establishment of a competitive labor market."[100] Polanyi is optimistic that most "of the massive suffering inseparable from this transition is already behind us," and that the debris of the old liberal laisse-faire economic order contains within itself the "makeshifts" of "great and permanent institutions."[101] Polanyi's *great transformation* of de-commodification, needless to say, did not happen.

Given the global retrenchment of neo-liberal ideology in the last quarter of the twentieth century, we continue to operate on what Tony Judt (†2010) calls "the political autism of Hayek."[102] Any movement for a common good is socialism. All varieties of socialism are *roads to serfdom* for individuals and societies that are delusional enough to take them. The project

98. Polanyi, Great Transformation, 157.
99. Polanyi, Great Transformation, 170, 258.
100. Polanyi, Great Transformation, 259.
101. Polanyi, Great Transformation, 258–59.
102. Judt, Thinking the Twentieth Century, 345.

and process of universal commodification by the global market order is not the sickness; it is the cure. F. A. Hayek (†1992) claims, "our civilization depends, not only for its origin but also for its preservation, on what can be precisely described only as the extended order of human cooperation, an order more commonly, if somewhat misleadingly, known as capitalism."[103] To abolish it is to simultaneously abolish the individual freedoms that it gave rise to. To prevent its spread is to prevent eventual emancipation in cultures that are adopting it. There is no alternative. Whatever freedom there is for individuals owes its existence to the self-regulating market. But if Polanyi, prefigured by Aristotle, is right about the need to de-commodify, nature specifically, the *massive suffering* that may move us to transform our system appears to be just beginning. The contradictions continue to multiply. More de-regulated free trade agreements, transferring economic sovereignty to international corporations, accompany ever more global warming and other environmental agreements. We must trust green global capitalism to self-regulate.[104] There is, again, no alternative—yet.

Nomos is a category of *physis*. We belong to it, not it to us.

What *price* will have to be paid before we rediscover this *priceless* truth?

Holism

Environmental amendments have been added to three principal ethical theories: Consequentialism, deontology, and virtue. As we have seen, the latter is, at best, an ethics and politics in the making. The former two center their attention on the emancipation of select species of animals on the grounds of shared capacities, which has a controversial scientific basis.[105] As C. S. Lewis (†1963) understood it, animals experience "a succession of perceptions," but not "a perception of succession" to confer meaning on suffering.[106] The latter *conscious* ability distinguishes human pain from the suffering of other animals. We are truly different in this respect. Any cross-species ethics that overlooks this difference of consciousness has a shaky, anthropomorphic foundation. There may be cause for humanistic concern because the misanthropic tendency of animal rights has been linked with fascist regimes.[107] As

---

103. Hayek, *Fatal Conceit*, 6.

104. On the apparent collapse of this world order and its ensuing—even more socially and ecologically problematic—division of the world into competing *civilizational states*, see Pabst, *Liberal World Order and Its Critics*, 81–98.

105. See Budiansky, *If a Lion Could Talk*, 194.

106. Lewis, *Problem of Pain*, 133.

107. See Ferry, *New Ecological Order*, 93–107; Sax, *Animals in the Third Reich*, 110–23; Closmann, "Nazi Germany's Reich Nature Protection Law," 18–42.

certain other elect species go up in value as legal persons, rights and value go down for certain categories of human beings.[108] This guilt by association is, for the most part, reactionary hysteria, fueled by increasingly questionable scientific presuppositions, but the historical precedent does not help animal rights' current credibility as a political experiment.

Even if we reject the foundations of animal ethics on behalf of humanism, we still judge our morality by the extension of its merciful inclusion. We still must reject despotic anthropocentrism. Our progress will be measured by our treatment of the poor, weak, damaged, and excluded. Regarding other animals, a change of heart seems well underway across a broad spectrum of worldviews. *True humanists* may still be rightfully required to be vegan and animal advocates.[109] Given the suffering and injustice exposed by Singer, Regan, and a growing chorus of activists, the call to mercy may be enough for rights and protections. The real problem emerging here is the high eco-political hopes attached to applied environmental ethics, e.g., Monbiot, to mobilize and save the planet. The politics of de-commodification could be a vital project for virtue ethics, but at present there seems little movement in this direction. Utilitarian and deontological applied ethics remain basic conceptual tools for environmental management and public policy beyond the animal rights question.[110] The latter two traditions have tremendous difficulties, though, expanding ethical consideration beyond certain individual animals within select or higher species. Duties to lower creatures, flora, and systems of air, water and land are only indirect. Moral concern arises only insofar as their condition adversely affects other individual creatures that are owed moral consideration. Managerial ethics of *our resources* offers scant critique of the presuppositions of current political economy.

Many theorists and activists claim we need a new prescriptive ethic for the environmental question. Our inherited ethical traditions are part of the problem because they are saturated with individualistic and human-centric notions that cannot address the ethical status of the Earth as a whole. The present crisis is unprecedented. It calls for an innovation beyond accepted ethical forms. This view is put forward by the movement known as *deep ecology*. Ethics must not only include other animals; it must encompass the whole Earth. This self-regulating global sum of all ecosystems is named

---

108. See Proctor, *Nazi War on Cancer*, 129.
109. See Scully, *Dominion*, 95–100.
110. See DesJardins, *Environmental Ethics*, 38–124.

Gaia by James Lovelock.[111] Its physical components are atmosphere, cryosphere, hydrosphere, and lithosphere. The Earth is our largest and most complex moral subject.

The moral philosophy of Deep Ecology claims it can address a truly planetary crisis. Since its publication in 1949, Aldo Leopold's (†1948) *A Sand County Almanac* remains a core text for Deep Ecology. Leopold, professor of wildlife management at the University of Wisconsin, develops a philosophical position known as biotic holism. The entire ecosystem of the Earth has moral status. *Holism* means individual members are morally derivative to the welfare of the whole species, or ecosystem; what Leopold calls the community of energy or, simply, *land*. For example, wild-life managers conserve species and ecosystems. The sacrifice of individuals can be justified for the health of both. Species count, specimens not so much. Leopold's position is evolutionary. The environmental crisis is an opportunity for advancing ethics from human beings to the land. The land includes all elemental processes and the flora and fauna that depend on them. To Leopold, moral evolution means the enslavement of property relations is replaced by ethical consideration and rights. He, too, along with Aristotle, calls for de-commodification on a planetary scale:

> The first ethics dealt with the relations between individuals; the Mosaic Decalogue is an example. Later accretions dealt with the relation between the individual and society. The Golden Rule tries to integrate the individual to society; democracy to integrate social organization to the individual.
>
> There is as yet no ethic dealing with man's relation to land and to the animals and plants which grow upon it. Land, like Odysseus's slave-girls, is still property. The land-relation is still strictly economic, entailing privileges but not obligations.
>
> The extension of ethics to this third element in human environment is, if I read the evidence correctly, an evolutionary possibility and an ecological necessity.[112]

Both human history and the natural world reveal progressive co-operation or symbioses as the engine of mutual survival. We must now evolve ethically. "The land ethic," Leopold claims, "simply enlarges the boundaries of the community to include soils, waters, plants, and animals, or collectively, the land."[113] We move from conqueror of the Earth, with no obligations, to being a biotic citizen of the planet. Leopold says, "The conqueror

---

111. See Lovelock, "Gaia as Seen through the Atmosphere," 579–80.
112. Leopold, *Sand County Almanac*, 218.
113. Leopold, *Sand County Almanac*, 219.

role is eventually self-defeating."[114] We are kicking to pieces the hill of which we are king, destroyed and enslaved by our own destruction and enslavement: "Land-use ethics are still governed wholly by economic self-interest, just as social ethics were a century ago."[115] Leopold calls to our ecological conscience. An ethical relation to our environment must establish biotic rights regardless of the presence or absence of economic advantage for us. The land must be emancipated from being mere property to rights bearing agency. What is the nature of this new relation? Leopold advocates an ethical relationship with the biotic pyramid of energy—the lines of complex and inter-dependent uplifts of energy distribution—the total ecosystem, Gaia, whose functioning depends on the co-operation and competition of its diverse parts. One of these parts is the human species. We must act in a way that recognizes the biotic rights of all other species and processes that constitute the whole planet. This new ethics is "a kind of community instinct in-the-making."[116]

Leopold's land ethic, however, has been accused of eco-fascism. The ecological system, the ecosphere, is the reality of which we are only one part. We are embedded in it and totally dependent on it. The welfare of all creatures is subordinated to the integrity, stability, and beauty of the biotic community. One subordinates individual human welfare, in all cases, to the welfare of the biotic community. The reduction of individual value to a function of the collective makes the land ethic, according to Tom Regan, a type of "environmental fascism."[117] From the point of view of the land ethic, continues William Aiken, "massive human diebacks would be good. It is our duty to cause them. It is our species' duty, relative to the whole, to eliminate 90 percent of our numbers."[118] "Anything we do to exterminate excess people," Frederick Ferré exclaims, "would be morally 'right'! To refrain from such extermination would be 'wrong'!"[119] "Taken as a guide for human culture," he concludes, "the land ethic—despite the best intentions of its supporters—would lead to classical fascism, the submergence of the individual person in the glorification of the collectivity, race, tribe, or nation."[120]

---

114. Leopold, *Sand County Almanac*, 220.
115. Leopold, *Sand County Almanac*, 224.
116. Leopold, *Sand County Almanac*, 219.
117. Regan, *Case for Animal Rights*, 362.
118. Aiken, "Ethical Issues in Agriculture," 269.
119. Ferré, "Persons in Nature," 18.
120. Ferré, "Persons in Nature," 18.

J. Baird Callicott defends Leopold's land ethic: "The holistic Leopold land ethic is not a case of ecofascism."[121] He does admit, though, that conservationists like Leopold are "professionally concerned about biological and ecological wholes—populations, species, communities, ecosystems—not their individual constituents."[122] And Leopold's planetary moral imperative does define right and wrong in, strictly, holistic terms: "A thing is right when it tends to preserve the integrity, stability, and beauty of the biotic community. It is wrong when it tends otherwise."[123] Leopold's holism is a community of energy. Human beings are one part; a problematic one right now. If right and wrong action relate only to the well-being of the biotic whole, human claims to exception and preservation at all costs must be denied. We must become more natural and join the rest of the community of energy, where "the only truth is that its members must suck hard, live fast, and die often."[124] "In the biotic community," Callicott informs us, "there are producers and consumers; predators and prey. One might say that the integrity and stability of the biotic community depends upon death as well as life; indeed, one might say further, that the life of one member is premised on the death of another."[125] Thus, we cannot argue that "killing of fellow members of the biotic community is, prima facie, land ethically wrong. It depends on who is killed, for what reasons, under what circumstances, and how."[126] This kind of description is very troubling. If death is an imperative for biotic survival, does it entail allowing the necessary steps to eliminate masses of human beings in the name of planetary integrity and stability?

Callicott defends Leopold on the grounds that the land ethic is an accretion. The land ethic amends or extends our accumulated social ethics; it does not replace them: "With the advent of each new stage in the development of ethics, the old stages are not erased or replaced, but added to."[127] Callicott concludes: "The duties attendant upon citizenship in the biotic community (to preserve its integrity, stability, and beauty) do not cancel or replace the duties attendant on membership in the human global village (to respect human rights)."[128] But whose rights take priority in the conflict between competing communities of interest, regarding the health of the

---

121. Callicott, "Holistic Environmental Ethics," 128.
122. Callicott, "Holistic Environmental Ethics," 123.
123. Leopold, *Sand County Almanac*, 240.
124. Leopold quoted in Callicott, "Holistic Environmental Ethics," 124.
125. Callicott, "Holistic Environmental Ethics," 124.
126. Callicott, "Holistic Environmental Ethics," 124.
127. Callicott, "Holistic Environmental Ethics," 125.
128. Callicott, "Holistic Environmental Ethics," 125.

biotic whole? For example, there are over six billion people on the Earth that exist at the increasingly unsustainable expense of all other communities within the biotic whole. Callicott says the *ranking of interests problem* can be resolved by recognizing that the land ethic is a first order principle, needing further supplements for operational clarity.

There is a key distinction between the first second-order principle (SOP-1) and the second second-order principle (SOP-2) within the idea of moral pluralism. SOP-1: "Obligations generated by membership in more venerable and intimate communities take precedence over those generated in more recently emerged and impersonal communities."[129] For example, caring for family usually takes precedence over the performance of civic duties. However, there is the supervening condition of SOP-2: "That stronger interests generate duties that take precedence over duties generated by weaker interests."[130] For example, if an enemy invades your country, your obligation to sacrifice for the collective would override your obligations to family. So, by extension, if, in a time of environmental crisis, the health of the biotic community is stronger than strictly human or personal concern, SOP-2 overrides SOP-1. "Thus, when holistic environment-oriented duties are in conflict with individualistic human-oriented duties," Callicott reaffirms, "and the holistic environmental interests at issue are significantly stronger than individualistic human interests, the former take priority."[131] Still, this perspective should raise considerable concern. Who gets to decide when biotic interests should override human interests, i.e., SOP-2 overrides SOP-1? When individuals are not recognized as having inherent value, what are the limits on overriding human interests? Unlike an exceptional political crisis, like invasion, the environmental crisis is so dispersed, multifaceted and complex that permitting sacrifice of living individual human beings is truly extreme. Less overtly, this point of view may stop humanitarian aid in order to decrease human numbers among the already weak and vulnerable on behalf of the biotic whole.

Callicott's second order principles works out Leopold's position. It is undecided whether he succeeds in sufficiently amending what he elsewhere admits may be its "inhumane or antihumanitarian consequences," flowing from "a logically consistent deduction" of the land ethic's premises.[132] If he has not succeeded, Callicott admits the "magnitude and monstrosity" of

---

129. Callicott, "Holistic Environmental Ethics," 126.
130. Callicott, "Holistic Environmental Ethics," 126.
131. Callicott, "Holistic Environmental Ethics," 128.
132. Callicott, "Conceptual Foundations of the Land Ethic," 206.

what follows: "If this is what membership in the biotic community entails, then all but the most radical misanthropes would surely what to opt-out."[133]

ENVIRONMENTAL COSMOLOGY

Not surprisingly, perhaps, many thinkers are extremely critical of deep ecology and applied environmental ethics and rights in general. "Contemporary ecological sensibilities," David Harvey argues, "have their roots in traditions that also prompted the Nazis to be the first radical environmentalists in charge of a state."[134] As indicated previously, Luc Ferry draws the questionable conclusion that there is a direct correlation between the ascendancy of the inherent rights of nature and the descent of inherent human rights. He claims that it is not an accident that the Nazi regime passed laws in the 1930s to protect and enfranchise with rights animals and natural places while at the same time rescinding rights to certain different types of people.[135] Whether or not there is a direct link, a causal relationship, or merely guilt by coincidence, between extending the franchise of rights to animals and wild places and the demise of millions of human beings will not be decided here. The situation maintains a complex and particularized political history that is not easily extended to our current situation.[136]

Having environmental concern does not mean you are a fascist. Far from it. Defending the status quo is not an option. But the specter of the relationship, accompanied by growing and intense conceptual critique, surrounding current offerings in this category of environmental philosophy, has led some environmental thinkers within the deep ecology movement to reject the land ethic along with doctrines of animal rights. There is recognition that this crisis is rooted much deeper than any well-intentioned but, possibility, dangerous ethical manifesto can easily address. Arne Naess (†2009) is right to call for a radical change in our philosophical outlook, affecting "basic economic and ideological structures."[137] But just because it is needed does not mean you can simply call it into being and, more problematically, will such a doctrine on a world not prepared for it. Ideas, like everything else, must find their way in life of their own accord. Consequently,

---

133. Callicott, "Conceptual Foundations of the Land Ethic," 206.

134. Harvey, *Justice, Nature, and the Geography of Difference*, 171.

135. See Ferry, *New Ecological Order*, 99.

136. See Uekoetter, "Nazis and the Environment," 1–16; Dominick III, "Völkisch Temptation," 81–115.

137. Naess, "Defense of the Deep, Long-Range Ecology Movement," 264.

there is a strong inclination towards *ecological metaphysics*; what I inelegantly call *environmental cosmology*. Joseph R. DesJardins tells us:

> Inspired by ecology, Deep Ecologists seek to develop alternative worldviews that echo ecological insights into such issues as diversity, holism, interdependence, and relations. Deep ecology traces the roots of our environmental crisis to fundamental philosophical causes. Solutions can only come from a transformation of our fundamental worldview and practices. These fundamental questions include what is human nature? What is the relation of humans to the rest of nature? What is the nature of reality? These questions are traditionally identified as *metaphysical* questions. Deep Ecology, therefore, is as concerned with questions of metaphysics and ontology (the study of what is) as it is with the question of ethics.
>
> Deep Ecologists trace the cause of many problems presupposed by the dominant philosophy of modern industrial society. The transformation that we have mentioned involves a shift away from the dominant model and onto an alternative worldview that takes its inspiration from ecology. Deep Ecology is concerned with a *metaphysical ecology* rather than a scientific one.[138]

Metaphysical ecology, according to Bill Devall and George Sessions, is not so much a creation of something new as it is a "reawakening of something very old."[139]

Cosmology is the third category of philosophy of environment. The Greek term *kosmos* means the order of things. *Logos* means sign, disclosing an intelligible pattern of relationships. When we grasp the logos of something, we understand it. Cosmology, then, is what we know as the common organization of things. This category examines potent and embedded operating principles of culture. Environmental cosmologies place the order between human being and the rest of being: Ethics depends on them, not them on ethics. They are collectively given horizons of meaning, which drive, shape, and legitimate what we do. Such cosmologies impart our sense of sacred and profane; they define what is and is not permitted in our relationship with the environment. A destructive order will not easily go away just because we suddenly perceive its effects. The main lines of current thought are narrative and theogony.

---

138. DesJardins, *Environmental Ethics*, 218.
139. Devall and Sessions, *Deep Ecology*, ix.

Narrative

Many thinkers argue environmental cosmologies are consequent upon social practices. They are not antecedent, directive, and operational. Their function is to justify the human transformation of the environment. Human action to secure the material conditions of life requires a cultural script to normalize such production. We need a therapeutic story to tell us what we are doing is both expected and right. An environmental cosmology is a legitimating metanarrative.[140] This perspective assumes a certain claim about human nature, which is not a contingent metanarrative.

Humanity is a productive force, not merely a passive evolutionary product. The transformation of our surroundings, according to Karl Marx, is "only the manifestation of a force of nature."[141] Environment is "the primary source of all instruments and objects of labour."[142] Human mediation divests environment of its estrangement and externality. We create ourselves in and through what environs us; it is what we do *by nature*. The social production of environment satisfies the demands of a community, existing in a distinctive time and place. At different stages in the development of social production, we will encounter different types of environmental cosmologies, legitimating certain practices and de-legitimating others. For example, hunter-gathering societies tend toward animism and pantheism, whereas industrial societies often embrace a world-picture of disenchanted mechanism.

Environmental metanarratives are arbitrary communal adaptations. They evolve to justify novel, hence unsettling, social actions as they contingently arise in the production of the material conditions of life. Narratives adapt themselves to shifts in social production. For example, the *Genesis* account of creation can be understood as marking the transition from the relative innocence of hunter-gathering to the dominance of nature and animals required for agriculture. These cultural accounts are neutral. Any cultural narrative can be adapted to legitimate any social practice as the need arises. An environmental cosmology is a pragmatic metaphor, which Richard Rorty (†2007) well describes as "a tool which can be used by many different hands," for equally as many projects; it offers a "way of using reality," which amounts to "justification which meets the demands of that community."[143] Therefore, metaphysical ecologists work under the assumption that the

---

140. See Sessions, "Deep Ecology as Worldview," 207–23.
141. Marx quoted in Schmidt, *Concept of Nature in Marx*, 16.
142. Marx quoted in Schmidt, *Concept of Nature in Marx*, 15.
143. Rorty, "Truth without Correspondence to Reality," 23, 33, 37.

environmental crisis requires the deconstruction of prior metanarratives now deemed harmful. In this free place, we must elevate cross-cultural alternatives, rehabilitate older metanarratives, and create new ones to meet the current *demands of that community* envisioned by the sustainable social production of life.[144]

Theogony

Another school of thought portrays environmental cosmologies as active. They set the order of relations between humanity and the environment. We do not produce them through our action on environment. Our action on environment is determined by environmental cosmologies. The prior narrative position of human self-creation still assumes we are authors of our own nature. Self-production depends on re-translating narratives of our place in nature. But we are still humanizing the world with the projection of our ideas. Environment is a canvas wiped clean. We are painting something different, but we remain the creator. Nature is still a social category. Therefore, nothing much has changed. It is still all about us and our imposition of a collective will to create a new environmental world-picture. What has emerged in metaphysical ecology is a competition over guiding images. New or rehabilitated metanarratives are offered in order to topple the old environmental cosmology and, consequently, install themselves as the new metanarratives of sustainable production. Narrative environmental cosmology is green ideology. It is another banner or brand for yet another utopian, anthropocentric project. "The postulation of a planetary ecological crisis," to David Harvey, "repeats in negative form the hubristic claims of those who aspire to planetary domination."[145]

The alternative view presents environmental cosmologies as *tautegorical events*.[146] They come as themselves. The cosmological process repeats, recreates, and realizes itself through human consciousness. These autonomous configurations order our representations and actions. They encompass not only our past, but also our present and future. Environmental cosmologies are operational and deeply rooted, which is evidenced by the logic of the same offered by narrative activists advocating more human willpower and better technology to *fix* the environmental situation. Our crisis

---

144. See Merchant, *Reinventing Eden*, 201–4; Gare, *Postmodernism and the Environmental Crisis*, 139–51.

145. Harvey, *Justice, Nature, and the Geography of Difference*, 194. See also Geus, *Ecological Utopias*, 247–61.

146. See Cassirer, *Mythic Thought*, 1–26.

re-enacts an anthropocentric *theogony* (origin and genealogy of the gods) of unfettered will to re-create the world in our image. Evil, in Christian and other traditions, is excess of self-assertion. Humanity's independent power seeks to replace God by attempting to be our own creator and savior. Human selfhood strives to be the ground of the whole. "Self-will can elevate itself above everything," Martin Heidegger (†1976) remarks, "and only will to determine the unity of the principles in terms of evil."[147] Humanity has become "a reversed god, of the counterspirit."[148] There are disastrous consequences for the community of being: "But reversal and upheaval are nothing merely negative and nugatory, but negation placing itself in dominance. Negation now transposes all forces in such a way that they turn against nature and creatures. The consequence of this is the ruin of beings."[149] The rage of human independency eclipses all things, severing and refusing all relations, binding us to its destiny. Humanity as self-grounding subject leads to the annihilation of all that is not the subject and, ultimately, to our own destruction. This nihilistic cosmology is the *radix* of our environmental crisis.

Heidegger claims we are currently *enframed* by technology. The historical epoch marked by technology is the endgame of nihilistic cosmology; its essence is the full matrix mastery, transformation, and destruction of the planet. Everything (and everyone) is conscripted as standing-reserve resources. The modern centrality of the human subject collapses; we join the sway of all Earthly things: Commodities on behalf of global projects beyond our control. Within this frenzy of determination, philosophy's role is therapeutic preparation and intimation. Humanity is swept along in the undertow of *post*-modernity's cosmological process. We are not in command of this unfolding. We cannot significantly amend its vector and momentum by more of the same. Individual freedom in the face of such inevitability becomes an event of willing not to will. *The will that wills nothing* is an awakening from within. The negation of the will by the will absolves the self of its compulsive drive for technological actualization. The self is re-potentialized. Freedom gives re-potentialization. Such comportment situates an individual's existence. One is now beyond the modern environmental cosmology of domination. In this cleared place, the open, we await, enduring the end of collective evil.

We prepare for the event to come, which may give our new way of being with the Earth, or something else entirely. The coming order between humanity and the Earth cannot be willed into existence. "Freedom," Heidegger

---

147. Heidegger, *Schelling's Treatise on the Essence of Human Freedom*, 142.
148. Heidegger, *Schelling's Treatise on the Essence of Human Freedom*, 143.
149. Heidegger, *Schelling's Treatise on the Essence of Human Freedom*, 143.

says, "governs the open"; it is not the property of beings: "The essence of freedom is *originally* not connected with the will or even the causality of the human will."[150] Freedom is submission to the event to come, where only the pure, those with "the quiet heart of opening," may be given a sign, a hint, of the next cosmos, as this one continues to disintegrate.[151] Heidegger speaks of *the future ones*: "Those strangers alike in heart, equally decided for the bestowal and refusal that have been assigned to them. The ones who bear the staff of the truth of beyng."[152] The future poem of place is a whisper on the wind, a gentle incantation of the fourfold to come: Earth, sky, divinities, and mortals.[153] Things are restored to their proper needful relationships—beyond the dark night of the commodity. Again, we hear Aristotle's call for the goodness of limits within our use (*chresis*) of the world.[154] Our way of embracing being returns to sacramental giving, *the immanent grace of the Charities*. We, if we are the future ones, may be able to go home, again.

There may be an alternative to the narrative activist's naïve faith in the same and the quietest submission to the apocalypse of *beyng*. Prior traditions of environmental meaning are certainly more deeply rooted than a quick and intentional change of metanarratives can effectively address. Current environmental visions do appear to be just another call to our utopian will-to-power; another modern wolf in new age sheep's clothing. But we are not beyond reasonable amendment and responsible action; this, too, seems an overly hasty and self-serving conclusion. The depth of the problem requires a counter-depth of analysis. The tradition from which it sprang can be identified; its poisonous streams critiqued and avoided. Other tributaries must be discovered, and carefully surveyed for travel. As Heidegger once *hinted* through the voice of Friedrich von Hölderlin (†1843), "But where danger is, grows / The saving power also."[155]

---

150. Heidegger, "Question Concerning Technology," 25.
151. Heidegger, "End of Philosophy," 68.
152. Heidegger, *Contributions to Philosophy (Of the Event)*, 313.
153. See Mitchell, *Fourfold*, 3–23.
154. See Mitchell, *Fourfold*, 294.
155. Heidegger, "Question Concerning Technology," 34.

TWO

Metaphysics and Preliminary Statement of the Problem

This chapter examines R. G. Collingwood's *An Essay on Metaphysics* (1940). Metaphysics is critico-historical thinking on absolute presuppositions. This approach is then employed as philosophy of environment. The environmental crisis emerges from a certain coalescence of cultural assumptions. A preliminary examination of these presuppositions is given through the pioneering work of Lynn White Jr. and John Passmore.

COLLINGWOOD'S *ESSAY*

Collingwood claims metaphysics is the science of absolute presuppositions. This idea finds its ground in Aristotle's *Metaphysics*. It is well known that Aristotle presents the science of pure being as first philosophy. Metaphysics is presupposed by every other science, but it is the last one from a student's perspective because it requires a comprehensive mastery of many other sciences—temporally posterior and ontologically prior. Collingwood, however, rejects Aristotle's science of pure being. A science must have a subject matter to think about in an orderly way. The subject matter of ontology is the limiting case of complete abstraction from the contents of the real: Nothing. He concludes that a science without a determinate subject matter is no science at all. There cannot be a presuppositionless science of pure being. Metaphysics without ontology must restrict itself to Aristotle's less familiar second definition of metaphysics as "the science which deals with the presuppositions underlying ordinary science."[1] What are *underlying presuppositions*?

Aristotle's *second way* directs Collingwood back to Plato's (†347 BCE) *first way*, which is found in the latter's *Republic* (533c).[2] Plato distinguishes between two ways of thinking: Mathematical (*reasoning from*) and dialectical (*reasoning to*). To presuppose is to place one thing beneath another. To *reason from* an opening condition is an act of hypothetical confidence because what is presupposed must be simply accepted as self-evident. A presupposition cannot be conceivably reduced to another that is more primary. From this trusted *given*, we place one thing atop another—we construct our configurations of derived suppositions. Presuppositions, therefore, are logically prior to suppositions that depend on them. They are foundational for inferences: If this presupposition is held, then that supposition follows. Unlike presuppositions, suppositions are subject to truth values. Does this supposition necessarily follow from its presupposition or not? If the presuppositions are accepted, the suppositions rightfully drawn from them are true. Mathematical reasoning leaves no room for alternative conclusions; it is logically compulsive, where the nature of inference is such that nobody can affirm the premises without being required to affirm the conclusion. Freedom of choice, nonetheless, is still conserved by deductive inference in two ways: We are not compelled to make the initial assumption because the starting-points of demonstrative reasoning are not themselves demonstrable; and if we do make a choice on a starting-point, we are still at liberty to stop thinking whenever we like. What we cannot do is to make the initial assumption, to go on thinking, and to arrive at a conclusion different from that which is demonstratively correct.

Dialectic reverses the mathematical order of thinking; it is a process of destabilizing privation, ceasing to presuppose accepted hypotheses: "It means causing the non-supposal of what has been supposed."[3] *Reasoning to* a better presupposition requires rational demolition, undercutting various candidate presuppositions: Un-giving demonstrates contradictions, consequences, and limitations. Taking presuppositions away means the suppositions built upon them crash, like a house of cards, into unintelligibility. By bringing to light presuppositions and then removing them, a fertile breach is enacted. In this open place of non-presupposing, reflective thought and its dialectical amendment can occur. *We* are free to follow what happens when we cancel presuppositions or presuppose their opposite.

1. Collingwood, *Essay on Metaphysics*, 11.
2. See Collingwood, *Essay on Metaphysics*, 156.
3. Collingwood, *Essay on Metaphysics*, 158.

There is a responsibility placed upon us to move past one presupposition to another more worth having. Dialectical advance means probationary and divergent presuppositions undergo a series of transformations by affirmation, denial, and revision, converging on a closure presupposition, behind which no more basic one can be found. Plato's realism means the path of inquiry must be relied upon to reach its own unimpeded and spontaneous conclusion: *The Good* of the thing under review is self-displayed, expediting an encounter with its reality and, if required, action on behalf of its truth. Ultimate reality communicates itself to our collective intuition. There is an undistorted reception of that which is being and truth. If, in order to begin, mathematics must assume a presupposition, then dialectic, in order to end, must reach a decisive presupposition. Bedrock or absolute presuppositions open and close, respectively, mathematics and dialectic.

Collingwood follows Plato by accepting that knowledge of presuppositions provides us with a means to disentangle our "knot of thoughts" and, accordingly, provides the basis for the "systematic thinking we call science."[4] The neglect of Aristotle's second way in favor of ontology has resulted in widespread confusion and disdain regarding metaphysics; it also exposes us to significant cultural risk because we lack a serious science dedicated to finding and understanding the basic presuppositions of human action. A presupposition is a constitutive relationship to a world. The employment of assumptions without challenge and reflection signals unwarranted obedience to current authority. It often creates a toxic atmosphere of ignorance and illusion that is unable to either recognize or change its principles of action, particularly when our educational formation "cannot or will not" provide us with a science to distinguish "what people are doing" from "what they think they are doing."[5] Our regulating blind spots may lead us to social and, now, ecological perdition because we know not what we do.

Collingwood presents a logic of question and answer as a fresh start for metaphysics. A skilled dialectician can ask the right questions in the right order. Questions and their answers create patterns, demonstrating the logical operation of presuppositions. Every statement, every proposition, answers a question. Every question rests upon a presupposition, without which the question could not arise. For example, when a medical doctor asks, "What does this symptom mean?" she presupposes that the symptom has a meaning. Such a presupposition is considered relative because it, too, can be the answer to a question; namely, "Has this symptom a meaning?"

---

4. Collingwood, *Essay on Metaphysics*, 22.
5. Collingwood, *Essay on Metaphysics*, 19.

Relative presuppositions are subject to being confirmed or denied. An *absolute presupposition*, by contrast, "is one which stands, relatively to all questions to which it is related, as a presupposition, never as an answer."[6] Collingwood employs *a* sense of cause to illustrate an absolute presupposition for "the *practical sciences of nature*," which include "engineering or medicine."[7] Cause means an antecedent condition that can be directed either to enable or avert a certain consequent. This meaning of cause comprises "control of nature."[8] In full form: "Here that which is 'caused' is an event in nature, and its 'cause' is an event or state of things by producing or preventing which we can produce or prevent that whose cause it is said to be."[9] In her diagnosis of a certain symptom, a medical practitioner will determine if it is a cause of a specific illness. The primary concern of the doctor is to cure and prevent diseases. A presupposition is relative if it can be abandoned without undermining the area of practice within which it is formulated. A diagnostic test of a symptom, for example, can fail to be confirmed, to have an identifiable medical meaning, without endangering the practice of medicine itself. But an absolute presupposition, by contrast, cannot be forsaken without overthrowing the very foundations of this practical science. An absolute presupposition—like causation above—grounds its conditions of possibility, the very form of investigation that makes it what it is. It must be presupposed if medicine is to be possible. We can still, of course, form the logically trivial grammatical question, "Does this symptom have a cause?" But an affirmative answer must be presupposed; a denial dissolves the system of regulative and constitutive rules that define medical practice.

An absolute presupposition is a basic condition that founds and sustains a course of investigation; it cannot be identified with any question or answer because it indicates that which accounts for the whole process. This generalized antecedent, then, sets the boundaries on a consequent domain of analysis. Within the limitations that it places, an absolute presupposition functions as a common integrating principle of thought and action: A game's rule. Certain questions can be pursued for answers; certain others are excluded. An absolute presupposition is that by which correct judgments on propositions may be formed. It is the measure of what is measured. It is a rule that obtains and assembles the internal order of propositional sets. We distinguish and unite on its basis. The art of weaving similarity and distinction at their precise jointures, distinguishing the part that combines from

6. Collingwood, *Essay on Metaphysics*, 31.
7. Collingwood, *Essay on Metaphysics*, 286, 287.
8. Collingwood, *Essay on Metaphysics*, 286.
9. Collingwood, *Essay on Metaphysics*, 285.

the part that separates—truth from falsity, sense from nonsense—depends on its ground of meaning.

An absolute presupposition can never be made an answer to a question because it is what makes questions possible: "Metaphysics is concerned with absolute presuppositions. We do not acquire absolute presuppositions by arguing; on the contrary, unless we have them already arguing is impossible for us. Nor can we change them by arguing; unless they remain constant all our arguments would fall to pieces. We cannot confirm ourselves in them by 'proving' them; it is proof that depends on them, not they on proof."[10] Absolute presuppositions are logically prior to our experience of reality; they cannot be proven true or false from observations within a reality they presuppose. They are not derived from experience because experience depends on them for intelligibility: "An absolute presupposition cannot be undermined by the verdict of 'experience,' because it is the yard-stick by which experience is judged."[11] It governs experience, but not as a different conception of the same set of independent things, but as a different conception of a different set of things. Absolute presuppositions will logically determine the being of things under their domain of analysis. They structure an area of experience or knowledge. The way we know makes a constitutive difference to the thing known. We are, therefore, not involved in an eliminative competition of explanations on the nature of the same reality. We cannot consistently claim to know things as they are in themselves. Each domain of inquiry and endeavor maintains itself as a complementary expression of reality with its own distinctive set of principles and intentional objects for investigation.

As Giuseppina D'Oro rightly concludes, Collingwood's metaphysical method concerns the detection and demonstration "that certain absolute presuppositions are explanatorily necessary," which, "involves showing that such presuppositions are logically related to the form of experience they make possible."[12] *Explanatory necessity* refers to a criterion (or a set of criteria) *needed* to explain a feature of experience within a domain of inquiry; it governs entities internally, providing a field of significance or propositional framework that has the power to give rise to an exact and relevant set of questions. There are rules for forming significant statements and for testing, accepting, and rejecting these bounded statements. Metaphysics is a "criteriological discipline," whereby, "the philosopher does not discover some

---

10. Collingwood, *Essay on Metaphysics*, 173.
11. Collingwood, *Essay on Metaphysics*, 193–94.
12. D'Oro, *Collingwood and the Metaphysics of Experience*, 6.

ultimate truth about reality, but the principles that govern experience."[13] "The attempt to verify absolute presuppositions by assigning them a truth value," D'Oro contends, "would be as nonsensical as the attempt to answer the question 'how long is the standard metre?'"[14] Different explanatory contexts require different criteria. The criteria of one form of investigation are not universally applicable in all explanatory contexts. The rules of chess, for example, are not applicable to hockey.

Collingwood's idea of metaphysical analysis is a second-order undertaking to excavate, identify, and clarify the ideas absolutely presupposed by first-order practitioners: "The analysis which detects absolute presuppositions I call metaphysical analysis."[15] To A. W. Moore, this approach to knowledge indicates "that making sense of things, at the highest level of generality, involves making sense of making sense of things."[16] Moore draws a "direct connection" between his conception of metaphysics and "metaphysics as Collingwood conceives it"—that is, both acknowledge the science of absolute presuppositions presents *metaphysics as history*.[17] Absolute presuppositions should not, then, be misunderstood as static and timeless, and it is on this decisive point that Collingwood breaks with Plato's real presence method of dialectical exposure, removal, and progression towards a collective experience of timeless being. Progress through contradiction is a purely temporal affair. Emil L. Fackenheim (†2003) points out the radical nature of Collingwood's claim: "R. G. Collingwood said nothing new when he affirmed that metaphysical presuppositions are unprovable. But that the validity of these presuppositions depends on their historical setting was a revolutionary assertion on his part."[18] The *historicizing of Plato* means Collingwood unsettles classical dialectic with a logic of question and answer that can investigate past ideas in the present. Real presence dialectical participants, who embody their innate presuppositions, are exchanged, to a great extent, for historical investigations into the absolute presuppositions of people no longer in existence.

Absolute presuppositions occur in a dynamic complex of "historical facts," which Collingwood calls "a constellation."[19] Absolute presuppositions hold internal logical relations between each other as categories in a

---

13. D'Oro, *Collingwood and the Metaphysics of Experience*, 17.
14. D'Oro, "Unlikely Bedfellows?," 813.
15. Collingwood, *Essay on Metaphysics*, 40.
16. Moore, *Evolution of Modern Metaphysics*, 496.
17. Moore, *Evolution of Modern Metaphysics*, 496.
18. Fackenheim, "Metaphysics and Historicity," 124.
19. Collingwood, *Essay on Metaphysics*, 66.

constellation, signifying that "each must be *consupponible* with all others; that is, it must be logically possible for a person who supposes any one of them to suppose concurrently all the rest."[20] A constellation is the categorical structure of our thinking, or the thought we are studying. To be the possessor of a constellation is not necessarily to be aware of its underlying configuration. For the most part, absolute presuppositions "are doing their work in darkness, the light of consciousness never falling on them."[21] Metaphysics is an endeavor to identify and interpret these deeply rooted preconceptions, casting some light on the creeds that commit us to certain kinds of action. It is the difference between an investigation into phenomena and an investigation into the principles that generate and govern phenomena.

In Collingwood's meaning of the word, *metaphysics* is the exploration of the historical constitution and transmission of absolute presuppositions: "An absolute presupposition" is not "a presupposition innate in the human mind. It belongs to the mental furniture of a certain age."[22] Metaphysics must take time seriously. We need to dispense with the idea that temporality is an impediment to be removed, allowing access to a fully unhidden realm of eternal verities. Time, development, and novelty are dynamic factors of constellations and their absolute presuppositions. Collingwood is quite clear: "Metaphysics is an historical science," "metaphysics is the science of absolute presuppositions," and "the metaphysician is a special kind of historian."[23] Analysis disentangles a constellation's absolute presuppositions during a particular period—in art, ethics, politics, science, and religion. Aristotle's second way must sever its ties to ontology, and "abandon once and for all the hope of being a 'deductive' or quasi-mathematical science."[24] The sister ship is free to set sail. The scope of its discovery is to be greatly expanded, encompassing "the past in its entirety."[25]

Metaphysics emphasizes study of the categorical stresses or "strains" within constellations that give rise to change—to history itself: "Where there is no strain there is no history."[26] This kind of investigation claims a special kind of insight. Metaphysical historians expose, classify, and analyze constellational strains found in the relational configurations of absolute presuppositions; they are made available to the intellect for understanding,

---

20. Collingwood, *Essay on Metaphysics*, 66.
21. Collingwood, *Essay on Metaphysics*, 43.
22. Collingwood, *Essay on Metaphysics*, 265.
23. Collingwood, *Essay on Metaphysics*, 60–62.
24. Collingwood, *Essay on Metaphysics*, 67.
25. Collingwood, *Essay on Metaphysics*, 71.
26. Collingwood, *Essay on Metaphysics*, 75.

but their discovery and logical examination cannot be subject to value claims. Constellations set the place or horizon where value claims can be legitimate answers to questions. Rex Martin, for instance, claims absolute presuppositions "are neither right nor wrong, true nor false; they just are."[27] To Errol E. Harris (†2009), the metaphysician's proper attitude is descriptive neutrality: "Evidence is sifted, marshaled and systematized and the facts are determined, not merely on hearsay or authority, but by direct scientific research," and, moreover, the practice of metaphysics "is not the study of a closed system. Its task is not system building. The metaphysician should not aim at completeness."[28] Open systems of thought are understood as they are, when and where they are; they are not to be closed by intentional revision, overlaying prescriptions that corrupt scientific data.

The metaphysician's object of analysis is constellational metamorphosis. The internal dynamics of change among historically situated absolute presuppositions are most evident during what Collingwood calls *phases*: "The essential thing about historical 'phases' is that each of them gives place to another; not because one is violently destroyed by alien forces impinging on its fabric from without by revolution, but because each of them while it lives is working at turning itself into the next. To trace the process by which one historical phase turns into the next is the business of every historian who concerns himself with that phase. The metaphysician's business, therefore, when he has identified several different constellations of absolute presuppositions, is not only to study their likenesses and unlikenesses but also to find out on what occasions and by what processes one of them has turned into another."[29] The movement of history is a subtle relationship between process, phase, and strain: "The dynamics of history is not yet completely understood when it is grasped that each phase is converted into the next by a process of change. The relation between phase and process is more intimate than that. One phase changes into another because the first phase was in unstable equilibrium and had in itself the seeds of change, and indeed of that change. Its fabric was not at rest; it was always under strain. If the world of history is a world in which *tout passe, tout lasse, tout casse*, the analysis of internal strains to which a given constellation of historical facts is subjected, and of the means by which it 'takes up' these strains, or prevents them from breaking it in pieces, is not the least part of an historian's work."[30] Collingwood's philosophy of history appears to operate as a directed system,

---

27. Martin, "Collingwood's Doctrine," 93–94.
28. Harris, "Collingwood on Eternal Problems," 232.
29. Collingwood, *Essay on Metaphysics*, 73.
30. Collingwood, *Essay on Metaphysics*, 74.

having a defined end and teleological process of some kind. Adepts of the design can comprehend the active and invisible form of history; it subsumes and guides all seemingly particular and contingent instances of strain and change towards its necessary conclusion. For the uninitiated comprehension is not possible. History is a disjointed and arbitrary process. Its interpretation is just as idiosyncratic and relative as the process itself.

Collingwood's thinking, however, takes a different turn than the above; he distances himself from both esoteric (necessary design) and relative historicism (no design), presenting an original *via media* between formulaic repetition and will to power imposition. Ordered relations amid constellational categories of absolute presuppositions are underdetermined and creative ways of life; these *civilizations* communicate their own recognizable structures. Collingwood's model of history is an evolutionary drama of human action: "A reformed metaphysics will conceive any given constellation of absolute presuppositions as having in its structure not the simplicity and calm that characterize the subject matter of mathematics but the intricacy and restlessness that characterize the subject matter, say, of legal or constitutional history."[31] Sources of change burst forth of their own accord within a particular phase. Proper metaphysical analysis can clearly and securely identify historical strains within constellations. Therefore, it can answer the question, "Why did they change?" But such an answer cannot claim to be a discovery of a complete plan. The results of metaphysical analysis do not translate beyond their limited province of study. Moreover, strains within the tissue of history are never fully reconciled. There remains a suspended residue, what Collingwood calls a "minority report," which may be the agent of change in another phase: "A civilization does not work out its own details by a kind of static logic in which every detail exemplifies in its own way one and the same formula. It works itself out by a dynamic logic in which different and at first sight incompatible formulae somehow contrive a precarious existence; one dominant here, another there; the recessive formula never ceasing to operate, but functioning as a kind of minority report which, though the superficial historian may ignore it, serves to a more acute eye as evidence of tendencies actually existing which may have been dominant in the past and may be dominant in the future."[32] Strains are variable. What counts as a recessive strain in one era or phase of history may not in another; it may govern as a normal rule within a constellation. A once hegemonic absolute presupposition can be rendered a minority report or recessive presupposition in yet another phase. History is the fragile and complex motion

---

31. Collingwood, *Essay on Metaphysics*, 77.
32. Collingwood, *Essay on Metaphysics*, 75.

of human action; the debris from one era becomes the building material of another.

Strains are contradictory remainders that can only be temporarily ameliorated. Unless a constellation collapses completely and is replaced by another, strains are never fully extricated from relations amongst its absolute presuppositions; they explain a constellation's historical development, distortion, and extinction: "Why, asks my friend, do such changes happen? Briefly, because the absolute presuppositions of any given society, at any given phase in its history, form a structure which is subject to 'strains' of greater or lesser intensity, which are 'taken up' in various ways but never annihilated. If the strains are too great, the structure collapses and is replaced by another, which will be a modification of the old with the destructive strain removed; a modification not consciously devised but created by a process of unconscious thought."[33] The visible or external site of historical change is merely the outward result of an inner transformation that is mostly unknown to those affected. The factually given variation is an outcome of its antecedent strain.

Collingwood claims we are not usually aware of our absolute presuppositions. We are not ordinarily mindful of changes in them. He concludes, such changes "cannot be a matter of free choice."[34] The creative motion of the unconscious accounts for change, but it is not an autonomous and occult faculty within the individual or collective psyche. Being unconscious of our presuppositions simply means not being aware of the logical foundation upon which we commit to an order of things. James Connelly makes the key corrective point: "For Collingwood, presupposing is a *logical* relation: we are unaware of our presuppositions in so far as we do not realize to what our statements logically commit us—the relation between our thought and its presuppositions is logical, not psychological or temporal."[35] Unconscious change is understood as a course of logical variance: "There is no 'process of unconscious thought' understood as the actions of an autonomous faculty (the 'unconscious') which works out the logical implications of these principles. Rather, the picture is of conscious thought working out in detail the consequences of principles of which it is unaware but nonetheless logically committed to by its inquiry and questions asked in the course of its inquiry. Similarly, change in absolute presuppositions is change resulting not from the activities of a supposed 'unconscious' but resulting from the activity of people thinking systematically according to certain presuppositions of

33. Collingwood, *Essay on Metaphysics*, 48.
34. Collingwood, *Essay on Metaphysics*, 48.
35. Connelly, *Metaphysics, Method, and Politics*, 105.

which they are ordinarily unaware but to which they are nevertheless logically committed."[36] This kind of determinism is tempered by a certain kind of reflective freedom available to individuals. We can comprehend our logical commitments and their accompanying strains, by proper metaphysics, but value judgment on the current motion of civilizational change is, for the most part, beyond the scope of metaphysics as a descriptive science.

Changes affecting presuppositions, in any case, are consequent upon "changes in the course of inquiry"—"in the sense that those committed to the form of inquiry in question were not consciously aware of changing or seeking to change those presuppositions, but *were* aware of the structure of their thought and its modifications, which modifications logically presuppose different presuppositions and thereby effect a change in those presuppositions."[37] But what changes the course of inquiry? Connelly does not directly address the question. An answer could be novel experiences. Systems of thought encounter certain impasses because of unique occurrences. These exceptions cannot be accommodated within a constellation as it is presently situated. The resulting strain amplifies until we are aware of it. We are aware of strain, not necessarily of the presuppositions themselves, still less of other candidates that may replace them. We are aware of the fact of undergoing modification. Sometimes it is a cataclysmic transition from an old to a new constellation; sometimes it is a minor adjustment of a constellation's absolute presuppositions.

Collingwood claims the metaphysician's task is to think the historical strain, making presuppositions visible. The metaphysician, however, occupies a historical moment within a constellation. Does this kind of thinking influence her present constellation? Furthermore, since the metaphysician is supposed to be the only one proficient enough to identify absolute presuppositions, it would seem to follow that she can propose an alternative presupposition. Collingwood would accept that a metaphysician might very well be affecting her own constellation, but not prescriptively with her metaphysics. Metaphysics is an exacting method, maintaining descriptivist ethics as its modus operandi. Normative judgments on the better or worse are outside its undertaking. The business of historical metaphysics, like other sciences, is proof; its aim is to establish evidence of the existence, effects, and transmission patterns of absolute presuppositions. Methodological neutrality must be practiced, or it ceases to be metaphysics. A metaphysician demonstrates absolute presuppositions, showing they are presupposed by a branch of human action. She suspends judgment, refusing to debate

---

36. Connelly, *Metaphysics, Method, and Politics*, 106.
37. Connelly, *Metaphysics, Method, and Politics*, 107.

Metaphysics and Preliminary Statement of the Problem

questions on why one presupposition is preferable over another. The role of metaphysics is limited to exact historical analysis; it enables specific disciplines to make their own progress in their own way, and in their own time. Science is given a clearer picture of its own nature.

We are usually not aware of the principles that inform our ways of life. Metaphysics provides inquirers with self-understanding, pinpointing and clarifying what we actually presuppose, as opposed to what we often mistakenly think we do. In an earlier essay, Collingwood tells us, "The business of sound theory, in relation to practice is not to solve practical problems, but to clear them of misunderstandings which make their solution impossible."[38] Even without value judgment placed upon them as either right or wrong, the correct depiction of presuppositions can still cause great disturbance: When our principles are exposed to simple conscious awareness, *the surprising fact that we actually have them*, we can anticipate that "people are apt to be ticklish in their absolute presuppositions."[39] 'Ticklishness' indicates that a deep existential nerve has been affected. "When an absolute presupposition is touched," Collingwood expects, "the invitation will be rejected, even with a certain degree of violence."[40] What goes without saying, when said, will not usually be welcomed. Without a science to familiarize ourselves with the grounds of our commitments, we tend to exempt these principles from criticism or even explicit statement, while assuming their truth and sufficiency to be confirmed without presumptions. Collingwood defines irrationalism as the tacit claim that "scientific thought has no presuppositions."[41] We refuse to answer questions upon what presuppositions our action rests and whether they can be justified because we take such things to be common sense, auto-explanatory or, simply, given. Instantaneous experience denies all reality to intercession by absolute presuppositions. There is immediate inference: If *this* given event or fact, then *that* spontaneous judgment. We could not draw the inference unless it was already there in the experience itself; we find or receive the implication, not make it. A rule of logical inference is enfolded in the facts of experience, and the mind merely unfolds its truth by way of observational generalization.

Collingwood, of course, criticizes "the positive faith in natural science" and, on the basis of the historical production of absolute presuppositions, reverses the "the first principle of positivistic metaphysics, the principle that all the presuppositions we can detect underlying our thought must be

---

38. Collingwood, "Political Action," 158.
39. Collingwood, *Essay on Metaphysics*, 31.
40. Collingwood, *Essay on Metaphysics*, 44.
41. Collingwood, *Essay on Metaphysics*, 146.

justified, and justified by an appeal to observed facts."[42] The given does not validate the rule. The rule validates the given. In his posthumously published lectures on history, we encounter a key statement: "Philosophy is reflective. The philosophizing mind never simply thinks about an object, it always, while thinking about an object, thinks also about its own thought about that object."[43] First degree thought involves an object or fact in the sense above. "Thought about thought" is "second degree" reflection.[44] In his work on method, Collingwood describes thinking of this kind as a "search not of facts to be accepted on authority but of conceptions in whose light the facts may be understood."[45] A metaphysician never simply accepts a fact; she relentlessly, while thinking about a fact, thinks also about her own thoughts about that fact. A fact is not intelligible without knowledge of its historical emergence and contextual enactment: The constellational contraction of its presuppositions. What underlying presumptions make this fact a fact? In advance of any observation, an inquirer's range of interpretation is fixed by a system of postulates, charting the limits of significant experience. Rules govern what makes sense. Prescribed theoretical conditions define an area for argument and research. As Richard Campbell well summarizes, within any form of human action, "many of the presuppositions remain unstated, but they powerfully influence the course of the investigation none the less, not least by defining the range of possibilities in accordance with which the inquiry can proceed."[46] Without metaphysics, no clear line can be drawn between the evidence and what is presupposed to generate the evidence. Collingwood's metaphysics, as portrayed here, presents a rule as logically prior to experience. Instead of forming a rule because we have observed it amid the facts, to have the capacity to recognize it is already to have the rule in some sense, but we usually cannot account for it because we lack an apt science to figure out the character of this *in some sense*—this absence leads to a crisis of irrationalism, denying the intercession of experience by historically saturated absolute presuppositions.

The claim of unmediated sense certainty of physical experiences is one thing, but to extend this justification to societal cases is quite another. Social facts do not impute on the senses the same way as physical facts do. The latter tend to be involuntary reactions of the body; the way, for example, light triggers a species-normative, biogenetic series of responses by the human eye.

42. Collingwood, *Essay on Metaphysics*, 151, 154.
43. Collingwood, *Idea of History*, 1.
44. Collingwood, *Idea of History*, 1.
45. Collingwood, *Essay on Philosophical Method*, 16.
46. Campbell, *Truth and Historicity*, 13.

Social facts may *enfold* physical properties as part of their reality, but they are *unfolded* by something else besides bare sensation. Murder, for instance, is a category of social experience that is proven by biological remains, a weapon, and so on, but unless another level is satisfied of its prescribed conditions for interpretation—concepts, laws, and procedures—the aggregate of physical evidence on its own is incapable of demonstrating the social fact of murder. It has no determinate sense. There is an overlapping and hierarchical distinction between sociality and physicality. The higher social level necessarily and always affirms the lower physical level. The lower level only partially affirms that higher level. The lower level includes one part of the higher level within itself, but disallows another part. A difference of degree gives way to a difference in kind. The *immediate* physical order of the senses remains intact, surely, but the meaning of what they give as evidence is governed by socially *mediated* rules. The social framework, to Collingwood, is coextensive with the historical motion of constellations, which is the object of metaphysics: "All metaphysical questions are historical questions, and all metaphysical propositions are historical propositions."[47]

Collingwood's *Essay* criticizes many theories for their lack of reflection on absolute presuppositions. In particular, the chapter entitled "The Suicide of Positivistic Metaphysics" answers the charges leveled against metaphysics by logical positivism; especially those found in the first chapter of A. J. Ayer's (†1989) *Language, Truth, and Logic* (1936), "The Elimination of Metaphysics."[48] Ayer's characterization of metaphysics consists of a "faculty of intuition," giving special access to "a reality which transcended the phenomenal world," which "leads to the view that the sensible world is unreal"; or that it is ontology, whose object is "Nothing."[49] Either way, metaphysical claims are "beyond the limits of experience," and "have no literal meaning" because "they are not subject to any criteria of truth or falsehood."[50] Therefore, metaphysicians are "devoted to the production of nonsense"; they are "duped by grammar" and "primitive superstition."[51] At best, metaphysics may express something "emotionally significant" for the author, but "until he makes us understand how the proposition that he wishes to express would be verified, he fails to communicate to us."[52] Much seems to hang on the *presupposition* of verification.

47. Collingwood, *Essay on Metaphysics*, 49.
48. See Ayer, *Language, Truth, and Logic*, 33–45.
49. Ayer, *Language, Truth, and Logic*, 33, 45, 44.
50. Ayer, *Language, Truth, and Logic*, 33, 44.
51. Ayer, *Language, Truth, and Logic*, 34, 45, 42.
52. Ayer, *Language, Truth, and Logic*, 36.

Verification is the process a proposition undergoes to assess its truth or falsity. A proposition that fails this test is false; if it passes, it is true. If a statement cannot be verified as being either true or false by an appeal to observed facts, it is a pseudo-proposition and, therefore, philosophical nonsense. Governing this process are the rules of empirical observation about "matters of fact" within the bounds of "sense-experience."[53] Verification can be strong or weak. The strong variety assumes the truth of a proposition "could be conclusively established in experience"; in the weak sense it means "if it is possible for experience to render it probable."[54] Ayer's broadside against what he depicts as metaphysics hinges on the experiential status of the rules of verification: Can they be verified by observation? If not, then, by Ayer's own definition, they are pseudo-propositions of metaphysics because these rules are 'not subject to any criteria of truth or falsehood.' That which can be true or false depends on that which cannot be empirically confirmed or falsified.

Ayer's visceral tone is fittingly explained by Collingwood: "In my own experience I have found that when natural scientists express hatred of 'metaphysics' they are usually expressing dislike of having their absolute presuppositions touched."[55] However, if metaphysics is what Collingwood says it is, Ayer's description of metaphysics misses the mark. Metaphysics is not ontology; it deals with this world, which is a historical world. Verification, then, is not unproblematic or unaffected by history. Collingwood demonstrates that the rules by which verification establishes truth or falsity, proposition from pseudo-proposition, sense from nonsense, cannot be verified from within simple observation itself. The facts of sense experience are historically positioned; they reveal nothing at an isolated instant. Observation is saturated with unobservable convictions by which verifiability is established or not established. Verification depends on these convictions, not they on verification. Ayer and others who put forward the view that "thinking involves no presuppositions at all, and therefore no absolute presuppositions," "reduces all thought to the standard of thinking at its most confused and unscientific level."[56] Collingwood concludes: "Any attack on metaphysics is an attack on the foundations of science; any attack on the foundations of science is an attack on science itself."[57] Although he is not directly acknowledged, Collingwood's defense of metaphysics, or at least the

---

53. Ayer, *Language, Truth, and Logic*, 35.
54. Ayer, *Language, Truth, and Logic*, 37.
55. Collingwood, *Essay on Metaphysics*, 44.
56. Collingwood, *Essay on Metaphysics*, 170–71.
57. Collingwood, *Essay on Metaphysics*, 170.

kind of criticism Collingwood puts forward on verification's higher order rules, appears to have had a significant impact on Ayer's later views, admitting "the principle of verification itself to be regarded, not as an empirical hypothesis," but as a special kind of methodological rule or "convention" that can be "neither true nor false."[58] The verification of experience, then, depends on what Collingwood calls an absolute presupposition. A methodological rule cannot be argued for, or argued against; neither demonstrated, nor tested—if we ask for reasons to believe it, or whether it is true or false, we commit a basic error of understanding. From whence rules?

Collingwood's Pragmatism

Ayer eventually rejects radical empiricism, taking "a pragmatic view of ontology. It is pragmatic in the sense that once it has been established by the appropriate criteria that a given set of propositions is true, and there is no means of translating out the entities which figure in them, the question whether these entities are to be reified is treated as a matter of convenience."[59] The criteria for a set of propositions, consequently, cannot be true or false, conceding their function, in Collingwood's vocabulary, as absolute presuppositions. Criteria create and order propositional environments. A proposition's reality—its meaning and role in relation to itself and all other propositions—belongs to its unique environment. External to its context, a proposition ceases to have significance. What, now, in Ayer's terms, is at issue, for Collingwood, is to explain the origination and task of *appropriate criteria*. If sets of propositions are governed by their criteria, what kind of principle or activity gives rise to criteria? More clearly, perhaps, is there a concept of *external reality* that accounts for the generation, preservation, and demise of criteriological frameworks? Ayer points us to pragmatic expediency.

Pragmatic criteria are often depicted as varieties of conventional apparatus. Rules are tools: Institutions of practice. Criteria are generalized commitments to act certain ways on certain kinds of occasions. Conventions embody procedural orientations in one's environment, emerging as suitable theories-methods of dealing with reality. These *habits of action* are determined by the ways in which they enable us to meet our needs. Different rules define different forms of subsisting. The existence of so many diverse frameworks of practice leads to the view that they are modes of adaptation. A rule's efficacy is tested by adjustments to meet needs. A convention holds

58. Ayer, *Language, Truth, and Logic*, 16–17.
59. Ayer, *Origins of Pragmatism*, 323.

only as long as it beneficially serves an individual and community. Just as needs are variable and multiple, so with criteria. When a rule becomes ill-adapted or in*convenient*, it must be abandoned for another.

Pragmatism is an experimentalist philosophy of novelty and invention in light of the future. Propositional truth is consequent upon criteria, criteria upon the efficacy of practical action. *Praxis is the radix of truth*. The present structure of our beliefs is provisional; it is a temporary fashion of thought and practice that must perpetually accommodate itself to different circumstances. A principle we live by today is not infallible. We must be ready to call it unjustified tomorrow. A thing's place in a system of purposes can be re-interpreted and employed for new ends. There is no necessary implication between origination and present (and future) utility. New experiences require the creation of new criteria. A good pragmatic theory or concept contains within itself a capacity to anticipate the future consequences of holding it to be warranted. A concept's full meaning includes the future tense. The ideal pragmatic framework is modelled on evolutionary mutation; it can adapt itself to an indefinite series of changing situations and purposes: A meta-apparatus of habit taking *per se*, readjusting old beliefs and constructing new ones. The present sheds a forward light on the world's expedient processes. We must learn to think and practice in the same prospective way.

The pragmatism suggested by Ayer's mature outlook does intersect many of Collingwood's historicist views. Reality manifests an irreducible temporal structure; it is not identified with essential presence. The absolute presuppositions that comprise reality are exhaustively tensed in their contexts. Structure is a result of temporal process. For believers in essential presence, by contrast, being is fully disclosed, but hiding itself, such that we must locate its constant replication by removing the veils of becoming's temporal distortion; occasioned by language, perception, authority, and so forth. The truly real is typically alike in all the manifold profusion of temporal worlds. Reality is complete and necessary, achieving its end at every single moment. We can, therefore, access its static structure of imperishable essences at any place and time because unchanged values forever repeat the same meaning. *Collingwood's metaphysics repudiates this interminable view: Reality is unfinished and contingent.* Meaning and historical process cannot be separated from one another. A meaning is a practical habit of life—an implicit vow or covenant—a measure by which a responsible structuring of our world is measured. History becomes the ground of justification for our invested confidence in someone or something. A prior allegiance will be continually tested by present and future circumstances, entailing a succession of different conventions. We can and often should lose faith *in criteria* because our trust has been violated. The trustworthiness of a thing is its reasonableness, which is ultimately decided by what becomes of it in the future. *Pragmatic truth*, like trust, is created, preserved, and lost in time.

Collingwood unties absolute presuppositions from unchanging forms, achieving pragmatic social pluralism: "It may help us to realize the arbitrary character of our own classifications if we study the very different classifications of the same material which other people have practised in the past or indeed still practise in the present."[60] Absolute presuppositions are merely parts of the *mental furniture* of a particular time and place, held for a limited period by an equally limited number of people. *Civilizations* are the results of diverse processes of change. Each civilization will have a distinct adaptive history—the invention, preservation, and disappearance of different practical rules—because each must respond to a unique sequence of events. Again, concerning ways of life, Collingwood would most likely approve these pragmatic conclusions because a "civilization is a way in which people live, and if the way in which people live is an impracticable way there can be no question of saving it. What has to be saved is not the way of living but the people who live in that way; and saving them means inducing them to live in a different way, a way that is not impracticable."[61] Metaphysics must veer away from the synchronic ontology of identity, of substance, and open itself to the primacy and richness of relational becoming: History. It can serve future adaptation by shining an intense and targeted *backward light* on our presuppositions.

Metaphysics is offered as a science of human action, communicating sufficient logical clarity, such that unviable presuppositions can be identified and exposed. In this cleared place, an affected community can evaluate replacements. In this pragmatic sense, Collingwood answers Michael Beaney's question on absolute presuppositions: "Can they not be verified by the success—in some relevant way—of the system as a whole?"[62] A form of life or civilization comprises a "system of thought," which is defined by "its constitutive rules, which cannot themselves by 'verified' but which play a role in the 'verification' of propositions within that system."[63] A civilization's pragmatic structure of absolute presuppositions can adapt or it can fail to do so. It is this *second degree* meaning of *verification* by human action that concerns metaphysics.

---

60. Collingwood, *Essay on Metaphysics*, 195.
61. Collingwood, *Essay on Metaphysics*, 226.
62. Beaney, "Collingwood's Conception of Presuppositional Analysis," 51.
63. Beaney, "Collingwood's Conception of Presuppositional Analysis," 57–58.

As reported in his *An Autobiography* (1939), the *rapprochement* between metaphysics and history stems from Collingwood's search for a humane science capable of overseeing the tremendous power of modern natural science being handed to increasingly volatile sectors of humanity. His internationally recognized contribution to the science of archeology informs the claim that, "historical problems arise out of practical problems. We study history in order to see more clearly into the situation in which we are called to act."[64] To understand what we did, we must understand why we did it: "For the archaeologist this means that all objects must be interpreted in terms of purposes."[65] Human actions express the intentions of agents capable of making decisions on rule following. "And when I speak of action according to a rule," Collingwood clarifies, "I shall be referring to that kind of action in which the agent, knowing or believing that there is a certain rule, applicable to the situation in which he knows or believes himself to be, decides to act in accordance with it. I shall not be referring to any kind of action in which the agent, though actually obeying a rule, is unaware that he is doing so."[66] *An Essay on Philosophical Method* (1933) also resonates with a pragmatic tone: "A principle of method is necessarily provisional," which "means constantly revising one's starting-point in light of one's conclusions and never allowing oneself to be controlled by any cast-iron rule whatsoever."[67] Present rules may be preserved but, depending on circumstances, they may also be changed; either by the emergence of new rules, or the resurrection of old ones. The gap between rule and situation requires practical judgment because "action according to rules always involves a certain misfit between yourself and the situation."[68] Agents, situations, and relations between the two manifest unique features. We have to choose between alternatives. The rules themselves cannot do this for us. Our decisions may not match the circumstances. These free or *pragmatic* actions make up the tissue of metaphysics as a historical science: The study of the human spectacle of successful variation and maladaptive disaster.

With great prescience, Collingwood identifies *a certain misfit* between modern natural science and a science of human action: "It seemed almost as if man's power to control 'Nature' had been increasing *pari passu* with a decrease in his power to control human affairs," and there is, consequently, "a plain fact that the ill effects of any failure to control a human situation

64. Collingwood, *Autobiography*, 114.
65. Collingwood, *Autobiography*, 128.
66. Collingwood, *Autobiography*, 102.
67. Collingwood, *Essay on Philosophical Method*, 52.
68. Collingwood, *Autobiography*, 104.

were more serious now than they had been before, in direct proportion to the magnitude of the new powers put by natural science, with divine indifference, into the hands of the evil and the good, the fool and the wise man."[69] Collingwood's proposed remedy, however, cuts directly against the grain of the received faith of many of his contemporaries: Scientism. The latter's program extends the reach of modern natural sciences; that is, to better understand ourselves, offsetting the power of the natural sciences that we possess, human sciences must become more, not less, united with methods of measure and mastery. We move the modern machinery of *problem solving* from nature to human nature. To Collingwood, this is a catastrophic mistake of methodology because we turn on ourselves the same techniques that drive the modern domination of nature. The positive program can only serve to unleash more ominous forms of violence (physical, biological, and social) into the domain of human relationships. The dangerous illusion of scientism is that "improvements in transport, in sanitation, in surgery, medicine, and psychiatry, in commerce and industry," resulting from past wars, can ameliorate or even sever their connections, "to the next war."[70] Now, of course, we factor in ecology, which multiplies the effects of the war-machine logic, expanding its list of past, present, and future casualties. Collingwood refuses to make this basic category mistake of scientism. He will not throw humanity into the crushing jaws of maximal efficiency; irrationally expecting an outcome of peace and enlightenment instead of the advance of domination.

Progress in the natural sciences threatens to overwhelm the adaptability of human action. Scientism's civilizational shipwreck is demonstrated by the First World War and, as Collingwood correctly anticipates in the late nineteen-thirties, its impending sequel promises to reach the limits of our capabilities for total war: A technological power to destroy the *all in all*—civilization itself. A new science not modelled on the natural sciences must be built, but what is this different undertaking, exactly? After a prolonged period of intense reflection, Collingwood recounts his breakthrough, "I completed my answer to the question that had haunted me ever since the War. How do we construct a science of human affairs, so to call it, from which men could learn to deal with human situations as skillfully as natural science had taught them to deal with situations in the world of Nature? The answer was now clear and certain. The science of human affairs was

---

69. Collingwood, *Autobiography*, 91.
70. Collingwood, *Autobiography*, 90.

history."[71] Collingwood takes certain elements of the contemporary Italian school of historical metaphysics in a progressive direction.[72]

With significant *archaeological* amendments, he positions himself to be the inheritor of Giambattista Vico's (†1744) original strange fusion of philosophy and history.[73] Vico founds the true modern science of human action. Many students remember Collingwood saying it was Vico who influenced him the most.[74] The Italian philosopher presents humanity as self-constituting; history is no longer viewed as the actualization of a pre-given form, but of our actually making that form by free activity. Human nature is not unchanging, simply received and repeated, whose goals and properties are knowable independent of temporal experience. Human nature is conventional; it is built in time. We are the molder and maker of ourselves—*verum et factum convertuntur*. To truly know something is to create it. Human beings are granted the power to freely create our own worlds, but we must also understand the proper use (again, Aristotle's *chresis*) of this power. If we do not, we will be destroyed by it.

Time as Freedom

Vico finds a zealous disciple in Collingwood. There is a fundamental divide between studying nature and human beings. Unlike nature, the world of civil society has certainly been made by human beings, and that its principles are, therefore, to be found within the pragmatic process of human history. Historical metaphysics is to the study of humanity what mathematics is to the study of the natural world. The humane science of historical metaphysics concerns the internal relations of free actions. Natural science directs itself to understanding the external relations of events. Astronomy, for example, presents us with a system of physical, cosmic events, but history presents us with a series of social acts. The external logical structure of events is different from the internal logical structure of actions. Natural

---

71. Collingwood, *Autobiography*, 115.

72. On Collingwood's controversial association with this philosophical school—Benedetto Croce (†1952), Giovanni Gentile (†1944), and Guido de Ruggiero (†1948)—see Connelly, "Collingwood, Gentile, and Italian Neo-Idealism in Britain," 205–34; Harris, "Introduction," 8, 18–19; Peters, *History as Thought and Action*, 481–559. As a young philosopher, Collingwood translated Benedetto Croce's *The Philosophy of Giambattista Vico* (1913).

73. For a synoptic background on Vico, see Verene, *Metaphysics*, 51–71.

74. See Boucher, *Social and Political Thought of R. G. Collingwood*, 11. Collingwood also recognizes a resonance with Confucianism's pedagogical "union of history with philosophy" (60).

science and historical metaphysics, then, give their own answers to different questions about two different worlds: Nature and society, respectively. There is a science that best describes the world of externally related events, and there is a science appropriate to internally related actions. Historically situated absolute presuppositions impart continuous and constitutive meaning-structures, contextualizing present free activity. We can, and must, to preserve our interiority of freedom, connect to the vast historical sweep of human action. *Human freedom is interchangeable with historical consciousness of a certain kind; one capable of providing a hermeneutical framework, shouldering the practical governance of our natural scientific power.*

The natural sciences concern objects not of our own creation. Despite our best reconstructions, usually in the laboratory, in order to find out how things have been made, and what principles govern their operation, our knowledge can only be externally related to physical nature. Our knowledge of the *external* world, therefore, will always retain immense intractability. The more we know, the more we realize we do not know. Although knowledge of physical nature offers great potential for the betterment of the human estate, the essentially alien quality of the object of our knowledge exposes us to colossal vulnerabilities by amplifying the uncontrollability of unintended (and intended) consequences. This risk situation is compounded when we make the methodological mistake that this is the best way to comprehend ourselves: We turn ourselves inside out, becoming estranged from our humanity along with the rest of creation.

An internal relation holds among parts of a whole; it is the common principle grounded in the parts themselves. The parts are not independent of each other—they are not self-supporting, having external relations between them. Put another way, occurrences and their common relation are not individually real. We cannot conceivably think of these occurrences without them being related by this very relation and no other; that by which a series is ordered is *convertible* with the operation that creates one action from another. Knowledge of one part will exhibit this relation to every other part and to the continuous whole. We should not accept that an internal relation is something that we can either grant or not grant, nor admit to it as tentative, because it remains the most comprehensive fact underlying our experience. A change in it signifies a change in us. Nor should we examine the question as though we were in a position either to assent to it or reject it by explicit individual decision; for it is the case that *we* are enveloped by its presence, and we are filled with it, even if we are unaware (or deny) its existence. We possess our very essence by virtue of our integral bond to it. Knowledge, after all, is separated from its object by some degree of otherness. But prior to that knowledge, which knows another as being itself other, there is a unitary connection with a constitutive relation, giving an indivisible form of belonging, of each to the other. In this way, the reality of free human action in the past is internally related to its repetition in present existence; as that which comes to be as actuality's condition and principle. The past gives meaning to the present and sets it free. Therefore, our self-creation of social form can and, more to the point, *should be* our most intimate object of knowledge.

History alone is known internally because we have enacted it by free activity. The rest of nature or, more exactly, our knowledge of it, can only be external because we have not made it ourselves. Only God can comprehend the whole of creation internally. Natural sciences can only give us power to master nature, but not the wisdom to govern our power. The intoxication of dominance fills us with the vain hope of penetrating to an inside knowledge of creation reserved only for God. Exteriorization means imposition by means of representational fields of our own construction, trespassing current limitations in pursuit of a perpetually elusive goal: To know the natural world as God knows it. Instead of being a steward of our history—the interior way of metaphysics and wisdom—we are caught in an asymptotic logic of accelerated power. We must change our scientific orientation from outer power to inner wisdom to govern our power. Civil societies are our most well-known object of analysis. By reflecting on how our actions contribute to the course of history, we can come to understand the presuppositions of our ways of life. Human institutions are the result of diverse human choices on values, needs, and utilities, undergoing constant adaptation in changing environments.

The conjoint course of human civilization, however, is not modelled on a timeless form of human nature, of which history is merely a moving shadow; but the autonomy of historical process does not fall victim to relativism either. To avoid both snares, historical action relies upon a deeper criterion—the motion and pattern of freedom on another level of time. Human action in time signifies the work neither of fate nor of chance, but of the necessity which is not determination and the liberty which is not accident. This kind of history, does not, properly speaking, have a *cause* at all; it is a creative activity, of free and intelligent minds. Civil institutions embody human freedom in a variety of ways, but they are also linked in their unfolding to a shared ground. The exact nature of this association remains vague and controversial in the thought of Collingwood, but its social role is more precisely defined: Decisions on needs and utilities that manifest a plurality of nations do not cut us off from our internal relationship with one another. The heterogeneity of self-made social ends does not erase the basic internal relatedness of human beings to one another. The progressive civilization of humanity, like nature within the natural sciences, can be grasped by a properly trained intellect, one trained in historical metaphysics. The diversity of human civilizations also means an ongoing drama of success and failure: Pragmatic adaptation and maladaptation. With the science of historical metaphysics, we are given a method to read our story of free creation; to become wiser in our societies by doing so.

Theologically considered, the process of free-pragmatic action occurs in the *economic*, not divine, order of time, requiring a philosophy founded and proved in *economic history*. Thus, we must grasp something of Collingwood's complex and fragmentary idea of time because it underpins his metaphysics of absolute presuppositions. History concerns the past, and the past is, in one sense, settled because its occurrence cannot be altered; it is a place of disappearance, where present appearance deposits itself. In another sense, though, the past's remnants are firmly embedded in the present's ongoing activity. The present is porous, open to the past's communication without being determined by it, connecting to it by means of the historical forms called *absolute presuppositions*. In a recently discovered set of manuscripts, Collingwood tells us, "the past is the substantial being of the present," but "the past is only known by analyzing its traces (evidence) in the present."[75] A "trace" is a "schema of the past, not the past in its full concrete existence."[76] A historicized concept (*'schema'*) relates to the present by being "the existentializing of this concept into individual spatio-temporal form."[77] "The notion of trace," Paul Ricoeur (†2005) explains, "is *left* by the past, it *stands for* the past, it 'represents' the past."[78] "The trace" is a symbol or schema because it "takes the place of *(Vertretung)* the past, absent from historical discourse."[79] Past reality is communicated by absolute presuppositions to an interpreter's present actuality. Historical metaphysicians can detect and decipher these deeply coded frameworks. The trace of an absolute presupposition, then, is a "special form of activity," constituting a "unique and non-recurrent culmination"—"the genesis of a being which at every moment is but the presence of its own past."[80] But the repetition of the past does not determine present *action* as a closed pattern.

---

75. Collingwood, *Principles of History*, 140–41.
76. Collingwood, *Principles of History*, 135.
77. Collingwood, *Principles of History*, 135.
78. Ricoeur, *Reality of the Historical Past*, 2.
79. Ricoeur, *Reality of the Historical Past*, 2.
80. Collingwood, *Principles of History*, 200–201.

Collingwood claims *historical reality* is the pre-condition of free action in the present: "The gates of the future are open."[81] Further: "History is this gathering-up of the whole past into the present, as determining that novelty which the present, by thus being itself, creates."[82] The past's concrescence of presuppositions in the present is a "power both liberating and constraining"; it "consists in the resolution of existing into happening," where "happening" is creative autonomy in the present.[83] The present's "*pure act posits itself and its own presupposition at once. The past belongs to the present, not the present to the past.*"[84] To be determined means "the present is the caused effect of the past," but in the human mind, "the past is the analysed content of the present. Thus what the mind is and what it does are its past and present respectively."[85] What we are includes all that we have done and all that has happened to us, but the present moment is not a mere determined result of these past things. "The past living in the present" is not the cause of a "fixed and unchangeable" effect called "the present"; it is the emancipating *form* of present action.[86] The logical motion from antecedent to consequent provides the worldview, the determinate range of possibilities offered by absolute presuppositions, within which self-determination takes place. Historical time is liberated time, releasing its own autonomous sphere of actualization.

Today's action is free *because* it emerges from yesterday's reality. *History* means the reality of the past establishes the free activity of the present. The present "is always *more than what it is*. It is this (i.e., past) as to content: as to form, it is free activity."[87] "The past," Collingwood maintains, "does not possess the present, the present possesses its own past. The possessive act by which the present affirms itself affirms its own past."[88] The primacy of the present means "this *positedness* of the past is part of the selfpositingness of the present. This selfpositing of the present is what always and necessarily escapes the historian."[89] "The 'free will'" that chooses a course of action "only becomes a reality," Collingwood observes, "when it has ceased to be

---

81. Collingwood, *Principles of History*, 194.
82. Collingwood, *Principles of History*, 204.
83. Collingwood, *Principles of History*, 204.
84. Collingwood, *Principles of History*, 220.
85. Collingwood, *Principles of History*, 220.
86. Collingwood, *Principles of History*, 193. On the German idealist tradition of freedom as form, which Collingwood follows in many significant respects, see Schindler, *Perfection of Freedom*, xiii–xxvi.
87. Collingwood, *Principles of History*, 193.
88. Collingwood, *Principles of History*, 193.
89. Collingwood, *Principles of History*, 141–42.

an act and has passed into fact."[90] *Facts are re-potentiated acts.* Lastly: "This limitation appears as a *contingency*: i.e., an incomplete determination of the present by the past"—the past "only determines *possibilities* between which the present may choose."[91] The dependence of past reality upon present action is the principal property of history. The past is the product of judgment, a modification of present experience, setting into place historical reality: The historical schema of facts and their absolute presuppositions. The freedom of present action means something new is set free, something not repeated and not to be repeated by any cyclic revolution arriving from the reality of the past; then something has come into being which has never been before.

Human action is the distinctive object of metaphysical investigation, requiring its own system of analysis. It is not to be understood as some kind of rival to natural sciences—a charlatan or pseudo-science. It concerns our knowledge of the *internal* world. As envisioned by Collingwood, metaphysics is a humanistic practice—a study of free people in the past by free people in the present. The penalties for neglecting Vico's humane science have reached a tipping-point: The modern sway of domination remains substantively unchallenged, but is it unchallengeable? We must find out, and soon. Metaphysics is an attempt to counterbalance the rapidly expanding power of natural science by questioning its presuppositions. In light of the history of consequences for human action, can modern natural science's presuppositions still be justified? Are they even properly identified and understood? Further, if we wager that scientific power can serve civilization instead of destroying it, what principles are required to distinguish *the hands* of the evil from the good, the wise from the foolish?

To Collingwood, an undertaking of this kind must first deal with historical relativism, establishing a criterion of unity that accounts for (not erases) the diversity of pragmatic systems. Then, modern natural science must become aware of its true absolute presupposition. Finally, a conversion from descriptive metaphysics to prescriptive political theology is required to demonstrate natural science's proper role in the way of nations. All of these elements intersect in the crucial middle chapter of *An Essay on Metaphysics*: "Quicunque Vult."

Relativism

Historical pluralism is the uncontroversial recognition that different peoples at different times have enacted different processes to achieve different

---

90. Collingwood, *Principles of History*, 142.
91. Collingwood, *Principles of History*, 142.

ends. It is the commonplace claim that what is the case for one individual or social group may not be the case for another. Yet, liberal-minded pluralism takes a more sinister turn when the position of skeptical equivocation is taken. Historical *relativism* means there is no semantic leakage between forms of life: Divergence without convergence. As Collingwood phrases it, in an exceedingly important late essay, "for any given society the proposition 'we are civilized' has a sense peculiar to that society; for 'civilized' has no constant meaning in such propositions."[92] What is the case is always relative to a conceptual, cultural, or linguistic framework. Alternative systems of reality maintain their own symbolic independence, individuating truly distinct subjects.

Experience is mediated in a variety of ways. Internally related strata of signification belong to various social modes of development, influence, and decline. Individuation of social identity requires symbolic enclosure. Meaning is uniquely evolving and culturally intransitive. There is no higher level by which any one way of life can be critically assessed by any other. Without a univocal union between representational systems, relating them to a shared *criterion*, no standard of judgment can command validity beyond the limits of the worldview in which it originates and operates. There is no possible vantage point to adjudicate the right and good between differences.

Societies are isolated singularities. A disruption of *sense* exists between them. A shared descriptor may be temporarily achievable, denoting the same object, but it cannot be trusted to connote the same thing. We must remain skeptical. An equivocal opening of difference will erase all our efforts to stabilize a unified meaning—a criterion or *common sense*—because social forms of life have their own exclusive histories and, therefore, their own internally related, dynamically evolving fields of significance. An ideal held in one place and time is incommensurate with any other; it does not communicate beyond its sealed sphere. According to Enno Rudolph, this criterion crisis stems from the presumption that "there are no metahistorical structures of meaning by which the course of history can be critically assessed."[93] Collingwood detects the consequences of this stance: Paralyzed détente before *the other* denies a historical metaphysician's "ability to grasp any process by which one stage of human affairs turned into another."[94] To be clear, historical transformation within one's own system is comprehensible. Outside this very specific domain of identity, it is not. There is no common history, only *histories*. Our knowledge of other cultures becomes

---

92. Collingwood, "What 'Civilization' Means," 489.
93. Rudolph, "Symbol and History," 9.
94. Collingwood, "What 'Civilization' Means," 486.

the same as our knowledge of nature; it is external and estranged, driven by domination as appropriation, seeking an inside that forever eludes it, destroying its object.

A different society's vista of meaning is exterior to our understanding. We simply cannot think that. To believe that we can indicates our colonizing mentality. We miss the crucial communication of difference itself, as *that which* eludes our framework of categories, providing equivalence of existence and value. All societies have equally incomparable and incompatible frameworks. None of which can be justly condemned or universalized. We are spoken into being by different voices. There is no outer point or standard of reciprocal evaluation. Legitimate judgments on better and worse—on kind and intensity—are impossible. All social systems are equal simply by being held by someone at some time. History consists of an anarchy of externally related singular forms. As they appear and disappear, coalesce and disperse, each is dedicated to their own unaffected, solitary way of life; oblivious to the interior reality of other forms. At their boundaries, discontinuous ideals mutually repel and neutralize each other's domain of representation. Criterions break this peaceful symmetry. The parallax ethics of relativism requires the preservation of this equilibrium between authentic identities.

From a recent lexicon, criterions are socially transitive *metanarratives*. They are tricks of ideological interpellation by the oppressor against the oppressed—Trojan Horses of the soul. To take in the outward gift of mutuality is a catastrophic mistake; it unleashes violence against a culture's internal form, ending in its elimination and enslavement. The work of *critical thought* is the exposure and destruction of all metanarratives. The very idea of a higher order internal relationship is an act of deception by the strong. A criterion trespasses the territories between equally different societies of unequal power. There can be no standard without the hidden hand of domination. To turn externally related societal ideals into an internally related unity means the destruction and absorption of many by one. There is no alternative conclusion. To assume that there is merely signifies your society's hegemony and its unchallenged right to absorb other forms of life. Universalization is assimilation; it cannot be anything but the raiding, seizure, and breaking up of another society's internally related structure. One symbolic order is strengthened by its victory over others. Devoted *in*difference for the many is the only protection from the deceptive force of the same: Let be, let difference be different.

The traditional response to relativism centers on the logical charge of self-refutation. To claim, "what is right for you is not the same as what is right for me," presents itself as a non-relative truth. So, the statement is a counterexample of the universal claim it makes. The relativist can only avoid self-refutation by accepting that relativism cannot be proven true in any universal or non-relative sense. It can only be true in a singular context, relative to its own domain of sense. Relativism could be false *and oppressive* in other frameworks of meaning. In simpler terms, relativism exposes itself as the very thing it claims to be against; namely, universalization of a merely local and arbitrary idea. The proposition that there is no non-oppressive criterion erases itself. If it is true that all universal ideals are oppressive, this proposition is also oppressive because it must assume universal extension. If it makes an exception for itself, it negates itself, collapsing by internal contradiction. Yet, to isolate this perspective, to relativize relativism, by denying its commensurability, applicable to other societies, condemns the skeptical-relativist viewpoint to the local site of its formation and enactment.

A *differentist* may respond to this kind of argument by saying it, too, depends on presumptions from a specific logical framework. One that a differentist does not recognize as being other than context dependent. Demonstration of self-refutation requires the universalization of a particular logic, holding it to be absolute across other symbolic territories. What the argument of self-refutation really demonstrates is the erasure of symbolic independency by an absolute logic, enacting a many-to-one act of domination. In Collingwood's vocabulary, the absolute presupposition of indivisible difference—being as difference—frees up a space for diverse logical worlds.

In terms of linguistic-propositional analysis, a world is a frame of reference; it sets in place an internally related field of representation or propositional context: A grammatical *situs*. A linguistic framework is understood as a set of rules for forming propositions for verification, determining how we represent things without itself representing anything—the adoption of which is a matter of pragmatic utility, not truth and falsity. This principle of integration operates such that the truth and falsity of one proposition follows from the truth and falsity of others; it is that in virtue of which its propositions achieve existence, meaning, and function, without which they cease to manifest what they are. For every proposition, for example, that can give a fact, *P-F*—an affirmation or denial of a feature of experience—there must be a framework to ultimately account for why *P-F* is the case. The rules of a framework mark the limits of propositional analysis. Rules of a propositional system cannot be true or false, and they are externally related to their practice. Embodied actions end the regress chain of linguistic propositions that can be true or false, beginning the pragmatic valuation of the framework. To test its validity, we must play by the current rules of the game. For practical purposes, therefore, we must accept, *this is just what we do*.

Existence exhibits the features of external relations between atomic objects. Language is an internally related system of concepts or propositions. An outside utility bestows a contingent pattern of rules, arising from the naturalist selection of advantage. An adaptable framework determines the limit-conditions whereby an inside individuates a distinctive form or *world* of meaningful activity. Contingent external relations direct a form of life's pragmatic fitness. Viability depends, in due course, on a wild and inexplicable whirl of physical, biological, and social factors. The exterior pragmatic environment of objects is characterized by randomness, discontinuity, and diachronic meaninglessness. Even so, this nihilistic place constantly gives rise to, preserves, and destroys various internally related forms of life because, every internal relation presupposes an external relation. The traumatic truth about origination and destination—*void-nothing*—appears to compel each conceptual framework to present itself as synchronically necessary, continuous, and meaning-*filled*. Universality is merely a local façade; temporarily protecting a fragile system of internal meaning from the external realities of force and chance. It is an essentially tragic outlook on existence.

We are all incarcerated in our mythopoeic cells of representation. But somehow, as generous commentators conclude, this realization liberates a pluralistic ethic of tolerance and equality, regarding all other forms of life. David K. Naugle, for example, claims, for Ludwig Wittgenstein's (†1951) philosophy, "the fact of a multiplicity of mutually exclusive world pictures, forms of life, and language games" leads to the post-modern presupposition, "in which the struggle for worldviews over one and the same world is replaced by a variety of noncompetitive, linguistic constructions of reality . . . all of which are relative and none of which is privileged over another. In this way his goal is to enable people to see the world differently, not as it really is, but as it is given to them in their sociolinguistic context."[95] Just why relativism leads to "noncompetitive" mutual recognition rather than its opposite is unclear. The idea here, I think, is that philosophy is best practiced as therapy, treating us for the post-modern trauma of skepticism and nihilism that accompanies relativism. The problem is to realize the groundlessness of all our believing. To understand that our form of life is thoroughly conventional—historically and pragmatically arbitrary—is to be first thrown into the epistemological abyss of pure difference but, after the therapeutic process of philosophy, a viable, pluralistic subject can emerge; one able to live and flourish without foundational certainties. Tragic-therapeutic philosophy seeks to amend the fact, as Donald Phillip Verene rightly observes,

---

95. Naugle, *Worldview*, 152–53.

that externally related world systems "often sharply confront each other. In fact, each symbolic form has within it a drive to dominate culture itself and subordinate all other forms to itself."⁹⁶ Philosophy must deal with the reality of incommensurate forms of life and their *universal* meaninglessness.

Outside decides inside. Contingent activity creates conceptual necessity. Embodied performances in the realm of independent objects can succeed or fail, governing the *pragmatic* adoption, preservation, and abandonment of frameworks. This exterior place is the origin of interiorly related forms or frames of reference that individuate genuine identities—the players of a game. It appears as a site of contested dominance, defined by the properties of lawlessness, *senseless* clash, leading to the spontaneous generation of order beyond the influence of free human action's interior relatedness. Human society is reducible to nature of a certain eristic characterization; that the freedom of human action *should* be of concern is a mere peculiarity of one arbitrarily arising and sequestered worldview. External relations account for relativism and the criteria that institute the multitude of internal relations that make up symbolic regimes. The naturalistic sway of fate and chance determines all things. But is this our only reasonable option for dealing with affinity and diversity?

Self-Differentiating Unity

In the *Essay*, Collingwood argues for the need of an *absolute* presupposition, not of itself true or false, to account for relative expediencies between frameworks: Do they have a right and good absolute presupposition of a *third degree*, adjusting the worth and movement of all others, not open to further inquiry because no principle of pragmatic convenience more temporally basic can ever be expected to be found? But without Plato's transcendent lure of the Good, beyond being and becoming, how do we avoid the traditional implications of historical relativism—skepticism, nihilism, and force of perspective? The properties of this third level of historical process are not entirely clear in the *Essay*. Leslie Armour (†2014), for example, calls this situation a "Collingwood mystery."⁹⁷ As Michael Beaney accurately remarks, in the task "of describing how one absolute presupposition changes into another, Collingwood is assuming" that "we can in some sense understand both. But this would imply there is some deeper (even more absolute) presupposition underlying the conceptualization that makes this possible."⁹⁸

---

96. Verene, *Metaphysics*, 98.
97. Armour, "Speculative versus Critical Philosophy of History," 158.
98. Beaney, "Collingwood's Conception of Presuppositional Analysis," 93.

Metaphysics and Preliminary Statement of the Problem

For his part, Armour deciphers the enigma of Beaney's *in some sense* as having "to do with how the framework of the emerging universal as a set of real particulars is to be understood as an historical process," and, "thus the logical background of the intelligible world. It is the process embedded in it that makes historical knowledge possible."[99] Since all presuppositions are subject to historical strain and change, they are all contingent. There is no Archimedean point outside history, but the claim here is that historical metaphysics can reveal the logical and conceptual architecture of its own claim on the real. Metaphysics of this kind can trace (detect and describe) its own irreducible layer or *form of time*; enough to provide an answer to the question, "What is the 'emerging universal' that makes historical understanding possible?"

To solve his metaphysical mystery, Collingwood leaves a suggestive series of clues. To follow them we must first return to his reading of Aristotle's three senses of metaphysics. Most commentators agree that he thoroughly rejects Aristotle's first sense of metaphysics as the science of pure being. Collingwood accepts the second sense: The analysis of absolute presuppositions underlying ordinary knowledge. Unlike Aristotle's conception, though, this type of metaphysics presents history as its ground. But what is usually overlooked is that Collingwood also accepts—in the light of the latter modification—Aristotle's third sense of metaphysics as *wisdom* or *theology*. Metaphysics, so amended, is still the "First and Last Science," but the First Science now pursues historically constituted absolute presuppositions, not pure being: "The First Science in the sense that it is logically presupposed by every other science."[100] "As the Last Science," Collingwood tells us, "it will be the ultimate goal of the scientist's pilgrimage through the realms of knowledge."[101] Metaphysics is the descriptive science of specific sub-universals called absolute presuppositions, but it is also the pursuit of their generic logical ground. Metaphysicians seek "the ground of all other universals, and the First and Last Science is therefore the science of that which stands as ultimate logical ground to everything that is studied by any other science."[102] Clearly expressed, "The ordinary name for that which is the logical ground of everything is God," and, "the name which tells us what it is about, is therefore Theology."[103] Collingwood claims to work "in accordance with the Aristotelian principle that metaphysics and theology

---

99. Armour, "Speculative versus Critical Philosophy of History," 158.
100. Collingwood, *Essay on Metaphysics*, 9.
101. Collingwood, *Essay on Metaphysics*, 9.
102. Collingwood, *Essay on Metaphysics*, 10.
103. Collingwood, *Essay on Metaphysics*, 10.

are the same."[104] Theology grasps the basic principles of action that govern becoming. "The act by which we hold such presuppositions," Collingwood explains, "is religious faith; and God is that in which we believe by faith."[105] Pragmatic systems of belief depend on some kind of third level ground, "therefore all our absolute presuppositions must be presuppositions in holding which we believe something about God."[106] Theology is the science of judgment on utmost *explanatorily necessary* principles. Deity—as ultimate absolute presupposition—must secure an *explanation* for "the oneness of things and their manyness."[107]

In the *Essay*, Collingwood emphasizes the relation between modern natural sciences and their theological *radix*. Again, he follows the Philosopher: "Aristotle's *Metaphysics*, openly and professedly a theology, reminds the reader by this fact of the intimate connexion that there must always be between the doctrines of religion and the foundations of natural science."[108] The prevailing concern here appears to be re-introducing the present variety of natural sciences to their ultimate absolute presupposition: The principle of "self-differentiating unity" that establishes a system for understanding the natural world.[109] Modern natural science has slipped its mooring, endangering human action. Chapter 21 is Collingwood's theological attempt to civilize science, to re-anchor the Promethean power of this activity to its proper sphere of service to creation: "The business of metaphysics is to state the absolute presuppositions of natural science."[110] The chapter is entitled, "Quicunque Vult," which are the first two words of the Athanasian Creed: "Whosoever will be saved." The phrase is also used to refer to the Creed as a whole, which professes the absolute presupposition of the Catholic Faith. Christianity is a constellation that arises in response to a problem. That problem is the existence of the world of nature and the failure of ancient Greek science to adequately account for it. Christianity is an undertaking that sets out to *save the phenomena*: The historical appearance of things.

Collingwood positions both Plato and Aristotle as advancing beyond polytheism's logic of "departmental gods"—that is, deities practice independent governance of the many realms of nature, precluding "the oneness

---

104. Collingwood, *Essay on Metaphysics*, 221.
105. Collingwood, *Essay on Metaphysics*, 216.
106. Collingwood, *Essay on Metaphysics*, 216.
107. Collingwood, *Essay on Metaphysics*, 210–11.
108. Collingwood, *Essay on Metaphysics*, 211.
109. See Collingwood, *Essay on Metaphysics*, 6, 212, 219, 220.
110. Collingwood, *Essay on Metaphysics*, 216.

of natural science."[111] To offset these rival and incommensurate domains of difference, they propose theologies of unity. *Monotheism* must now articulate, "the one activity of the one God as a self-differentiating activity," offering explanations of "how a single activity differentiates itself into various activities."[112] But their progress is incomplete. Particularly, Aristotle's one God with many logical modes does not include a doctrine of creation. The existence of nature is discovered with the senses; no God (or *theogony of gods*) created it. He falls into error because, as we have seen with Ayer, sense experience is saturated with prior convictions about the content of the observed; it is neither self-explanatory, nor self-justifying of itself. The given is not unmediated. Its origination must be theologically accounted for. The unified existence of the world is an absolute presupposition, not simply an observed fact. To Aristotle, nevertheless, the existence of the natural world and the existence of God remain unrelated propositions. The absence of a theological opening principle affects his physics of motion. Sense experience, once more, accounts for our knowledge that there is motion in the natural world. Collingwood denies that motion can be a concept that we obtain through the senses because, "It is an idea which we bring with us in the shape of an absolute presupposition to the work of interpreting what we get by using our senses."[113] Like the existence of nature, motion is "an attribute or activity of God," which means, "that to be the creator of movement in the natural world is just as much a part of God's nature as to be the source of diversified orderliness in the natural world."[114]

Aristotle's denial of divine ground for the existence and movement of nature relaxes the logical tie between the sacred and the natural. The divine in things is intelligible order. Motion is a mimetic attraction a thing has to its inherent good, reflecting God's thought of itself. But in a significant and practical respect, nature is a disenchanted and independent realm of immanent phenomena that can be scientifically investigated with the senses. Study of potency, energy, growth, and so on, require little reflection on a thing's ultimate significance. Things in nature happen of themselves through a fourfold *aitia*. Supplementary theological explanations can offer support for formal and final causes, but the parsimony of reason reduces their needful inclusion in the practice of empirical science.

---

111. Collingwood, *Essay on Metaphysics*, 213.
112. Collingwood, *Essay on Metaphysics*, 213.
113. Collingwood, *Essay on Metaphysics*, 217.
114. Collingwood, *Essay on Metaphysics*, 216, 218.

To Collingwood, the empirical immanence of existence and motion is a "metaphysical error," which "was corrected by Christianity."[115] Metaphysics is not a hollow façade—an ideological result—that merely reflects the inner change of a society driven by other historical forces. It is certainly not, as it is commonly characterized, "a mere luxury of the intellect," afforded to idle, Ivory Tower elites.[116] Change in the outward structure of society is related to underlying change in metaphysics. The relationship is not causal in a strict unidirectional sense; for example, in necessary entailment from antecedent to consequent. But there is a *material implication* found in the complex interior dialectic that a society experiences in times of fundamental change of absolute presuppositions. During these tipping points, the practice of metaphysics can take the decisive initiative in the creation of a new order of things. On the change from classical Greco-Roman society to Christian society, Collingwood makes some strong claims in this regard: "The breakdown of Greek science implied a breakdown of Greek civilization."[117] A flaw or crack in the foundation of knowledge creeps into civilization itself, taking root in an expansively corruptive manner "because metaphysical analysis is an integral part of scientific thought, an obstinate error in metaphysical analysis is fatal to the science with which it is concerned. And because science and civilization, organized thought in its theoretical and practical forms, stand or fall together, the metaphysical error which killed pagan science killed pagan civilization with it."[118] The ancient world did not decline and fall because of barbarian invasions. Collingwood accepts the "Patristic diagnosis"—namely, "the 'pagan' world died because of its failure to keep alive its own fundamental convictions."[119] Barbarian invasions are symptomatic of a much deeper fragility of absolute presuppositions, a *constellational* crisis.

Since the disease of Greco-Roman civilization is metaphysical in origin, Patristic writers propose a radical "metaphysical remedy."[120] Our understanding of God must change. "In order to understand what the Christian metaphysicians were doing," Collingwood continues, "and why the thing they did was ultimately accepted by the Greco-Roman world, in other words why that world converted to Christianity, it is necessary to bear in mind that at this point they are correcting a metaphysical error on the part of the

---

115. Collingwood, *Essay on Metaphysics*, 215.
116. Collingwood, *Essay on Metaphysics*, 224.
117. Collingwood, *Essay on Metaphysics*, 218.
118. Collingwood, *Essay on Metaphysics*, 224.
119. Collingwood, *Essay on Metaphysics*, 225.
120. Collingwood, *Essay on Metaphysics*, 225.

Greek philosophers."[121] He lists four basic principles that amend the foundation of natural science: "I. *There is one God*," "II. *God created the world*," "III. *The activity of God is a self-differentiating activity, which is why there are diverse realms of nature*," and "IV. *The creative activity of God is the source of motion in the world of nature*."[122] The central (but not only) presuppositions of natural science ever since take their constellational bearing from a new metaphysical analysis. The Patristics call it "the 'Catholic Faith.'"[123] God as Trinity presupposes the existence and motion of nature and, consequently, science as we have known it for two millennia. What we know as *history* is a record of the strains within the constellation of divine economy. The Trinity names the absolute presupposition of Occidental civilization; it is foreshadowed by certain elements of Greco-Roman thought but systematically worked out in the fourth and fifth centuries by the Patristic Fathers.

What is the Catholic faith? To the Patristics, it presupposes, "that we worship one God in trinity, and trinity in unity," whereby trinitarian plurality is preserved without reduction to unity and, conversely, unity is preserved without reduction to trinitarian plurality.[124] Through much struggle and controversy, Patristic theology worked its way towards a world-creating first principle of sameness, difference, and co-equality: Three-in-One, One-in-Three. As a principle of unity, it is not One in the sense familiar to the Greeks. Multiplicity is not opposed to wholeness, rendered other than or alien to it. The Many is somehow constitutive of primordial unity. Even more important for a social and ecological ethic, the One and the Many relate to each other without hierarchy. The Trinity's three terms have been traditionally called the Father, the Son, and the Holy Ghost. Unlike the various systems of Greek theology, i.e., the hypostases of One, mind, life, henads, and so on, their distinctions do not result in a scale of greater and lesser being. Difference does not imply subordination. Divinity abhors domination. Trinitarian co-equality, Hans Urs von Balthasar (†1988) even suggests, "is in truth the most conspicuous victory of Christian thought over Greek thought."[125] The One and the Many form a dynamic and creative internal relationship. Diversity and unity belong to each other in a creative and egalitarian way.

Collingwood stresses this principle's transformation of Greek natural science: "By believing in the Father they meant (always with reference solely

---

121. Collingwood, *Essay on Metaphysics*, 219.
122. Collingwood, *Essay on Metaphysics*, 219–21.
123. Collingwood, *Essay on Metaphysics*, 225.
124. Collingwood, *Essay on Metaphysics*, 225.
125. Balthasar, *Presence and Thought*, 19n16.

to the procedure of natural science) absolutely presupposing that there is a world of nature which is always and indivisibly one world. By believing in the Son they meant absolutely presupposing that this one natural world is nevertheless a multiplicity of natural realms. By believing in the Holy Ghost they meant absolutely presupposing that the world of nature, throughout its entire fabric, is a world not merely of things but of events or movements."[126] Christian natural science, then, liberates human action to further liberate creation, thereby serving our common creator. This kind of science presumes the temporal openness of reality. Historicity requires a different approach to knowledge. *The Trinity is the 'emerging universal' that makes historical understanding possible.*[127] The Father provides an irreducible unity to temporal process; there is one history, not many incommensurate histories. But this does not dissolve diversity into an empty uniformity of time because the Son (λογος) is the *hypostasis* that pluralizes unity. Temporality is the self-differentiation of the divine creative activity. The Holy Ghost is the principle of historicity that encompasses humanistic and, conceivably, naturalistic realities of free activity. As Saint Augustine reminds us, "novelties are possible, things which have not happened before and yet are not at variance with the ordering of the world."[128] *The gates* of the present and future are unlocked by the past, by the continuous diversity of time. Time is prospectively open as the Holy Ghost but retrospectively unified and determined as the Father; the oscillating intersection between the two is the Son: The incarnational time of the present—*Et verbum caro factum est*.

The role of the Son is fundamental to Christian historicity. To Michael Hinz, for instance, "The doctrine of the Incarnation corresponds to the realization that the source of all value is historical process itself, through which all value is generate. Thus, the activity of historical process brings about *the realization that the justifying grounds for all systems of thought and value are historically constituted.*"[129] Again, from Von Balthasar, we get an extraordinary series of radiances on incarnational time. We have never been fully Christian, but if we were, herein this circle of brief light lies a glimpse of *fully converted* reality: "If any philosophy regards time as in some way mere appearance, as a 'mode of perception,' as something to be explained or explained away so as to attain to a supposedly supratemporal sphere in which we can withdraw into supposed security in the castle of eternity, then

---

126. Collingwood, *Essay on Metaphysics*, 225–26.

127. In am indebted to James Bradley for pointing out the crucial role of the Trinity in Collingwood's metaphysics and, as I (not Bradley) extend it in the concluding *Supplement*, in his political theology. See Bradley's "Philosophy and Trinity," 155–78.

128. Augustine, *City of God* XII.21 (500).

129. Hinz, *Self-Creation and History*, 198.

Metaphysics and Preliminary Statement of the Problem

that philosophy must be rejected" because this is the "precise thing we do when we sin, which is to break out of time, within which is contained God's dispositions for us, in order to arrogate to ourselves a sort of eternity."[130] The human ambition to eternalize some self-empowering feature of the finite order is the source of sin; therefore, "all sin, consists essentially in breaking out of time."[131] Balthasar claims that "original sin consisted in anticipation of this kind."[132] To view, as with the Greek perennial version of truth, "actions in time from some vantage point of eternity," "would be to do away with his [Christ's] temporality" because "he would no longer be the model of Christian existence and of Christian faith."[133] "If we think of escaping from time," Balthasar cautions, "that is an attack on the basic phenomenon of Christian existence."[134] For a historically reconfigured person, "something timeless is not inherent in the real character of his existence in the world."[135] "He must live in time, and not attempt to rise above it," "not imposing upon time a meaning he himself has evolved. He must accept the content and meaning of his life, that is, precisely, accept *his time*, as a gift from God," and above all, avoiding sin by "not making the Promethean attempt to be master of it himself."[136] The root of human violence is the domination of time. The tender gift becomes weaponized for impossible projects of self-creation.

Fully converted time, by contrast, signifies "making present of the life of the Trinity."[137] This is "a kind of time that is sacramental," "becoming a living sacrament of the triune life."[138] The Christian criterion "communicates to existence both its supreme Idea and the inner strength to seek it and attain a proper relation to it."[139] Balthasar presents it in terms of "the foundation of a future freedom," "giving space and scope to the freedom of man," and the criterion must "form the vessel of a content yet to come."[140] The truth of freedom is love; it is the only "event of total originality," an unconditional "pledge of eternity" that requires of humanity "a surrender of itself, and thus of all its own truth, all its own evidence, in a love which

---

130. Balthasar, *Theology of History*, 34, 36.
131. Balthasar, *Theology of History*, 37.
132. Balthasar, *Theology of History*, 36.
133. Balthasar, *Theology of History*, 38–39.
134. Balthasar, *Theology of History*, 47.
135. Balthasar, *Theology of History*, 40.
136. Balthasar, *Theology of History*, 120.
137. Balthasar, *Theology of History*, 49.
138. Balthasar, *Theology of History*, 98, 75.
139. Balthasar, *Theology of History*, 70–71.
140. Balthasar, *Theology of History*, 58.

prefers God's invariably greater truth to its own."[141] In this breakthrough of "eternal love, time, as the creature's form of being, is not annihilated but consummated and filled to overflowing with the eternal dimensions of divine life."[142] The criterion of love surrenders itself to us as its unconditional "time-dimension" such that in our acceptance of it, our surrendering of ourselves to it, "the criterion passes over to God."[143] The economy of mutual renunciation changes the meaning of *sacrifice* as a foundation for community. Self-sacrifice *for* others begins to replace the collective sacrifice *of* others. The way out of an archaic world is finally glimpsed. By renouncing all sacred and retributive violence as perversions of a more primordial relationality, the criterion of history is revealed as an unconditional love to be gained. Guy G. Stroumsa, for example, argues that this "new covenant" overthrows "the sacrificial system" of an archaic world.[144] A universal beloved community is to be founded on a "spiritualized religion, or a religion without blood."[145] With the Christian Eschaton, the Promethean rage for timelessness—for the sacrifice of others *given the gift* of time—is weakened, but certainly not extinguished. In Collingwood's terms, this historical tendency remains an unreconciled *minority report*. In times of intense constellational strain, it can reemerge as *barbaric* phenomena. Atavistic social forces and presuppositions are unleashed, serving as a catalyst for further constellational development or ruin.

Why the Christian metaphysical alternative occurred rather than another is not for metaphysics to determine. A metaphysician can only demonstrate the change, content, and effects of constellations. But *Quicunque Vult* also marks Collingwood's transition from what P. F. Strawson (†2006) calls "descriptive metaphysics" to "revisionary metaphysics" or *political theology*, where "descriptive metaphysics is content to describe the actual structure of our thought about the world, [while] revisionary metaphysics is concerned to produce a better structure."[146] *The civilization of the natural sciences* begins with a *description* of their absolute presupposition: The Trinity. However, its regressive (barbarous) element of overwhelming power will not simply be corrected by descriptive reminders of their ground in *Deus caritas est*. David Boucher observes that Collingwood gradually changed his view on the problem of civilization, "It was not only the separation of the forms

---

141. Balthasar, *Theology of History*, 39, 99, 45.
142. Balthasar, *Theology of History*, 46.
143. Balthasar, *Theology of History*, 25, 47.
144. Stroumsa, *End of Sacrifice*, 79, 78.
145. Stroumsa, *End of Sacrifice*, 65.
146. Strawson, *Individuals*, 9.

of experience from one another," which is the view of Collingwood's early work, *Speculum Mentis* (1924), "but the emergence of one which threatened to obliterate the rest."[147] We cannot presume an equilibrium of differences in our approach to the evaluation of enquiry because we are put at immense risk—made socially and ecologically vulnerable—by one *form of experience*: "Natural science, although invaluable in the civilizing process, threatened to destroy civilization because of its denial of any form of knowledge that was not its own."[148] To preserve and advance civilization, the natural sciences must *serve* human action. This historical occurrence means a "new way of living would involve a new science and a new civilization."[149] Properly re-constituted, the absolute presuppositions of the emergent civilization known as Christianity can overcome the return of *Promethean nihilism*, but it requires an innovative politics of human action.[150] This orientation will be sketched in the *Supplement* that follows the metaphysical investigation, ending this work.

HISTORICAL METAPHYSICS OF ENVIRONMENT

There is much more to clarify and learn from Collingwood's *Essay*. Metaphysical analysis, however, is the appropriate orientation to proceed with our study.[151] How does this historical science accommodate itself to the

---

147. Boucher, *Social and Political Thought of R. G. Collingwood*, 233.
148. Boucher, *Social and Political Thought of R. G. Collingwood*, 233.
149. Collingwood, *Essay on Metaphysics*, 227.
150. See Hinz, *Self-Creation and History*, 199.

151. Influential thought with an acknowledged debt to Collingwood's pioneering approach to historical metaphysics, the fusion of historical and philosophical questions, include Hans-Georg Gadamer's (†2002) philosophical hermeneutics (see Gadamer, *Truth and Method*, 333–41, 467–69, 486); Hans Robert Jauss's (†1997) theory of literary reception (see Jauss, "Literary History as a Challenge to Literary Theory," 9–11); and, most directly, the political thought of Michael Oakeshott (†1990). For the convergences and divergences between Collingwood and Oakeshott, see Boucher, "Human Conduct, History, and Social Science," 607–717.

Other leading thinkers maintain an antagonistic or mostly unacknowledged debt to Collingwood. These include Leo Strauss (†1973) (see Strauss, "On Collingwood's Philosophy of History," 559–86); Thomas S. Kuhn (†1996) (see Kuhn, *Structure of Scientific Revolutions*); and Michel Foucault (see Foucault, *Les Mots et les choses*). For Strauss, the dispute with Collingwood centers less on the validity of historico-philosophical method than it does on which strain of thought—i.e., Greek, Roman, Christian, Enlightenment, Romantic, Arab, or Jewish—is said to define, or should define, contemporary political experience. Collingwood thinks there is continuity within the Occident based on the Trinity. As our politics becomes more in tune with the doctrine of the Trinity, the more civilized we become. Conversely, the less we acknowledge our Occidental debt

problem of environment? Thankfully, we are not completely in the dark. The two thinkers we will now examine accept implicitly much of what Collingwood has put forward. The absolute presuppositions of our crisis have been identified. They are Occidental strains. As Charles Norris Cochrane (and Balthasar) suggests, the crisis is consequent upon the return of *Promethean* science. There is an idolatrous self-worship of our workings and power, "the prostitution of the mind to its own fancies."[152] The environmental crisis emerges from a certain minority report within the constellation of the West.

Lynn White Jr.

In his justly celebrated essay, "The Historical Roots of Our Ecologic Crisis" (1967), Lynn White Jr. traces the source of our present environmental crisis to the presuppositions that informed the industrial revolution of the midnineteenth century: Principally, "the emergence in widespread practice of the Baconian creed that scientific knowledge means technical power over nature."[153] The "acceptance" of this relation of domination "as a normal pattern of action may mark the greatest event in human history since the invention of agriculture, and perhaps in nonhuman terrestrial history as well."[154] In a century and a half, "the impact of our race upon the environment has so increased in force that it has changed its essence."[155] The

---

to the Trinity, the more barbaric we become (see Collingwood's "Fascism and Nazism," 168–76). Strauss disagrees, and he draws his lines of strain differently. With Kuhn and Foucault, the issue with Collingwood is, again, not so much the linking together of history and philosophy as it is a struggle with incommensurability. Collingwood thinks the West has a clear constellation upon which to do metaphysical analysis, reaching from the formation of the Trinity to the present, inclusive of nature, politics, science and religion. Kuhn and Foucault, however, tend to emphasize the *archeological* asymmetries of interpretation found between one age and another, one institutional form and another, one community of inquirers and another. For the latter two, the region of constellational analysis, *episteme* in Foucault's sense and *normal science* in Kuhn's, is much more limited and epistemologically problematic. Perpetual discontinuities or irruptive breaks occur in the multiple chains of continuity among various communities of inquiry. This situation makes commensurate translation between epistemes extremely complicated, if not impossible. On the similarities and differences between Collingwood, Kuhn, and Foucault, see Forrester, "On Kuhn's Case," 782–819.

For the purpose of environmental-historical analysis, this work assumes that Collingwood's Occidental continuity is valid. Its validity is established by the accumulated historical evidence constituting the problem, and its proposed amendment.

152. Cochrane, *Christianity and Classical Culture*, 462.
153. White Jr., "Historical Roots of Our Ecologic Crisis," 8.
154. White Jr., "Historical Roots of Our Ecologic Crisis," 8.
155. White Jr., "Historical Roots of Our Ecologic Crisis," 8.

prospects for nuclear annihilation are now well recognized, "but our present combustion of fossil fuels threatens to change the chemistry of the globe's atmosphere as a whole, with consequences which we are only beginning to guess."[156] This energy choice combined with "the population explosion, the carcinoma of planless urbanism, the now geological deposits of sewage and garbage," leads White Jr. to conclude that "surely no creature other than man has managed to foul its nest in such short order."[157] The *Anthropocene Age* has arrived.

Like Collingwood, White Jr. is suspicious of quick and ready prescriptions: "What shall we do? No one yet knows."[158] Furthermore, "Unless we think about fundamentals, our specific measures may produce new backlashes more serious than those they are designed to remedy."[159] *Thinking about fundamentals* means metaphysical analysis, "clarifying our thinking by looking, in some historical depth, at the presuppositions that underlie modern technology and science."[160] Again, in tune with Collingwood, White Jr. employs the science of absolute presuppositions within the *continuity* of the Occidental constellation: "We continue today to live, as we have lived for about 1,700 years, very largely in a context of Christian axioms."[161] What historical strains give rise to the environmental crisis?

Christianity's triumph over Greco-Roman animism is a sound departure point. This event leads to the disenchantment and devaluation of nature. Although Greco-Roman animism is not the same at different times and places, there is a common denominator within pagan animism that guards the natural world. Each place (and its creatures) is experienced as having an indwelling sacredness—a *genius loci*—which serves to instill an intricate and potent web of taboos and restrictions that protects it from excessive human exploitation. "By destroying pagan animism," White Jr. claims, "Christianity made it possible to exploit nature in a mood of indifference to the feelings of natural objects"—that is, "The spirits *in* natural objects, which formally had protected nature from man, evaporated. Man's effective monopoly on spirit in the world was confirmed, and the old inhibitions to the exploitation of nature crumbled."[162] God is no longer present in nature. "God does not manifest himself in the forces and rhythms of nature,"

---

156. White Jr., "Historical Roots of Our Ecologic Crisis," 8.
157. White Jr., "Historical Roots of Our Ecologic Crisis," 8.
158. White Jr., "Historical Roots of Our Ecologic Crisis," 8.
159. White Jr., "Historical Roots of Our Ecologic Crisis," 8–9.
160. White Jr., "Historical Roots of Our Ecologic Crisis," 9.
161. White Jr., "Historical Roots of Our Ecologic Crisis," 11.
162. White Jr., "Historical Roots of Our Ecologic Crisis," 11.

Jürgen Moltmann observes, "he reveals himself in human history."[163] The absconded God means, "Nature is stripped of her divinity."[164] God creates nature, but God is not nature. Our relation to the natural world is not sacrosanct in any significant way. It is simply there for us to use, explore, and modify by our lights, as we are able. "It is clear," to M. B. Foster (†1959), "that Christianity, by eliminating this pagan doctrine from theology, supplied the condition of the development of modern natural science."[165] The historical fact of disenchantment is a necessary but not sufficient condition for either the rise of modern science or its consequent industrial offspring. This absolute presupposition is subsumed by others within the constellation of the Occident.

White Jr. asks, "What did Christianity tell people about their relationship to the environment?"[166] The Book of Genesis comprises the Occidental creation myth. It tells humanity we have dominion over all creation, signifying "no item in the physical creation had any purpose save to serve man's purposes."[167] We are created in God's image (*imago Dei*) and, therefore, we are not simply part of nature. We are God's second. Human beings are an exception; discontinuous and superior to all other creatures. As God transcends the celestial universe, so we transcend terrestrial nature. "Especially in its Western form," White Jr. concludes, "Christianity is the most anthropocentric religion the world has seen" because "Man shares, in great measure, God's transcendence of nature," and this asymmetry "not only established a dualism of man and nature but also insisted that it is God's will that man exploit nature for his proper ends."[168] White Jr., however, acknowledges that his presentation of Christianity is a common caricature, requiring additional metaphysical refinement: "Christianity is a complex faith, and its consequences differ in differing contexts."[169] Christianity in the Greek East, for example, tends toward a sacramental relationship of participation with the natural world. The study of nature or natural theology is "primarily a symbolic system through which God speaks to men."[170] Sin is intellectual blindness. Salvation is found in right knowledge. To achieve this end, contemplation of God's traces in the world (*vestigia trinitatis in*

---

163. Moltmann, *God in Creation*, 13.
164. Moltmann, *God in Creation*, 13.
165. Foster, "Christian Theology and Modern Science of Nature," 451.
166. White Jr., "Historical Roots of Our Ecologic Crisis," 11.
167. White Jr., "Historical Roots of Our Ecologic Crisis," 11.
168. White Jr., "Historical Roots of Our Ecologic Crisis," 11.
169. White Jr., "Historical Roots of Our Ecologic Crisis," 11.
170. White Jr., "Historical Roots of Our Ecologic Crisis," 12.

creatura) is required. But Christianity in the Latin West emphasizes activity over contemplation. Sin and salvation are matters of right and wrong action. This strain is known as voluntarism. The environment is not a contemplative object of divine symbols. Rather, the environment is a stage for self-determination through action. This difference in orientation translates into technological self-help programs to act on the environment.

As it develops in the medieval period, the approach to nature of the Latin Church "was ceasing to be the decoding of the physical symbols of God's communication with man and was becoming the effort to understand God's mind by discovering how his creation operates."[171] Thinking God's ideas after Him becomes the ground of scientific law. Knowledge of laws furthers capacity for universal quantification, increasing the efficiency of technological action on an environment assumed to lack any religious significance. This constellation of cerebral absolute presuppositions coalesces with the material aspirations of an emerging secular culture, the raw hand of colonial expansion, and capitalism. Although capitalism's greatest known critic, in his *Grundrisse*, Karl Marx still admires its "great civilizing influence," which lies in capitalism's definitive rejection of the deification of nature: "Nature becomes for the first time simply an object for mankind, purely a matter of utility."[172] This complex of presuppositions provides the conditions, the combustible atmosphere, for the industrial ignition of the mid-nineteenth century.

We have come full circle. The originating condition of nature without divinity is drawn up into a political economy that continues to expand across the globe. White Jr. summarizes his argument in two propositions: "First, viewed historically, modern science is an extrapolation of natural theology and, second, that modern technology is at least partly to be explained as an Occidental, voluntarist realization of the Christian dogma of man's transcendence of and rightful mastery over nature."[173] In his brief prescriptive statements at the end of his article, White Jr. also appears very much attuned to Collingwood's (and Cochrane's) Christian political theology.

Against the growing grain of proposed ecological solutions, White Jr. maintains, "More science and technology are not going to get us out of our present ecological crisis until we find a new religion, or rethink our old one."[174] Further, "Since the roots of our trouble are so largely religious, the remedy must also be essentially religious, whether we call it that or not. We

---

171. White Jr., "Historical Roots of Our Ecologic Crisis," 12.
172. Marx, *Grundrisse*, 94.
173. White Jr., "Historical Roots of Our Ecologic Crisis," 12–13.
174. White Jr., "Historical Roots of Our Ecologic Crisis," 13.

must rethink and refeel our nature and destiny."¹⁷⁵ White Jr.'s sense of religious is, I think, closer to Collingwood's idea of historicized metaphysical theology than a call for another version of organized religion. An alternative Christian view is needed. White Jr. puts forward Saint Francis of Assisi (†1226) as his candidate of choice; he is "the greatest spiritual revolutionary in Western history," who "tried to substitute the idea of the equality of all creatures, including man, for the idea of man's limitless rule of creation."¹⁷⁶ The whole of creation will be set free—*Soteria*.

John Passmore

White Jr.'s remarkable sketch is mostly on target. But further qualifications are required to sufficiently identify this Occidental strain. In *Man's Responsibility for Nature* (1974), John Passmore extends White Jr.'s thesis. The origin of our crisis resides in the environmental cosmology of dominion; specifically, its interpretation within certain voluntarist streams of Western Christianity. Passmore begins his historical analysis with the Ur-text of Jewish, Christian, and Islamic civilizations. The Book of Genesis tells us the Lord God created humanity to have "dominion over the fish of the sea, and over the fowl of the air, and over the cattle, and over all the earth and over every creeping thing that creepeth upon the earth (Gen 1:26)."¹⁷⁷ Further, God not only tells us what we can do, but what we should do. God issues a mandate to humanity: "Be fruitful and multiply and replenish the earth and subdue it (Gen 1:28)."¹⁷⁸ This absolute presupposition influences contingent developments in social practice. The antecedent power of this cosmology makes the consequent ecological crisis a viable historical option.

"Uniquely Judaic, only," Passmore asserts, "is the suggestion that even before the Fall man *ruled over* his fellow creatures."¹⁷⁹ Unlike most creation narratives, humanity has dominion from the very beginning. Yet, original dominion of itself does not suggest that whatever exists is created for us to do with as we please. Hedwig Wahle, for instance, offers a sound explanation of the Hebrew idea of dominion. To Wahle, there is a moral calculus built into the concept, "The Hebrew word used here for dominion may imply real 'dominion,' but it also means 'descending.' Therefore, if man is worthy he dominates over the beasts and cattle; if he is not worthy," though,

---

175. White Jr., "Historical Roots of Our Ecologic Crisis," 14.
176. White Jr., "Historical Roots of Our Ecologic Crisis," 14.
177. Passmore, *Man's Responsibility for Nature*, 6.
178. Passmore, *Man's Responsibility for Nature*, 6.
179. Passmore, *Man's Responsibility for Nature*, 7.

"he will sink to a level lower than that of an animal."[180] A relationship of authentic dominion, then, must recognize that creation "belongs to God and not to man."[181] We are "guardians of that which is not" essentially ours; consequently, we have a duty to repay this "loan of nature" by "handing it over to our children in a perfect state so they in turn can bequeath it to posterity."[182]

The Old Testament may not explicitly license unfettered domination or squandering of *our trust fund*, but "there is one point on which it is absolutely clear: nature is not sacred."[183] The rejection of the view that nature is holy does not necessarily justify an irresponsible attitude, but it leaves the way open to that attitude, and does not condemn it as sacrilegious. Like White Jr., Moltmann, and Foster, Passmore claims the crucial cosmological move is the radical distinction between God and nature, which is "the striking peculiarity of the religion of the Hebrews."[184] "The Hebrew God," he continues, "to put the difference technically, is transcendent, not immanent; he creates and rules nature but is not to be identified with it."[185] The lack of a divine sense in our relationship to the natural world "left man free to exploit it with none of the qualms which, in many other societies, he would have felt when he cut down a tree or killed an animal."[186] Consequently, two traditions of interpretation emerge on dominion.

(1) *Despotism*: Humanity is a "ruler who cares for the world God made subject to him only in so far as he profits from doing so."[187] There are no moral obligations toward creatures and places. We can exploit them at will. Our immortal salvation does not depend on our mortal treatment of other species and elemental systems. (2) *Stewardship*: "He takes care of the living things over which he rules for their own sake, governing them not 'with force and with cruelty' but in the manner of the good shepherd, anxious to preserve them in the best possible condition for his master, in whose hands alone their final fate will rest."[188] The difference between this kind of responsibility position and that found among other immanent traditions, e.g., Jains, Hindus, Alchemical/Magical, Original Peoples, and so on, is the

---

180. Wahle, "Human Responsibility for God's Creation," 62.
181. Wahle, "Human Responsibility for God's Creation," 62.
182. Wahle, "Human Responsibility for God's Creation," 63.
183. Passmore, *Man's Responsibility for Nature*, 9.
184. Passmore, *Man's Responsibility for Nature*, 10.
185. Passmore, *Man's Responsibility for Nature*, 10.
186. Passmore, *Man's Responsibility for Nature*, 10.
187. Passmore, *Man's Responsibility for Nature*, 9.
188. Passmore, *Man's Responsibility for Nature*, 9.

lack of supervening sacrilege in the relationship between us and the extra-human content of nature. For example, the moral sacrilege of human murder is not equivalent to killing animals, cutting down trees, or ripping up the Earth. The intuitional conscience is just not affected or attuned in the same way. The despotic tradition informs our environmental crisis. Stewardship requires considerable rethinking. "Of these two ways of interpreting the Biblical view," Passmore rightly detects, "the second has recently come into favor. But the first view, that man is entitled to rule as an absolute despot, was for long predominant."[189] *Passmore's contribution to White Jr.'s general thesis is to establish which strain of Western Christianity informs the tyrannical position.* It would be a mistake to attribute the despotic tradition to Hebrew teaching because "it originates with the Greeks."[190] Specifically, it originates with the Christian appropriation of ancient Stoic philosophy.

Stoicism first appears in Athens in the Hellenistic period; it is introduced by Zeno of Citium (†262 BCE). Western Christianity's tyrannical cosmology originates from the syncretism between Hebraic dominion and Stoic anthropocentrism. The Stoic view, in its Roman version, prevails during Christianity's early formation. "It is one thing to say, following Genesis, that man has dominion over nature in the sense that he has the right to make use of it," Passmore states, and "quite another to say, following the Stoics, nature exists only to serve his interests."[191] One of the fundamental and lasting effects of this doctrine is to render humanity, on the ground of superior rationality, morally discontinuous with the rest of being. The limit of our moral consideration is the limit set by superior reason; we are only morally responsible to rational members of our species.

Stoic influenced Christianity can be taken as a guide to environmental practice in two distinct ways. (1) *Conservative*: Although God has designed everything for our use, it would be impious for us to alter it; this would imply that we can do better than God. The emphasis should be on leading good lives; being open to God's grace for eternal salvation: "What men had to transform was not nature, but themselves."[192] We cannot elevate ourselves to grace, to perfection, through our own *creative* hand; in short, we cannot save ourselves. We are free to use nature to secure the necessary material conditions of life without worshiping it, but otherwise it is best left alone. Passmore notes that cultivation of wilderness is the one exception; we are encouraged to transform wild spaces into farm and pasture. Conservatism dominates nearly three quarters of Christianity history: "Christianity, at

---

189. Passmore, *Man's Responsibility for Nature*, 9.
190. Passmore, *Man's Responsibility for Nature*, 13.
191. Passmore, *Man's Responsibility for Nature*, 17.
192. Passmore, *Man's Responsibility for Nature*, 17.

Metaphysics and Preliminary Statement of the Problem 93

least in its Hellenistic and medieval forms, certainly did not encourage man to undertake the transformation of the environment."[193] The conservative or quietest position is still prominent, as already noted, within the Eastern Church. Quietism denies the Promethean independency of self-making. Nature is a contemplative *subject* to be conserved because it manifests signs and symbols of Divinity. Through surrendering to the love of God, fount of life and freedom, we open ourselves to the event of saving grace. Grace cannot be willed into being by our own acts; it must be freely given by God. (2) *Radical*: This interpretation is the crucial one; the driving engine, according to Passmore, of our ecological crisis—as first indicated by White Jr., in rough outline, as *Occidental voluntarism*. Like the first, we are at liberty to transform nature, but unlike the first, we modify nature as a self-help program to save ourselves: *God only helps those who help themselves. God punishes those who do not help themselves.* The Roman Stoic Cicero (†43 BCE) foreshadows the prevailing spirit of what would become the environmental cosmology operative at the core of industrial-technological society. "By means of our hands," the great Roman voice encourages, "we try to create as it were a second nature within the world of Nature by applying the 'hand of man' to the discoveries of thought."[194] Dominion in this sense clearly means domination of nature through uniting knowledge with technical power. The idea is that we can save ourselves through our own independent and *creative* power. The means of salvation is the humanization of nature, *the construction of a second creation*; our only impediment is the lack of scientific knowledge and technical power to implement it.

The absolute presupposition informing our environmental crisis is the radical interpretation of Stoic Christianity. Stoicism's anthropocentrism and view of knowledge as technical mastery of nature combines with the Hebraic mandate of dominion. The world is designed for us to use; it exists for no other purpose. Since it has no divinity in it, the environment is not subject to moral consideration; rather, God commands us to replenish and subdue it. The ancient radical view is supplemented by the theological views of Pelagius, who claimed we can achieve God's grace through our own moral efforts. This minority report carries through the Christian underground by way of monastic practices and traditions. Pelagianism is revived in the Renaissance and Reformation, enshrined as socially normative by Enlightenment thinkers, and it is modified as a scientific project by Francis Bacon (†1626) and René Descartes (†1650). The way to self-made salvation is the unfettered humanization of nature. Modern life is presented as a secular program of liberation through mastery of the environment.

193. Passmore, *Man's Responsibility for Nature*, 18.
194. Cicero quoted in Passmore, *Man's Responsibility for Nature*, 18.

THREE

Pelagianism, Nature, Politics

THIS CHAPTER DEVELOPS THE strain of thought presented in the preceding chapter. The idea of self-salvation is traced from its theological origin to its transformation into modern politics. Salvation is made through right action. Mastery of self eventually translates into mastery of what surrounds the self: The social and natural environments. The environmental crisis arises from a Western Christian dispute on salvation. The essence of the conflict emerges as a theological clash of doctrines between Pelagius and Augustine. The debate between Pelagius and Augustine is not only a significant moment by which to understand the origin of our environmental crisis but, in many ways, it is a contest over Western civilization itself, the Christian idea of human nature, and the consequences for the world that flow from it.[1]

PELAGIUS VERSUS AUGUSTINE

Pelagius calls on us to reform ourselves by our own efforts. Our faculty for good and evil is what makes us God's "image and likeness," and what makes "all animals subject to man and set him as lord over creatures."[2] "Man alone,"

---

1. Peter Brown, for instance, calls the disagreement between Augustine and Pelagius "one of the most dramatic crises in the Christian church in the West" (Brown, *Augustine of Hippo*, 346). If Collingwood and Cochrane are right, however, Christian institutions carry the constellation of absolute presuppositions that constitute the historical tissue of Western culture; therefore, this crisis carries forward in a much wider, i.e., secular, and influential historical process than the obscure and archaic theological dispute it first appears. In this respect, Pelagius and Augustine are our ecological contemporaries.

2. Pelagius, "Letter to Demetrias," 37.

Pelagius continues, "was able to recognize the maker of all things and to serve God by using those same faculties which enabled him to hold sway over the rest."[3] "Pelagius," Stuart Squires verifies, propagates an anthropocentric theology, whereby "the dignity of the human person clearly becomes manifest in the dominion over the rest of God's creation."[4] Our right to rule creation is grounded in freedom, "There is no ground for preferring the rational creature to the others except that, while all the others possess only the good derived from their own circumstances and necessity, it alone possesses the good of free will also."[5] Further:

> The Lord of Justice wished man to be free to act and not under compulsion; it was for this reason that "he left him free to make his own decisions" and set before him life and death, good and evil and he shall be given whatever pleases him . . . that man has not been created truly good simply because he is able to do evil and is not obligated by the overpowering inclination of his own nature to do good on compulsion and without possibility of variation. . . . It is this choice between two ways, on this freedom to choose either alternative, that the glory of the rational mind is based, it is in this that the whole honor of our nature consists, it is from this that its dignity is derived and all good men win others' praise and their own reward. Nor would there be any virtue at all in the good done by the man who perseveres, if he could not at any time cross over to the path of evil.[6]

We are born indeterminate—open—without a substantial nature, with the capacity to self-*create* through the choices we make. To Pelagius, "It was because God wished to bestow on the rational creature the gift of doing good of his own free will and the capacity to exercise free choice, by implanting in man the possibility of choosing either alternative, that he made it his peculiar right to be what he wanted to be, so that with his capacity for good and evil he could do either quite naturally and then bend his will in the other direction too."[7] Evil is not a metaphysical substance that we inherit; it does not irrevocably stain or eclipse the capacity for goodness found in human nature. Evil is a matter of habit, "Nor is there any reason why it is made difficult for us to do good other than long habit of doing wrong which has infected us from childhood and corrupted us little by little over many

---

3. Pelagius, "Letter to Demetrias," 37.
4. Squires, *Pelagian Controversy*, 183.
5. Pelagius, "Letter to Demetrias," 37.
6. Pelagius, "Letter to Demetrias," 38.
7. Pelagius, "Letter to Demetrias," 38.

years and ever after holds us in bondage and slavery to itself, so that it seems somehow to have acquired the force of nature."[8] Evil is *good* in the sense that it makes good action autonomous, "He could not claim to possess the good of his own volition, unless he was the kind of creature that could also have possessed evil."[9] The power that determines our decision is our trace of divinity, "Our most excellent creator wished us to be able to do either but actually to do only one, that is, good, which he also commanded, giving us the capacity to do evil only so that we might do his will by exercising our own."[10] "That being so," Pelagius concludes, "this very capacity to do evil is also good—good, I say, because it makes the good part better by making it voluntary and independent, not bound by necessity but free to decide by itself."[11] If anything is said to define us, therefore, it is freedom, "the capacity for either direction," the donation of God's activity—what Pelagius means by *natural grace*.[12]

Humanity is an autonomous chooser. We have the capacity of freely deciding between good and evil. This grace is natural because it is the faculty of freedom given to all human beings; it is an original endowment that remains intact and unaltered by habitual evil. The potential for salvation, to become sinless, is open to the whole human race by faith and the works which actualize faith. God calls on us to be perfect; to be sharers of divine substance, the freedom of God. God would not command us to do what lies beyond our powers, placing on us commandments we could not bear, and then punishing us for something we cannot do. What kind of a God would command laws nobody could obey, and then punish us for not obeying them? "He has not willed to command anything impossible," Pelagius argues, "for he is righteous; and he will not condemn a man for what he could not help, for he is holy."[13] Through His supernatural grace, God may help those who help themselves, but it is not a necessary condition for self-perfecting goodness. We can achieve salvation on our own through activating our potential natural grace given equally to all. Free choice is natural grace, and it is powerful enough to enable a person to perform acts that will merit either Heaven or Hell. Free will must be granted to justify God's condemnation of us for doing evil. We are condemned by God because we have misused our freedom. Since perfection is naturally possible, it is

---

8. Pelagius, "Letter to Demetrias," 44.
9. Pelagius, "Letter to Demetrias," 38.
10. Pelagius, "Letter to Demetrias," 38.
11. Pelagius, "Letter to Demetrias," 38.
12. Pelagius quoted in Evans, *Pelagius*, 95. On natural grace, see Rees, *Pelagius*, 91.
13. Pelagius, "Letter to Demetrias," quoted in Passmore, *Perfectibility of Man*, 94.

obligatory. To Peter Brown, "the Pelagians placed the terrifying weight of complete freedom on the individual: he was responsible for his every action; every sin, therefore, could only be a deliberate act of contempt for God."[14] Evil habits can, and must, be reformed. We win or lose our salvation by what we decide to do or don't do. The Christian church, so conceived, is an institution made up of such self-perfected persons.

To Pelagius, human merit can achieve divine election. Conversely, divine election is impossible without human merit. Yet, the doctrine that anyone may be saved—whatever our merits—has been one of the great attractions of Christianity. Further, according to Passmore, "If all men can be perfect, given only that we seriously try, it is only a short step to the conclusion that they deserve damnation—or execution—for not being perfect."[15] Augustine, and the whole central tradition in Christian theology, insists that divine grace is essential for the performance of good action. In Pelagian terms, *supernatural* grace is needed to actualize natural or potential grace. Such an intervention cannot be merited by any preceding act of humanity. Divine grace is a gift of love to humanity. No action on our part can petition it in advance. *There is no salvation calculus of human merits and demerits that we can comprehend and, certainly, no set of self-perfecting techniques that can be practiced, qualifying us for salvation. I cannot be holier than Thou. Nobody can live without sin. To be is to be a sinner.*

The doctrine of Pelagius "blur[s] the distinction between the Catholic church and the good pagans," and Brown rightly observes, "No matter how self-consciously Christian the Pelagian movement had been, it rested firmly on a bed rock of the old ethical ideals of paganism, especially on Stoicism."[16] Ancient Stoic practice is directed to individual self-sufficiency and autonomy, getting a person to free herself in relation to others, to events, and to everything else. This kind of self-mastery means one is no longer subject to the impulses of the passions; that she no longer experiences anything that disturbs her rational equilibrium: *Apatheia*. She has *potestas* over herself. The cosmos communicates to those trained to listen. By obeying her own reason, an autonomous sage comprises the reason that rules the cosmos. Rational identification signifies that an individual wills what the entire world itself wills; by being master of herself, she is in *a certain way* master of the universe. She has achieved true freedom of the will.

---

14. Brown, *Augustine of Hippo*, 350–51.

15. Passmore, *Perfectibility of Man*, 95.

16. Brown, *Augustine of Hippo*, 351. For the Stoic setting of the Pelagian movement, see Chadwick, *Sentences of Sextus*, 118–22, 138; Ferguson, *Backgrounds of Early Christianity*, 354–69; Fransen, "Augustine, Pelagius, and the Controversy," 179–80.

Stoicism, then, provides Pelagius with his theory of human nature. Human beings are rational by nature. We can discover the cosmic natural law, governing us and all things and, thereby, act in ways determined by nature's reason to be right. Divine intervention and assistance are not required for moral improvement because *divine rationality* is already immanent in the structure of the cosmos. The natural law of cosmic reason directs human willing and deciding toward the right course of action and enactment. Rational persons are also moral persons because they live according to their natures. To Pelagius, God's principal gift of grace is nature itself (*bonum naturae*). The image of God in human beings is this capacity for moral choice and performance. God created moral nature in human beings so they can know and do what is right. If we have such a nature, we must be able *not* to sin all on our own. Choosing and doing the good do not require a further gift of divine assistance. A vertical or transcendental break is not needed to fulfill the ambitions of *autarkic-apathetic* individualism,

To Augustine, being a good pagan-Christian is an affront to the *patientia* faith.[17] Natural salvation is a fallacy of nonrelational being. Pagan *apatheia* fundamentally obstructs the truth of Christian *caritas*. The rational ideal of perfection requires that we sever all emotional ties to things: The cosmic order on which one depends. Autonomous individuals are presented as all-powerful and perfect; they are needless gods, sages, or angelic beings. Since they are truly rational, *perfecti* are self-sufficient, having to care for nothing or nobody but themselves. To believe that we can somehow free ourselves from our relations to others is a lie that shuts us off from their suffering and struggles. We then consider ourselves as being part of a self-created and sinless elect; all others are damned because they have failed to *self-actualize* after being given equal opportunity by the rational cosmos, deserving their self-caused misery or, even, our intentional maltreatment.[18] It also appears to make Christ unnecessary for salvation. The grace of nature's rational law is enough. Augustine, consequently, anathematizes the proposition that we could, without special grace from God, be without sin by the exercise of our free will.

Human beings do not have the natural power to do what is right by human will alone. Pagan independency must give way, completely, to Christian dependency. Salvation requires the surrender of power and pride, not

---

17. On Stoic and Christian variations of *patientia*, see Pap, "Stoic Virtues in Tertullian's Works," 7–16.

18. This strain of thought continues to permeate our lives. In *Neoliberalism's Demons*, for instance, Adam Kotsko gives a startling account of the current economic variation of this generic, Pelagian logic, "using freedom as a mechanism to generate blameworthiness. If you fail, it is your fault, and yours alone" (95).

their assertion on behalf of a divine reward, "And should he consent that we receive love from the grace of God, he must not suppose that any merits of our own preceded our reception of the gift. For what merits could we possibly have had at the time we loved not God? In order, indeed, that we might receive that love whereby we might love, we were loved while as yet we had no love ourselves."[19] At its core, Christianity is the message of the gift of God's grace through Christ, "nothing whatever in the way of goodness pertaining to godliness and real holiness can be accomplished without it."[20] To further distinguish himself from Pelagius, and the Classical aftermath of perfectionism that he represents, Augustine develops (and radicalizes) his doctrine of original sin.[21]

The Pelagian person is basically a separate individual, an enlightened and autonomous Christian in touch with natural reason. The Augustinian is engulfed in immense, enigmatic solidarities: Afflicted events of co-transformation between human beings, creation, and God. To Pelagius, sin is a matter of habit and choice. Sinners choose to imitate Adam, the first sinner and, crucially, it is within their power to choose not to. By the light of reason, we can save ourselves by willing the good. Augustine also proposes that humankind receives its disposition for malevolence from the sin of Adam. But it is not a question of an individual's habitual choices; it is an *ontological* (and historical) matter of the deepest concern. In the most intimate and irreversible mode of being, we are an Adamic race or species, a carrier and transmitter of an inherited darkness that we cannot *enlighten* of our own accord. As Michel Foucault explains, what is at issue here for the early Christian pastorate is the fundamental configuration of "the relations between salvation and perfection. Does salvation imply perfection? Does the act that saves us make us perfect, or do we have to be perfect to be saved?"[22]

Pelagius presents human nature as the indeterminate potential of natural grace, having no predisposition for either good or evil. He preserves the need for perfection and the natural capacity to achieve it. Superhuman Christians can achieve their own salvation through their *habitual* practice of various techniques of self-mastery. Augustine grounds salvation in *essential* human imperfection; this non-Classical absolute presupposition indicates, "Christianity is a religion of salvation in non-perfection."[23] He separates perfection from salvation: We "can be saved without being

---

19. Augustine, "What True Grace Is," 178.
20. Augustine, "What True Grace Is," 178.
21. See Wiley, *Original Sin*, 56–75.
22. Foucault, *On the Government of the Living*, 258–59.
23. Foucault, *On the Government of the Living*, 259.

perfect."[24] Foucault accurately reads this moment as decisive for Western ideas of *governmentality*, "that two institutions developed that are both close and in a sense parallel, but go in opposite and opposed directions."[25] The two orientations pursue different questions: "What does it mean to still want perfection in a system of salvation? You can see that this question is opposite and symmetrical to the question: how can one preserve salvation if one continues to sin?"[26] Augustine achieves the medieval majority report with the latter question, but Pelagius eventually triumphs in modernity. Their overlap and distinction require further clarity.

Pelagius claims to be inspired by Augustine's early work entitled *On Free Choice of the Will* (*De Libero Arbitrio*) (387–395 CE). Although Augustine eventually (and vehemently) denies he held comparable views in his early career (*Retractationes* 1.9.2–6), many passages in Book One of this work are enough to justify at least some of the theological incitement of Pelagius and his followers. The moral tones of Stoic willpower are certainly detectable as Augustine argues against the Manichees, seeking "to refute those who deny that the origin of evil lies in the free choice of the will and therefore contend that we should blame evil on God, the Creator of all natures," those who "assert the existence of an unchangeable principle of evil coeternal with God."[27] Augustine's theodicean challenge to the Manichees places the root of evil in the individual human will. God is not to blame. We are. Radical freedom is required to secure this new site. On the independency of the human will, we read, for example, "only its own will and free choice can make the mind a companion to cupidity" and, concerning people who take this path to perdition, "that it is by their own will that they have fallen from happiness into the hardships of mortal life."[28] More directly, "it is by the will that we lead and deserve a praiseworthy life and happy life, or a contemptible and unhappy one," which Augustine ascribes to an "eternal law" that "has established with unshakable firmness that the will is rewarded with happiness or punished with unhappiness depending on its merit."[29] All of this sounds very Pelagian. In Book Two, however, the difference between his theology and that of Pelagius begins to surface quite distinctly.

---

24. Foucault, *On the Government of the Living*, 259.
25. Foucault, *On the Government of the Living*, 259.
26. Foucault, *On the Government of the Living*, 259.
27. Augustine, "Excerpt: *Reconsiderations*," 124–25.
28. Augustine, *On Free Choice of the Will*, 17, 18.
29. Augustine, *On Free Choice of the Will*, 22, 23.

Augustine presents his doctrine of the will as an *intermediate good* in God's well-ordered hierarchy of goods, capable of accommodating and explaining the presence of evil in such a cosmos. Evil is permitted by God because the creature responsible for it is the hinge of creation, an intermediary more in being than the innocents of nature that cannot do otherwise, but less than the perfection of the angels who, also, cannot do otherwise. "There is no blame involved," Augustine stresses, "when nature and necessity determine an action."[30] If something is "compelled by its own nature" to do something, it is beyond fault.[31] The free creature exists to complete the whole cosmos. Without a voluntary creature that can act, "either rightly or wrongly," the cosmos becomes something diminished, something less perfect, less worthy of its creator.[32] In this sense, Dominic Keech points out, "Augustine begins to explore the possibility that the presence of evil in the world may in fact be a constitutive part of the well-ordered hierarchy of goods."[33] But can, as Pelagius argues, a human being achieve moral merit and perfection by her own natural power, "when the will cleaves to the common and unchangeable good," and, conversely, damnation, when the will turns, "away from the unchangeable good and toward changeable goods?"[34]

To Augustine, in order to preserve the core of Christianity, only the latter case can be true. Moral "movement is voluntary," but "we cannot pick ourselves up voluntarily as we fell voluntarily, let us hold with confident faith the right hand of God—that is, our Lord Jesus Christ—which has been held out from on high. Let us await him with resolute hope and desire him with ardent charity."[35] To Pelagius, sin is superficial; it is a matter of choice and habit. Wrong choices can simply be reversed. Augustine makes sin a permanent, ontological *discordia*. To be a human being is *to be* a sinner. The cure must be something far deeper than mere voluntary change of habit. Only the Christ event can open the way to the "highest good"—that which "is not used up in the course of time; it does not move from place to place. Night does not cover it, and no shadow hides it."[36]

Keech is, once more, correct in his analysis. The central problem for Augustine with Pelagianism's "gospel of autonomy"—the "claim that humans could attain to a sinless life through free will"—is its sidelining of the

30. Augustine, *On Free Choice of the Will*, 71.
31. Augustine, *On Free Choice of the Will*, 71.
32. Augustine, *On Free Choice of the Will*, 67.
33. Keech, *Anti-Pelagian Christology of Augustine*, 73.
34. Augustine, *On Free Choice of the Will*, 68.
35. Augustine, *On Free Choice of the Will*, 69.
36. Augustine, *On Free Choice of the Will*, 59, 58.

essential truth of Christianity: If we can save ourselves, why is the Incarnation needed at all?[37] To preserve the integrity of the faith, consequently, "any suggestion of meriting grace by isolated human will is entirely done away with."[38] Brown also demonstrates that Pelagian ideas "cut at the roots of episcopal authority," "that by appeasing the Pelagians the Catholic church would lose the vast authority it had begun to wield as the only force that could 'liberate' men from themselves."[39] Tatha Wiley coincides with both commentators. Augustine's anti-Pelagian doctrine of original sin arises as a "desire to ground the universal necessity of Christ's redemption," and to secure "the church as mediator of salvation."[40] To achieve these things, he must deny, for every aspect of experience, that human nature is neutrally open to good and evil. It is biased towards evil.

The theologically mature Augustine is clear and militant. Christ fulfills both the necessary *and sufficient* conditions for salvation: "Nobody, absolutely no one at all, has been, is being or will be freed, without the grace of the liberator" (*Pecc. Orig.* 34.29).[41] In this salvific event, an individual will's self-achieved merits count for naught: "For their hearts too were cleansed by the faith of the mediator, and love was poured into them by the Holy Spirit; he blows where he wills without following an individual's merits, but creates merit itself" (*Pecc. Orig.* 1.1–25.22).[42] In order to further emphasize the necessity for divine grace over the capacity of natural grace for salvation, Augustine claims the human will has an inevitable tendency towards evil. Through the first sin of Adam, the whole human race bears the transmission of substantive evil. The corruption of the will, i.e., *concupiscence*, is an inherited part of our Adamic being. We are fallen creatures: *Massa peccati*. Augustine writes that "the seed of our common human nature was present in Adam and thus we in him. By birth all men belong to Adam and his sin, just as all who are reborn belong to Christ."[43] The liberation offered by the Incarnate Christ, the Mediator, can only be salvific for *all* humankind because *all* human beings are *massa peccati*. Therefore, the will needs the Incarnate Christ's divine grace even more to *free* it from its inherited disposition.

---

37. Keech, *Anti-Pelagian Christology of Augustine*, 3, 43.
38. Keech, *Anti-Pelagian Christology of Augustine*, 80.
39. Brown, *Augustine of Hippo*, 359.
40. Wiley, *Original Sin*, 57, 56.
41. Augustine quoted in Keech, *Anti-Pelagian Christology of Augustine*, 91.
42. Augustine quoted in Keech, *Anti-Pelagian Christology of Augustine*, 90.
43. Augustine quoted in Vandervelde, *Original Sin*, 16.

Augustine distinguishes between human free choice (*liberum arbitrium*), what Pelagius calls natural grace, and higher freedom (*libertas*). Only the latter—as a result of divine grace—can properly situate the activity of the former. The former left to its own tendencies cannot escape the gravity of substantial evil. Human beings retain freedom of choice (*liberum arbitrium*) after Adam's sin, but it is free choice in inescapable servitude to sin. In fallen human nature, what free choice does easily is choose evil. More difficult, perhaps even impossible for Augustine, is choosing and doing good. By Adam's sin, human beings lose true freedom (*libertas*), the freedom to direct ourselves wholly toward our true good. Freedom is diminished by Adam's sin, causing the will to be misguided. In terms of Augustine's trinitarian theology of *imago Dei*, original sin renders the human image "deformed and discolored" and, while our image is corrupted by our own will, it cannot be "reformed and renovated" except through the power and mercy of God's grace (*Trin.* 14.16.22).[44] To Gerald P. Boersma, "The distinction between the 'image' and 'likeness' becomes concretized in Augustine's dealings with the Pelagians. The image is iterated as a type of *capacity* for union with God, but it requires the operations of grace and the free movement of the will to achieve its end."[45] The critical question centers on agency: Can we—in any sense, under any circumstances—make the initial *free movement of the will*? Or does the operation of grace also account for the activation of our capacity for movement?

Pelagius thought Augustine's portrayal of sin as effectively inevitable would contribute to moral irresponsibility. If sin is fated, why should we try to pursue a moral life? Further, if grace is required to always precede and, therefore, activate the will's motion to accept the grace that is also given, then we seem to be doubly helpless: Grace requires the annihilation of agency in order to supposedly rehabilitate it. To accept the gift of grace, our hand must also be lifted by grace. We are the paralyzed middle term in the syllogism of salvation. The early Augustine of *On Free Choice of the Will* (*De Libero Arbitrio*), however, seems more accommodating to free human initiative. God orders and foreknows all things, but He creates a distinct space for autonomous activity. "God's foreknowledge," Augustine claims, "does not force the future to happen."[46] Human agency exists in the ontological gap between foreknowledge and causation: "God's foreknowledge does not cause everything he foreknows."[47] God's acausal foreknowl-

---

44. Augustine quoted in Boersma, *Augustine's Early Theology of Image*, 261.
45. Boersma, *Augustine's Early Theology of Image*, 261n18.
46. Augustine, *On Free Choice of the Will*, 78.
47. Augustine, *On Free Choice of the Will*, 78.

edge leaves us free to act without being determined by anything external to our will and, hence, in this sense, we can understand the morality of Augustine's statement, "God justly punishes the sins he foreknows but does not cause."[48] In Book Three, Augustine does say human beings are "born under the penalty of that sin," taking away "their power to be good," but he does leave a crucial remainder—a drive or initiative of the will—so that "it must implore its Creator for help in the struggle."[49] We are neither helpless nor self-sufficient. Grace may arrive without our merit, certainly, but sincere faith that turns the will to God from our side of things, opening it to the absolute need for grace, *for help in the struggle*, is not to be condemned as mere pride either.

For Augustine of later works, though, in full battle with Pelagian theological forces, he appears to close the gap on human agency—that is, predestination and grace form a doubly causal framework for salvation. Grace must precede the will's turning to God; it *causes* an individual's act of faith. To Augustine, "it is indeed by the will that we sin or live rightly. But unless the will is liberated by grace from its bondage to sin and is helped to overcome its vices, mortals cannot live pious and righteous lives. And unless the divine grace by which the will is freed preceded the act of the will, it would not be grace at all. It would be given in accordance with the will's merits, whereas grace is given freely."[50] The will is not free to choose God, and God does not choose us because there is an established, self-achieved worthiness. He then speaks "of the grace of God, by which he so predestines his chosen people that he himself prepares the wills of those who are already using their free choice."[51] By free choice he means (*liberum arbitrium*). On its own, the human will cannot achieve the *libertas* of grace in any conceivable way. In his *Anti-Pelagian Writings*, we read Augustine's double causal doctrine, "between grace and predestination there is only this difference, that predestination is the preparation for grace, while grace is the donation itself."[52] Therefore, God's causal foreknowledge or predestination is the "preparation of grace; which grace is the effect of that predestination."[53] Acausal "foreknowledge may exist without predestination" because it

---

48. Augustine, *On Free Choice of the Will*, 78.

49. Augustine, *On Free Choice of the Will*, 78, 108, 106, 110. On this early version, see Levering, *Predestination*, 44–49.

50. Augustine, "Excerpt: *Reconsiderations*," 127.

51. Augustine, "Excerpt: *Reconsiderations*," 125.

52. Augustine, "In What Respects Predestination and Grace Differ," 19.

53. Augustine, "In What Respects Predestination and Grace Differ," 19.

concerns things God does not do.[54] God's causal foreknowledge, "by predestination," concerns "those things which He was about to do."[55] The act of faith necessary for grace does not originate from "the power of our will but from His own predestination. For He promised what He Himself would do, not what men would do. Because, although men do those good things which pertain to God's worship, He Himself makes them to do what He has commanded; it is not they that cause Him to do what He has promised. Otherwise the fulfilment of God's promises would not be in the power of God, but in that of men."[56] The power and the glory totally belong to God, acting to select, i.e., predestine, an elite section of humanity for saving grace, leaving the rest as *massa damnata*, *massa peccati*, and so on—the irredeemable debris of salvation history.

Augustine's position, then, may have its own difficulties. His alleged doctrine of a predestined elect doubly cements in the uselessness of human striving. Salvation by divine grace alone is not universal. God has casually preordained certain individuals for salvation; the rest of humanity is damned. It appears that it doesn't matter what we do, or how we live, because our merits do not count in the calculus of God's grace or His providence. The moral struggle is valueless if the rejected cannot be saved no matter how hard they try, and the saved cannot fall no matter how bad they behave. Does this doctrine, by informing us that our efforts are worthless, meritless, weaken or even abolish the will to do good over evil? On the nature of human freedom, an enduring and volatile aporia rises on the horizon of Western culture.

JOHN CASSIAN

Between Pelagius and Augustine stands John Cassian (†435). Born in the ancient Scythian region—what is now mostly Romania—Cassian is the principal founder of the Western Christian ascetic movement.[57] His career involves travel, study, and priestly duties in Egypt, Constantinople, Rome, and Antioch. He eventually settles in Marseilles, where he founds two monasteries and composes three treatises (*The Institutes of the Cenobia and the Remedies for the Eight Principle Vices*; *The Conferences*; and *On the Incarnation of Christ against Nestorius*). Cassian brings Occidental stability to the intensifying, and increasingly heterodox, ascetic movements being

---

54. Augustine, "In What Respects Predestination and Grace Differ" 19.
55. Augustine, "In What Respects Predestination and Grace Differ" 19.
56. Augustine, "In What Respects Predestination and Grace Differ" 19.
57. See Foucault, *On the Government of the Living*, 261, 279n28.

imported from the Greek East and the Orient. Western monasticism is a reaction to the latter's escalation of radical austerities and, even, immolations; all on behalf of the precept that one can achieve divinity through these practices. Nevertheless—and despite his achievements tempering extreme perfectionism—Cassian is also the crucial figure in a vague tradition (called the *Massilian*: Men of Marseilles) that is held responsible for transmitting Pelagianism through the underground strains of Western history.[58]

Cassian's project establishes an orthodox regulation of Christian ascesis. "In short," Foucault explains, "ascesis and the rules of ascesis had to be brought back into the system of the Church itself."[59] Against the "divine man, the perfect man" of the self-saved ascetic, Cassian lays the "foundation of the first great practice of *discretio*, of moderation."[60] A. M. C. Casiday similarly depicts Cassian's approach to ascetic practice: It is marked by a "certain moderation, even humaneness," which implies that he "judged the forms of self-mortification associated with the fathers of Syria and Egypt to be out of place and inappropriate in the Occident."[61] Both Foucault and Casiday agree that Cassian's central achievement is (in Foucault's words) to successfully "distinguish the system of salvation and the requirement of perfection. The task of salvation does entail a work of striving for perfection; it does not postulate the existence of perfection."[62] *Cassian is not a Pelagian, and his version of Christianity is "a religion of salvation uncoupled from the presumption of perfection."*[63] Yet, Cassian's account of how divine grace and human effort are related must still assure the *work of striving for perfection* is still worthwhile, even though its goal of sinlessness is impossible to achieve for mortals. He must steer a middle course between the Scylla of perfectionism and the Charybdis of fatalism. This event of theological navigation occurs in *Conference* 13 and it remains deeply controversial.

Cassian's monastic ideal does effectively fend off the forces of Eastern perfectionism, but it must also counter the undertow of *Provençal fatalism*.

---

58. See Hanby, "Augustine And Descartes," 466–68; *Augustine and Modernity*, 117–26.

59. Foucault, *On the Government of the Living*, 292.

60. Foucault, *On the Government of the Living*, 292, 293. The development of Cassian's *discretio* becomes "the schema of Christian subjectivation," which is a foundational absolute presupposition, "for the history of the relationships between truth and subjectivity in the Christian West" (309, 308).

61. Casiday, *Tradition and Theology in St. John Cassian*, 57.

62. Foucault, *On the Government of the Living*, 293.

63. Foucault, *On the Government of the Living*, 309. On Cassian as an anti-Pelagian, see Casiday, *Tradition and Theology in St. John Cassian*, 73–118.

Cassian must deal with the local—Augustine enthused—Predestinationists.[64] The Gallic reception of Augustine's double causal doctrine of grace and predestination is understandably problematic for those who dedicate their lives to mastery of the will, i.e., *ascesis*. Some people are created for salvation. Some are created for damnation. All are saved or damned regardless of their action. If, as the Provençal fatalists argue, ascetic *discretio* cannot of itself secure even the increased possibility of post-mortem divine election because all things are causally preordained, the Western monastic movement faces a significant crisis, to say the least. To be blunt, if the fatalists are correct, asceticism can claim no exceptional path to salvation over any other way of life. One could just as well be a herdsman, shopkeeper, servant, or even soldier, thief, or murderer. Causal necessity subtracts choice and effort from the world. The former is an illusion. The latter is useless. Cassian, then, is faced with the subtle task of answering the fatalists in such a way as to secure the theological legitimacy of the ascetic way of life while, at the same time, not falling into perfectionism. He defends the authenticity of the Christian struggle to be, if not perfect, then, in some significant way, morally and spiritually *better*—not *holier than thou* but *holier than I*—that is, a human being can, with the aid of ascetic practice, elevate themselves from a previous condition. To improve is not to be perfect.

Conference 13 attempts to mediate between extremes, and it relies exclusively on arguments from the authority of scripture. What emerges is an affirmation of the aporia on human freedom. Cassian exhibits scripture that supports salvation that depends on initiating acts of human will and salvation that does not, where the grace of God begins, accompanies, and ends the process of salvation. He concludes that the Christian faith requires we affirm both human free will and divine grace. To deny one or the other is an act of prideful contradiction. To Cassian, "These things are mixed together and fused so indistinguishably that which is dependent on which is a greater question as far as many people are concerned—that is, whether God has mercy on us because we manifest the beginnings of a good will, or we acquire the beginnings of a good will because God is merciful. For many who hold to one of these alternatives and assert it more freely than is right have fallen into different self-contradictory errors" (XI.1).[65] He is quite clear: "These two things—that is, the grace of God and free will—certainly seem mutually opposed to one another, but both are in accord, and we understand that we must accept both in like manner by reason of our religion,

---

64. On the Predestinationists of fifth-century southern Gaul, see Casiday, *Tradition and Theology in St. John Cassian*, 43–44.

65. Cassian, *Conferences*, 476.

lest by removing one of them from the human being we contravene the rule of the Church's faith" (XI.4).[66] But how, exactly, are we to understand and affirm the harmony of grace and free will?

Cassian provides an ingenious, *dialectical* alternative. His calculus of salvation affirms the gratuitous nature of divine grace *and* the worthiness of free human faith and good works. Cassian refuses to make the stark choice between the radical optimism of self-salvation and the equally as radical counter-position of pessimistic fatalism. We cannot save ourselves, but we are not simply saved by preordained ordinance no matter what we do. How God confers salvation is not something we can claim to know with the degree of certainty put forward by both radical positions. How and who God saves is ultimately up to God. Any person that claims to know God's ways with complete surety falls into hubris, using such claims for purely mortal ends and imposing a false limitation on God's absolute freedom and unconditional love. What is lost in such disputes on the mode of deliverance is the miracle of salvation as such; that there is such giving and elevation at all.

To Cassian there is a continuum: $0 \leq df \leq 1$, where df stands for *degree of faith*, 0 for no faith and 1 for complete faith. In our mortal lives, 0 and 1 are absolute limits. A person cannot be created totally without faith or achieve perfect faith. God gives salvation to each according to their circumstances, abilities, and degree of faith. "And so the manifold wisdom of God," Cassian claims, "dispenses the salvation of human beings by numerous and inscrutable kindnesses and imparts its generous grace according to the capacity of each person, so that he wills to administer healing not according to the uniform power of his majesty but according to the degree of faith that he finds in each person or that he himself has bestowed on each person" (XV.2).[67] The ways of God's salvation are multiple and, for the most part, enigmatic: "Hence it is quite clear that 'inscrutable are the judgments of God and unsearchable his ways' by which he draws the human race" (XV.1).[68] Salvation reflects the "manifold bounty of God's design," and, "Whoever believes that he can sound the depths of that immeasurable abyss by human reason is trying to nullify the marvelous aspect of this knowledge" (XVII.2–3).[69] Cassian gives a strong implication here that both extreme perfectionists and extreme fatalists are "declaring with impious audacity that the judgments of God are not inscrutable and that his ways are traceable" (XVII.3).[70] Both

---

66. Cassian, *Conferences*, 477.
67. Cassian, *Conferences*, 486.
68. Cassian, *Conferences*, 485–86.
69. Cassian, *Conferences*, 489.
70. Cassian, *Conferences*, 489.

maximums dispense with humility before the divine infinite, overstepping their appropriate, reasonable limitations.

In His intellect, freedom, and generosity, only God is perfect; perhaps, saving each and all because God loves unconditionally. Christianity demands a double affirmation of both sides of the aporia. We must not erase the worthiness of human striving or put restrictions on God's grace. *Sometimes* we are saved by our faith alone; sometimes accompanied by works, demonstrating faith. But *sometimes* we are saved by God conferring the faith by which we are saved, when we have next to no faith, good works, or even deeply mired in the most heinous of sins, believing ourselves to be without the possibility of salvation—an *Amazing Grace*. Cassian upholds the priority of salvific difference, "And God's generosity is shaped according to the capacity of human faith," but, "no one should think that we have suggested these things in an attempt to say that the whole of salvation is entirely dependent on our faith, according to the godless opinion of some, who ascribe everything to free will and understand that the grace of God is dispensed to each person in conformity with his deserts. We, however, declare firmly and clearly that the grace of God sometimes even overflows and surpasses the limits of human faithlessness" (XVI.5; XVII.1).[71] Moreover, the authority of scripture sanctions multiplicity: "From these examples which we have produced from the gospel writings we shall be able to perceive very clearly that God provides for the salvation of the human race in numberless different manners and in inscrutable ways" (XVII.1).[72] Sometimes grace precedes the free human will. Sometimes the will precedes grace. Cassian writes, "He inspires some who wish it and thirst for it, to a greater ardor, while some others, who do not even wish it, he compels against their will. Sometimes he helps to accomplish the things that he sees we desire for our own good, and at other times he inspires the beginnings of that holy desire and bestows both the commencement of a good work and perseverance in it" (XVII.1).[73]

In the economy of God's grace, then, there is equality of distribution: From each according to her degree of faith, to each according to her need of salvation. At certain times, within certain events, we fall somewhere on the continuum, where our degree of faith can be very high, or near non-existent. The lower our degree of faith, the higher our degree of need becomes. What Cassian seems to be saying is that while God does not guarantee us salvation for our faith and works, the less we need him for these things, the more we can increase towards the possibility of salvation by our own

---

71. Cassian, *Conferences*, 487.
72. Cassian, *Conferences*, 488.
73. Cassian, *Conferences*, 488.

abilities. We can become *much better* human beings, but not perfect: Therefore, the ascetic way of life is a legitimate undertaking. Legitimacy is supremely qualified. Although not arbitrary from God's perspective, salvation is still a very contingent affair from our limited view. No matter how high our abilities for faith and good works, no one can truly claim to know they are saved in this life. No one can become sinless. Further, no matter what limited degree of ability we may have, we are never to be completely written off as not savable—especially by the prideful and righteous pretensions of the self-perfected.

Cassian compares God to a father who works as a gracious physician. Sin in the soul, like disease in the body, individuates our human condition—that is, like disease, everyone will manifest sin differently, requiring an *equally different* way of healing, of saving: "Therefore it is evident from indubitable faith and from—as I would say—palpable experience that the God of the universe, like a most loving father and a most gracious physician, works all things evenhandedly in everyone, according to the Apostle" (XVIII.2).[74] *Evenhandedness* signifies equality of salvific distribution, taking contingency and context into consideration. The mode of salvation depends, like a prescription for a patient, on the specific nature of the individual affliction. "Sometimes," Cassian repeats with daring precision, "he inspires the beginnings of salvation and places in each person a fervent good will, while sometimes he grants the performance of the work and the perfection of virtuousness. Sometimes he calls back from near ruin and a sudden fall even the unwilling and the unaware, while sometimes he provides occasions and opportunities for salvation and withholds heedless and violent efforts from deadly outcomes. Some he supports as they hasten and run, while others he draws unwillingly and resisting and compels them to a good will" (XVIII.2).[75]

Cassian's *evenhandedness* in dealing with the dispute between perfectionists and fatalists is complicated by his position as Abbott of twin monasteries. Predictably, the practice of ascesis leads to stressing the responsibilities of the human will. *Cut away the passions, then grace will flow.* First the will acts, then grace is given. In his *Institutes*, Cassian's call to Christian perfection often sounds very Pelagian: "When we say that human efforts cannot of themselves secure perfection without the aid of God, we thus insist that God's mercy and grace are bestowed *only* upon those who labor and exert themselves" (XII.14).[76] He instructs the novices on the

---

74. Cassian, *Conferences*, 489–90.

75. Cassian, *Conferences*, 490.

76. Cassian, *Institutes*. For the full measure of this disciplinary regime, see Foucault, *On the Government of the Living*, 261–75.

originating power of their wills, "It is given to them that ask, and opened to them that knock, and found by them that seek" (XII.14).[77] Salvation, in this case, seems to depend on an inviolable human will that has the power to voluntarily open itself to God: "For he is at hand to bestow all these things, if only the opportunity is given to him by our good will" (XII.14).[78]

Owen Chadwick (†2015) explains Cassian's dilemma: "Because he was writing for the novices and the inexperienced; because he felt impelled to push the monks into the fight—he turned with inconsistency to state the successive theory of freewill and grace."[79] Cassian's English translator, Boniface Ramsey, is more measured in his interpretation. Cassian is not preaching salvation by the merit of the will alone; rather, in his *The Institutes*, especially, he seeks "to reassure his monastic audience in southern Gaul that their arduous life counted for something and that somehow grace and human effort could meet each other partway."[80] Emendation of the will is co-operative. To do God's will, the prideful will must be fundamentally altered, and, in this respect, Cassian does not think the will is totally debilitated. *Conference* 13 offers a more developed outlook and, perhaps, a way to reconcile this apparent inconsistency. If, as is the case with a novice Sister or Brother, one is granted the opportunity and ability to increase your *degree of faith*, you are compelled to do so. In these circumstances, to not do so is to consciously renege on your potential to actualize a higher degree of faith and good effort. In the economy of salvation this *laziness*, as Cassian calls it, is a much worse moral condition than that found in those with little ability or opportunity and, therefore, a higher degree of need. To not *knock* when you are at the door, and have the ability to do so, is much more detrimental to your prospects for salvation than those whose need is so great, whose degree of faith so little, that they have to be brought by God to the door of salvation, and whose hand must be held or, in some cases, pushed to knock against their will.

OCKHAM VERSUS BRADWARDINE

Within the Western monastic tradition, however, Cassian's theological subtleties carry the minority report of Pelagianism or *semi-Pelagianism* down through the centuries.[81] From the sixth to the fourteenth century, the nature

77. Cassian, *Institutes*.
78. Cassian, *Institutes*.
79. Chadwick, *John Cassian*, 113.
80. Ramsey, "John Cassian and Augustine," 129.
81. The controversy continues to follow Cassian. Even Thomas Merton claims

of this transmission and the general historical trail of figures and ideas are unclear (at least within the author's incomplete research). What emerges in the fourteenth century is better documented, but it is still historically controversial.[82] The reappearance of Pelagianism marks the break between *via antiqua* and *via moderna*. Pelagianism is an absolute presupposition of *via moderna*. In the first part of the fourteenth century, Oxford master Thomas Bradwardine (†1349) launches a formidable offensive "Contra Pelagium," in a massive work completed in 1344: *De causa Dei*. What occasions such an immense effort? Bradwardine's antagonist is William of Ockham (†1347/49). Ockham and his followers are referred to as the "Moderni," which Bradwardine identifies with Pelagianism: "Sicut antiqui Pelagiani . . . ita et moderni."[83]

What makes Ockham's ideas Pelagian is the exultation of will and reason, which are given an autonomous domain of their own. *Nature* replaces God's creation. Ockham performs a double untying of real relations between things: (a) God from creation, and (b) the human mind from things in that creation. (a) The realm of the senses ceases to impart any rational knowledge of God. Since neither God nor His traces in creation are available to sense experience, they cease to belong to the region of reason because they are outside the terms of possible reference. God belongs to the supernatural realm of faith. Natural knowledge and the exercise of the practical will are divorced from matters of faith, which cannot be proven or enlightened by reason. Adrian Pabst provides an accurate metaphysical summary: Ockham forsakes the Christian-Neoplatonic "emphasis on God's free gift of being and the divine act of being binding together all individual things in favor of God's absolute, unmediated power (*potentia Dei absoluta*) that keeps all being in separate existence, without any unifying bond of being."[84] Within "the temporal-spatial realm of the *saeculum*," common creation is replaced by individualistic nature.[85]

Cassian seems to commit a *Pelagian* error because Cassian claims "the first beginnings of salvation *sometimes* come from God and sometimes from man." Cassian is wrong here on *sometimes from man* because he "actually deviated from the true doctrine (of St. Augustine)" (Merton, *Cassian and the Fathers*, 105).

82. See Gilbert, "Ockham, Wyclif, and the 'Via Moderna,'" 85–125; Courtenay, "Antiqui and Moderni," 3–10; Oberman, "*Via Antiqua* and *Via Moderna*," 23–40.

83. Bradwardine quoted in Oberman, "*Via Antiqua* and *Via Moderna*," 23.

84. Pabst, *Metaphysics*, 291. On Ockham's theory of relations, see Brower, "Aristotelian versus Contemporary Perspectives," 47–54; Henninger, *Relations*, 119–49; Spade, "Ockham's Nominalist Metaphysics," 100–117. On Ockham's non-relational theory of cognition and signification, see Rayman, "Ockham's Theory of Natural Signification," 289–323.

85. Pabst, *Metaphysics*, 291.

There can be no metaphysical relationship "between God and world. This absence of real relations extends to all beings within creation."[86] The link between God and creation is broken; in *nature* there is no means of tracing God's attributes of mercy, goodness, justice and so on. Creation communicates divinity; nature does not. (b) The abstraction of concepts from the senses transcend, have a radical independence from, the things that originally occasioned their formation. Accordingly, all our concepts, abstractions, and values derive from the mind and not from things themselves. Natural knowledge is nominal, of the logic of terms, not of the being of things. The new nature is a logical taxonomy of terms, propositions, and syllogisms. The order of things in God's creation is replaced by the order of words, which are (more or less) arbitrary products of various communities of minds. The world reveals our signatures, not God's.

To Gordon Leff, Ockham's double removal of real relations "seemed inevitably to lead to partisanship for men and the natural."[87] It is not surprising, then, that the ascendancy of such a purely human world would induce a theological crisis; the scale of which had not be been experienced "since the Pelagian controversy of the fourth century."[88] Ockham divides God from nature, revelation from sense experience, and faith from reason. This radical partition poses a formidable challenge to traditional Christian cosmology: "It is evidence of the breakdown in the old harmony between the divine and the created that, instead of ascertaining God through His traces in the world, His existence had to be reconciled with man's. The unity between the divine and the created which formed the starting-point of the thirteenth-century systems had given place to a one-sided attitude in which the two were not apprehended as part of one another."[89] Something fundamental has shifted—an incommensurate inversion of things, priorities, and values. More simply, the Ockhamists see humanity where Bradwardine says they should see God; they see nature where they should see creation: "Free will for them came before grace; they measured the nature of the future and of contingency in human not divine terms."[90] Ockham is eventually called to account for his views by the *magistri* of Avignon in 1326. Of the fifty-one articles extracted from his work the first four are called Pelagian. In defending these articles Ockham comes closest to articulating the classical views of Pelagius; we earn merit or condemnation only if our wills are free to move

---

86. Pabst, *Metaphysics*, 291.
87. Leff, *Bradwardine and the Pelagians*, 127.
88. Leff, *Bradwardine and the Pelagians*, 10.
89. Leff, *Bradwardine and the Pelagians*, 10–11.
90. Leff, *Bradwardine and the Pelagians*, 13.

in either direction. Ockham's Pelagianism is a complex similitude of the original, dealing with different theological concerns.[91] What is important here is that the transmission of this historical strain has been established and, despite the efforts of Bradwardine and others, this persona of modernity continues to spread its influence.

RENAISSANCE AND REFORMATION VARIATIONS

In the Italian Renaissance, Pelagianism breaks free from Christian asceticism and scholastic theology, leaning more toward its Greco-Roman origins. Anthropocentric optimism gathers momentum; its salvation project evolves from moral mastery of self to merit eternal salvation into artistic endeavor, the revolutionary transformation of society, and the technological mastery of nature. For leading writers such as Giannozzo Manetti (†1459), Giovanni Pico della Mirandola (†1494), and Marsilio Ficino (†1499), being created in the image of God no longer means free moral capacity to perfect ourselves; it means unlimited freedom *to create* beauty, truth, and goodness—not merely to construct them in the light of creation's pre-established and divine forms. We can still save ourselves independent of God's divine grace; but this time perfection depends on dominion over nature. Natural grace means we can merit salvation by *perfecting* the given environment. Human aspiration to divinity is connected to human manipulation and subjugation of all things. The humanization of nature has begun.

The tyrannical reading of dominion is latent in the mostly aesthetic ambitions of Renaissance humanism to complete God's gift of creation. Manetti, for instance, is typical in his remarks. "The world and all its beauties," he declares, "have been first invented and established by Almighty God for the use of man, and afterwards gratefully received by man and rendered much more beautiful, much more ornate and far more refined."[92] Manetti's seemingly benevolent views are radicalized by Ficino: "Therefore man who universally provides for all things living is a certain god. He is god without doubt of the animals since he uses all of them, rules them, and teaches some of them. He is established also god of the elements since he inhabits and cultivates them."[93] The project to be "master of all," Ficino continues, "will not permit anything to be left out and excluded from his rule," and the

---

91. For Ockham's theological preoccupations, see Leff, *Bradwardine and the Pelagians*, 188–210; Spade, "Ockham's Nominalist Metaphysics," 105–11
92. Manetti quoted in Trinkaus, *In Our Image and Likeness*, 247.
93. Ficino quoted in Trinkaus, *In Our Image and Likeness*, 484.

reason for this project is to "seek a divine condition."[94] Pico echoes Pelagius by claiming humanity is "a creature of indeterminate nature," whose independent choice it is "to degenerate into the lower forms of life," or, to "be reborn into the higher forms, which are divine."[95]

In his (still) authoritative reading on the presuppositions comprising the Renaissance, Ernst Cassirer (†1945) claims—when it comes to salvation—leading thinkers offer a united doctrine that "differs from Augustine."[96] "The effectiveness of grace" is ascertained by a human soul's "capacity for self-movement and self-determination"—"The choice, the final decision, rests with man."[97] Beauty is the key preoccupation, the crack or fissure through which Pelagianism flows into modernity; first as a seductive trickle, then as a torrent that covers an entire world system. Beauty is considered a co-equal transcendental with goodness and truth, but it is not, as supposedly truth and goodness are, simply given by God as a perfect creation. Beauty requires human beings to give it form, "the medium *through which* the free creative force of man acts and becomes conscious of itself."[98] Human freedom is not something opposed to grace, to the creative efficacy of God; rather, in its manifestation as the creator of beauty, it "becomes a moment of the religious process itself," a way of self-redemption through aesthetic (*not ascetic*) practice.[99] The aesthetic innovation is initially restricted; it is presented as a prospective ecclesiastical order dedicated to art. But humanistic intervention eventually slips its church moorings, spreading from beauty to the other transcendentals: Truth (science) and goodness (ethics and politics) can also be reworked in our many freedom projects for—increasingly secular—immediate, worldly salvation. "Science," Cassirer claims, "is a second creation brought about by reason, and art is a second creation brought about by the imagination."[100] The humanistic drive for *second creation* also grounds the transcendental of goodness. *Creative*

---

94. Ficino quoted in Trinkaus, *In Our Image and Likeness*, 483.

95. Pico quoted in Trinkaus, *In Our Image and Likeness*, 341.

96. Cassirer, *Individual and the Cosmos*, 65. Some recent commentators, however, have defended the more Orthodox, Augustinian foundations of Renaissance Christianity and ideas, generally considered; in Ficino's case especially, Anthony Levi argues, there is an attempt to reconcile the aporia between human freedom and God's grace that is not a vulgar return to Pelagianism but, in the spirit of both Neoplatonism and Cassian, a unique "Christian apologetic" that makes a "hugely important contribution" to Christianity and "the development of western culture" (Levi, "Ficino, Augustine, and the Pagans," 99).

97. Cassirer, *Individual and the Cosmos*, 65.

98. Cassirer, *Individual and the Cosmos*, 67.

99. Cassirer, *Individual and the Cosmos*, 67.

100. Cassirer, *Individual and the Cosmos*, 67.

politics is non-moral and successful politics: The art of achieving and keeping power by any means necessary, even good means. Ficino's contemporary and fellow Florentine, Niccolò di Bernardo dei Machiavelli (†1527), is usually ascribed responsibility for this innovation. If we trust to divine justice as the proper end to politics, then it also defines the means by which it is to be attained. This idea of politics will doom its followers to enslavement by other princes or nations that trust only to power, violence, perfidy, and so on. On this crash of transcendentals into the *saeculum novum*, Cassirer is dramatic and effective in his theological criticisms: Christ is converted "into the idea of humanity in the ancient Stoic sense of the word," and, thereby, "the Christian philosophy of history created in Augustine's *De civitate Dei* is shattered."[101] Pelagian Christendom re-begins.

What starts in artistic endeavor, then, quickly spreads to other, more insidious, forms of Pelagian will-to-power. The second creation project sets its sights on nature. French mathematician and humanist Charles de Bovelles (Carolus Bovillus) (†1566), for instance, links human freedom to self-perfection by appropriating the whole of nature for our utility.[102] Giordano Bruno (†1600) explicitly articulates a Pelagian program of dominion. Freedom means refashioning the world into whatever we desire without moral impediment:

> The gods have given man intelligence and hands, and have made him in their image, endowing him with a capacity superior to other animals. This capacity consists not only in the power to work in accordance with nature and the usual course of things, but beyond that and outside her laws, to the end that by fashioning, or having the power to fashion, other natures, other courses, other orders by means of his intelligence, with that freedom without which his resemblance to the deity would not exist, he might in the end make himself god of the earth.[103]

By Bruno's time, the Pelagian, heretical nature of the Renaissance spirit is clearly understood by religious authorities on both sides of the Reformation and Counter-Reformation. Although opposed on most things, both sides attempt to stem the secular and religious flood of Pelagianism; often, and in the case of Bruno, through violent means. At the core of the cultural maelstrom is Augustine's doctrine of original sin. Pelagian humanism revives fundamental questions on Christian human nature, providing fresh alternatives. At this historical hinge-moment, Cassirer (again) accurately

---

101. Cassirer, *Individual and the Cosmos*, 71.
102. See Rice, *Renaissance Idea of Wisdom*, 106–23.
103. Bruno quoted in Farrington, *Philosophy of Francis Bacon*, 27.

claims, "The influence of Pelagianism in the religious position of humanism becomes increasingly evident; efforts to throw off the hard yoke of Augustinian tradition become more and more deliberate."[104] Pelagian forces infiltrate both Protestantism and Catholicism.

B. B. Warfield (†1921) gives a simplistic summary of the theological situation. But it remains instructive. "The Reformation," Warfield writes, "inwardly considered, was just the ultimate triumph of Augustine's doctrine of Grace over Augustine's doctrine of the Church."[105] The ways of dealing with Pelagianism break along similar Augustinian lines. Martin Luther (†1546) writes *The Bondage of the Will* (1525) in response to his arch-rival, the Catholic theologian Erasmus (†1536), whom Luther accuses of Pelagianism. Luther reasserts salvation by divine grace alone, but in individual hearts, the true citadel of salvation, not in the external institutions of the *Roman* church:

> For so long as a man is convinced that he can do something for his own salvation, he retains his self-confidence and does not completely despair; for this reason he does not humble himself before God, but asserts himself, or at least hopes and wishes for opportunity, time, and work in order finally to attain his salvation. But he who never doubts that all depends on the will of God, despairs completely of helping himself, does not choose us, but awaits an act of God; he is nearest to Grace and salvation.[106]

Some Cassian concessions on salvation are granted during the Council(s) of Trent (1545–1563) as the Roman church affirms its own mediatory, sacramental role in the event of divine grace: *Extra Ecclesiam nulla salus*.

ENLIGHTENED REVOLT

Fractured Christianity puts forward a unified front against Pelagianism. According to Diarmaid MacCulloch, both Catholic and Protestant authorities are "horrified at the thought of *Wildwuchs*, spontaneous movements of the people which lacked the control of God's properly chosen representatives."[107] Theological proclamations and condemnations do little to stop its spread. If anything, Pelagianism becomes even more sweeping as a program of *enlightened secularization*. Cassirer argues that the "concept of

---

104. Cassirer, *Philosophy of the Enlightenment*, 139–40.
105. Warfield, *Calvin and Augustine*, 332.
106. Luther quoted in Cassirer, *Philosophy of the Enlightenment*, 139–40.
107. MacCulloch, *Reformation*, 156.

original sin is the common opponent against which all the different trends of the philosophy of the Enlightenment join forces," signifying "the unity of the goal seems for a time to outweigh all differences as to the means of attaining it."[108] Secular politics replaces theology as the proper intellectual site for disputes on human nature. The *state of nature* plays the role once attributed to the Christian doctrine of original sin.

In *Leviathan* (1651), for example, Thomas Hobbes (†1679) presents human nature as a condition of unremitting fear and violence, i.e., "of every man, against every man."[109] We are inherently and permanently flawed: "I put forward a generall inclination of all mankind, a perpetuall and restlesse desire for Power after power, that ceaseth onely in Death."[110] *The state of nature arises from human nature left to its own inclinations.* Only the construction of civil society and its absolute state can rescue us from this incessant strife. Mutual fear and the consequent need for self-preservation direct us to renounce our natural right to dominate everything and everyone. We transfer this right by contract. This social contract creates a sovereign or *Leviathan*. The sovereign can protect us from regressing to a state of nature. In order to save us from ourselves, the sovereign must have unlimited power; she is not answerable to the laws by which she governs and keeps the peace. The sovereign is unrestricted because she must have the absolute power to induce fear, "to over-awe them all."[111] Fear of the sovereign is essential for collective security because it is the ground for renouncing our natural right. The less we are afraid of the sovereign, the more we slip towards a state of nature. This fear generating capacity is only ensured if the sovereign can act arbitrarily and completely unfettered to meet the challenge of security in changing circumstances.

Hobbes is by no means a Pelagian optimist, but his theory thoroughly pushes aside Christian narrative. Human nature claims shift from assumed religion to disputed politics. *Leviathan* declares independence in the name of conservative materialism. Hobbes secularizes and radicalizes Augustine's qualified pessimism. Human nature does not *Fall* from innocence. We were never innocent. Hobbes substitutes total war for prelapsarian Eden. Human nature is constituted by self-interested domination from the beginning. Transformation in this life is not a realistic expectation; it certainly cannot be assumed as the ground of social order. Human evil is normative in the present and future. All we can do is to make the best of a bad lot. The

---

108. Cassirer, *Philosophy of the Enlightenment*, 141.
109. Hobbes, *Leviathan*, 185.
110. Hobbes, *Leviathan*, 161.
111. Hobbes, *Leviathan*, 185.

sovereign must be given the power to terrify us into obedience. Its mechanics of fear produce the outward mask of goodness that keeps our natural inclination in check, i.e., *falling* back into a state of nature. Fear of God's judgment in the afterlife just won't do the trick. Therefore, the *Leviathan* functions as God's deputy. Hobbes speaks of, "That mortal God, to which we owe under the immortal God, our peace and defence."[112] A fake God ensures a fake salvation for civil society.

For the progressively minded, however, Hobbes has let the worldly Genii out of its hallowed bottle. Scriptural tradition is open to significant amendment or total substitution. Enlightened meditations on the state of nature reach very different conclusions on human nature and its political possibilities. "The *Philosophes*," Carl L. Becker (†1945) writes, "demolished the Heavenly City of St. Augustine only to rebuild it with more up-to-date materials."[113] Enlightenment thinkers construct their earthly utopias on foundations of Pelagian Stoicism. The dismantling of Christian dogma is contemporaneous with the retrieval and reinterpretation of ancient, especially Roman, figures and ideas. Tellingly, the Stoic Emperor, Marcus Aurelius (†180 CE), provides the celebrated quotation of the period: "There is nothing evil which is according to Nature."[114] Nature is conceptualized as a great leveler. Instead of the equality of essentialist evil we find in Hobbes, the state of nature provides a normative condition of pre-societal indeterminacy or innocence.

John Locke answers Hobbes in *An Essay Concerning Human Understanding* (1690). Locke's denial of innate ideas demonstrates that the mind owes nothing to inherited dispositions and everything to environment. Locke claims the mind is a *tabula rasa*; it starts as a "white paper, void of all characters," or an "empty cabinet."[115] Like the tenets of Pelagius, then, we are pure indeterminate potential *for either direction*; habits learned from experience account for our good and evil. Again, following Pelagius, Locke's empiricism—that there is nothing in the mind that was not previously in the senses—finds its direct inspiration in Stoic doctrine.[116] According to the ancient doxographer Aetius (†454 CE), "When a man is born, the Stoics say, he has the commanding part of his soul like a sheet of paper ready for writing upon. On this he inscribes each one of his conceptions. The first

---

112. Hobbes, *Leviathan*, 192.
113. Becker, *Heavenly City*, 31.
114. Marcus Aurelius, *Meditations*, 2.17.
115. Locke, *Essay Concerning Human Understanding*, 89, 72.
116. See Sellars, *Stoicism*, 74–77.

method of inscription is through the senses."[117] Locke successfully counters Hobbes and, for the enlightened, he removes the stain of original sin once and for all. "What Locke aimed at no doubt, what the eighteenth century acclaimed him for having demolished," Becker contends, "was the Christian doctrine of total depravity, a black, spreading cloud which for centuries had depressed the human spirit."[118] The political translation of this original equality of indeterminate potentiality remains controversial.

Locke's epistemological position implies that inequities are unnatural; society accounts for the negative environments that produce evil. It would seem reasonable to draw the conclusion that civil society should be constructed to reflect this axiom of human nature. Locke's *Second Treatise of Government* (1690) presents a state of nature that, at first, coheres with this assumption. He says, "*That all Men by Nature are equal*," which includes "that *equal Right* that every Man hath, *to his Natural Freedom*, without being subjected to the Will or Authority of any other Man."[119] From this first premise, however, Locke goes on, in the name of property, with a remarkable argument that has been used to legitimate slavery, deny the rights of *wives, children, and servants*,[120] and justify the unconditional expropriation of Native Americans, and colonization by force.[121]

Labor accounts for property. The consequent movement out of the egalitarian communism of a state of nature is justified on behalf of "the Regulating and Preserving of Property."[122] "Every man has a *Property* in his own Person," Locke writes, so that "the *labour* of his own Body, and the *Work* of his Hands" are his, and therefore, whatever "he removes out of the State that Nature hath provided, and left it in, he hath mixed his *Labour* with . . . and thereby makes it his property."[123] Even though "'tis *Labour* indeed that *puts the difference of value* on every thing," the invention of money negates current claims by laborers to ownership over what they produce.[124] In a state of nature, before money, the creation of individual property through labor is a kind of theft from the commons: "Individual property did not arise from the common consent of all mankind."[125] To give workers in civil

---

117. Aetius quoted in Sellars, *Stoicism*, 75.
118. Becker, *Heavenly City*, 64–65.
119. Locke, *Two Treatises of Government* II.54 (304).
120. See Locke, *Two Treatises of Government* II.86 (323).
121. Duchrow and Hinkelammert, *Property*, 43–76.
122. Locke, *Two Treatises of Government* II.3 (268).
123. Locke, *Two Treatises of Government* II.27 (287–88).
124. Locke, *Two Treatises of Government* II.40 (296).
125. Laslett, "Introduction," 101–2.

society property rights over what they produce means returning to this state of noncompliant inequality. Such a proposition is the enemy of civil society because it leads to resentment, poverty, and perpetual violent competition.

Money is the great miracle of civil society; it restores common consent to the inequality of property distribution found in a state of nature. The *common* market of commodity exchange, i.e., money, replaces the original commons. Just as "different degrees of Industry were apt to give Men possessions in different Proportions, so this *Invention of Money* gave them the opportunity to continue and enlarge them," and since money has "its *value* only from the consent of Men," we have in effect "agreed to disproportionate and unequal Possession of the Earth."[126] In other words, civil society means accepting the common value of money; laborers thereby relinquish ownership over what they produce. Further, along with other commodities, the labor of paid servants and unpaid slaves is then priced, bought, and sold for profit. Sir William Petty (†1687) captures the spirit of Locke's civil society: "The Labour of Seaman, and the Freight of Ships, is always of the nature of an Exported Commodity, the overplus whereof above what is imported, brings home money. The accession of Negroes to the American plantations (being all Men of great labour and little expense) is not inconsiderable."[127] Civil society exists to protect property; more specifically, the common value of money, those with it, and the things that they own, which includes the labor that goes into the production and exchange of things that can be owned; the surplus thereof creates more money for the owner.

What are we to make of Locke's argument? Even his most sympathetic of readers find it hard to argue against what "looks like an uncompromising defence of wealth and power."[128] Locke's "symbolic system seems to express all human rights as market commodities," and he is essentially "the spokesman of a rising class . . . the capitalists, the bourgeoisie."[129] The proper perception of Locke is obscured by the fact that many of us still live under a political regime founded on his *absolute presupposition*, and which still evolves therein. "The Lockian system," Collingwood accurately detects, "is based on private property, and therefore logically presupposes a 'state of nature' in which property is already a factor. Property is conceived not as a product of political activity in the past (in which case it would have been for political history a relative presupposition) but as a 'natural' basis,

---

126. Locke, *Two Treatises of Government* II.48, 50 (301, 302).
127. Petty, *Economic Writings*, 259–60.
128. Laslett, "Introduction," 105.
129. Laslett, "Introduction," 105.

an absolute presupposition, of all political activity whatever."[130] Our bourgeoisie schools still maintain Locke's heroic hagiography. He is praised for his political doctrine because it denies the arbitrary exception claimed by the Divine Right of Kings.[131] Against the doctrine of Hobbes, Locke argues as follows: "He that thinks absolute power purifies men's blood and corrects the baseness of human nature but read the history of this or any age to be convinced of the contrary."[132] The terrifying arbitrariness of another human being's unfettered liberty to dominate in a state of nature is to be remedied by setting up a sovereign whose unfettered liberty to dominate is both arbitrary and backed up with overwhelming force. Locke finds it hard to understand why anyone would leave a state of nature at all. "He being in a much worse condition," Locke, claims, "that is exposed to the arbitrary power of one man who has command of 100,000, than he that is opposed to the arbitrary power of 100,000 single men."[133] Such an unlimited sovereign as argued for by Hobbes keeps the peace by establishing a reign of terror that makes his state of nature appear as a paradise.

Locke argues for a limited sovereign under a constitution, its laws, answerable to adversarial and democratically representative institutions (checks and balances). In times of crisis, which threaten the existence of the State, extraordinary, but temporary powers can be given to an executive. The executive's temporary *prerogative* is the "power to act according to discretion for the public good, without the prescription of the law and sometimes even against it."[134] The powers of executive prerogative are to be clearly defined. The period of time that the prerogative reigns is limited, open to review, and grounded in the events of a clear and present emergency. If the executive uses the power of emergency, or even manufactures emergencies, to seize power and abolish constitutional freedom, to "enslave or destroy" a people, citizens have the right to "appeal to Heaven," and take up arms to reclaim their liberty by abolishing the tyrant.[135] The ultimate arbitrator of sovereignty abides with the ruled, not the ruler.

What is meant by the rights of citizens, however, is defined by money and individual property. Internal to civil society, those mostly without either have no right to *appeal to heaven* and fight against the representative powers, laws, and constitutions that legitimate and police these *human* rights.

130. Collingwood, *Essay on Metaphysics*, 97.
131. See Ignatieff, *Lesser Evil*, 27, 43.
132. Locke, *Two Treatises of Government* II.92 (327).
133. Locke, *Two Treatises of Government* II.137 (359–60).
134. Locke, *Two Treatises of Government* II.160 (375).
135. Locke, *Two Treatises of Government* II.168 (379).

Under this régime, revolutionary action on behalf of a common redistribution of concentrated individual wealth overturns civil society. The elected rulers can claim the *temporary prerogative* to restore order on behalf of the threatened public good. Externally considered, for those on the receiving end of this absolute presupposition, it is one long nightmare of slaughter, oppression, and expropriation in the name of bourgeoisie human rights. As Ulrich Duchrow and Franz J. Hinkelammert conclude, "The West has conquered, colonized, enslaved and humiliated the world, annihilating whole cultures and civilizations. It has carried out unprecedented genocide but has always done it in the name of human rights. For this reason, the blood spilled by the West leaves no stain. On the contrary, it is this blood which washes the West white and gives it the guise of the guarantor of human rights."[136] Jean-Jacques Rousseau (†1778) sets a more consistent political course from the post-Augustinian theological mark.

To Rousseau, human nature is not originally stained by the evil of our freedom. In a state of nature, natural humanity (*l'homme naturel*) is innocent of all sin. Moral evil only emerges for civilized humanity (*l'homme artificial*). Rousseau's *Émile* (1762) begins with the words, "All is well when it leaves the hands of the Creator of things; all degenerates in the hands of man."[137] This phrase is a variation on the Stoic maxim of Marcus Aurelius. Responsibility for the corruption of the human will, its tendency for arrogance, resides in the inherent evil of society. Society alone is liable for the "egoism which causes man to turn tyrant against nature and even against himself."[138] To Cassirer, the source of evil moves from the mythology of original sin to present society; salvation from an event of grace to *creative* politics:

> No God can bring it about for us; man must rather become his own deliverer and in the ethical sense his own creator. Society heretofore has inflicted the deepest wounds on mankind; yet it is society too which through a transformation and reformation can and should heal these wounds. Such is Rousseau's solution to the problem of theodicy. . . . And he has in fact placed this problem on an entirely new footing, removing it from the sphere of metaphysics and making it the focal point of ethics and politics. . . . A new norm for human existence appears here; instead of the mere desire for happiness, the idea of law and

---

136. Duchrow and Hinkelammert, *Property*, 43.
137. Rousseau quoted in Cassirer, *Philosophy of the Enlightenment*, 156–57.
138. Cassirer, *Philosophy of the Enlightenment*, 157.

social justice is made the standard by which human existence is to be measured and tested.[139]

Only social modification can repair what society corrupts. To end evil, political emancipation is an imperative; especially against the inequalities of property within a civil society. *Lockean civilization* is a trick perpetrated by the strong on the weak in order to maintain and increase their power and wealth. Such a civil society eventually undermines itself because, "Man is born free, and everywhere he is in chains. He who believes himself master of others does not escape being more of a slave than they."[140] To overcome the evils of human nature, we must attack its source in inequitable arrangements of social power. Liberation encompasses both private and public spheres of life. *Wives, children, servants, and slaves* confront their husbands, parents, employers, and owners—along with the impositions of kings, priests, and merchants. Revolt continues until all forms of coercion are abolished. Social utopia means an end to evil. Hierarchies of dominance collapse. Human nature returns to its original freedom. We are born again through revolution. In a purely secular place, "The disciple is not above his master, but every one when he is perfected shall be as his master" (Luke 6:40 KJV).

---

139. Cassirer, *Philosophy of the Enlightenment*, 158, 154.
140. Rousseau, *Social Contract*.

FOUR

The Ontology of Mastery

THIS CHAPTER PRESENTS THE Pelagian spirit of modern science through two of its founding figures: Francis Bacon and René Descartes. Extricating Christian pessimism is just as important for science as it is for politics. Both eventually reinforce each other; the latter as end, the former as means. The celestial heaven is to be dismantled in order to be rebuilt on Earth. Humanity is free to play with utopia, projecting it as something to be practically realized in this life. Science provides the power to master nature. This *science of order* has defined our relationship to environment for centuries.

PROMETHEUS REDUX

In *De Sapientia Veterum* (1609), Francis Bacon names the anthropocentric declaration of independence, "Prometheus, that is of Human Nature."[1] Humanity "may be regarded as the center of the world."[2] Nature derives its purpose only "in usefulness towards man."[3] Bacon repeats the rebellion of Aeschylus's (†c. 456 BCE) Prometheus: "In a single word, I am the enemy of all the Gods that gave me ill for good."[4] We can save ourselves. Our knowledge and labors should be directed to improving this temporal life. To achieve this goal, there will be a new science, combining the speculative and the mechanical arts into one—*scientia propter potentiam* (knowledge

---

1. Bacon, *Philosophical Works of Francis Bacon*, 848.
2. Bacon, *Philosophical Works of Francis Bacon*, 849.
3. Bacon, *Philosophical Works of Francis Bacon*, 850.
4. Aeschylus, *Prometheus Bound*, 45.

for the sake of power). The project to transform nature for human benefit is the *way of mastery*. "Man, by the Fall," Bacon writes, "fell at the same time from his state of innocency and from his dominion over creation. Both of these losses, however, can even in this life be in some part repaired, the former by religion and faith, the latter by arts and sciences."[5] To restore our lost dominion, Bacon envisions a *Promethean Church of the New Science*. This novel social organization is dedicated to human betterment through command of nature. It, supposedly, can partner with established Christian institutions. Through our own scientific effort and ingenuity, accompanied by faith, we can re-inscribe the prospects for human nature.

Augustine, as we have seen, presents original sin as a hereditary stain that marks humanity—one *we* cannot remove. Our created state cannot be altered by our mere constructions: Descent from Adam means humanity cannot confer salvation on itself. Only God's grace can elevate us above sin's inescapable gravity, enough to change freedom of domination to freedom of liberation. Bacon, though, intends to restore our lost dominion through a new science that secures only the former freedom, "Let the human race recover that right over nature which belongs to it by divine bequest."[6] His project is correctly identified and defined by John Passmore as "Pelagian, not Augustinian, heretical in a manner that was essential if Christianity was to be reconciled with technological optimism. With Pelagius, that is, Bacon emphasized what man can achieve by his own efforts; against Augustine, he reduces to a minimum the corrupting effects of Adam's sin."[7] One aspect of original sin is our alienation from creation. We lose our lordship of dominion. Bacon's *techno-Pelagianism* intends to amend this feature of postlapsarian existence: "What sin had shattered science could in large part repair: man could become not only the titular but the actual lord of nature. This was by no means the orthodox Christian teaching; it amounted to saying that *man*, as distinct from God, could bring the world into the ideal state which Isaiah has prophesized."[8] Humanity is now presented, "not as essentially corrupt but as having a duty to create, by his own efforts, a second nature—identified in the Christian West, with a second Garden of Eden—that can either provoke or be used to justify a scientific-technological revolution."[9] We are, as is the pattern, not merely *constructors* that

---

5. Bacon, *Philosophical Works of Francis Bacon*, 247–48.
6. Bacon, *Philosophical Works of Francis Bacon*, 115.
7. Passmore, *Man's Responsibility for Nature*, 19.
8. Passmore, *Man's Responsibility for Nature*, 19.
9. Passmore, *Man's Responsibility for Nature*, 19.

participate in the goodness, truth, and beauty of creation; we are portrayed as *creators* of ourselves through the renewed lordship of nature.

It is our cosmos to bring to perfection. Self-salvation by Promethean (pace Pelagian) science, then, has as its end the recreation of the Earth; it is the power to liberate humanity through the improvement of the practical conditions of life: The progress of health and wealth. Joseph Priestly (†1804) captures the essence of the Baconian program:

> Thus all knowledge will be subdivided and extended; and *knowledge*, as Lord Bacon observes, being *power*, the human powers will, in fact, be enlarged; nature, including both its materials, and its laws, will be more at our command; men will make their situation in this world abundantly more easy and comfortable; they will probably prolong their existence in it, and will grow daily more happy, each in himself, and more able (and, I believe more disposed) to communicate happiness to others. Thus, whatever was the beginning of this world, the end will be glorious and paradisiacal, beyond what our imaginations can now conceive. Extravagant as some may suppose these views to be, I think I could show them to be fairly suggested by the true theory of human nature.[10]

Human nature is not a fixed essence ruined by original sin. As Pelagius has intimated, it is an indeterminate capacity. We will our own form of life. Bacon supplements the ancient perfectionist drive to become godlike through moral right action with the fusion of commonplace practical techniques and eminent sciences. He also presents a method to implement his program.

Scientific practitioners are schooled in the empirics of induction and natural history. Nature is known through experiment, requiring surveillance under controlled conditions. Observations are recorded in elaborate registers or tables. Scientists sift through data tables until they infer likely conclusions—axioms on the order of nature. Since axioms are only probable, they are open to revision by further experiments. With each turn in the self-reinforcing scientific wheel, we have a natural history that acts as the foundation for future discoveries. Past errors are detected, then they are corrected by new experiments, and more of nature's secrets are revealed. Bacon welcomes the advancement of his experiments:

> There will be found, no doubt, when my history and tables of discovery are read, some things in the experiments themselves that are not quite certain, or perhaps are quite false, which may make a man think that the foundations and principles upon

10. Priestly, *Essay on the First Principles*, 4–5.

> which my discoveries rest are false and doubtful. But this is of no consequence, for such things must needs happen first. It is only like the occurrence in a written or printed page of a letter or two mistaken or misplaced, which does not hinder the reader, because such errors are easily corrected by sense. So likewise may there occur in my natural history many experiments which are mistaken and falsely set down, and yet they will presently, by the discovery of causes and axioms, be easily expunged and rejected.[11]

Moreover, he speaks of the many secrets still contained within "the womb of nature," which will be revealed "only by the method of which we are now treating."[12] Bacon's Promethean Church also requires faith. Scientific progress depends on an economy of trust. A community of inquirers must trust their senses, the observational data, the hypothetical axioms that emerge from experiments, the integrity of their fellow researchers who assess their claims, and so on. If any link in the chain is corrupted, healthy skepticism turns into cynicism, undermining the advancement of knowledge.[13]

Bacon's approach to science and nature is still usually hailed as a great breakthrough for human progress. Some commentators, though, have accused Bacon of modeling his experimental method on trial and torture. The scientist is an interrogator. Nature is the accused. The experimental laboratory is a chamber filled with a vast array of devious devices, which are designed to extract facts. Nature is forced to confess its secrets. Dominion is to be reestablished through inventive techniques of violence. Ernst Cassirer, for instance, claims Bacon's approach to science is modeled on forced confession:

> The very style of Bacon's writings evinces this spirit. Bacon sits as a judge over reality, questioning it as one examines the accused. Not infrequently he says that one must resort to force to obtain the answer desired, that nature must be "put to the rack." His procedure is not simply observational but strictly inquisitorial. The witnesses are heard and brought face to face; the negative instances confront the affirmative ones, just as the witnesses for the defence confront those for the prosecution. After all the available bits of evidence have been gathered together and evaluated, then it is a matter of obtaining the confession which

---

11. Bacon, *New Organon*, 108.
12. Bacon, *New Organon*, 102.
13. See Shapin, *Social History of Truth*, 3–41.

The Ontology of Mastery

finally decides the issue. But such a confession is not obtainable without resorting to coercive measures.[14]

A more recent critic explains Bacon's metaphorical transfer of torture to experiment as the key to understanding the misogynistic founding principles of scientific methodology, and the consequent *death of nature*. To Carolyn Merchant:

> The use of torture rhetoric condones a transfer of methodological approaches used to extract information from the accused to extracting secrets from nature. The method of confining, controlling, and interrogating the human being becomes the method of the confined, controlled experiment used to interrogate nature. Torture should not be used on witches but on nature itself. The experimental method is superior to that developed by magicians to control nature. A question must be asked and an experiment designed to answer it. For the experimental method to succeed, the experiment must be a closed, isolated system in which variables are controlled and extraneous influences excluded. Witnessing is crucial to the process. The trial—that is, the experiment—must be witnessed by others. Indeed, it was one of Bacon's singular contributions to realize that to be understood, nature must be studied under constrained conditions that must be both witnessed and verified by others. Bacon used metaphor, rhetoric, and myth to develop his new method of interrogating nature.[15]

The Promethean-Pelagian fallacy promises salvific re-creation of humanity through techniques that can control the forces of nature, but there can only be violent re-*construction* of the environment and, ultimately, ourselves. The freedom of domination can become more and more powerful, but it cannot deliver what it promises: The *creative* liberation of truth, goodness, and beauty.

---

14. Cassirer, *Platonic Renaissance in England*, 47–48.

15. Merchant, "Scientific Revolution," 524. The *misogyny environmental thesis* draws together the historical depiction and treatment of gender and nature. Attitudes are correlated between the former and latter and, insofar as systems of dominance oppress non-masculine genders, so with nature. Science in its modern form is said to be misogynistic and thus destructive of nature. Conversely, gender liberation correlates with better treatment of the environment and a different idea of science. For two significant works, see Merchant, *Death of Nature*; Midgley, *Science as Salvation*.

DESCARTES'S NEW WORLD ORDER

René Descartes accepts Bacon's ambitions, but he does not adopt Bacon's dramatic and Biblical manner of expression, or Bacon's sense and trust based experimental method. "There is nothing created," Descartes tells us, "from which we cannot derive some use."[16] He aspires to radical dominion through "a practical philosophy by means of which, knowing the force and the action of fire, water, the stars, heavens, and all the other bodies that environ us, as distinctly as we know the different crafts of our artisans, we can in the same way employ them in all those uses to which they are adapted, and thus render ourselves the masters and possessors of nature."[17] The practical way to dominance is found in the quantitative method of investigation. Bernard Williams (†2003) maintains that Descartes's "study of nature is just, in the purest sense possible, applied mathematics."[18] Mathematical first principles can be discovered by specially trained individual minds and, unlike Bacon's experimental axioms, they are not subject to the fallibility of the senses, or the corruption of a community of inquirers. Descartes's dream of a *mathesis universalis* intends "great changes in the order of things. The whole world would have to be a terrestrial paradise—something one might propose only in the realm of fiction."[19] Given the power of quantification, he envisions a *New World Order* for those that hold such knowledge.

Descartes presents the triad of self, God, and idea as the metaphysical underpinning of certain mathematical knowledge. Is there anything that cannot be doubted? In his *Meditations on First Philosophy* (1641), Descartes argues that he has an innate and indubitable idea of himself. Along with the idea of himself, he also finds the spontaneous idea of God because the self cannot be the source of its own being. If the idea of himself signifies the certainty of his existence, then the idea of God means God exists as its ground, as being itself: "The mere fact that I exist and have within me an idea of a most perfect being, that is, God, provides a very clear proof that God indeed exists."[20] There are, then, only two ideas beyond doubt; namely, himself and God: "The only remaining alternative is that it [God] is innate in me, just as the idea of myself is innate in me."[21] The idea of the self establishes the domain of pure mind—*res cogitans*. The coexistent innate idea

---

16. Descartes, "Principles of Philosophy [Haldane]," 271.
17. Descartes, "Discourse on the Method," 119.
18. Williams, *Descartes*, 260.
19. Descartes, "Letter to Mersenne," 6.
20. Descartes, "Meditations on First Philosophy," 97.
21. Descartes, "Meditations on First Philosophy," 97.

of God provides the certain cause for the effect that is pure mind. God is uncreated—*actually infinite*—intellectual substance that creates the self. The created human subject is also defined as intellectual substance. God also guarantees the truth of other necessary ideas present to a human being's pure mind, concerning the mathematical properties of the physical order. Nature is now defined by the mind (thus God) absconded machinery of the second created substance: *Res extensa*.

To Descartes, introspective analysis signifies "when I turn the mind's eye upon myself."[22] Introspection presents the relationship between his idea of himself and God as one of effect and cause, respectively. The created bears the mark of the creator. *Imago Dei* means "I understand that I am a thing which is incomplete and dependent on another and which aspires without limit to even greater and better things; but I also understand at the same time that he on whom I depend has within him all those greater things, not just indefinitely and potentially but actually and infinitely, and hence that he is God."[23] Descartes concludes, "The whole force of the argument lies in this: I recognize that it would be impossible for me to exist with the kind of nature I have—that is, having within me the idea of God—were it not the case that God really existed."[24] A series of controversial questions arises on the character of this human trace of divinity: Do we have the capacity to become actually infinite, or *perfect*, like God? Or are we limited to a *fallen* or *indefinite life*? What is our relationship to res extensa supposed to be? Are we defined by power or love? In short, is Descartes a Pelagian or an Augustinian? Or *something other* altogether?

Some contemporary interpreters claim Descartes does provide a correction to the traditional divisive or dualistic reading of his work by incorporating actual infinity and the passions into his moral theory found in *Les Passions de l'âme* (1649).[25] The infinitude of the passions provides the interceding third element—i.e., between mind and body, and between the human subject and the physical world—without becoming a substance in its own right. Intercession between isolated created substances is an occasionalist event of God's grace. These commonplace integrations that make up the world are created and preserved in being by the fiat of divinity, demonstrating the perfect infinitude of God's love or passion. Descartes's consequent *ethics of generosity* prefigures a philosophy that challenges duality and totality; it is not a Pelagian-perfectionist philosophy that leads to

22. Descartes, "Meditations on First Philosophy," 97.
23. Descartes, "Meditations on First Philosophy," 98.
24. Descartes, "Meditations on First Philosophy," 98.
25. See Marion, *On Descartes's Passive Thought*.

domination of each other or nature: The actual infinite has an overflowing nature of emancipatory passion.[26] Finite being, as Descartes has stated, always has a kind of infinitude about it, but any claim to perfect knowledge or interpretation, i.e., to be God, is invalidated. Therefore, the meaning of things is always open. Violence against beings in the name of any closed concept is not justifiable. In its place is a kind of non-relative pluralism. We are to recognize an open reality of passionate infinitude in our relations with others; to become infinitely responsible for the liberation of *the other*.[27] To touch the infinite mind of God is to be transformed by His infinite passion.

Descartes's ethical doctrine is his bright essence; one that has been traditionally misunderstood and undeveloped. God's actual infinity turns out to be goodness, love, and generosity, not merely power. To truly understand Descartes's philosophy requires the retrospective light of his infinite ethics.[28] Regarding nature, however, there seems to be an undeniable dark essence to the reception of his ideas. *Infinite generosity to the other* does not extend to beings outside our species. In the name of the only *mindfully* created substance in the cosmos—the human subject—res extensa is set up as a place of unrestricted violence. The tradition of mastery by mathematical method shadows his work. To be the image of God means to ascend to His infinite power, reconstructing the material world by our criteria of truth, goodness, and beauty. The material world exhibits none of these things by its own existence. Power is the meta-predicate of divine existence, making all others a function of it. As God's *imago Dei*, we are called to participate in the power of actual infinity by making a second world.

Descartes proposes a *New World Order*, but it no longer signifies creation. His terrestrial paradise is a human artifact or construction that can be totally ours. Based on a self-creating I (*ego cogito ergo sum*), his philosophy sets out to expropriate nature. There is a conception of God as absolute will. God gives up entitlement to creation, but He guarantees the certainty of a science that makes our mastery possible.[29] There is no unmediated communicative relationship between divinity and creation. God is known in nature *only* through his human mediator; the specially trained human mind has within it "a sort of spark of the divine, in which the first seeds of useful ways of thinking are sown."[30] Descartes's God is radically voluntarist. He creates necessary truths by sheer will; they are true because he willed them, not

---

26. See Armour, "Descartes and the Ethics of Generosity," 79–102.
27. See Levinas, *Totality and Infinity*, 24–32.
28. See Marion, "Descartes and Onto-Theology," 67–106.
29. See Gillespie, *Nihilism Before Nietzsche*, 59–63.
30. Descartes, "Rules for the Direction of our Native Intelligence," 4.

willed because they are true: "It is because he willed to create the world in time that it is better this way than if he had created it from eternity; and it is because he willed that the three angles of a triangle should necessarily equal two right angles that this is true and cannot be otherwise; and so on in other cases."[31] "Whatever God knows," Anthony Kenny abbreviates, "he wills it."[32] Mathematical truths are distinct from God's essence; they are something God creates, and these truths remain under His control. Eternal truths stand in a relationship to God defined by efficient causality. "God can be called the efficient cause (of the eternal truths)," Descartes claims, "in the same way the King is the maker of the law, even though the law is not a physically existent thing."[33] God is a cosmic lawgiver. Richard S. Westfall confirms that the relationship between God and nature has "to do overwhelmingly with the maintenance of law."[34] Noninterventionist preservation of physical laws is discrete from the individual things that gain their existence through these laws. As Gary B. Deason points out, "Although God was sovereign over a world that He created and, in principle, could suspend or change natural laws to accomplish a special purpose, in practice He did not tamper with the laws of nature."[35] Descartes's God is a God of general providence and, only *occasionally*, as in the case of the *ethical miracles* of generosity, a God of special providence. The being of individual creatures "are thus subordinated to the general laws by which God maintains the common good."[36] Rules, algorithms, and mathematical formulas have maximal being; their instances are diminished of worth, if not eliminated of it altogether.

A properly directed mind learns to recognize God's perpetual laws as clear and distinct ideas. "It is very clear," Descartes directs us, "that the best path to follow when we philosophize will be to start from knowledge of God himself and try to deduce an explanation of the things created by him. This is the way to acquire the most perfect scientific knowledge, that is, knowledge of effects through their causes."[37] The *things created by him*, however, are not the physically existent things found in sense experience. God's effects or traces are the necessary ideas he has willed. Necessary ideas are stamped on the human mind along with the mind's idea of itself and God as their mutual efficient cause. Sense perception cannot reveal any trace of God.

31. Descartes, "Objections and Replies," 135.
32. Kenny, *God of the Philosophers*, 19.
33. Descartes quoted in Kenny, *God of the Philosophers*, 20.
34. Westfall, "Rise of Science," 233.
35. Deason, "Reformation Theology," 187.
36. Deason, "Reformation Theology," 187.
37. Descartes, "Principles of Philosophy [Cottingham]," 168.

To Cartesians, as Paula Findlen accurately perceives, mathematics becomes the ultimate "means of communion with the Deity."[38] God's eternal mathematical ideas are that *through which* we are to produce a new world; they are divine principles by which we create and sustain things in their very being. An idea is not something known, and by being known, it makes known something outside the mind. Ideas are not forms of things said to be in the knower whereby she knows things. The knowing subject immediately attains only her own ideas. Knowledge through the senses is denied. The being of creation is replaced by construction of being.[39] The sensible realm outside the mind does not directly participate in God's rationality. But this world is not merely unknowable; it is a night of deceitful and Godless chaos—a nothing, *nihil*. "I realize that I am, as it were," Descartes confesses, "something intermediate between God and nothingness."[40] Only the spark of human reason has access to God's clear and distinct ideas, offering "*a priori* demonstrations of everything that can be produced in this new world."[41] The world as it is, as it is received from its creator, then, must be remade. Reconstruction means *rationalization* founded on God's divine ideas. Rationalization is mathematization. Descartes's *new world* is a blank canvas of pure extension. And he aspires to something well beyond humble construction that seeks to participate in creation's pregiven divine pattern. Since we are the *imago Dei* of the actually infinite power, we get to play the role of a second God by implementing a second *ex nihilo creation*. This creation of a new world is the redemption of the nothingness presented by the senses.[42] The goal is to win back the Earth through mathematical representation and the purely practical activity of the will. *This nihilistic-messianic reading of Descartes emerges from his creationist conception of mathematics.*

The First *Mathesis Universalis*

Descartes transforms the mathematical ideas of the Neoplatonic philosopher, Proclus Diadochus (†485).[43] In *A Commentary on the First Book of*

---

38. Findlen, "Janus Faces of Science," 240.

39. On the modern way of ideas, which denies the reception of being in favor of its production, see Dewan, "St. Thomas, Ideas, and Immediate Knowledge," 392–404; Peifer, *Concept in Thomism*, 9–28.

40. Descartes, "Meditations on First Philosophy," 99.

41. Descartes, "World," 97.

42. See Rotman, *Signifying Nothing*, 60–66.

43. See Sasaki, *Descartes's Mathematical Thought*, 333–57. On Proclus's philosophy of mathematics, see Charles-Saget, *L'architecture du divin*; Mueller, "Mathematics and Philosophy," 305–18; Schmitz, *Euklids Geometrie*; MacIsaac, "Soul and Discursive Reason," 115–85.

Euclid's Elements, Proclus (like Descartes) speaks of one all-encompassing science as *mathesis universalis*; it "embraces alike all forms of mathematical knowledge."[44] Proclus enfolds mathematical forms within the active intellect. They are the basic types *by which* the soul shapes and illuminates sensible reality. "We must therefore," Proclus concludes, "posit the soul as the generatrix of mathematical forms and ideas."[45] Forms are genetically rooted in the soul. We have essential knowledge, already inscribed, that continually rewrites itself as it is actualized by experience. By accepting this presupposition, Proclus claims to be a faithful disciple of Plato: "And if we say that the soul produces them by having their patterns in her own essence and that these offspring are the projections of forms previously existing in her, we shall be in agreement with Plato and shall have found the truth with regard to mathematical being."[46] The operation of *mathematical being* in the soul has a distinctive process.

The active intellect (*nous poiētikos*) projects (*probolē*) forms or structuring presuppositions (*logoi*) onto the passive intellect—the screen of imagination (*nous pathētikos, phantasia*).[47] There is a motion in the soul that accounts for the transformation of the undividable and immobile forms into the divisible and mobile types (*typoi*). "We invoke the imagination and the intervals that it furnishes," Proclus explains, "since the form itself is without motion or genesis, indivisible and free of all underlying matter, though the elements latent in the form are produced distinctly and individually on the screen of the imagination."[48] What appears on the imaginative *screen* are primordial image-types, displaying what Gottfried Wilhelm von Leibniz (†1716) later calls *virtualité*.[49] A *virtual image*, then, is a specific gap by which *this form* (and no other) is spatialized-materialized. It does not, however, contain the same spatial materiality as sensible things. Proclus describes this receptive place as noetic matter (*hylē noētē*); it is an interval or receptacle (*khôra*) that exists between, i.e., external to but permeable by, sensible matter and the indivisible purity of ideal forms. We can, for example, contemplate the properties of ideal geometric figures, e.g., triangles, with or without their sensible extension. The pure mathematical being of a triangle can reside in noetic matter alone. The imagination also makes possible the event of fusion between the permanency of form and the flux

---

44. Proclus, *Commentary on the First Book* 7 (6).
45. Proclus, *Commentary on the First Book* 13 (10).
46. Proclus, *Commentary on the First Book* 13 (10).
47. On Proclus's theory of projection, see Steel, "Breathing Thought," 293–307.
48. Proclus, *Commentary on the First Book* 56 (45).
49. See Leibniz, *Monadology and Other Philosophical Writing*, 367.

of sensible appearance. The projective relation between the imagination and the active intellect opens a creature to sense experience.

The power that projects is the active intellect. The contents of this projection are the *logoi*. The receptive screen for the projected logoi is the imagination. *Nous pathētikos* is a dual power. It can *internally reflect* the matter of projected pure forms, allowing contemplation of fundamental formal properties without sensible matter, and it also has the formal power of *external projection*. The imagination externally constitutes sensible matter through its formal feature. This double interval-function follows the causal model of emanation. This universal structure has three moments: Remaining (*monē*), procession (*prohodos*), and reversion (*epistrophe*).[50] To Proclus, "What projects the images is the understanding; the source of what is projected is the form in the understanding; and what they are projected in is this 'passive nous' that unfolds in revolution about the partlessness of genuine Nous, setting a distance between itself and that indivisible source of pure thought, shaping itself after the unshaped forms, and becoming all the things that constitute the understanding and the unitary ideas in us."[51] The higher level of pure, nonextended *logoi remains* in itself, but this very preservation of identity occasions the second moment. Noetic *projection proceeds* by materializing the form as the imagination's primordial symbol. The third moment *reverts* this noetic matter back to its source, producing the necessary substratum for any conscious reflection whatsoever. This cyclic process can continue indefinitely as a purely internal affair of thought's reflection on the contents of itself. But the imagination is now a solidly structured lower level, imitating the higher level it has come from—that is, it has an externally projective power all its own. As it arranges sensible matter, the imagination *re-projects* or *re-presents* the active intellect's formal irradiation.

By the external mode of imaginative projection, we comprise appearances, which are the sensible likenesses of the forms. "For Proclus," Radek Chlup summarizes, "all sense-perception presupposes an unconscious projection of *logoi* organizing the sensible qualities we receive through the senses."[52] The forms *remain* as a stable feature of the imagination's noetic matter; they then *proceed* externally to organize the data of perception, *reverting* back to noetic matter to deliver experience to its internal reflective function. *Our imaginations, however, do not create the sensible real.* "The positive role of *phantasia* might evoke the concept of creative imagination,"

---

50. See Proclus, *Elements of Theology* 25–43.
51. Proclus, *Commentary on the First Book* 56 (45).
52. Chlup, *Proclus*, 151.

Chlup claims, "however, Proclus never gets this far."[53] Appearances are projected by forms independent from the activity of the human mind. But these sensible appearances are only knowable by the active intellect's projection of these self-same forms upon our imagination, serving to organize sensible matter. The imagination ties together our internal world with the external world: We *participate* (methexis) in a shared formal reality, common to all things. The generative source of being is elsewhere than the human intellect. Physical forms and cognitive forms derive from the same origin: The Cosmic Soul and, ultimately, The One, The Good.

Perception's sensible matter fills out the imagination's formally projected interval. "The understanding sees them by virtue of what it has within," Proclus clarifies, "and through employing projections of its ideas, it is moved by itself to make them external."[54] There is a *virtual identity* between our projected forms and the external forms that account for the matter of sensible appearance: "In going forth into this matter and shaping it, our ideas are plausibly said to resemble acts of production; for the movements of our thoughts in projecting its own ideas is a production."[55] "Prior to sense objects, therefore," Proclus precisely summarizes, "are the self-moving intelligible and divine ideas of the figures. Although we are stirred to activity by sense objects, we project the ideas within us, which are images of things other than themselves; and by their means we understand sensible things of which they are paradigms and intelligible and divine things of which they are likenesses."[56] To Proclus, mathematics is a fundamental study of formal reality as it initially manifests itself from the intersection of mind and world. It is the crucial foundation for the symbolic emendation of the soul; the first rung on the ladder of ascent, leading to the Real.

Mathematical forms in the *external* realm of nature have the power of organizing appearances, but they are devoid of *internal* knowledge and intelligent comprehension. Active intellects have immaterial thought and spontaneous knowledge, *but not the generative and activating cause*. Mathematical knowledge occupies "a middle position between the intelligible and the sense worlds."[57] The latter world is the domain of physics—the realm of change, probability, and opinion. The former world, which is of primary concern for Proclus, eventually leaves mathematics for the soul's dialectical ascent through the multiple henads to the undivided One, the source and

---

53. Chlup, *Proclus*, 154n25.
54. Proclus, *Commentary on the First Book* 55 (44).
55. Proclus, *Commentary on the First Book* 78 (64).
56. Proclus, *Commentary on the First Book* 140 (112).
57. Proclus, *Commentary on the First Book* 35 (29).

destination of all—the divine substance of the world. The division between intellect and nature collapses in an event of *symbolic reunion*. Reality is holy:

> Therefore just as nature stands creatively above the visible figures, so the soul, exercising her capacity to know, projects on the imagination, as on a mirror, the ideas of the figures; and the imagination, receiving in pictorial form these impressions of the ideas within the soul, by their means affords the soul an opportunity to turn inward from the pictures and attend to herself. It is as if a man looking at himself in a mirror and marveling at the power of nature and at his own appearance should wish to look upon himself directly and possess such a power as would enable him to become at the same time the seer and the object seen . . . to behold the secret and ineffable figures in the inaccessible places and shrines of the gods. . . . For all figures attain consummation in the henads, the source from which they all enter being.[58]

Proclus imparts a sacramental view of the world, investing divine presence in its very sinews, its corporeal substance. There is no *real* chasm of separation between the sacred and the sensible world. Material appearance can provide access to its inner symbolic realm; it is a site of spiritual transformation, a stage whereupon we can achieve the presence of true being. Since *formal traces* of the divine are already infused throughout the flesh of the cosmos, we are provided with resources for the recovery of its divine nature. The self can attain transcendental consciousness because the gods are present in its immanent, material structure. But the dividedness of embodiment makes this level of wholeness faint, illusory. We must recover the material world's sacred unity. *Mathematics grasps the first formal trace of divine reality. It is a decisive opening—a preparatory link—to the higher stages of dialectic and theurgy.* Mathematics has limits of divine comprehension. It requires the next level of dialectic. But dialectic has limits, too. Mind must re-incarnate itself, *return* to itself from its extreme noetic universalism, in and through the matter of the world.

Dialectic leads to theurgy; an embodied ritual process to realize self-unification with the gods. Gregory Shaw captures the phenomenon with elegant concision: "Theurgic rites transformed the soul from being its own idol, in an inverted attitude of self-interest, into an icon of the divine, with its very corporeality changed into a vehicle of transcendence."[59] No aspect of our nature is simply given as divine. The idolatry of our material lives

---

58. Proclus, *Commentary on the First Book* 141–42 (113).
59. Shaw, "Theurgy," 21.

The Ontology of Mastery 139

must be transformed into an iconic or symbolic form of life. Conversion is made possible by actions informed by nature's sacred codes. As Pierre Hadot († 2010) explains, "We thus witness the development in late Neoplatonism of a certain kind of sacramentalism: certain signs, or 'symbols,' and certain material rites can, in Neoplatonic theurgy, enable the soul's return to its divine origin."[60] "In the process," Hadot continues, "it was admitted that certain material substances possess divine energy within them, and an effort was made to decipher the code of universal sympathy, to reconstruct the chains that connect all the degrees of reality, down to the lowest one, with the gods."[61] The capacity for salvific change, then, is present in matter, not opposed to it.

In his *Platonic Theology* (1.29), Proclus says, "And as the theurgic art through certain symbols calls forth the exuberant and unenvying goodness of the Gods into the illumination of artificial statues, thus also the intellectual science of divine concerns, by the compositions and divisions of sounds, unfolds the occult essence of the Gods."[62] Theurgic art enacts a tangible sense of the transcendent, divine *symbola*. It "installs the soul in the cause of all things, and by some sort of ineffable unification it makes the one that is being filled identical to the one that is filling . . . setting up a unifying mixture and a single divine bond between the participant and the participated."[63] The gods can be persuaded to open themselves to us. Reality's sacred dimension is called into being by our symbolic action. Reunion is brought about by a recital of the gods' divine names (*voces mysticae*). We invite them to join our chorus, "For the gods rejoice whenever they hear these symbols, and they readily listen to those who evoke them, revealing their own specific individuality through these tokens (*synthēmata*), since they regard them as especially familiar and appropriate to themselves."[64] Theurgy is a transfiguration of our encounter with the material world, revealing its divine interior. Matter is not a principle of alienation. It is the source of salvation.

Henry Corbin calls this innermost experience "an Event of soul," which "transmutes all cosmic realities and relations and restores them to symbols."[65] And, as Algis Uždavinys († 2010) well describes, "the divine symbols have a transformative and elevating power" because "they are regarded

---

60. Hadot, *Veil of Isis*, 111.
61. Hadot, *Veil of Isis*, 111.
62. Proclus, *Theology of Plato*, 125.
63. Proclus quoted in Chlup, *Proclus*, 192.
64. Proclus quoted in Chlup, *Proclus*, 192.
65. Corbin, *Avicenna and the Visionary Recital*, 236.

as the things demiurgically woven into the very fabric of being and therefore directly attached to, and united with, the gods themselves, the principles of being."[66] Theurgic symbols are unusual signs; "they do not simply stand for invisible and divine things, but are inherently connected with them: in a sense, they *are* 'gods.'"[67] Plotinus (†270 CE) even goes as far as to posit a homecoming of the undescended soul; now, liberated from its material estrangement. A part of us is already symbolic. A true self *is* a god. A self, touched by transcendence, is a "self glorified, full of intelligible light—but rather itself pure light—weightless, floating free, having become—but rather being—a god."[68] But, for Proclus, the soul has descended fully into sensible matter, and its search for transcendence depends on sacred corporeality. Embodiment is not an obstacle to becoming symbolic, it is a requirement.

Theurgy is essential for a salvific transition. From a profane (idolatrous, self-seeking) way of life, we attain a divine one. To *reenchant* the self, consequently, one must first find, and then perform, the original enchantment patterns that make up the texture of the world. Patricia Cox Miller maintains, "For Proclus the self was always in a world marked by division, it could not achieve its own channels of connection to the divine apart from the material world and the ritual procedures whereby elements of the world provided pathways to spiritual communication."[69] The theurgic symbol has the capacity to bring together meaning and being. The result of a symbolic event is a genuine human being. In the profane time of incompleteness, she is temporarily beyond it—unbroken, made whole, in accord with her true nature. From our side of the fracture between being and appearance, we can call upon divinity, or at least take the lead, to remove the mythopoetic veils of representation (*synthēma*) that separate us from reality.

Through a performative symbol (*symbolon*), we can enact a sacramental co-creation, re-bonding all the lost pieces of our essence. The recognition of being uncompleted is a divine provocation to search for that which can make us whole. We are known to the gods through our distinctive wounds: To mend is to remake a person, anew. Just as we are not whole in different ways, so the curative symbolic experience individuates lives. Paradoxically, we only become authentically distinct, true to our essence, by a transfiguring experience of unity. *Theurgy enables us to step beyond our fields of partial representation in mathematics and dialectic and, by reaching their ground,*

---

66. Uždavinys, *Philosophy and Theurgy*, 205.
67. Uždavinys, *Philosophy and Theurgy*, 221.
68. Plotinus, *Enneads*, 6.9.9.57–59.
69. Cox Miller, *Corporeal Imagination*, 34–35.

find our hidden connection to deity. In this sense, mathematics is a necessary lower moment in a sequence of higher, divinatory arts.

The Second *Mathesis Universalis*

Descartes's *way of mastery*, by contrast, denies dialectic and pagan theurgy, presenting a creationist mathematical physics in the service of our godlike power. His *mathesis universalis* not only embraces all forms of mathematical knowledge, it intends to make all *legitimate* forms of knowledge mathematical: Whomever measures the world correctly, can master it accordingly. The Platonic tradition (reaching to Collingwood and beyond), though, teaches that there must be cooperation between mathematics and dialectic because mathematical demonstrations cannot prove the principles upon which they rest; they must be presupposed without demonstration.[70] Mathematics can draw systematic conclusions from the starting points it posits, but it is unable to validate these foundations. First principles or axioms cannot be proven within the domain of mathematics itself; they must be accepted as undemonstrated hypotheses. Thus, mathematics cannot stand autonomously as a science, having no choice but to remain incomplete.[71] To escape the purely arbitrary selection of ground, it needs another rational science: Dialectic.

First principles, argue the Platonists, must be *chosen* in the course of dialectic from a range of candidates. Each choice must be rigorously vetted for its *truth*. Truth includes a full range of anticipated social and ecological effects; not just internalist criteria, e.g., pragmatic warrant, systematic adequacy, and coherence. Only the science of dialectic can examine mathematical hypotheses, using them as steps to ascend to the non-hypothetical principle of being: The Good. Regarding all number and mathematics, to Proclus, dialectical progression *necessarily* leads to the precondition of determinate unity, identity, or *oneness*. For Descartes, however, any mathematical foundation must align itself with the Christian maxim of *voluntary creation from nothing*.[72]

---

70. See Plato, *Rep.* 533b–c; 510c. For Plato's idea of dialectic, see Gadamer, "Dialectic and Sophism," 93–123.

71. See Sasaki, *Descartes's Mathematical Thought*, 360–62. On Proclus's role for dialectic, see Chlup, *Proclus*, 155–58. For a contemporary debate on the same issue, see Dummett, "Philosophical Significance of Gödel's Theorem," 140–55.

72. On the basic differences between Neoplatonic (necessary) and Christian (voluntary) versions of emanation, see Bonin, *Creation as Emanation*, 1–21.

Descartes no longer needs dialectic to provide principles for mathematics because his innate idea of himself, backed by God as pure existence, provides a self-explanatory, regress-stopping ground for truth. The everlasting axioms of mathematics are created by God's will. God initially created them, and He continues to will these axioms as true. Knowledge of mathematical principles occurs through intuition, which is described as "the indubitable conception of a clear and attentive mind."[73] Intuition is self-reflexivity, enfolding content into itself. Reflection certifies the self-evident certainty of the content: "Thus everyone can mentally intuit that he exists, that he is thinking, that a triangle is bounded by just three lines, and a sphere by a single surface, and the like."[74] Doubting mathematical axioms is to doubt the existence of the self. Doubting the existence of the self means doubting God as actually infinite existence itself: "The light of nature or faculty of knowledge which God gave us can never encompass any object which is not true in so far as it is clearly and distinctly perceived."[75] Therefore, Descartes asserts, "Mathematical truths should no longer be suspect, since they are utterly clear to us."[76] Dialectic under these presuppositions would indicate either skeptical atheism or a return to the theurgic practices of Neoplatonic paganism.

One is incapable of having clear and certain knowledge about anything until she knows the true God. Chikara Sasaki draws the following remarkable conclusion: "In Descartes's opinion, only the Christian can possess the true knowledge of mathematics."[77] A true Christian mathematics, then, must have an appropriate conception of number, which is something other than the determinate unity of the pagan Platonists. It must also have creative, *theurgic* power. Mathematics is not conceived as a derivative link in the intellect's ascent of the chain of being; it is not given a receptive and secondarily constructive role in an already divine and complete reality. As is well known, Descartes inaugurates modern mathematics by collapsing the distinction between geometry and algebra (*La Géométrie*, 1637). The theory of number underlying his analytic geometry overturns the determinate monad of the Platonists and their geometrically bounded, closed order of its demonstration. Descartes places a zero-based symbolic algebra onto an unbounded and homogenous geometrical plane: *Res Extensa*. Pure nature is a created potential infinity—(0, 0)—a spatial-nothing, a blank canvas given

---

73. Descartes, "Rules for the Direction of Our Native Intelligence," 3.
74. Descartes, "Rules for the Direction of Our Native Intelligence," 3.
75. Descartes, "Principles of Philosophy [Cottingham]," 170.
76. Descartes, "Principles of Philosophy [Cottingham]," 170.
77. Sasaki, *Descartes's Mathematical Thought*, 367.

to us by God: The space to recreate our new world order through God's mathematical ideas.

The Symbol of Zero

Descartes's number theory radicalizes the prior work of François Viète (†1603) and Simon Stevin (†1620). According to Jacob Klein (†1978), from Viète, Descartes appropriates "logistice speciosa," transforming it into "an *Organon* in the realm of all possible knowledge whatever."[78] *Logistice speciosa* are signs of possible givenness. Indeterminate symbols are not tied to individual instances of figures, motions, or numbers; they are grasped as pure numeric possibility. A symbol "intends *directly the general character of being a number* which belongs to every possible number, that is to say, it intends 'number in general' immediately, but the things or units which are at hand in each number only mediately."[79] The symbolic formulation of number is the decisive break from ancient and scholastic ontology; it heralds the beginning of the modern scientific project, where order and measure (*ordo et mensura*) are placed at the heart of our relation to things. In Klein's definitive study, this crucial (but complex) change is described as follows:

> In the language of the schools: The letter sign designates the intentional object of a "second intention" (intentio secunda), namely of a concept which itself directly intends another *concept* and not a *being*. Furthermore—and this is the decisive turn—this general character of number or, what amounts to the same thing, this "general number" in all its indeterminateness, that is, in its merely possible determinateness, is accorded a certain independence which permits it to be the subject of "calculational" operations. This is achieved by adjoining the "rung" designations, whose interconnections according to precise rules indicates the particular homogeneous field underlying each equation which is constructed. The "rung" designation, which taken independently corresponds to the Diophantine *eidos, thus transforms the object of the* intentio secunda, namely the "general number" intended by the letter sign, *into the object of an* intentio prima, of a "*first intention*," namely of a "being" which is directly apprehensible and whose counterpart in the realm of ordinary calculation is, for instance, "two monads," "three monads."[80]

---

78. Klein, *Greek Mathematical Thought*, 169.
79. Klein, *Greek Mathematical Thought*, 174.
80. Klein, *Greek Mathematical Thought*, 174–75.

With the Viète-Cartesian advent, being does not merely *have* a mathematical structure—it is its mathematical structure. The assumption of the world's ontological independence is not so much denied as it is enfolded into the symbolic being of the intellect. This new method is fundamentally different than its ancient and scholastic inheritance. As we have established, Platonists hunt for the thing itself through the communal labors of dialectical recollection. Plato's *Republic*, for instance, presents the ideas of mathematics as having a degree of ontological independence; they are a bridge or ladder that reaches from the sense world to the intelligible realm of moral ideas and, ultimately, the Good.[81] Mathematical forms occupy a separate reality apart from the realm of the senses, but they are only lower links in the dialectical chain of being. Aristotelians consider mathematical form via its abstraction, separation, or subtraction from sensible matter.[82] Forms are taken into the soul from physical nature, but mathematical forms have no real being apart from the things in the world. They do, however, have a conceptual existence. Thus, because the mind is immaterial, the natures of material things exist in the mind in a way suitable to the mind, i.e., they have an immaterial existence in the mind. There is a hard and fast distinction between being as materialized in the sensible world (*first intention*) and being as dematerialized in the mind (*second intention*). Mathematical abstraction considers only the quantitative features of physical things within second intention, i.e., lines, planes, and so on, without attending to other non-quantitative aspects of physical things within the realm of nature. Mathematical aspects do not exist independently (as first intention) from their physical objects.

Viète's enclosure of being within the symbolic intellect is truly revolutionary. On the one hand, he accepts the Platonic separateness of mathematical form from sensible matter, but he denies its status as a lower link in the dialectical chain of being—*it is being itself*. Dialectic is no longer needed to establish the truth of things. Symbolic mathematics communicates what is universally intelligible as *formulas*: The true (and only) language of being. In its Aristotelian sense, mathematical concepts within second intention have a symbolic aspect that is being as first intention. All other features of actual being are consequent upon symbolic being; insofar as they are subject to being symbolized, they are real. If something cannot to be symbolized, it is not a property of actual being in first intention. What defies quantification

---

81. For Plato's theory of mathematics and dialectic, see Cornford, "Mathematics and Dialectic in the *Republic* VI–VII (I)," 37–52; "(II)," 173–90.

82. On the subtleties and controversies of abstraction, see Koninck's three-part analysis, "Abstraction from Matter"; Weinberg, "Abstraction in the Formation of Concepts," 1–9; Cleary, "On the Terminology of 'Abstraction' in Aristotle," 13–45.

is an attribute of second intention within the mind. Symbolic existence is existence proper because it is *objective*. What cannot be quantified is *subjective*. "This heralds a general conceptual transformation," Klein writes, "which extends over the whole of modern science."[83] Further:

> This means that the "being" of the species in Viète, i.e., the "being" of the objects of a "general analytic," is to be understood neither as independent in the Pythagorean and Platonic sense nor as attained by "abstraction" (ἐξ ἀφαιρέσεως), i.e., as "reduced" in the Aristotelian sense, but as *symbolic*. *The species are in themselves symbolic formations—namely formations whose merely potential objectivity is understood as an actual objectivity.* They are, therefore, comprehensible only within the language of *symbolic formulations*, which is fully enunciated first in Viète as alone capable of representing the *"finding of finding,"* namely "zetetic." Therewith the most important tool of mathematical natural science, the *"formula,"* first becomes possible, but, above all, a new way of "understanding," inaccessible to ancient *episteme* is thus opened up.[84]

Ancient dialectic and theurgy, along with scholastic ontology and syllogistic logic, are all made redundant. The true science of *being qua being* is the symbolic calculus of mathematics. Guided by algebraic signs, Viète opens the pathway to modern science; something unavailable for both ancient and medieval philosophers.

Klein stresses Viète's novel breakthrough:

> But above all—and it is this which gives Viète his tremendous role in the history of the origin of modern science—he was the first to assign to "algebra," to this "ars magna," a *fundamental place in the system of knowledge in general*. From now on the fundamental *ontological* science of the ancients is replaced by a *symbolic* discipline whose ontological presuppositions are left unclarified. This science, which aims from the first at a comprehension of the totality of the world, slowly broadens into the system of modern mathematical physics. Within this discipline the things in this world are no longer understood as countable beings, nor the world itself as a *taxis* determined by the order of numbers; it is rather the *structure* of the world which is grasped by means of a symbolic calculus and understood as a *"lawfully"* ordered course of *"events."* The very nature of man's understanding of the world is henceforth governed by the symbolic

---

83. Klein, *Greek Mathematical Thought*, 175.
84. Klein, *Greek Mathematical Thought*, 175.

"number" concept, a concept which determines the modern idea of science in general.[85]

Other forms of knowledge are not really *knowledge* at all because they cannot grasp the structure of reality. Insofar as human knowledge is just that, knowledge, it must align itself with the symbolic language of being willed by God—*algorithmic formulas* that reveal themselves to the specially trained intellect.

Descartes recognizes Viète's symbolic method as *the* way to reform Proclus's idea of universal mathematics. In this sense, science is a general approach to all things that can be investigated in deference to *ordo et mensura*: "And thence it became clear that there ought to be *some general science* which would explain everything that could by investigated in respect to order and measure when these are not ascribed to any special material, and that this same science was named—*using a word not newly appropriated but old and of accepted usage—Universal Mathematics*, since in it was contained everything on account of which other sciences are called *parts* of mathematics."[86] Viète's overturning of ancient mathematical ontology is, however, incomplete—that is, if identity (the determinate unit or oneness) is not the principle of the symbolic conception of number, what is? Simon Stevin provides an answer, which Descartes accepts; namely, the *arche* of number is zero. According to Definition II of Stevin's *Arithmetique* (1585): "Number is that by which *the quantity* of each thing is revealed."[87] The *principium* of number—the *that by which* numbers come to be—cannot be the unit or monad because "*the unit is a number.*"[88] Stevin accepts the classical definition of number as "a multitude consisting of units," but he conceives of number as having a form and matter distinction.[89] The principle, beginning, or *form of number* cannot itself be any material number. The unit is part of a multitude of units; therefore, the unit is "of the same material" as the multitude.[90] The monad, then, is a number like any other.

The *absolute presupposition* that underlies Stevin's form and matter distinction is Viète's symbolic enfoldment of being into the intellect. The problem of the mind's knowledge of things in the world is sidestepped by shutting out the sensory world altogether. In Aristotelian terms, the individual thing (form and matter identity) is now irrelevant to both being and

85. Klein, *Greek Mathematical Thought*, 184–85.
86. Descartes quoted in Klein, *Greek Mathematical Thought*, 182–83.
87. Stevin quoted in Klein, *Greek Mathematical Thought*, 191.
88. Stevin quoted in Klein, *Greek Mathematical Thought*, 191.
89. Stevin quoted in Klein, *Greek Mathematical Thought*, 191
90. Stevin quoted in Klein, *Greek Mathematical Thought*, 191.

knowledge. The senses do not communicate being. The mind does not receive form from matter. What can be known of reality is already available to a properly trained intellect. Symbolic concepts, form*ulas*, or *ciphers* operate as being in first intention; they do not need what is communicated by the senses. Symbolic concepts in first intention have their own objects or matter to work on: Numbers and their properties. More simply, being is purely a mathematical affair of the mind:

> The fundamental *presupposition* which underlies his understanding—although he hardly recognizes it as such—is precisely the identification of the mode of being of the *object* with the mode of being of the *concept* related to the object. This means that the one immense difficulty within ancient ontology, namely, to determine the relation between the "being" of the object itself and the "being" of the object in thought, is here (and elsewhere) accorded a "matter-of-course" solution whose presupposition and the extent of whose significance are simply bypassed in the discussion. The *consequence* of this solution is the *symbolic* understanding of the object intended, an understanding in which its *actual* objectivity is posited as identical with the mode of being of a "general object," or, in other words, in which the object of an "*intentio secunda*" (second intention), namely the concept as such, is turned into the object of an "*intentio prima*" (first intention).[91]

The symbolic *general object*, i.e., the formula of formulas, expressively exhausts the meaning of being. The Aristotelian *and Neoplatonic* presupposition of autonomous forms in the natural world—abstracted and projected (respectively) by the intellect—is thoroughly pushed aside as an archaic impediment to science. Being is united in the symbolic general object. There is nothing more outside or inside. No other method of inquiry, therefore, besides mathematics is really needed for apprehending truth. This radical idea presupposes an equally as radical idea of number.

The ancients hold the monad as the principle of number because mathematics is consequent upon the truth and experience of unitary being. Wholeness is first in the order of reality. The things we encounter in the world are determinate and monadic entities, governed by nature's forms and their ultimate principle: The One, the Good. Mathematics reflects this actuality. If it deviates from this actuality, mathematics falls into a fantasy world of its own devices. Stevin says this presupposition is fatal in its consequences for the development of mathematics, giving the whole "barbarous age" its

---

91. Klein, *Greek Mathematical Thought*, 192.

puerile character.[92] The Greeks, subsequently, did not progress because they lacked "the necessary equipment, namely of *ciphers*."[93] In order to attain a symbolic understanding of things, though, the tie to determinate being, to the Good, must be severed. A symbolic principle of number is possible only on the presupposition of indeterminate being.

"Zero," Stevin declares, "is the true and *natural* beginning" (le o est le vrai et naturel commencement).[94] *Zero symbolizes creatio ex nihilo*—the *genus* of number, thus reality itself. It is spatial continuity that is both unbounded and undifferentiated. Zero is the origin of symbolic ciphers. These *specific* or *formulaic differences* are continuous structures that embody reality. Mathematics is liberated from purely determinate operations. Stevin no longer deals with numbers of units in each case. Symbolic mathematics maintains the unlimited possibility of combining ciphers according to determinate rules of calculation. Symbolic formulations and their operations on *material* numbers constitute the new concept of mathematics.

Zero overturns the determinate monad. The sign of nothing opens frontiers previously unimagined for mathematics, but Stevin leaves its ontological consequences vague and unexplored—for if, as he claims, real being is only presented symbolically, what does it mean to assume that the ground of that presentation is *ontological zero*? In Aristotelian terms, for instance, mental concepts presume the independent presence of things in the world. Things communicate their forms to a receptive intellect. The realm of the senses (*sensus communis*), the subject matter of *physics*, is the transmission medium of these forms. But being is not an exclusive domain of mathematical *form*ulas because being will then lack *embodiment, real motion, and change*. A real thing is a determinate unity of form and matter, having its own generating principle: Just this entity. Reduction of a thing to its abstracted mathematical properties, especially zero, destroys a thing; it is a violent process from *a* divine, embodied limit to the chaos of the unlimited, from something (*this* one thing in the world) to nothing. To Descartes, nonetheless, zero appears to operate as a *Christian* generating principle of some mysterious kind and, in Proclus's sense, as the primordial *gap* that accounts for the screen of the imagination. This virtual space is a featureless desert of the real: The indefinitely extended plane of res extensa. It makes room—gives place of presence—for symbols, objects, properties, and their algorithmic order. But, simply put, is this lifeless, abstracted location *nature*?

---

92. Stevin quoted in Klein, *Greek Mathematical Thought*, 193.
93. Stevin quoted in Klein, *Greek Mathematical Thought*, 192–93.
94. Stevin quoted in Klein, *Greek Mathematical Thought*, 193.

The Ontology of Mastery 149

Descartes dispels Stevin's ontological ambiguity. True physical being is identical with its symbolic-mathematical *general object*. The substantial corporeality of the world is identified with extension: "Only by virtue of this identification did symbolic mathematics gain that fundamental position in the system of knowledge which it has never since lost."[95] Thus, the being of things in totally subsumed by the mind: "That the *intellectus* is assigned the role not only of the *eidos* (form) but also the *hyle* (material). In other words, the 'extraworldliness' of the *intellectus* does *not determine its mode of being*."[96] In reference to his assertion that "extension is not body," Descartes affirms, "no special idea corresponds to this word 'extension' in the imagination"; rather, "this whole assertion is effected by the *pure intellect* which alone has the ability of *separating abstract beings* of that sort."[97] In other words, the absolute presupposition of an indeterminate spatial plane underpins the intellectual level of pure symbols. This space is no place in particular; it is abstracted space in general, the real substance of the material world—*res extensa*. This kind of abstractive reflexivity is Descartes's unique contribution to the mathematical appropriation of being. He ingeniously incorporates Proclus's double movement of projection into his method. Like Proclus, there is projection or *emanation* (*prohodos*) of God's complete, mathematical ideas (*monē*) on the imagination and then abstraction-reversion (*epistrophe*) from sensible matter, constituting a purely internal reflection on the symbolic structure of the world: Intuitive introspection. Unlike Proclus, however, the symbolic second projection onto the sense world recreates it from nothing into something. The human intellect is the generative source of being.

Following Proclus, then, Descartes accepts the intellect's projection of mathematical ideas, virtual interval-forms, onto the screen of the imagination. Formal projections give place to the impressions of the world. This process occurs in such a way that the sensing parts of the body affected, including the imagination, take on the mathematical *figure* of that part of the world which is making the impression. Unlike scholastic Aristotelians, however, Descartes denies the possibility of taking in the formal being of things through the senses: "Nor, in general, do we recognize those beings of the philosophers which really cannot come before the imagination."[98] And, contrary to Proclus and most ancient Platonists, mathematical forms have no independent reality in the realm of nature. The power of creating

95. Klein, *Greek Mathematical Thought*, 198.
96. Klein, *Greek Mathematical Thought*, 298.
97. Descartes quoted in Klein, *Greek Mathematical Thought*, 198.
98. Descartes quoted in Klein, *Greek Mathematical Thought*, 203.

appearances, their procreant and activating cause, resides in the same site as their knowledge and intelligent comprehension; explicitly, the intellect—*res cogitans*.

What the intellect abstracts are the symbolic mathematical ideas that it initially projects for itself in order to structure bodily impressions. What is knowable as the matter for abstraction is already reduced to the mathematical aspects of determinate objects. This noetic-numeric matter pre*figures* sense experience in the imagination, but it cannot be experienced by the senses. To Klein, "the Cartesian conception of this process is completely original in reducing everything perceptible by the (external) senses, that is, besides the 'things' themselves also their colors, warmth, coldness, hardness, roughness, sweetness, etc., to 'figures,' which are supposed to represent the *true* 'nature' of the 'things' or 'forces' or 'properties' in question, namely precisely that nature which is inaccessible to the external senses."[99] Secondary qualities are presupposed by their primary quantities. The former are properties of sense experience. The latter obtain through the intellect.

The event of pure intellect, Descartes explains, occurs when the mind "turns *itself toward itself*," and thereupon, "beholds some one of the ideas that are *within itself*."[100] Symbolic entities are the ideas that the pure intellect brings back to itself from the imagination. Mathematical figures are initially projected upon the imagination to order sense impressions. These determinate figures are then abstracted by the intellect. Abstraction transforms figures within the sense saturated imagination into symbols at the level of the intellect. The pure intellect, therefore, is "divorced from the aid of any bodily image."[101] "Here the constant presupposition," Klein observes, "is that *the 'pure' intellect in itself has no relation at all to the being of the world and the things of the world*."[102] Reality is revealed when it has thoroughly removed its sensory obstructions.

Symbols are generated when mathematical figures, i.e., numbers, lines, planes, shapes, and so on, are taken from their embodied particularity, and elevated to indeterminate continuities: "*Thus the imaginative power makes possible a symbolic representation of the indeterminate content which has been 'separated' by the 'naked' intellect.*"[103] For example, the imaginative power that allows us to envisage *five units* enters the service of the pure intellect, which, being bare of any immediate reference to the world, comprehends

---

99. Klein, *Greek Mathematical Thought*, 307.
100. Descartes quoted in Klein, *Greek Mathematical Thought*, 200–201.
101. Descartes quoted in Klein, *Greek Mathematical Thought*, 200.
102. Klein, *Greek Mathematical Thought*, 202.
103. Klein, *Greek Mathematical Thought*, 202.

fiveness as something separate from both *five* (idea of the imagination that structures impressions), and the *five sensory things* in my immediate presence. Extension, then, is the foundational abstraction of abstractions. At the level of the imagination, each determinate figure is bounded to its singular place, gap, or virtual interval. Therefore, at the symbolic level, this translates into *placelessness*. Extension is indeterminate continuity as such because it is free of all its enveloping places, i.e., imaginative figures that enclose sense impressions. Symbolic extension is homogeneous and unbounded; it is the clean slate prepared for mathematical physics—upon which Descartes writes his new *science of order* by symbol-generating abstraction.

The realm of being qua being is symbolic objectivity. Knowledge is the mind's reflexive movement from itself onto the imagination and, then, back to itself from the imagination. The middle term of sensory content provides no clear and certain knowledge. Rather, to Descartes, the contents of the senses "are without us and *very much foreign*."[104] The intellect first unknowingly projects determinate figures to order impressions, and then abstracts them back as known indeterminate symbols—ciphers, formulas, or mechanical laws. Any and every sensory content can be reduced to its symbolically ordered quantities. Real being maintains quantificational equivalence, admitting mathematical properties, within a homogeneous continuum of extension that provides discrete location.

Sensory bodies in mindless extension, which includes all flora and fauna, are considered *automata*.[105] The universe is a great machine, where the artifacts produced by artisans are no different (in kind, not complexity) than the other things we find in nature because they are simply products of the same mechanical laws. Descartes places human-made and God-made automata upon the same mechanistic plane. The distinction between human construction and divine creation begins to collapse. God's presence to things is only through His symbolic laws; mediated and known by the human mind as clear and distinct ideas. Descartes's repressed premise here is that we are free to manipulate, explore, and *recreate* the world without theological impediment. God's communication is restricted to His symbolic ideas; they run the machine and keep it going, but do not reach to the individual, sensorially embodied being of natural things. Science, in this sense, claims for itself the *aesthetic right* to recreate the universe in the image of its creator. *Imago Dei* means the indefinite power of human creativity. Humanity, the sole subject in a mechanical universe, is given the world as a kind of extended artist's palette of pure potentiality; something to actualize by

---

104. Descartes quoted in Klein, *Greek Mathematical Thought*, 202.
105. See Rosenfield, *From Beast-Machine to Man-Machine*, 3–26.

human ingenuity and power. Through divine symbols, laws, or ciphers, we can constantly create a new world order. The novel role for imagination, then, is its *second projection* that, contrary to Proclus, turns the mirror outward onto the sensible appearances themselves.[106] Sensible objects have no intrinsic being apart from serving our creationist project. Descartes, in Proclus's sense, projects the idolatry of species-selfish power: Salvation through fake recreation leads to the domination of all things.

On Descartes's project, Stanley Rosen (†2014) concludes: "Having no determinate objects, the Cartesian *mathesis universalis* deals solely with 'order and measure,' regardless of whether such measure be sought in 'numbers, figures, stars, sounds, or any other object.' Nevertheless, although it has no determinate object, *mathesis universalis* determines order, measure, or proportion on the basis of the operation of imagination upon the perception of extended or material things."[107] Appearances are to conform to the *order and measure* projected upon them. Experienced phenomena have no intelligible existence or independent value. Given the divine ciphers of the intellect, we are summoned to create new reality from nothing; to make useful things out of the chaotic and threatening flux given to the senses.

Descartes's Dualistic Reception

The immediate reception of Descartes's doctrine as a way of thinking and being in the world, with the things of the world, splits into two opposed camps. The first, *the enlightened and triumphant*, claims for Descartes what is also attributed to Locke and Bacon: The overcoming of original sin. More in keeping with the political philosophy of Hobbes, however, Descartes's endeavor is less a response to the Fall than a case of marginalizing its significance. *Conversion to Cartesianism* means embracing humanistic optimism of a rather extreme kind; it proposes to restore prelapsarian knowledge and its consequent power to return this world to its Edenic state. "By adopting the procedures set out by Descartes," Peter Harrison claims, "the Cartesian method offered a means of overcoming the limitations of the fallen intellectual faculties of Adam's seventeenth-century descendants, and thus of restoring the fabled encyclopedic knowledge of the first man."[108] The necessary reform of the fallen mind can be accomplished through *clear and distinct ideas*; their attainment returns the mind to its original Adamic condition. There can be pure, uncorrupted knowledge of God's ideas.

106. See Nikulin, *Matter, Imagination, and Geometry*, xiv–xvi.
107. Rosen, "Central Ambiguity in Descartes," 26–27.
108. Harrison, "Original Sin and the Problem of Knowledge," 239.

The natural light of the intellect can provide the foundation of a complete and certain science. "Descartes's confident assertion," Harrison informs us, "presupposed the persistence of the natural light and the divine image even in fallen human beings."[109] For those who believed the Fall substantially diminishes the natural light and the divine image, knowledge "did not penetrate to the essences of things and was at best probable rather than certain."[110] "The optimism of the rationalist tradition," Harrison rightly concludes, "is thus related to a view of the Fall which considers it effects to be serious, yet reversible—a privation rather than a complete corruption, and hence a condition amenable to therapy."[111] Properly trained intellects can restore humanity's lost dominion.

Although, "Descartes avoids making reference to the revealed truths of Christianity, including the doctrine of original sin," his thought is theologically received as an implicit assessment of the Fall.[112] Descartes's philosophy is interpreted as a method to re-establish prelapsarian conditions in the present world. Nicolas Malebranche (†1715), for example, identifies the Cartesian project as the recovery of Adamic science: "It is not the philosophy received from Adam that teaches these things; it is that received from the serpent; for since Original Sin, the mind of man is quite pagan. It is this philosophy that, together with the errors of the senses, made men adore the sun, and that today is still the universal cause of disorder of men's minds and the corruption of men's hearts."[113] The mind's fallen state, then, is self-repairable, not irretrievably corrupted. The bodily senses are the source of error and sin. Therefore, "the mind must judge all things according to its inner lights, paying no heed to the false and confused testimony of its senses and imagination," and further, "when a man judges all things only by the mind's pure ideas, when he carefully avoids the noisy confusion of the creatures, and, when entering into himself, he listens to his sovereign Master with his senses and passions silent, it is impossible for him to fall into error."[114] The mind is capable of making infallible judgments when it functions in the way originally intended by God; namely, by getting to know God's ideas on the *symbolic* level of mathematical form: The basic structure of creation.

---

109. Harrison, *Fall of Man and the Foundations of Science*, 6.

110. Harrison, *Fall of Man and the Foundations of Science*, 7. On this key and complex distinction, separating rationalists from experimentalists, see 10–16.

111. Harrison, "Original Sin and the Problem of Knowledge," 257.

112. Harrison, "Original Sin and the Problem of Knowledge," 9.

113. Malebranche, *Search after Truth*, 451.

114. Malebranche, *Search after Truth*, xxxvii.

In his Gifford Lectures (2011), Harrison claims, "the new sciences entailed an explicit rejection of the symbolic significance of nature."[115] In its medieval, sacramental sense, this is undoubtably a true statement.[116] However, a further amendment is needed—that is, Descartes's philosophy is not an erasure of symbolic presence altogether; it is a thorough anthropocentric appropriation on behalf of a literal reading of dominion over the self and natural world.[117] In simpler terms, the symbolic domain belongs to the human intellect, alone. We, it appears, can repair the effects of the Fall, but the cosmos is left in an unredeemable state. Thus, our redemption depends on nature's re-creation, reinstating human dominion over all things. The true end of philosophy is the emendation of the soul through transformation of the world. Descartes's tacit remedy for original sin is a double movement of inwardness and exteriorization.

Contrary to the earlier presentation of his infinite ethics being based on the Christian God's diffusive passion for the liberation of others, Descartes takes the now familiar Stoic-Pelagian stance of *apatheia*. Self-mastery means *controlling the passions* generated by the senses. Enslavement to immediate desire is overcome by reaching the purely inward and *unaffected* symbolic level of ideas. Knowledge of ideas frees the soul and sanctions an exteriorization of self-mastery: The endeavor to control the unruly forces or *passions* of nature. To alleviate the human estate, we are to master and possess the world through first knowing God's symbolic ideas, then projecting them onto the chaotic realm of the senses. "Descartes's science," Michael Allen Gillespie clarifies, "achieves this end by reconstructing the chaos of the world in representation, by transforming the flux of experience into the motion of objects in a mathematically analyzable space."[118] Salvation can be achieved through mastery of self and world. Not surprisingly, therefore, the reception of this doctrine among traditionally minded Christians is less than sympathetic. Richard S. Westfall claims Descartes denies the full doctrine of the Christian Trinity: "There were no vestiges of a triune God."[119] The world outside the intellect ceases to communicate the symbols of God's triune nature. Descartes's philosophy is theistic; it requires the existence of God but, as Westfall perceives, "It is difficult to find in it anything specifically Christian. His God was the God of the philosophers, necessary to call the world into being and necessary to sustain it. He was not the God who

---

115. Harrison, *Territories of Science and Religion*, 136.
116. See Harrison, *Territories of Science and Religion*, 55–81.
117. See Harrison, *Territories of Science and Religion*, 136–44.
118. Gillespie, "Descartes and the Origin of Modernity," 23.
119. Westfall, "Rise of Science," 226.

redeemed mankind with his blood."[120] Descartes emphasizes, "God the Creator and Sustainer at the expense of God the Redeemer."[121] This reduction carries over into his ethical philosophy and, predictably, the theologians of his time have just cause to complain of his *Pelagianism* (the view that we can save ourselves without the aid of divine grace).

The role of redeemer is transferred from Christ's blood and love to human being's scientific power. Self-redemption is contingent on *our* restoration of the world. Pelagius's doctrine of natural grace is transformed from mere Christian *ascesis*—the moral mastery of the will which, Michael Hanby describes as "a Stoic conception of volition that identifies freedom primarily with the capacity to withhold assent from the biddings of desire"—to a positive program of self-making through commanding the forces of nature.[122] Descartes thoroughly pushes aside the medieval Christian doctrine of *sacramental creation* by denying any vestige of God in the sensory world. In its place, he adopts the Stoic attitude towards *nature—Homo faber*. Appius Claudius Caecus (†273 BCE), Roman statesman and architect of great public works, presents the apt maxim: *Homo faber suae quisque fortunae* ("Man is the creator of his own fortune"). For *Homo sapiens*, knowledge is for its own sake. The things of creation are contemplative signs, occasioning wonder, love, and wisdom. For *Homo faber*, by contrast, knowledge is for the sake of making technological instruments that control and transform nature for human advantage. Human being is a self-making project through technological appropriation; this doctrine is further reinforced and advanced by its incorporation within the Hebraic injunction to subdue and rule the Earth. "The Biblical God," Emil L. Fackenheim reminds us, "places no limitation upon the exercise of human reason; His gift of the Earth to man is radical."[123] The *radical gift*, however, entails equally as radical responsibility. Fackenheim distinguishes "our conquest, either in scientific understanding or technological control" of the universe in the contemporary age, from the doctrine of gift, of creation, which it misrepresents.[124] The former pursues a path of power; liberation without obligation to the *natural means* of this emancipation. The latter doctrine is "the gift of existence—the world's and our own."[125] For Fackenheim, "creation is a gift whenever there

---

120. Westfall, "Rise of Science," 226–27.
121. Westfall, "Rise of Science," 227.
122. Hanby, "Reconsiderations," para. 18.
123. Fackenheim, "Man and His World," 57.
124. Fackenheim, "Man and His World," 57.
125. Fackenheim, "Man and His World," 57.

is human acceptance of it," which "makes inescapable the acceptance of its burden"—we are called "to be responsible for the world."[126]

On Descartes's alleged Stoic-Christian (*pace* Pelagian) worldview, many commentators are unusually penetrating in their critiques. Hans Jonas (†1993), for instance, remarks:

> There remained, then, the time-honored—Stoic as well as Christian—idea that plants and animals are for the benefit of Man. Indeed, since the existence of a living world is the necessary condition of any of its members, the self-justifying nature of at least one such member (=species) would justify the existence of the whole. In Stoicism, Man provided this end by his possession of reason, which makes him the culmination of a terrestrial scale of being that is also self-justifying throughout all its grades (the end as the best of many that are good in degrees); in Christianity, by his possession of an immortal soul, which makes him the sole *imago Dei* in creation (the end as the sole issue at stake); and Cartesian dualism radicalized this latter position by making man even the sole possessor of inwardness of "soul" of any kind, thus the only one of whom "end" can meaningfully be predicated as he alone can entertain ends. All other life then, the product of physical necessity, can be considered his means.[127]

As the singular subject of value in an otherwise uncommunicative, de-inscribed universe, humanity is depicted as a kind of second god; a Platonic demiurge that literally makes order from the chaos of the given world. The moral aspect, then, of Pelagian natural grace, which emphasizes the freedom given to all human beings (as *imago Dei*) to choose good or evil, is replaced by freedom as the power to create, not merely to *responsibly construct*. God still calls on us to be perfect; to be sharers of divine substance, the freedom of God, but we have at the core of our being an ontological zero, a void, that the will transforms into something through ordering the machinery of the world towards our *end*. Like God, we work with nothing in order to create. But, unlike God's nothing, our nothing is all the beauty of the world already created and laid out before our eyes!

The net effect of Descartes's "Pelagian grace is to sacrifice the entire trinitarian economy and to set divine and human agency in opposition. Such opposition puts divine and human agency, as it were, on the same level."[128] We are to the world what God, supposedly, is to us: A wild principle

---

126. Fackenheim, "Man and His World," 58.
127. Jonas, "Meaning of Cartesianism," 59–60.
128. Hanby, "Augustine and Descartes," 462.

The Ontology of Mastery

of absolute freedom beyond the physical mechanics of natural laws. "Like the Stoa," Michael Hanby claims for Descartes, "the freedom of the will is utterly uncharacterizable, except as sheer spontaneous power. It is this power, alone among the divine predicates to transcend hyperbolic doubt, which makes possible the Cartesian *époche*. It is this power that Descartes's *res cogitans* appropriates to itself as the mark of the *imago Dei*."[129] The human will is sheer power; not subordinate to reason, law, or rule. We are free to create heaven or hell on Earth. To Gillespie, "God's infinite and all-powerful will proves in the end not to endanger human will and power but, on the contrary, to enable it to achieve a universal mastery of nature."[130] We, like God, are self-creators from nothing.

God is pure freedom to be. As *imago Dei*, we too are characterized by this theological presupposition. Fackenheim calls this heterodox view the *meontological tradition*. In a rich and dense passage, he explains its characteristic *emanationist* process: "The God of meontological metaphysics would have to be described as a process which (i) because it is pure *making* proceeds from the indifference of sheer possibility of nothingness (μὴ ὄν), into the differentiation of actuality—*ex nihilo in aliquid*; (ii) because it is *self*-making establishes its own identity throughout this process by returning upon itself; or, otherwise put, proceeds into otherness, yet cancels this otherness and in so doing establishes itself; (iii) because it is *absolute* self-making, actualizes *ex nihilo* the totality of possibilities."[131] Freedom is *me on*: The Nothing; it is infinite potentiality, becoming without complete essence. The Nothing must, nevertheless, make itself be, be something. Identity, then, is not given; it is progressively created by the will—a shadow seeking its substance. In the case of Descartes, the self-making subject establishes itself by projecting its order upon the sensory world. The otherness of the world is cancelled. Our essence is achieved by mastering and possessing what environs us, treating it as a mere receptacle for the symbolic impositions of our will. Unlike God, however, we are not really creators of anything; we cancel, annihilate created things (something, not nothing) to merely *construct* ourselves, turning creatures into reconstructed machines for our use. This mistake of species redemption will turn to perdition for all truly created things.

---

129. Hanby, "Augustine and Descartes," 474.
130. Gillespie, *Nihilism Before Nietzsche*, 62.
131. Fackenheim, "Metaphysics and Historicity," 129.

Pelagian Persecution

The immediate cultural influence of Cartesianism is profound; especially, on the nature of truth as disseminated by educational institutions. The audacity of Descartes's project eventually catches up with him. His continued residency in The Netherlands deepens an ongoing theo-political crisis between orthodox Calvinists and Pelagian leaning Protestant reformers.[132] Calvinists of this variety affirm Augustine's triple doctrine of original sin, predestination, and divine grace, which they integrate into Aristotelian natural philosophy. In 1639 the physician Henri Regius (†1679) begins teaching Cartesian views at the University of Utrecht. This infiltration into the University curriculum is viewed by Calvinist professors as an attack on both their Augustinian and Aristotelian presuppositions. In the 1640s a pedagogical war ensues that spills over onto Descartes himself; he is eventually drawn into a fierce controversy with the Calvinist theologian and Rector of Utrecht University Gisbertus Voetius (†1676). Voetius accuses Descartes of atheism and Pelagianism, reviving the ideas of the reform minded Jacob Arminius (†1609). The University of Leiden eventually joins the academic posse of public condemnation.[133]

Descartes is charged, like Pelagius and Arminius before him, with maintaining that grace is *naturally* distributed among all human beings. Human beings are able to achieve salvation through their own works. With Pelagius, Descartes affirms that free will is the indifferent capacity for either direction (*liberum arbitrium*). This freedom is the sign of God in human nature, and human beings can be praised or blamed according to their use of it. Self-conferring natural grace does not need the supernatural and predetermined grace of God to elevate arbitrary free will to true *libertas*. People are good, he believes, only to the extent that they act freely for the good of others; such generosity is the highest virtue. Choosing goodness over evil is mostly assured when people do their best to find, and act upon, the truth. Human reason can find the truth. Descartes claims to have developed *the* method for accessing God's clear and distinct symbolic ideas. Truth automatically induces right action in the world.

Voetius also criticizes Descartes's natural philosophy. The assumption of a purely mechanical universe leads to atheism. Voetius argues that reducing the conception of natural causality to self-operational efficiency makes it impossible for theologians to explain the relationship between God and creation in philosophical terms. Descartes's natural philosophy is atheistic

---

132. See Verbeek, *Descartes and the Dutch*.
133. See Kenny, *Rise of Modern Philosophy*, 37–40.

because he denies God-as-Trinity's causal relation to creation through substantial form.[134] The heterogeneous nature of substantial forms is replaced by homogeneous matter; more accurately, by a mathematically analyzable extension (*res extensa*). To Descartes, beyond the symbolic physical laws intelligible to the mind, God does not interfere, nor can He be reasonably experienced as otherwise revealed, in the order of nature. This doctrine undermines the status of theology as a scientific discipline of the rational knowledge of God through the senses; it also threatens to either deify humanity as a god on Earth (principle of divine mind) or reduce human beings to soulless mechanisms in an equally as soulless universe (principle of res extensa).[135]

Descartes defends himself with a public letter to Voetius (*Epistola at Voetium*) in 1643.[136] Surprisingly, though, he does not attempt to refute the charges; rather, Descartes heaps abuse back on his accusers, affirming his right to hold such views under the liberal religious laws of Holland. In defending his method against the Calvinists' Aristotelian natural philosophy, Descartes (more or less) confirms their accusations. His method, not theirs, can access truth. Universal mathematical science is the modus operandi of natural grace; the way to self-made salvation:

> The philosophy against which you rail with such violence . . . aims at the knowledge of the truths which are acquired by means of natural light, and which promote the benefit of the human race; by contrast the dominant philosophy, which is taught in the schools and the universities, is merely a muddled collection of opinions which are mostly open to doubts, as is proved by the debates that they occasion day after day, and which are entirely without practical benefit, as centuries of experience have proved only too well.[137]

Descartes's *Open Letter* leads Voetius to have him summoned before the town council of Utrecht to answer the charge of slandering a clergyman.[138] The magistrates threaten Descartes with expulsion from the Netherlands and the public burning of his books. Descartes, however, avoids capture by fleeing to The Hague, where he convinces Frederick Henry (†1647)—Prince of Orange and stadtholder of Holland, Zeeland, Utrecht, Guelders, and Overijsse—to intervene on his behalf. Descartes avoids

---

134. See Van Ruler, *Crisis of Causality*, 305–20.
135. See Verbeek, *Descartes and the Dutch*, 33–45.
136. See Cottingham, *Descartes*, 15–17.
137. Descartes quoted in Cottingham, *Descartes*, 15–16.
138. See Gaukroger, *Descartes*, 359–61.

persecution, spending the next half decade developing his ethical and scientific work under the protection of various powerful courts. Tired of the strife, incessant movement, and academic squabbling, in the autumn of 1649, at the invitation of Queen Christina of Sweden (†1689), Descartes moves to Stockholm. After taking up the early morning tutelage of the young Queen, he dies on February 11, 1650, leaving the fulfillment of his vision for a new world order to succeeding generations.

FIVE

From Mastery to Stewardship

THIS CHAPTER FIRST PRESENTS some contemporary criticisms of the Cartesian inspired idea that the domination of nature is a pre-requisite for human liberation. Then, based on the evidence gathered from the preceding three chapters, historical metaphysics of environment is defended as the appropriate *phenomenological* method against its critics. The concluding sections of this chapter examine the paradoxical and mostly unrecognized tradition of attachment, coinciding with the modern *master*-narrative. The drive for human independence demonstrates overwhelming evidence of dependence. The radical deafness towards environment reveals openness to its intricate structures of communication. The professed mentality of domination of nature is overtaken by its repressed premise—stewardship as the liberation of creation. Criticisms of stewardship are presented. Stewardship is then defended as an activist type of distributive justice that includes the environment.

CARTESIANISM NOW

On the cultural influence of Descartes's worldview, Michael Allen Gillespie holds, "For better and for worse, we are the heirs of this Cartesian vision."[1] Gillespie draws a continuous Pelagian line of thought from Ockham to Descartes. The domains of world and revelation are divorced from one another. Revelation is a purely subjective affair of faith. Anthropocentric nature replaces God's creation: "Nature thus can be mastered by the human

---

1. Gillespie, "Descartes and the Question of Toleration," 120.

will through the application of science to secure human freedom and well-being."² This *way of mastery*, however, is supposedly embedded in social ethics of some kind. Descartes seeks a new path to human welfare. He finds it in his dream of a universal symbolic science placed in the hands of a tolerant and generous humanity, making itself *master and possessor* of nature. The central tension in Descartes's philosophy is reconciling his ambition of making humanity *more perfect* through the appropriation of nature with the immense capacity for dominance that it entails. Put otherwise, why should we trust that the *science of order* will not turn on ourselves? Can a despotic relation to nature make human being more benevolent? Or is it simply a recipe for tyrannical relations all the way up the scale of being?

Time, events, and a growing chorus of commentators have not been kind to Descartes's gamble on the therapeutic effects of nature reduced to symbolic extension and knowledge committed to mastery. "Of Descartes's dream," James J. Bono argues, "are made the sciences and the follies, the noble aspirations and obsessive nightmares, of the modern world."³ Cost, it seems, is overwhelming its cornucopia of temporal benefits; more apocalyptic nightmare than saintly vision. Gillespie even claims the Cartesian project lies at the heart of modern totalitarianism:

> The God that Descartes first imagined and feared was a titanic God, beyond reason and nature, beyond good and evil. Descartes wins his struggle with this fearsome God, however, only by taking this God's power upon himself. He thereby opens up the hope and aspiration for human omnipotence, a hope that has manifested itself repeatedly in often monstrous forms, especially in the twentieth century. Despite his liberal impulses, Descartes should thus not be counted among the fathers or forefathers of liberalism, but among those who unwittingly gave birth to an apocalyptic politics that aimed to make a god of man and a heaven of earth but that ultimately produced not the overman but the beast and not paradise but the inferno.⁴

On this reading, power is returned to its pagan throne as the most divine of all properties. As we are to God, nature is to us—that is, nature is put at our arbitrary mercy. But unlike God's ways, we have demonstrated only systematic mercilessness.

To Jürgen Moltmann, divine power is the theological midwife of modern science:

2. Gillespie, "Descartes and the Question of Toleration," 119.
3. Bono, *Ficino to Descartes*, 271.
4. Gillespie, "Descartes and the Origin of Modernity," 24.

> This was the new picture of God offered by the Renaissance and by nominalism: God is almighty, and *potentia absoluta* is the pre-eminent attribute of his divinity. Consequently God's image on human being (which in actual practice meant the man) had to strive for power and domination so that he might acquire *his* divinity. Power became the foremost predicate of the deity, not goodness and truth. But how can the human being acquire power, so that he may resemble his God? Through science and technology; for "knowledge is power," as Francis Bacon exultantly proclaimed. The goal of the scientific knowledge of natural laws is power over nature, and with that the restoration earth, the of the human being's resemblance to God and his hegemony. In his theory of science, *Discours de la méthode*, Descartes also declared that the aim of the exact sciences was to make men "maîtres et possesseurs de la nature."[5]

The Cartesian dualism of *res cogitans* and *res extensa* prompts the modern process of differentiation between humanity and nature, the purposes behind that process, and its increasingly disastrous consequences.

The methodological aspect of dominance is the key to understanding the specific difference of modern societies. To dislodge its normativity, Moltmann distinguishes between societies dedicated to equilibrium and those dedicated to imperial conquest:

> The earlier civilizations were by no means "primitive," let alone "under-developed." They were highly complicated systems of equilibrium—equilibrium in the relationship between human beings and nature, equilibrium in the relationship between human being and human being, and equilibrium in the relationship between human beings and "the gods." It is only the modern civilizations which, for the first time, have set their sights on development, expansion and conquest. The acquisition of power, the increase of power, and the securing of power: these, together with "the pursuit of happiness," may be termed the values that actually prevail in modern civilizations.[6]

Surely, though, the historical record demonstrates ample examples of ancient civilizations that *set their sights on development, expansion, and conquest*. If I am understanding him here, Moltmann is not denying these obvious facts, but pointing to a unique and defining property of modern civilization as it has emerged in the secular West—that is, for many ancient

---

5. Moltmann, *God in Creation*, 26–27.
6. Moltmann, *God in Creation*, 26.

civilizations, essential equilibrium (divine) is punctuated by accidental *development, expansion, and conquest* (worldly). The latter exception is a constant threat to the former's sacred pattern of life. What seems to occur for the first time in modern Europe is a civilization essentially dedicated to domination (worldly). Only accidentally are their periods of peace and equilibrium (divine). Material progress is relentless, innovative profanation. This *modernization* process is not an anomaly. It is the new globalized norm. All will be subject to its logic.

If this interpretation of Moltmann's text is acceptable, the modern European *switch of essences* seems to be well documented by the colonial and post-colonial experience of Western modernization. Complaining of his country's backwardness, and otherworldly fatalism, the Indian novelist and satirist Bankimchandra Chattopadhyay (†1894), for example, observes that the difference between Indian and European civilizations rests in the latter's insatiable quest for power:

> "Knowledge is power": that is the slogan of Western civilization. "Knowledge is salvation" is the slogan of Hindu civilization. . . . Europeans are devotees of power. That is the key to their advancement. We are negligent towards power; that is the key to our downfall. Europeans pursue a goal which they must reach in this world: they are victorious on earth. We pursue a goal which lies in the world beyond, which is why we have failed to win the earth. Whether we will win in the life beyond is a question on which there are differences of opinion.[7]

Indians require a different kind of knowledge for temporal salvation—one that unlocks the secrets of nature, enabling mastery of the Earth. Chattopadhyay, though, understands the European drive for victory over nature is connected to domination over other peoples. European colonization of the world is obvious proof. Power as means, then, is simply power as end: Power for power's sake. Mastery of nature as a means for increasing human generosity is, at best, a historically tenuous assumption.

The list of significant critics continues to grow. "What men want to learn from nature," Max Horkheimer (†1973) and Theodor W. Adorno (†1969) reason, "is how to use it in order to wholly dominate it and other men."[8] Étienne Gilson (†1978) calls Descartes's project "a recklessly conducted experiment to see what becomes of human knowledge when molded into conformity with the pattern of mathematical evidence."[9] To Hans Jonas,

---

7. Chattopadhyay quoted in Chatterjee, *Nationalist Thought*, 56–57.
8. Horkheimer and Adorno, *Dialectic of Enlightenment*, 5.
9. Gilson, *Unity of Philosophical Experience*, 133.

"It is a formal fact that the countering of power with power is the sole relation to the totality of nature left for man."[10] Cartesianism leaves only domination as our relationship to the world: "For extension, or the quantitative, is the one essential attribute left to the world, and therefore, if the world has anything to tell us it is through this property: and what magnitude can tell of is power. But a world reduced to a mere manifestation of power admits toward itself—once the transcendent reference has fallen away and man is left with himself alone—nothing but the relation of power, that is mastery."[11] To lay all of these apocalyptic charges on Descartes's doorstep seems more than a bit extreme, overstated, scapegoating his ideas for the horrors of modernity. Most likely, aspects of Descartes's thought are taken up into a historical process already well underway, developing from multiple philosophical sources and practical endeavors. *Cartesian ideology* must be carefully distinguished from the perennial fertility of Descartes's philosophy. The complex nature of ideas in their historical contexts is examined in the next section.

REPLY TO EXPECTED CRITICISM OF HISTORICAL METAPHYSICS OF ENVIRONMENT

Edmund Husserl (†1938) calls Cartesian ideology, "the surreptitious substitution of the mathematically substructed world of idealities for the only real world, the one that is actually given through perception, that is ever experienced and experienceable—our everyday life-world. This substitution was promptly passed on to . . . the physicists of all the succeeding centuries."[12] As a counter-movement, *phenomenology* seeks to recover the life-world (*Lebenswelt*) from its symbolic reduction. Husserl's maxim of turning "back to things themselves" (*Zurück zu den Sachen selbst*) has kindled a plurality of philosophical endeavors.[13] Such multiplicity makes phenomenology notoriously hard to grasp as a thing itself but, perhaps, this is the point. Phenomenology casts fresh light on the great themes and problems of philosophy; it reopens, pluralizes, and returns to our contact with things as they present themselves from themselves. In a negative sense, you are a phenomenologist if you deny enclosure of the life-world on any set of assumptions. In a more problematic and positive sense, you remain faithful to the things themselves as an inexhaustible, multifaceted, and independent source, placing

---

10. Jonas, "Epilogue," 324.
11. Jonas, "Epilogue," 327.
12. Husserl, *Crisis of European Sciences*, 48–49.
13. For an *orientation* to recent critical phenomenology, encompassing gender and race, see Ahmed, *Queer Phenomenology*, 1–24.

themselves into the light of your experience. The giving of the perceptual given is not a nihilistic threat—a tissue of lies—requiring mastery and idolatrous re-creation. The perceptual world is full of significance: Independent, perspectival, and communicative. Phenomenology is a meta-method for letting things present themselves from their own natures. Instead of violent construction based on immovable presuppositions, we have an approach to reality as openness, as beloved reception of its irreducible multiplicity. Josef Seifert well captures its character:

> A phenomenological grasp of things themselves ought to be the goal of any good philosophy. The phenomenological method, interpreted in this way, is not a single or a narrow method of philosophy, but *the* method and the broadest possible method of philosophy which is open to every meaning and being and seeks out the appropriate form of givenness, knowledge, experience, and so on, in which each being discloses itself. This method opposes itself to any sense of distancing one's theories from being, to any failure to listen to the voice of things, to any putting of obstacles into the way of their presenting their own intelligibility to our minds.[14]

Method, then, follows phenomena. Contrary to Descartes's symbolic reduction, phenomena are not forced to conform to the *mathematically substructed world of idealities*. Phenomenal methodologies that do not maintain quantificational equivalence are not figments of idiosyncratic imaginations: Unscientific opinion (conventional stipulation) on secondary qualities. The symbolic method, the "finding of finding," reduces experience to homogeneous ideality; it entails a heteronomous relationship of many-to-one. The phenomenological method, by contrast, is the *letting of letting be* from a thing's own being. The world communicates itself with many voices. This heterogeneous meta-method maintains a many-to-many relationship. Casually put, one size does not fit all, and acting as if it did causes immense damage to the thing under consideration.

Descartes's symbolic ontology, however, is not wrong; it is simply an immense overreach of what is best suited to the things themselves. Many things can be mathematically grasped, but not all things are reducible to symbolic representations. Truth is not convertible with primary quantities: *Substructed* mathematical symbols. Instead of being assumed, method must develop with phenomena. Following a thing's immanent necessity means not interfering with it by imposing a pre-established schema. The subject matter legitimates the method. What is an appropriate method for one

---

14. Seifert, *Back to "Things in Themselves*," 14.

phenomenon may not be appropriate for another phenomenon; learning to recognize the difference is a crucial element of phenomenology. "True method," to Hans-Georg Gadamer, is not "alien to the thing" because it is "an activity performed by the thing itself," in which, "certainly, the thing does not go its own course without our thinking being involved, but thinking means unfolding the proper logic of the thing itself."[15] Phenomenology maintains itself as a rigorously open approach to things and their schemas of representation; it is a project that informs many disciples of study and life in general: *Being-with* does not necessarily mean being in control.

Thus far in the analysis, historical metaphysics is assumed to be the appropriate method. It grows out of the phenomenon of the environmental crisis itself. Martin Heidegger, for instance, puts Collingwood's science of absolute presuppositions into phenomenological terms. "Philosophical cognition," Heidegger says, "is essentially at the same time, in a certain sense, historical cognition."[16] Historicized phenomenology is "a de-constructing of traditional concepts carried out in an historical recursion to the tradition. And this is not a negation of the tradition or a condemnation of it as worthless; quite the reverse, it signifies precisely a positive appropriation of tradition."[17] One may, of course, argue that the critical *appropriation* of absolute presuppositions is not the appropriate method. Historical metaphysics does not fit the phenomenon. Eco-politics and ethics are more in tune with the thing itself. This may in fact be true but, given the peculiar nature of the phenomenon, the onus of justification for dismantling historical metaphysics in favor of eco-politics or ethics is placed on the dismantler. But here, thankfully, phenomenology helps us out; it is more a matter of affirming all three and their appropriate relationship to each other (*dialectic*), than a contest of elimination (*eristic*). Eco-politics needs ethics, and ethics, since it is dealing with such a novel phenomenon, needs the historical science of absolute presuppositions to critique its constitutive ideas, mapping other territories for ethical thought. Instead of opposing and competing for the phenomenon, all three methods are appropriate and interpenetrating. This work affirms a priority for historical metaphysics of environment because, although the elder approach, it is the least developed and, I think, appreciated of the categories of philosophy of environment. This type of *critical-historical phenomenology* may also prove to be appropriate—an edifying, *learned ethos*—for those who contemplate, enact, and govern

---

15. Gadamer, *Truth and Method*, 421.
16. Heidegger, *Basic Problems of Phenomenology*, 23.
17. Heidegger, *Basic Problems of Phenomenology*, 23.

experiments on behalf of the fundamental change of social and ecological presuppositions.

Apart from justifying historical metaphysics of environment as such, a more troubling problem emerges from within the discipline itself. Environmental historiography tends to present certain taboo subjects as being at the root of the crisis. Western religion, science, and politics—a potent cluster of dearly cherished absolute presuppositions—are all held up to critical historical analysis, i.e., *de-construction*. Not surprisingly, then, historical metaphysics of environment has occasioned considerable retrenchment among philosophical historians. For example, to present the development of modern science as being something other than a miraculous light that overcomes a dark age of ignorance and superstition is still a distinct challenge to established views.[18] What seems to be at stake in this dispute, for Carolyn Merchant, are "perceptions of the Scientific Revolution as a grand narrative of progress and hope versus one of decline and disaster."[19] Defenders of the scientific faith and its saints challenge the whole project of environmental historical metaphysics; it is nothing more than an arbitrary witch hunt, an ideologically driven "projection of grievance and complaint onto the past."[20] This accusation is, methodologically speaking, very disquieting; it seems to suggest that historical metaphysics is doing something very different than following a phenomenon's logic of self-emergence. Historical metaphysics is not phenomenological; rather, it acts as covert ideology, imposing certain nonrevocable presuppositions on the phenomenon. This criticism must be taken seriously, but it is the risk any historical metaphysics must take. Thankfully, though, Collingwood has already prepared us, as much as is possible, for how to distinguish history as selective ideology from true phenomenology.

The ethics of historical metaphysical analysis means any kind of moral judgment on history is suspended in favor of increased identification, clarification, and reenactment of the historical motion that continues to shape us and the Earth. Through compiling historical sources, and commentators, we can identify a certain coalescence of absolute presuppositions as having its event. For historical metaphysics, however, merely identifying a phase of change through figures, dates, and events is not enough. One must also map the processes, thinking the internal dynamics of change. The assumption here is that history is an underdetermined process, iteratively nonlinear. The idea of recessive minority reports from one time becoming the

---

18. See Vickers, "Francis Bacon, Feminist Historiography," 117–141, esp. 117–18n2.
19. Merchant, "Secrets of Nature," 148.
20. Merchant, "Secrets of Nature," 147.

dominant presupposition of another means such an analysis admits degrees of continuity and discontinuity. History is not to be reduced to a formulaic logic of the same, draining its contingency and innovation, but neither are events *sui generis*; original in such a way as to make the gap between historical planes of meaning incommensurate. The whole point of historical metaphysics is identifying and reenacting the gap. The gap contains a shape of historical motion by which absolute presuppositions are repositioned into a new order of things.

The debate over modern science, therefore, appears to be a clash of judgments on the influence of the scientific revolution on culture and nature. One group defends the traditional idea that it is the birth of light and progress over the forces of darkness and reaction. The other side claims it is the beginning of apocalyptic domination. Proper environmental metaphysics cannot really decide the issue; both sides seem to be, to some extent, intentionally projecting ideological judgments back into the past. It may even be appropriate to affirm both absolute presuppositions. This analysis presented and developed the minority report that makes modern science just one moment in a much older set of theological ideas on salvation. Description and reenactment may appear to be mere ideological cover for the same process of selection by presupposition; complete ideological neutrality may not be possible. The burden of proof for this charge is on the accuser, not the defendant. The openness of phenomenological environmental history does not necessarily mean ideological driven arbitrariness.

Historical metaphysics of environment is a subtle and exacting task; it must be undertaken in good faith and be open to further amendments by the progress of inquiry. Margaret J. Osler explains the reflexive relationship between history and the historian: "Questioning the canon leads us to inquire why and how it was formed. And this inquiry, in turn, causes us to interrogate our own presuppositions as historians and how those presuppositions affect what we see in the past."[21] The present ecological crisis motivates considerable identification and reappraisal of past absolute presuppositions. It is true that there has been a tendency to assign blame to specific figures and ideas even though other influences played an equally, if not more, significant part. Historically saturated ideas may not be that influential at all; they merely project an illusory order over multiple practices in the localized development of the social production of life. Regarding the emergence of what is called modern science, Steven Shapin, for example, argues against the very idea of a scientific revolution and, further, "any

---

21. Osler, "Canonical Imperative," 4.

single coherent cultural entity called 'science.'"[22] Instead of the Grand Narratives of modern science, environmentally critical or otherwise in favor, he presents a pluralistic and embedded *phenomenological* approach to the "diverse array of cultural practices aimed at understanding, explaining, and controlling the natural world, each with different characteristics and each experiencing different modes of change."[23] A unified description merely maps over these practices as a *pragmatic heuristic*. Descriptors are ways of coping with the reality of multiplicity, existing without a reference to a common relationship. There is no commensurate and intelligible significance between differences. But unities must always be imposed by various fields of representation to achieve some sense of things, but they are not essential relations that determine the order of the many things they describe.

This analysis, nonetheless, maintains many of these risky preferences; it assumes a qualified Grand Narrative from certain theological strains. A minority report reaches across centuries, preserving a coherent, but non-necessary, unity of development. This undertaking is a conceptual *description* of a pattern of life that continues to be *commonly directive* of harmful ecological practices. While it is certainly true that environmental historical metaphysics of the formulaic and judgmental variety must become more ethical in Collingwood's sense—conclusions more tempered—a purely localized approach quickly assumes the appearance of what it professes to be against. The practically embedded construction of *different histories* is still an absolute presupposition, suspending all meaningful common explanations on historical process. Reflective analysis on its nature leads to the problem of accounting for the reality of any unified social activity whatsoever, no matter how small or large the scale: The *ensemble des ensembles*.[24] There is nothing there to explain. We are merely explaining our past and present explanations: The differences found in our discourses about things, not *the things themselves*.

To portray history as an accidental aggregate of incommunicable practices without the possibility of a common referent is itself something that must be justified, explained, not simply *ideologically* given. The materialist hypothesis, for instance, traditionally presumes order is the accidental outcome of cycles of integration and disintegration. The cycles themselves are just as random, meaningless, and diverse as their contents. The theory of history supposed here, by contrast, is a modified Christian progressive one. It is linear: Continuous in an *iterative-emanative* sense, generating novel

---

22. Shapin, *Scientific Revolution*, 3.
23. Shapin, *Scientific Revolution*, 3.
24. See Braudel, "Society," 458–61; Latour, *Reassembling the Social*, 159–64.

constellational patterns by freely proceeding from and returning upon itself. Self-envelopment presents unique historical regions linked by the common struggle for emancipation. Difference is part of historical order; it does not threaten a structure that evolves by freedom rather than necessity or chance. Plurality is the *intelligible* result, not contrary, of history's *self-differentiating unity*.

Instead of assuming ready-made interpretive categories without explanation, the science of absolute presuppositions demands identification and explanation for that which makes any preference preferable and, more generally, what makes any intelligible explanation of a certain kind possible. The latter view has the advantage of not leaving its absolute presuppositions untouched; it is not a view from nowhere or everywhere. To engage absolute presuppositions is to contact the productive site, genus, or *idea* of history itself. For example, which is more insightful, more attuned to the thing itself, for historical reenactment of attitudes to nature in seventeenth-century France: The material practices of a humble village artisan or the works of Descartes and the texts of those that react to his philosophy? Which explanation is more revealing of the era? But there is no real eristic competition to be found here. The turn to multiplying power through various bottom-up cultural endeavors—given in the embedded hermeneutic—is the absolute presupposition under analysis; one that provides a coherent unity of explanation for multiple, localized *phenomenologies*. It answers the question of why there is such a *common* revolution in many local regimes of practice. Absolute presuppositions do more than reflect diverse practical processes; they are directive in the dynamic and fallible sense already described by Collingwood and others. *Directive* does not mean a simple cause to effect relation where one element (idea) makes the other (practice) a derivative outcome. Practically embedded ways of life and their governing ideas maintain co-equal identities, but in a way that is open and interpenetrating, affecting reciprocal modification in each element.[25] So, with warts and all, this analysis holds firm to the measured conclusion that the historical development of self-salvation through dominance of nature is a conceptually essential (but not *materially sufficient*) aspect of any explanation of the antecedents that inform our environmental crisis.

---

25. For an excellent analysis that achieves a place for both ideas and embedded practices—without subjecting one element to be a causal outcome of the other—see White Jr., "Cultural Climates and Technological Advance," 171–201.

CREATION GRASPED OTHERWISE

The first three chapters of Michel Foucault's *Les Mots et les choses* (1966) are an elegant expression of the themes we have been tracing. In their pages, we discover the modern *science of order*.[26] The multiplicity of jointures between mind and world produce an equally as manifold variety of sign systems. The open signatures of the world are eventually enclosed by what Foucault describes as the lattice of *genesis*, *mathesis*, and *taxinomia*.[27] Creation *ex nihilo* moves from God to human subjectivity (0, 0). Ontological zero is "the blank space that separates between the presence of representation and the 're-' of its repetition."[28] "This genesis," Foucault continues, "functioned exactly instead of and in place of *Genesis* itself."[29] Second creation by representation is a sequential and interlocking order of calculation and empirical classification: "The region of signs."[30] What cannot be signified symbolically by algebraic-algorithmic relations, variables, equations, formulas, operations, and so on is constituted by a qualitative order of taxonomy: "On the one hand, we have the utilization of the symbols of possible operations upon identities and differences; on the other, we have an analysis of the marks progressively imprinted in the mind by the resemblances between things and the retrospective action of imagination."[31] The lattice of representation encloses the commons it creates for itself; it is a self-referential system of transferable planes of signification, encompassing all possible meaning and value—*mathesis universalis*. "Representations," to Foucault, "are not rooted in a world that gives them meaning; they open of themselves on to a space that is their own, whose internal network gives rise to meaning. And language exists in the gap that representation creates for itself."[32] There is no outside to get in anymore. As Michel Serres also witnesses: "We communicate irrepressibly. We busy ourselves only with our own networks. Those who share power today have forgotten nature, which could be said to be taking its revenge but which, more to the point, is reminding us of its existence."[33] We only speak ourselves. Anthropocentric monism, not dual-

---

26. See Foucault, *Order of Things*, 3–85.
27. See Foucault, *Order of Things*, 51–85.
28. Foucault, *Order of Things*, 78.
29. Foucault, *Order of Things*, 78.
30. Foucault, *Order of Things*, 81.
31. Foucault, *Order of Things*, 81–82.
32. Foucault, *Order of Things*, 86–87.
33. Serres, *Natural Contract*, 29.

ism, is a better description of things. For another four hundred years our strange deafness to what surrounds only increases.

The global progress of the science of order, however, reveals a paradox: The professed trajectory of liberation from essential relations has deepened, not severed, our connections to things and people.[34] The more we struggle to be free from the world, the more we entangle ourselves in a constant process of ever greater attachment and responsibility. The way to self-made salvation opens onto an archaic path, leading back to salvation for all things. "We had Nature, we had nurture," Bruno Latour explains, "but we don't know what it would mean for Nature itself to be nurtured. The problem is, we don't know how to deal with this gigantic dissonance: everywhere attachments and yet no other option than emancipation. We seem to be stuck."[35] For an anthropologist of modern science, Latour makes a surprising proposal to get *unstuck*. His orientation for confronting the ecological crisis is directed towards reclaiming the Christian doctrine of creation, i.e., "to grasp it otherwise."[36] As *nature* gains scientific traction, Christianity gradually abandons *creation*; it retreats "to the inner sanctum of the soul," or flees "into the supernatural."[37] This absconding turn hands the Earth over to the full spectrum dominance of the science of order. Latour condemns this desertion as theological cowardice: "A religion that has abandoned the cosmos has made itself irrelevant from the start."[38] He then provides an ecological reversal of a traditional theological question: "What use is it to save your soul, if you forfeit the world?"[39]

Contemporary creationism recognizes the problem but, in its attempt to imitate science on its own ground of nature, creationism makes a counter-productive category mistake. Interpreting the Bible as if it were a geology book "is really the end of the play: *Exit* religion."[40] Latour attempts to clarify and realign the proper categories for *creationists*, who need "to encounter something other than nature."[41] Science is primarily defined by *reference chains* in nature: Symbolic representation in *res extensa*. Science allows us to safely access otherworldly domains defined by ever increasing remoteness; from the sub-atomic realm to the outer reaches of space.

---

34. See Latour, "It's Development, Stupid!," 5–9; *Pandora's Hope*, 145–216.
35. Latour, "It's Development, Stupid!," 6–7.
36. Latour, "Will Non-Humans Be Saved?," 17.
37. Latour, "Will Non-Humans Be Saved?," 8.
38. Latour, "Will Non-Humans Be Saved?," 13.
39. Latour, "Will Non-Humans Be Saved?," 6.
40. Latour, "Will Non-Humans Be Saved?," 8.
41. Latour, "Will Non-Humans Be Saved?," 9.

Religion, though, "attempts to access the this-worldly in its most radical *presence*."[42] The missing modern middle term between religion and science, detachment and neighborliness, reference and presence, has been available since Charles Darwin's (†1882) attempt to reintroduce creativity back into science.

Latour claims both religion and science, in the above sense, miss their conceptual marks. Science presents creativity as mere "REProduction"—being is mapped onto reference chains in the deadening remoteness of *res extensa*.[43] Religion counters the *blind watchmaker* of science with an intelligent creator, "But they are still two engineers who master what they do."[44] The autonomous creativity of things—their environment (*Umwelt*)—is erased: "Individual actors are transformed into carriers of indisputable necessities. The creativity which seeps in at the gaps and discontinuities faced by each organism as it sustains, perpetrates and reproduces itself has all but disappeared."[45] Latour claims A. N. Whitehead (†1947) is the first thinker to fully grasp creation's declaration of independence from both scientific and theological necessities: "Organisms create their own meaning."[46] A creature is an entity "for whom there is no overall narrative, no controlling divinity: each individual organism is alone with its own risk, goes nowhere, comes from nowhere: it is creativity all the way down. To be sure, each organism has antecedents and consequents, but between the causes and the consequences, there is always a little gap, a little hiatus: evolution is this hiatus."[47] A connection can be made between creativity and creation that is impossible with nature. *Creationists* must reestablish this tie by recovering the history of Christian theology because "it was the whole of Creation that was in the throes of salvation."[48] Any Western ecological movement must "retrieve these resources which have been covered by so many layers of modernism that they seem as lost as the bones of our ancestors."[49] But, "Can they be resurrected?"[50]

---

42. Latour, "Will Non-Humans Be Saved?," 7.
43. Latour, "Will Non-Humans Be Saved?," 13.
44. Latour, "Will Non-Humans Be Saved?," 13.
45. Latour, "Will Non-Humans Be Saved?," 13.
46. Latour, "Will Non-Humans Be Saved?," 13.
47. Latour, "Will Non-Humans Be Saved?," 13. On Whitehead's notion of creativity, see Bradley, "Speculative Generalization of the Function," 253–71. On the *hiatus* idea in evolutionary biology, see Gould, *Structure of Evolutionary Theory*, 1214–18.
48. Latour, "Will Non-Humans Be Saved?," 6.
49. Latour, "Will Non-Humans Be Saved?," 6–7.
50. Latour, "Will Non-Humans Be Saved?," 7.

THE GOOD SHEPHERD AND HER CRITICS

A responsible engagement with creation appears to depend on proper reclamation of the Christian tradition, integrating it into current ecological concern. Latour's surprising direction of thought is a variation on what is usually called the *stewardship* view of Christian dominion. The stewardship interpretation of dominion is clearly articulated by the Anglican Bishop Hugh Montefiore (†2005): "Men hold their dominion over all nature as stewards and trustees for God."[51] Human beings have "an inalienable duty towards and concern for their total environment, present and future; and this duty towards environment does not merely include their fellow-men, but all nature and all life."[52] Stewardship still maintains human sovereignty over creation because we are created in God's image (*imago Dei*). As God is to humanity, so humanity is to creation which, in this sense, is not a Cartesian relation of absolute power. Rather, it is an economy of unconditional care and radical responsibility. Stewardship is a kind of custodial guardianship of God's creation; it is a trustee arrangement. That we have a legitimate claim to govern remains unquestioned. What is contested is *the way* we should rule.

If dominion is interpreted as domination, Francis Bacon says, the *lord of nature* is a dictator who maintains the power to "conquer and subdue her, to shake her to her foundations."[53] If we rule as proper stewards, however, the lord of nature is replaced by the *good shepherd of creation*. John Passmore explains the pastoral metaphor of governance: "He takes care of the living things over which he rules for their own sake, governing them not 'with force and with cruelty' but in the manner of the good shepherd, anxious to preserve them in the best possible condition for his master, in whose hands alone their final fate will rest."[54] Unlike the one sided self-interest of domination, the interests of the flock and ourselves maintain a symbiotic relationship: The well-being of the shepherd depends on keeping the flock in good health. Stewardship, then, presupposes a reciprocal relationship of mutual interdependence between humanity and environment. Michel Serres updates the distinction between domination and stewardship. It is a difference between, respectively, parasitic and symbiotic relations:

> A symbiont recognizes the host's rights, whereas a parasite— which is what we are now—condemns to death the one he

---

51. Montefiore, *Can Man Survive?*, 55.
52. Montefiore, *Can Man Survive?*, 55.
53. Bacon, "Thoughts and Conclusions," 93.
54. Passmore, *Man's Responsibility for Nature*, 9.

pillages and inhabits, not realizing that in the long run he's condemning himself to death too. The parasite takes all and gives nothing; the host gives all and takes nothing. Rights of mastery and property come down to parasitism. Conversely, rights of symbiosis are defined by reciprocity: however much nature gives man, man must give that much back to nature.[55]

The stewardship model appears to have much to recommend it. Unlike parasitic domination, we enter a relationship of exchange; of give as well as take. Symbiotic stewardship takes responsibility for human maltreatment, attempting to make amends as we are able. However, the traditionalism that makes stewardship appealing as a way forward also leaves it open to severe criticism. Critics claim it fails to provoke enough change in our absolute presuppositions. Stewardship is a distinction without a difference from despotism; it is a mask, covering the fountainhead of the totalitarian science of order—the same old poison in a new bottle.

Stewardship has its problems. John Passmore asks, "What evidence is there in support of such an interpretation of Christian teaching?"[56] He readily admits, "Very little, I should say."[57] In the Western tradition, human stewardship "relates to the Church, not to nature."[58] Clare Palmer is even more pointed in her criticism: "There is no 'biblical concept of stewardship of nature,'" which raises the question "of why stewardship of nature is so popular among Christian writers, given the lack of actual biblical support for it?"[59] Stewardship has recently entered the political discourse as the leading conceptual ground of action on the environmental crisis. The reason for its popularity is that it doesn't challenge or change much of anything beyond business as usual. To Palmer, "Stewardship can be used without mounting a challenge to the status quo," which means "that the rest of the natural world is there for our use. It is our resource."[60] The stewardship version of dominion upholds that the "reason for the existence of minerals in the soil, trees in the forest, fish in the sea, is for the benefit of humanity. Thus, Pope John Paul II could say, 'all created goods are directed to the good of humanity.'"[61] The only change from despotism is the idea we should manage God's creation, our inheritance, more prudently. We have acted like squandering trust-fund

---

55. Serres, *Natural Contract*, 38.
56. Passmore, *Man's Responsibility for Nature*, 29.
57. Passmore, *Man's Responsibility for Nature*, 29.
58. Passmore, *Man's Responsibility for Nature*, 29.
59. Palmer, "Stewardship," 65.
60. Palmer, "Stewardship," 69, 72.
61. Palmer, "Stewardship," 73.

kids; it is time to grow up and manage our entitlement as grownups. "Nature," Palmer writes, "resembles a trust account, which must be allowed to accrue interest for future generations, rather than selfishly spent in an orgy of present luxury."[62] Further:

> One could almost compare the natural world to a giant, all-embracing bank account, containing food, clothes, riches, medicines, companions, leisure facilities, landscapes, views and climate regulators! We are here to look after it, cultivate it, develop it, use it—but prudently, as we have it in trust. We must not destroy it by "spending it all at once." This perception of stewardship portrays God as a rich man who has handed his riches over to humanity to use to its greatest advantage. Thus humanity is a kind of investor—intended to use the resources to the master's and its own best advantage, to make them grow. The master is thus no longer involved with his possessions, although there will be a reckoning when the steward has to account for the way in which he has used the finances entrusted to him.[63]

Instead of the accent being on symbiotic exchange, "the primary emphasis is the steward and the use of resources."[64] It can come as no surprise, Palmer concludes, "the financial world is one of the strongest associations behind the concept of stewardship. When humans are described as stewards of the natural world, the language in which this is embedded is usually associated with money. Again and again, the idea of resources, which we must use carefully, look after as if for someone else, encourage to grow, recurs in both Christian and secular writing."[65] The stewardship version of dominion is domination with a humanistic and ecological face.

Palmer's critique is stinging, near devastating. She argues that current ideas of stewardship amount to little more than environmental public relations; it is a way for vested and moneyed interests to change their brand, deceiving and hiding their actual behavior behind a carefully constructed façade of advertising. By following the "green trend," the concept of stewardship is also way for us, the public, to lose some guilt from our consumptive *lifestyle*. Stewardship is also criticized for maintaining the same sense of supremacy as domination. From an evolutionary perspective, humanity's illusory hubris of stewardship is defied by the vast time scale of nature. We

---

62. Palmer, "Stewardship," 67.
63. Palmer, "Stewardship," 67–68.
64. Palmer, "Stewardship," 68.
65. Palmer, "Stewardship," 66–67.

might not like the consequences, but the Earth will take good care of itself. Stephen Jay Gould (†2002) puts the objection as follows:

> The view that we live on a fragile planet now subject to permanent derailment and disruption by human intervention and that humans must learn to act as stewards for this threatened world, however well-intentioned, are rooted in the old sin of pride and exaggerated self-importance. We are among millions of species, stewards of nothing. By what argument could we, arising just a geological microsecond ago, become responsible for the affairs of a world 4.5 billion years old, teeming with life that has been evolving and diversifying for at least three-quarters of that immense span? Nature does not exist for us, had no idea we were coming, and doesn't give a damn about us.... We are virtually powerless over the earth at our planet's own geological time scale.... On geological scales, our planet will take good care of itself and let time clear the impact of any human malfeasance. ... All the megatonnage in our nuclear arsenals yield but one ten-thousandth the power of the asteroid that might have triggered the Cretaceous mass extinction. Yet the earth survived that large shock and, in wiping out dinosaurs, paved the road for the evolution of large mammals, including humans.[66]

However, Gould goes on to suggest that thinking on a geological scale is mostly irrelevant to human concerns. "We cannot threaten at geological scales," Gould claims,

> but such vastness has no impact upon us. We have a legitimately parochial interest in our own lives, the happiness and prosperity of our children, the suffering of our fellows. The planet will recover from a nuclear holocaust, but we will be killed and maimed by billions, and our culture will perish. The earth will prosper if polar icecaps melt under a global greenhouse, but most of our major cities, built at sea level as ports and harbors, will founder, and changing agricultural patterns will uproot our populations.[67]

Gould's perspective is informed by science before the arrival of the *Anthropocene's geological scales*. He would have undoubtedly modified his position in view of new evidence.

Peter Singer tells us the entire concept of dominion is rotten. Stewardship in the image of God is just as bad as despotism. "The Bible tells us,"

---

66. Gould, "Golden Rule," 30.
67. Gould, "Golden Rule," 30.

Singer states, "that God made man in his image. We may regard this as man making God in his own image."[68] Stewardship is the same old selfish and spiritually vain wolf; not dressed up in sheep's clothing, but the shepherd's. Finally, ecological historian David Worster claims, "Christian pastoralism" is responsible for creating the modern imperial tradition of mastery.[69] The original pagan *Arcadian* tradition of the Good Shepherd portrays humanity as a protector of nature and rural life from the encroaching corruption of urbanism. Over time, the influence of city-centered Christianity inverts the vision of pagan Arcadia. It is urbane humanity that the Shepherd must protect "*against* the hostile forces of nature."[70] Stewardship means technical rationality. Nature and her wild rustics must be tamed, converted, and ordered—made useful for city folk.

OMNES ET SINGULATIM: FOUCAULT'S CRITIQUE OF PASTORAL POWER

At least part of the problem with the stewardship position is its lack of historical and philosophical grounding. We simply do not know enough about it. Environmentally minded theologians have been left scrambling for secure footing. Scholarly claims of Christian liability have provoked a mostly apologetic rush to press mentality, falling easy prey to critics. There is a disconnection between simply professing a green faith and demonstrating that the faith is really, and primarily, green. The most prolonged and insightful study of stewardship is found in the later writings of Michel Foucault; it is also the most critical. Foucault's analysis stresses the dark side of *pastoral power*. However, there is another aspect to the Christian care of creation, a minority report, a distinction with a difference from domination that will hopefully reveal itself in this analysis.

Foucault presents pastoral power as the key to understanding the formation of the socioeconomic institutions of the modern state.[71] The Christian pastorate is characterized by a unique *gouvernementalité*: "Pastoral power is a power of care. The essential objective of pastoral power is salvation of the flock."[72] The economy of human souls (*oikonomia psuchōn*) is an elaborate social commerce: "The pastor guides to salvation, prescribes

68. Singer, *Animal Liberation*, 187.
69. Worster, *Nature's Economy*, 14.
70. Worster, *Nature's Economy*, 26.
71. See Foucault, *Security, Territory, Population*, 115–253; "Omnes et Singulatim," 225–54.
72. Foucault, *Security, Territory, Population*, 126–27.

the law, and teaches the truth."[73] The shepherd requires the flock's complete submission and obedience. The pastoral technology of the Christian church is different from its Greek and Roman antecedents. The shepherd's power is essentially exercised over a "multiplicity in movement," a human population, not a territory.[74] This kind of power totalizes and individuates, all and each—*omnes et singulatim*. The salvation of the whole of humanity is equally the salvation of each human soul. Christianity introduces the revolutionary social idea that individuals count as wholes themselves, not as parts expendable for a higher unity. Equality of being overturns social identity. The soteriological model of shepherd and flock "is a power directed at all and each in their paradoxical equivalence, and not at the higher unity formed by the whole."[75] To save the whole is to save each. To save each is to save the whole. Conversely, salvation cannot occur if individuals are destroyed on behalf of the whole or if individuals destroy the whole on behalf of themselves.

The paradox of the shepherd is the problem of "sacrifice of one for all, and the sacrifice of all for one, which will be at the absolute heart of the Christian problematic of the pastorate."[76] The cleric-shepherd owes everything to her flock, agreeing to sacrifice herself for its salvation. She is prepared to sacrifice herself for the whole flock and each sheep. The shepherd finds her own salvation by saving *all and each*. She agrees to sacrifice herself for the whole: Community *and* individual. Since she must save each sheep, however, she must be willing to risk the remaining members of the flock. The paradoxical distribution of salvation means *the whole* is saved by the fact that she is prepared to sacrifice the rest of the flock for a single lost sheep. Each is worth the whole or none is, *especially lost individuals*: The marginal that are easily scapegoated and disposed of by the remaining majority. These outsiders count equally (if not more) or there is no salvation for all. To achieve its salvation, the beloved community depends on the extension of belonging to the limit cases, the most vulnerable and ostracized; they count equally, if we do. We must risk all for each and each for all: *Soteria*. Foucault traces how this principle of mutual self-sacrifice for others is transformed by the modern state. The history of how the Christian pastorate combines with its opposite, the state, is a "decisive phenomenon, no doubt unique in the history of societies, and civilizations."[77] The produc-

---

73. Foucault, *Security, Territory, Population*, 167.
74. Foucault, *Security, Territory, Population*, 125.
75. Foucault, *Security, Territory, Population*, 129.
76. Foucault, *Security, Territory, Population*, 129.
77. Foucault, *Security, Territory, Population*, 173.

tion of salvation moves from the representatives of the pastorate of God to the functionaries of the totalitarian state.

In the Christian tradition, the shepherd's tie to her flock includes the details of each of their lives, enfolding "all their actions, all the good or evil they are liable to do, all that happens to them."[78] The pastoral cleric's prescription individuates each soul. Right thought and conduct are produced through a calculus of material and moral distribution of goods. The shepherd acts to fulfill an individual's bodily and social needs and, most importantly, to fulfil the spiritual needs of each, inducing "self-examination and the guidance of conscience."[79] Food, shelter, and employment are offered along with confessions, rituals, and penances. To be made whole, everyone receives a prescribed calculus uniquely tailored to their circumstances. In this relationship of absolute exposure, a new self is created. By saving each, the shepherd saves herself and all. Each new subject, so created, is open to others with the same passion for self-sacrifice—for all and each.

The pastorate is eventually appropriated by the modern *raison d'État*. The object of the state's *science of order* is life itself. Pastoralization is the rational administration of all relationships: Between human beings, between human beings and nature. The state poses as the church; police and government officials as its cleric-shepherds. The state is Janus-faced, presenting itself as Christ, acting like Caesar. Unconditional pastoral care becomes absolute control of each and all. "Right from the start," Foucault claims, "the state is both individuating and totalitarian."[80] His location of modern totalitarian forms of governance in a *genealogy* of pastoral power is in one way accurate but, as he admits, it is an incomplete analysis: "All of these reflections on governmentality, this very vague sketch of the pastorate, should not be taken as gospel truth. This is not a finished work, it is not even work that's done; it is work in progress, with all that this involves in the way of inaccuracies and hypotheses—in short, it amounts to possible tracks for you, if you wish, and maybe for myself, to follow."[81] Let us follow Foucault's *tracks* a bit further.

It is true that the totalitarian horrors of the past century (and this one) find considerable traction on the appropriated ground of salvation. The mutation of political and pastoral power is especially horrific among regimes that abandon Christianity altogether for rationalistic atheism (Communism) and irrational neopaganism (Nazism). As we have seen in

78. Foucault, "Omnes et Singulatim," 236.
79. Foucault, "Omnes et Singulatim," 238.
80. Foucault, "Omnes et Singulatim," 254.
81. Foucault, *Security, Territory, Population*, 135–36.

the preceding chapters, the problematic theological strain of Christianity unique to Pelagianism is transmitted by certain ascetic practices into the maelström of modernity's political and scientific formation. At first, this historical identification seems in line with Foucault's account. He grounds his totalitarian pastoral critique in early monastic orders.[82] For example, he claims that John Cassian's *Coenobiticul Institutions* is clear evidence of the assumption of salvation through submission: "Obedience is a virtue."[83] Foucault even tracks the drive for self-perfection to its proper pre-Christian antecedents:

> In order to ensure this individual knowledge, Christianity appropriated two essential instruments at work in the Hellenistic world: self-examination and the guidance of conscience. It took them over, but not without altering them considerably. It is well known that self-examination was widespread among the Pythagoreans, the Stoics, and the Epicureans as a means of daily taking stock of the good or evil performed in regard to one's duties. One's progress on the way to perfection, i.e., self-mastery and the domination of one's passions, could thus be measured.[84]

Foucault presents Christianity as *corrupting* the ancient tradition of self-mastery. By accepting this presupposition, he implicitly accepts Pelagian Christianity as essential Christianity; it is an inevitably totalitarian tradition because of its founding first principle, requiring unconditional sacrifice for others—*omnes et singulatim*. The individual is saved through complete submission to pastoral power. The autonomous self is erased by the techniques of inspection, instruction, and discipline. A collective soul rises from the ruins. This new communal self is completely exposed to the community; it is totally obedient, willing to sacrifice itself for all and each. Foucault's project, then, is to preserve the pre-Christian autonomous self, and he takes his orientation from the later Stoics; most notably, Seneca (†65 CE) and the public moral combat of the Cynics.[85] He resurrects the radically individualistic ancient tradition of self-mastery as an alternative to the Christian and communal variety of the same thing. Therefore, Foucault fails to recognize and exorcize the strain. Instead of non-Stoic Christianity, communalism without domination—self-sacrifice as an alternative to the sacrifice of others to preserve and enhance the *autonomy* of the self—he opts for an apologetics of the totalitarian self. By favoring later Stoicism over what I have hoped

---

82. See Foucault, *Security, Territory, Population*, 165–90.
83. Foucault, "Omnes et Singulatim," 237.
84. Foucault, "Omnes et Singulatim," 238.
85. See Miller, *Passion of Michel Foucault*, 359–64.

to have confirmed as Stoic-Pelagian Christianity, *Foucault's alternative is a distinction without much of a difference.* The remedy for totalitarian communalism is the totalitarian individualism from which it originated.

This direction of thought continues to have profound political consequences, re-inscribing the foundations of progressive politics. Foucault seems to place the bureaucracies and institutions of democratic welfare states on the same *track* as the political technologies developed by Nazism and Communism. The ultimate destination for all is the "concentration camps."[86] He gives immense credibility to the neo-liberal ethic of autonomy unencumbered by social responsibility. We must dismantle the welfare state to protect ourselves from inevitable catastrophe. The revolution continues, however, but this time it is not ours, only mine—alone. We must throw off the heavy chains of care for others and begin caring for ourselves. These are wide and seemingly polemical claims. They seem to mischaracterize Foucault's activist mystique; especially his alleged critique of neo-liberal *gouvernementalité*.[87] Market totalitarianism is a science of order dedicated to engineering a new human being—*homo œconomicus*. Global corporate capitalism subsumes all difference in a mono-consumer culture; it individuates by consumer brands, invading the mind through ever more invasive techno-diffusions, e.g., advertising. We are obedient to the logic of pure market. To Foucault, though, this kind of liberalism supposedly misrepresents the true ethic of *laissez-faire*, individualism, nominalism, autonomy, and so on; it is not its ideological fulfillment. Rather, market totalitarianism is still somehow pastoral power through the rhetoric of individual freedom and liberation. The vast and resilient tentacles of *omnes et singulatim* claim yet another victim; first the church, then the state and, finally, the *stewardship* of the multi-national corporation. It is still the essence of pastoral power found in Christianity that must be abolished in order to achieve human freedom.

In his last interview, Foucault tells us, "In Christianity, salvation is obtained by renunciation of self."[88] There is no alternative but to preserve the "care of self" by releasing the self, "from the care of others."[89] Foucault's position is more nuanced than crude egoism, certainly, but he still maintains his characterization of Christianity as *the* road to totalitarian serfdom. In its place, he believes, "that in Greek and Roman thought the care for self cannot in itself tend to this exaggerated love of self which would, in time, come to neglect others or worse still, abuse the power that one can have over

---

86. Foucault, "Omnes et Singulatim," 226.
87. See Foucault, *Birth of Biopolitics*, 129–59.
88. Foucault, "Ethic of Care for the Self," 119.
89. Foucault, "Ethic of Care for the Self," 119.

them."⁹⁰ Surprisingly, he omits the ancient institution of slavery. Imperial masters are portrayed as the true models of liberated individuals. As should be apparent by now, however, this analysis claims that these exemplars are the root of the science of order that Foucault seeks to abolish.

Foucault, echoing Adam Smith (†1790), believes in "a care of one's self which will be beneficial to others."⁹¹ But, unlike Smith, a prior obligation to others is absent in order to protect them from the tyranny of your care. Sacrifice for others is merely an arbitrary preference in a society of pluralistic ends; it is one choice in the market commerce of individual values. Self-perfected autonomous selves must always volunteer willingly, but it is hard to see why they will ever bother doing so if they have reached total sufficiency. They do not *need* anything from anyone else. Rather, such totalitarian selves demand the same self-perfection from others. Whether others have the resources and abilities to do so is of complete indifference for the self-made who owe nothing to anyone else. Like Pelagius before him, Foucault repeats the same logic of self-perfecting hubris. If all people can be perfect, given only that we seriously try—*if I did it, so can you*—it is only a short step to the conclusion that non-perfected persons deserve to stay in their destitute condition for not achieving autonomy or, in its ancient sense, slaves deserve to remain slaves. The poor are responsible for their own hardship. Redistribution of resources from the haves to the have nots is now anathema to social order; it takes from merited, self-perfected individuals and undermines the less motivated even further. Charity is not social justice. Self-perfected individuals get to decide, by their own criteria, who is deserving and undeserving of their help.

It can come as no surprise, then, that Foucault finds "the same spiritual care" of self while "reading Descartes."⁹² The Cartesian mastery of self that sets its sights on nature fulfills "the functions of spirituality on an ideal based on scientificity."⁹³ Finally, he denies the very possibility of love without a hidden totalitarian hand: "Power is always present: I mean the relationship in which one wishes to direct the behavior of another."⁹⁴ Thus, Foucault presents love in general and institutional altruism in particular as a façade through which the fist of pastoral power seeks to control the mind and body of all and each. *Society must be defended* from the despotism of assumed responsibility for each other. "The well-known 'welfare-state'

---

90. Foucault, "Ethic of Care for the Self," 119.
91. Foucault, "Ethic of Care for the Self," 120.
92. Foucault, "Ethic of Care for the Self," 125.
93. Foucault, "Ethic of Care for the Self," 125.
94. Foucault, "Ethic of Care for the Self," 122.

problem," Foucault writes, "must be recognized for what it is: one of the extremely numerous appearances of the tricky adjustment between political power wielded over legal subjects and the pastoral power wielded over live individuals."[95] Foucault denies the difference in kind of democratic pastoral power from its tyrannical version. It is pastoral power as such that threatens the democratic rights and freedoms of citizens.

Foucault joins the ranks of other Cold War philosophers in attacking the very idea of communal obligation as anything other than an inevitable *track* to the camps.[96] Stewardship is a system of complete domination which, unlike ancient systems of oppression, invades the interior self and leads from within. Pastoral power tricks a person into thinking they are free when they have completely abandoned any semblance of authentic selfhood. Foucault's primary example of totalitarian stewardship is the history of the Orthodox Christian Russian Empire continuing, without a real change in social form, under Soviet Communism.[97] He abandons collective responsibility for an individualistic identity politics: Autonomy. Unlike collective identity politics, e.g., fascism, evidently, this kind of identity politics can be progressive—that is, emancipation continues but, this time, it is on the ground of me first. What oppresses me?

Liberation is individuated and multiplied across a much broader spectrum of social (and ecological) categories of oppression. Struggle, yes, but not necessarily class or, primarily, without a collective economic meta-narrative, confronting property relations as *meta*-oppression. My fight for authentic selfhood, i.e., autonomy, may involve race, history, language, gender, disability, age, environment, or cultural/geographical displacement. Therefore, my struggle may be very different from yours, but it is just as valid. *Intersectional* formations of collective liberation depend on shared individual oppressions, which may or may not be economic in origin; they are temporary, non-binding (*fluid*) expressions of the aggregate autonomies of individuals. In simpler terms, the whole has no reality. There is an equilibrium of oppressions: The individual struggles of the rich are just as authentic as those of the poor. The net effect of *progressive* identity politics over the past four decades is to either factor out economic exploitation and class-conflict altogether or make it one variable among many in

---

95. Foucault, "Omnes et Singulatim," 235.

96. See Hayek, *Road to Serfdom*, 37–48. James Miller claims Foucault maintains "unprecedented sympathy" for the neo-liberalism of Hayek; the free market is a "citadel of individual liberty and a bulwark against the power of the state. A market economy is the chief means 'to repair the effects of an excess of governmentality'" (Miller, *Passion of Michel Foucault*, 310–11).

97. See Foucault, *Security, Territory, Population*, 154–56.

various intersectional formulas for liberation. Progressive identity politics celebrates advancement of individual autonomy, difference, and *negative freedom*. Being-in-common (*ens in communi*)—the *we*—is reduced to an intersection of individual concerns; made a useful fiction, a means to further self-realization. All is social resource for each. There is an absolute presupposition of perspectival moral equivalency—that is, like all other activities, the social whole is an arena, a marketplace, of competing individual narratives (and their intersectional allies) of oppression and liberation. Liberation is still essentially about rivalry for social dominance: Whose version of oppression and liberation will dominate the marketplace? There is no outside of—no liberation from—social relations constituted by power.

Foucault's project fits perfectly, hand-in-glove, with neo-liberal *gouvernementalité*: "As much as any figure of his generation," James Miller argues, "Foucault helped inspire a resurgent neo-liberalism in France in the 1980s."[98] Progressive politics is about struggle for authentic identity; it is no longer defined by collective socioeconomic equality and responsibility. Class, for the most part, is left without voice or struggle: The liberal rhetoric of *human rights* presumes autonomy seeking individuals, factoring out economic concerns. It is bait and switch. For example, if you are employed, you have an *individual* right not to be discriminated against because of your gender, but you do not have a *common* labor right to be employed in the first place. The bizarre logic of this world continues to mutate. If you are truly authentic, free from all personal oppressions, your socioeconomic concerns will just magically resolve themselves in a free market, which actualizes and rewards your true self: Your true *brand*. You will become an *authentic entrepreneur* of realized potentialities. Instead of being subject to an intrinsically oppressive external commodification process, made an employee of an employer, you are obligated to self-commodify, to become both employee and employer: An authentic *self-brand*. Wealth will simply find you. If you are poor, you have only yourself to blame. You have failed to be authentic, to self-actualize. The problem cannot be the *free market system*; it is your lack of will-to-self-perfection that (*pace* Pelagius and Foucault) legitimately condemns you to your socioeconomic condition. The long delusion is that identity politics—in its individual and intersectional configurations—can be progressive. It cannot. What it really does is erode the moral and socioeconomic fabric to such an extent that it conjures its true ancestor and inheritor: Collective identity politics. But is Foucault really saying there is *no alternative* besides the social default found in the neo-liberal form of

---

98. Miller, *Passion of Michel Foucault*, 315.

gouvernementalité? The fascism of the *authentic self* versus *authentic fascism*? Can another model be articulated?

Foucault does gloss Plato's analogy of dialectical weaving of a political commonplace in the *Statesman*. Plato rejects the shepherd analogy because it is not commensurate with the governance of human beings. The *close woven* community has a source of authority that "is not made, as an instrument is, with a view to the production of something but in order to preserve a thing once it has been produced."[99] *Dialectical governmentality* preserves difference in a common tissue of the same, but it is an open and revisable site of communication and mediation; it does not seek to engineer the same and eliminate difference. Foucault also presents alternative nonhierarchical formations of pastoral power from *Wyclif to Wesley*, which seem more in line with the thinking behind democratic welfare state institutions than a track to the camps![100] But, in the end, neither Plato's dialectical weaver nor the experiments of Christian reformers are to be trusted. It is the tacit reality of the common tie—*omnes et singulatim* or *positive freedom*—as such, "from which we have still not freed ourselves."[101]

Foucault is a fellow traveler in Isaiah Berlin's (†1997) neo-liberal movement.[102] "The essence of men," Berlin decrees, "is that they are autonomous beings."[103] Therefore, it is unfair, "to coerce men in the name of something less ultimate than themselves."[104] With the noted anomalies of "British Idealism," "some Christian and utilitarian, and all socialist, doctrines," Berlin claims, "the desire not to be impinged upon, to be left to oneself, has been a mark of high civilization of both individuals and communities."[105] Exploitation and poverty are not real experiences in the sense they exist "only if I accept the theory," which makes me perceive myself as exploited and impoverished.[106] Socio-economic concerns certainly do not supervene other "ends equally ultimate, and claims equally absolute, the realization of some of which must inevitably involve the sacrifice of others."[107] Sacrificial culture

---

99. Plato, *Statesman* 287e (53).

100. See Foucault, *Security, Territory, Population*, 140–48; "Omnes et Singulatim," 232–34.

101. Foucault, *Security, Territory, Population*, 148.

102. On Foucault's rejection of pastoral or *positive* freedom for negative freedom and his belated interest in liberalism and Berlin, see Miller, *Passion of Michel Foucault*, 311–12.

103. Berlin, "Two Concepts of Liberty," 183.

104. Berlin, "Two Concepts of Liberty," 184.

105. Berlin, "Two Concepts of Liberty," 170n1, 194n3, 176.

106. Berlin, "Two Concepts of Liberty," 170.

107. Berlin, "Two Concepts of Liberty," 213–14.

regresses from *for others* to *of others* as the legitimate ground of community. The *common* moral preference for the poor, weak, damaged, and so on is replaced by what John Gray calls Berlin's (and Foucault's) individual value-pluralism; *agonistic liberalism* maintains "ultimate human values are objective but irreducibly diverse, that they are conflicting and often uncombinable, and that sometimes when they come into conflict with one another they are incommensurate; that is, they are not comparable by any rational measure."[108] Most tellingly, "Berlin's is a stoical and tragic liberalism."[109] That such a theory is much more *agonistic* and *tragic* for the *values* of the weak, e.g., food, shelter, and health, is of no real consequence in a political order of professed neutrality: Moral equivalency of oppressions.

This kind of order really advantages the strong. An a priori social détente that levels values presents a society modeled on skeptical indifference, posing as tolerance, and arbitrary preference, posing as pluralistic freedom; all of which is typical of Roman Stoicism with its illusions of contented slaves serving their masters.[110] Even his apologetic biographer, Michael Ignatieff, admits that, at best, Berlin "left his commitments to social justice unspecified."[111] *At worst*, such a schema is a fundamental retrenchment of social stratification and privilege; it is reactionary politics wrapped in pagan nostalgia for the natural right of the master class against the Christian bias for the weak—against the *rational measure* of values grounded in equality as mutual sacrifice for *all and each*. Friedrich Nietzsche (†1900) is much more honest and forthright on the nature of this position. He dramatizes the raw origination of the Christian alternative to the Roman version of *agonistic liberalism*:

> And one ends by discovering that there is *virtue* also among the lowly and subjugated, the poor in spirit, and that *before God* men are equal—which has so far been the *non plus ultra* of nonsense on earth! For ultimately, the higher men measured themselves according to the standard of virtue of slaves—found they were "proud," etc., found all their higher qualities reprehensible.
>
> When Nero and Caracalla sat up there, the paradox arose: "the lowest man is worth more than that man up there!" And the way was prepared for an image of God that was as remote

---

108. Gray, *Berlin*, 1. For Foucault's similar version of the agonistic society, see Miller, *Passion of Michel Foucault*, 317–18.

109. Gray, *Berlin*, 1.

110. On Berlin's problem with the "contented slave," see Flikschuh, *Freedom*, 28–36.

111. Ignatieff, *Isaiah Berlin*, 229.

as possible from the image of the most powerful—the god on the cross!¹¹²

STEWARDSHIP AS DISTRIBUTIONAL JUSTICE

In the sights of certain, contemporary political ideas, then, stewardship is the enemy. This set of positions presents a caricature, drawn under the influence of updated Stoic doctrines of mastery; it is pastoral power in the hands of residual pagan imperialism that becomes integrated into the church when Constantine (†337 CE) makes Christianity the official religion of the Roman Empire.¹¹³ It is this tension between *imperial Christianity* as a system of dominance and *multitude Christianity* as a liberating spirit on behalf of the poor, enslaved, and weak that plays out dialectically throughout the history of the religion; stewardship as domination, posing as care, versus *true* stewardship as liberation of the dominated. Imperial closure on the interpretative commons creates the conditions where the spirit of the multitude overflows and wars against the legitimacy of its authority: "The Spirit is anarchy."¹¹⁴ Modernity complicates this historical dialectic. The Protestant Reformation marks the appropriation of pastoral authority (*auctoritas*) on salvation by state power (*potestas*).¹¹⁵ Stewardship's ground is first occupied by the state and, now, by the multinational corporation. The authoritative discourse on economic-historical salvation now belongs to secular capital.

Carl Schmitt (†1985) is a key thinker on European sovereignty in a post-medieval world. He puts forward the following thesis: "All significant concepts of the modern theory of the state are secularized theological concepts."¹¹⁶ The theological presuppositions involved in our political situation reveal the logic of a form of life on its most axiomatic level. Schmitt's general thesis finds abundant historical support. "That temporal government," Martin Luther (†1546) proclaims, "is God's ordinance."¹¹⁷ Without the divine referent of love, the state's *secularized pastoral authority* is a uniquely terrifying phenomenon. The state is two steps removed from original stewardship; it is pastoral authority as pure force—that is, voluntary

---

112. Nietzsche, *Will to Power*, 468.
113. See Drake, *Constantine and the Bishops*, 201–10.
114. Drake, *Constantine and the Bishops*, 104.
115. For an excellent overview of this basic historical change of *governmentality*, see Moltmann, "European Political Theology," 3–22.
116. Schmitt, *Political Theology*, 36.
117. Luther, *Luther's Works*, 46:104.

re-creation of new subjects (church political theology/authority) turns to involuntary re-construction of new subjects (state political religion/power). Ernst Bloch (†1977) calls the modern state an "apotheosis of force for the sake of force, of authority for the sake of authority."[118] State force is holy. It can bring secular salvation and deliver us from evil—*to katechon* (κατέχων).[119]

The neo-liberal idea is that only the corporate market can free us from the clutches of the totalitarian pastoral state. Secular salvation moves from state force to the mysterious sway of *market forces*. The actors and apparatus of global liberal economics are positioned as *to katechon*. This hegemonic historical reality is another post-medieval displacement of sovereign order and multitude stewardship, perverting human freedom and destroying creation. With neo-liberal stewardship, we have the commodification of all things. Modern nature overthrows medieval creation. Post-modern envirocapital erases modern nature; all semblance of existence value—independent of the enforced schemas of capital—*melt into the air*. Enforcement of the rights of corporations creates a regime of accumulation that systematically impoverishes the multitude, generating profound inequality.[120] The great expropriation of wealth also depends on the destruction of the environment on a radically accelerated global pace. "If we are entering the danger zone of transforming the global environment, particularly its climate," David Harvey warns, "as to make the earth unfit for human habitation, then further embrace of the neoliberal ethic and of neoliberalizing practices will prove nothing short of deadly."[121] But, if Schmitt is right, when we envision liberationist alternatives to state and corporate power, we are in even deeper trouble than we usually think.

Schmitt carefully distinguishes "between the *anarchy* of the Middle Ages and the *nihilism* of the twentieth century."[122] The "wars and feuds" of the former are still securely rooted in a spatialized cosmology of heaven and earth, "the fundamental unity of order and orientation."[123] The right of liberationist resistance against a designated oppressor, i.e., *anarchy*, "occurred within the framework of one and the same total order encompassing both warring parties. This means they did not negate this total order. Therefore, they not only allowed, but necessitated a moral-theological evaluation of the

---

118. Bloch, *Natural Law and Human Dignity*, 31.
119. See Schmitt, "Three Possibilities," 167–70.
120. See Piketty, *Capital*, 1–45.
121. Harvey, *Brief History of Neoliberalism*, 173.
122. Schmitt, *Nomos of the Earth*, 57.
123. Schmitt, *Nomos of the Earth*, 57.

question of whether they were just or unjust."[124] The "anarchistic methods of the Middle Ages were not nihilistic" because a true act of anarchism "must neither destroy nor disavow the spatial structure as a whole."[125] Anarchistic conflicts occur within a revealed religion's cosmos. Nihilistic conflicts occur between secular-ideological worldviews. The former phenomena share a binding ground of place and time where peace and progress are possible. The moderns, by contrast, drift upon a sea that is de-spatialized, de-temporalized, a political chasm of perpetual war.

Secular emergency measures are constantly required—"the *tabula rasa* of nihilistic legalizations, of salvaging the possibilities of concrete orders."[126] Internal to a sovereign state, these make-shifts are designed to temporarily fend off "nihilism, and to cover the abyss with legitimist or legalitarian, conservative or constitutional facades."[127] Externally, between states, legalizations become "nothing more than a facade for the internal nihilism of traditional European international law."[128] Necessity is a noble lie, a hollow and fleeting concept designed to keep a hollow and fleeting order of things. To Schmitt, true liberation from oppression can only occur within a cosmos that grounds itself in a criterion of the common good that makes this claim significant and legitimate. The collapse of the medieval *pluralistic framework* results in an interminable clash *between* autistic ideologies, each claiming its own criterion of the good. Agreements are rag-tag and *ad hoc*. Modern anarchism can only be a nihilistic force of perdition, ripping to pieces what is left of the delicate and temporary threads of political order. In the context of relativism, emancipation from any and all hierarchical configuration leads to ideological perdition, violence without end.

Emil L. Fackenheim is once again instructive. He appears to concur with Schmitt's nihilistic assessment of the modern predicament. Fackenheim summarizes the effects of the secular "view that history discloses a variety of conflicting *Weltanschauungen*, with no criterion for choice between them anywhere in sight" as *skeptical paralysis, pragmatic make-believe*, and *ideological fanaticism*.[129] The last is particularly problematic because "it knows itself to be not truth, but merely one specific product of history," and "in order to resolve its internal conflict," "it must engage in a total war from

---

124. Schmitt, *Nomos of the Earth*, 58–59.
125. Schmitt, *Nomos of the Earth*, 187, 188.
126. Schmitt, *Nomos of the Earth*, 188.
127. Schmitt, *Nomos of the Earth*, 292.
128. Schmitt, *Nomos of the Earth*, 300.
129. Fackenheim, "Metaphysics and Historicity," 123.

which it hopes to emerge as the only ideology left on earth."[130] *Modern totalitarianism*, consequently, is not, as Foucault argues, something *essentially* operative within Christian stewardship; it is one minority strain with a long and horrible history of successful *secular* mutations. According to Katrin Flikschuh, even Isaiah Berlin eventually admits the problem with pastoral power, stewardship, or *positive freedom* is "the political misuse of the positive concept."[131] *What, then, is the positive concept of stewardship? What is the alternative reading of* omnes et singulatim *that is conducive to dealing with the environmental crisis?*

Given the analyses of Schmitt and Fackenheim, does it even make sense to attempt to *grasp this archaic concept otherwise* than as another modern nihilistic form of totalitarian ideology? Perhaps, just perhaps— as Latour also seems to wager, too—creation has never really gone away; that the global spectacle of modern domination by misrepresentation, i.e., nature and enviro-capital, is literally exposing its deep symbolic structure: Reality. This event, this *eschaton* is conceived *otherwise* than the medieval experience, but it retains a continuity of repetition with up to date theories, evidence, and methods, especially in the life sciences, carrying forth with renewed emancipatory energy in a new context. In the lengthening shadow of ecological collapse, Nathan Lyons suggests the same *paradoxically joyful* sentiment: "But perhaps Trinitarian theology needed evolutionary theory to help it unearth this possibility buried in the logic of its own tradition."[132] Beneath the excavated Christian structure we also rediscover the heart of Neoplatonism. For the Platonists, Pierre Hadot reminds us, "reality and divinity are identical."[133] We cannot, and will not, lose creation just as we are beginning to truly know it, not for the first time, but at the end of the first time, where we now have to begin again.

LOGICAL REDUX: *OMNES ET SINGULATIM*

Stewardship is a distributional principle of individuation through community: From capacity, to need. For the "multitude," we read in the Acts of the Apostles, "distribution was made unto everyman according as he had need" (Acts 4:35 KJV). The capacities of individuals are directed to meeting the needs of community and, conversely, the capacities of community are directed to meeting the needs of individuals, which further enables and frees individual

130. Fackenheim, "Metaphysics and Historicity," 123.
131. Flikschuh, *Freedom*, 34.
132. Lyons, *Signs in the Dust*, 153.
133. Hadot, *Veil of Isis*, 54.

capacities to meet the needs of community. A virtuous circle is created by an ever-increasing horizon of individual independency in and through its symbiotic relationship to community. The community gives individuals what they need to be independent, to actualize their abilities on behalf of themselves, which translates into their increased capacity to meet the needs of community. Thus, all and each (*omnes et singulatim*) are equally real and operationally constitutive of one another. Both are distributed *wholes* in a triadic relationship of reciprocal giving. The gap of mutual elevation allows cooperative wealth and creativity to flow more abundantly as more needs are met and more abilities are actualized.

Logically considered, distribution refers to the terms of a proposition. A term is said to be distributed if the whole of it is covered by predication; if only part of it is covered by predication, it is said to be undistributed. Logical quantity of distribution is not concerned with numbers, which implies sub-sets, parts, or *particulars* in the traditional logic of class inclusion (some). Rather, only universal (all or *omnes*) and singular (this or *singulatim*) propositions are said to be distributed because they are wholes; they are not aggregates (some) partly covered by predication. For example, in the universal affirmative proposition, "all humans are animals," the acceptation is distributed if you take this man Bill, or Ted, and you discover him to be an animal. The distributive logical principle concerns itself with whole potentially-distributed kinds and actualized-distributed singulars, and not with the extension of finite aggregates, or denumerable collections. All singulars are given once the all (*omnes*) is given, but this does not mean it is complete in the sense that actual distributed singulars can exhaust the distributional potentiality of the kind. Further, this does not imply that the mind is able to survey all the actualized distributed singulars. Nor can a whole distributed kind be considered a finite aggregate collection—a numerical particular (some).

Distribution is a relational feature of *omnes et singulatim*; community and individuals are continuous. Between existing singulars there is an inexhaustible possibility of intermediaries between them, which is their continuity—all. There is distributional continuity between actualized finite singulars and the inexhaustible potential of the whole kind. Singulars are products of an inexhaustible, *all*-comprehensive, continuum of possibilities, where all things would exist if that were possible. Or, potentially, all things possible can emerge into actuality. There is more reason for existing than not existing. In short, the idea of a distributed whole kind involves possible variations of creativity that no multitude of existing singulars could exhaust. Between any two singulars there are not merely possibilities, but possibilities beyond all multitude, which can never be fully actualized by any existing set of singulars. Creativity, then, seeps in through the relational gap between *omnes et singulatim*—the communicative order demonstrates continuous mediation of capacity and need: To be made whole.

Distributional continuity is a triadic relation. If there is to be an ordered series, relations must be assumed as something coextensive between elements. Bertrand Russell (†1970) explains, "Two terms alone cannot have an order, we must not assume that order is possible except where there are relations between two terms."[134] Further, Russell says there are the two ways in which order may arise, but "the second way is reducible to the first," which is a triadic relation basic to the generation of any series: "In the *first*, what may be called the ordinal element consists of three terms *a*, *b*, *c*, one of which (*b* say) is *between* the other two. This happens whenever there is a relation of *a* to *b* and of *b* to *c*, which is not a relation of *b* to *a*, of *c* to *b*, or of *c* to *a*. This is the definition, or better perhaps, the necessary and sufficient condition, of the proposition '*b* is between *a* and *c*.'"[135] The hypothesis of a serial order, therefore, requires the iteration of a triadic relation. The self-returning repetition of the relation between elements expands continuously and indefinitely. Order can be reduced to dyadic relations. Elements can be viewed as origins and termini of relations; they are discontinuous from each other and self-sufficient through their own being. Continuity, however, cannot be generated from an aggregate of dyadic elements. A series can be broken or halted, but it cannot be created. Therefore, the triadic relation must be assumed as the formative principle for any series of elements. Russell is reluctant to acknowledge this *logical communalism*, but he is "ultimately forced to accept" the triadic "relation of *between* by which order is to be constituted."[136] Whatever the mathematical merits of logical communalism, to Russell, it is incommensurate with social life, where *elements* are assumed to be primary. Logic is one thing, politics quite another. Russell, like Berlin, is highly critical of Christian and communitarian assumptions; their political expression has a long history of overriding the primacy of individual well-being.[137]

What happens if we take the logical irreducibility of the triadic relation as commensurate with social-ecological associations? To suspend its extension may be philosophically disingenuous; a negation for all the right political reasons. Unlike Russell, Jean-Paul Sartre (†1980) *eventually* follows

---

134. Russell, *Principles of Mathematics*, 200.
135. Russell, *Principles of Mathematics*, 200.
136. Russell, *Principles of Mathematics*, 211.
137. See Russell, *Why I Am Not a Christian*, 13–28; *Power*, 165–73.

its validity into social life.¹³⁸ Sartre revises the radical individualism of his earlier work. In *L'Être et le Néant* (1943), for example, community is, at best, a term that merely signifies "an infinite variety of experiences" and, consequently, the relation to others (the presumption of responsibility) is an arbitrary construct of individual freedom (*liberum arbitrium*): "This humanistic 'Us' remains an empty concept."¹³⁹ Community is often portrayed as a monstrous threat. The *totalitarian Other* is a great vampire, draining individuals of their authenticity; we must be free to self-create without preconditions, without ties that bind. The Other's fiction of relations imprisons us.¹⁴⁰

The Sartre of *Critique de la Raison Dialectique* (1960), however, accepts the presupposition of tri-relational logic as the *irreducible ground* for any account of individuals and collectives. The "mere aggregation" of elements, Sartre argues, "*already has* a serial structure."¹⁴¹ *Elements* are presupposed by serial relations. Each *element* is still an irreducibly unique and whole place in a series, but this difference does not mean isolation from the series. Rather, this difference, "this alterity, as a principle of ordering, naturally produces itself as a *link*."¹⁴² Serial difference—not the power of an *elemental* will—is the site of relational production: "In other words, *a series is a mode of being for individuals both in relation to one another and in relation to their common being* and this mode of being transforms all their structure."¹⁴³ In the series, "everyone becomes himself (*as Other than self*) in so far as he is other than the Others, and so, in so far as the Others are other than him."¹⁴⁴ The common difference or "*common being* produces seriality as its own practico-inert being-outside-itself in the plurality of practical organisms; everyone realizes himself outside himself in the objective unity of interpretation in so far as he constitutes himself in the gathering as an objective element of a series."¹⁴⁵ But does this *common being* override the wholeness of individuals, making them mere functions of a pre-given order? Do the congruencies between logic and social life lead, ultimately, as Russell indicated, down a path to the totalitarian erasure of individuals on behalf of the serial order of the collective?

---

138. See Sartre, *Critique of Dialectical Reason*, 256–69.
139. Sartre, *Being and Nothingness*, 413, 423.
140. See Sartre, *Being and Nothingness*, 433–42.
141. Sartre, *Critique of Dialectical Reason*, 265.
142. Sartre, *Critique of Dialectical Reason*, 263.
143. Sartre, *Critique of Dialectical Reason*, 266.
144. Sartre, *Critique of Dialectical Reason*, 262.
145. Sartre, *Critique of Dialectical Reason*, 265–66.

Sartre is aware of the problem of totality, but he refuses the default position of individualism; it is logically and socially fallacious. What emerges in the *Dialectique* is a double movement of structuring and de-structuring. As the various collective formations enfold into one another, the order of relations does become enclosed. The aliveness, spontaneity, and radical openness that defines their initial formation, as a meeting of individual capacity and communal need, is totalized into a rule: Technocratic proceduralism, legalism, and managerialism. The wholeness of *elements* is reduced to a complex of dehumanized collective functions, but this danger does not occasion retreat to individualism. Building a *total* ideological wall around individuals is not an answer to the question of community. The priority of collective serial structure cannot be justifiably ignored; this means abandoning society for the mythology of *elemental* self-sufficiency. Defending the wholeness of individuals is defending the wholeness of society.

Sartre's liberationist program is the simultaneous building up and tearing down of serial collectives. Novel formations are structured as a mediation of capacity and need; oppressive collectives are de-structured. Perpetual *praxis* is continuous definition, redefinition, creation, and destruction of the meaning and existence of serial orders; they can never be abandoned, and they can never, in this life at least, be constructed such that individuals and communities are made perfectly whole. Sartre places the burden of responsibility for the Sisyphean labor of structuring and de-structuring on the individual. We do not get to hide behind the illusory walls of our private sphere or the impersonal public duties of our organizational functions: "So since *praxis*, when considered at the level of each function, is still individual action and, as such, a moment of constituent dialectic—regardless of readjustments and the relation of common individuals elsewhere, this very action is done through the mediation of individual *praxis*."[146] Sartre's relational-liberationist view of social reality is a profound breakthrough in thought, but it is left undeveloped by his contemporaries for various, mostly parochial, reasons.[147] In the context of ecological concern, Arran Gare even claims, "there is no reason why Sartre's concepts could not be further developed to characterize the longer term social dynamics that give rise to new eras and even civilizations, and then to situate these in the dynamics of nature."[148] Dialectically considered, creation means nature as a social category collapses into society as a natural category; each belongs as a whole, not as a part, to *the Other*.

---

146. Sartre, *Critique of Dialectical Reason*, 505.
147. See Gare, *Philosophical Foundations of Ecological Civilization*, 72–99.
148. Gare, *Philosophical Foundations of Ecological Civilization*, 99.

In the vocabulary of our earlier terminology, *omnes* without *singulatim* is slavery and brutality perpetrated by the collective against the individual, but *singulatim* without *omnes* is individual privilege, injustice, and alienation at the expense of the community. Put otherwise, the *et* between is the place where individuals are constituted and preserved in and through community, but community is simultaneously constituted and preserved by individuals. Individuals do not belong to a community as parts to a whole; we are not simply expendable for the continuity of the community. The triadic distributive principle of *stewardship* affirms individuals and community; they are different, yet equal, aspects of the same whole. The distinction between individual and community is a *formal* one.[149] The formal distinction of community from an individual means they are conceptually different and, so, susceptible of definition independently of each other, but what the mind discovers as non-identical and discrete is whole in reality. Individual and community are not really two separable things; they are distinct *formalitates* of the same triadic relation. Community cannot be without individuals and individuals cannot exist without community. The continuous whole potential is distinct from the equally as whole actual singularities. Community is not something more real than individuals, making them undistributed means to its end. Individuals are not self-sufficient atoms capable of generating community. Community and individuals are convertible features of the same whole when viewed from two conceptually independent perspectives.[150]

However, as a social-ecological principle, wholeness cannot be assumed. Stewardship is a process of making whole. *Distributive justice* means mending what is broken, integrating what is isolated, and dismantling what is oppressive—to give what is needed, to all, and to each. Stewardship is equality of distribution; each answers for all and all for each. As Willis Jenkins rightly advocates, "The ecological task of stewardship is the dispensation of justice, giving each its due."[151] In the definitive words of Saint Thomas Aquinas, "The essential character of justice consists in rendering to another his due according to equality."[152] Distributive equality does

---

149. See Grajewski, "Formal Distinction of Duns Scotus," 121–43; Cross, *Duns Scotus*, 149.

150. The analogy with light in modern physics is, perhaps, a good one; that is, when viewed one way, light is a continuous wave and, from another, it is a particle. The best way to deal with this apparent paradoxical dualism is, following Russell, through the primacy of tri-relational continuity over the assumption of discrete units. See Rovelli, "Relational Quantum Mechanics," 1637–78

151. Jenkins, "Biodiversity and Salvation," 414.

152. Aquinas quoted in Benzoni, "Thomas Aquinas," 456.

not mean to treat others the same despite differences; it is equality of consideration for differences. Difference, as Sartre indicates, is the productive source of relationships that individuates (singular wholes) and unites (communal wholes). Stewardship is a moral idea of how we should treat others to meet their needs, freeing their capacities to meet the needs of community. Equal consideration for different beings, communities, and systems requires modification of the calculus of capacity to need; it is *custom-made* to fit difference.

Stewardship is the power of unconditional care that ensures a certain kind of freedom. According to Gerald C. MacCallum Jr. (†1987):

> Whenever the freedom of some agent or agents is in question, it is always freedom from some constraint or restriction on, interference with, or barrier to doing, not doing, becoming or not becoming something. Such freedom is thus always *of* something (an agent or agents), *from* something, *to* do, not do, become or not become something; it is a triadic relation. Taking the format "*x* is (is not) free from *y* to do (not do, become, not become) *z*," *x* ranges over agents, *y* ranges over such "preventing conditions" as constraints, restrictions, interferences, and barriers, and *z* ranges over actions or conditions of character or circumstance.[153]

MacCallum Jr. rejects the reduction of freedom to dyadic relations, along with the assumption that individuals can be free *simpliciter*.[154] Freedom is not some antecedently given and metaphysical state of being. On this *nominalist-Pelagian* view, the capacity for freedom is a property of the uncaused spontaneity of will found within self-sufficient individuals. Against this idea, MacCallum argues that freedom specifies relations between persons; it is a continuous state of affairs in the world. We have relational commitments to each other—freedom is a *triadic relation*.

Freedom is freedom *from* impediments, allowing an agent *to* actualize a potentiality; freedom is also freedom *through* a community's institutions. This latter *being-in-common* is symbolized by the *z* variable; it ranges over social-ecological collectives, bringing about what Thomas Hill Green (†1882) calls the "positive equality of conditions."[155] Individual freedom, in this sense, is less about being left alone to make our private choices as it is the recognition and exercise of our capacities to meet social-ecological need. We are called to build collectives that reform and replace institutions

---

153. MacCallum Jr., "Negative and Positive Freedom," 314.
154. See MacCallum Jr., "Negative and Positive Freedom," 330–31.
155. Green, *Prolegomena to Ethics* 267.

that continue to perpetrate what Johan Galtung calls *cultural violence*.[156] Proper stewardship collectives, z, then, provide concrete enabling conditions to agents by meeting different needs, helping them make the most of their capabilities. All creation must be made whole; the death, not of self, but of selfishness and violence: *Agape-z*.

---

156. See Galtung, "Cultural Violence," 291–305.

SIX

Stewardship of Sign

> Creation itself will be set free.
> —Romans 8:21

> Our Earth is communicating to us.
> If we want to survive,
> We must listen to it and decipher its message.
> —Benedict XVI

ANTHROPOCENE. HUMANITY IS AN elemental force. We join the colossal motions of water, air, land, and fire; an insatiable climate of flesh, moving upon the Earth. This chapter concludes the overview of philosophy of environment. The violent logic of dominance returns to its human sender. Stewardship is an ecological variation on agapistic traditions for overcoming violence. Nature grasped ethically is creation. Creation is environment; it is a system of communication—signs in need of liberation. Stewardship is developed from its initial presentation as a form of distributive justice to an ethic of communication. An *eco-agapistic* ethic is passion for the poor, including the suffering of the whole environmental domain and its creatures. Creation lies beyond the violent dualism of nature and culture. The absolute presupposition of being as communication becomes the subject matter for historical metaphysics of sign theory.

NATURAL CONSTRUCTIVISM

Collectivization is a process of habituation. The relationships between human beings and their environment (social/natural) transcend the immediacy of here and now and, over time, form serial patterns.[1] Serial patterns are systems of signs, incorporating the institutional reserve of knowledge from prior generations. John R. Searle calls these cultural deposits, "collective intentionalities."[2] They repeat themselves through subsequent generations; it is inherited reality, predating an individual's birth. "Language," to Peter L. Berger and Thomas Luckmann, "becomes the depository of a large aggregate of collective sedimentations, which can be acquired monothetically, that is, as collective wholes without reconstructing their original process of formation."[3] Inherited sign systems are *social deontologies*: The rules and conventions of the antecedently given. This legislative power structures the consequent thought and behavior of each new member of a culture.[4]

As Sartre has already shown, the repetition of *collective intentionalities* means ever more complex and rigid totalization. "Symbolic universes" present themselves as "inevitable totalities."[5] They explain and justify the order of things presented to an individual consciousness; it is "the sphere to which all forms of institutional conduct and roles belong, the symbolic universe provides the ultimate legitimation of the institutional order by bestowing upon it the primacy in the hierarchy of human experience."[6] Symbolic universes are inherently conservative—that is, they tend to be reactionary in relation to the new. Change, except in something evil, is very dangerous. But symbolic universes change, must change, so appropriating novel collective formations is the source of its continued existence. Symbolic universes that do not adapt, that continually chose nihilation over invention, collapse. They become dualistic processes of cultural violence: "Legitimation maintains the reality of the socially constructed universe; nihilation *denies* reality of whatever phenomena or interpretations of phenomena do not fit that

---

1. See Berger and Luckmann, *Social Construction of Reality*, 33–118.
2. Searle, "What Is an Institution?," 6–7.
3. Berger and Luckmann, *Social Construction of Reality*, 65.
4. See Searle, "What Is an Institution?," 10–14; Berger and Luckmann, *Social Construction of Reality*, 52–67.
5. Berger and Luckmann, *Social Construction of Reality*, 85.
6. Berger and Luckmann, *Social Construction of Reality*, 89–90.

universe."[7] The greatest cultural violence confronting the Earth is ecocide: We must change *something evil*.

Human induced collapse of ecosystems may bring the Earth to the point where life as we know it becomes impossible. At least part of its dynamic pervades with the denial that *creation* (or at least some of it, especially life) means the presence of independent sign systems. Creatures and places exist by their own right. *Nature* (and enviro-capital) is purely a function of human sign systems: A variable social category. Sign activity is the exclusive preserve of human cultures' collective intentionalities. Nature, then, is constructed in the dialectical gap between inherited symbolic universes, and their perpetual transformation; it is a contingent product of social history—a culturally embedded set of pragmatic metaphors (*metanarratives*). Such metaphors are not reducible to physical quantities, but they nonetheless operate within the social atmosphere to direct our relationship with environment. Examples of socially constructed metaphors include nature as mother, machine, or self-sustaining organism (Gaia). *Real* nature, however, is subject to quantification; somehow escaping the contingent vagaries of social construction. To claim that sign activity is an objective feature of nature, even though it not always measurable, is to commit an anthropomorphic projection. Human qualities are attributed to non-human beings and processes. Human culture is a symbolic solipsism; it is limited in its understanding of nature to what is communicated to us by the algorithmic order of physical quantities. Whatever does not fit this bifurcation of metaphoric culture and quantifiable nature is subject to institutional, specifically *natural* scientific, nihilation. *Cartesianism's symbolic universe, then, still stands mostly unchallenged.*[8]

A recent movement within the natural sciences, though, has put forward the supposition that sign activity is an objective—but non-quantificational feature—of living things. Signing is a continuous and *emergent* property of life and, perhaps, of the universe in general as the ground of physical information. There is a breach, or reversal, in the meaning of physical order. Instead of the translation of physical quantities into signs, quantities are considered conversions of signs. Signs make quantitative instantiation possible, but their range of logical extension is not limited to quantification.[9] Not unexpectedly, this idea has been met with skepticism;

---

7. Berger and Luckmann, *Social Construction of Reality*, 106.

8. On the navigation—i.e., avoidance—of incorporating quantifiable-physical (ahistorical, asymbolic, and observer independent) science into social construction theory, see Berger and Luckmann, *Social Construction of Reality*, 8; Searle, "What Is an Institution?," 3–5; *Construction of Social Reality*, 1–31.

9. See Hintikka, *Lingua Universalis vs. Calculus Ratiocinator*, 140–61.

Stewardship of Sign 203

it goes against the grain of mainstream, i.e., Cartesian, presuppositions.[10] The door is opened to non-verifiable (quantifiable) claims about the nature of things. Reified occult entities may reappear in this world beyond measure. But, at present, such a reaction seems premature and unfounded. The movement towards sign systems amongst natural scientists appears to be more *phenomenological practice* in search of an appropriate theory than it is an a priori imposition of a presupposition on their results. It is often in the laboratories where this idea is gaining its ground, dealing with the objective *metaphor* of irreducible (to physical quantities) organic codes.[11]

To take nature and culture as an overlapping, communicative, and evolutionary structure offers a better way to save the phenomena. This semiotic exchange is neither nature nor culture; it is creation. Just how this shift of interpretation cashes out in innovative methods and results is yet to be fully determined, as is its repositioning of the priority and role of quantification.[12] For example, a recent movement called *panarchy* offers a way "to integrate across disciplines to better understand systems of linked ecological, economic and institutional processes."[13] The panarchic approach assumes communication as constitutive of both culture and nature; it transforms this presupposition into an experimental hypothesis "for tough specific predictions that can be tested empirically."[14] Sign theory is an intriguing possibility for natural sciences. However, the idea of shared communicative presence is an imperative for any possibility of ecological forms of ethics and politics; especially regarding other animals and physical systems.[15]

Being and sign are convertible identities. This absolute presupposition reconfigures the opposition between culture and nature. Ecological violence can be mediated: A system of communication and symbiotic exchange can temper the necessities of human appropriation so that they need not be self-annihilating.[16] The question that haunts our future is whether we are truly capable, as a species, of developing an institution, a novel collective intentionality—an *agape-z* variable—that can overcome the violence within

---

10. On the problem with organic *codes* and their irreducibility, see Barbieri, "Biosemiotics," 577–99; *Organic Codes*. For emergent symbols in mathematical logic and physics, see Neumann, *Theory of Self-Reproducing Automata*, 121–23; Polanyi, "Life's Irreducible Structure," 1308–12; Pattee, "Physics of Symbols," 5–21.

11. See Ji, "Semiotics of Life."

12. See Witzany, "Review," 104–9.

13. Gunderson and Holling, *Panarchy*, 21

14. Gunderson and Holling, *Panarchy*, 14.

15. See Apel, "Ecological Crisis," 220–24.

16. See Wheeler, *Whole Creature*, 45–160.

human being and its cultural constructions, that surrounding us in the natural world, and the amplifying clash between the two? Can we move from the violent dichotomy of nature and culture to creation? Donald Favareau describes the *naturally strange* project of biopolitical correction:

> The principles of natural organization are often brutal in ways that are almost inconceivable to us, even *after* the horrors of the twentieth century. Programmed cell death, the hyper-hierarchical order of the insect hive, cannibalism of one's newborns, never-ending warlike territoriality, parasitism, role definition rigidly assigned by sex and age, violently maintained tribal enmity—*all* of these "ensure the health and fullest flourishing" of the collective in nature . . . as, of course, do cooperation, altruism, and symbiosis. If it is our human attempt to achieve our survival *only* (or even primarily) by the means of the latter, and *not* by the means of the former, then this is something "new" in nature—and thus the template for what form of human "government" would be best suited to bringing this strange new way of being in nature to fruition may have to be devised in *contravention* of some of nature's principles, and not just in accordance with them (as, indeed, we do when we protect the weak and disabled).[17]

However, those familiar with the history and doctrines of Christianity will find Favareau's *strange new way of being in nature* neither strange nor new. The struggle to overcome violence is its revolutionary heart. As Charles Taylor observes, "Thus we can point to the Gospel picture of a Christian counter-violence: a transformation of the energy that usually goes into scapegoat purification, transformation that reaches to overcome the fear of violence not by becoming lord of it, by directing it as an annihilating force against evil, but that aims rather to overcome fear by offering oneself to it, responding with love and forgiveness, thereby tapping a source of goodness and healing."[18] *Stewardship*, in the sense developed here, is a variation on this core social principle. What does it mean to extend it to environment? What does it mean to liberate creation?

IS HUMAN VIOLENCE NATURAL?

Favareau claims that, along with mutual aid, forms of violence are necessary for common evolutionary success. If this is true, why is humanity an

17. Favareau, "Understanding Natural Constructivism," 520.
18. Taylor, "Notes on the Sources of Violence," 38.

exception? Why not simply accept that we are like any other species: Violence is a part of our makeup that helps ensure survival? Why is it something to overcome? Would eliminating violence undermine our chances for survival? The claim here, then, is that it is not, ultimately, in the interest of our collective survival. Human violence is maladaptive to social and ecological flourishing. Why is this *contravention* of nature particular to humanity? The answer seems to be a matter of both kind and scale.

On kind. The human phenomenon of violence involves radical escalation of retributive justice. We can *intentionally violate* others; for the most part, this is the specific difference that separates us from the rest of nature. *Antagonism* in the natural world is inevitable and necessary, but it is often (but not always) factored into limits.[19] It is the unlimited, or totalizing, nature of human violence that is the key concern, distinguishing it from the aggressive struggles for survival found amongst our fellow creatures. Human *crime*, for example, is considered neither necessary nor inevitable. Violation means to knowingly desecrate someone or something belonging to someone. Within the victim's space of violation, a sacred debt is created. Justice is born of injustice. The principle of retaliation (*lex talionis*) demands an equivalent repayment for crimes committed, punishing the transgressor in proportion to the crime. The debt is repaid; in Exodus we read: "Life for life, eye for eye, tooth for tooth" (Exod 21:23 KJV). *On scale.* The problem with retributive justice is that the agent of retribution creates more violations and victims. The dark angels of vengeance demand retribution for past crimes, but acts of revenge create more crimes, demanding more retribution. Every correction is a bloodbath, calling for a new correction. An exponential cycle of amplifying intensity is unleashed. Technology increases the capacity to destroy in the name of justice. The vendetta spreads like a firestorm beyond mortal containment. In its wake, individuals, families, communities, kingdoms, republics, civilizations and, perhaps, the Earth are annihilated. In Aeschylus's *Oresteia*, we encounter the logic of retribution and its incomplete overcoming. The Chorus seeks a new form of justice to replace retribution; but one that must still answer the same profound question as vengeance once did: "What can wash off the blood once spilled upon the ground?"[20] They demand an end to the cycle of ever amplifying violence in the name

---

19. There is substantial evidence of retributive violence and reconciliation among many primates. See the work of primatologist and ethologist Frans B. M. de Waal (esp. Waal, *Peacemaking among Primates*, 9–34). The human difference from our fellow primates, though, breaks with the adaptive function of violence. The source of this maladaptive discontinuity is a complex knot of intelligence, language, intentionality, institutional forms, and technology, accompanying violation.

20. Aeschylus, *Oresteia*, line 48 (94).

of justice: "Must he give blood for generations gone / die for those slain and in death pile up / more death to come for the blood shed / what mortal else who hears shall claim / he was born clear of the dark angel?"[21]

René Girard (†2015) propounds that the traditional social mechanism for halting the cycle is through sacrificial displacement. Legitimate violence is inflicted on the least capable of retribution—*the scapegoat*. All against all shifts to all against one. The sacrifice secures "the safety of the group by checking the impulse for revenge."[22] Social validation of this transfer of collective antagonism to a defenseless singular takes the form of religious practice: "Violence is the heart and secret soul of the sacred."[23] Sacrificial religion, nonetheless, can become ineffective, especially during conflict amongst the higher levels of political power. In the *Oresteia*, for example, several sacrifices are made to halt the slaughter, but it does little to prevent the next wave of revenge killing. An independent legal authority is created to replace religion; the laws and its officers will hold the monopoly on retribution. In the *Oresteia*, this transition is described in mythological terms. The Furies (*angels of vengeance*) eventually relinquish their call for the personal vendetta; they take a new place in the impersonal judicial order as police and punisher. Vengeance cannot be abolished entirely. Without fear of retribution, human nature will gravitate to unlimited crime: "There are times when fear is good. / It must keep a watchful place / at the heart's controls."[24] The problem of retribution, then, which the new system of public vengeance hopes to resolve, is that revenge leads to more revenge, but without retribution as an *aspect* (not the heart) of justice, crime seems inevitable. The Furies are reluctant to give up their place at the center of holy justice. The new gods, Apollo and Athena—associated with reason, enlightenment, civilization, and communal love—convince them by honoring their past service to community, enshrining them in the new order as adjuncts. The Furies are the strong arm of justice. Their new role is pre and post justice. The Furies apprehend and bring the accused to face justice, punishing the guilty after justice is determined. But they are no longer the divine instruments of the essence of justice.

Apollo and Athena preside over the new institution of justice: The court, which is professionally detached from the private affairs of its citizens. Persuasion through law, evidence, and reasoned argument will decide the guilt or innocence of the accused. The court must be careful because

---

21. Aeschylus, *Oresteia*, lines 1336–42 (78).
22. Girard, *Violence and the Sacred*, 21.
23. Girard, *Violence and the Sacred*, 25.
24. Aeschylus, *Oresteia*, lines 517–18 (153).

convicting the wrong person creates a victim, who will seek revenge, but acquitting the guilty leaves a victim without justice. The properly convicted, then, must face a judgment that renders proper retribution on behalf of the victim. The court must clear the debt to the victim, who is the volatile reactor that continues the cycle of reciprocal violence. The aim of the new justice is to bring internal security to the community by removing the right for personal vendetta, avoiding civil war:

> *Chorus*
> This my prayer: Civil War
> fattening on men's ruin shall
> not thunder in our city. Let
> not the dry dust that drinks
> the black blood of citizens
> through passion for revenge
> and bloodshed for bloodshed
> be given our state to prey upon.
> Let them render grace for grace.
> Let love be their common will;
> Let them hate with a single heart.
> Much wrong in the world is thereby healed.[25]

The economy of public vengeance is asymmetrical. The system has the monopoly on impersonal retribution, acting on behalf of victims. We forfeit the right to private revenge. Further, we have no right to seek vengeance on persons who act for the impersonal system. To Girard. the judicial system frees us "from the terrible obligations of vengeance."[26] "Fear of reciprocal violence," he claims, "provides our judicial system with its structure."[27] Violence can be now properly understood through the dichotomies of public/private, legal/illegal, and legitimate/illegitimate. The function of the first half of each pair is to remove the threat of the second half. The semantics are changed. In the first half of each pair, force can be good, enacted by public defenders, who are sanctioned by the laws and institutions of a community; the second half is violent and evil. *Criminalities* arise from private maladies and projects that employ violence. Therefore, murder is an act of violence, but capital punishment by a legitimate authority is not. The former is a threat to the community, evoking the specter of reciprocal violence. The latter restores the integrity of the community by repaying the debt to the victim; it halts the amplification of vengeance.

---

25. Aeschylus, *Oresteia*, lines 976–87 (169).
26. Girard, *Violence and the Sacred*, 21.
27. Girard, *Violence and the Sacred*, 27.

Legal force, then, constrains us from the initiatives and consequences of the private vendetta, but not the collective vendetta. In the hands of the state, legality can be used as a weapon to intensify scapegoating. To Girard, a system of public vengeance "eventually wears thin."[28] Social solidarity can be manipulated by the doctrine that it requires an enemy; the capacity for retribution on its behalf increases exponentially. The abundant resources and technologies available to the public structure can "oppress as well as liberate."[29] Legal political forms may be inherently biased or break down during crisis situations. The impersonal monopoly on vengeance can regress to the scapegoat mechanism that it replaced. Whole races, genders, classes, religions, and cultures may be targeted for sacrifice as legitimate enemies—both internal and external. Capacity for mobilization and technological efficiency ensure destruction on a scale unimaginable for private individuals under the spell of revenge. Girard speaks of "unlimited violence—a violence that knows no bounds."[30] The problem of retribution is not resolved by a system of public vengeance; it grows much more subtle, covert, and dangerous under the cloak of legal legitimacy.[31]

The ecological adjustment to this general logic of violence seems to consist in a certain idea of progress: The Cartesian project of dominating nature for human betterment. In the nuclear age of total violence, large scale wars of retribution must be left behind. Mutual reconciliation of humanity is now predicated on accelerating global economic development; this involves a massive technological appropriation of nature through rapidly expanding regions of production, circulation, consumption, and waste—*Growth. Nature becomes the scapegoat.* To overcome our impulse for vengeance against each other on a total scale, the building up of social tensions through the works of fear and resentment, we sacrifice the environment for mutual economic growth.

Nature is thought the least capable of reciprocal violence because it is merely a collection of unintentional and impersonal mechanisms. This sacrifice provides a cornucopia of wealth, however ill-distributed, which is still said to be the master-key for unlocking a lasting human peace. Our violence against the Earth substitutes for mass human violence. This displacement seemed like a sensible idea when the alternative was mutually assured nuclear destruction. In Isaiah, we hear that peace between rival

---

28. Girard, *Violence and the Sacred*, 23.
29. Girard, *Violence and the Sacred*, 23.
30. Girard, *Violence and the Sacred*, 24–25.
31. See Benjamin, "Critique of Violence," 277–300; Wolff, "On Violence," 601–16; Arendt, *On Violence*, 35–60; Derrida, "Force of Law," 927–45.

nations means "they shall beat their swords into ploughshares, and spears into pruning hooks; nation shall not lift up sword against nation; neither shall they learn war any more" (Isa 2:4 KJV). Now, though, we are beginning to realize that ploughshares and pruning hooks are not so benevolent. They, too, can become a way of war with the Earth. To treat the Earth as our species' scapegoat is not without its consequences. We have profoundly misjudged our situation. *Scapegoat-Earth* has its own powers of retribution. It is the most, not least, capable of retribution. In a metaphoric sense, with terrifying literal consequences, the Earth is seeking its revenge.[32] The Furies now seem to be driving elemental forces in our direction. We begin to see the maladaptive nature of human violence on a global and ecological scale; the same cycle of unsustainable excess with the same consequences. In the human case, then, *cooperation, altruism, and symbiosis are the only ways to ensure the health and fullest flourishing of the collective in nature.*

Martin Luther King Jr. (†1968) poses the existential decision to be made: "The choice today is not between violence or non-violence; it is either non-violence or non-existence."[33] And Girard presents us with Christianity's perennial challenge to the legitimacy of violence:

> To leave violence behind, it is necessary to give up the idea of retribution; it is therefore necessary to give up forms of conduct that have always seemed to be natural and legitimate. For example, we think it quite fair to respond to good dealings with good dealings, and to evil dealings with evil, but this is precisely what all the communities on the planet have always done, with familiar results. People imagine that to escape from violence it is sufficient to give up the violent *initiative*, but since no one in fact thinks of himself as taking the initiative—since all violence has a mimetic character, and derives or can be thought to derive from a first violence that is always perceived as originating with the opponent—this act of renunciation is no more than a sham, and cannot bring about any kind of change at all. Violence is always perceived as being a legitimate reprisal or even self-defense. So, what must be given up is the right to reprisals and even the right to what passes, in several cases, for legitimate defense. Since violence is mimetic, and no one ever feels responsible for triggering it initially, only by an unconditional renunciation can we arrive at the desired result:
>
> *And if you do good to those who do good to you, what credit is that to you? For even sinners do the same. And if you lend to*

---

32. See Lovelock, *Revenge of Gaia*, 1–66.
33. King Jr. quoted in Ceric, "Judaism, Christianity, Islam," 54.

> those from whom you hope to receive, what credit is that to you?
> Even sinners lend to sinners, to receive as much again. But love
> your enemies, and do good, and lend, expecting nothing in return
> (Luke 6:33–35).[34]

Blood cannot wipe away blood. Love must go beyond violence, beyond friends against enemies, so that blood no longer runs in the name of justice. Only forgiveness casts out vengeance. The social-ecological dynamics of the scapegoat must end. *Nature* ceases to be an enemy. *Creation* is an ethical subject for mutual repair.

These presuppositions can no longer be considered arbitrary preferences in a marketplace of individual *spiritual* values; they are features of human nature that reveal our prospects for survival. Although their radical Christian form may be the most familiar, such moral gravitations are certainly not unique to this religion or exhaustive of its cross-cultural potentialities and adaptabilities.[35] The ability to recognize and follow the stewardship ethic is not, as some Christian theologians argue, predicated *entirely* on the reception of divine grace or being specifically Christian in the sense of professed faith; it may not even depend on belief in a supernatural deity.[36] Many people reject organized (and spontaneous) religion because they see it as the prime mover of violence. There are sound reasons for holding such a view. History is marked by perpetual atrocity in the name of religion. Apocalyptic eschatology, common to the great monotheistic theological systems, especially Christianity, may even be founded upon the logic of total violence.[37] However, these critics still tend to reject the violence they perceive as characterizing religion in favor of a secular and atheistic version of a similar set of nonviolent principles. The religion free future that supposedly brings them into reality is entrusted to human reason and science: *Neoenlightenment*.[38] But the consequent *secular* commitment to progress by scientism and rationalization has an equally as violent political and environmental history in its name (if not more).[39] Religion, though, like the con-

---

34. Girard, *Things Hidden since the Foundation of the World*, 198.

35. See Heft, "Introduction," 1–14; Sharma, *Ethical Philosophies of India*, 52–69.

36. On this debate, see Jenkins, "Biodiversity and Salvation," 410; Benzoni, "Thomas Aquinas," 449–50; and, more generally, on grace for transformative goodness, Nygren, *Agape and Eros*, 50–67

37. For this view, see Moore, "Revolting Revelations," 183–200; Moyise, "Does the Lion Lie down with the Lamb?," 181–94. For rebuttals, see Toole, "Divine Ecology and the Apocalypse," 547–61; Dunham, "Ecological Violence of Apocalyptic Eschatology," 101–12. On current ecopolitical manifestations, see Gray, *Black Mass*, 1–35.

38. See Hitchens, *God Is Not Great*, 277–84.

39. See Eagleton, *Reason, Faith, and Revolution*, 85–108; Murphy, *Rationality and Nature*, 27–42.

tradition of human *nature* it reflects, may contain the driving impulse for both mutual aid and violence. It may even evolve and favor certain *mutualist memes* over their *toxic* brethren.[40] The former memes are more conducive to the adaptations we need to survive. The engine of natural selection, so far modeled, seems to favor communication, cooperation, and forgiveness.[41] At this critical stage, it is necessary to understand our evolutionary prospects in terms of what Peter Kropotkin (†1921) calls *solidarity*:

> Thus by an unprejudiced observation of the animal kingdom, we reach the conclusion that wherever society exists at all, this principle may be found: *Treat others as you would like them to treat you under similar circumstances.*
>
> And when we study closely the evolution of the animal world, we discover that the aforesaid principle, translated by the one word *Solidarity*, has played an infinitely larger part in the development of the animal kingdom than all the adaptations that have resulted from a struggle between individuals to acquire personal advantages.[42]

There is an ethical gap between origin and present utility—the open presence of communication—creation. Girard proclaims that we are now in the place of "instantaneous *conversion*," where we must decide "between the evil reciprocity of violence and the benevolent reciprocity of love," between abyss and the kingdom to come.[43] Be it by theological presupposition, literary hermeneutics, or scientific evidence, how you arrived in this gap is not as important as having recognized the decision to be made: Nature or creation?

CAN DIONYSUS RETIRE?

It can be argued that *pluralistic eco-agapism* is neither possible nor preferable. We belong to the Earth. Like all other living creatures, aggression, egoism, cruelty, and so on are programmed into our very being. We cannot, and should not, attempt to make ourselves an exception. Conversion

---

40. See Dennett, *Breaking the Spell*, 328–39.
41. On the science of this hypothesis, see Axelrod and Dion, "Further Evolution of Cooperation," 1385–90; Grim, "Spatialization and Greater Generosity," 3–17; Nowak and Sigmund, "Tit for Tat in Heterogeneous Populations," 250–52; Nowak, "Five Rules for the Evolution of Cooperation," 1560–63; McCullough, *Beyond Revenge*, 1–19; Coakley and Nowak, "Introduction," 1–34.
42. Kropotkin, "Anarchist Morality," 97.
43. Girard, *Things Hidden since the Foundation of the World*, 215.

is an illusion that interferes with the natural course of things. Moral impediments are contrary to life; they repress and delay biological necessity. Christianized Occidental civilization seeks to redeem our nature, creating a new human being. All it really does is dam up vital energies until the levies overflow. Such events occasion massive displays of misdirected violence. If we are true to our *animal being*, the scale and extent of our violence will be factored into a more harmonious balance. Measured function in tune with need restrains self-annihilating excess. In Euripides's (†406 BCE) *The Bacchae*, Dionysus admonishes repressed humanity: "Too late to know me now. You did not when you should. / I am a God. And when insulted, Gods do not forgive."[44]

Violence, too, is holy. It is the fiery essence of the will-to-life. The worship of an otherworldly, non-violent God devalues this existence, especially the conflict required for its creation and preservation. Nihilism is aversion to existence. Another kind of human being must be created to overcome it. We should fight for this life, not the one to come because this life is all there is. Beyond here, the void. "The hero," Max Stirner (†1856) declares, "wants not to go into the other world, but to draw the other world to him, and compel it to become this world! What he has the power to do, he also has the right to do."[45] When I am existentially challenged by social and natural forces, I, like the gods, *do not forgive*. I do not forfeit my life. A hero battles onward until her life is taken. A life of pure immanence obeys the warrior ethic. Strife, struggle, and death are celebrated as sublime. Pagan glory—life as the *naturalist* affirmation and celebration of superior power over weakness—is put forward, again, to replace agape's moral economy of love.

Destruction is required for new creation; the pulverization of the fixed and eternal by the vital and temporal. Friedrich Nietzsche, for instance, proposes a rapprochement between humanity and violence on this basis. He intends "to translate man back into nature."[46] This *anti-conversion* is a clash between basic life and its abolition: "*Dionysus against the Crucified.*"[47] For Nietzsche, "Life itself, its eternal fruitfulness and recurrence, creates torment, destruction, the will to annihilation."[48] Re-paganization signifies that the "god on the cross is a curse on life, a signpost to seek redemption from life; Dionysus cut to pieces is a *promise* of life: it will be eternally reborn and

---

44. Euripides, *Bacchae*, 82–83.
45. Stirner, *Ego and His Own*, 40.
46. Nietzsche, *Beyond Good and Evil*, 230.
47. Nietzsche, "Ecce Homo," 262.
48. Nietzsche, *Will to Power*, 543.

return again from destruction."⁴⁹ In order for life to be reclaimed from the deadening clutches of Christian morality, the *Crucified* must be purged from culture: "In denying God, we deny accountability," Nietzsche claims, "only by doing *that* do we redeem the world."⁵⁰ A renewed Dionysian *life-faith* will emerge from the ashes of the old God: "Is this pagan cult not a form of thanksgiving and affirmation of life?"⁵¹ This revived cult is "a joyful and trusting fatalism," "beyond pity and terror, *to realize in oneself* the eternal joy of becoming—that joy which also encompasses *joy in destruction*," and "such a faith is the highest of all possible faiths: I have baptized it with the name *Dionysus*."⁵² Tragic optimism is an aesthetic generalization, encompassing the entirety of human endeavor: "The tragic artist is no pessimist: he is precisely the one who says Yes to everything questionable, even the terrible—he is *Dionysian*."⁵³ De-Christianization is a total cultural program. Along with music, literature, and plastic arts, the Dionysian Passion enfolds politics, science, and ethics.

All is will-to-power. Existence is simply the space of appearance; it is from nowhere, going nowhere, pure flux without meaning, or universal categories for common interpretation. The heroic aesthete, the Dionysian Superman, however, can accept these facts and not be destroyed by the scandal of meaninglessness. By sheer force of will, she creates order from chaos, imprinting her icon of Being on becoming. The "Dionysian experience" reinstates "the immovable order of rank and inequality of value between man and man."⁵⁴ Nietzsche's Dionysian faith is radically elitist. It does not go all the way down. But the Christian ethic of agape is not replaced. Rather, it is strategically repositioned as *herd morality*. Christianity is slave will-to-power; it is an expression of *ressentiment*—a way of levelling the strong. The weak create another world *to come* in order to triumph over their powerlessness in this one. "One cannot sufficiently condemn Christianity," Nietzsche writes, "for having devalued the value of such a great purifying nihilistic movement, which was perhaps already being formed, through the idea of the immortal private person: likewise through the hope of resurrection: in short, through continual deterrence from the *deed of nihilism*, which is suicide."⁵⁵ The Christian triumph means, "It substituted slow suicide: gradu-

---

49. Nietzsche, *Will to Power*, 543.
50. Nietzsche, "Twilight of the Idols," 212.
51. Nietzsche, *Will to Power*, 542.
52. Nietzsche, "Ecce Homo," 260–61.
53. Nietzsche, "Twilight of the Idols," 256.
54. Nietzsche, *Will to Power*, 540.
55. Nietzsche, *Will to Power*, 143.

ally a petty, poor, but durable life; gradually a quite ordinary, bourgeois, mediocre life, etc."[56]

The ethic of mediocrity is not abolished. The Dionysian *political* elite seek to master the herd. A master needs spiritually healthy slaves in order to be master. She must appear to fulfil herd values while undermining them: A true wolf in shepherd's clothing. A Dionysian ruler oppresses, kills, and enslaves in the name of liberty, life, and prosperity. Properly ordered slaves are commanded from within by unwittingly consenting to their own domination, having their morality used against them. *Morality* has come to an end because it is now a weapon used to impose the natural order of subordination and exploitation. The multitude, *the last men*, must be made compliant and comfortable with their inferior place in the hierarchy. Nietzsche's project seems quite clear: "My philosophy aims at an ordering of rank: not at an individualistic morality. The ideas of the herd should rule in the herd—but not reach out beyond it: the leaders of the herd require a fundamentally different valuation for their actions, as do the independent, or 'the beasts of prey,' etc."[57] The politics practiced by the *beasts of prey* is mostly hidden, manipulating general Christian feelings and views:

> I have declared war on the anemic Christian ideal (together with what is closely related to it), not with the aim of destroying it but only of putting an end to its tyranny and clearing the way for new ideals, for *more robust* ideals.—The continuance of the Christian ideal is one of the most desirable things there are—even for the sake of the ideals that want to stand beside it and perhaps above it—they must have opponents, strong opponents, if they are to become strong.—Thus we immoralists require the power of morality: our drive for self-preservation wants our *opponents* to retain their strength—it only wants to become *master over them*.[58]

René Girard praises Nietzsche for his unprecedented insight into the cycle of redemptive violence that characterizes pagan religion: "The death of God is also his birth."[59] Moreover, "The consequences of God's murder are religious, therefore, purely religious. The very deed that seems to put an end to the religious process is really the origin of that process, the sum

---

56. Nietzsche, *Will to Power*, 143.
57. Nietzsche, *Will to Power*, 162.
58. Nietzsche, *Will to Power*, 197. On Nietzsche's alleged influence on Neoconservative politics, see Drury, *Political Ideas of Leo Strauss*, 170–81.
59. Girard, "Dionysus versus the Crucified," 831.

total of it, really, the religious process par excellence."[60] Nietzsche's judgment on Christianity is also partially correct: "The Christian passion is not anti-Jewish as the vulgar anti-Semites believe; it is anti-pagan."[61] Girard's admiration is severely qualified; even though Nietzsche is more aware of the role of violence at the fount of religion than most thinkers, "nevertheless there is blindness in him."[62] Nietzsche is rightly attuned to Christianity's radical break with what Girard calls the "evil sacred" of paganism—that is, the notion that "violence alone is able to master violence, because the sacred is at once the evil and the remedy."[63] Nietzsche's blindness emerges from reading the Christian deviation as a denial of life because it attempts to de-legitimate violence. He becomes an evangelist for the cult of Dionysus, heralding the modern return of the *evil sacred* that supposedly revitalizes human existence.

There is an essential difference between Christianity and pagan mythologies. The sacredness of Dionysian violence is cancelled by Christianity. On this point both Nietzsche and Girard agree. The adepts of Dionysus interpret his martyrdom in a manner quite different from the Christian interpretation of the passion of Jesus. In the latter case, "the emphasis lies on the *innocence* of the victim and, as a consequence, on the guilt of the murderers."[64] This absolute condemnation of the *evil sacred* marks a revolutionary break with Dionysian duality: "The god can be the victim and he can also be the chief murder. He can be victimized and he can be the victimizer."[65] "It is inconceivable," Girard says, "that Jesus would become the instigator of some *holy lynching*."[66] Nietzsche is the first to perceive (at least in the modern period) that Christianity topples the evil sacred. The genesis of a fundamentally distinct idea of *the good* for humanity rejects violence as the ground of terrestrial order. The crucifixion, like the killing of Abel by Cain before it in the Jewish Bible, is a founding murder like no other: "It is not the same thing to interpret the same murder as a glorious deed with the Romans and to interpret it as a crime with the Bible."[67] Praise of the crucifixion "points to a violent origin of human society passively reflected and assumed by mythological cultures whereas it is denounced by the Bible and

---

60. Girard, "Dionysus versus the Crucified," 831.
61. Girard, "Dionysus versus the Crucified," 823.
62. Girard, "Dionysus versus the Crucified," 825.
63. Girard, "Dionysus and the Violent Genesis of the Sacred," 496.
64. Girard, "Dionysus versus the Crucified," 821.
65. Girard, "Dionysus versus the Crucified," 822.
66. Girard, "Dionysus versus the Crucified," 822.
67. Girard, "Dionysus versus the Crucified," 823.

Christian gospels."[68] Nietzsche sees clearly that Jesus died not as a Dionysian victim, self-resurrected as victimizer, but against all cyclic sacrifices of this type. The crucifixion is "a silent but definitive condemnation of pagan order, of all human order really."[69] To side with the victims, instead of the victimizers—to cleave off the holy victimizer element, denying cyclic polarity—is the moral and political antithesis of sacrificial civilization.

The anti-sacrifice of Jesus exposes the evil sacred as *the big lie*. To Nietzsche, this reversal denies the victors their rightful glory and elite status; thus, it denies the order of life itself. Social leveling undermines a culture's vigor and dynamism. The strong and exceptional are caught in an undertow of banality and weakness that inhibits the full expression of their powers. The protection, even deification, of victims threatens the *health* of a community. The death and resurrection of Jesus overturns *the natural* pagan order. On Girard's interpretation, "Nietzsche accused this death of being a hidden act of *ressentiment* because it reveals the injustice of all such deaths and the 'absurdity' not of one specific mob only but of all 'Dionysian' mobs the world over. The word 'absurdity' is Nietzsche's own."[70] Further, "When Nietzsche keeps repeating that the passion of Jesus is an 'objection to life,' or 'a formula for its condemnation,' he understands that the Christian passion is a rejection and an indictment of everything upon which the old pagan religions were founded and with them all human societies worth their salt, in Nietzsche's estimation, the societies in which 'the strong and the victorious' were not prevented by the down-trodden masses from enjoying the fruits of the superiority."[71] Nietzsche's illumination of the decisive stakes involved in the Christian moment is truly remarkable, but equally as extraordinary is his misinterpretation of its significance.

Christian *ressentiment* does not weaken communities by undermining the potentialities of the strong. The iterative cycles of vengeance destroy societies, which are perpetuated by the contests of the powerful. "*Ressentiment*," Girard claims, "is the interiorization of weakened vengeance."[72] Nietzsche misreads the essence of his own analysis:

> *Ressentiment* flourishes in a world where real vengeance (Dionysus) has been weakened. The Bible and the gospels have diminished the violence of vengeance and turned it to *ressentiment* not because they originate in the latter but because their

68. Girard, "Dionysus versus the Crucified," 823.
69. Girard, "Dionysus versus the Crucified," 823.
70. Girard, "Dionysus versus the Crucified," 822.
71. Girard, "Dionysus versus the Crucified," 822–23.
72. Girard, "Dionysus versus the Crucified," 825.

real target is vengeance in all its forms, and they have succeeded in wounding vengeance, not in eliminating it. The gospels are indirectly responsible; we alone are directly responsible. *Ressentiment* is the way the spirit of vengeance survives the impact of Christianity and turns the gospels to its own use.

Nietzsche analyzed *ressentiment* and all its works with enormous power. He did not see that the evil he was fighting was a relatively minor evil compared to the more violent forms of vengeance.[73]

It is sacred violence that wrecks culture: "The sacred is quite real since it is violence in its entirety. What men desire when they give themselves up to desire against one another in the loss of all community, which is to say of all communal adoration, is always violence, the same violence to which the sacred remains indefatigably attached and follows as its shadow."[74] A civilization must eventually decide on its absolute presupposition. We seem to be stuck, caught between worlds; powerless to decide on the nature of the sacred.

Ressentiment is a waystation between vengeance and agape. But it is not *ressentiment* that somehow dams up vengeance until it overflows *to get it out of our system*. The tracks back to sacred violence are open for travel, but going back is neither inevitable nor preferable. *Ressentiment* means Christian presuppositions first become ossified, corrupted, fail to advance, and then cultural energies regress to atavistic mythological forms of divine violence: "*Ressentiment* is intense enough to generate more and more intellectual nihilism but not intense enough so far to annihilate real being."[75] Nietzsche makes a choice; the spiritual doldrums of *ressentiment* can only be overcome by a Dionysian whirlwind, not an agapistic progression. Such a wish can only emerge within a spoiled, bored bourgeoisie culture where vengeance has ceased to terrify as an operative social force. Girard argues, "He could afford the luxury of resenting *ressentiment* so much that it appeared as a fate worse than real vengeance. Being absent from the scene, real vengeance was never seriously apprehended. Unthinkingly, like so many thinkers of his age and ours, Nietzsche called on Dionysus, begging him to bring back real vengeance as a cure for what seemed to him the worst of all possible fates, *ressentiment*."[76] All violence is vengeance at heart; it is the regressive destination; once agapistic energies for progress collapse, creating

---

73. Girard, "Dionysus versus the Crucified," 825.
74. Girard, "Dionysus and the Violent Genesis of the Sacred," 496.
75. Girard, "Dionysus versus the Crucified," 826.
76. Girard, "Dionysus versus the Crucified," 825–26.

more scapegoats to halt what cannot be truly halted until the evil sacred is overthrown again.

Violence is not holy. It is Nietzsche who emerges as absurd; he is another *Zauberlehrling* (Sorcerer's Apprentice), inciting dark spirits he cannot command: "At more and more levels of reality, the urgency of the gospel message can no longer be disregarded with impunity. Those thinkers, like Nietzsche, unthinkingly appealed to real vengeance in their itch to get rid of *ressentiment* resemble these foolish characters in fairytales who make the wrong wish and come to grief when it comes true."[77] Not only Nietzsche is seduced by the lie of a *progressive* return to pagan forms of power and civilization, but, as we have prefigured, it infects *Nietzsche's Apprentice*: Foucault.[78] Surely, if it posits that there is no truth outside of historicity's *different* cyclic struggles for dominance, a philosophy cannot be described as progressive! No other kind of common liberation is possible here besides the temporary triumph of the variously dispersed centers of competing wills to dominate; each with an equally as incommensurate liberation narrative as its *will-to-power*. It is just another covert operation by *different Dionysian birds of prey*—multiplied across the complex registrars of class, race, and gender—to dismantle and obscure the true threat to its perpetration: Civilizational advancement to agape.

John Gray observes that Nietzsche's (and, to a certain extent, Foucault's) progressive schema for translating humanity back into nature never truly leaves "Christianity behind."[79] What you get is a lethal hybrid of Christian aspirations and neo-pagan barbarism in the age of technology. Humanity is still considered capable of transforming its nature. Instead of faith in an eternal love that can redeem our violence, however, we have a counter faith in human liberation through the immanent joy of destruction, hardheartedness, cruelty, and the will to annihilate inferior sorts of human beings through eugenics, euthanasia, and industrial slaughter. Unleashing Dionysian hordes to transfigure humanity is, perhaps, the worst idea of all time: "He was trapped in the chalk circle of Christian hopes. A believer to the end, he never gave up the absurd faith that something could be made of the human animal. He invented the ridiculous figure of the Superman to give history meaning it had not had before. He hoped that humankind would thereby be awakened from its sleep. As could have been foreseen, he succeeded only in adding further nightmares to its confused dream."[80]

---

77. Girard, "Dionysus versus the Crucified," 826.
78. See Foucault, *Lectures on the Will to Know*, 202–28.
79. Gray, *Straw Dogs*, 47.
80. Gray, *Straw Dogs*, 49.

Gray sets out to correct Nietzsche's error. Instead of optimistic naturalism that turns tragic, the proper view of humanity is pessimistic naturalism that can, against the odds, turn *fortunate*.

The environmental crisis, especially, is something best left to take its own course without any new conversion programs for human nature; this can only make things worse. The Earth will correct our numbers, one way or another, through the usual pogroms of famine, disease, disaster, and genocide: "The destruction of the natural world is not the result of global capitalism, industrialization, 'Western civilization,' or any flaw of human institutions. It is a consequence of the evolutionary success of an exceptionally rapacious primate."[81] "Throughout all of history and prehistory, human advance has coincided with ecological devastation," Gray claims, and "humans are like any other plague animal. They cannot destroy the Earth, but they can wreck the environment that sustains them."[82] But Gray's biological variety of determinism denies that we are completely fated. He cites James Lovelock's four possible outcomes of *disseminated primatemaia*: "Destruction of the invading disease organisms; chronic infection; destruction of the host; or symbiosis—a lasting relationship of mutual benefit to the host and invader."[83] Of the four, the first is the most likely. The last is the least probable outcome, but as bleak, frightening, and uncompromising as his analysis tends to be, even Gray hints at an opportunity for symbiosis through our *animal virtues*.[84]

Gray's ecological ethic, if it is that, is certainly not a prospectus for creating a new human being; it is recognition of our solidarity with other creatures. Between humans and other animals no dissimilarity can be found so great but that the similarity is always greater. Communication underpins our analogical virtues; it is our basic tie to other lifeforms: "The calls of birds and the traces left by wolves to mark off their territories are no less forms of language than the songs of humans. What is distinctively human is not the capacity for language. It is the crystallization in writing."[85] Gray condemns the *solipsism of anthropocentrism* because it denies the scientific validity of interspecies communication. This enclosure of the commons is an erroneous, ecocidal conceit of Western thought, enduring as an orthodox foundation of higher education. Anthropocentrism is disseminated as "Idealism

---

81. Gray, *Straw Dogs*, 7.

82. Gray, *Straw Dogs*, 7, 12. On this naturalist thesis, see Crosby, *Ecological Imperialism*, 1–40.

83. Lovelock quoted in Gray, *Straw Dogs*, 8.

84. See Gray, *Straw Dogs*, 110–16; *Silence of Animals*, 147–210.

85. Gray, *Straw Dogs*, 56.

stated in linguistic terms," and this philosophy of obliviousness pervades both the dominant traditions of analysis and postmodernism:

> "If a lion could talk, we could not understand him," the philosopher Ludwig Wittgenstein once said. "It's clear that Wittgenstein hadn't spent much time with lions," commented the gambler and conservationist John Aspinall. . . . By the time he had formulated his second philosophy, most clearly expressed in his *Philosophical Investigations*, Wittgenstein had given up the idea that language could mirror the world. Instead he denied that any sense could be given to the idea of a world existing apart from language. . . . He wrote: "The common behavior of mankind is the system of reference by means of which we interpret an unknown language." We might more truly say: The common behavior of animals is the system of reference by means of which we interpret the brute noises of humans.[86]

The suggestion here, I think, is that an environmental crisis is an evolutionary feature we share with all forms of flourishing life; it is a predicable outcome of natural history. The Earth will eventually check this species boom with an ecological bust. Our species' overreach, though, is exacerbated by its *culture* of deafness with regards to the rest of the natural world. We inhabit a vicious intraspecies circle, opening only for raiding and polluting.

The most extreme example of this phenomenon of Western enclosure is found in modern economic theories. Nature is considered an infinitely regenerative gift: The *free* origin of all property, labor, commodities, and use/exchange value. Nature is also the destination for waste created in production, circulation, and consumption—a profit making externality.[87] A promising theoretical movement is proposing a reconstruction of nature within commensurate ecological and economic models.[88] Nature's free goods and services are quantified and priced. This *natural capital* is then integrated into existing market mechanisms that enable us to calculate the *true ecological price* of commodities. By any measure, our current system is incredibly unaffordable and incommensurate. Further compounding the problem is the lack of viable options among current economic models. They reflect human aspirations that are anything but symbiotic.

---

86. Gray, *Straw Dogs*, 53–54.

87. See Karsten, "Nature in Economic Theories," 61–70; Immler, *Natur in der ökonomischen Theorie*.

88. See Costanza et al., "Value of the World's Ecosystem," 253–60; Hawken et al., *Natural Capitalism*, 1–21.

George Monbiot makes a startling observation on contemporary economic alternatives:

> Modern economics, whether informed by Marx or Keynes or Hayek, is premised on the notion that the planet has an infinite capacity to supply us with wealth and absorb our pollution. The cure to all ills is endless growth. Yet endless growth, in a finite world, is impossible. Pull this rug from under the dominant economic theories, and the whole system of thought collapses. And this, of course, is beyond contemplation. It mocks the dreams of both left and right, of every child and parent and worker. It destroys all notions of progress. If the engines of progress—technology and its amplification of human endeavor—have merely accelerated our rush to the brink, then everything we thought was true is false. Brought up to believe that it is better to light a candle than to curse the darkness, we are now discovering that it is better to curse the darkness than to burn your house down.[89]

These things may all be true, but added to them is perpetual political subterfuge, shutting out any discussion of economic presuppositions other than continued *growth*. We must trust capitalism to undo the immense damage it has a major hand in inflicting. Cleaning up must be made just as profitable (or more so) than messing up. There must be all gain, more *sustainable* growth, and no pain. Not surprisingly, direct confrontation with the problem continues to be elusive. "Scientific expertise," as Jay Foster points out, "cannot act as a surrogate for political will and moral commitment."[90] There are, and will be more, well-advertised, placebo ideas and programs, reinforcing (not challenging) the existing order of things. For example, what is emerging in the *Western Guilt Market* of carbon offsets is yet to be determined, but it seems to be falling into the all too familiar pattern of the rich visiting the consequences of their interests on the poor.[91] Without the will for reciprocal sacrifice, with the rich (within and between societies) relinquishing much more than the poor, symbiosis by way of natural capitalism is merely wishful thinking; it is a deceptive pretense for further immiseration and expropriation of the already vulnerable.

There are specific differences, then, that we do not share with other animals, vices all our own. Self-deception, sloth, and gluttony color our instincts much more than disproportionate violence. Like other animals, Gray concludes, we have an "itch for violence," but we are not "a uniquely

---

89. Monbiot, "Mocking Our Dreams," para. 7.
90. Foster, "Between Economics and Capital," 73.
91. See Checker, "Double Jeopardy," para. 1–6.

aggressive species," or even the most violent primate: "E. O. Wilson observes, 'if hamdryas baboons had nuclear weapons, they would destroy the world in a week.' Mass murder is a side effect of technological progress."[92] Human beings are primarily "peace-loving animals," and, "they are drawn to thinking, but at the same time they hate and fear the unsettling thinking brings."[93] *So, can Dionysus retire? Can the violent element of our evolutionary heritage withdraw from our relationship with the Earth? And, in that departure, open a communicative space of co-liberation?* The surprising answer is "YES." But we must somehow get beyond the absolute presuppositions that reinforce our complacent natures, our seductive illusions.

GREEN ANTHROPOCENTRISM REVISITED

Ecological pessimism is unexpectedly qualified. Ecological perdition may not be inevitable. Orientation to creation's symbiotic communication could possibly reroute our present course. John Gray calls it a long shot but, in the absence of any other plausible option, it seems to be the only one worth pursuing. Environmental violence is rooted in a vast and complex network of expedient practices. There must be disruption of established habits and moral inertias. Instinctual inclinations for comfort and thoughtlessness must be simultaneously challenged across multiple cultural strata and, perhaps, philosophy is just as good a place to start as any other. Can we meaningfully speak about communication between human beings and other creatures? Further, is it possible to develop a credible theory of communication that includes nonhuman beings and processes within an ethical community? Where the liberation from violence and the meeting of need through capacity is an operative feature of our renewed *animal virtues*?

Advocates of an anthropocentric view deny that such a project is possible. The gap between humans and the rest of nature is just too great. There are tremendous problems with *intra*human translation of often incommensurate languages. The problems of translation and interpretation with *inter*species communication undermine it as a workable option. The best we can do is to develop a moral accommodation. A more *humane* anthropocentrism ensures we impose only minimal damage on the environment; we get to preserve our exclusive species interests. This comfortable philosophical habit is no longer tenable. Anthropocentrism is neither symbiotic nor intercommunicative because it is fixed within a constellation of absolute presuppositions that exclude these options. Incommensurability is not just

---

92. Gray, *Straw Dogs*, 116, 91–92.
93. Gray, *Straw Dogs*, 116.

Stewardship of Sign

a matter of degree but of kind.[94] Green anthropocentrism, then, makes our *long shot* impossible; not just highly improbable. Modern *nature* has been considered many things, but it can never be *creation*: A semiotic presence included in our ethical considerations. Moral value depends on language as the ground of having intelligible ethical interests. In an otherwise silent universe, the human subject is the only being capable of language. Therefore, we are the lone center of value. On this view, human language is not a calculus—*zetetic*, *heuristic*, or *finding of finding*—that seeks commensurate vocabularies between us and creation. Human language is an impregnable wall that separates us from the rest of being. As Jaakko Hintikka (†2015) explains, in a cosmos like this "You are virtually a prisoner of your language."[95] There is no intelligible outside.

In *A Secular Age* (2007), Charles Taylor gives an account of the rise of the linguistically incarcerated human.[96] Modernity is characterized by the development of the "buffered self," which is part of a greater cultural drive "to produce some substitute for agape."[97] Stoic foundations underlie our modern socio-ecological formation. The centuries-long transformation produces a hybrid called, "Christianized Stoicism," and this phenomenon functions as a middle term between Christian and secular concepts of civilization.[98] On this bearing of thought, Taylor amplifies and clarifies many premises already put forward in this work.[99] With extraordinary mastery, he navigates a wild sea of cultural distinctions, theological knots, political aspirations, and historical contingencies. Still, on the human and environment relationship, certain persistent patterns arise within this period of hybridization. Like Christianity, Stoicism is pan-humanistic; the Stoics "really did conceive of solidarity as species wide," "seeing us as part of the great cosmopolis of all Gods and humans."[100] Unlike medieval creation, though, modern nature is not included in the universal city of Gods and humans. This crucial ethical change is a consequence of the difference between Stoic *ataraxia* and Christian agape. Moral *indifference to nature* becomes a basic attitude of this system of life. In his discussion of the most influential

---

94. See Williams, "Must a Concern," 233–40.
95. Hintikka, *Lingua Universalis vs. Calculus Ratiocinator*, 141.
96. See Taylor, *Secular Age*, 27–42.
97. Taylor, *Secular Age*, 27.
98. Taylor, *Secular Age*, 115. Taylor's magisterial account of the rise of neo-Stoic Christianity seems to confirm and deepen the author's limited sketch of the influence of modern mutations of Pelagianism. See Taylor, *Secular Age*, 114–58.
99. See Taylor, *Secular Age*, 27–376.
100. Taylor, *Secular Age*, 246.

neo-Stoic of the sixteenth century, Justus Lipsius (†1606), Taylor explains this key distinction:

> (a) Christianity sees us as in need of God's grace to liberate our good will, which is only potentially ours; where Stoicism appeals purely to our powers of reason and self-control; (b) Christianity sees the fullest realization of the good will in us in agape, our love of neighbor. Stoicism sees the wise person as having attained apatheia, a condition beyond passion. Now these two are not necessarily incompatible; agape could be conceived as a kind of passionless condition of strenuous benevolence. But Christian theology has steered away from this Stoicised reading, and with good Biblical reason. Christ of the Gospels is portrayed as being moved "in the bowels" by compassion (*splangnizesthai*); and his cries on the cross were hardly manifestations of apatheia. This has given the greatest difficulty to Christian theology in the early centuries, precisely because of the force of the Greek-derived idea that God is apathes; Jesus' obvious failure to meet this standard even became an argument for Arianism. But in the end orthodoxy refused the Stoicised solution.
>
> But this is just what Lipsius espouses. He rejects miseratio, or misericordia, the compassion of feeling, in favor of the compassion of active intervention, but on the basis of a full inner detachment.[101]

Stoic Christianity's idea of a more perfect human nature stresses detached interiority, control, and reasoned reflection over emotional expressions of solidarity, spontaneous action, and self-giving—love. This change of emphasis shapes a subtly gradual, but profound, reversal of ethical meaning. Being ethical is primarily *being for self, not being for others*. Selfishness, then, not selflessness, becomes the primary virtue. On the ground of being for others, Lipsius's idea of compassion through complete inner detachment is an ethical enigma. Why would a thoroughly disconnected, emotionally neutered, and needless self, move towards the other? The motivator would have to be either an arbitrary impulse or, most likely, instrumental reasons to further maximize self-sufficiency and control. Either way, ethics is first and foremost for me, here and now, and not for others, or any kind of abstract ideal: "Its notion of human flourishing makes no reference to something higher which humans should reverence, love or acknowledge."[102] For practitioners of *enlightened* self-love, being for others is still an option, but it is only preferable if it is reasonable to assume that my temporal welfare

---

101. Taylor, *Secular Age*, 115.
102. Taylor, *Secular Age*, 245.

will also be enhanced. Self-interest is presumed to be the rational ground of ethics.

Taylor depicts a revolution of *innocent self-love*. This great reversal of traditional Christian ethics "consists in a rehabilitation of ordinary, untransformed human desire and self-love, previously seen as an obstacle to universal justice/benevolence, which now is cast either as innocent, or as a positive force for good. The 'innocentizing' strategy paints human motivation as neutral; always a mode of self-love, it can either be well or badly, irrationally or rationally directed. Guided by reason it leads to justice and mutual aid."[103] The idea that I should sacrifice beyond what is maximizing for my benefit, or even against it, is irrational; it is against my solidarity with all other ethical self-seekers. For the Stoic Christian elite of the sixteenth and seventeenth centuries, who first took this view, it is also very bad taste, going against civilized refinement, and even proper cosmopolitan civilization itself.[104] Why would anyone with present wealth, status, and power intentionally inflict pain, impoverishment, and exclusion upon themselves for the sake of others who have none of these things? The idea of selflessness is no longer viewed as the basis of ethics, certainly, but it is also considered an irrational threat to the socio-ecological order to be built: "The successor to agape was to be held strictly within the bounds of measure, instrumental reason, and perhaps also good taste."[105] Without a prospect for a reciprocal benefit, an enlightened person simply does not risk herself for others.

Within this developing Stoic-Christian framework, temporal utopia replaces the heavenly kingdom to come. The ethical ideal changes from *being for others*: Enlightened people participate in *being for themselves*. If their self-love is truly rational, it will have the same mutually elevating side effect as previously ascribed to being for others. This cosmopolis is an ethical economy between humanity and the gods. The rest of being is excluded because reason (*language*) is the "spark of God within us."[106] Its fire resides nowhere else in the universe. This exceptional divine property makes us discontinuous with the rest of nature; it also provides the power to become the lords of nature: "The power to impose order on self and the world is God's power in us, which we have to recognize and nurture."[107] The cosmos of communication, "a universe of ordered signs," is now "a domain of asemeiotic

---

103. Taylor, *Secular Age*, 253.
104. See Taylor, *Secular Age*, 240–55.
105. Taylor, *Secular Age*, 247.
106. Taylor, *Secular Age*, 252.
107. Taylor, *Secular Age*, 235.

things."[108] Nature is a wild, dark, and mute profusion of disconnected bits and pieces. An ethical stance towards it is as nonsensical as it is irrational. The absence of reason-language signifies the nonexistence of autonomous order and moral value. There is no possibility for symbiotic partnership. This purely one-sided relationship is unobstructed by moral impediments. Nature is simply raw chaotic stuff. This unintelligible sphere is the precondition for human mediation. Our constructions produce something we can both understand and capitalize on. Amoral and incomprehensible natural objects easily become commodities; they can be exchanged by linguistic subjects in their ethical calculus for advancing mutual flourishing.

Green anthropocentrism is a change from these modern absolute presuppositions only in the sense that the selfish *individual* within the species is simply writ large as our individual species *per se*. We must unite to maximize our species wellbeing. Linguistic isolation is still assumed, as is anthropocentric mastery, and the impossibility of an ethical alliance with silent nature. However, our porous scientific models have somehow revealed that we are acting irrationally because we are undermining our welfare. We must become more rational by knowing where our true interests are found, using our technological powers to achieve them. The environment will be benefited as a spin-off of our *detached compassion*. Present selfishness must be sacrificed to further future selfishness. These environmental absolute presuppositions undermine our prospects for symbiosis. Stoic-Christian foundations must be unsettled; they are no *substitute* for agape.

ECO-AGAPISM

Ecclesia . . . nos sumus. Agapism is rarely in *good taste*, opposing and exposing the subtly vicious game of self-interest beneath the fine manners of the elite. Agapism sides with the crude, sweating, struggling, and dying multitude; it seeks expansive union—unlimited neighborliness finds its ground in the tragic nature of *all* life: Intrasocial, interspecies, and the physical universe that supports all things. Ethics becomes a multifaceted network of commensurate responses to need from com*passionate* capacity. Those that need are *the poor*. Their need communicates itself to those attuned by a receptivity mostly defined in nonlinguistic terms: *Animal virtues* in Gray's sense. The reality of suffering demands liberation—*soteria* (σωτηρία). To project an image of liberation in the postmodern context seems thoroughly passé. All narratives of liberation, supposedly, have been exposed as vehicles of power and oppression. Every postulate of another state of being is

---

108. Taylor, *Secular Age*, 98, 330.

a veiled attempt to rule over others. Nevertheless, discourses about the anthropogenic environmental crisis (and struggles of gender, race, economic inequality, and so on) are driven by images of liberation. Perhaps, if we are asking a near impossible thing, getting out of the environmental crisis, an equally improbable ethical principle is required.

We need to carefully revisit ideas of liberation: *Soteriologies*. The postmodern critique is not wrong, but it is a fallacy of accent on one type of soteriology. Edward Schillebeeckx (†2009) provides a helpful threefold distinction: "To sum up, one can speak of (i) horizontal and future soteriologies (which look for completely different social structures); (ii) vertical soteriologies (often apolitical in their, perhaps well-intended, religious liberation); (iii) religious and political soteriologies (in which progressive and political meaning of the religious is stressed)."[109] Many postmodern thinkers rightly condemn the first type's tendency to totalize a finite sociopolitical movement as the absolute disclosure of historical salvation. Horizontal soteriologies present transient forms of culture as definitive agents of closure on the meaning of historical process. In the extreme, whether Marxist-Leninist, fascist, or neo-liberal, these soteriologies legitimate and normalize various kinds of systemic violence to attain preconceived ideals, benefiting the priorities of minority elites. Horizontal soteriologies are instrumental: Calculating rationality renders most people and creaturely forms of life servile subjects of exploitation by dominant interests. Human communities and the biosphere are sacrificed on behalf of the interests of a dominant group.

Vertical soteriologies, by contrast, are fideistic, isolating salvation within a disembodied and apolitical interiority; withdrawn from social and ecological responsibilities, yearning for a post-historical event. Professed neutrality translates into passive participation in dominant systems of oppression. The *third type* attempts to avoid the excesses of immanence and transcendence characteristic of the instrumental and fideistic types, respectively: Neither totalizing nor renouncing the political. Emancipation without salvation is totalitarian. Salvation without emancipation is alienation. The present environmental crisis is the result of centuries of horizontal soteriologies, preying on nature as an instrumental means. During the same time, vertical soteriologies surrender creation. The environmental question, too, must seek a third way to liberation, integrating historical emancipation with divine salvation: *Freedom in the image of agape*.

Sigurd Bergmann recognizes this apparent fit of environmentalism with Christian doctrine. Creation is the subject of liberation; it is defined by

109. Schillebeeckx, *Christ*, 907.

communication and symbiosis. In *Geist der Natur befreit* (1995), he begins, in Latour's sense, the *resurrection* of Christian tradition in light of ecological concern, "where love for the poor is at the heart not only of ethics but also of theology and anthropology."[110] Bergmann's work is original, expansive, and very exploratory. He presents a common framework for the poor of creation: "The place where creatures struggle for the right of survival is just as holy as the place where the poor struggle for their human rights."[111] The ethical viability of this project depends on the development of a theory of communication that makes it meaningful to speak about a community of suffering and hope shared by different subjects of creation:

> One cannot develop a comprehensive theory of communication of this sort within utilitarian understanding of reality because the latter views only the more complex animals as physiologically capable of suffering in the first place. Nor is it possible within an anthropocentric construction, since such a perspective views only human beings as subjects. Within a sympathetic ecological understanding of nature, however, it is quite possible to view the relational patterns between organisms and their environment in this comprehensive fashion from the perspective of the experience of suffering.
>
> Here we no longer narrowly understand the concept of "suffering" merely as the physical pain of subjects, but rather more broadly as the "mutual exchange of suffering subjects with respect to ecological violence." Within this broader understanding, "suffering" applies not only to the algae that simply dies from lack of acidity, but also the heath whose botanical makeup is altered by air pollution, to the Indian child injured in the Bhopal, and to the small farmers in a Third World country who are robbed of their economic and cultural potential by the global financial policies of the rich.[112]

What Is the Agapist Meaning of Communication?

The language of other living creatures is a "wordless voice," a "silent song," distinguishing it from communication among human beings.[113] The focus on delineating a boundary between human beings and other creatures is

---

110. Bergmann, *Creation Set Free*, xiii.
111. Bergmann, *Creation Set Free*, 296.
112. Bergmann, *Creation Set Free*, 297.
113. Bergmann, *Creation Set Free*, 108.

based on the capacity for rational language: "The Stoics maintained that human beings alone possessed reason (logos)."[114] To complicate this presumed border, Bergmann develops the concept of *natural communication*. There is sign exchange within the cosmos in general and between sensuous creatures in particular. Natural communication, unlike the intrahuman kind, is unconditionally surrendered: "In that sense heaven, sunlight, and sea air all communicate themselves to all things in unrestricted love lacking all envy."[115] What Bergmann means by the capacity of physical creation for communication is this power to issue cogent signals: To guide, instruct, and even to silently proclaim. Creation is construed as a nexus of evolving texts. The "language of nature" does not necessarily assume the use of letters, sentences, and writing, but rather the exchange of information and meaning by signs: "Through its very existence before us, corporeal nature posits signs."[116] Even the etymology of the term *stoicheia* suggests that this is how the concept was understood—that is, the basic elements of the cosmos are signs; they form ever more intricate, dynamic, and wondrous arrangements, comprising our common sense (*sensus communis*) of things.[117]

Bergmann presents a fertile direction for socio-ecological *praxis*. The semiotic doctrine of creation authorizes common action for liberation, enfolding the poor of the world, not just our species. The presupposition of symbiotic mutuality becomes the human project of building proper institutions. We attempt, as we have before in human terms, to liberate the poor from need through the self-donation of our capacities. Bergmann draws from the deep well of certain, perhaps unfamiliar or unacceptable, theological concepts. Along with the non-propositional openings to communication found in perception, emotion, recognition, and physical performance, he includes spirit, soul, and will.[118] He rejects, however, the theological idea that perceiving creation as a semiotic partner in common struggle is (pre)determined by the bestowal of supernatural grace. Bergmann builds his ecological theology on the thought of Gregory of Nazianzus (†389 CE): "The world with its [communicative] presence" is grasped "through nature rather than through grace."[119] Put in Augustinian terms, the natural gift (*datum*) of communication is disclosed by all existents; the granting (*donum*)

---

114. Bergmann, *Creation Set Free*, 108.
115. Bergmann, *Creation Set Free*, 108.
116. Bergmann, *Creation Set Free*, 110.
117. See Bergmann, *Creation Set Free*, 109–10.
118. See Bergmann, *Creation Set Free*, 108–11.
119. Bergmann, *Creation Set Free*, 106.

of divine grace is an addition, raising some exceptional existents to God.[120] Acknowledging the validity of the former does not depend on the event of the latter. The *donum* reveals the transcendental ground of the *datum* but, in Bergmann's interpretation of Nazianzus, the purely immanent and autotelic *datum* is enough for the recognition of communication as a primary feature of the world. Graced and un-graced humanity, then, is still one exemplary creature in a far greater epistemic network:

> The adjective "epistemic" in Greek refers to the capacity to understand something. Living beings perceive various phenomena and processes in their surroundings, react to these perceptions, and communicate with their surroundings through various signs. All living beings can come to understand something external to themselves. Theological reference to the aesthetic-epistemological capacity of creatures implies that living beings are capable of perceiving their existence as that of creatures—as that of created beings. Although this assertion seems utterly meaningless under the conditions of Western rationality, it is well documented in the theological understanding of nature throughout the history of Christianity.[121]

Bergmann's proposal is not so much a full theory of communication, ethics, and liberation as it is a suggestive path within the context of specifically Christian concerns on environment. This agapist *return* to creation is a revision on much more *horizontal*, activist, and temporal grounds than what Alfred Edward Taylor (†1945) cites (in *vertical*, idealist, and contemplative terms) as the principal doctrine of the West before the ascent of Stoic Christian nature in the modern era: "The main doctrine, then, may be stated thus. Sense and thought are radically disparate, yet everywhere connected. Nature, the realm revealed to our senses, is only half-real, but it suggests a further reality which lies beyond itself. *It is a system of symbols*, and we ascend to truth by learning to pass from the symbols to the non-sensuous realities symbolized. Christian thought was dominated by this view of nature from St. Augustine to St. Thomas, and it has never really outgrown it."[122] Bergmann sidesteps the central Christian idealist tradition. He emphasizes the socio-ecological potentialities of alternatives present during the founding of Christianity. Love for the poor is the axiom of engagement, rehabilitating the fourth-century Cappadocian Fathers of Asia Minor—most notably, Nazianzus. Based on the Trinity, Gregory seeks to connect God's suffering

---

120. See Rorem, *Eriugena's Commentary*, 99–121.
121. Bergmann, *Creation Set Free*, 275.
122. Taylor, *Platonism and Its Influence*, 41–42.

with all creation. His cosmology transforms the *apatheia* of the Greek god into the passionate *pathos* of the Christian God who is intent on setting the entirety of creation free: Emancipation and salvation. Unlike Taylor's symbolic idealism, then, where what is important is *beyond* the visible world, Nazianzus (like Proclus) presents material creation as the principal site for liberation. "His focus is the connection between the life of society and the life of creation," Bergmann explains, "since nature and society are parts of *one* community: the fellowship of all fellow creatures."[123] Historical emancipation and divine salvation are coequal moments in the same process of liberation for all creation: "The goal of this liberation, however, is not freedom *from* the corporeal, but rather the freeing *of* the corporeal itself to a new life free from the power of evil. For Gregory the corporeal is not merely an instrument the human spirit uses for encountering God, but rather is itself an object of liberation by God. Gregory's theology associates the corporeal and spiritual in a necessary and mutually beneficial relationship such that both strive upward to God and both are set free together."[124]

Stewardship is an ethical praxis. The poor communicate their *corporeal* need—the *datum*. Their suffering and struggle (*agôn*) cry to our capacities for common action—the *donum*. Liberation means liberation *from* something (violence), *to* something (increased freedom and potential for flourishing), and *by* something (institutions of distributive socio-ecological justice—stewardship). Violence is involuntary privation; it is a restriction of free will (humans) and, more generally considered, intentional deprivation of potentiality by the structures of greed and domination (humans and creation). Gregory attributes a decisive role to human beings in mediating the redemption of the material world because we are the exceptional "seat of the image (*eikon*)" of God and, contrary to the moderns, the image is not defined by power: It is agape.[125] Such a perspective positions asceticism against the accumulation of wealth, truth against power, and love of the poor against self-love.

These complex threads require further clarification and development. The tradition of *creation as sign* is still not clearly understood. The convertibility of being and communication in the context of struggle for liberation is a revolutionary metaphysics, giving an ethical heart for a different kind of community. This fountainhead can serve as a source of mobilization, integrating, and transforming social and ecological aspects of signs and struggle—a rebirth of semiotic creation, liberation by and for the poor.

---

123. Bergmann, *Creation Set Free*, 142.
124. Bergmann, *Creation Set Free*, 141.
125. Bergmann, *Creation Set Free*, 141.

SEVEN

The Language of the Real
Classical and Christian

THIS CHAPTER FIRST EXPLORES the Classical antecedents of the Christian semiotic worldview; then, the formation of the Trinity, and its amendment of the concept of relationship. Finally, Christian commitment to relational divinity and reality retranslates the ontological status of the sign. In Classical presentations, signs are, for the most part, devalued as derivative representations of an archetypical reality: Transcendent (Plato) and immanent (Aristotle). Signs are also construed as raw events of sensory appearances within becoming without being (Stoics). Trinitarian and Incarnational theology presents the communication of signs as the imaging forth of the continual act of God's love, fulfilling itself in creation. The redemption of appearances institutes the symbolist worldview—a dynamic hermeneutics of *vestigia trinitatis*. We are called to love the world's communication just as God loves and communicates it. The world is a divine text, a *codex Dei* that humanity must learn to worthily interpret in order to be in the Trinity's image (*imago Dei*).

SIGNS OF BECOMING AND BEING

The philosophy of Heraclitus of Ephesus (†475 BCE) offers the initial waypoint. Plato gives us an influential characterization of Heraclitus as a philosopher of radical and multidimensional flux: "For no thing ever *is* but is always *coming to be*."[1] Becoming produces no being. Plato's interpretation of Heraclitus is heavily indebted to Cratylus (mid to late fifth century BCE), his former teacher and proponent of Heraclitean ideas. There is a double priority of process and strife; becoming is continuous transmutation of all things into one another. There are ceaseless cycles of opposition into reconciliation, and reconciliation into opposition, alternating creation and destruction.

Out of difference and accord come individual things. Within this process there are no absolute things. Everything is only a transition—a continuously perishing limit—between coming-to-be and passing away. The birth of Y is the death of X. The birth of Z is the death of Y. To be is to be a point between appearance and disappearance. Everything is established and sustained by a principle of transient order. Unities are common gatherings of oppositions; they display a temporary balance of forces and processes. Heraclitus calls an intelligible structural pattern by the name of *Logos* (Λόγος): "Therefore it is necessary to follow the common; but although the Logos is common the many live as though they had a private understanding" [Fr. 2].[2] Although apparently plural and discreet, all things are a confluence of relationships; they express the *common* (ξυνός) Logos. A regularity accounts for the recognition of something *different* from anything else—that is, a thing's unique principle of unity is what makes it identifiable as that thing and, by extension, not anything other than what it is. Paradoxically, then, in order to be different, unity must be presumed. When I recognize this glass as being a glass, for example, it is because a common type of conceptual-linguistic denotator is operational, but its operation must exclude all other conceptual-linguistic denotators. The event of identity (*is*) is also the event of difference (*is not*). Identity is an inseparable occasion of difference.

The Logos is not transparent communication; it shows and conceals itself through the medium of signs: "Nature," Heraclitus says, "loves to hide herself"; she is like, "the lord whose oracle is in Delphi, who neither declares plainly nor yet conceals, but gives a sign" [Fr. 123, 93].[3] Signs (semainei, σημαίνει) communicate the Logos in an enigmatic manner; they are double-edged enticements. Signs may stand for reality or they may lead us to error and illusion. Following Heraclitus's semiotics, Martin Heidegger captures the enigmatic, double-edged nature of signs: "Being-a-sign-for can itself be formalized as a *universal kind of relation*, so that the sign structure itself

---

1. Plato, "Theaetetus," 152d2–e8 (857). Translation revised by the author.
2. Kirk and Raven, *Presocratic Philosophers*, 188.
3. Kirk and Raven, *Presocratic Philosophers*, 193, 211.

provides an ontological clue for 'characterizing' any entity whatsoever."[4] The universe speaks clearly to us, inviting us to follow its trail of signs to the truth, but we are mostly confused and distracted by the wrong signs; they force, intoxicate, and deceive. We are never fully awake. We never encounter the pure disclosure of reality. Heraclitus [Fr. 1] uses the analogy of consciousness and sleep to distinguish, respectively, the Logos (truth) from *semainei* (perception). He delivers a severe verdict on our usual condition: Most human beings are sleepwalkers, existing in an atmosphere of dreams. Most lives are lived on behalf of lies, partial truths, without much connection to the real.

The Logos and its signs enfold cosmic, social, and psychological levels of communication and interpretation. *Heraclitus introduces the semiotic worldview into Western thought.* Thomas M. Robinson calls his doctrine, "the language of the real."[5] "For Heraclitus," Robinson explains, "the real in its rational respect, could have been conceived of as actually *uttering*, analogously to a human rational agent, on a cosmic scale and everlasting a (true) account of its own structure and operations that is periodically and no doubt imperfectly captured in language by people like Heraclitus."[6] Further, "That the real qua rational is conceived of by Heraclitus as eternally uttering an account of itself seems clear from his understanding of *logos* concerning the real as something to which one *listens* (Fr. 5)."[7] The universe may speak itself clearly, but we hear it through tangled knots of signs. Multivocity and complication indicate "that the very density of language itself can very frequently be an indicator of the density of the real itself and its operations."[8] The universe is "meaningful communication with a complex order," which Daniel W. Graham compares to "the modern distinction between objective and subjective interpretation," with the middle term of mediation being the crucial social element.[9] "All particular things are merely symbols; no one of them is a complete and independent expression of *the logos*," Francis M. Cornford (†1943) claims, and "this is true of the universe, no less than human society; it is *common* (ξυνός) to all things."[10] From Heraclitus, we get a convergence of ideas on the cosmos as a common *environment*.

4. Heidegger, *Being and Time*, 107–8.
5. Robinson, *Logos and Cosmos*, 41.
6. Robinson, *Logos and Cosmos*, 43.
7. Robinson, *Logos and Cosmos*, 43.
8. Robinson, *Logos and Cosmos*, 44.
9. Graham, *Texts of Early Greek Philosophy*, 18.
10. Cornford, *From Religion to Philosophy*, 186–87.

The Language of the Real

Environment is communication. The cosmos is a complex of cyclic relationships across multiple scales of being, enfolding and unfolding in dynamic events of, respectively, integration and disintegration. However, this *pluriverse* is not simply a bustling confusion of order and change with a few scattered signs to guide the perplexed. It is not arbitrarily arranged. Heraclitus presents justice as governing the order of communication between nomos (signs as appearances) and cosmos (logos as reality). Justice (dikē, δίκαιον) is not the exclusive preserve of human societies; it is a common feature of the cosmic Logos. Justice does not have to involve conflict, but it is a bipolar concept: Without strife (*is not*) there cannot be agreement (*is*). Conversely, without agreement (*is*) there cannot be strife (*is not*). Justice can be the mutual interpenetration of polarities; an exchange between contrary movements is temporarily achieved: Peace. The discord between human and natural orders of communication arises from static polarities. The normative (νόμος) and the actual (φύσις) orders of things are isolated from one another, conflicting with one another. This condition ought to give way to the *passing through* (διαϊόν) of one into the other.[11] Environmental justice is the constancy of proportion and intercommunication; the attunement that emerges when barriers are lifted between oppositions. The pursuit of common signs must follow the Logos. The consequences of not doing so are severe. The force of primal justice will be visited upon our world [Fr. 53, 80]. The Logos is a structure that "can support opposite processes," and our world's destruction is just as reasonable and just as its preservation through attunement.[12]

Heraclitean polarities and cycles are received by the Greeks with profound unease. The rule of Strife speaks darkly: Cosmic communication cannot (ultimately) escape retribution, force (*deinos*).[13] Self-revealing (*phusis*) is faithful to its self-concealing origination. Common signs of attunement all disintegrate before the primeval womb of violence from whence they emerged. For example, finding a way to cope with the communicative force of the world marks Plato's dialectical struggle to stabilize and enact the fragility of goodness.[14] According to Robinson, the Heraclitean notion of *the language of the real* is "taken over by Plato."[15] Catherine Pickstock also claims that Plato agrees with Heraclitus—that is, "The sensible realm is made up of signs," "all components of the phenomenal world are themselves

---

11. See Cornford, *From Religion to Philosophy*, 189.
12. Graham, *Texts of Early Greek Philosophy*, 190.
13. See Lloyd, *Polarity and Analogy*, 214–16.
14. See Bruns, *Hermeneutics*, 21–45
15. Robinson, *Logos and Cosmos*, 41.

signs," which form "a continuum on a single but variously-articulated plane."[16] Signs, though, are not irrevocably caught in the universal cycles of attunement and dissolution, characterizing becoming without being. They are invitations to "the higher realities in which they participate."[17] The kernel of the Good, not violence, is the vital thing itself. This cosmic substratum lies beneath the layers of signifying force occasioned by appearances.[18]

The *Logos* is not something that can be assumed; it is something to be realized or enacted (*praxis*) through dialectic. Signs are wild and equivocal, but dialectical decoding through recollection (*anamnesis*) tames the sign, reducing conflict as it leads us to the Logos. This process requires common *desire* (ἔρως) to disclose the "excellence of things in light of the form of the Good."[19] Λόγος is constantly being born. Desire is the energy that creates and holds together the assemblages of our concept-words, inscriptions, and icons; they are heuristic actions of pursuit and courtship. Signs are thoroughly relational because they *desire* something other than themselves, something other than signs—the Good, the True, and the Beautiful. Plato tells us the very name for "name" (ὄὄνομα) means "a being for which there is a search (*on hou masma estin*)."[20] Knowing, like loving, is a perilous affair of fantasy, intoxication, deceit, and infidelity. Through the close companionship of rigorous dialectic, however, right desiring is possible. The unbroken and iterative chain of signs is lured by the thing itself, becoming coterminous with true reality. Plato describes the experience as a "leaping spark" from the fourfold limit of signs to *the fifth*:

> There is a true doctrine, which I have often stated before, that stands in the way of the man who would dare to write even the least thing on such matters, and which it seems I am now called upon to repeat.
>
> For everything that exists there are three classes of objects through which knowledge about it must come; the knowledge itself is a fourth, and we must put as a fifth entity the actual object of knowledge which is the true reality. We have then, first, a name, second, a description, third, an image, and fourth, a knowledge of the object. Take a particular case if you want to understand the meaning of what I have just said; then apply the theory to every object in the same way.[21]

16. Pickstock, "Late Arrival of Language," 247.
17. Pickstock, "Late Arrival of Language," 247.
18. See Gadamer, *Plato's Dialectical Ethics*, 17–99.
19. Pickstock, "Late Arrival of Language," 248.
20. Plato, "Cratylus," 421a–c (138).
21. Plato, "Letters: VII," 341d–342c (1589).

Common dialectical minding (*synousia*) may, for a time, reveal the *oikeios logos ousias*: The order of the thing itself. Inhabiting the good (*aretē*) of a thing remains a place illuminated by a momentary fire. Initiates to *the fifth* are called to carefully, often secretly, guard its embers. Plato compares his adepts to "good helmsmen," and he warns them not to be "caught napping" on a darkening sea of signs.[22] If the flame extinguish itself, the approach of the storm is left unseen; they will face the "unexpected magnitude of the tempest and be so overwhelmed by its violence."[23]

The Stoic alternative reverses Plato's ontological priority of good ideas, returning to Heraclitus's cycles and polarities.[24] The Logos, though, is replaced by the void. Surface reality is the only communicative reality: Appearances are signs (*sōma*) open to the senses. They exist as events (*evenit*) that comprise the world. Only the void, not the Logos or the Good, exists beneath their relentless shifts of becoming. Plato's *words of being* are merely useful human conventions of speech and writing; what the Stoics call *lekta*: Ways of organizing and predicating occasions of perceptual communication, e.g., *pragma* (actions and passions), *katēgorēma* (types), and *axiōma* (propositions).[25] But, for the Stoics, Jeffrey Barnouw claims, "The propositional character of perceptions does not arrive from language."[26] It arrives from perception itself—that is, "What we perceive is real in the mode of fact, event, state of affairs."[27] There is no essential substratum: The senses are the only mediums of significance. It is always best to let our predicative powers follow the logic of experience; to let "*lekta* subsist in accordance with perception."[28] The study of signs is called semiotics and, to Galen (†c. 200 CE), for instance, it informs the practice of medicine: "Semiotics has for its parts the diagnosis of what is present and the prognosis of what is to come."[29] In the unstable world of becoming, the *logic of sense* communicates that which can be understood about what is and what will be.

In this kind of semiotic universe there are no moral absolutes, neither lies nor truth. There are adjustments to what happens within various régimes of signs. The indifference of the void's cosmic justice plays itself out. There

---

22. Plato, "Letters: VII," 351d (1589).

23. Plato, "Letters: VII," 351d (1589).

24. Aristotle's theory of language will be examined throughout the remaining analysis; it is a fundamental aspect of the semiotic worldview embedded in other topics of concern.

25. See Nuchelmans, *Theories of the Proposition*, 45–88.

26. Barnouw, *Propositional Perception*, 1.

27. Barnouw, *Propositional Perception*, 3.

28. Barnouw, *Propositional Perception*, 289.

29. Galen, *Three Treatises on the Natural Sciences*, 28.

is communication of sensual affects one must endure and welcome (*amor fati*), ceaselessly differentiating planes of auto-creation and auto-destruction perpetually interlock and disband. At the vital edge of immanence, the vanguard of becoming exists in harmony with the will of fate, constituting the event. To Gilles Deleuze (†1995), it means "willing that which occurs (*vouloir ce qui arrive*) insofar as it does occur."[30] What is, is also what ought to be. Welcome *all* experience as a gift: Beyond this lies nothing.

THE CHRISTIAN CONCEPT OF RELATIONSHIP

The Heraclitean atmosphere never lifts from the ancients. Nature as sign remains a poem of destabilizing lies and force to ameliorate or indifferent affects to courageously affirm. The Christian amendment offers something fundamentally different; it rehabilitates the universe, which is also a world of communication, of signs. The Trinity transfigures the very marrow of ancient presuppositions. Λόγος is love's communication: Creation.[31] Christ is the Sign of signs; He is a cosmic hermeneutical principle. Edward Morgan claims the Incarnation "entails a transformation of the material order at the behest of a transformation of the symbolic one."[32] The Christian *Weltanschauung* is a semiotic metaphysics of love. Everything that exists proclaims the Trinity. "He placed Himself in the order of signs, in the order of symbols," Maurice de la Taille (†1933) proclaims, "to have the joy of symbolizing and, by symbolizing it, of building up the mystical Body of which we are the members."[33] The Christian revelation shows that the sign subsists within the Godhead Itself. The sign is not an imitation (or *intimation*) of a more perfect reality; it is not inferior, duplicitous, violent, or indifferent. Semiotic redemption expresses the personal image, located in the creative economy of the world. Creation is also something we do. "This is the communication of the image," Dorothy L. Sayers (†1957) says, "something that puts new knowledge of ourselves in our grasp."[34] Divine information creates a person, "the very image in which reality knows itself and communicates itself in power."[35] Creativity in the image of love liberates the realm of signs,

---

30. Deleuze, *Logic of Sense*, 143.

31. On the *real distinction* between the Heraclitean Logos of violence and the Johannine Logos of love, see Girard, *Things Hidden since the Foundation of the World*, 263–80.

32. Morgan, *Incarnation of the Word*, 70.

33. Taille, *Mystery of Faith*, 179.

34. Sayers, "Toward a Christian Esthetic," 40, 42.

35. Sayers, "Toward a Christian Esthetic," 42.

redeeming their affliction; it reveals their true symbolic face, instituting a novel kind of *relationship*.

Aristotle's Accidental Category of Relation

Relations are of prime theological importance. The Christian doctrine of the Trinity appropriates Aristotle's substance-accident ontology. The category of relation moves from the *least of all things* (*Metaphysics* 14.1, 1088a20) to the most important thing because the God of Christianity is a *relational God*.[36] "The only category applicable to God other than substance," Julius R. Weinberg (†1971) confirms, "is, accordingly, relation."[37] The elevation of relation from an Aristotelian accident of finite substance to Christian Godhead raises the ontological status of its sacred and secular vehicle: The sign. An accident is defined as *being in another* or *inherence* in a substance. Substance is *being in itself*. Relation, though, is primarily identified as *being to another*. To *pros ti* means (literally) *that which is towards something*; it is the order of one thing to another.

Relation is an accident of substance that reveals the connections between things, but it depends on substance and other accidents for its degree of reality. "The relative," to Aristotle, "is least of all things a real thing or substance" (*Metaphysics* 14.1, 1088a20).[38] Accidents gain existence through their inherence in a substance. Relations are defined through other categorical accidents; they are doubly removed from the source of existence, having minimal reality. There is nothing "relative without being so as something else" (*Metaphysics* 14.1, 1088a27). These relations are called *categorical* because of their derivative standing. Relation is unique because it is the syncategorical division of being; it enjoins the universe of things, both *ad intra* and *ad extra*. For example, there are relations between quantities (*ad intra*) and between quantities and qualities (*ad extra*).

Aristotle has two definitions of relation: (1) discursive—that which is said to be to another; and (2) ontological—that which really connects one

---

36. See Cooper, *Panentheism*, 13–30.

37. Weinberg, *Abstraction, Relation, and Induction*, 87. Weinberg's Western Christian claim must be qualified with Eastern Christianity's development of Aristotle's category of activity. Eastern Christianity posits divine activities—*energeiai* or operations—as distinct from divine relations and divine substance. Western Christianity denies the Eastern doctrine of divine energies, but there is an appropriation of many of their functions into the doctrine of divine relations and divine *esse*. See Bradshaw, *Aristotle East and West*, xi–xii, 164–165, 242–277, esp. 251.

38. All quotations of Aristotle's *Metaphysics* are from vol. 2 of Aristotle, *Complete Works*.

thing to another.[39] According to the first definition, "Things are called relative, which, being either said to be of something else or related to something else, are explained by reference to that other thing" (*Categories* 7, 6a37).[40] Aristotle alters this first definition to keep substance from being relational—that is, he intentionally excludes substance from the ontological category of relation, i.e., *essential relativity*, upholding the dialectical gap between the merely said and the independently real: "Indeed, if our definition of that which is relative was complete, it is very difficult, if not impossible to prove that no substance is relative. If, however, our definition was not complete, if those things only are properly called relative in the case of which relation to an external object is a necessary condition of existence, perhaps some explanation of the dilemma can be found. The former definition does indeed apply to all relatives, but the fact that a thing is explained with reference to something else does not make it essentially relative" (*Categories* 7, 8a28). There are two ways, then, in which something can be relative: In the order of discourse and in the order of real being. Substance can *be said* to be relative. Yet, to Aristotle, this claim is only a manner of speaking; it does not obtain to the way things have existence. Just because a substantial thing can be explained in relative terms does not mean it is essentially relative. Any entity, including substance, can be explained in terms of its relations to others, but not all entities are essentially relative to others. Essential relativity is a property of accidents, not substance. Legitimate discursive claims refer to the ties between them.

Even if we accept that relation is in fact an exceptional accident—both *in and to another*—it seems to be something other than the least significant category. Even though it is posterior in the order of being to substance and all other accidents, Aristotle admits relation is an ultimate condition of accidental being. Relations, however, are not dynamically operative; they are not capable of constructing things. The actualizing function of a thing is the exclusive preserve of substantial form. "Therefore," Aristotle says, "what we seek is the cause, i.e., the form, by reason of which the matter is some definite thing" (*Metaphysics* 7.17, 1041b5). He explicitly recoils from the category of relation; it is denied entry to the domain of potential and actual substance. Aristotle is, I think, quite clear:

> A sign that the relative is least of all a substance and a real thing
> is the fact that it alone has no proper generation or destruction
> or movement, as in quantity there is increase and diminution,

---

39. On this key distinction, see Cavarnos, *Classical Theory of Relations*, 41–45.

40. All quotations of Aristotle's *Categories* are from vol. 1 of Aristotle, *Complete Works*.

in quality alteration, in place locomotion, in substance simple generation and destruction. The relative has no proper change; for, without changing, a thing will be now greater and now less or equal, if that with which it is compared has changed in quantity. And the matter of each thing, and therefore of substance, must be that which is potentially of the nature in question; but the relative is neither potentially nor actually substance. It is strange, then, or rather impossible, to make non-substance an element in, and prior to, substance; for all the categories are posterior (*Metaphysics* 14.1, 1088a30).

In his *Nicomachean Ethics*, Aristotle restates this position to deny the reality and *relatability* of Plato's Form of the Good: "A thing-as-such, i.e., a substance, is by nature prior to a relation into which it can enter: relatedness is, as it were, an offshoot or logical accident of substance. Consequently, there cannot be a Form common to the good-as-such and the good as relation" (*Ethics* 1.6, 1096a20–22).[41] Forms and their relations cannot be separate (*chorista*) from actually existing singulars upon which they depend for their minimal being. To defend the separability and relatedness of forms is to fall into irrationality: Contradiction and regress. If the Form of the Good is itself, it is unrelatable, thus unintelligible. But if it is relatable to several singulars, each one being good by participating in it, then it ceases being inseparable; stops being just itself to be communicable to its members: It is and is not separable (*contradiction*). Furthermore, if the Form of the Good is relatable, we now have the separable Form of the Good and its good things to account for as a new collection: Separable Form + its things, which itself will need participation in the unrelatable Form of the Good. But if it can participate, then the Form of the Good ceases to be just itself, creating yet another new collection of things in need of participation in the same contradictory ground *ad infinitum*.

For these reasons (and more), Aristotle holds to the primacy of singular substances. His syllogism is perfectly valid: All accidents are posterior to substance. / Relation is an accident. / Therefore, relation is posterior to substance. But what if relation is included in the domain of substance? It is a question posed, for precise theological reasons, by the Church Fathers.

---

41. Aristotle, *Nicomachean Ethics*, 11.

Substantial Relationships & The Trinity

Substantial relations are primary features of the Christian God.[42] These relations account for the Persons of the Trinity—their unity and difference. "God," in the Christian sense, Maximus Confessor (†662 CE) explains, "is identically Monad and Triad."[43] Further, according to Gregory of Nyssa (†394 CE), the theological revolution of the Trinity preserves "the middle between the two conceptions [of polytheism and undifferentiated unity], destroying each heresy and yet accepting everything useful from each."[44] When speaking of the Trinity, we are "speaking of the same thing as being both conjoined and parted."[45] The doctrine of the Trinity cannot be three Gods, but the divine substance has to consist of the Father, the Son, and the Holy Spirit, and they have to be understood as singular. Communion and distinction must be systematically accounted for. But how?

To the fourth-century Cappadocian Fathers of Asia Minor, the answer to the riddle lies in further appropriation and displacement of Aristotle's *Categories*. Formal substance (οὐσια) is the principal category the early Church Fathers adopt to understand the nature of the Trinity. Substance is *being through itself*, not through another; it is that which subsists by itself, in itself, and does not have its being in another. A substance has no need of another for its unity, existing independently of its connections to other things. Self-identical immediacy means a substance is *essentially discontinuous* with the rest of being. Aristotle describes primary substance as "that which everything is predicated, while it is itself not predicated of anything else" (*Metaphysics* 7.3, 1028b36). To be a finite singular thing is to be a substance. Self-subsistent actuality determines its own particularization—to be *this* entity and no other. The principle of its generation is not common to anything else; *it is not owed elsewhere*. When transposed to the Christian Godhead, formal substance provides a foundation for comprehending divine singularity and uniqueness. God is pure actuality (*actus purus*), containing no potentiality. However, divine unity is achieved at the expense of undermining the reality and the plurality of Persons—their belonging to each other, and to the created world. The Persons of the Trinity must be accounted for.

The exceptional properties of relation already noted (and devalued) by Aristotle, i.e., *having no proper generation, destruction, movement, or change*, present themselves in a promising theological light. After substance, relation

---

42. See Stead, *Divine Substance*, 164–66.
43. Maximus Confessor, *Selected Writings*, 14.
44. Gregory of Nyssa quoted in Pelikan, *Christianity and Classical Culture*, 32–33.
45. Gregory of Nyssa quoted in Pelikan, *Christianity and Classical Culture*, 33.

appears to be the least temporally constrained; it seems to escape the limitations of the other accidental categories, applying to finite being. Relation, like substance, can circumscribe divine infinity: Pure existence through which all existents depend for their creation and finite preservation. Aristotle's enigmatic division of reality becomes the foremost conceptual fabric of the Trinity, but it is a substantial category, and not an accidental one. The Christian sense of relationship also draws from other sources: Stoic ethics and Neoplatonic metaphysics. This worldview founding *theologoumenon* is primarily attributed to Gregory Nazianzus.[46] He reaches this insight while engaging in a dispute with the Eunomian brand of Arianism. In a highly charged political atmosphere, Nazianzus defends the Trinity against a Post-Nicene, Arian counter-offensive.

Roman Emperor Flavius Valerius Constantinus (†337 CE) converts to Christianity in 312 CE. His vision for a unified Christian empire requires a program of theological syncretism. H. A. Drake claims Constantine's goal is "divinely favored, monotheistic empire."[47] If the empire is to be unified and sectarian conflict avoided, Christianity must have a common doctrine. Ralph Martin Novak draws the connection between theological and political agendas: "Constantine appears to have believed that Christianity could be made to serve as a source of unity and strength for Rome's empire by establishing a strong common bond among its many peoples. Such a purpose would explain why after his conversion Constantine was so troubled by the ferocious doctrinal disputes of the early fourth-century CE Christian Church."[48] Constantine attempts to establish a unified voice for *imperial Christianity*; he supervises its creation at the Council of Nicaea in the summer of 325 CE. The central theological dispute dividing the Christian community concerns the relation between the Father and the Son in the Godhead. The tradition represented by Arius (†336 CE) denies the co-eternality and equality of the Son with the Father. Trinitarians claim the opposite view. According to Rowan Williams, "Imperial authority intervenes to make possible a universal, 'ecumenical' solution, in accord with Constantine's own goal of homogenizing his potentially chaotic empire," and,

---

46. See Chevalier, *S. Augustin*, 141–59; TeSelle, *Augustine the Theologian*, 294–96; Lossky, *Mystical Theology of the Eastern Church*, 44–54. There are clear intimations of this theological move in the work of fellow Cappadocian, Trinitarian, and contemporary of Gregory, Basil of Caesarea, and another concurrent version of *subsistent-relations* in the theology of Gaius Marius Victorinus. On the former, see Basil of Caesarea, *Against Eunomius*, 121, 142–43; Wolfson, *Faith, Trinity, Incarnation*, 340–42. On the latter, see Clark, "Introduction," 13–17.

47. Drake, *Constantine and the Bishops*, 205.

48. Novak, *Christianity and the Roman Empire*, 171.

consequently, "We are witnessing a new development in Christian reflection on the boundaries and definition of the Church."[49] In the end, the Trinitarians prevail: The Son is declared *consubstantial* (ὁμοούσιος; homoousias) with the Father.[50] Richard Paul Vaggione explains the problem that follows the victorious Nicene *homoousians*: "The mediating formulae do not define the grounds on which they are to be accepted," which leads to "a larger and more systematic discussion of the meaning of relationship as such."[51] In a foundational sense, the legitimacy and survival of Nicene Christianity depends upon a successful doctrine of divine relations.

This lack of conceptual ground leads to a second and more radical version of Arianism. Eunomius (†c. 394 CE), also a Cappadocian, represents the second generation and most extreme version of Arian thought. Together with his teacher, Aëtius (†367 CE), Eunomius denies the equality (*homoiousios*) and identity (*homoousios*) of substance between the Father and the Son. Only the Father is God because He is a complete and undivided infinite substance:

> This Only-begotten God is not to be compared either with the one who begot him or with the Holy Spirit who was made through him, for he is less than the one in being "a thing made," and greater than the other in being a maker. . . . For we confess that only the Son was begotten of the Father and that he is subject to him in essence and in will, believing him to be neither *homoousios* nor *homoiousios*, since one implies a generation and division of essence and the other an equality. . . . Anything derived from a source is secondary to the source; therefore the Son is secondary to the Father, not *homoousios*. If he is *homoousios*, the one Godhead must be cut in two; the Son cannot be *homoousios*. We neither believe that the Father is begotten or that the Son is unbegotten, but that what the Son is everlastingly is what he is also rightly called: Offspring, obedient Son, most perfect Minister of the whole creation and will of the Father, ministering for the maintenance and preservation of all existing things, for the giving of the Law to mankind, for the ordering of the world and for providential care. . . . In all these things the pre-eminence and sole supremacy of God is preserved, for the Holy spirit is clearly subject to Christ, as are all things, while the Son himself is subject to his "God and Father."[52]

49. Williams, *Arius*, 86–87.
50. For the history of the term before Nicaea, see Stead, *Divine Substance*, 190–91.
51. Vaggione, *Eunomius of Cyzicus*, 205, 71.
52. Eunomius, *Eunomius*, 69, 182, 71.

The Language of the Real

Nazianzus's crucial adjustment for the development of the Trinity seems to have come in response to the Eunomian argument that whatever is said of God must be said according to substance or *essence* and not according to accident. The Father and the Son cannot be equal (*homoiousios*) because equality is a quality—an accident of substance—and God is free of all accidents of essence. Substance is that which is in itself, and not in another; therefore, if the substance of the Father is ungenerated, the Son, who is generated, cannot be the same substance (*homoousios*) as the Father. The Son is a different substance than the Father because he is begotten. The Son is a distinct, subordinate, or *secondary substance*. Eugene TeSelle tells us, "Gregory saw that the only solution was to transcend the opposition between substance and accident and speak of relation (σχέσις [*Or.* 29, 16])."[53] "God (Θέος)," Nazianzus asserts, "is a relational, not an absolute term."[54] Gregory gives us an example, "'Father' designates neither the substance nor the activity, but the relationship, the manner of being which holds good between the Father and the Son."[55] There is difference within the Trinity, but it is not a hierarchical ontological difference between discreet substances; it is a difference of "relationship," σχέσεως, within one substance.[56] The Father is ranked prior to the Son in terms of relationship; not in terms of difference of substance. Relational difference makes consubstantiality intelligible and defensible. As Nazianzus explains, "The aim is to safeguard the distinctiveness of the three persons within the single nature and quality of the Godhead. The Son is not the Father; there is one Father. Yet he is whatever the Father is. The Spirit is not the Son because he is from God; there is only one Only-begotten. Yet whatever the Son is, he is. The three are a single whole in their Godhead and the single whole is three in its individual distinctions."[57] The divine concept of equality has difference as its ground. Difference does not mean subordination or division of essence. The Persons are equal and different Relationships.

Skhesis or σχέσις derives from the Greek verb ἔχω, to have. In this sense, having means making something one's own. The act of appropriation

---

53. TeSelle, *Augustine the Theologian*, 295. Nazianzus's usage of σχέσις seems to be derived from his teacher, Didymus the Blind (see Norris, *Faith gives Fullness to Reasoning*, 151). On the Alexandrine, Neoplatonic influence, see Plaxco, "Didymus the Blind." Other traditions attribute the original use of relation as an explanation of the meaning of the terms "Father" and "Son" to Basil of Ancyra and Epiphanius of Salamis (see Chevalier, *S. Augustin*, 117–26, 161).

54. Nazianzus, *Oration* 30.18, in Norris, *Faith Gives Fullness to Reasoning*, 274.

55. Nazianzus, *Oration* 29.16, in Norris, *Faith Gives Fullness to Reasoning*, 255.

56. Nazianzus, *Oration* 31.9, in Norris, *Faith Gives Fullness to Reasoning*, 283.

57. Nazianzus, *Oration* 31.9, in Norris, *Faith Gives Fullness to Reasoning*, 283.

enjoins one thing to another. This tie constitutes the very being of a thing. *Skhesis* connotes an intimate kind of relationship to another. Having is liberating something to its own place of self-determination. This *communication of difference* is an event of relationship, belonging to essence. In other words, σχέσις is substantial relationship, securing real diversity without division of essence. Each Person of the Trinity belongs equally to the other two as one substance, but each Person gains its distinctive autonomy in and through mutual belonging. The inseparability of the divine Persons entails dynamic three-way reciprocity between the Father, the Son, and the Holy Spirit. *Skhesis means this essential triadic relationship*. Nazianzus adopts the term περιχώρησις (*perichoresis*) to clarify the properties of triadic relationships. *Perichoral differences* proceed through one another, resolving themselves into one another—simultaneous coalescence of difference through unity and unity through difference. Verna Harrison claims this tri-interpenetration "genuinely unites while preserving distinctness, and thus stands at the heart of a Christian ontology of Love."[58] Therefore, perichoresis is the foe of totalizing homogeneity. Individual uniqueness is not diminished by the beloved community. The Trinity is the principle of heterogeneity—*personality*.

To Nazianzus, divine differentiating (διαφέρω) suggests parental generation. "What he had in mind," TeSelle concludes, "was the relationship of parent and offspring, which involves both an identity of nature and a distinction between begetter and begotten; thus 'unbegottenness' is not a characteristic of the essence of God but of the relation of the Father to the Son, and the begetter and the begotten must be both distinct (because of the relation) and of the same nature (*Or.* 29, 10–12)."[59] Gregory's "relationship of generation in finite life is transitory, coming into play for a time and then ceasing to have reality after the offspring has become a distinct being, while in God there is neither beginning nor cessation of a real relation between begetter and begotten."[60] *Skhesis* continues even when its terms (ground and terminus) disappear. Within this life of inevitable loss, there is a remainder: A loving touch of divinity. In one of Nazianzus's most beautiful passages, we read the following: "We also stem from a pair, not a single being, making us be divided and become human beings, gradually, and maybe not even human beings of the kind we are intended to be. The ties are dissolved by one side or the other, so that only the relationships remain, bereft of the realities."[61]

58. Harrison, "Perichoresis in the Greek Fathers," 65.
59. TeSelle, *Augustine the Theologian*, 295.
60. TeSelle, *Augustine the Theologian*, 296.
61. Nazianzus, *Oration* 29.5, in Norris, *Faith Gives Fullness to Reasoning*, 247.

Relativities: Ta Pros Ti and Skhesis

The Trinity imparts a relational *Weltanschauung*. Denis Edwards puts forward the proposition that "Once the nature of God is understood as relational, then this suggests that the fundamental nature of all reality is relational."[62] The principal ontological category is "being-in-relation."[63] Joseph Ratzinger agrees, and he develops the notion considerably:

> Therein lies concealed a revolution in man's view of the world: the sole dominion of thinking in terms of substance has ended; relation is discovered as an equally valid primordial reality. It becomes possible to surmount what we call today 'objectifying thought'; a new plane of being comes into view. It is probably true to say that the task imposed on philosophy as a result of these facts is far from being completed—so much does modern thought depend on the possibilities thus disclosed, without which it would be inconceivable.[64]

Skhesis is the triadic fountainhead of this tradition. This essential relation of the Trinity communicates itself to creation, communicating communicativity. The origin and features of this kind of relationship are still not well understood. They are often confused with (and reduced to) relation presented in Aristotle's substance-accident ontology.

Aristotle's Aporetic Relatives

To Aristotle, "categorical predicates indicate distinct ways in which things exist" but, for the most part, he reserves *pros ti* (πρός τι) to denote terms of discourse.[65] Aristotle preserves an *aporia* (Ἀπορία; "not passable") between relation in the orders of discourse and real being. Learning how to navigate past aporetic obstructions, to untie their *knots*, as Joseph Owens (†2005) best describes it, is the proper *dialectical modus operandi* of his (and Plato's) philosophy.[66] The aim of Aristotle's dialectical logic, then, is not to subsume or erase either side of the gap between discursive and real relations. Dialectical progress on the nature of relation is not possible without this division; it is required for provisional integration. Edward Booth deepens Owens's

---

62. Edwards, *God of Evolution*, 26–27.
63. Edwards, *God of Evolution*, 28.
64. Ratzinger, *Introduction to Christianity*, 184.
65. Weinberg, *Abstraction, Relation, and Induction*, 68.
66. See Owens, *Doctrine of Being in Aristotelian Metaphysics*, 107–14.

insight: "At first sight the acknowledged and unacknowledged aporias seem to be nothing but a statement of insoluble difficulties; but this is not the case."[67] Rather, "To appreciate the aporia from within is a mark of competence; like an initiate he then perceives what kind of problem the philosopher again and again attempts to resolve, what limits the factors that refuse to come together, their area of operation and their area of independence; and what kind of a partial answer is temporarily tolerable."[68] As envisioned by Aristotle, logic is evaluative and heuristic training for living dialectic. Discursive formalization is a precise locating device for judicious recollection, necessitating shared or *joint* action.[69]

Hans-Georg Gadamer (†2002) claims "*reciprocal koinonia* (fellowship, kinship)" is indispensable for dialectic.[70] But *cooperation* (eirene) cannot give the final account on relation. The medium of the *Logos* (the proper order of being in discourse) can bring us to the leap-off point. The logical precipice is the present dialectical limit of signification enough to be enacted by the good of a thing. The dialectical and aporetic course of questioning seeks to possess the right path, the way of clear passage, to where we *participate* (methexis) in the real presencing of things themselves. Aristotle's methodological procedure is a process of commensurate integration of signs and reality. He turns from the terms that are said to the things that are. Aristotle provides a classification scheme for predicates, an ontological framework for things, and a medium of their integration, holding true for the bond between language and world. Linguistic entities are divided into ultimate subjects that denote the actual things *that are said* to comprise ultimate subjects—that is, kinds of existents naturally separate into subjects and predicates. The conceptual structure of language reveals the structure of reality. There is an exchange of communication. Meaning (*pragma*) is securely anchored in the world, sharing itself with our naturally occurring concepts (*pathema*).

Linguistic relatives can interweave with their actual counterparts without diminishing the reality of singular substances. Each side reflects the other, needing and belonging to the other. Knowledge is joyful reunion of language and world. Linguistic and real relatives integrate, and, by this integration, they communicate the formal actuality of substances as concepts (*pathema*). John Herman Randall Jr. (†1980) provides a graceful summary: "The *ousia* expressed in statement leads beyond statement to the

---

67. Booth, *Aristotelian Aporetic Ontology*, 2.
68. Booth, *Aristotelian Aporetic Ontology*, 2.
69. See Scott, "Problem of Demonstration in Aristotle."
70. Gadamer, *Plato's Dialectical Ethics*, 91.

ousia encountered in its natural operations. Starting with the things that are said, *ta legomena*, what things can be said to be, we are led to *ta onta*, to things themselves."[71] Humans are capable of real knowledge. However, the correlation of terms with the categories of existents, i.e., extralinguistic states of affairs, cannot simply be assumed; it must be carefully achieved in the breach between word and world. This place is always just beyond the limit of articulation, but *we* can inhabit and enact it. The dialectical process is perpetually open and revisable. For example, a future dialectic on relation will navigate under different conditions, locating different integration points; they are places of the Good in the aporetic gap.

The goal of logically audited dialectic is not sophistical refutation, reducing difference to same, the many to the closure of the one. The *rhetorical eristic* of eliminating opposing viewpoints is, for Gadamer, replaced by "liberating opponents for a shared substantive enquiry."[72] The discursive action of one to many and many to one "progressively discloses the object, continually addressing it as something different, despite the contradiction between one and the many which is inherent in so doing."[73] Common dialectical desire is driven by singular fragility and *need* (agôn). Aristotle, like Plato, recognizes the destructive communicative power of aporetic difference. We either learn *to sign* together, letting difference and the Logos liberate us, or we face social and ecological shipwreck.

The Aristotelian *aporia* on relation provides the ground for influential Latin debates between *nominalists* and *realists*.[74] The former position affirms logical and cognitive relations, denying their extra-mental being; the latter maintain the reality of both. The *dialectical and aporetic ethics* of the ancients is caught in *knots of eristic* theo-political conflicts within Christendom. This obscure and highly technical dispute conveys significant implications for the philosophical direction of Western culture. A thinker's position on relations indicates his loyalties to certain ideas about power, community, and individuality; along with the current figures and movements said to embody them. The fallout of this dispute, favoring nominalism, forms the atmosphere of modernity.[75] What this narrative tends to overlook is the relationship-semiotic tradition; it is lost in the debris.

71. Randall Jr., *Aristotle*, 113.

72. Gadamer, *Plato's Dialectical Ethics*, 57.

73. Gadamer, *Plato's Dialectical Ethics*, 19.

74. See Henninger, *Relations*, 1–12; Weinberg, *Abstraction, Relation, and Induction*, 86–119. For the overlapping debate on universals, see Spade, "Introduction," vii–xviii.

75. See Gilson, *History of Christian Philosophy*, 491–94; Heidegger, *Fundamental Concepts of Metaphysics*, 51–52; Doyle, "Introduction," 9–29; Deely, *Four Ages of Understanding*, 394–407.

Simplicius and Constitutive Relationships

The triadic communicative ontology of *skhesis* has a genealogy distinct from Aristotle's substance-accident ontology of *pros ti*. Scholastic attempts to integrate both frameworks complicate and obscure *being-in-relation*. Unhinged from its ancient aporetic milieu, Aristotelian philosophy has a compelling nominalist orientation: The priority of individualistic substance and the treatment of relation as the least real accident, which is primarily intelligible within the realm of mind-discourse. An *eristic* philosophy of refutation seems to favor the elimination of extra-mental relations as an unnecessary hypothesis or ontological commitment. Being is its proper logical structure.

Skhesis (σχέσις) is the term for *relationship* or relation in itself; it emerges from the Stoic categorical framework: Substratum (ὑποκείμενον), quality (ποιός), disposition (πὼς ἔχον) and relative disposition (πρός τί πως ἔχον or σχέσις).[76] Although the categories are found separately in various fragments of Stoic writers, there is scant evidence of a *fourfold* ontological system.[77] They do not seem to be listed together any earlier than Simplicius (†c. 560 CE) and Plotinus.[78] The primary Stoic sources on *skhesis* are Zeno and his student Aristo (†c. 260 BCE). To Zeno, relative disposition is dependent on our judgment; it is defined in terms of four virtues: Wisdom, courage, moderation, and justice. Virtues are internal compartments; they are correlative and interchangeable powers to relate to an external world. Plutarch (†c. 120 CE) attributes to Zeno the view that "virtue is one, and only differs in its relations (*scheseis*) to things according to its actions."[79] According to Margaret E. Reesor, Aristo "recognized one virtue called by several names according to their relation."[80] The division between internal and external governs Stoic ethical logic. *Skhesis* is the internal differentiation of the virtues, which are regarded as several, but they are inseparable aspects of wisdom. For example, courage is wisdom in things to be endured, and justice is wisdom in things to be distributed. The entities of the external world impinge on us. The Stoic Sage affects the appropriate virtuous response; this internal relationship translates into an external disposition (πὼς ἔχον) towards the world of substratum (ὑποκείμενον) and quality (ποιός).

---

76. See Weinberg, *Abstraction, Relation, and Induction*, 79–80; Gerson, "Categories and the Tradition," 79–83.

77. On the "intractable" problem of sources, see Colish, *Stoic Tradition*, 21–22.

78. See Reesor, "Stoic Categories," 63.

79. Pearson, *Fragments of Zeno and Cleanthes*, 173–74, quoted in Cavarnos, *Hellenic-Christian Philosophical Tradition*, 77.

80. Reesor, "Stoic Categories," 65.

It is the Neoplatonist, Simplicius, however, who positions relationship as the non-derivative, essentially constitutive, category of reality. *Being is the concrescence of relationship.* In his *Commentaries On Aristotle's Categories,* Simplicius reorders Aristotelian and Stoic categorization. Unlike Aristotle's "horizontal" categories, where a thing's essence is distinguished from its accidental being, Marcia L. Colish claims, Stoic categories are "vertical"—a thing is understood according to degrees of concreteness.[81] None of the categories is accidental: "All must be present if reality is to be grasped in all its individuality."[82] In both the Aristotelian and Stoic categories, relation is the least real. Aristotle maintains its modicum of real being within his aporetic treatment, but the Stoics subtract relation from the realm of external reality altogether. Relation is an internal moral disposition, having its operation restricted to the logical "sayables" or *lekta*.[83]

Simplicius critiques and supplements Aristotle's notion of a relative. *Ta pros ti* denote singular things that stand in certain relationships. Richard Sorabji makes a key assertion: "For Aristotle a relative is not a relationship but the thing related."[84] Like the Stoics, Simplicius uses the term *skhesis* to refer to relationships themselves. Aristotle speaks of "the things that partake of the relationship, and not the relationship itself."[85] The two vocabularies often overlap but, according to Constantine Cavarnos, Simplicius tends to use the expression *ta pros ti* for denoting relative terms, such as "lover" and "beloved," and *skhesis* to refer to Relationship, such as "lover of," "beloved of," and "love."[86] The "priority" of "the Relationship (*skhesis*) of relatives (*ta pros ti*)," means "the connate Relationship of relatives is prior to acquired relationships."[87] Relationship is prior in the order of being to the things that have relationships, but the implication here is much stronger: Things are essentially relational (*skhetikê*). Love, for instance, must somehow be before lovers and beloveds. Love constitutes what lovers are and what beloveds are. Relative things (*ta pros ti*) acquire or instance the triadic structure of Relationship (*skhesis*). For example, this individual Jane (*to pros ti*) acquires the Relationship (*skhesis*) of love for this individual John (*to pros ti*). Jane is then the *lover of* John, and John is the *beloved of* Jane.

81. Colish, *Stoic Tradition*, 55.

82. Colish, *Stoic Tradition*, 55. On Stoic categorical *concrescence*, see Rist, "Categories and Their Uses," 40–51.

83. See Rist, "Categories and Their Uses," 44.

84. Sorabji, "Preface," ix.

85. Simplicius, *On Aristotle's "Categories 7–8,"* 14.

86. Cavarnos, *Hellenic-Christian Philosophical Tradition*, 78.

87. Simplicius, *On Aristotle's "Categories 7–8,"* 11.

Against the Stoics, and with Aristotle, he is arguing for the real being of relation. Simplicius, however, rejects Aristotle's horizontal-binary ontology of substance and accident. He upholds Stoicism's vertical fourfold with the radical qualification of universal Relationship. The Stoic categories are transformed; they are relational modes or *concrescent* divisions, partaking of "the form of Relationship" (*metaskhesis*).[88] Simplicius does not simply reshuffle the Stoic categories, putting the bottom on top. He preserves their vertical priority. Simplicius denies Relationship can be derived from the other categories.[89] All categories obtain their reality from Relationship. Barrie Fleet gives a precise synopsis: "Simplicius's conclusion is that Relationship underpins all the other categories, both Intelligible and Sensible."[90] There is Relationship between the intentional and the natural. Although not directly explored by Simplicius, a further amendment on signs is implied from his relational ontology. The Stoics maintain the category of relation (both *skhesis* and *ta pros ti*) is an Intelligible; it is a feature of virtuous disposition and mind-discourse (*Lekta*). In his treatise on Stoic logic, Sextus Empircus (†c. 210 CE) tells us, the sign belongs "to the relative class."[91] If, to Simplicius, Relationship is syn-categorical and triadic, it would seem to follow that the sign is, too. Being as Relationship infers the manifold concrescence of sign activity—communication.

From the perspective of tracing the semiotic Weltanschauung, the primacy of Relationship is significant. In his Commentary on Epictetus's (†c.135) *Enchiridion*, Simplicius gives *skhesis* a more secure definitional footing: "*Skhesis* in general terms is the linking (*suntaxis*) of certain things together; it is either natural (*phusikê*) or intentional (*proairetikê*) of either like or unlike; sometimes it unites (*sunagôgos*), sometimes it separates (*diastatikê*), although the individuality (*perigraphê*) of the items in the relationship endures."[92] Further: "Relationship is found between the items that have the relationship; it contains (or rather is contained by) both, by being the relationship so that, even if they are separated and change, they are not completely torn apart, but continue to belong to each other."[93] It is this continuance, this irreducible belonging, bereft of its terms, Nazianzus also speaks of: *Skhesis* melts away, revealing a world of things, lone to alone.

88. Simplicius, *On Aristotle's "Categories 7–8,"* 29.

89. See Simplicius, *On Aristotle's "Categories 7–8,"* 20–29.

90. Fleet, "Introduction," 2.

91. Sextus Empiricus, *Against Logicians*, 323. On this influential Stoic placement of the sign, see Markus, "St. Augustine on Signs," 74; Manetti, *Theories of the Sign*, 92–100.

92. Simplicius, *On Aristotle's "Categories 7–8,"* 158–59n7. Translation in Hadot, *Simplicius*, 31.

93. Simplicius, *On Aristotle's "Categories 7–8,"* 158–59n7.

Relationship returns, disappears into the sea of infinite potentiality from which it first emerged; but it is never really exhausted of its reality, of actually having been, creating ripples, waves of affects, crossing over each other, giving rise to another Relationship, and enfolding other things.

Simplicius struggles to explain and defend the form of Relationship. This *metaskhesis* of social and ecological Relationship Christians eventually call the Trinity. David Cunningham, for example, describes the Trinity as a relational whole: "Relation without remainder."[94] The logic of a new world is put in motion.

THE SYMBOLIST WORLDVIEW

The bond between Relationship and the sign is initially realized in the Trinitarian doctrine of *vestigia Dei, imago Dei*. Humanity's capacity for becoming the image relies firmly on the recognition of the traces of God in the physical universe. The Trinity is ecological by nature. Between human intentions and the rest of creation, there is communication. The dynamic of Relationship (*skhéseôs*) is symmetrical, reciprocal, and simultaneous—a personal dwelling place (*oikos*). To behold God as threefold being, we turn to the beings on which the Trinity has set its mark. The Christian's path of salvation is an elevation of awareness, moving from the disconnected aggregate of things to triadic communicative signs, which opens the prospect for the sacramental experience of the symbol. The latter restores to the universe its original signification. What was broken by the fall is now mended forever by the Logos of Christ. The truth of the thing is the sign. The truth of the sign is the symbol.

The ontological movement from thing to sign is a matter for the intellect; it is capable of demonstrative acceptance as a change in the principle of reason.[95] The transition from sign to symbol, though, requires the living Relationship. Marie-José Mondzain depicts Relationship as, "love or grace that ties the image to its model."[96] Relationship "is called *skhésis*, not *pros ti*," and in this Trinitarian gaze of human *imago*, "matter becomes a mirror for the Word, aiming in its orientation for the blind spot in the eye that catches only the divine *vestigium*."[97] To see symbolically is to become one's image. We see and love the world as God sees and loves us, knowing the world as God knows it. In the First Epistle to the Corinthians, we read: "For

---

94. Cunningham, *These Three are One*, 165.
95. For the dynamics of this transition, see the following chapter on Augustine.
96. Mondzain, *Image, Icon, Economy*, 78.
97. Mondzain, *Image, Icon, Economy*, 78, 98.

now we see through a glass, darkly; but then face to face: now I know in part; but then shall I know even as also I am known" (1 Cor 13:12 KJV). Étienne Gilson (†1978) provides a valuable exegesis of this passage: "In this sense the likeness a man produces of himself in a mirror is truly his image because he produces it, and for the same reason the Word can rightly be called God's image because the Father begets Him as the perfect likeness of himself. This initial relation of God to Himself whereby He is fully expressed in Image-in-itself, i.e. in the Word, is the source and model of every relation which will enable creatures to come to be and to subsist."[98] By destroying the *vestigia* of creation, its *oikonomia* or *economy*, we diminish the light of the Trinity reflected therein. We eclipse our potential for *imago*.

Bonaventure of Bagnoregio (†1274), for instance, links the soteriological aspects of the "Trinitarian structure of history," or economy, and "the true sign value of things"—a *liberation* semiology of creation.[99] Bonaventure explains the triadic-semiotic cosmos as a "being toward something—relation," an emblem of the Triune God.[100] Economic existence, then, is a moving or evolving inscription, a signature, of the Trinity or, as Gilson phrases it, "a community of relations," diffusing "the very power of communication," where all creatures therein "can be interpreted either as things, or as signs: *creaturae possunt considerari ut res vel ut signa*."[101] The error of philosophers is to interpret creation as an aggregate of things. Creation is a system of intelligible signs on their way to symbolic liberation. The world is a love letter from God. For Bonaventure, "Every creature is a divine word which God speaks."[102] Moreover, "He who does not allow himself to be illumined by the glory of created things is blind; he who does not awaken to their call is deaf; he who does not praise God for all his works is mute; he who does not discover the First Principle from all these signs is a fool."[103]

The Trinity has revealed itself in three ways or books: The Book of Creation, the Book of Scripture, and the Book of Life. William B. Ashworth Jr. calls this pan-hermeneutical approach to existence, the "emblematic world view."[104] Reality is a *physico-theological* palimpsest. The complementary overlay of sacred texts derives its inspiration from the Epistle to the Romans: "For since the creation of the world, God's invisible qualities—his

---

98. Gilson, *Christian Philosophy of Saint Augustine*, 211.
99. Ratzinger, *Theology of History in Bonaventure*, 48, 84.
100. Bonaventure quoted in Miller, "Cosmic Semiosis," 304.
101. Gilson, *Philosophy of St. Bonaventure*, 189, 183, 198.
102. Bonaventure quoted in Cullen, *Bonaventure*, 108.
103. Bonaventure quoted in Cullen, *Bonaventure*, 25.
104. Ashworth Jr., "Natural History and the Emblematic World View," 303.

eternal power and divine nature—have been clearly seen, being understood from which has been made, so that men are without excuse" (Rom 1:20 KJV). The God who reveals himself in scripture is also communicated throughout the rest of creation. The cosmos came forth from God in signs, and the way back is by means of signs. The light of the Word shines forth, revealing a relational and symbolic economy at the heart of creation and scripture. "The symbolic," Paul Ricoeur explains, "is rather between the symbols, as relation and as the economy of their relating."[105] Relationship (*skhesis*) enraptures our perception; it frees us from outward visible things, and signs, initiating the vision of what makes them intelligible: The veiled Trinitarian signature as symbol. To Ricoeur, "This system of symbolics is nowhere more apparent than in Christianity, where the natural symbolism is at once freed and ordered entirely in the light of the Word," and, the "symbolic resides, then, in this ordered play of natural symbolism, of abstract allegorism, and of historical typology: signs of nature, figures of virtues, Christ's acts, are mutually interpreted in this dialectic of the mirror and the book which is continued in every creature."[106] Everything is potentially a *sacramentum* because all things have a symbolic inner reality.

Giorgio Agamben observes, "The aporias in the theory of the signature repeat those of the Trinity: just as God was able to conceive and give shape to all things by means of the Word alone, as both model and the effective instrument of creation, the signature is what makes the mute signs of creation, in which it dwells, efficacious and expressive."[107] The Trinity communicates its divine realities to creation. "The early Church," Klemens Richter claims, "applied the world *sacramentum* to the whole of God's saving activity."[108] The *things* of creation, however, are not sacred in and of themselves. The Trinity is inscribed onto the world. Joseph Martos says, "seals of the Spirit" are present everywhere and open to everyone: "They are signs of sacred realities that God wants to communicate to people for their own benefit."[109] When a common sign is recognized as a divine signature it becomes a symbol. "The *sumbolon*," to Mondzain, is everywhere "involved with the universe of profane signs."[110] Signs "are kept in the confusion of the sacredness without a 'symbol,' which lacks the economy of the 'relative' (*katà skhésin*)."[111] "In

---

105. Ricoeur, "Structure and Hermeneutics," 59–60.
106. Ricoeur, "Structure and Hermeneutics," 60.
107. Agamben, *Signature of All Things*, 43.
108. Richter, *Meaning of the Sacramental Symbols*, 16.
109. Martos, *Doors to the Sacred*, 83.
110. Mondzain, *Image, Icon, Economy*, 141.
111. Mondzain, *Image, Icon, Economy*, 121.

the concrete world," Louis-Marie Chauvet confirms, "sign and symbol are always mixed together."[112] How are they distinguished?

In Chauvet's remarkable study, we are told that sign and symbol only maintain a "mutual relationship of differences"—that is, each region of reality is "governed by a different principle, the symbol cannot be understood as an offshoot of the sign, as if it were only a more 'aesthetic' or complex realization of the latter."[113] The sign relates to, reveals, an order of meaning other than itself to an interpreter. Paradoxically, the sign is itself only by emptying its identity to manifest something else. The symbol, as contrary, maintains its power as "a *mediator of identity*."[114] It has the power to make whole. The symbol marries the lost and alienated aspects of subjects. We are broken, incomplete, but we can return home again, a place where we truly belong. Chauvet guides us to a definitive passage by Edmond Ortigues (†2005): "The symbol does not refer, as does the sign, to something of another order than itself; rather, its function is to introduce us into an order to which itself belongs, an order presupposed to be an order of meaning in its radical otherness."[115] The symbol marks the dissolution of false alterity; that which is assumed to be irrevocably Other is revealed as co-essential for identity. "The primary function of the symbol," Chauvet explains, "is to *join* the persons who produce or receive it," and this "mutual recognition" is not the sign's "representation of objects, but of communication between subjects."[116] The symbol operates "as witness to this vacant place of the Other" and, in this inauthentic void or gap, "the symbol gathers together entities into a significant world."[117] The symbol reunites the most real feature of ourselves and our world; it merges what truly belongs together. All estrangement and isolation fall. Ortigues is once more instructive on *its triadic signature*: "The whole problem of symbolization is in this transition from the dualistic opposition to the threefold relation."[118] The medium of this transition is, for Christians, found in sacramental experience. Sacramentality is a complex opening, overlapping liturgical, natural, and social expressions of the symbol.

---

112. Chauvet, *Symbol and Sacrament*, 111.

113. Chauvet, *Symbol and Sacrament*, 111.

114. Chauvet, *Symbol and Sacrament*, 112.

115. Ortigues, *Le discours et le symbole*, 65, quoted in Chauvet, *Symbol and Sacrament*, 113.

116. Chauvet, *Symbol and Sacrament*, 120–21.

117. Chauvet, *Symbol and Sacrament*, 118.

118. Ortigues, *Le discours et le symbole*, 205, quoted in Chauvet, *Symbol and Sacrament*, 118.

The Language of the Real 257

Symbols (*sumbola*), then, occasion sacramental events of redemption. Michael G. Lawler writes that symbols "make present what they signify and arouse in the person who lives into them an entire range of personal, sensitive, imaginative, intuitive, emotional, conceptual information, action and reaction that affects the participant's total being. Symbols represent a personal way of knowing, as distinct from a logical one."[119] Martos provides an insightful (and affecting) summary:

> The meaning that is experienced in the sacramental event is experienced as discovered, as encountered. It is not felt to be artificial or imposed on the symbol. The meaning seems to come not from us but from or through the sacrament. It radiates out of the sacramental object or illuminates the sacramental ritual from within. It is experienced as something that is simply given, within the sacramental event. In that sense it is gratuitous: the sacred meaning does not have to appear, it does not have to be experienced. So when it does appear it is felt to be a gift, a grace. The experienced effect of the sacrament is experienced as somehow caused by something or someone else than the person who is having the experience.[120]

A person is recreated from what was, previously, merely a human individual. Being-a-symbol is an event of Relationship. The sacramental subject lives into its communion. Communication between God and humanity is experienced in and through the figure of the symbol.

The symbol is a form of presentation with *complete indifference* such that the signified is completely the signifier. Jaroslav Pelikan (†2003) claims, "The sign and what the sign represents are identical."[121] A symbol does not endlessly defer or arbitrarily refer; it is what it means. The whole being of a sign communicates something other than itself (*significate*) to an interpretive power; it is erased to present what it is not. Mondzain makes the distinction clear: "It is therefore a sign rather than a symbol, because it refers to something other than itself."[122] The *sacramentum* elevates the participant by revealing the divine signature, enfolding the initiate in "the economic relation (*skhésis*) that links the word, the thing signified, and the image."[123] There is mediation between substantial being, the thing, and relational being, the sign. Substance is in itself; it is what it is and cannot be related or

119. Lawler, *Symbol and Sacrament*, 25.
120. Martos, *Doors to the Sacred*, 20–21.
121. Pelikan, *Imago Dei*, 59.
122. Mondzain, *Image, Icon, Economy*, 114.
123. Mondzain, *Image, Icon, Economy*, 30.

represented. A sign cannot be an identity because it is something other than itself. A sign cannot coincide with itself and still be a sign. *A symbol is a substantial sign.* What cannot be transitive is communicated. What cannot be intransitive is identical with itself. The visible and horizontal experience of the profane sign is transfigured. Spiritual seals are broken. The sign is baptized by the invisible and vertical dimension of sacred substance.

The sacramental cosmos requires a method of interpretation, a hermeneutic, to provide the condition of its possibility. In Greek, "symbolon" (συμβολον) denotes, "drawing together," the re-integration of the whole that has been fragmented, lost as separate things, now reunited in a matching relationship.[124] The method of drawing together scripture and creation is developed by the Alexandrine Platonists over the first three centuries of the Christian era; it is brought to full fruition with the third-century Church Father, Origen (†c. 254 CE). According to Patricia Cox, Origen depicts creation as "a living text, an explosive constellation of divine designs, a record of mysteries like holy scriptures themselves."[125] The elements of creation, then, are signs to be read, "alive with feathers, scales, roots, and minerals."[126] Gerald L. Bruns claims, in this tradition, creatures "are sheer living signs and words of God."[127] Scripture and creation have a common method of interpretation. This hermeneutic is designed to open the seals of the invisible inscribed on the visible world of signs. The *literal* meaning is the body of scripture and creation; its historical and empirical sense. The *moral* sense is the soul of scripture and creation, which teaches us how life should be lived. The spirit of scripture and creation is the highest level of meaning. The *allegorical* sense contains timeless theological truths, which repeat the patterns of heavenly things. Origen is not saying, however, that *all* events depicted by scripture, and occurring in creation, are open to non-literal interpretation.

Origen uses the Greek term "enoptic" to mark the transition to symbolic interpretation.[128] The prefix 'en' suggests entry or conversion into a specified state, and 'optic' pertains to the visible. An *enoptic* interpretation deciphers the heavenly symbols beneath signs. Origen calls a mere sign, "the outer covering of the letter."[129] The interpreter seeks the Trinitarian *ichnos*, trace, or signature. Hermeneutical practice is a sacrament. Entry into the

---

124. Ladner, "Medieval and Modern Understanding of Symbolism," 23. See also Struck, *Birth of the Symbol*, 78–110.

125. Cox, "Origen and the Bestial Soul," 117.

126. Cox, "Physiologus," 437.

127. Bruns, *Hermeneutics*, 143.

128. Cox Miller, "Pleasure of the Text, Text of Pleasure," 244–45.

129. Origen, *On First Principles* 4.2.8 (285).

soul and spirit of scripture and creation is not open to all readers. Enoptic vision depends on the gift of inspiration. To Cox Miller, it is granted to lovers of the text: "For to contemplate is to desire. The name of love is the substance of language itself."[130] Symbols are not merely a tissue of analogies, a doctrine of homonyms, or natural metaphors; rather, they provide the possibility for sacramental communion. "Allegory," Bruns reminds us, "is a mode of appropriation in which one reinterprets another's text as if it were one's own."[131] There is a union, a fusion, a mélange of knower and known, which become one without ceasing to be two.

Origen's hermeneutics is ultimately concerned with the third text that integrates the other two: The soul. The process of reading the language of creation, the spiritual overlay of scripture and world, Henri Crouzel says, is an "evangelization of our being," which "must not be limited to univocal consciousness but extends itself also to psychic depths, the mark of our animality, which contemporary psychology is discovering more and more."[132] Origen speaks of confronting and transforming the intimate self. The *hospitium* is the guest-chamber for an-*other*, darker self—the unconscious; it is a haunted place of dreams, desire, and violence, containing the raw power, the raw symbolic flesh of our animal nature. Symbolic mentality is the metamorphosis of soul from damnation to salvation. The texts of creation and scripture are enveloped in a *psychic-aesthetic* drama of the soul's liberation from the night within. This event of sacramental tri-textuality is an enoptic vision, seeing and naming our beasts and demons, and being released from their control. We gain dominion over the primal animal symbols, directing our *literal* perception and action. Symbolic events are healing traumas. The semiotic power of love, of the Word, the Christ, "breaks through the 'iron bars' of our literalisms."[133]

The world is embraced as the enigmatic bearer of the kingdom of heaven itself. For Origen, according to Cox Miller, the bodily senses are the "windows" through which the Word of God enters the soul; they are transformed into "senses of the heart"—*ta aisthērēria tēs kardias*.[134] "It is a heart which is burning with love for the whole of creation," Vladimir Lossky (†1958) witnesses, whereby, "a few drops of blood recreate the whole

---

130. Cox Miller, "Pleasure of the Text, Text of Pleasure," 244.

131. Bruns, *Hermeneutics*, 143.

132. Crouzel, *Théologie de l'Image de Dieu chez Origène*, 206, quoted in Cox, "Origen and the Bestial Soul," 132.

133. Cox, "Origen and the Bestial Soul," 133.

134. Cox, "Origen and the Bestial Soul," 120.

world."[135] Sensible signs are experienced as symbolic realities. Enoptic interpretation lives into the sensuous dimensions of the Trinity, lying hidden beneath the appearance of the world. Bernard of Clairvaux (†1153) later tells us, "Believe one who knows: You will find something greater in woods than in books. Trees and stones will teach you that which you can never learn from masters."[136]

---

135. Lossky, *Mystical Theology*, 110, 111.
136. Bernard of Clairvaux, *Letters*, 106–7.

EIGHT

Augustine on Symbols, Signs, and Things

THE CULTURAL MOVEMENT THAT gives rise to modern nature is, at least in part, a reaction against the excesses of the symbolist mentality. Semiotic creation stands between nature and symbol. This chapter examines Augustine's views on language, presenting his distinctions between symbols, signs, and things. The language of the real is articulated within a complex set of theological presuppositions. What seems to emerge is the secular space-time of the world as a communicative system of triadic signs. Signs are neither wholly excluded from symbolic experience, nor are they reduced to instrumental and impersonal nature.

THE COLLAPSE OF THE SYMBOLIST WORLDVIEW

Symbolic experience does not translate into rational categories. Marie-Dominique Chenu (†1990) claims it is beyond the intellect's comprehension: "To bring symbolism into play was not to extend or supplement a previous act of reason; it was to give primary expression to a reality which reason could not attain and which reason, even afterwards, could not conceptualize."[1] The symbolist mentality's tendency for otherworldly enthusiasm—its intersection with idolatrous, magical, alchemical, divinatory, or astrological practices, and generalized esteem of esotericism and irrationalism—eventually

---

1. Chenu, "Symbolist Mentality," 103.

lead to its discredit.² The collapse of the *emblematic worldview* gives rise to the depersonalized outlook on *nature*. Sacramental creation fades from its central position on the cultural horizon. Outside the strict limits of *private* religious experience, symbolic preoccupation becomes a minority view, reemerging within the influential margins of the aesthetic imaginary: The work of art, mythology, and the ethereal *hospitium* of psychoanalysis.³ Our approach to nature becomes radically instrumental and, above all, *literal*: Empirics, logical analytics, legalistic naturalism, and the quantification and domination of all things on behalf of human being—the sole point of communicative value in an otherwise silent universe.⁴ The language of the real is a metaphor exclusively tied to the order of number and measure. Galileo Galilei (†1642), in many ways, closes the Book of Creation and opens the Book of Nature; symbolist experience other than mathematics is "a dark labyrinth."⁵

The sweeping extrication of literal experience partially accounts for the demise of this aspect of the semiotic worldview. Everything exists on an enchanted plane of concealed symbols. The invisible orders the visible. Ordinary signs and experiences are seemingly diminished, emptied of their worldly reality and agency.⁶ The shift from things to signs precedes the sacramental transfiguration of signs by symbols. Things or substances have accidental relations. Signs *are* triadic relationships. In Christian terms, signs are *literal* traces of the Trinity. Ratzinger's transition from thinking in terms of relationship instead of substance is, in a fundamental sense, a change from things to signs: Creation as communicative liberation and rationality. John Milbank explains this transition: "Christian theology has begun to be a metaphysics/metasemiotics of relation, rather than a metaphysics of substance."⁷ The Christian symbol may be the truth of the sign, but the truth of the thing, the sign, must first be explained. The terrestrial spaces of possible symbolic experience also seem to require restraint.

---

2. See Chenu, "Symbolist Mentality," 127, 134.

3. See Todorov, "Romantic Crisis," 147–221; Schelling, *Philosophy of Art*, 45–60; Losev, *Dialectics of Myth*, 18–32; Eagleton, *Ideology of the Aesthetic*, 262–87; McGrath, *Dark Ground of Spirit*, 1–43.

4. See Bono, "From Paracelsus to Newton," 45–76; Leiss, *Domination of Nature*, 3–101.

5. Galilei, "Assayer," 238.

6. On the simultaneous and co-reinforcing turn to the literal in Christian theology, scientific endeavors, and European culture, generally considered, see Bruns, *Hermeneutics*, 139–58.

7. Milbank, "Theology Without Substance," 146.

SACRAMENTAL ENCLOSURE

Augustine is a decisive figure on symbols, signs, and things for the Latin West. Unlike the tradition of the Greek East, Augustine tends to limit symbolic life to exegetical readings of scripture and, then gradually and ultimately, liturgical rites, especially the Eucharist. To Klemens Richter, this limitation means sacramental events "can be experienced only in this way in the liturgy or else not at all."[8] Oliver Davies, however, puts forward an argument for sacramental continuity between church and creation: "Eucharistic semiotics is not something other than Christian semiotics more generally, but it is a particularly intensive instance of it."[9] The Eucharist is the deepest symbol, reading, or "inhabiting of the text of Scripture which has at its heart Jesus' own indwelling of Scripture."[10] The true reality of the Trinity is "not to be found in the sign" because its communicative self-evacuation, as being other than itself, precludes real presence of the thing in itself; it is a pregnant expectation that is fulfilled by the Eucharistic symbol or sacrament.[11] The ostensible "Real Presence" "of Christ" becomes "'substantially' present," drawing together "*signum et res*: the material sign and the divine reality it signifies in combination."[12]

Augustine does not eliminate the Trinitarian value of creation. He still, at times, upholds the symbolic view, "or, in other words, to ascertain what is eternal and spiritual from corporeal and temporal things."[13] "The term sacrament," Davies says, "as we find it in Augustine, expresses the belief that the things of creation have some kind of signifying relation to the Creator; only gradually did the term come to be restricted to the seven sacraments we know today."[14] For Davies, the superabundant and embodied "life of the Trinity is therefore present all around us" and, as C. C. Pecknold also *reaffirms*, "to refer to 'the Word made flesh' is to refer not only to the incarnation of God in Christ but also to the semiotic universe in which such an incarnation occurs," but there is a distinct humanistic shift of emphasis.[15] Symbolic life is increasingly intra-scriptural, social, and liturgical. Edward Morgan clarifies Augustine's transition: The "means by which the process of

---

8. Richter, *Meaning of the Sacramental Symbols*, 9.
9. Davies, "Sign Redeemed," 220.
10. Davies, "Sign Redeemed," 220.
11. Davies, "Sign Redeemed," 235.
12. Davies, "Sign Redeemed," 230.
13. Augustine, *De Doctrina Christiana*, 1.9, 17.
14. Davies, "Sign Redeemed," 230.
15. Davies, "Sign Redeemed," 239; Pecknold, *Transforming Postliberal Theology*, 43–44.

transformation in God's image can be continued" within the triadic interiorities[16] of the human soul is positioned on a plane of scriptural interpretation, which exteriorizes itself, gives its evidence, within the transformation of social relationships.[17] Put otherwise, the symbolic breakthrough of divine love (*aedificatum in caritate*), uplifting human *imago*, is occasioned by the *vestigia trinitatis* of scripture, and its social translation. On Augustine's theolinguistic turn to social relationships, Pecknold tells us, "Words must do what the Word made flesh does, namely, *love*, and therefore save the world by indwelling."[18] The human relationship with God is a continuum, relating to the emendation of human signification, which is gradually subsumed and consummated within the *sacramenta* of the church. The soul is a ship; adrift, divorced (*alienaremur*) from its homeland, but the sea of signs leads to the church's home port. In Augustine's *De doctrina Christiana*, we read: "Instead of many signs there are now but a few signs, simple when performed, inspiring when understood, and holy when practiced, given to us by the teaching of our Lord himself and the apostles, such as the sacrament of baptism and the celebration of our Lord's body and blood."[19]

If not, at worst, explicitly hostile towards creation's symbolic expression, Augustine becomes only incidentally concerned with the creatures, systems, and spaces that sustain humanity in time. A Christian should be a good steward of creation, but the outcome of sacramental enclosure is not without a degrading effect on the meaning and value of nonhuman creation.[20] "It is," John Donne (†1631) reminds us, "a lovely and religious thing, to finde out *Vestigia Trinitatis*, Impressions of the Trinity, in as many things as we can. Let us therefore, with S. *Bernard*, consider *Trinitatem Creatricem*, and *Trinitatem Createm*, a Creating, and a Created Trinity."[21] If the structure and power (*Trinitatem Createm*) of our creative operations (*Trinitatem Creatricem*) should turn from the power of love to love of power, communication with creation (created/creating) will only command; it will not hear. Outside the Trinitarian framework, our capacity to order all enslaves all; namely, the creative processes upon which we ultimately derive our existence.[22]

---

16. On Augustine's "innumerable" triads, see Jaspers, *Plato And Augustine*, 87.
17. Morgan, *Incarnation of the Word*, 11; see also 17.
18. Pecknold, *Transforming Postliberal Theology*, 50.
19. Augustine, *De Doctrina Christiana*, 3.31, 147.
20. See Brown, *God and Enchantment of Place*, 5–36.
21. Donne, *Sermons of John Donne*, 3:144–45.
22. See Hanby, "Reconsiderations," para. 1–29.

THE COMMUNICATIVE LOGIC OF SIGNS

Augustine's displacement of the symbolist mentality greatly amends the fascination with the Trinity's similitudes; it inaugurates an alternative between symbolic and tyrannical mentalities. *Trinitarian communicative rationality* begins to define the pre-symbolic space-time of the *saeculum*: An economic realm of signs without things. The literal understanding of the order of communication carries its own freedom for ground: *Principium rationis*.[23] To R. A. Markus (†2010), "The triadic relation of signification is the key to Augustine's entire hermeneutical theory."[24] The language of the real is defined by the triadic logic of interpropositional semiotic events and their relationships to interpreters.

In the context of Christian education on scripture (*De doctrina christiana*), Peter Ochs claims that Augustine appropriates "Stoic logic into the triadic semiotic that, alone, can diagram the mediatory movement of intra-Scriptural."[25] The Stoics define the sign (*sēmeîon*; "stands for") as a tri-termed relationship (*skhesis*) which, Giovanni Manetti argues, already presumes a shift from "substance to events, with respect to their ontological point of view."[26] Aristotle's categorical logic follows his metaphysics of formal substance.[27] His *intra*propositional logic describes relations (*ta pros ti*) between specially vetted signs (*sēmaínei*) or terms, serving as subjects and predicates in types of propositions. Propositions constitute a syllogism, which is a triad of connected propositions, so related that the one of them, the conclusion, necessarily follows the other two, which are called premises. A syllogism is an argument to demonstrate that two terms which are each related, as subject or as predicate, to the same third term, are necessarily related, as subject or as predicate, to one another. Relations (*ta*

---

23. On the principle of reason, *Weltanschauung* as order of Relationship, and the freedom of reason, see Heidegger, *Essence of Reasons*, 80–85, 123–31.

24. Markus, "Signs, Communication, and Communities," 103.

25. Ochs, "Reparative Reasoning," 201.

26. Manetti, *Theories of the Sign in Classical Antiquity*, 98.

27. Aristotle maintains an oftentimes vague distinction between the sign and the symbol. The latter is employed, for the most part, to investigate the meaningful affections, intentions, and actions of the soul; and the ultimate grounding of signification in concepts. The former is mostly restricted to the logical analysis of the *aporetic* ratio, or gap, of being between what is said and the things themselves. See Manetti, *Theories of the Sign in Classical Antiquity*, 70–91. Deborah K. W. Modrak is correct in pointing out that the symbol mediates "the relation between the spoken word and the associated mental state"—that is, the symbol *translates* signs within a conventional language, e.g., English, conveying them into intelligible, naturally common concepts (*pathema*) (Modrak, *Aristotle's Theory of Meaning and Language*, 44; see also 27–51).

pros ti), though, are not logically relevant. To Aristotle, a relation is not a relationship (*skhesis*); neither a generating principle of order nor an operation independent of its terms. Modern logic, for example, changes its metaphysical presuppositions from accidental relations of substantial things to relationships between events. As Bertrand Russell notes, "Traditional logic, since it holds that all propositions have the subject-predicate form, is unable to admit the reality of relations: all relations must be reduced to properties of the apparently related terms."[28]

Aristotle seeks the necessary sign (*tekmêrion*) of irrefutable deductive proof. *The word of being* is causal knowledge (*dióti*; why) of the substance of things. In his *Nichomachean Ethics* (1139b20), for example, scientific knowledge (*epistēmē*) is defined as that which *does not admit of being otherwise*. To know scientifically is to know necessarily, not contingently. Necessary knowledge brings forth intelligence (*phronesis*), understanding (*nous*), and wisdom (*Sophia*) (1140a25–1141b25). The generic *semeion*, contrastingly, refers to less trustworthy ways of knowledge; it is associated with production (*poiesis* and *technē*) and action (*praxis*) (1140a1–20). Reasoning from the becoming of things is inference from effects (*hóti*; "that"): The hypothetical and the probable. Aristotle distinguishes the real knower from someone who is merely observant of passing signs—*sēmeiōtikos*. Knowledge of appearances is knowledge of things that *admit of being otherwise*. Social life, especially, must navigate volatile atmospheres of opinion. We are vulnerable to regimes of persuasion.

Due to the ontological priority of individual substances (mirrored in the logical-linguistic priority of subjects) and its necessary science, the logic of becoming by common relation, i.e., *function*, is left undeveloped.[29] Russell is, again, helpful: "Here the traditional logic failed completely: it believed that there was only one form of simple proposition (i.e., of proposition not stating a relation between two or more propositions), namely, the form which ascribes a predicate to a subject."[30] "Thus," he concludes, "propositions stating that two things have a certain relation have a different form from subject-predicate propositions, and the failure to perceive this difference or to allow for it has been the source of many errors in traditional metaphysics."[31] Unlike the majority, Aristotelian tradition, however, the Sto-

---

28. Russell, *Our Knowledge of the External World*, 56.
29. See Cassirer, "Concept of Thing," 3–26.
30. Russell, *Our Knowledge of the External World*, 54.
31. Russell, *Our Knowledge of the External World*, 54. As we have already noted, despite's Russell's logical and mathematical commitment to the "reality of relations," he remains hesitant, possibly for good political reasons, to connect this commitment with a social one, favoring individual freedom (of terms) over mutual control (by an

ics practice *inter*propositional logic. There is becoming without being. There are facts, events, or effects (*hóti*; "that") without causes; only the *form* of relationship (*skhesis*) between the propositions in the conditional statement counts. To Tzvetan Todorov (†2017), "The fact that we are moving from one proposition to another (from 'this woman has milk' to 'this woman has given birth') and not from one predicate to another (from 'mortals' to 'men') is crucial, for we are passing by the same token from substance to event."[32] Stoic, "propositional logic, for its part, grasps facts in their becoming, facts as events. Now it is precisely events (and not substances) that come to be treated as signs."[33] The logic of relational process—*states of affairs*—imparts a unique structure of signification.

Sextus Empiricus gives the Stoic tripartite definition of the sign: "[The Stoics claim] that three things are linked together: what is signified (*tò sēmainómenon*) [*lektón*, 'the said'], that which signifies (*tò sēmaînon*), and the [external] object of reference (*tò tynchánon*)."[34] Todorov traces Augustine's definitional development of the sign and its consequent transformation of the Stoic triadic relational structure. Augustine's "insistence on the communicative dimension is new," as is his emphasis on "interpretation," which leads to "the disappearance of the 'thing' [external object of reference (*tò tynchánon*)], or referent."[35] Along the same trail of definitions, culminating in *De doctrina christiana*, R. A. Markus notes the replacement of the Stoic third term, the referent, with the perspectives of the communicative subject: First, sign giver (or user), and second, sign receiver. Augustine gives priority to the sign receiver because "not all signs are *given*, though all—because a thing is a sign insofar as it stands for something to somebody; to be a sign, a thing must necessarily be experienced by some subject—are received."[36] To Markus, "The sign, to be a sign, in all cases has a relation to two other terms: the signified and the giver or perceiver; which of the two classes it falls into will, however, be determined by whether it depends on the giver/

---

assumed social "form" of Relationship) (60). Oftentimes, he, like Nazianzus and Simplicius—who do commit to *skhesis* as ontologically prior to terms that instance a particular Relationship—presents a constitutive relationship as essentially enigmatic: "It is neither in space nor time, neither material nor mental; yet it is something" (Russell, *Problems of Philosophy*, 78).

32. Todorov, *Theories of the Symbol*, 21.
33. Todorov, *Theories of the Symbol*, 23.
34. Sextus Empiricus quoted in Manetti, *Theories of the Sign in Classical Antiquity*, 93–94.
35. Todorov, *Theories of the Symbol*, 36, 39, 40.
36. Markus, "Signs, Communication, and Communities," 98.

perceiver or on the signified."[37] The important thing to note here is that both "the definitions given in *De doctrina christiana* are, in other words, triadic, though this triadic relation presupposes a (dyadic) relation of dependence between the sign and either the signified or the giver/perceiver."[38] Semiotic logic takes its ground.

Communication is a relationship with three terms: X (sign) stands for Y (signified) to Z (interpreter). The communicative subject can be a giver or a perceiver of signs. The perceiver, however, must be present for an *act of communication*. The dyadic relation of sign-signified is neither significant nor communicative without a giver/perceiver; as is the sign-giver/perceiver dyad without a signified. The sign-signified-giver triad transmits significance, but it is only potentially communicative. The act of significance is not consummated; it does not communicate without a perceiver. Signs can be present to a perceiver with or without a giver. The logic of communication requires a perceiver. The event of reception and interpretation resides with the third term. The *interpreter* completes the semiotic circuit of communication.

THE SYMBOLIC INTERPRETER AND SCRIPTURE

Todorov asserts that Augustine's triadic "schema remains entirely within the realm of communication."[39] The Stoic third term of external designation is replaced by the interpreter: "We are dealing only with the relation of communication."[40] Augustine restricts this relationship to the community of scriptural interpreters: Those "whom we desire to be educated for the good of the church."[41] Future teachers and preachers of divine scripture "must communicate what is good and eradicate what is bad."[42] Guiding interpretation is Augustine's *principium rationis*. The rule of faith (*regula fidei*) uplifts to the rule of love. God's authority "opens the door" to "a will to believe," and "prepares man for reason."[43] Divine authority "not only transcends all human capability, but taking on the actual form of man, shows man to what

---

37. Markus, "Signs, Communication, and Communities," 98.
38. Markus, "Signs, Communication, and Communities," 98–99.
39. Todorov, *Theories of the Symbol*, 43.
40. Todorov, *Theories of the Symbol*, 42.
41. Augustine, *De Doctrina Christiana*, 4.8, 199.
42. Augustine, *De Doctrina Christiana*, 4.14, 201.
43. Augustine, *De ord.* II, ix, 26; *De spir. et litt.*, xxi, 54; *De vera relig.* xxiv, 45, quoted in Przywara, *Augustine Synthesis*, 54, 56.

depth It has condescended for man's sake."⁴⁴ It is "the function of our own will" to consent or to dissent; if we yield our trust to divine authority, we begin to learn.⁴⁵

The Word made flesh (Et verbum caro factum est) is the absolute presupposition for meaningful reading. The Incarnational rule of trust in God's Word in the world is an essential heuristic for interpretation. Everything in scripture is read in relation to it. The Word made flesh is the Word made legible. The semiotic universe is paradigmatically encoded in holy writ; it is the privileged and exclusive *symbolic* site for the Christian interpretive community. According to Michael Cameron:

> The Word made flesh (John 1:14) discloses the capacity of the uncreated and supratemporal to 'dwell' in the created and temporal. Because of the symbiotic relationship between Christology and language (*doc. Chr.* 1.13.12), the incarnation constitutes the basis for a renewed sacramental understanding of signification whereby the sign not only represents but contains and mediates the reality it signifies. The sign incarnates meaning before it is understood to point the way to meaning.⁴⁶

For the initiate, Paolo Virno claims, "The simple enunciation of the divine word institutes a protective proximity between creature and creator" because "the incarnated God neither explains nor describes: it realizes the presence of the Word in the world, a presence that is both the promise and the fulfillment of salvation."⁴⁷ To enter the symbolic order there must be *fleshed* interpretation; performance in liturgy, song, confession, prayer, charity, and so on. For Virno, "the voice is sacred," and "only the fact of speaking is *redemptive*."⁴⁸ Symbolic experience follows upon faith and understanding.

Faith gives the understanding access to scripture's sacramental symbols. Unbelief closes the door to them. *Regula fidei*, as Augustine describes it, is more a "starting point for knowledge," a "disposition to seek the truth" of divine things, which cannot yet be understood, than "that which presumes things unknown to be known."⁴⁹ The rule of faith is the semiotic logic of trust, of love, for reading and living. Faith seeks. Understanding finds. The embodied voice experiences the symbolic presence. Eating of the

---

44. Augustine, *De ord.* II, ix, 27, quoted in Przywara, *Augustine Synthesis*, 54.
45. Augustine, *De spir. et litt.*, xxi, 54, quoted in Przywara, *Augustine Synthesis*, 56.
46. Cameron, "Signs," 795.
47. Virno, *When the Word Becomes Flesh*, 76.
48. Virno, *When the Word Becomes Flesh*, 83.
49. Augustine, *De Trin.*, IX, i, 1, quoted in Przywara, *Augustine Synthesis*, 63.

tree of life precedes eating of *the tree of knowledge*. Augustine distinguishes symbolic reasoning from other kinds of understanding:

> There are three classes of credible things. Some there are which are always believed, and never understood; such is all history, ranging over the temporal doings of man. Others are understood as soon as they are believed; such are all human reasonings, whether on number or any other branch of science you please. Thirdly, there are those which are believed and afterwards understood; such are those dealing with divine things, which cannot be understood except by those who are pure of heart.[50]

The signs of scripture are shaped by the Word of God, which is not "utterly hidden from the rational creature, once it makes use of its reason."[51] "Understanding," Augustine tells us, "is the reward of faith. Therefore, seek not to understand that thou mayest believe, but believe that thou mayest understand."[52] Once you have understood, speak the Word in the world.

Scriptural interpretation is the opening for the *Pentecostal experience* of the Trinity. Interpreters indwell or replicate the Word in their flesh; lives become texts of salvific action. C. C. Pecknold explains the link between *signum* and *sacramentum* as "the divine self-giving of God in the Word made flesh and the ongoing communication of this God in scriptural signification."[53] "The relationality of the 'third,'" Pecknold claims, "is both the gift of the Holy Spirit (Pentecost having sign interpretation at its very heart), which is the bond of love between the Father and the Son, and simultaneously the gift of meaning to a community of readers."[54] What is communicated is pure communicativeness itself—love of God and neighbor. In Augustine, we read, "The love of God is first in the order of enjoining but love of our neighbor is first in the order of doing."[55] The gift of love (*donum caritatis*) is the gift of knowledge (*donum scientiae*). On Augustine's scriptural semiotics, Derek J. Simon verifies that "Love is the ultimate referent, the practical outcome, and the formal principle of semiotic discernment in

---

50. Augustine, *De div. quaest.*, XLVIII, quoted in Przywara, *Augustine Synthesis*, 63.

51. Augustine, *In Joan. Evang.*, CVI, 4, quoted in Przywara, *Augustine Synthesis*, 74.

52. Augustine, *In Joan. Evang.*, XXIX, 6, quoted in Przywara, *Augustine Synthesis*, 58.

53. Pecknold, *Transforming Postliberal Theology*, 56.

54. Pecknold, *Transforming Postliberal Theology*, 57.

55. Augustine, *In Joan. Evang.*, XVII, 9, quoted in Przywara, *Augustine Synthesis*, 353.

the ecclesial activity of biblical interpretation."[56] *Love and do what thou wilt.* William S. Babcock also affirms that the rule of love is "the *terminus* of all biblical signification."[57]

THE TRINITY AND THE SIGN'S SPACE-TIME

The Holy Spirit is the divine relationship that *enjoins* the eternal and the temporal. When articulating the Persons of the Trinity, Augustine says, "The Spirit is the gift eternally, but has been given in time."[58] He elsewhere (*De Civitate Dei* 11.6) cautions our understanding of the phrase *given in time*. From the perspective of an interpreter of scripture within an already created world, the Holy Spirit is given *in* time; but the world "was not created *in* time but *with* time"—that is, "The world was in fact made *with* time."[59] The universe is a free, creative, and loving act of God. The Word by which all things are made is not an event *in* time; it is the event of time itself. God did not create the world from preexistent temporal matter. The movement, change, iteration, and serial succession of temporal order is the divine *economy* of the Trinity. As we read in the Book of Genesis, this original communication is attributed to the workings of the Holy Spirit in and through creation: "The Spirit of God moved upon the face of the waters" (Gen 1:2 KJV).

The Holy Spirit is generated as love of the Father and the Son. Love, time, and the sign are correlative economic terms. Profane time is a moving and empty vessel—*the sign or form of love is the self-erasing non-identity of the present; always other than itself, accounting for movement from past to future. The sign signifies the past to the future.* This horizontal and impersonal time of the sign (*hic temporis*) is punctuated by the Holy Spirit's vertical *inpouring* of symbolic communication. The gift of the unredeemed sign is time's spatialization; it is still, as Mondzain insists, "a uterine *khôra* traversed by divine breath," but, to Augustine, "in the symbol of the cross every Christian act is inscribed."[60] Christian love is simultaneously symbol, and liberated time—*kairòs*—to come. *Christiana libertas*, Morgan explains, "enables the mind to see signs as directed towards the final end of human existence," and "love in the eschatological future, becomes the icon of this future."[61] The

56. Simon, "Ad Regnum Caritatis," 118.
57. Babcock, "*Caritas* and Signification," 155.
58. Augustine, *Trinity*, 5.16.17, 195.
59. Augustine, *City of God*, 436.
60. Mondzain, *Image, Icon, Economy*, 101; Augustine, *De Doctrina Christiana*, 2.150, 129.
61. Morgan, *Incarnation of the Word*, 69, 57.

future is the symbol, drawing the profane signs of past and present to itself as a spatialized process of liberation found in time's completion: *Eschaton*.

On the Trinity, Augustine follows the Greek Fathers, but he distances himself from Aristotle's ontological vocabulary of finite being. The term *substance* (ousia) has enduring associations as a singular entity that is a correlate of accidents. Therefore, Augustine prefers the Latin term, *essentia*, being itself; it escapes the limitations of Aristotle's finite categories, denying relationship into the realm of substance.[62] The pursuit of a proper theological vocabulary—the category of predicament suitable for God—is distinct from Aristotelian ontology. Augustine defines the self-communicative *logic* of the Trinity in Stoic terms: Entirely based on "the category of relationship."[63] There is semantic continuation and modification of the Greek *skhesis* by the Latin *relativum*.[64] What the Greek Fathers posit as three subsisting realities or *hypostases*, divine operations with discrete relationships, Augustine contracts to relational Persons; or, more clearly, the essence of God is understood by relative predication alone—Persons subsist in the self-relating being of God. "In other words," as Karl Rahner (†1984) stresses, "these three self-communications are the self-communication of the one God in the three relative ways in which God subsists," and, "these persons do not differ from their own way of communicating themselves."[65] The difference, then, between the Father, the Son, and the Holy Spirit is not one of essence or operation, but of the expression of mutual relation only (*quae relative dicuntur ad invicem*):

> Wherefore, let us hold fast above all to this principle: whatever in that divine and exalted sublimity is said in reference to Himself is said according to substance; but what is said in reference to something does not refer to a substance but to a relationship. ... The things in the same Trinity that are properly predicated of each person are by no means predicated of them as they are in themselves, but in their relations either to one another or to the creature; it is obvious that such things are predicated of them relatively, and not in regard to their substance ... if by the Holy Spirit is meant the person to whom it properly belongs, then it denotes a relation. ... Hence, the Holy Spirit is in a certain sense the ineffable communion of the Father and the Son. ... For He is called properly what they are called in common, because the

---

62. See TeSelle, *Augustine the Theologian*, 296; Augustine, *Trinity*, 5.5.3, 177; 5.8.9, 187.

63. Augustine, *Trinity*, 5.7, 185.

64. See Emery, *Trinitarian Theology of St. Thomas Aquinas*, 79–84.

65. Rahner, *Trinity*, 35–36.

> Father is a spirit and the Son is a spirit, and the Father is holy and the Son is holy. In order that the communion between them might be signified by a name which is appropriate to both, the Holy Spirit is called the gift of both.[66]

Augustine continues with his description of the Spirit's sacred, relational properties; summarized as pure love:

> Wherefore, the Holy Spirit also subsists in this same unity and equality of substance. For whether He is the unity between both of them, or their holiness, or their love, or whether the unity, therefore, because He is the love, and the love, therefore, because He is the holiness, it is obvious that He is not one of the two. Through him both are joined together; through him the begotten is loved by the begetter, and in turn loves Him who begot him; in Him they preserve the unity of spirit through the bond of peace, not by participation but by their own essence, not by the gift of anyone superior to themselves but by their own gift. And we are commanded by grace to imitate this unity, both in our relations with God as well as among ourselves.... The Holy Spirit is, therefore, something common, whatever it is, between the Father and the Son. But this communion itself can be appropriately designated as friendship, let it be so called, but it is more aptly called love. And this again is a substance, because God is a substance, and "God is love," as it is written [1 John 4:16].[67]

The only essence, or substantial thing, is God, who is love. Love, therefore, is the tri-termed model of creation/communication: The Father (Lover), the Son (Beloved), and the Holy Spirit (Love). The Son is the *symbol* of the Father communicated through the Holy Spirit *to* creation *in* time which, in Augustine's constraint, incarnates itself in scripture for sacramental interpretation. Symbolic interpretation of creation is often associated with the path to idolatry. Morgan points out that Augustine devalues creation's profane signs because they direct "the mind to worship the creation rather than the creator. For that reason, such signs are useless (*inutilia*), no matter how we use them."[68] Outside scripture, semiotic creation, nevertheless, still maintains its spatiotemporal structure as the embodied trace of the Word made *with* time; it is still a realm of *unfulfilled* signs that only refer because they are constituted as the issue or outflow of an act of donation within the

---

66. Augustine, *Trinity*, 5.8.9, 185; 11.12, 189–90.
67. Augustine, *Trinity*, 6.5.7, 206–7.
68. Morgan, *Incarnation of the Word*, 68.

Trinity. Be it diminished and symbolically incomplete without scripture and liturgy, the world still preserves its triadic *vestigia* as a system of profane or secular signs. The extreme plenitude of divine self-giving defines creation as communication all the way down without remainder; each part is concurrently signifier, signified, and interpreter. Rowan Williams admits that the mature Augustine "is more inclined to see terror and mystery in the natural world than to sense God in it," but he is not always so derisive in his attitude.[69] In an earlier, more *trusting*, moment, Augustine encourages us to "arouse the reason of the heart, awaken the interior inhabitant of thy interior eyes, let it take to its windows, let it examine God's creation."[70]

The environment is a text of triadic signs; it is not a realm of substantial things. The former is not mapped onto the latter as a mystical or enthusiastic product of symbolic vision. The latter is illusion, error, and sin. The former is reality as constitutive relationship. There are no real external referents, or finite things in themselves. Only God is true substantial being—creation's ultimate referent. There seems to be no reason why *the thirdness* of the interpreter should be restricted to exegetes or rational creatures in general. For Christians, scriptural interpreters and liturgical participants can be viewed as the highest symbolic grade on a comprehensive semiotic continuum of interpretation. The universe includes physical and life signs, and conventional (instituted) signs of human culture; they all belong to the supervening relationship of divine communication: *Relativum*. Each type requires an interpreter to make signs communicative. A sign is only a sign if it communicates something other than itself to an interpretative power. Differentiation of interpretative power encompasses the entire continuum. Outside the symbolic fulfillment of scripture and liturgy, there also seems to be no reason to restrict the transposition (*translata*) of triadic signs. A sign is transposed when the signifier becomes the signified, the signified becomes the interpreter, or the interpreter becomes the signified. Each term is interchangeable with the other two. There is a dynamic three in one and one in three relationship. Communication is perspectival; each position or term is defined by the changing pluriverse of contextualized semiotic standpoints—physical, ecological, and social.

The profane space-time of the *saeculum* communicates patterns of meaning. Systems of signification are drifting regimes of triadic signs within becoming; they stand in need of redemption, of symbolic waypoints, directing them to the home port of divine love—origin and destination.

---

69. Williams, "Language, Reality, and Desire," 140.

70. Augustine, *Serm.* (*de Script. Nov. Test.*) CXXVI, ii, 3, quoted in Przywara, *Augustine Synthesis*, 52.

The world has changed its base.

SIGNUM & RES

The difference between God and creation is the difference between the thing (*res*) and the sign (*signum*). God is *res*. All else is *signum*. To comprehend this ontological difference, as Rowan Williams points out, is "to know the difference of God, and be so equipped for life in God's image, the unending expansion of love."[71] God—as Triune love—is the only substance (*res*). God is eternal life *in itself* as ontological Trinity (*ad intra*), but the Triune God is dynamic relational substance, or *essentia*. God freely communicates communication *with* and *in* time. This *economic* Trinity (*ad extra*) accounts for a cosmos consisting primarily of triadic signs. Nevertheless, there are not two Trinities. Ontological Trinity is economic Trinity. Creation's economy is the only content of divine ontology, but the significance of the economy is nothing other than its relationship to the divine end. The hiatus between being and becoming, God and creation, finds its resolution in the Word made flesh: Both wholly man and wholly God—the meta-symbol, sign of signs— love, that for which heaven is torn open. The Word made flesh renders all fleshy being as word, as sign. *Ordo ad finem* (order of economic process) and *ordo ad invicem* (order of divine being) refer to one another, found themselves on one another, in perpetual semiotic transposition. The Christian, therefore, is called to convert *from the thing mentality to sign reality*.

In *De doctrina christiana*, what Augustine means by things is not, at first, straightforward. Finite things are understood in the broadest sense of everything that exists. A sign is a thing because "what is not a thing does not exist."[72] All signs are things, but not all things are signs. In another more problematic sense, things are still things when they "are not employed to signify something."[73] Augustine also speaks of "the fact that things exist, not that they signify something else besides themselves."[74] This distinction seems to imply the primary reality of self-determining substances. Intransitive identities are only secondarily and accidentally signs. Individual beings do not belong to systems of signification. To Augustine, however, this view is a mistake. *The only substance wholly not a sign is God*. Only God is not determined by relations to others. God is the lone self-sufficient reality, requiring no context or interpretation, belonging to no field of representation, and

---

71. Williams, "Language, Reality, and Desire," 147.
72. Augustine, *De Doctrina Christiana*, 1.5, 15.
73. Augustine, *De Doctrina Christiana*, 1.4, 13.
74. Augustine, *De Doctrina Christiana*, 1.5, 15.

gaining no meaning by virtue of its signification of something else. *There are no finite things in this substantial sense.* We live entirely in a world of profane signs, the outer inscription of the creative Word, in need of sacramental redemption. The opposition between the thing and the sign must be reconstituted at another level; namely, at the level of function, not substance. A sign may be considered from two points of view: As thing and as sign. On things: "When I was writing about things I began with the warning that attention should be paid solely to the fact that they existed, and to anything besides themselves that they might signify."[75] On signs: "Now that I am discussing signs, I must say, conversely, that attention should not be paid to the fact that they exist, but rather to the fact that they are signs, or, in other words, that they signify. For a sign is a thing which of itself makes some other thing come to mind, besides the impression it makes on the senses."[76] But further conceptual clarity is needed here.

To Tzvetan Todorov, "The opposition does not lie between things and signs, but between pure things and sign-things."[77] There are sign-things, but not all things owe their existence entirely to the fact that they are signs. To Augustine, it turns out that the only pure thing is God. Creation is an *economic* set of sign-things without exception. "It would be clearer," Todorov explains, "to oppose signs that *already exist* as things to those that are *deliberately created* for signification."[78] Human beings, for example, are divinely instituted sign-things. We are created *with* time and we create language *in* time. We are the product of communication and we produce communication. The truth of the temporal thing, or bare entity, is its *existence* as the sign. More clearly, that which truly signifies is existence itself. God *speaks* a sign-thing into being from nothing. The problem is the failure to recognize this fact. We relate to our environs in a confused way, enjoying and using the wrong things.

The distinction between *frui* (enjoyment) and *uti* (use) is superimposed on the distinction between *res* and *signum*. *Res* is enjoyed as an end. *Signum* is used as a means to an end. For Augustine, the only true thing to be enjoyed is the Trinity: "The things which are to be enjoyed, then, are the Father and the Son and the Holy Spirit, and the Trinity comprised by them, which is a kind of single, supreme thing, shared by all who enjoy it—if indeed it is a thing and not the cause of all things, and if indeed it is a cause. It is not easy to find a suitable name for such excellence, but perhaps

---

75. Augustine, *De Doctrina Christiana*, 2.1, 57.
76. Augustine, *De Doctrina Christiana*, 2.1, 57.
77. Todorov, *Theories of the Symbol*, 46.
78. Todorov, *Theories of the Symbol*, 48.

the Trinity is better called the one God from whom, through whom, and in whom everything is."[79] Augustine introduces two key and interconnected ideas; the first, most explicit and well covered by commentators, is the unique moral and spiritual instrumentalization of creation. "Creaturely reality," Susannah Ticciati clarifies, "is a means to the end of the enjoyment of God."[80] God alone is to be enjoyed. In respect of God, all else is to be used. The second, subtle, but perhaps more significant ontological point, antecedent to the first, is the circumvention of the relationship of cause and effect. Morgan detects Augustine's metaphysical difference: "The language of thing (*res*) and the more explicitly metaphysical language of cause (*causa*) begin to fall apart."[81] Augustine imparts a diverse cosmos of events and signs.

When describing the relationship between God and sign-things, and between sign-things, relating ultimately to God, Augustine hesitates to speak of cause and effect. Sign-things are not simply derivative and determined effects of a divine cause or, it appears to follow, accidents of divine essence. Perhaps, as a weak hypothesis, not usually made explicit by commentators, but aligned with the logic of Augustine's sign theory so far presented, it is best to think of sign-things in a Stoic manner. Todorov, for instance, does acknowledge (but does not develop) Augustine's "point of departure, namely, Stoic sign theory."[82] Augustine's portrayal of the Trinity as creator, preserver, and redeemer—that *from, through*, and *in* all sign-things exist—suggests the intimate and loving relationship (*skhesis*; *relativum*) between parent and offspring, much more than the impersonal mechanisms of cause and effect, substance and accident. Creation is characterized by the predicates of becoming, contingency, and indeterminacy. Economic sign-things, then, appear to operate as self-determining and relational bodies, facts, or non-substantial events. Sign-things are *significant affects* (*hóti*; that); although they are initially truncated and intoxicated by the wild plurality of mere arbitrary freedom (*liberum arbitrium*), and its illusion of self-making emancipation, sign-things are to be liberated by the higher freedom of God's grace (*libertas*).[83] The relationship between God and humanity, in particular, reflects a parent's unconditional love for lost or prodigal children. The latter's freedom, in the sense we have tracing here, is corrupted, but it can be restored by the homeward direction offered by the symbolic experience of scripture.

79. Augustine, *De Doctrina Christiana*, 1.10, 17.
80. Ticciati, "Castration of Signs," 165.
81. Morgan, *Incarnation of the Word*, 49.
82. Todorov, *Theories of the Symbol*, 56.
83. See Gilson, *Christian Philosophy of Saint Augustine*, 143–64.

Entry into a "properly triadic relation" with the other sign-things of the world must be free, but freely given by God's grace, a redeemed freedom, not a forceful effect of the will's power.[84] Interpretation of scripture is an opening for grace. The insatiable desire (*cupiditas*) of arbitrary freedom (*liberum arbitrium*) is redeemed by the love (*caritas*) of higher freedom (*libertas*). To enjoy (*frui*) sign-things *as if* they were substantial-things is, simultaneously, domination and idolatry:

> A person enslaved by a sign is one who worships (*veneratur*) that which is meaningful but remains unaware of its meaning. But the person who attends to or worships a useful sign, one divinely instituted, and does realize its force and significance, does not worship a thing which is only apparent and transitory but rather the thing to which all such things are to be related. Such a person is spiritual and free—and this was true even in the era of slavery when the time was not yet ripe for carnal minds to receive the clarification of the signs by which they had to be disciplined, like oxen beneath a yoke.[85]

The enjoyment or worship of *signum* as *res* imparts closure on the meaning of creation; its true *uti* in God. In theo-linguistic terms, Rowan Williams beautifully articulates the stakes of the issue:

> The language of *uti* is designed to warn against an attitude towards any finite person or object that terminates their meaning in their capacity to satisfy my desire, that treats them as the end of desire, conceiving my meaning in terms of them and theirs in terms of me . . . that the whole creation is uttered and "meant" by God, and therefore has no meaning in itself. If we do not understand this, we seek for or invent finalities within the created order, ways of blocking off the processes of learning and desiring. Only when, by the Grace of Christ, we know that we live entirely in a world of signs are we set free for the restlessness that is our destiny as rational creatures. . . . That is to say, we live in a world of restless fluidities in meaning: all terms and all the objects they name are capable of opening out beyond themselves, coming to speak of a wider context, and so refusing to stay still under our attempts to comprehend or systematize or (for these go together) idolize. . . . The Christian life itself, as we have seen, is in constant danger of premature closure.[86]

---

84. Ticciati, "Castration of Signs," 165.
85. Augustine, *De Doctrina Christiana*, 3.30, 145–46.
86. Williams, "Language, Reality, and Desire," 140–42.

Williams continues onward with his *de-constructive* sacramental semiology. The breakthrough from signs to the Word transforms the profane life to something suggestive of a better, whole one; another level of signs—what we have called *the symbolic*:

> The omnipresence of metaphor, then, is "controlled," not by a breakthrough into clear metaphysical knowledge . . . but by a central metaphor to which the whole world of signs can be related, a sign of what all signs are. The Word incarnate and crucified represents the absence and deferral that is basic to *signum* as such, and represents also, crucially, the fact that absence and deferral are the means whereby God engages our desire so that it is freed from its own pull towards finishing, towards presence and possession. Christ can only be shown to be the enactment of God if, as bearer of ultimate promise, he at the same time defers and transforms that promise by a death that presages our baptismal death as believers (and our daily losing of and longing for the face of God in the practice we call faith), and a resurrection that does not destroy our creatureliness but at least strips it of creaturely "attachment."[87]

The death of one semiotic way of life is the birth of another. It is to be properly orientated in our desires, in our love for the right things.

To enjoy sign-things as ends in themselves is a *dyadic relation*. Creaturely realities are not to be enjoyed because it diminishes their true signification—*frui* amounts to *use* as *abuse*. The asymmetrical relation of oppression is evoked. If I enjoy a sign-thing, treat it as a *res*, I totally define and expend its significance. By intending a *signum* for the fulfillment of my desire (*cupiditas*), and only this end, a sign-thing's meaning is essentially dependent on me. This sign-thing has no other possible *existence* beyond the satisfaction of my desire. I am the terminus of its signifying activity. Conversely, treating *signum* as *res* exhausts my significance; my desire needs no completion by anything else. I am reduced to my meaning for it and it is reduced to its meaning for me. If, however, a *signum* has significance in relation to another, it reaches beyond what it is in relation to me. Through my recognition that sign-things are there for my use (*uti*) rather than enjoyment, other creatures gain their true significance; sign-things are more than ends for my desire. All creaturely activity is *essentially* significatory, maintaining different and inexhaustible ways of signifying.

What is involved in the enjoyment of the Trinity? How does this singular *frui* emancipate us from the dyadic domination of our fellow

---

87. Williams, "Language, Reality, and Desire," 148.

sign-things? God is truly *res*, needing no further *environment* of interpretation. My enjoyment of the Trinity cannot work in the same way as my intended enjoyment of sign-things, mistakenly taken as *res*. God, in no way, is dependent on me for definition. The Trinity's significance cannot be closed by fulfillment of *my* desire. I cannot circumscribe, contain, or suppress the infinite existence of God. To desire God for my own end is to find myself defined wholly in terms of God's end. I am the Trinity's means, discovering that I am a sign-thing, like all other creatures, for God's use (*uti*). Egalitarian neighborliness replaces subjugation. To Ticciati, "True enjoyment of God, therefore, is incompatible with self-interested activity; as self-dispossessing, it prevents my use of finite creatures purely for my own end. Both my own desire and that of my fellow creature are placed in the greater context of God as end."[88] But the vital thing is *the conversion* of the principal form of relationship: "The dyadic relation is converted into a triadic one in which God is the third term. My 'use' of other creatures is therefore precisely not their use for my own end, but their 'use' for our shared end in God."[89] Enjoyment of God reveals an ever-present thirdness, *defining* the temporal economy. Existence, the sign's *thingness*, refers to the interpreter of interpreters. The chains of dominance and desire dissolve before the univocal thirdness of God; this precludes the dyadic reduction and exploitation of *signum*—my neighbor. "In other words," Augustine says, "that his love of his neighbor, like his own self-love, should be totally related to God."[90] Restoring the third term imparts symbolic fusion of the scriptural interpreter with the ultimate referent of interpretation: "In this state he extricates himself from all the fatal charms of transient things; turning away from these, he turns to the love of eternal things, namely the unchangeable unity which is also the Trinity."[91]

In a mostly dormant and implicit sense, love of neighbor still includes the created world outside the human community. Love's liberation from the violence of domination can also be extended to creatures and places in need of it. Augustine's inclination to blend off the sacramental commons as useless (*inutilia*) signs need not be a justification for anthropocentrism. Creation communicates itself, calling for the end of partition; it, too, is an interpreter of our existence—equally meaningful and *useful* within the love of God.

---

88. Ticciati, "Castration of Signs," 166.
89. Ticciati, "Castration of Signs," 166.
90. Augustine, *De Doctrina Christiana*, 2.18, 65.
91. Augustine, *De Doctrina Christiana*, 2.18, 65.

NINE

Aquinas and Poinsot
Semiotics of Being

AUGUSTINE INTRODUCES THE SEMIOTIC priority of the interpreter, completing the triadic circuit of communication. This chapter presents John Poinsot's sign theory.[1] Following Augustine, Poinsot accepts the interpreter as the key feature of the sign; unlike Augustine, however, signs communicate substantial things, not merely *sign-things*, and Poinsot does not restrict communication to Christian interpreters of scripture. Triadic communication is a natural (and divine) feature of the being of essential relationship. Poinsot enriches the thought of Thomas Aquinas; further integrating Trinitarian theology with Aristotelian substance-accident ontology. Poinsot's semiotics emphasizes the epistemological being of the sign. The primary site of actuality is the intellect's *real* relationship to the world through *formal signs*. *Esse*, substance-accident, and relationship are foundational metaphysical priorities. Poinsot harmonizes all three categories. As Jacques Maritain (†1973) points out, a follower of Aquinas does not think a choice has to be made between the "relation of identity" and the "relation of sign."[2]

---

1. John Poinsot is also known as John of St. Thomas, reflecting his renown as a Dominican in the tradition of St. Thomas Aquinas.
2. Maritain, "Appendix I," 387.

AQUINAS'S METAPHYSICS

Poinsot's sign theory is best understood as a *precise* extension of Aquinas's philosophy, deepening the latter's presuppositions on certain matters. This section first examines Aquinas's articulation of the Trinity and its consequent ideas on accidental relatives and constitutive relationships. Then, with a renewed doctrine of *vestigia trinitatis*, Aquinas characterizes an entity as a marriage of *esse* (trace of the Father) and form (trace of the Son). A supplementary analysis on matter, actuality, and communication is also given. Finally, Aquinas's idea of relationship (trace of the Holy Spirit) is articulated as a preparation for Poinsot's development of communicative relationship within his sign theory. His work on signs and relations extends his articulation of the gifts of the Holy Spirit.[3]

Aquinas gives the relational God of Christianity its definitive articulation as Pure Being (*Actus Purus*). Theological fidelity to the Trinity as creator means commitment to God's creation. Protection of this *divine concordat* will require different undertakings: Ontological, semiotic-epistemological, moral, and so on. A basic presupposition of Aquinas's thought is *operatio sequitur esse*.[4] The *operation* of creation follows from its creator's *esse*. Aquinas accepts Aristotle's primacy of formal substance, but he presents form as the mediatory principle of divine *esse*—that is, a creature's form *is not* the self-grounding, independent source of its own act of existing.[5] Every created being's form participates in God's *esse*. God alone is *esse*. The act of being of every creature is participated because no thing outside God is its own *esse*. A creature *gains its independency* through its participation in the gift of the Father. As Anthony J. Lisska argues, Aquinas is still committed "to the fundamental and foundational category in his metaphysics, which is primary substance."[6] To account for the independency of form *in and*

---

3. See Poinsot, *Gifts of the Holy Spirit*, 35–102.

4. See Aquinas, *Summa Theologiae*, I, q. 75.

5. There is a longstanding debate on the ontological status of Aristotle's formal substance: Is singular, formal substance the immanent source of its own being or does the doctrine of the Unmoved Mover (Actus Purus) prefigure and, thus, justify Thomas's Christian *correction* of The Philosopher because the latter's metaphysics implies a relationship of dependency of some kind between a singular form and its ground in the Unmoved Mover? To a limited extent, this question will be examined in the next chapter but, at best, due to his minimization of the being of relations, it is a crucial aporia of Aristotle's thought, appearing to side (for the most part) with the radical independency of individuals. Aquinas, of course, navigates the aporia differently; dependency on the Trinity must be secured, but without erasing the value and independency of singular creatures.

6. Lisska, *Aquinas's Theory of Perception*, 11.

through dependency on *esse*, Aquinas achieves a double composition of act and potentiality. *Singular form is to God what matter is to singular form: Potentiality.* In relation to its own embodied potentiality, a creature's form *is* the principle of actualization, i.e., matter *participates* in its form to gain realization. However, a creature's form derives its actualizing capacity of matter from elsewhere: From *participation* in God's *esse*. *Esse* is a creature's act of being. This gift of the Father is a creature's prime trace of divinity that actualizes a creature's *form*—a gift of the Son. In relation to its *esse*, a creature's form participates as a potentiality in the highest actuality: God as pure being.

To secure his metaphysics, Aquinas also adjusts Aristotle's presentation of accidental relatives. Thomas grants relationships independence and constitutive power within finite existence. This presupposition is the intricate and rich ground of Poinsot's theory of signs. Relationships are traces of the Holy Spirit, accounting for the reality of communication. A sign is a triadic relationship that communicates the actuality of a thing to an interpretative power. The source of creation's semiosis is the Trinity's divine communication. Temporal semiosis is *vestigium trinitatis*: The Father (lover/sign) reveals the Son (beloved/significate or image) to the Holy Spirit (love/interpreter): "The procession of love, by which the beloved is in the lover, like the reality spoken or understood through the conception of a word is in the understanding" (*ST* Ia, q. 27, a. 3). The Holy Spirit is thus love in person. Primordial, infinite communication is the nexus and mutual love of the Father and the Son. The Holy Spirit is First Gift from which all others proceed in time. The procession of love comprises the communication of the world's historical mission. Inscribed in each and all is the promise of a new way of life, in which the Person, Love, is made present in the Word's faithful liberation, drawing us into the joyful Triune life as its interpreters, its co-lovers, and fundamentally changing the cyclic arc of time to fulfill its Eschaton.[7]

The Trinity and Its Relationships

Aquinas is unambiguous on the Persons of the Trinity: "*Persona est relatio*" (*ST* Ia, q. 29, a. 4). The Persons are *subsistent* relations: "[*Personae*] *sunt ipsae relationis*" (*ST* Ia, q. 40, a. 2). To support his claim, Aquinas cites Boethius (†524/25): "In God the substance contains the unity; and relation multiplies the Trinity" (*ST* Ia, q. 29, a. 4). Relations do not exist *between* the Persons; they are the Trinitarian Persons. Aquinas first borrows the definition of

---

7. See Legge, *Trinitarian Christology of St. Thomas Aquinas*, 211–31.

relation from Aristotle. Relation is the "order of one thing to another," and, then, following the *relationship* tradition of Nazianzus (*skhesis*) and Augustine (*relativum*), Aquinas makes the distinction between *relation* as an accident of finite substance and *relationship* within the Godhead: "Whatever has an accidental existence in creatures, when considered as transferred to God, has a substantial existence; for there is no accident in God; since all in Him is His essence" (*ST* Ia, q. 28, a. 2). Aquinas defines relationship in the divine order; it "is not predicated of God according to its proper and formal meaning, that is to say, in so far as its proper meaning denotes comparison to that in which relation is inherent, but only as denoting regard to another" (*ST* Ia, q. 28, a. 1).

Aristotle's problematic presentation of relation as an accident of finite substance finds its root in the tension between the dual properties of inherence and to another. Even as an accident, Aquinas claims, relationship is not primarily something inhering *in* a thing; rather, it is an ordering *to* something external: "But relation in its own proper meaning signifies only what refers to another" (*ST* Ia, q. 28, a. 1). And elsewhere, "But the true idea of relation is not taken from its respect to that in which it is, but from its respect to something outside" (*ST* Ia, q. 28, a. 2). By emphasizing this aspect of relationship, the categorical elevation to divine substance is uncomplicated. In the realm of finite entities, relationship is also principally reference to another; therefore, it is "more than a perfection in the subject, [but] is a reference to the terminus, and its essential characteristic lies precisely in that reference (*esse ad*), while its inherence in the subject (*esse in*) is secondary, and may be real or only logical."[8] Relationship is ontologically independent of its realization in either reality or intellect. *Being-to-another* is first in the order of temporal beings. Inherence as an accident is secondary. In the order of divine essence, though, relationships are purely to another. Relationships do not inhere in the Persons—they are the Persons. The Persons are distinct *subsistent relationships*. As Aquinas tells us, "[Relation] enters into the notion of the Person," and he cites Boethius's affirmation that "every word that refers to the Persons signifies relation" (*ST* Ia, q. 29, a. 4). Person and relation are drawn into joyful identity.

Aquinas then expands the Trinitarian concept of relationship. Why must relative opposition be posited within the Trinity? "The very nature of relative opposition includes distinction," Aquinas argues, "hence, there must be real distinction in God, not, indeed, according to that which is absolute, namely, essence, wherein there is supreme unity and simplicity—but according to that which is relative" (*ST* Ia, q. 28, a. 3). In other words, we

---

8. Parente et al., *Dictionary of Dogmatic Theology*, 239.

cannot distinguish the Persons at all without relative opposition. In a series of lucid formulations, we read, "Therefore person in any nature signifies what is distinct in that nature," and, "distinction in God is only by relation of origin," "while relation in God is not as an accident in a subject, but is the divine essence itself; and so it is subsistent, for the divine essence subsists" (*ST* Ia, q. 28, a. 3). "Therefore," Aquinas concludes, "a divine person signifies a relation as subsisting. And this is to signify relation by way of substance, and as such a relation is a hypostasis subsisting in the divine nature" (*ST* Ia, q. 28, a. 3). When we say, "the Father," "the Son," and "the Holy Spirit," we name three distinct subsistent relationships. *The God of Christianity is Triune Relationship*. The divine essence subsists as three relata. Since each relatum is purely *being-to-another*, all three Persons are irreducibly triadic. Each Person is what it is by virtue of its *relationships to* the other two. The three Persons cannot be understood as isolated monads or dyads; they subsist through one another. Their eternal reality lies as equal and triply communicative relationships; each Person gains its singular personality in and through identity with the other two.

Tri-relational actuality is complicated by the Latin doctrine of the *filioque* (*and from the Son*). The mutual generation of the Holy Spirit by the Father *and the Son* separates Western from Eastern Christianity. Eastern critics claim their Western brethren confuse the constitution of the economic Trinity with the divine Trinity. The economic Trinity of the created order maintains the *filioque* structure, but the divine Trinity does not. Vladimir Lossky explains the distinction: "The Eastern Church has criticized western theology for confounding the exterior aspect of God's manifesting activity in the world (an activity in which the Holy Spirit, as a consubstantial Person sent by the Father and the Son, reveals the Son), and the interior aspect of the Trinity, in which the Person of the Holy Spirit proceeds from the Father alone without having any relation of origin with the Son."[9] The Western tradition tends to uphold the identical process of generation of the Holy Spirit in both economic and divine presentations of the Trinity so as not to spread conceptual confusion, i.e., two distinct Trinities because of two distinct processes. But, in doing so, this tradition has conceptual problems of its own.

Aquinas maintains that the three *divine* Persons *are* the subsistent relationships of paternity (the Father), filiation (the Son), and procession (the Holy Spirit). Western filioquism introduces a fourth divine relationship into the Godhead. The co-origination of the Holy Spirit is a relationship that

---

9. Lossky, *Mystical Theology*, 85. For an excellent historical and conceptual overview, see also, Siecienski, *Filioque*, 3–72.

must be accounted for. The generation of the Holy Spirit *from* the Father and the Son is called *active spiration*. Since it belongs to both the Father and the Son, active spiration is regarded as a unique relative distinction that does not constitute another Person of the Trinity. The essential relationship that subsists as the Holy Spirit is known as *passive spiration*; it is the relationship *to* the Father and the Son. Aquinas explains the *filioque* relationship within the Trinity:

> Although there are four relations in God, one of them, [active] spiration, is not separated from the person of the Father and of the Son, but belongs to both; thus, although it is a relation, it is not called a property, because it does not belong to only one person; nor is it a personal relation—i.e., constituting a person. The three relations—paternity, filiation, and procession—are called personal properties, constituting as it were the persons; for paternity is the person of the Father, filiation is the person of the Son, procession [passive spiration] is the person of the Holy Ghost proceeding. (*ST* Ia, q. 30, a. 2)

Essential relationships can be distinguished as follows: (1) the Father to the Son (Paternity—relationship of generation); (2) the Son to the Father (Filiation—relationship of procession); and (3) *filioque* relationships: (3.1) the Father and the Son to the Holy Spirit (Active spiration—relationship of generation), and (3.2) the Holy Spirit to the Father *and* the Son (Passive spiration—relationship of procession). Active spiration appears to maintain a relative opposition to passive spiration. This opposition implies a fourth Person of the Trinity. Are the Father and the Son, when taken together as a generational unity, a distinct Person? The answer must be negative, but how is this refutation to be understood?

Active spiration opposes passive spiration. This opposition does not denote another Person because the one *Spirator* is two Persons. The Father and the Son spirate the Holy Ghost. Active spiration is identical with paternity and filiation; it completes paternity and filiation. Their principles are perfected. In paternity, active spiration is from the Father, whereas, in filiation, it is received from the Father. This dyadic relationship requires a third relatum: The Holy Spirit. Further, of the four divine relationships, only three are in opposition to one another. Therefore, only three are really distinct: Fatherhood, Sonship, and Passive spiration (Holy Spirit). Active spiration stands in opposition to passive spiration only; it is not opposed to Fatherhood and Sonship. Therefore, active spiration is not distinct from the Father and the Son. There are only three really distinct relationships in God. There are only three Persons. Finally, without active spiration there can be no relative opposition between the Holy Spirit (passive spiration) and the Son. On their own, filiation and passive spiration do not establish a distinction between the Person of the Son and the Person of the Holy Spirit. Without the *filioque* the relationship between the Son and the Holy Spirit is not intelligible. The *filioque* makes the Trinity whole.

The fourth relationship is not really an *oppositional* relative; it cannot be properly definitive of a divine Person. Rather, as Karl Rahner upholds, this relationship is to be viewed as the communion of essential love because, "and insofar as the Father and the Son (receiving from the Father), welcoming each other in love, drawn and returning to each other, communicate themselves *in this way*, as received in mutual love, that is, as Holy Spirit."[10] The Holy Spirit is love. Loving (active spiration) and its return (passive spiration) are a singular union and exchange of divine self-communication—God's essence, love. God is love and the Person of the Holy Spirit is that nexus, the divine relationship of pure communication. The Holy Spirit is the rule of love. The unimaginable Father (lover and sign) communicates, images, or reveals Himself as The Son (beloved and significate) to the Holy Spirit (love and interpreter). The communication and interpretation of that love is creation *with* and *in* time. "That which is experienced first," Eugene TeSelle insists, "is the love of the Spirit."[11]

Trinitarian Anthropology and Ecology

Potentiality is not attributable to the Trinity. Trinitarian relationships arise out of God's infinite perfection; they are the overflowing of what God is essentially and absolutely. Triadic multiplication is not a *synthetic* process, adding to God something more than He had before. The Triune God is not a composite between the potential and the perfectly actual. There is no potentiality or composition in God. Therefore, relationships do not compromise divine simplicity, or add any growth, or novelty within God's essence. In finitude, however, there is potentiality, and there is communication *with* and *in* time. Aquinas develops an elaborate Trinitarian anthropology, drawing together previous Christian thought on human being. Here we reencounter the doctrine of *vestigia trinitatis*. All things are traces of the Trinitarian Creator. The Christian humanist tradition of Augustine and Aquinas develops *vestigia trinitatis* in terms of *imago Dei*. *Imago Dei* refers to both the creation of human beings *in* the image of God and the self-actualization of humanity *through* God's image: Christ, the Word.

10. Rahner, *Trinity*, 35.
11. TeSelle, *Augustine the Theologian*, 309.

The Trinity is a *semiotic substance*.¹² Therefore, all things are signs in the sense of being reflections of God. All things also bear a causal dependency upon God. But only human beings can conform themselves to the divine will and have the divine as the object of their activities. The human aspect of *vestigia trinitatis* is emphasized to the neglect of the created order. Like Augustine's, Aquinas's reason for this avoidance is probably due to a combination of ignorance of the physical order, fear of re-introducing pagan, occult powers back into creation, and the need to preserve the transcendence of God. Aquinas does, however, renew the theological ground of *vestigia trinitatis* as a complete doctrine of creation. The exceptional relationship of God to humanity is preserved, but the rest of the created order is not abandoned. The relationship of the Trinitarian God to creation is further clarified. Each entity is a triunity: (1) *Esse*, or act of being, is the *generative* gift of the Father's paternal expression; (2) individual nature (form or *species*) is the expressed Word, or *filiated* gift of the Son or Logos; and (3) the *relationship* to other things, the *spirated* gift of love, communication, or community is given by the Holy Spirit (*ST* Ia, q. 45, a. 7).

Imago Dei is a divine semiotic process. We are created in the image of God, and we fully realize our symbolic image by understanding, loving, and liberating the community of being. Neighborly love *is* the actualization of divine love, enfolding the entirety of creation.

Esse: Actuality and Potentiality

As the *vestigia* of the Father and the Son, a created entity is an embodied unity: Form and matter are unified by *esse*. *Esse* is an entity's act of being. Form is the principle of *esse*. "Form," Lawrence Dewan (†2015) says, is "something divine in things."¹³ Aquinas explains the distinction between *esse*, form, and matter in *De veritate* (27.1.ad 3): "God causes in us natural *esse* by creation, without the mediation of any efficient cause, but nevertheless through the mediation of a formal cause: because natural form is the principle of natural *esse*."¹⁴ In *Quaestiones disputatae de anima* (q. 6), we read, "In substances composed out of matter and form we find three [items], viz. matter, and form, and, [as a] third, *esse*, whose principle is form."¹⁵ Moreover, "For matter, by the fact that it receives form, participates in *esse*. Thus, therefore, *esse* follows upon form itself, nor nevertheless

---

12. See Lyons, *Signs in the Dust*, 39–62.
13. Dewan, *St. Thomas and Form*, 12.
14. Aquinas quoted in Dewan, "St. Thomas and the Distinction," 189.
15. Aquinas quoted in Dewan, "St. Thomas and the Distinction," 189.

is form its own *esse*, since it is its principle. And though matter does not attain to *esse* save through form, form nevertheless, inasmuch as it is form, does not need matter for its *esse*, since *esse* follows upon form itself; but it needs matter since it is such form as does not subsist by itself."[16] "*Esse*," Christopher Hughes maintains, "so construed applies to Aristotelian first substances."[17] Matter and accidents are ontologically thin traces of *esse*; their degree of being depends on their *formal* actualization. For Stephen L. Brock, Aquinas presents substantial form as that which "holds a thing in being" (*ST* I, q. 59, a. 2).[18] That which holds substantial form in being is God's *esse*. Dewan concludes that the ontological priority of form is the "doctrine which will prevail" for created things.[19] Aquinas (*Quodlibetum 9, 2, 2, responsio.*) seems quite clear on the point: "*Esse* is attributed only to a substance which subsists *per se*: everything which does not subsist *per se* but in another and with another, whether it is an accident, or a substantial form, or any part, does not have *esse* as though it truly were."[20] Each created entity, then, is a triunity *held in being* by its *esse*. An entity's act of being is *from elsewhere* than the entity itself: The gift of the Father through the Son.

What is ultimate, in Aquinas's system, is actuality. Actuality is explanatorily basic because it is ontologically basic. Intelligibility and actuality are interchangeable terms. Privation (*potentiality/matter*), accidents (*in another*), and relationship (*with and to another*) are types of actuality. To be either as matter, accident, or relation is first and foremost *to be*. Aquinas's *hylomorphism*, for example, is a conceptual distinction on a diminished feature of actuality: Potentiality. Potential matter is not something that a form is literally joined to, or that it somehow dwells within. Entities are not compositions of actuality plus mysterious stuff known as potentiality. According to Robert Pasnau, an entity is "various forms of actuality, bundled together in a certain way," and unified "around a single substantial form."[21] Potentiality exists as embodied levels of privation and reality; greater and lesser degrees of *formal* actuality. The matter of a substance is not something over and above its form. Matter does not have any autonomous causal powers not attributed to form. Actuality discloses matter in different ways; there is motion, alternation, generation, and corruption. Potentiality also exists as hierarchical intensities of being.

16. Aquinas quoted in Dewan, "St. Thomas and the Distinction," 189.
17. Hughes, "Matter and Actuality in Aquinas," 65.
18. Brock, *Philosophy of Saint Thomas Aquinas*, 49.
19. Dewan, "St. Thomas and the Distinction," 189.
20. Aquinas quoted in Hughes, "Matter and Actuality in Aquinas," 65.
21. Pasnau, *Thomas Aquinas on Human Nature*, 135.

Pasnau calls Aquinas's ontology a "monism" of actuality but, perhaps, because Aquinas is not reducing everything to *form*, it is more accurate to view his ontology as the expansion, multiplication, or pluralizing of actuality.[22] More and more reality is grasped by the intellect. Privation is reduced. Further participatory strata reveal more traces of divine *esse*. There is first actuality—form *per se* as the principle of *esse*. There is second actuality. Form's operational typology mediates privation (potential or matter), contingent categories (accidents), and communication (relationships). As Joseph Owens indicates, Aquinas is simply being a consistent student of Aristotle:

> The matter is indeed a constitutive part of the corporeal composite, yet it is not the source of any new intelligibility for it. The intelligibility, even in regard to the matter, has to come entirely from the thing's other constituent, that is, from the form. This will mean, then, that the matter and the composite are knowable only in virtue of the form. Aristotle expresses that tenet concisely in saying that what is to be expressed in concept or word is the form and the individual insofar as it has the form, but never the material constituent just as itself. Only through the form is the matter or composite thing knowable.[23]

Behind one layer of being there is another, and behind that one is yet another. If all actuality is stripped away, there is nothing left. More precisely, there is *prime matter*.

The only outside of actuality is privation-in-itself, marking ontological difference between being and nothing. Aquinas states, "[Only] that matter which is construed without any form or privation, but is subject to form and privation, is called prime matter, inasmuch as there is no other matter prior to it (*De Principiis Naturae* 2)."[24] Prime matter is the term that marks the edge of intelligibility. Beyond the limit of being there is no degree of actuality—ontological zero. Prime matter is "that at which the analysis of natural bodies ultimately stops (II SENT 12.1.4c)."[25] Aquinas takes himself to be following Aristotle when he insists prime matter does not exist in its own right; the existence of non-existence, the form of formlessness, is a logical absurdity, a contradiction. "Matter," Thomas claims, "is never stripped of form and privation, because at one time it exists under one form, at another time under another. But in itself (*per se*) it can never exist, because given

---

22. Pasnau, *Thomas Aquinas on Human Nature*, 135.
23. Owens, *Aristotle's Gradation of Being*, 141–42.
24. Aquinas quoted in Hughes, "Matter and Actuality in Aquinas," 70.
25. Aquinas quoted in Pasnau, *Thomas Aquinas on Human Nature*, 43.

that by its nature it has no form, it has no actual existence, since actual existence comes only through form, whereas it is solely in potentiality" (*De Principiis Naturae* 2.112–18).²⁶ Prime matter defies containment by operational actuality; it has no motion, alternation, generation, or corruption. Thinking the *Nothing* is thinking the limit of being. Prime matter is the place where nothing stops and actuality begins. Pasnau concludes, "In a sense, then, Aquinas's theory of matter is eliminative. His talk of prime matter does not introduce some primitive, mysterious stuff. It does just the opposite, because it entails the complete rejection of matter as any kind of stuff having independent ontological status."²⁷

Commentators on Aquinas seem at a loss to pin down prime matter's exact role in his metaphysics, but it is usually associated with contingency and becoming.²⁸ It may not exist, but prime matter still may affect the constitution of *finite* creatures. Lawrence Dewan directs us to an extraordinary series of passages by Charles de Koninck (†1965). The latter philosopher presents his view on prime matter through an analysis of *contingent form*: "Natural beings are contingent because there is in them a real potency for not-being: prime matter."²⁹ Koninck asks the question, "Precisely what do we mean by the contingency of the form?"³⁰ In his answer, though, he appears to recoil from his initial position:

> Indeed, the form is not contingent because its co-principle is for it a potency toward not-being; the composite is corruptible because its form is contingent. It is the contingency of the form which is the intrinsic reason for the precariousness and the uncertainty of its [the composite's] existence. That is why we can conceive of a form which would not be contingent, in spite of its union with matter—the human form after the resurrection, where the composite is incorruptible."³¹

Koninck confesses prime matter as an explanation for the contingency of creatures but, then, he subtracts it, leaving the *principle* that accounts for the contingency of form unexplained. Prime matter as a principle of contingency resembles Aristotle's indeterminate potentiality (*sterēsis*, *adynamia*, and *mē ontos*): "[The] coming-to-be of what is not" (*De Generatione* 1.3,

---

26. Aquinas quoted in Pasnau, *Thomas Aquinas on Human Nature*, 43.
27. Pasnau, *Thomas Aquinas on Human Nature*, 43.
28. See Pasnau, *Thomas Aquinas on Human Nature*, 130–32.
29. Koninck quoted in Dewan, "Importance of Substance," 122.
30. Koninck quoted in Dewan, "Importance of Substance," 122.
31. Koninck quoted in Dewan, "Importance of Substance," 122.

319a26–28).[32] Indeterminate potentiality may be related to the determinate potentiality found in a finite entity's form and matter composite. How?

We will revisit Aristotle's answer in the next chapter but, for Aquinas, as Brock argues, "prime matter is only potency, and it has no form of its own. This is why Thomas holds that not even God can make it exist by itself."[33] But if matter cannot *be* without becoming actual, is it not then a variety of form? The being of non-being must be form, being that erases non-being; otherwise it falls into a contradiction, abhorred by God. Being is (and cannot not be). Non-being is not (and cannot be). But the conceptual *reality* and *role* of matter, not-being, seems deferred rather than answered here. For his part, Brock does risk a very Aristotelian explanation of "prime matter, which is potency to all forms. But matter, as we have said, has no actuality or identity of its own. It simply is all things, though only in potency."[34] Form and the privation of form deserve a more comprehensive analysis.

Prime Matter, Knowledge, and Communication

Prime matter may suggest Aristotle's negative principle of vital process but, to Aquinas, it seems to function epistemologically rather than ontologically. Prime matter marks the limit of *our* current comprehension of being. This limit is not fixed; it extends across domains previously thought to be nonexistent. Extending the limit brings additional knowledge, more actuality. Aquinas uses bronze as an analogy for prime matter (II Sent. 17.1.1 ad. 4). Thinking bronze's prime matter may lead to further discoveries beyond the limits of our current knowledge. Modern physical science, for example, shows bronze has more layers of actuality at the atomic and sub-atomic levels. Bronze's present prime matter denotes further unknown levels of actuality. What was thought to be an unalterable boundary, separating the actual from non-existence, shifts to uncover more degrees of being. This progression indicates prime matter has more to do with our ignorance of reality than being a true principle of reality.

Aquinas's analysis of prime matter may not mean ontological recoil from the constitutive power of absolute privation. A more generous reading suggests its epistemological role is mostly consistent with what Michael Polanyi (†1976) later calls *tacit knowledge*: "I shall reconsider human knowledge by starting from the fact that we can know more than we can

---

32. All quotations of Aristotle's *On Generation and Corruption* are from vol. 1 of Aristotle, *Complete Works*.

33. Brock, *Philosophy of Saint Thomas Aquinas*, 42.

34. Brock, *Philosophy of Saint Thomas Aquinas*, 68.

tell."[35] Actuality is the current state of the known, but it *emerges* from an unknown, indeterminate, or *tacit* dimension, which is always just past the limit of present knowledge. Polanyi, like Aquinas, assumes only the actual is knowable. The *tacit* dimension is fully actualized, but it is unknown; otherwise, we could never know it. Indetermination is unknown determination. As presently known as unknown, however, the *tacit* dimension can only be *the Nothing*. More clearly, in Aquinas's sense, the *tacit* dimension is prime matter. Un-pre-thinkable prime matter marks known actuality from other unknown tiers of being; it is the sign of our present conceptual limitation: "It embodies the *metaphysical claim* of tacit knowing. The act of tacit knowing thus implies the claim that its result is an aspect of reality which, as such, may yet reveal its truth in an inexhaustible range of unknown and perhaps still unthinkable ways."[36] "My definition of reality, as that which may yet inexhaustibly manifest itself," Polanyi explains, "implies the presence of an *indeterminate* range of *anticipations* in any knowledge bearing on reality. But besides this indeterminacy of its prospects, tacit knowing contains also an *actual knowledge* that is indeterminate, in the sense that its content *cannot be explicitly stated*."[37] Tacit knowing is the movement from the known *to* and *through* the unknown dimension, unveiling more actuality.

Polanyi calls the actualization of knowledge, "communication"; it is surprisingly, or unsurprisingly, a triadic process of interpretation: "A stands for B to C."[38] A (sign) stands for B (significate) to C (interpretant). Communication is triadic in form. It is always *personalized*—socially embedded, and biologically embodied—*indwelt*. Knowledge actualization depends on the interpretant. Polanyi commentator, Harry Prosch (†2005), claims, "'Meaning' is, therefore, really a triadic term"—that is, "there must also always be a person, a user, an intender involved."[39] The universe, then, is meaningful, triadic actuality. Life is its most active and demonstrable achievement, of which the human being is life's most complex and, perhaps, dangerous occurrence. Communication is "a triad of triads," which is "a sequence of three integrations," namely, sense-reading, sense-giving, and sense-reading again.[40] To illustrate this rich semiotic structure, he uses the *human* example of travel and letter writing:

---

35. Polanyi, *Tacit Dimension*, 4.
36. Polanyi, "Logic of Tacit Inference," 4.
37. Polanyi, "Logic of Tacit Inference," 4.
38. Polanyi, "Sense-Giving and Sense-Reading," 301
39. Prosch, *Michael Polanyi*, 69.
40. Polanyi, "Sense-Giving and Sense-Reading," 305.

Suppose we travel in a country we have not visited before. By the end of the morning we will be full of new experiences and may report them by letter to a friend so that he may read our message and try to understand our experiences. This is a sequence of three integrations. The *first* is an intelligent understanding of sights and events, the *second* the composing of a verbal account of this experience and the *third* the interpretation of this verbal account with a view to reproducing the experience which is reported. The first two integrations are the work of one person, while the third is done by another person, the friend addressed by the first. We may note also some variation in the character of the three consecutive integrations. The first triad is mainly cognitive; it has the structure we met in the process of perception and, more strikingly perhaps, in the identification of a specimen by an expert. The second triad, which puts the result of the first into words, resembles more the performance of a practical skill, while the third returns once more to the cognitive type which integrates clues to a meaningful experience. The *first* triad is more a sense-*reading*, while the *second* more a sense-*giving* and the *third*, once more, a sense-*reading*.[41]

Being is convertible with sense. The appearance of the original three integrations initiates unlimited semiosis. The universe manifests a continuity of meaning. Triadic sense relations have an indefinitely generative character.

All creation is meaningful actuality. Aquinas tells us there is a trace of the divine in it. If it is properly interpreted, creation will be saved. To understand is to liberate a thing's divine essence, recognizing that its significance belongs to God: Soteria of the Holy Spirit. "When it came night," Stephen Crane (†1900) writes of shipwreck survivors, "the white waves paced to and fro in the moonlight, and the wind brought the sound of the great sea's voice to the men on the shore, and they felt that they could then be interpreters."[42]

The Relationship between Creator and Created

Even with his emphasis on the gifts of the Father and the Son, Aquinas provides a secure foundation for understanding the Holy Spirit's gift of Relationship in the created order. A created entity's *esse* is the relationship of causal dependence on God. "For [passive] creation is not a change," Aquinas says, "but that dependence of created being (*esse creati*) on its source from which it is set forth. And so it [creation] is of the category of relation"

---

41. Polanyi, "Sense-Giving and Sense-Reading," 305–6.
42. Crane, *Open Boat*, 77.

(*Summa contra Gentiles* II, c. 18).[43] The God to creature relationship is non-mutual and asymmetrical. The creature is related to God by a constitutive relationship of dependence. We exist *because* we participate in God's *esse*. God is related to the creature only by a logical relationship, being completely independent, uncreated substance; it is a relationship of the intellect only.[44] "The creature-to-God relation is real," Mark G. Henninger verifies, and "the God-to-creature relation is only of reason."[45] It must be rational because two things cannot be mutually and *really* related if their foundations are incommensurable. God transcends the genus of created being (*extra genus esse creati*). God, to Aquinas, is "altogether outside the genus of created being by which the creature is really referred to God" (*De Potentia*, q. 7, a. 10).[46] God and creatures are of radically different ontological orders. Any relationship between different orders of being is termed asymmetrical.[47]

Creatures depend on God for existence, but God does not depend on creatures for existence. This relationship of ontological dependence constitutes an entity's intrinsic form (*formae intrinsecae*). Created *esse* always entails a relationship to its creator. According to Rudi A. Te Velde, "No created essence *exists* without a relation to its good creator."[48] A creature's act of existence is the foundation for both its abiding limitation that subsists as its own being and its participation in divine substance. Henninger clarifies Aquinas's position: "Specifically, Aquinas expands the Aristotelian notion of action-as-foundation from its original meaning as a determination of an already existing substance to the creature's created act of existence which serves as the foundation of the real relation of dependence on God."[49] The relationship between divine cause and creation is a hierarchical distribution of dependent effects. Each tier is a form, a species. Horizontal planes of being have the capacity for mutual and symmetrical relationships. Vertical planes do not. The structure of hierarchy means ascending and descending grades of being. Incommensurable orders of being lack the common ground for real relationships. Relationships between species levels are non-mutual and asymmetrical. Everything that is caused by God, however, participates by way of a certain likeness in God, not according to the same species, but in

---

43. Aquinas quoted in Henninger, *Relations*, 38
44. See Cavarnos, *Classical Theory of Relations*, 89–92.
45. Henninger, *Relations*, 33.
46. Aquinas quoted in Henninger, *Relations*, 36.
47. See Cavarnos, *Classical Theory of Relations*, 89–92.
48. TeVelde, *Participation and Substantiality in Thomas Aquinas*, 49.
49. Henninger, *Relations*, 38.

respect to the *esse* that is common to all things. Structured hierarchy retains an egalitarian property: Dependence on God for being.

The unique presence of finite *esse* in humanity as *imago Dei* does not mean we are lesser, or second gods. Just because a creature is illuminated and heated by the sun does not mean a creature is the sun. Creation is the outpouring of the infinite love of the Trinity into a multitude of various things. Each entity reflects the Trinity's simple and perfect love in its own way. The similarity between God and creation is an analogical one. God communicates his likeness to His *effects*. A real similarity exists between God and creatures because God has caused creatures. The similarity between Creator and created is *derived* from the Creator. There is an ontological difference between God and creation. The first Being differs from finite beings by its different relationship to the same. The Trinity exists *by its perfect relational essence*. The finite creature exists *by participation* in its essential relationship of dependence on God. Divine cause and contingent effect possess the same characteristic of being in accordance with its own distinct ontological order.

Relationships between species, then, have a commensurate ground. Participation in *esse* means the hierarchy of species is not immutable, static, or the model for domination. What is common to all species is causal dependence on God. Essential relationship suggests being communicates a dimension of univocal equality. All things depend on the Trinity for their existence. All divinely dependent things also depend on each other. Our participation in *esse* is how we comprehend God's relationship to us. This *rational* relationship encourages us to understand the Trinity's communication of actuality to the rest of creation. We understand God's rational relationship to us through understanding our relationship to others. Human self-actualization (*imago Dei*) is through the intellect's comprehension of the community of being. We read in Thomas, "That which the intellect first conceives as most known, and into which it resolves all other concepts, is being" (*De Veritate*, q.1, a.1).[50] Further layers of actuality are discovered by the intellect; more interdependent species are comprehended. In the created order, between the human creature and other creatures (not creatures and God), a rational relation is interchangeable with a real one. "This whole doctrine of knowledge," Étienne Gilson summarizes, "can be summed up in a few words: every cognition of an object other than ourselves is a real relationship between our own being and another being."[51] To be is to be in relationship with creation's self-communicative actuality. Our knowledge is

---

50. Aquinas quoted in Peifer, *Concept in Thomism*, 32.
51. Gilson, *Elements of Christian Philosophy*, 261.

only limited by our present interpretation of being; it is revisable, opening onto more and more actuality. Being in the order of knowing is the gift of the Holy Spirit. Communication signifies *mutual actualization, divine dependency, plurality, and equality.*

POINSOT ON RELATIONSHIPS

Aquinas's ontology of the Trinity emphasizes the gifts of the Father (*esse*) and the Son (form). The gift of the Holy Spirit is relationship. *Relationships are a unique kind of actuality. They communicate other kinds of actuality. Being in the order of communication is the realm of the sign. Signification is a species of relationship.* John Poinsot develops the communicative aspect of Aquinas's ontology; he is not, however, innovating on Aquinas's thought. Poinsot keeps the ontological supremacy of *esse* and form, working out Aquinas's ideas on relationships in the context of our knowledge of created things.[52] In his articulation of the Trinity, Aquinas has given us a crucial set of distinctions and priorities. Relationship is *essentially to another*. In his *Tractatus de Signis*, Poinsot repeats Aquinas's position on relationships, "Relatives are those things whose entire being consists in bearing toward another."[53] Only secondarily do relatives function as inherent accidents. Poinsot's advance is, as John Deely tells us, "the discovery that relations are fundamental realities *alongside* substances."[54] Reality is a relational order of essential things.

There is an essential relationship to the Trinity. Relationship, though, is not the principle of *esse*. Relationship is a type of actuality. Actuality is not a type of relationship. Relationship to the Trinity does not overturn the priority of the *first* principle of *esse*. *Essential form* is not a bundle of relationships. The kind of actuality that communicates divine actuality between God and created *esse* does not subsume its terms. Actuality is not a monism of communication. Essential relationships communicate actual things through their formal signs; they do not replace things. There are relationships between entities and between their species divisions of being—ecological and cultural types of communication. Relationships are dynamic, symbiotic and, above all, open to the interpretive intellect. As well as being *alongside*, relationships also communicate many secondary formal operations internal

---

52. Poinsot's restriction of semiosis to the created order is challenged, I think successfully, by Nathan Lyons. For Aquinas, semiosis belongs to the Trinity. See Lyons, *Signs in the Dust*, 13–62.

53. Poinsot, *Tractatus de Signis*, 81 (hereafter, *TDS* with page numbers following).

54. Deely, "Postmodernity as the Unmasking of Objectivity," 46.

to an entity. Accidents and matter, in many respects, are intelligible through *formal relationships*.

The *intrinsic form of essential relationship* accounts for the participatory communication of an entity's first actuality—form's relationship to *esse* and, through *esse*, to God. This relationship is common to all finite creatures. Second actuality also admits relationship. Forms have an *operational* relationship to matter and its accidents. Poinsot, for example, claims, (1) Aquinas's principle of individuation is *matter designated by quantity*, and (2) this principle "*is produced by an intrinsic relation of matter to quantity considered as dividing and separating form.*"[55] The principle of individuation is distinguishable from the individual or numerical unity as a cause is distinguished from its effect: "But the formal individuality caused by the principle of individuation is metaphysically the individual difference itself and physically it is the numerical and individual unity whereby a being is one so that it is not further divisible or communicable through other contracting differences."[56] Potentiality is *formally* communicated to accidental quantity. There is a contraction of differences. The degrees of privation and quantitative indeterminateness are radically reduced, reaching a singular limit point of *this* individual's determinate dimensions. Poinsot claims, "*The principle of individuation of material substances is matter considered as radically related to indeterminate dimensions.*"[57] From matter to quantity, there is actualization of relationship—*information* that accounts for singular difference.

John Poinsot, then, clarifies the role of relationship within the secondary formal operations of a singular entity. For his theory of signs, Poinsot refines the concept of *essential relationship*. Relativum secundum esse is "an adventitious order, which consists in pure respect, or *whose whole being is to hold itself towards another entity.*"[58] In *relativum secundum esse*, we find the continuation of Augustine's *relativum*, and Nazianzus's *skhesis*. Relationship is a *vestigium* of the Holy Spirit. *Relativum secundum esse* is the expression "used to denote the relation in itself only, not also the ground of the relation."[59] Without *essential* relationships, we have no way of understanding our relationship with God and the community of being. However, if communication with another site of awareness (divine and created) is real, essential relationship is real, too.

---

55. Poinsot quoted in Gracia and Kronen, "John of Saint Thomas," 522.
56. Poinsot quoted in Gracia and Kronen, "John of Saint Thomas," 514.
57. Poinsot quoted in Gracia and Kronen, "John of Saint Thomas," 526.
58. Poinsot quoted in Cavarnos, *Classical Theory of Relations*, 79
59. Poinsot quoted in Cavarnos, *Classical Theory of Relations*, 80.

Essential relativity is not reducible to *ens reale* or *ens rationis*. *Relativum secundum esse* is independent of its realization in both thing and concept. Reality and mind are two types of relative actuality. *Relativum secundum esse* also ensures each order is *essentially communicative and commensurable* with the other. Each type grounds itself in the other as communicational exchange of information. Symmetrical, mutual, and *essential* relationships constitute distinct categorical identities. Essential relativity simultaneously preserves and resolves the *aporia* between mind and world. The tie between the two issues a concept. *Ens rationis* is the intellect's conceptual being. Concepts receive and express the things communicated by *rerum natura*'s essential relativity, obtaining independently of the considerations of the intellect. Real things communicate their *formal signs*. These communiqués are received by the intellect as the basis of its concepts.

Aristotle divides *ens* into *ens rationis* and *ens reale* before he divides *ens reale* into the ten categories; therefore, *ens rationis*, properly considered, is the order of actuality external to categorical reality. The actuality of the intellect admits the distinction between concepts (*relativium secundum esse in first intention*) and conventional languages (*relativum secundum dici in second intention*). The latter is founded on the former—that is, the latter is grounded in the reality (*ens reale*) that the former reveals to the latter through its concepts. Conceptual unity diffuses itself through an indefinite series of conventional languages. A concept is formed by the first or direct application of the intellect to a thing's essential relationship to the mind. This process is known as *first intention*. "In first intention," Edward J. Furton maintains, "the intellect directs its gaze to the thing as it exists in the real."[60] Things communicate themselves as formal signs through essential relativity, securing the reality of the intellect's concept formation.

The apparent autonomy of human discourse is the outcome of the formal convertibility of concepts and things. Conventional communicability, then, depends on the medium of *relativum secundum esse*. The ontological independence of essential relativity is not reducible to intellectual concepts or categorical reality. The relationship that ties together the rational and the real, producing a concept, is essentially distinct from the intellect and reality: *Being-to-another*. Conventional signification depends on the reality of concepts as its condition of possibility. Stipulated terms (*relativum secundum dici*) do not require an extra-linguistic referent except for the occasional here and now practicalities of discourse. A real cat, for example, shows itself here and now, and I say the English term, "cat." Primary signification is not to existing things, but to other terms, grounded in their concepts, e.g.,

---

60. Furton, "Constitution of the Object in Kant and Poinsot," 64n28.

concept of cat. Systems of reference appear enclosed, arbitrary, and disconnected from immediate experience.

To Poinsot, though, all conventional languages are grounded in the prior reality of universal concepts, liberating language to its internally self-referential discrete infinity—its perpetual, deferred, and different series of signifiers. In other words, conventional signification does not need a direct tie to reality to provide the conditions for describing and understanding something. I do not require the presence of a cat to write a novel about a cat; just the concept of *catness*. Only *secondarily*, then, is reference to existing entities a requisite condition for intelligibility. Real concepts from *first intention* serve as the substrate, the conceptual point of real presence, for linguistic invocation of the orders of actuality that conventional languages signify. *Relativum secundum esse* communicates homogenous and synchronic formal signs that turn into the concepts of a *species* intellect—that is, *first intention* provides the unity of intelligibility that pervades common humanity. Despite conventional differences, we can *really* communicate to one another because we have normative concepts rooted in the real. The languages of *second intention* depend on the universality and reality of formal concepts in *first intention* for their operation. Conventional languages assume real ties to things through the latter's communication of their *formal signs*.

Conventional terms maintain their being as transcendental (not categorically real) relationships of the intellect. "A relation is transcendental," Furton explains, "when its being is not found within (and so when it 'transcends') the ten categories. A transcendental relation, therefore, does not properly belong to the Aristotelian category of relation, but is a way of describing the constitution of finite being—substance and accidents."[61] The knowing subject immediately attains only her own system of predication. These immanent products of the intellect are called *second intentions*. The doctrine that posits only transcendental relationships is known as *nominalism* [nominalis; "of or pertaining to names"]. Constitutive relationships—*relativum secundum esse*—are reduced to accidental properties of terms, denying their mind-independent and constitutive being. Transcendental relatives are useful connections that the intellect imputes between predicated terms. If the referent to essential relativity is dropped, however, logical-conceptual actuality (*ens rationis*) does not have a ground in *ens reale*. There is no outside the mind. Concepts are our own variable constructions: Meta-conventions. A conventional term no longer assumes a concept's tie to

---

61. Furton, "Constitution of the Object in Kant and Poinsot," 65.

an extra-mental reality. Fields of representation encounter only themselves. We encounter only ourselves.

Nominal relationships are transcendental relationships only; the order of being known as *relationes secundum dici seu transcendentales*. Concepts are denied their direct relationship with things. There is only second intention. Language is an exclusive affair of transcendental relatives and terms. Poinsot defines *transcendental* relationship as "an order included in some absolute [or intrinsic] nature."[62] To Constantine Cavarnos (†2011), a transcendental relationship is a name "used to denote not only the relation itself, but the quality, or whatever it is, in which the relation is grounded."[63] Further, "Transcendental relations are distinguished sharply from relations *secundum esse*, because while the latter are nothing but relations, the former have a dual aspect, being not only relations, but having also an intrinsic nature."[64] Transcendental relations are "entities which are not really relations but are called relations because they bear a certain analogy to relations in the strict sense (*relationes secundum esse*), it holds that a relation may sometimes exist even though it has no relatum. It holds also that a certain class of relations which it calls 'logical' (*rationis*) do not have a ground."[65] Put otherwise, a transcendental term presumes Aristotle's accidental category of *ta pros ti*. Transcendental relatives inhere in their terms, denying *relativum secundum esse*—the Trinity's *relativum*. This crucial *vestigium* of the Holy Spirit no longer secures the independent and communicative presence of things in creation. The real and the conceptual distinction collapses. The human intellect's second intention also envelops first intention as the principle of actualization. *The place of formal signs* no longer receives and interprets reality; it constructs reality. We are only connected to a world we construct for ourselves. This self-referential closure of the real commons is cognitively and socially projective of a *virtual commons*—there is the imaginary and *the will* to contruct a world in its image. We only hear ourselves. Interpretation does not conform to the actualities of the world; it does not receive and reproduce them as a contemplating, mediating, and loving subject. There is *nothing* to interpret, understand, or love. The void outside requires we self-actualize through an image we posit for ourselves. The demise of the real, therefore, signifies never-ending conflict between bearers of world-pictures because the latter are without any legitimacy for truth besides temporary, superior power.

62. Poinsot quoted in Cavarnos, *Classical Theory of Relations*, 85.
63. Cavarnos, *Classical Theory of Relations*, 85.
64. Cavarnos, *Classical Theory of Relations*, 85.
65. Cavarnos, *Classical Theory of Relations*, 70.

To conserve the outside, creation itself, then, we must affirm ontological convertibility. *Ens rationis* is co-objective with *ens reale*. *Relativum secundum esse* preserves and integrates the relationally commensurate divisions of relative being—mind and world. Real things communicate their *formal signs* to an interpretative intellect. Poinsot reaffirms Aquinas's position "that relation is something mind-independent" [relationem esse aliquid reale].[66] Further: "There can be no doubt what the opinion of St. Thomas is, for he expressly argues against those who said that relation is not a thing of nature, but something of the mind."[67] Poinsot argues for the extra-mental reality of relationship. This position counters those who "have thought that relations are nothing but either extrinsic denominations or something mind-dependent," which are also, "those who do not distinguish mind-dependent relations from a fundament," leading to the fundamental error "that relations do not belong to things except according to objective being, and are only intentional affections or conditions by which we compare one thing to another. Whence they constitute relations [i.e., make them consist] not in a respect, but in a comparison."[68] For both Aquinas and Poinsot, the ultimate justification for *relativum secundum esse* is the Trinity: The Holy Spirit's *essential trace*.

To deny the independency of *relativum secundum esse* is to deny the Trinity is independently real—that is, creatures and their relations are *mind-independently real* because the Trinity and its Relationships are mind-independently real. If the Trinity's is actually distinct from the mind, creation's essential relativity is, too. Relationship is the divine heart of reality:

> This reason is often used by St. Thomas, and he indicates another in the first Book of the *Commentary on the Sentences Written for Annibald*, dist. 26, q. 2, art. 1, culled from the believed fact of there being divine relations, which, insofar as they are mutually distinguished, are given independently of the finite mind, for otherwise the relative persons would not be distinguished independently of the finite mind, which would be a heretical assertion. But the divine relations are not distinguished except as pure relations are according to the way they have their being. For if they were distinguished other than as pure relation, there would be not only relative things divided in God, but absolute

---

66. Poinsot, *TDS* 82.

67. Poinsot, *TDS* 81. Poinsot continues: "See the *Summa Theologica* I, q. 13, art. 7; q. 28, art. 2; q. 39, art. 1. See also the *Summa contra gentiles* Book II, chap. 12; the *Disputed Questions on the Power of God*, q. 7, arts. 8 and 9, and q. 8, art. 2. And in a thousand other passages, but particularly in these" (Poinsot, *TDS* 82).

68. Poinsot, *TDS* 82, 83.

ones also [which is impossible]. Therefore there exist in God relations independent of all finite minds, although on account of the supreme divine simplicity they are identified with substance. Why therefore should there be any reluctance to acknowledge a mind-independent existence of relations among created things, relations which are neither substance nor infinite?[69]

To deny the reality of relations in the created order diminishes the Trinity's reality of relations:

> Finally, those holding this opinion will find it most difficult to explain how there are three relative persons in the divine processions constituted and distinct independently of every finite mind, if relations are extrinsic denominations. They will likewise find it very difficult to explain from which absolute form such denominations derive. But if in God relations are not extrinsic denominations, but intrinsic forms, although substantial and identified with the divine substance, why would we say that such an order of relative being, although not identified with substance, is impossible in creatures? Created things have rather more the fundament of such a relation, because they are more dependent and ordered or subordinated to another.[70]

SIGNS AND COGNITION

In view of Aquinas's Trinitarian presuppositions on relationships, the project of Poinsot's *Tractatus* is to clarify the sign within logic and cognition. Terms, propositions, syllogisms, and all the machinery of logic presuppose the sign: "The universal instrument of Logic is the sign, from which all its instruments are constituted."[71] Signs are also basic to experience: Perception and the intelligibility of the world. To Poinsot, the sign is "That which represents something other than itself to a cognitive power" [Id, quod potentiae cognoscitivae aliquid aliud a se repraesentat].[72] Jacques Maritain enhances Poinsot's definition: "*Signum est quod repraesentat aliud a se potentiae cognoscenti*. A sign is something that makes something other than itself present to knowledge. A sign manifests and makes known something for which it stands vicariously and to which it is related as the measured is to

---

69. Poinsot, *TDS* 82–83.
70. Poinsot, *TDS* 83.
71. Poinsot, *TDS* 38.
72. Poinsot, *TDS* 25.

the measure."[73] However, Poinsot's recognition of the intrinsic relationality of the sign does little to transform the basic tenants of Aristotelian logic, i.e., subject-predicate/substance-accident. There is no revolutionary turn to the Stoic idea of a proposition or development of an alternative triadic-semiotic (Christianized) logic of becoming for the created order. Poinsot's achievement is restricted to the ontological aspects of representation—that is, his relational amendments are fundamentally epistemological in character.

The sign is a basic feature of reality and human knowledge. How do formal signs communicate real things as concepts within cognition's *first intention*? How do concepts communicate conventional (transcendental) signs within cognition's *second intention*? To answer these questions, Poinsot explains what signification means. "To signify," Poinsot claims, "is said of that by which something distinct from itself becomes present."[74] *Signs may be divided in two ways: (1) As they are ordered to a knowing power, and (2) as they are ordered to something signified.* In the former division, there is a twofold distinction between formal and instrumental signs. The formal sign has two aspects: Impressed species (sense) and expressed species (intellect). In the latter division, there is a threefold distinction between natural, stipulated, and customary signs. Poinsot's theory of signification emerges from his presentation of formal and stipulated signs.

(1) *As the sign is ordered to a knowing power.* (a) *Formal sign*: "The formal sign is formal awareness which represents of itself, not by means of another."[75] Formal signs are the relational means *by which* we know something, and *that which* a cognitive power knows as a *conceptual* something; they are the exclusive preserve of mental activity. Formal signs of *first intention* constitute the rationally real (*ens rationis*): The communicative actualization of *relativum secundum esse*. We have two kinds of knowing powers, namely, sense and intellect. There are, consequently, two aspects of formal signification to a cognitive power: (i) the *sign*-image (the *impressed species*/sense), and (ii) the *signified*-concept (*species intelligibilis* or *expressed species*/intellect). The former is *that by which* the intellect immediately understands something. An impressed species has its actuality as a communicative vehicle of objective reality; it delivers the objective being of an entity from outside to inside—*ens reale* to *ens rationis*. The latter is *that which* the cognitive power understands as first intentional interpretation: The species-concept as communicated and understood. An expressed species is separate

---

73. Maritain, "Language and the Theory of Sign," 86. See also Maritain, "Sign and Symbol," 191–224.

74. Poinsot, *TDS* 27.

75. Poinsot, *TDS* 27.

from the cognitive power *in se*. The transition from (i) to (ii), from the sign to the signified, marks the relationship from motive to terminative species. There is the tacitly known (impressed species) and the actually known (expressed species).

(i) An impressed species is the *medium quo*; the means by which objective entities outside the intellect are known. Inceptive sensation from things as they *immediately* exist (*ens reale*) is *mediated* by *sensus communis*: The internally tacit, brain/genetically embodied, or *motive* senses of imagination, judgment, estimative sense, and sense memory. An impressed (motive) species progressively exhibits more and more of an expressed (terminative) species. *As with any definition of the sign, the impressed species is a form of sacrificial de-actualization, presenting the known actualization (expressed species) by its disappearance. The sign of impressed species gives its entire being to convey that which is understood by a cognitive power.*[76] An impressed species is only tacitly known; it is known by the content it presents, which cannot be itself. All the being of an impressed species is self-evacuated, realized, and exhausted in signifying an expressed species to a cognitive power. The sign diminishes in being as the presentation of the signified content (expressed species) grows in being. In order to exercise its function as a sign, an impressed species is known not by appearing, but by disappearing before the expressed species: The typical gossamer or ghost like trace of absence. *The known is given actuality through the sacrifice of the sign's actuality.* An impressed mnemonic species or image is the first intentional form preserved in memory/brain; it is not *that which* is known when we remember. Rather, a mnemonic image is purely the means by which we tacitly retrieve an event experienced in the past. The impressed species by which we first seize an intelligible aspect of things is not *that which* is known when our intelligence is at work. These deep interior signs have a dynamic character as *pure bringing towards* that vanishes before the concept (expressed species) that is presented to a knowing power. An impressed species operates like a mooring of a boat. The activity of hauling (signifying) the mooring (the sign/impressed species) gradually shortens the amount of visible rope as the boat (concept/expressed species) moves across the water's surface, closer to the person on shore (knowing power). More and more of the mooring

---

76. On the *self-effacing* nature of Poinsot's epistemological semiosis, see Lyons, *Signs in the Dust*, 24–25; Paine, "Seven Signa," 51–62. My claim here is much stronger—that is, Christian semiotics presents reality as co-sacrificial communication, manifestation: The triadic relation of the sign is the antithesis of sacrificial violence. Created reality is *essentially* love. This line of thought strengthens, I think, Lyons's claim that semiosis belongs, for Aquinas, to the divine Trinity just as much as the economic, created order. The key feature, as will be explored, is the role of the Holy Spirit as the principle of communication for Creator and created.

disappears by passing back under the water in the opposite direction as the boat comes nearer the person hauling it.

(ii) The *expressed species* is the concept. The concept is *medium quod*; it is *that which* is first present in the soul as understood: The immediately present form of the thing distinct from the knowing power itself. The cognitive actuality of the knower is not identical with the concept, expressed species, or the thing known. The expressed species of the thing known is present to the knower as the *species intelligibilis* of the thing known. The expressed species in *first intention* is the terminus of the relationship from the proximate foundation of the existing entity in *ens reale* and its mediation, i.e., impressed species. *Esse significativum* is the real relationship of substitution of an objective entity's likeness in the ontological direction of *ens reale*. An expressed species *communicated* from the real also *communicates* in the ontological direction of transcendental cognition: *Relativum secundum dici*. The expressed species serves as the proximate foundation for the analogical denomination of significance in second intention (terminus): Second interpretation. *Esse manifestativum* is the virtual relationship of substitution of a concept for a transcendental term. Significative being connects the intellect to reality. Manifestative being connects the concept of first intention to the quasi-independent or transcendental planes of conventional representation: Second intention (*relationes secundum dici seu transcendentales*). The logico-mathematical being of signs is first in the order of second intention. Rationally real predicates express *relativium secundum esse in first intention*, i.e., irreducible conceptual attributes of type, genus, and so forth. Rationally real being is distinguished from what is second in the order of second intention: The purely conventional being of humanity's natural languages and cultural patterns of signification (*relativum secundum dici in second intention*). The formal sign's disappearance presents the rationally real and the virtually signified: Manifestative, transcendental actuality. In their operation between the real and the virtual, impressed and expressed species are doubly presenting, and doubly vanishing. *Ens signum—Janus*.

(b) *Instrumental sign*: "An instrumental sign is one that represents something other than itself from a pre-existing cognition of itself as an object."[77] An instrumental sign is a substitute or vicar for the presence of a thing. For example, the footprint of a horse represents a horse. An instrumental sign must be known first as a formal sign before we can know that it represents something else. All instrumental signs presuppose formal signs. The instrumental sign of the horse's footprint can only be known through a sense image, which is a formal sign (impressed species). The interpretation

---

77. Poinsot, *TDS* 27.

of the image depends on pre-existing concepts (expressed species) of what a print is, what a foot is, what a horse is, what kinds of horses there are, and the extension of the kinds of footprints there can and cannot be; for instance, the footprint cannot be of a unicorn.

(2) *As the sign is ordered to something signified.* (a) *Natural sign*: "A natural sign is one that represents from the nature of a thing, independently of any stipulation and custom whatever, and so it represents the same for all."[78] There is a real relationship between the sign and the thing it signifies. A natural sign has the same signification for all knowing powers. Examples: smoke signifies fire, thunder signifies a storm, wrinkles signify human age, and fever signifies illness. Natural signs constitute our common sense of things—the shared signified (*sensus communis*). (b) *Stipulated sign*: "A stipulated sign is one that represents something owing an imposition by the will of a community."[79] The stipulated sign is also known as the conventional sign—the transcendental sign of *second intention*. These signs are socially constructed human intentions and practices made *manifest* in linguistic expressions, both spoken and written. More simply, stipulated signs are what we commonly call languages (natural and artificial). The stipulated sign, because it signifies arbitrarily, requires agreement as to what it will represent. This agreement is an imposition of the collective will that is sanctioned by historical and social iteration, and/or professional or legal authority. English children learn the word "cat" through various social filters, e.g., family, schooling, and peers. Computer engineers use standardized languages; for example, HTML. Local laws dictate the meaning of traffic lights. Words have the dictionary as the authority for correct spelling and the grammatical range of imposition for a given meaning. International agreements define signs that apply universally. For example, for every mariner red means port (left) and green means starboard (right).

We have gone from reality's formal signs to concepts, and then from concepts to the virtual signs of conventional languages: *Relativum secundum esse* to *relationes secundum dici seu transcendentales*. Now, we will do the reverse, namely, going from virtual signs to concepts, and from concepts to reality's formal signs. The manifestative being of second intention connects transcendental planes of representation to the concepts of first intention. The significative being of first intention connects the intellect to reality. A transcendental term signifies other transcendental terms, but this virtual plane of significance is not closed; that is, a virtual term signifies or communicates its concept or formal term; as the likeness known (expressed

78. Poinsot, *TDS* 27.
79. Poinsot, *TDS* 27.

species), along with that through which the concept is known, i.e., the affective image (impressed species), giving rise to the concept by immediate sense impression and/or the mnemonic image formed by past immediate sensations of an objective entity's formal sign in reality. The conventional word "cat" (English/second intention), for example, conventionally signifies, *manifests* its formal concept (expressed species), and the affective image (impressed species) we have of a real animal. Virtual (conventional/transcendental) signs signify other like signs and to concepts (first intention) that signify reality's formal signs (*ens reale*). A knowing power is simultaneously an interpreter of arbitrary conventional signs, concepts, and the formal signs of real entities. The transcendental sign disappears to present the concept, which disappears to present the affective image of the formal sign communicated from reality—all can disappear to welcome a real entity, if *this* cat appears in the here and now.

A number is a sign of quantity. In second intention, the logic of number stands in first place as the rationally real. Number, it is argued, contains all possibility for the logical determination of the sensuous: All values for all its variable relationships. If there were no number, nothing could be understood. The underlying structure of nature is a mathematical language. Mathematical formulas express values and their relationships that are applicable to (interchangeable with) any existent. As we have examined previously, mathematical language maintains an atypical status as a transcendental sign system. The distinction between conventional and conceptual signification (second and first intention) appears to dissolve. The real sign of first intention and the conventional sign of second intention enfold one another; they relate as the actual sign to its virtual term—that which (*ens reale*) presents something other than itself (virtual) to a knowing power/interpreter can become the model of virtual construction. The interpreter of the rationally real is rendered the constructor of simulacra. Number comprises the universal analogical sign system (*mathesis universalis*) of second intention but, to Poinsot, it is not a transcendental *substitute* for our umbilical reception and connection to being in first intention (*ens reale*). Mathematics is a powerful way of interpreting things through concepts of first intention, marking the transcendental limit of language in second intention, but it does not exhaust the actuality of interpretation, extinguishing being's communication. To think this way makes all real things vanish before the virtual. We (and all things) are not virtual entities. *Environmental existence* obtains its own independency, value, and communicative power of self-representation. Existence, as Thomas teachers, is a common gift *really* owed elsewhere: The Trinity.

(c) *Customary sign*: "A customary sign is one that represents from use alone without any public imposition, as napkins upon the table signify a meal."[80] A sign is called *customary* when the relation between the sign and the thing is made through tradition. As traditions differ between cultures, so do the associations between signs and things. For example, a handshake may be an appropriate sign of greeting in one tradition, while kissing both cheeks may be the appropriate sign in another.

THINGS AND THEIR SIGNS.

The Trinitarian articulation of the sign begins with Augustine. Poinsot develops this tradition. Semiotic maturity is a consequence of Aquinas's doctrine of the Holy Spirit.[81] Unlike Augustine, semiotic activity is not restricted to scriptural exegetics. The sign operates in non-sacramental areas of reality and understanding. Love flows over all creation as a liberating force of essential communication. Human knowledge and creation itself repeat the Trinity's semiotic economy of divine love. Creation is the interpreter (the Holy Spirit) of the significate (the Son) revealed by the unconditional donation of the sign (the Father)—love of the beloved given by the lover. Procession of the Holy Spirit is communicative and liberating economy: Time.[82] The *esse* of relationship, signification, and interpretation are requisite elements of being, knowing, and loving. The triadic actuality of communication, however, does not replace the ontological priority of *esse* and form—*the thing*. The sign mediates the actuality of the thing through the thing's foundation; it makes the discrete entity the communicative object (*significate*) to the interpretative power. Objective appearance is actualization. Actualization requires disappearance—the sacrifice of the sign. The *sacrificate* is purely to another, erasing itself to present what it is not: The object to the interpreter. Giving. Absolute releasement creates presence—*ens sacrificium*—agape.

Signs are irreducible vehicles of essential relativity (*relativum secundum esse*). Relationships are *superordinate*. They remain intrinsically unaffected by their foundations in entities or the intellect. "Signs," John Deely

---

80. Poinsot, *TDS* 27.

81. See Margerie, *Christian Trinity in History*, 318–19.

82. On time and signs, see Deleuze, *Proust and Signs*, 3–25. Following the tradition of the Renaissance, especially Marsilio Ficino, for Deleuze's Proust, it is "in the absolute time of the work of art that all other dimensions are united" (25). The theological vocabulary of the Holy Spirit is replaced by aesthetics. Art is a sacramental event of time and sign.

claims, "act through their foundations, but the actual sign as such is not the foundation but the relation which exists over and above that foundation linking the foundation as sign-vehicle to some object signified."[83] The sign belongs to the relationship; it does not belong to the foundation. In human cognition, for example, purely relational signs are unavailable to the senses because they are the conditions of sensory communication. Objects of sense are revealed through their *sacrificates*. The formal sign transmits the impressed species from the thing to inner sensory faculties, forming the initial mnemonic image. The latter's communicative disappearance reveals the expressed species (concept). The concept then vanishes to present the transcendental sign to the interpretative power. Human symbolicity is a threefold act of unconditional donation, sacrifice, or love.

Things, however, are not signs. An entity is a foundation for communication; its form becomes an object to an interpreter through a sign. A thing retains its own substantive identity (*subjective structure*) outside any triadic field of signification (*objective structure*). Significant exchange does not create form, i.e., the principle of *esse*. Transmission of actuality does not exhaust a thing's principle of being. Form is nonetheless essentially communicative. Poinsot's achievement is to navigate this *aporia*. There is a safe passage (connection and communication) between the defined edges of immutable things. In a dense and definitive passage, Deely explains the Thomistic ontology of the sign:

> Thus, *things* are fundamentally distinct, in Poinsot's terms, from *objects*, in that the former (things) do not necessarily while the latter do necessarily involve a relation to a knower. Things may or may not also be objects, and objects may or may not also be things. But every object signified exists as such as the self-representing terminus of a sign relation. Whatever exists as a thing has a subjective structure, that is to say, a structure indifferent to being or not being known. But whatever exists as signified has an objective structure as terminus of a relation founded upon and correlated with some subjective structure of being, such as the psychological reality of a concept in the mind or the physical reality of a spoken, written, or gestured word. *Signs mediate between objects and things by giving rise to objects as significates and by the partial objectification of things in sensation as well as perception and intellection.*
>
> Whence objects participate in the indifference of sign relations to being based in cultural or natural constructions, inner and outer sign-vehicles; and sign-vehicles are distinct from

---

83. Deely, *Medieval Philosophy Redefined*, 366.

signs as the foundations of relations are distinct from the relations they found. The foundation as such may belong to subjective being or to objective being as terminus of another relation now founding yet another relation, whereas the relation as such is always suprasubjective pure and simple. So is the object as such which terminates the relation, but not purely and simply; for nothing prevents this object from coinciding materially with some actual structure of subjective being—again, either natural or cultural.[84]

Poinsot commits to *things* and the primacy of human cognition. Semiotic mediation does not construct being; it communicates being. Mind is *the* interpretative site. Formal presence terminates the process of significant actualization. The act of intellect completes the circuit of sign activity—*semiosis*. Finite interpretation receives the gift of being's self-communication. We bond with beloved creation and creator. To Poinsot, the sacrificial economy of the sign is the procession of the Holy Spirit. The communicative space of the *environment* is the expression of God's love. As Tracey Rowland indicates, the Trinity's gift of creation is "nourished by sovereign victimhood."[85] Paolo Virno seems to concur. For both Creator and created, the *"event of language"* involves a kind of actuality that "is incessantly *sacrificed.*"[86] The sacrifice of the sign defines creation; it is not violent or in vain.

We know, love, and liberate things through their signs.

What follows Poinsot, however, is secular nature. The *transcendental human subject* banishes "the hypostatic descent of the Holy Spirit inaugurated on earth."[87] Sacrificial donation of creation becomes violent appropriation of nature. Mute creation is stripped of its own communicative value, meaning, and divine love. Nature only *stands for* significates we impose upon it. Reception, interpretation, and love of creation are replaced by command, ruin, and theft of our common gift.

---

84. Deely, *Medieval Philosophy Redefined*, 367.
85. Rowland, "Globalization," 588.
86. Virno, *When the Word Becomes Flesh*, 59.
87. Rowland, "Globalization," 588.

TEN

Potentiality and Boehme
Semiotics of Becoming

AQUINAS AND POINSOT DEFEND the ontology of *the thing*. Signs communicate essential forms to interpretative powers. The real is complete and fully present to the intellect through its formal signs, but it is only partially known through conventional signification. This chapter introduces process semiotics, reversing the ontological priority between actuality and potentiality. Creation is a life of movement, evolution, and self-actualization—becoming through its relational potentialities. The real is the unfinished consequence of sign activity: *The productive and immanent semiotic drive for actuality precedes being itself.* Instead of actuality defining the epistemological function of the sign, there is cosmic semiosis. Signs are self-authoring vehicles of their own historical development. *Process semiotics* is first given its contemporary distinction from Poinsot's priority of form. This preface is followed by two initial steps in the reclamation of the tradition of semiotic potentiality, beginning with Aristotle's analysis of life and concluding with Jacob Boehme's Trinitarian theosophy.

FROM FORMAL SIGNS TO SEMIOSIS

Poinsot claims sign activity derives its actualization from the communication of complete forms to cognitive powers. To preserve the primacy of formal actuality and the cognitive subject, James Bernard Murphy alleges that Poinsot splits the semiotic triad into two dyads. "Instead of uniting sign, object, and mind within the triadic relation of semiosis," Murphy contends, "Poinsot unites sign to object by ontology, and unites sign to mind by cognition."[1] Formal actualization is not the principle of communication; rather, semiosis is the *principle* of actualization "once we see that the relation of any sign to mind is not cognitive, but *sui generis* semiotic."[2] Communication creates being. The real is not the fully actualized given that is communicated. Semiotic relationships do not transmit timeless and whole forms; they are no longer primarily bound to human cognition.

Creation is the triadic and egalitarian becoming of signs, replacing what Christopher P. Long calls the human subject's "hegemonic manner in which form sets beings in order."[3] The role of interpreter is generalized to all created and creating entities. Interpretation is a coequal moment in a continuous and triadic series, belonging to the whole cosmos. Human cognition is *a* (not *the*) distinct location within creation's open, fallible, and evolving semiotic process. Signs actualize themselves. Murphy seems to declare a manifesto for universal semiosis: "We must reject this hierarchy of dependence: all terms are equally relative within the semiotic relation."[4] Co-dependency and interchangeability are given as reasons for this view. "For in semiosis," he claims, "the object depends on the sign just as the sign depends on the object; and the sign depends on the mind just as the mind depends on the sign. Indeed the equality of terms is most easily grasped when we consider that, in semiosis, the object signified and the interpretative power may both be signs."[5] The *mind* encompasses any interpretative power—physical, vital, and cultural. Each term is threefold in nature and each term can occupy the place of the other. The *perichoretic* circuit means the interpreter becomes the sign, the sign becomes the object, and the object becomes the interpreter. There is progressive co-mediation of three inseparable elements; each element is what it is because of its interchangeable relationships to the other two. The relational circuit of sign-object-interpreter evolves and multiplies with constructive power.

Esse sequitur operationem and *ex nihilo in aliquid* are basic heuristic principles of becoming and potentiality. Actuality is something to be achieved through evolving communication. Potentiality has no essence; it is

1. Murphy, "Nature, Custom, and Stipulation," 40.
2. Murphy, "Nature, Custom, and Stipulation," 40.
3. Long, "Between the Universal and the Singular in Aristotle," 27.
4. Murphy, "Nature, Custom, and Stipulation," 41.
5. Murphy, "Nature, Custom, and Stipulation," 41.

the craving of nothing to be something, and contingent form follows upon its semiotic creativity. Signs have their own autonomous and innovative nature within a universe that is continuously being born; they overflow with new possibilities, tending toward their emergent actualization. The presupposition of semiotic potentiality also means we are not living in a totally actualized plane of being that is only partially or tacitly known. Full meaning is always to come; human cognition can only be the fractional actualization of the unremitting proliferation of signification.

Communication exists in the creative gap between antecedent and consequent. Change indicates self-renewing motion of semiotic systems. The iterative gap between prior and posterior is pregnant with new worlds—the spontaneous realization of novel possibilities. But just because a communicative event is new does not mean it is good. Evil exists, but its terms and conditions are what must be changed by the logic of self-renewing movement. Freedom in the image of love means each semiotic expansion diminishes the contractive power of selfish desire (monadic isolation) and violence (dyadic contests of elimination). Interminable, dynamic, and developmental process denotes the triadic movement's impossibility of closure until perfect communication is achieved: Liberation is restored to the whole of creation.

ARISTOTLE ON LIFE'S POTENTIALITY

The onto-theological dominance of substantial form is, for the most part, the accepted and propounded interpretation of Aristotle's thought, but this standard reading is complicated and supplemented by his analysis of potentiality within the domain of life. Aristotle examines desire, genesis, and destruction. Life's potentiality has many features that do not seem to be reducible to the passive and dependent privation of substantial form. What is the established view?

Onto-theology is attributed to Aristotle's metaphysical position: God is pure actuality without potentiality, accounting for the actualization of finite things through their substantial forms. The core of Aristotle's *Metaphysics* is the unmoved mover (12.6–7).[6] This *third substance* or *God* provides the principle of eternal motion and, through the latter, the actualization of things. *Actus purus* is "an eternal unmovable substance" (12.6, 1071b5). "There is a mover," Aristotle concludes, "which moves without being moved, being eternal, substance, and actuality" (12.7, 1072a25). "There is a substance

---

6. All quotations of Aristotle's *Metaphysics* are from vol. 2 of Aristotle, *Complete Works*.

which is eternal and unmovable and separate from sensible things," which he identifies with living thought: "[For] the actuality of thought is life, and God is that actuality; and God's essential actuality is life most good and eternal. We say therefore that God is a living being, eternal, most good, so that life and duration continuous and eternal belong to God; for this *is* God" (12.7, 1072b25–26). Although immobile, God draws everything, all potentiality, towards itself like a great cosmic magnet of pure *energeia*, realizing all things to an ever-increasing degree. Actualization processes depend on God. Formal actuality is the true, the good, and the beautiful—*the divine in things*. The life of the human mind participates in divinity by getting to know things through their formal signs.

Aristotle identifies matter with *potentiality* (dynamis); it is a thing's capacity to be or not to be: "The matter in each is capable of being and of not being" (*Metaphysics* 7.7, 1032a21–23). Potentiality is the capacity to be *actualized* (energeia) by substantial form. Aristotle's capacity to be is not pre-existent, eternal, or independent; it is completely dependent upon substantial form for its finite existence. The process of transition from the potential to be to its actualization is called *change* (kinēsis). To be a thing in-actualization is *to have its end in itself* (entelecheia). Substantial form is "the source from which the primary movement of each natural object is present in virtue of its own essence" (*Metaphysics* 5.4, 1014b18–20). Forms determine the order (*taxis*) of natural beings. Potentiality is the specified capacity to be actualized, but it only has *being in act*. In his *Metaphysics*, Aristotle argues for the primacy of form based on a thing's need for unity (*Metaphysics* 7.17). *Ousia* is stable and knowable form; it is the principle of continuous self-identity of *this* thing and no other (*to ti ēn einai*) through change. Aristotle uses the examples of a syllable and the flesh to illustrate his position (*Metaphysics* 7.17, 1041b10): "As regards that which is compounded out of something so that the whole is one—not like a heap, however, but like a syllable—the syllable is not its elements, *ba* is not the same as *b* and *a*, nor is flesh fire and earth; for when they are dissolved the wholes, i.e., the flesh and the syllable, no longer exist, but the elements of the syllable exist, and so do fire and earth." Matter cannot provide the principle of synthesis (*synkrisis*); it is only an inert aggregate: A *heap* of disconnected elements (*diakrisis*). A thing's principle of wholeness is its undivided being, which Lawrence Dewan describes as "the *one*, which is at the source."[7] Aristotle identifies the principle of unity with form, rejecting potentiality. Reality is formal actualization that grounds itself in the eternal actuality of God's living mind.

---

7. Dewan, "Importance of Substance," 114.

The onto-theologically triumphant view presents Aristotle's *Metaphysics* as the final word on potentiality. Ontology becomes ideological when it seeks an ultimate principle beyond all history: God legitimates a fixed natural and political order.[8] Just as matter derives its existence from form, so the power of the slave only has actuality through the mind of the master. Aristotle's investigation of living systems deviates from his metaphysical ideology of eternal actuality. Aporetic dialectical method and lifelong biological observations reveal a ceaselessly inquisitive, comprehensive, and revisable science in the making. There is no universal method: The inquiry must grow out of the subject matter itself. The phenomenon of life is a different topic than metaphysics, requiring renewed conceptual priorities. The "dynamic path of Aristotle's thinking, as opposed to his system of thought," Christopher P. Long, again, astutely observes, "does not easily fit into his metaphysical ideology of form."[9] Aristotle's *vital analysis*, then, is fertile ground for understanding potentiality. The capacity to be and not be actualized diverges in significant ways from his allegedly *final* onto-theological position of immutable dependency through form and God.

Life (*psychē*) is first and foremost the potentiality to be: "Life is the first entelechy of a natural body possessing the power to live (*dynamei zōēn echontos*)" (*De Anima* 2.1, 412a27–28).[10] *Entelechy* is the functioning of a living thing; it admits a conceptual distinction between potentiality (*dynamis*) and its operation (*energeia*). *Psychē*, as *first* entelechy, is potentiality. The sheer capacity to be is prior in the order of living time. Possessing life is antecedent to the consequent entelechy of actual living. Logically, *energeia* precedes *dynamis*; that is, potentiality is only understandable by its operation. For example, we understand the potentiality of sight through the activity of seeing. "'Life,' *psychē*," John Herman Randall Jr. claims, "is a function in both senses, but it is primarily the power to perform the function."[11] In this sense, *psyche*—life *per se*—maintains the priority of potentiality; it is not an *ousia* capable of existing independently by itself. Rather, *psychē*, as the *potential form* of any living body, requires co-operation between a "biological organism and an intelligible world."[12] *Psychē* is the end of all organisms; they exist for the sake of living, enduring in its raw power for

---

8. See Adorno, *Metaphysics*, 42–50.

9. Long, "Between the Universal and the Singular in Aristotle," 25.

10. Aristotle quoted in Randall Jr., *Aristotle*, 64. The author follows and, generally considered, accepts Randall's interpretation of Aristotle's vitalism.

11. Randall Jr., *Aristotle*, 65.

12. Randall Jr., *Aristotle*, 106.

further activity. Life is its own end: *Die Ros' ist ohn' Warum, sie blühet, weil sie blühet*—Angelus Silesius (†1677) (*Ohne Warum*).

Living is defined by desire (*orexis*). The potentiality of desiring (*to orektikon*) explains the transition to activity: "The ultimate mover, the ultimate spring of action, is the desired, *to orekton*."[13] Desire is the *moved mover* internal to a living process: Attraction (+), repulsion (-), and indifference (0). Sense (*aisthēsis*) is desire's vehicle; it is life's most general potential (*to aisthētikon*). An organism is the embodied specification of sensory potentialities. A living body is embedded within a limited range of desired objects—*an environment*. Orexis undergoes differentiation. A drive (*hormē*) is a distinctive type of desire. A specific drive motivates an organism to achieve its characteristic form of being. *Psychē* is directed towards the *unmoved mover*. The good of life is external to the specific operation of desire, sense, and drive by individual creatures; it is "some stimulus in the situation, some end of conduct, some practical good, which is not itself moved or affected by being desired, and is hence an 'unmoved' mover."[14] Life's common good is symbiotic fulfillment—*co*-operation within a shared *environment*.

As well as sense, human beings have the potential of *nous*. The mind defines our species desire. *Nous* is a unique drive (*hormē*) primarily concerned with reasoning on the future: Forechoice (*proairēsis*). Aristotle speaks of the mind's sense of time (*chronou aisthēsis*) and its resistance to immediate satiation of the flesh because of the future (*dia to mellon*) (See *De Anima* 3.10, 433a18–433b13). Deliberation (*boulēsis*) is desire in the light of time. The object of desire initiates reasoning: "Hence forechoice may be called either *nous* served by desire (*orektikos nous*), or desire served by reasoning (*orexis dianoētikē*), and just such an *archē* is man" (*Nichomach. Ethics* 6.2, 1139b5–7).[15] *Nous*, therefore, is not a potentiality found in all life; it defines only one kind of desiring life; namely, humanity's drive to know.

The mind is the receptacle of the forms; as *pathētikos nous*, the mind is the nearest thing to pure positive potentiality (*dynaton*) there is in nature, having the thorough capacity to be impregnated by any form. The mind is the ultimate organ of desire. Through the embodied motion of imagination (*phantasia*) and its sense-image memory (*phantasmata*), potential mind is capable of ingesting *impressed species* from sense experiences, actualizing universals (*expressed species*). Expressed forms are only the intelligible phase of sensible objects. Forms originate from what is immediately desired through sense. We know universals by physically embodied filtration of

13. Randall Jr., *Aristotle*, 70.
14. Randall Jr., *Aristotle*, 70.
15. Aristotle quoted in Randall Jr., *Aristotle*, 76.

sensory experience and socially embedded action (*praxis*). *Poiētikos nous* is the mind in operation; actualization is through the social practice of human *logos*. Signification is *psychē's* communicative operation. Sign potential (environmentally embodied and embedded) appears to be a key component of life, but Aristotle neglects "language and communication" on the level of *physikos*: "[He] never treats *logos* as a 'part' of the *psychē*, as one of the functions making up 'life.' Such a treatment is not in the *De Anima* at all, but it ought to be."[16] The potentiality and actuality of communication (*logos*) is consequent upon *nous*. Aristotle's analysis simply fails to cover life's communicative dimension. Other organisms are simply denied "the power of *nous*."[17] The species web (intra and inter) of environmental signification is left unexamined.

Aristotle's presentation of *psychē* explores the temporal priority of potentiality, process, and change. Living things and processes (*ousiai* and *kinēseis*) come-to-be, decline, and pass-away in time (*genesis kai phthora*). On Randall's remarkable interpretation, *vital* substance is the principle of continuous novelty:

> It is significant that when Descartes asked, "What is Substance?" he was asking for what persists unchanged throughout change, what it is in change that does not itself change. And in Locke and in Kant, in fact, throughout modern philosophy, "substance" has been taken as the unchanging, the permanent in change, whether Locke's "I know not what," or Kant's "permanent in relation to phenomena." But for Aristotle, who since he gave the technical meaning to the term *ousia* rendered into Latin as *substantia*, ought to know, *ousia* and *substantia* is defined precisely as that which undergoes change in change, what is at the end of any process is different from what it was at the outset. And in the most important and fundamental kind of change of all, *genesis kai phthora*, "generation" and "corruption," a new *ousia* or substance is present at the end that was not there at all in the beginning, or a substance has disappeared completely. Thus it is clear, Aristotle's pattern of motion and change is a pattern of novelty that emerges in process.[18]

Becoming an *ousia* (*hodos eis ousian*) is continuous disappearance and appearance. A living thing exists in the interval (*meden; den*) of passing-away and coming-to-be; it is the simultaneous outcome, rescission, and

---

16. Randall Jr., *Aristotle*, 102.
17. Randall Jr., *Aristotle*, 102.
18. Randall Jr., *Aristotle*, 112–13.

renewal of an end (*telos*) directed process of change. Organisms seek their ends within a contingent environment. Chance (*to automaton*) events and human art (*apo technēs*) are external influences on a living thing's hypothetical natural necessity. Good fortune (*tychē*) can enable an organism's achievement of its end, and violence (*bia*) can terminate the process (*energeia atelēs*). A living thing is an internally intended continuity that it is going-to-be, not that it will-be; that is, an organism's necessity is conditional on multiple factors being present and absent within an environment.

Aristotle recognizes the reality of non-being—*phthora*.[19] Life's potentiality to be (+P) is connected to its potentiality not to be (-P). Coming-to-be is the passing-away of what is not. Passing-away is the coming-to-be of what is not. There is light and dark matter. The latter is called *sterēsis*, *adynamia*, and *mē ontos*. Each term marks a further uncovering of the negative's role within *psychē*. *Sterēsis* is an irreducible factor, an *archē* of process. Any process is a change from *this* state to *that* state. Between antecedent and consequent there is an interval of creative motion (*genesis*). In this gap, certain absent characteristics are actualized. The passing-way of absence is the coming-to-be of actualization. Living things become toward something they are not-yet, but *this* not-yet is *something* they are implicitly determined with respect to; they are attracted to it by their uniquely occurring incompleteness that *desires* it. Absence, then, in a determinate process is not sheer nothingness. An absence (-P) is always coupled with a specific potentiality (+P) to acquire what is acquired. The negative is strictly defined by the intrinsic potential to be actualized. Absence, for a vital thing, is not *per se*; it is always an individuated property—a potential to be *this* actualized living thing (*to ti ēn einai*) and no other. For example, this red rose's bud that is currently lacking its red flower is not deficient of its white or pink flower. This red rose's flower (not an olive's) comes-to-be from this red rose's bud.

The process of change has three interconnected moments: (1) the subject, what changes; (2) what it is changed from; and (3) what it is changed to. The first is the material (*hē hylē*)—the something that is changed. The third is the form (*eidos*)—the specific character the subject acquires by actualization. The second is *sterēsis*—the initial absence (-P) of the form that the subject has the potentiality (+P) to acquire. A process's principle of actualization is not (ultimately) matter, *sterēsis*, or form; it is eternal motion (*Physics* 8.7 260a 26ff). Finite continuities have specific ends to achieve. A conditionally necessary process is a living thing's time of coming-to-be, which ends with its passing-away. All living things are defined by their

---

19. Aristotle's analysis of the *absential* features of life has recently been updated, incorporating contemporary biology. See Deacon, *Incomplete Nature*, 22–61.

measure of generation, corruption, and extinction. *Psychē* is desire's differentiation and duration in time. Aristotle attributes life to the necessary and continuous principle of motion (*De Generatione* 2.10–11). The principle of perishable process is perpetual motion.

The potentiality not to be (-P) seems thoroughly defined by the potentiality to be (+P). Coming-to-be is the passing-away of a specific absence. Passing-away, however, is its own reality; *it is the coming-to-be of what is not*. The distinction is difficult to detect and decipher. Giorgio Agamben places *sterēsis* within the setting of voluntary human action.[20] The potential not to be is an identifiable ingredient of our lives. A human being's potentiality to *intentionally* not actualize a capacity (*mē energein*) glimpses the visible darkness (*to skotos*); the form or face of *sterēsis* (*Physics* 2.1, 193b19–20). Agamben claims conceptual continuity and development from Aristotle's term *sterēsis* in *De Anima* and *Physics* to the term *adynamia* in *Metaphysics*. The coming-to-be of what is not is given a moral dimension: "[The] root of freedom is to be found in the abyss of potentiality."[21] The Greek terms *adynamia* and *adynaton* (*Metaphysics* 9.1, 1046a25–32; 9.3, 1047a24–26) signify *impotentiality*, which is the privation (-P) of privation (+P). The specific difference of human *psychē* is not Aristotle's *nous*, but Aristotle's *impotentiality*. Freedom, not the mind, sets us apart from all other forms of life.

Dynamis adynamia denotes a relationship between (+P) and (-P): "To be free is, in the sense we have seen, *to be in relation to one's own impotentiality*, to be in relation to one's own privation. This is why freedom is freedom for both good and evil."[22] To Agamben, Aristotle uncovers the principle of human freedom in *Metaphysics*: "[For] the same is potential both to be and not to be [*to auto ara dynaton kai einai kai mē einai*]" (*Metaphysics* 9.8, 1050b10).[23] The potential not to be is given its original figure as a bipolar identity. Impotential reality is a prime factor in human life because we know (*nous*), act (*praxis*), and produce (*technē*). More than any other species, human beings "exist in the mode of potentiality."[24] Human beings are liberated (*sōtēria*) from the totalizing process of actualization. Freedom is the capacity to know, do, and produce anything. We have this generalized *dynamis* because it is thoroughly *identified* with *adynamia*. This condition is the greatness and tragedy of our species: "Every human power is *adynamia*, impotentiality; every human potentiality is in relation to its own privation.

---

20. See Agamben, "On Potentiality," 177–84.
21. Agamben, "On Potentiality," 182.
22. Agamben, "On Potentiality," 183.
23. Aristotle quoted in Agamben, "On Potentiality," 182.
24. Agamben, "On Potentiality," 182.

Potentiality and Boehme

This is the origin (and abyss) of human power, which is so violent with respect to other living beings."[25] We are distinct from the rest of creation in this respect: "*Other living beings are capable only of their specific potentiality; they can only do this or that. But human beings are the animals who are capable of their own impotentiality. The greatness of human potentiality is measured by the abyss of human potentiality.*"[26] But, if there is a relationship between (+P) and (-P), how does it function during actualization?

Agamben suggests impotentiality is preserved by actualization—that is, negative potentiality ensures the inexhaustibility of actualization by continually *sacrificing* and receiving its own not-being in the operation of a positive power. Aristotle presents the negative in terms of living process, not good and evil. Actualization is the passing-away of a certain absence but change and *growth* also signify the coming-to-be of a certain absence: *This emergent attribute must supplant the present attribute that exists.* This and *that* cannot both be at the same time. The appearance of a red rose's flower, for example, is the simultaneous disappearance of its bud. Positive potentiality is specified and individuated: There is the coming-to-be of only *this* attribute from only *this* absence (red flower), replacing only *that* attribute (bud). Negative potentiality is *the not* as such (*ek mē ontos*); it is both *the determinate not from which* (+P) the new proceeds and *the indeterminate not to which* (-P) the old recedes. The motion of darkness to light is the motion of light to darkness.

To Aristotle, *impotentiality* seems to be a principle of eternal cyclic motion that secures ceaseless process (*De Generatione* 2.10, 336a15);[27] it provides an answer to the question of why the universe has not already been exhausted of its being by change? "Why, then, is this form of change necessarily ceaseless? Is it because the passing-away of *that* is a coming-to-being of *something else*, and the coming-to-be of *this* a passing away of *something else*?" (*De Generatione* 1.3, 318a23–25). Further: "[So] that a thing comes-to-be out of not-being just as much as it passes away into what is not. Hence it is reasonable enough that coming-to-be should never fail. For coming-to-be is a passing–away of what is not and passing-away is a coming-to-be of what is not" (*De Generatione* 1.3, 319a26–28).

Aristotle distinguishes between *qualified* non-being (*dynamis*) and *unqualified* non-being (*adynamia*): "For *qualified* coming-to-be is a process out of *qualified* not-being (e.g., out of not-white or not-beautiful), but

---

25. Agamben, "On Potentiality," 182.
26. Agamben, "On Potentiality," 182.
27. All quotations of Aristotle's *On Generation and Corruption* are from vol. 1 of Aristotle, *Complete Works*.

unqualified coming-to-be is a process out of *unqualified* not-being" (*De Generatione* 1.3, 317b4–6). *Adynamia* self-donates a positive power's (*dynamis*) qualified absence and it receives the unqualified absence brought about by the displacement of the old by the new. "In one sense," Aristotle tells us, "things come-to-be out of that which has no being without qualification; yet in another sense they come-to-be always out of what is. For there must pre-exist something which *potentially* is, but *actually* is not; and this something is spoken of both as being and as not-being" (*De Generatione* 1.3, 317b15–17). There are three transitions: (1) from unqualified to qualified potentiality; (2) from qualified potentiality to actualization of the new; and (3) from the de-actualized old to unqualified potentiality. Within this process the negative returns to itself; it *preserves* itself, and in preserving itself, saves the potential to be actualized within or without *this* particular actualization: "The constituents, therefore, neither *persist actually*, as body and white persist; nor are they *destroyed* (either one of them or both), for their potentiality is preserved" (*De Generatione* 1.10, 327b29–31). As Agamben recognizes, "This does not mean that it [impotentiality] disappears in actuality; on the contrary, it *preserves* itself as such in actuality. What is truly [positive] potential is thus what has exhausted all its impotentiality in bringing it wholly into the act as such."[28] Therefore, and seemingly in line with Aristotle's naturalist writings, he concludes, "Contrary to the traditional idea of potentiality that is annulled in actuality, here we are confronted with a potentiality that conserves itself and saves itself in actuality. Here potentiality, so to speak, survives actuality and, in this way, *gives itself to itself*."[29]

ARISTOTLE'S RECOIL FROM INFINITE POTENTIALITY

Through the vital dynamism of potentialities, Aristotle seems to suggest a cosmic life principle—a *moved mover*. Freedom of Agamben's description is the *archē* of eternal process. The insatiable desire (*orexis*) of nothing to be something pervades the universe as its principle of actualization. The negative is the heart of being—*the root of freedom*. Within Aristotle's shifting and *aporetic* planes of analysis, however, it is very questionable if this interpretation can be legitimately sustained. The claim that potentiality is relational implies that substantial form is relational, too. Actual substance is merely a moment in potential substance's mediation of indeterminate and determinate polarities. In short, potentiality takes operational priority over actuality. This implication is either completely and clearly rejected by Aristotle's

28. Agamben, "On Potentiality," 183.
29. Agamben, "On Potentiality," 184.

onto-theology (*Metaphysics*) or, more sympathetically, left as an unfulfilled intimation within his investigation of the temporal priority of potentiality within living processes (*De Anima*, *Physics*, and *De Generatione*).

Contraries cannot come together without a principle of relationship: Mediation. In Agamben's Aristotelian sense, freedom means (+P) is *in relationship* with (-P). *Hylē* provides the principle of its own self-actualization. On this reading, substantial form mediates with the negative pole of potentiality. The product of their union is the positive pole of potentiality. In other words, there is (-P), there is formal being, and their mediation is the pure capacity to be (+P): Becoming. If relational matter is the independent spring of activity, form is not operational. Substantial form is then, as Charles de Koninck cautions, *hollowed out*.[30] The onto-theological view can point to the fact that Aristotle does not have a substantial role for relationship; in fact, Aristotle does not have a concept of relationship (*skhesis*) at all. He has an accidental category of relatives (*ta pros ti*), which he explicitly excludes in his *Metaphysics* (14.1, 1088a30) from both potential and actual substance because an accident is posterior to substance. External relations happen to formal substances; the latter do not happen to be internally mediated relationships. If mediation, the principle of relationship, is excluded from substance in both ways, there is no cosmic or humanistic principle of freedom. Substantial form is operational. Relational potentiality is not. Substantial form actualizes qualified potentiality (determinate entity) and unqualified potentiality (indeterminate prime matter); it is not the product, the surface constituted by the dynamism of their relational polarities.

De Generatione hesitantly implies that potentiality can provide the principle for perpetual motion. The eternal return of the negative preserves itself and, in saving itself, saves continued actualization. This proposition defies Aristotle's onto-theological ideology. The *Metaphysics* is clear: God as pure being secures eternal motion. Aristotle identifies infinity (*apeiron*) with indeterminate potentiality but, despite its apparent dynamism in Aristotle's writings on life processes, it is merely passive prime matter that is enveloped by the determinate operation of finite being.[31] Infinite matter has no form of its own as a part of itself; it serves as potentiality for all substantial forms, having none that necessarily and always exists in it. Aristotle writes, "when distinguishing four kinds of causes, it is clear that the *apeiron* is a cause of matter," and, "also all other [physicists] clearly used the *apeiron* as matter; that is why it is absurd to make it what envelops but not what is

30. See Koninck, *Hollow Universe*, 60–63.
31. See Drozdek, *In the Beginning*, 11–12.

enveloped" (*Physics* 207b34–208a4).[32] Although it is uncreated, perpetual, and indestructible, indeterminate matter cannot be the prime cause: The *third substance* of the finite actualization of things. Substantial form has a hold on the infinite. Potentiality is the dependent subject of actualization; it is not actualization's autonomous source. Privation's determinate ($+P$) and indeterminate poles ($-P$) do not constitute a co-principle of being. Aristotle's God of pure and living *poiētikos nous* seems to cover its *relationship* to the divine potentiality of *pathētikos nous*.

There is only the motion from darkness to light without the motion of light to darkness. If potentiality does not preserve itself, however, eternal form will eventually exhaust all matter. Without a change of state from actuality to potentiality, matter is destroyed. Motion is finite, not eternal. The unmoved mover can also signify everything is already fully actualized, already light. The darkness is only our unknowing. The motion from light to dark is an illusion created by a limited human mind. The universe is complete and immobile like the unmoved mover. Aristotle, though, seeks to secure the real principle of actualization through eternal motion. It is difficult to understand how motion can be perpetual without the preservation of potentiality. Aristotle's treatment of potential infinity is atypically inelegant; it is so pronounced that Léon Robin (†1947) claims it "is one of the most embarrassing [problems] in Aristotle's philosophy."[33]

Potentiality opens an alternative direction for metaphysics. The negative has a constitutive place in life. But, without the substantial category of relationship, as Theodor W. Adorno confirms, in "Aristotle mediation is not itself mediated."[34] Agamben's signature of freedom lies elsewhere; namely, in the semiotic potentiality tradition of Jacob Boehme. Freedom is the relationship between determinate and indeterminate potentiality. Relationship, potentiality, and semiotic process all belong to the Triadic Godhead. Divine *psychē* is not pure mind: Freedom replaces intellectual essence; there is the priority of the will's drive, desire, and love. *Potentia Purus overturns Actus Purus as the principle of the Triune God*: "The will which is called God, which has freedom in itself generates itself in Nature—it is the universal power of Nature."[35] Boehme presents the living Trinity, emphasizing the *vestigium* of the Holy Spirit as the open triadic process of potentialities. Finite being is the simultaneous contraction and expansion of potentialities: The life-image or symbol reflects divine becoming.

32. Aristotle quoted in Drozdek, *In the Beginning*, 12.
33. Robin, *Aristote*, 144, quoted in Drozdek, *In the Beginning*, 101.
34. Adorno, *Metaphysics*, 44.
35. Boehme, *Six Theosophic Points*, 18.

Boehme is a traditional Christian symbolist; the language of the real is still *vestigia trinitatis*, but his doctrine of signatures mirrors the temporal characteristics of the Holy Spirit—ecological, evolutionary, and realist. Divine inscriptions bring creation's *potential existence* back to us from anthropocentric nature; revealing the Trinity's signatures liberates nature from our bondage. Creation's divine image of self-emergence is no longer eclipsed; it is something genuinely personal and precious in itself—far richer than impersonal mechanism, instantiation of a function, or material for self-salvation. But these symbols are not formal signs; they are free to develop themselves through their own historical processes (physically embodied and environmentally embedded), participating in a communicative perfection and liberation that is to be gained for the whole of creation. Evolution by *agape* is the cosmos' tendency to found habitudes of greater belonging which, as Thomas F. Torrance explains, "[Gives] rise to refined and subtle patterns of order in the ongoing spatio-temporal universe which we cannot anticipate but which constantly takes us by surprise."[36] It is a universe that admits and welcomes real novelty.

Reality is living communication of the Holy Spirit's drive toward self-revelation. This world of matter and time is necessary for the triadic process of divine self-constitution. Life is the passion of flesh and blood: Primal will signifies our animal *image*—raw, wild, and craving. Growth is from desire's embodied affliction to the plane of joy that *is* Spirit. We commend ourselves to the realization of a new life in the *image* of love. The latter is not something static or given. Love is achieved through intense struggle with the demonic gravity of our animal image. The dark and sacrificial fire of the Heraclitean *Logos* is becoming without hope of development. *Agape* is the true direction and end of life. The negative image of sacred violence is *to be* elevated to the semiotic light and life by the Johannine Word of Christ Liberator. Agonistic contradiction, however, is not denied or abolished; life depends on its spark. We can fail to transfigure freedom's primal and chaotic energies. Our divine image may never be complete.

Every human being, then, is a living confliction, a sign of travail between damnation and salvation. The opening of potentialities is a tormented mixture of animal and divine imagination. Since we are capable of *Nothing*, we are capable of anything—violence beyond animal, love beyond Angelic heaven—the freedom to inscribe, erase, and re-inscribe our own essential image.

---

36. Torrance, *Christian Doctrine of God*, 218.

INTRODUCING BOEHME

Jacob Boehme is a contemporary of René Descartes. Both figures are caught in the post-Reformation catastrophe of the Thirty Years War (1618–1648); for Boehme, it is near the end of his life, but it is the period (1619–1624) he writes all but one of his books while engaged in mercantile activities for Bohemia's Protestant side.[37] Descartes begins his philosophical career as an engineering adjunct in the army of the Roman Catholic Habsburgs. Like Boehme, Descartes claims to receive an epiphany near Prague around the time of the Battle of White Mountain (November 11, 1620).[38] Witnessing the triumph of the Habsburgs and the decimation of the Protestant Union has a bi-polar affect. Descartes claims to reach an intuition on method that would inspire the Enlightenment and scientific revolution. Boehme responds to the event with an equally as radical insight into the dark dynamics of the world created by the Trinity.[39]

Descartes inaugurates many of the central themes of modern thought, including liberal toleration, universal rationality, and the secular space of science. The Enlightenment supposedly breaks free from theology and the eccentric outpourings of hermetic theosophy, fueling the flames of religious strife. Boehme, by contrast, seems thoroughly of his time: The style and content of his narrative is typical of the emblematic worldview. Boehme's Christian symbolist thought is one of many meta-aesthetic, idiosyncratic, and anachronistic products of this turbulent age. The mania of *allegoresis* is given free reign. Enthusiastic mentalities propagate irrationalism and social havoc. Boehme's theosophy appears to be part of the *Schwärmerei*, sweeping across Germany in the post-Reformation period. Why, then, did significant post-Enlightenment thinkers consider his work revolutionary? Different than, but of the same radical order as, what follows Descartes? Additionally: Why is Boehme a significant moment for the *semiotic Weltanschauung*?

---

37. See Brown, *Later Philosophy of Schelling*, 36–37; Weeks, "Jacob Boehme and the Thirty Years' War," 213–21.

38. See Grayling, *Descartes*, 55–57; Weeks, *Boehme*, 157–84.

39. One way of understanding the similarity and difference between the two is the idea of zero. Descartes begins with the quantitative nothing. Boehme begins with the *qualitative nothing*. Both *nothings*, however, are infinite potentialities to be something; in the distinct and respective senses of imaginative human construction by signs and relations of quantity and divine imaginative construction by signs and relations of quality. The profound intuitions formed by White Mountain, then, are united by the idea of re-beginning a world from scratch. There are two distinct *freedom* projects: For Descartes, it is the heroic human overcoming of the dark and violent forces of external nature by technique; Boehme's mission directs us to love's victory over the turbulent nature within.

In its simplest terms, Boehme's original idea places potentiality at the heart of the Trinity. He introduces into the concept of God a dynamic principle of development. Life is the relationship between negative and positive potentiality—the self-actualization of divine freedom within the temporal order of creation. The becoming of the Holy Spirit's revelation (Offenbarung) is a familiar symbolist archetype but, unlike onto-theological symbolism, the sign of divine process (Bezeichnung) is, for the first time, given an independent and living triadic character. Signs grow and create—semiosis. A sign of the Trinity is an evolutionary, self-creating, and thoroughly communicative entity. Passive imitation and communication of an eternally actual model or formal sign is displaced by the moving triadic vestigia of semiotic innovation. Divine potentiality signifies an open historical process to be realized by the drive toward novel self-manifestation. The experience of a living God means the eternal overcoming of evil by love serves as the basis of cosmic integration of the Holy Spirit with and in time. Why is this obscure Christian theosophical presupposition so influential in its implications?

Nicolas Berdyaev (†1948) makes the sweeping claim, "Boehme is the fountainhead of the dynamism of German philosophy, one might even say of the dynamism of the entire thought of the nineteenth century."[40] Jacob Taubes (†1987) is more focused in defining Boehme's role in "the principle of history that becomes all important in modern times and the guide for scientific research."[41] Jacob Boehme is distilled "through the German Idealists," Taubes maintains, and the "the *imago trinitatis* of Christian theology turns into a principle of the historical process," which is, "a progressive succession of divine manifestation [as Spirit]."[42] From Boehme flows a plurality of historicisms. Thus, historicism can take the form of evolutionary semiotics. Self, society, life, and physical nature are triadic, inter-relational, and progressive systems of signs: The universe is communication in the making. Other versions deny tri-unity, divinity, continuity, semiotic constitution, teleological love, and so on. The key point, however, is that there are no permanent essences. Subjects and their principles of order are *created* by the immanent historical processes in which they are involved: The infection of time changes all things. Heraclitus is, finally, baptized.

We should not immediately view Boehme's Trinity as heterodox. This way of thinking presumes the onto-theological Trinity is the unquestionable

---

40. Berdyaev, "Unground and Freedom," xxxiii.
41. Taubes, "Dialectic and Analogy," 113.
42. Taubes, "Dialectic and Analogy," 113.

figure by which to judge any other version.⁴³ Variations on a complete model can only be deviant, an *innovation*. Despite its often crude, dark, and bizarre expression, Boehme's introduction of relational potentiality into the Godhead challenges the authenticity and, thus, cultural stability of Christianity's onto-theological Trinity. God is a life in motion, not a perfect ideal. The Trinity cannot be an *ideological* system of imitation, conformity, and obedience because the paradigm is not timeless and whole. The God of pure potentiality and becoming liberates being from its passive dependency on formal actualization. Univocal and egalitarian movement is always beyond relations of subordination. The Trinity radicalizes the open order of the Holy Spirit: "For here we have no continuing city, but we seek one to come" (Heb 13:14 KJV). All processes of becoming are manifestations of a single underlying divine process: The incompleteness of God *is* the freedom of the world. In the name of the *restoration* of the Bible's living God, Boehme initiates an inadvertent rupture within Christian tradition and Western thought. Offering an alternative *categorical* understanding of the Trinity is a revolution within the most potent archetype of Christendom. Boehme's Trinitarian theosophy of freedom complicates the eternal and economic distinction of the Trinity. He struggles to keep this difference in place, but in this creeping theological crack, according to John P. Dourley, we witness the beginning of "the collapse of the immanent or eternally self-sufficient Trinity into the economic Trinity," and what is "implied in Boehme" is "given philosophical formulation by Hegel in the nineteenth century."⁴⁴

The *Boehme legend* propounds his lack of Classical education in philosophy.⁴⁵ The *Philosophus Teutonicus* elicits a folk renewal of Christianity and philosophy on uniquely German ground. Boehme's unlettered instincts topple the Greek ideology of formal substance. Berdyaev argues that his theosophy is "free from the categories of the Greek gods."⁴⁶ The symbol of the Trinity revives the Hebrew life philosophy of historical immanence.⁴⁷ For nationalist reasons, the Greek influence is often portrayed as indirect and

---

43. Alexandre Koyré, for instance, claims *the* Trinity is poorly suited to Boehme's thought. See Koyré, *La philosophie de Jacob Boehme*, 410–13.

44. Dourley, "Jacob Boehme and Paul Tillich," 437. Despite Tillich's acknowledged and profound debt to Friedrich W. J. von Schelling, Dourley's otherwise excellent paper attributes the crucial philosophical rehabilitation of Boehme to Hegel only. In addition to Hegel and Schelling, we can also add the philosophy of Charles Sanders Peirce.

45. See Brown, *Later Philosophy of Schelling*, 32–35.

46. Berdyaev, "Unground and Freedom," xiii.

47. See Berdyaev, "Unground and Freedom," xii–xiv; McGrath, *Dark Ground of Spirit*, 180.

derivative, but it still signifies continuity of a still unclear kind.[48] Boehme is certainly not a scholastic philosopher, but his ideas on the Trinity are not without a clarifying connection to Greek categories. The first formation of Christian doctrine introduces triadic relationships within an analogue of Aristotle's unmoved mover of pure actuality, emphasizing the divine life of the mind. Boehme's second formulation can be viewed as divinizing Aristotle's intimation of cosmic life metaphysics. Positing a triadic relationship between determinate and indeterminate potentiality means the living God is radically voluntarist. The Trinity is the dialectical and developmental process of freedom's overcoming of its own contraries: Freedom in the image of love triumphs over the dark gravity of the will's own drive and desire.

Boehme's theosophy of the Holy Spirit is profound, rich, and original, but it is not truly sensed and seized upon as *the freedom to interpret* the Trinity until two centuries later.[49] Freedom enfolds and unfolds the core of Christian doctrine; alternative formulations can legitimately multiply. Christian growth is speculative engagement, experimentation, and application of the triadic principle—innovation is its good. The Trinity is a heuristic model for existence as self-communicative freedom. The Holy Spirit constitutes its own historical manifestation and evolution *by noetic, vital, and physical interpretation*. To be a true Trinitarian thinker is to be triadic without fixed theological presupposition: Progressive heterodoxy is orthodoxy. Boehme foreshadows onto-theological collapse. Theological contemporaries sense this implicit dissolution; both Protestant and Catholic condemn his *innovation* on the Trinity. For later triadic-historicist thinkers, however, Boehme is the unacknowledged *other father* of modern philosophy. For German Idealism, especially, Cyril O'Regan claims, "the topic of the relation of philosophy and the symbol of the Trinity was a crucial one."[50]

48. See Weeks, *Boehme*, 129–30.

49. At least part of the reason involves a cultural shift on the meaning of innovation, especially on a doctrine as fundamental as the Trinity. Prior to the Age of Romanticism, innovation tends to be portrayed as something threatening. Like many significant figures of his time, Boehme perceives his work in terms of *restoring* the true mimetic foundation of the Trinity, which has been obscured by centuries of theological sediment, an admixture of the false philosophies of the ancients and scholastics. In the wake of Romanticism, though, innovation means the creation of new foundations is positive, imitating a pre-given model is something negative: *Imago Dei* is the power of creativity *per se*. Thus, speculative innovation on the Trinity is, in some sense, the very essence of freedom. It is "in some sense" because without its onto-theological presupposition of pure actuality, the freedom to innovate on the Trinitarian principle is the *essence* of the living principle: Imitation is, paradoxically, innovation—essence erases essence—difference precedes unity. On this change of cultural attitude, see Girard, "Innovation and Repetition," 7–20.

50. O'Regan, "Trinity in Kant, Hegel, and Schelling," 256.

THE FINAL SIGNATURE

Boehme identifies communication with revelation and human essence. Humanity is called to be the revealer of divine *signatures*. But singular creatures are not themselves divine; they are communiqués, signing the hidden life of God. Signatures, however, are not fully actualized formal signs. Creatures are potentialities that develop themselves through the temporal process, reflecting what God, their source, is eternally. God is a life, not a fixed model or formal system: Life process *is* theogonic process. The temporal theatre is not the secondary replica of divine perfection. The world is the evolutionary series of free life-images. Creation's freedom is to be made whole through the human liberation of its divine signatures.

In place of static opposition and isolation, Boehme sees continuous development and growth, emerging from the constructive interpenetration of humanity, creation, and God. Because of our unique ability to *speak for* creation, the decisive indicator that humanity is the image of God, our own salvation depends upon the salvation of the cosmos. Humanity's role as the liberator of creation is the anticipation and the participation in the perfection that is to be gained for ourselves and the world. Becoming a person is not simply, from the offset, conferred on all human beings. Personality is achieved by the revelation of the divine *vestigia*, speaking on behalf of the subjugated creatures of the world. The liberation of creation implies the true interpretation of creatures through their divine signatures. The Spirit becomes realized through the human subject. As Alexandre Koyré (†1964) explains, "For [Boehme] to *be* means to realize one's potentialities actively, dynamically, and realization means manifestation, uncovering one's essential nature and deploying all inherent possibilities."[51] This characterization of existence finds its ground in God: "The perfect being is the one in whom this self-realization is most complete. Essential nature becomes conscious of itself within us in order to be revealed. Being as personal is thus the highest form of being because it achieves self-realization and self-revelation. Only by defining itself and manifesting itself is self-realization and self-manifestation fully achieved."[52]

The divine image in humanity, then—its characteristic feature that drives a thing to become itself (*Qualität*)—is not substantial form; rather, it is the dialectical potentiality for personality. The desires, forces, and conflicts

---

51. Koyré, *La philosophie de Jacob Boehme*, quoted in Boehme, *Essential Readings*, 36.

52. Koyré, *La philosophie de Jacob Boehme*, quoted in Boehme, *Essential Readings*, 36.

of life's embodied existence all manifest divine process.[53] The introduction of potentiality within the Christian Godhead challenges onto-theology by positing a constitutive relationship between materiality and divinity. There is also the progressive sense of God, allowing the world its own free space of emergence. Ernest B. Koenker makes several definitive points on Boehme's Trinity of Will:

> Nature, which had been excluded from God in the Hebrew encounter with the surrounding nature-gods, is brought into the Godhead once again. Potentiality is present within the Godhead, rather than the pure actuality of St. Thomas's conception of God. For St. Thomas there can be no potentiality in God because God supremely and eternally is everything he may become, but for Boehme the eternal will in God continually gives rise to all that is: will is the source of self-actualization in both God and in man. . . . Moreover, as has been indicated, Boehme's God is not absolutely simple, like the God of St. Thomas, but is guilty of composition: the totality of Being includes evil as well as good, darkness as well as light. For the classical theism of St. Augustine or St. Thomas such negativity within God is simply anathema: God is the sovereign exception to all negativities and potentialities. For Boehme the perfection of God simply demands that he is not altogether simple. Self-manifestation, self-consciousness, self-realization are all possible simply because there is dialectic within the divine.[54]

Creation still enchants as the onto-symbolic invention (*signatura*) of the divine imagination (*Magia*). The modern divorce of matter from mind is not present in Boehme's philosophy of nature; the cosmos is not ours to wantonly sacrifice for anthropocentric salvation. His view of creation is still liberationist, but it is not the quantitative vision of calculative control. The language of the real is *co*-evolutionary, symbiotic, and *qualitatively* semiotic: "This alphabet of the language of Nature is hidden among them all in black color," Boehme teaches, "save by him who possesses the language of Nature, to whom it is revealed by God's Spirit."[55] Creation is not silent, desacralized, and purposeless; it is something to be affected by, sensed, felt and, ultimately, loved. We speak, steward, in its interest, revealing our signature, not as master, but as *co*-liberator—willing the synergy of God, self, and other—WE. Boehme calls "life's image-like nature," "the embodied grace

---

53. See Boehme, *Aurora*, 76–86; Weeks, *Boehme*, 64–68.
54. Koenker, *Great Dialecticians in Modern Christian Thought*, 61.
55. Boehme, *Six Theosophic Points*, 154.

of God."[56] Divine self-constitution achieves personality: Life, light, and love triumph eternally over their dark ground. The achievement of human personality is an equivalent process, mirroring the struggles of divinity to harmonize its own wild, selfish, and evil nature (contractive force) with the contrary loss of the self by pure being-to-another (expansive force). As S. J. McGrath lucidly articulates, the "dark fire" of divinity also burns "in the heart of nature."[57] The *unpreconscious* "productive negative" communicates between sacred and temporal realms.[58] Boehme's dialectical conception of the *Ungrund* and the *Grund* emerges from the shadowy heart of God and nature.

The *Ungrund* is the everlasting, unoriginated, and undifferentiated source of the divine life; it is grounded in nothing whatsoever. In relation to particular and embodied creatures, the *Ungrund* can best be termed *No-thing*. Boehme's *No-thing* is the infinite power of being: "And thus we apprehend what God and Nature is; how the one and the other is from eternity without any ground or beginning. For it is an everlasting beginning. It begins itself perpetually and from eternity to eternity, where there is no number; for there is no ground."[59] The *Ungrund* must be distinguished from the nondialectical nothing of pure non-being, which the Greek language denominated *ouk on*. *Ouk on* is the nothing that has no relationship to being; it is absolute negation, existing outside of God as the complete absence of being. The traditional Christian doctrine of *creatio ex nihilo* rejects matter (potentiality) as the co-principle of creation, presenting the *nihil* out of which God (*Actus Purus*) creates as *ouk on*—the undialectical negation of being. Boehme's *Ungrund* is not *ouk on*; rather, it is the purely relational or modal *nihil*, having a dialectical relationship to being, which the Greeks termed *me on*. *Me on* is the divine *Prima Materia*, which is the infinite potentiality to create what can be, but is not. To Boehme, *creatio ex nihilo* means *creatio ex Deo*: God's nothingness, its freedom or dialectical potentiality, is implicit in, and part of, the divine life. Nothingness is not external to God—that is, potentiality is not that by which a perfectly actualized God freely chooses to create a world from. Nothingness is the very heart of God and the creation of the world is the naturalized, embodied phase of the divine life, inhering in the divine nature as the drive to manifest the contents of the divine imagination.

---

56. Boehme, *Six Theosophic Points*, 164.
57. McGrath, *Dark Ground of Spirit*, 75.
58. McGrath, *Dark Ground of Spirit*, 75.
59. Boehme, *Six Theosophic Points*, 146.

The *Ungrund* is replete with boundless freedom, which is the equilibrium (indifference) of endless and equal possibilities. The indeterminate capacity to be is described as being devoid of passion; nonetheless, to Boehme, the *principle* of being, the "*ewige Nichts*," is (inexplicably) teeming with the most profound drive (*Trieb*) to attain its *Grund*: "The unground is an eternal nothing, but makes an eternal beginning as a craving. For the nothing is a craving after something. But as there is nothing that can give anything, accordingly the craving itself is the giving of it, which yet also is nothing, or merely a desirous seeking."[60] Why did this transition from nullity and unity to difference take place? Why did the *Ungrund* interrupt its own infinity with the novelty of the Trinity—the symbolic passion for personality? Or the traditional question: Why something rather than *Nothing*? "The mystery," as Koenker detects, "is never 'explained,' other than to point to the actualization of the self, through opposition by an 'other,' into greater fullness—which nevertheless adds nothing to what is already present."[61] Further, for McGrath, "Why the unground wills self-revelation ultimately cannot be answered. To give an answer would be to ascribe a cause to that which has no ground, that which is absolutely unconditioned and free."[62] Boehme's God begins as a wild God. Eternal creation, then, need not have occurred because it is without precondition or motivating reason. Design, incompleteness, and desire to know itself cannot secure the reasons for God's self-creation. Life, eternal and temporal, is gift, not fate, spontaneity rather than necessity.

In *Signatura Rerum* (1622), Boehme, nevertheless, appears to offer some kind of an explanation for the creation of the cosmos: "For God did not give birth to Creation in order to become more complete, but rather for the purpose of His Self-Revelation, to his great joy and glory."[63] God generates the world that repeats in time and space the same process of freedom, affliction, and joy that is eternal in God. The *un*reason for something rather than nothing seems to be a kind of imaginative of love-play (*Liebesspiel*). Boehme employs the analogy of music to describe the communication of the eternal splendor of conscious personality. The divine music celebrates the achievement of light over darkness, life over death, and harmony over discord. The creation of the world is the hymn of praise to the glory of God who breaks the silence of the *No-thing* and triumphs over its own emergent and unconscious ground of opposing potencies. The creation of the world

60. Boehme, *Six Theosophic Points*, 141.
61. Koenker, *Great Dialecticians in Modern Christian Thought*, 59.
62. McGrath, *Dark Ground of Spirit*, 53.
63. Boehme, *Signature of All Things*, 115.

is "the Divine Extrication or Revelation, how God introduceth himself in the Eternal Nature, in Love and Wrath."[64] Creatures are given their own independent self-creativity as the outpouring of God's free personality: Personality means freedom. The musical play of ecstatic innovation embodies the world, seeking more players for the concert that begins as the dark and pregnant moment in eternity. Signatures are more like the divine traces of musical notation, eternal songs in the process of being played, than they are architectural blueprints; live repetition suggests embodied novelty rather than the formal and controlled imposition of divine design.

The procession from the *Ungrund* to the *Grund* is God's self-communication from Himself as nothing to Himself as something: Conscious personality. The *Grund* reflects God's pure potentiality as the eternal symbolic mirror (wisdom or *Sophia*). God's sighting of his own image as the *No-thing* generates the semiotic drive to create the world. Primordial reflexivity means consciousness. The *No-thing* that can recognize itself as the *No-thing* is conscious of itself: "Nothing without contrariety can become manifest to itself; for if it has nothing to resist it, it goes continually of itself outwards, and returns not again to itself. But if it return not again into itself, as into that out of which it originally went, it knows nothing of its primal being."[65] The *Grund's* mirror fractures the *Ungrund's* undifferentiated unity, enacting the eternal dialectic of identity and difference that creates life-images and their space-time continuum. The divine depth is reflected in the symbolic mirror, seeing itself, becoming the image standing over against itself as the knowing subject aware of its own *No-thingness*. The divine imagination's infinite symbolic potentiality is the *virtualized* passion for being:

> Seeing the first will is an ungroundedness, to be regarded as an eternal nothing, we recognize it to be like a mirror, wherein one sees his own image; like a life, and yet it is no life, but a figure of life and of the image belonging to life. Thus we recognize the eternal Unground out of Nature to be like a mirror. For it is an eye which sees, and yet conducts nothing in the seeing wherewith it sees; for seeing is without essence, although it is generated from essence, viz. from the essential life. We are able to recognize that the eternal Unground out of Nature is a will, like an eye wherein Nature is hidden; like a hidden fire that burns not, which exists and also exists not. It is not a spirit, but a form of spirit, like the reflection in the mirror. For all the form of a spirit is seen in the reflection or in the mirror, and yet there is nothing which the eye or mirror sees; but its seeing is in itself,

64. Boehme, "Appendix," 217.
65. Boehme, *Six Theosophic Points*, 167.

> for there is nothing before it that were deeper there. It is like a mirror which is a container of the aspect of Nature, and yet comprehends not Nature, as Nature comprehends not the form of the image in the mirror. And thus one is free from the other, and yet the mirror is truly the container of the image. It embraces the image, and yet is powerless in respect of the form, for it cannot retain it. For if the image depart from the mirror, the mirror is a clear brightness, and its brightness is a nothing; and yet all the form of Nature is hidden therein as a nothing; and yet veritably is, but not in essence.[66]

The unfathomable will within the divine mirror's *mysterium magnum* reveals God's wisdom and desire to create the world. He strives to actualize the vision of his splendor as reflected in the mirror. God's will acts upon the products of his imagination, and he craves to communicate his signatures to the world. "*Magia*," Boehme tells us, is "hunger after being."[67] God's desire "makes an imagination (*Einbildung*), and imagination is only the will of desire."[68] According to Robert F. Brown, "In creating, it is as if God projected images of his constituents onto a screen or an environment of space and time."[69] The eternal generation enters into space and time, constituting the visible world, by means of God's own fervent movement. Therefore, the creature is the symbolic repetition or likeness (*Gleichnis*) of the eternal process. Signatures manifest this same process temporally in their own development: "For this visible world with all its host and being is nothing but an objective representation of the spiritual world, which spiritual world is hidden in this material, elemental world, like as tincture in herbs and metals."[70]

Finite signatures in space and time embody all the qualities of the divine nature: The dark center of God (the eternal Abyss, Wrath, or No) is operative in creation as well as the light center (the eternal Byss, Love, or Yes). There is oscillation between the selfish contraction that cannot acknowledge the other and the expansive alterity that cannot acknowledge the self. The dialectic of contractive and expansive forces informs the whole of the created order as its evolutionary drive: Survival and salvation depend on the successful integration of the two opposing forces. But, to be clear, Boehme's ontological view of the world is *realistic*; its gravity tends toward

---

66. Boehme, *Six Theosophic Points*, 6–7.
67. Boehme, *Six Theosophic Points*, 119.
68. Boehme, *Six Theosophic Points*, 181.
69. Brown, *Later Philosophy of Schelling*, 66.
70. Boehme, *Six Theosophic Points*, 200–201.

the recognition of suffering, violence, and tragic failure—physical, moral, psychological, social, and ecological shipwreck on the rocks of the world's own freedom—for us and the creatures of the world. The embodied world of good and evil, the evolutionary engine of life, *can* end in the Kingdom of God, but the temporal theatre in which we are *thrown* and called upon to liberate is, first and foremost, a shadowy and monstrous place: "We find good and evil, and we find in all things the *centrum naturae*, or the torture-chamber."[71] *Hell on Earth* is the human norm. Brown well explains why this is the case:

> The creation consists of the same opposing forces that in God have a relationship of eternal harmony and order, now expressed in a process that involves temporal change and spatial extension. The creation is finite because its completion and goal are future, not simultaneously given with the process itself. Moreover, the creatures of the world are free. Therefore, whereas God and the world are alike in essence (have the same ontological constituents), God does not compel the world to realize the perfection of its essence in imitation of its own being. Whereas God wins an eternal victory over the destructive aspect of the dark center, the creatures of the world are free to either emulate God's victory, or succumb to the disintegrating influence of the pure *No* that is within them. When they succumb, the dark powers of God no longer function merely as vital forces, but appear as the wrath of God turned against them.[72]

The flow of the world out of the divine imagination is a Baroque mediation. The eternal generation of the bipolar Trinity is integrated within seven hermetic categories or processional stages.[73] The Trinitarian Persons are the three basic potencies or principles; the mirror's primordial symbols arise from the initial procession from the *Ungrund* to the *Grund*, constituting the One God: "[The] first *Magia*, which is God in his triad."[74] The Trinity, however, like all things in Boehme, goes through a process to fulfillment; it, too, emerges from "the foundation of the dark world."[75] The divine achievement of personality follows the sequence of growth: Seven energies or qualities operate through two triads, which mark the nadir (contraction, diffusion, and rotation/oscillation) and the acme (love, communication,

---

71. Boehme, *Six Theosophic Points*, 24.
72. Brown, *Later Philosophy of Schelling*, 68.
73. See Boehme, "Appendix," 215–39.
74. Boehme, *Six Theosophic Points*, 120.
75. Boehme, *Six Theosophic Points*, 94.

and harmonization) of the Trinity's development. Boehme associates the higher triad with the Persons of the Trinity; love is the Father, expression is the Son, and harmonization is the Holy Spirit.

The fully realized Trinity of Will has three aspects: "[There] is in God an Eternal Will, which He Himself is, [a Will] to give birth to His Son or Heart, and the same Will makes the impulse or issuance out of the Will of the Heart, which is a Spirit; so that eternity stands in three equal figures, which are called persons."[76] The Trinity's dynamics of creation balance contraction and expansion or, more precisely, the contraction of identity *is* the power of communicative expansion: "The divine will shuts itself in a place to selfhood, as to power, and becomes active in itself; but also by that activity goes forth, and makes itself an object, viz. wisdom, through which the ground and origin of all beings has arisen."[77] Wisdom (*Sophia*) is the mirror, reflecting God's harmony of identity (contraction) and alterity (expansion): Being for the self is being for the other and vice versa. In the dreamlike and musical play of divine imagination, all the possibilities that God could will are manifested as images in the infinite mind. The medium of the world's creation is the *impulse* of the Spirit, enacting and embodying the divine dream. The synthesized seventh energy communicates the divine imagination: "Magic is the activity in Will-spirit."[78] The symbolic flash (*Blitz*) creates the life-image or signature; it is like lightening from the buildup of static electricity—the reconciliation of the triads, constituting the One and Eternal Trinity. The higher triad overflows into the lower, elevating and harmonizing the lower, and generating the divine personality, the world, and the creatures of which it consists.

Unlike the divine life of God's pure harmonious creation, the embodied creature exists in a mixed state of torment between heaven and earth, divine signature and animal image. Other creatures, for the most part, cannot be otherwise than what they are. Humanity, however, is marked with the same radical freedom as God: "Man, moreover, has no law except he enkindle himself in the dark world's property, and walk according to this property. Independently of that, all is free to him."[79] The potentiality for personality is open to a human being, but it is an arduous project to accomplish. We exist as the hinge of freedom between two dominions, swinging to love or evil with the distinct inclination for the latter: "Two dominions, qualities and laws repose in him. The divine unto love and righteousness; whatsoever

76. Boehme, *Forty Questions of the Soul*, 34.
77. Boehme, *Six Theosophic Points*, 203.
78. Boehme, *Six Theosophic Points*, 135.
79. Boehme, *Six Theosophic Points*, 95.

he doth in meekness and love is without restriction for him, and is proper being; it consists not in any one's name or presumption; and the wrathful in the rising pride in the power of fire, in the stern, harsh, hellish covetousness, envy, anger and malice. The one to which the spirit unites itself, of that dominion it is."[80] Thus, Boehme concludes, "life is in a desperate strait between the two, and is at odds with itself."[81] Moreover, "Man must be at war against himself, if he wishes to become a heavenly citizen."[82]

Boehme offers his theosophy to those who seek emancipation from the bondage of their animal image: "Those who are often and much hindered by the contrarious life, and thus are involved in the mixed life, and travail in desire for the birth of holy life: for them are these writings written."[83] The event that occasions the human signature of personality is open to all: "God's word or heart has given itself to the shut up, dead, human essence; not to the earthly part, but to the heavenly part."[84] Further, "For an animal-man may attain the image [of God], if he turn round and suffer the Word that became man to draw him. If not, then he remains in his animal essence an evil beast."[85] We have the capacity for love or evil, something closed to our fellow creatures, but the refusal of personality gives us the potentiality to be more beastly or violent than any innocent animal. Other creatures can neither win personality nor lose their divine signature. The human being, by contrast, is caught in the conflict between the Spirit and Lucifer over "the soul (*Gemüth*) of man."[86] Our bare animal image can *fall* further than any other creature: "Thus the soul with the image falls unto the wrathful, dark world; and the image is brought into a hellish figure, into a form of its property which it had there. So it fared also with the devils, who had lost their first image."[87] But the restoration of our divine signature is also the greatest potentiality given to any creature.

The metamorphosis of the Spirit must first shatter the animal image that has turned to evil: "I come not to send peace, but a sword" (Matt 10:34 KJV):

> Since then both dominions are become powerful in him, and the dominion of wrath has overpowered love, he must wholly

---

80. Boehme, *Six Theosophic Points*, 97.
81. Boehme, *Six Theosophic Points*, 97.
82. Boehme, *Six Theosophic Points*, 111.
83. Boehme, *Six Theosophic Points*, 3.
84. Boehme, *Six Theosophic Points*, 81.
85. Boehme, *Six Theosophic Points*, 81.
86. Boehme, *Six Theosophic Points*, 170.
87. Boehme, *Six Theosophic Points*, 97.

break to pieces in substance, and be re-born again from the first root. And therefore he has in this twofold being laws, how he should conduct himself and generate a will-spirit unto eternal dominion. All this lies in his power. He may bring forth the spirit of wrath or the spirit of love, and in accordance with the same he is separated whither and into which he belongs; for he separates himself.[88]

To be born again, baptized by the Spirit, brings the spiritual war of liberation against "diabolized man"—dark forces "rob him of his noble image, and make of him a mask of the devil; that the individual, natural will may not enter again into a desire of its own for selfhood, and set itself up as the ruler over the inward ground, and destroy the true image of God."[89] The communication of the divine imagination through the Spirit accounts for creation. The path back to divinity is through the imaginative emancipation of the Spirit.

The natural language of liberation begins as the transubstantiation of the imagination: "It is spiritual blood, which outer nature cannot touch (*rügen*), but by imagination only."[90] The craving for individual power and mastery destroys others and the self by "earthly imagination (*Bildung*)," which Boehme describes as "[this] individual, image-like will [that] had arisen from its own ground, viz. from flesh and blood of the self-ful nature of man and woman, that is, in the separator of the emanated will, where the eternal will had confined itself in ownership and would go forth and rule in personal power and might."[91] The *lord of creation* "received not the eternal Word," remaining within *the devil's mask*.[92] To be our image is to speak for the divine image of the world and its creatures. "God is an eternal speaking," Boehme reveals, "for from God's speaking the life has proceeded and come into body, and is nothing else than an image-like will of God."[93] But Boehme's salvation project implies something beyond intellectual contemplation; it is radical and voluntarist, the active confrontation with the evils of our own nature, both within the psyche and in the outer theatre of world historical being. Love is the nexus of communication between divinity and creatures; humanity is charged with its freedom and preservation. The Trinity and the *whole* of creation must be reconciled.

88. Boehme, *Six Theosophic Points*, 96.
89. Boehme, *Six Theosophic Points*, 176.
90. Boehme, *Six Theosophic Points*, 118.
91. Boehme, *Six Theosophic Points*, 208.
92. Boehme, *Six Theosophic Points*, 208.
93. Boehme, *Six Theosophic Points*, 185.

Divine love brings the sword to fight the spread of hell on Earth. There must be direct conflict with temporal domination: Luciferian humanity is oblivious to the divine signature of its natural other, upon which it absolutely depends. The other pole must be also fought—the call for hysterical self-sacrifice of the self and the species for the good of the ecosystem is equally as evil. The actualization of the *ecological* Trinity, realizing the Kingdom of God, is the harmonization of the material, psychological, moral, political, economic, and so on. It is Boehme's original drive to encompass the natural world within the semiotic struggle for liberation that inspires Romanticism.[94] Ecological consciousness is born with the unified figure of human and natural emancipation. In Percy Bysshe Shelley's (†1822) *Prometheus Unbound* (1820), we read:

> Demogorgon.
> Spirits, whose homes are flesh: ye beasts and birds,
> Ye worms, and fish; ye living leaves and buds;
> Lightening and wind; and ye untameable herds,
> Meteors and mists, which throng air's solitudes:—
>
> A Voice.
> Thy voice to us is wind among still woods.
>
> Demogorgon.
> Man, who wert once a despot and a slave;
> A dupe and a deceiver; a decay;
> A traveler from the cradle to the grave
> Through the dim night of this immortal day:
>
> All.
> Speak: thy strong words may never pass away.
>
> Demogorgon.
> This is the day, which down the void abysm
> At the Earth-born's spell yawns for Heaven's despotism
> And Conquest is dragged captive through the deep:
> Love, from its awful throne of patient power
> In the wise heart, from the last giddy hour
> Of dread endurance, from the slippery, steep,
> And narrow verge of crag-like agony, springs
> And folds over the world its healing wings.
>
> Gentleness, Virtue, Wisdom, and Endurance,
> These are the seals of that most firm assurance
> Which bars the pit over Destruction's strength;

---

94. See Abrams, *Natural Supernaturalism*, 161–63.

And if, with infirm hand, Eternity
Mother of many acts and hours, should free
The serpent that would clasp her with his length;
These are the spells by which to reassume
An empire o'er the disentangled doom.

To suffer woes which Hope thinks infinite;
To forgive wrongs darker than death or night;
To defy power, which seems omnipotent;
To love, and bear; to hope till Hope creates
From its own wreck the thing it contemplates;
Neither to change, nor falter, nor repent;
This, like thy glory, Titan, is to be
Good, great, and joyous, beautiful and free;
This is alone Life, Joy, Empire, and Victory.[95]

---

95. Shelley, *Prometheus Unbound*, 152–53.

Supplement: *On Beloved Community*
Collingwood, Cochrane, and Ecological Civilization

DISTILLATIONS

FOR A CIVILIZATION TO thrive, there must be institutions for preserving and perpetrating its absolute presuppositions. In Europe it is Christian religious institutions that have traditionally fulfilled this role. Modern life has gradually eroded their power. David Boucher describes this process as an attempt "to distil from Christianity principles which relate to activities such as politics and scientific method."[1] Secular *distillations* eventually become "severed from their foundation, and the foundation was explained in other terms."[2] This obscuration of foundation can be problematic for a civilization in crisis. "If nothing remains to generate the will to preserve the absolute presuppositions upon which it rests," Boucher claims, this eclipse endangers not just European civilization but, in the ecological crisis, the Earth itself.[3] Unless this renewal occurs, we are increasingly defenseless—lacking connection to ground, to the means of repair, and to the very possibly of a common plan. Instead of the joyful labor for imaginative emancipation, we will be constantly visited by irrational cycles of reckless mutilation and domination.

We no longer believe in the logic of our world. There is a formless hunger for a new, unconditionally binding, commitment to a different kind of community, none that the fading politics of modernity approach. As secular

---

1. Boucher, *Social and Political Thought of R. G. Collingwood*, 236.
2. Boucher, *Social and Political Thought of R. G. Collingwood*, 236.
3. Boucher, *Social and Political Thought of R. G. Collingwood*, 237.

utopias demonstrate their insidious hollowness—especially liberalism's union with global capital, re-turning fascism to accompany ecological collapse—radical thought moves to present an alternative to modern systems in their entirety. Dispersed expectations converge on an event that will end our desert wanderings; yet, for such an exception to occur, we have been warned, it must not dispense a schematic, another prescriptive program; if it is to truly show itself openly in its otherness, it must negate itself as representation, as a real presence that can be used for domination. Surely, though, movement to a liberation mission of some kind is exactly what is needed; something that escapes the endless exercise of deconstructive, skeptical equivocations. Given our afflicted and restless predicament, we need a meaningful answer to the question: *What can restrain ecological perdition?*

There is, consequently, a revival of interest in theologically driven political ideas, arriving with our ecological crisis of civilization. This theoretical movement encompasses select thinkers on the European continent who were most active and influential between the two principal wars of the twentieth century. Political theology appears to center on the Christian form of life—that is, has modern secularization replaced it? If it has, how do we accommodate ourselves to the new situation of ideology without a transcendent referent? What is the politics, the worldview, announced by the claim *God is dead*? If not, how do we mobilize Christian absolute presuppositions to confront our various crises? Is it even theologically legitimate to attempt it? R. G. Collingwood and Charles Norris Cochrane are philosophers from this crucial era of ideas and events. They position themselves as defenders of the social and ecological prospects of the Christian constellation. The reality of Christian historicity requires further innovations in Christian forms of sovereignty. Secular experiments of ideology have proven disastrous. The Christian constellation still shines behind the dark clouds of war and environmental destruction, but the Earth itself has shifted to another position since then, revealing a different region of stars to guide us forward, homeward to the beloved community: A New Earth to be *re-grasped otherwise* in its angelic reality, in its historical communication of the Trinity, uniting *vestigia* (creation) and *imago* (human).

COLLINGWOOD AND POLITICAL THEOLOGY

Like many thinkers living between the two world wars of the last century, Collingwood is seeking to avoid another civilizational shipwreck. Modernity occasions a series of increasingly perilous waypoints that require faithful decisions. He would, for instance, no doubt agree with (his contemporary)

Carl Schmitt's definition of "Secularization," as naming the process, whereby "the state, perhaps, or the people, or even the individual subject—takes the place of God as the ultimate authority and decisive factor."[4] Agreement can also extend to the majority of Schmitt's brilliant and convincing diagnoses on our modern condition. But on the prescription, the two thinkers sharply diverge. Collingwood defends the prospect for institutional revitalisation of the Christian constellation. As Richard Murphy points out, for Collingwood, "Properly re-constituted, Christian principles can overcome nihilism."[5] Christianity "expresses in an allegorical form the solution to the crisis of Western civilization that Collingwood articulated in his metaphysics and philosophy of history."[6] Nihilism results from the distortion of Christian historicity by secular ideologies that cannot replace it. Schmitt initially takes up this position, but he eventually abandons this direction of ideas. The narrative of the differences between the two philosophers is instructive and pertinent for the proposed ecological variation of Christian political theology.

Throughout the nineteen-twenties, the German jurist's countermodern conservatism defends a rehabilitated Roman Catholic Church; it is capable of providing a viable political alternative to the "fundamental dualism" that pervades secular existence: "In this instance, too, she will be the *complexio* of all that survives. The inheritance will be hers."[7] The criterion "of the Trinity" means the "political power of Catholicism does not rest on economic or military power"—rather, it rests on the "representative capacity" of "*civitas humana*."[8] "The Church," accordingly, remains "the sole representative of political thought and political form."[9] The "cult of privacy" in religious life must be abolished, and "the Catholic Church" must reassert publicly its traditional "ecclesiastical authority" because it "goes hand in hand with the maintenance of justice."[10] If, in Collingwood's vocabulary, it is to keep its power to represent the Christian constellation, Catholicism must become something more than a "shadow of the past."[11] Schmitt then, apparently, loses faith in the "boundless adaptability" to the modern

---

4. Schmitt, *Political Romanticism*, 17.
5. Murphy, *Collingwood and the Crisis of Civilization*, 162.
6. Murphy, *Collingwood and the Crisis of Civilization*, 163.
7. Schmitt, *Necessity of Politics*, 40, 90.
8. Schmitt, *Necessity of Politics*, 37, 55, 56.
9. Schmitt, *Necessity of Politics*, 67.
10. Schmitt, *Necessity of Politics*, 72, 78.
11. Schmitt, *Necessity of Politics*, 85.

age found in "Christ's royal Bride."[12] As a perceptive biographer notes, he eventually rejects the Trinity and its church as an ineffectual "anachronism in the age of mass politics."[13] Medieval Christendom is a defunct political jurisdiction, and so are its absolute presuppositions. Tridentine personalism is abandoned along with its social conciliation of contraries; it cannot stand as an effective counterpoint to modern nihilism. The light of Christian civilization has darkened permanently. Many subjects simply refuse to accept it. But refusal does not make it any less true. An alternative must be found. *Post-Christendom* emergency measures are now required.

In the late 1920s and 1930s, Schmitt becomes, as a friend once described him, a "godless cleric" in search of a new church.[14] History, thankfully, sends a fresh dispensation by means of Germany's reactionary revolution. A messianic *sovereign* is revealed. His will can create an original constellational order of absolute presuppositions: A new civilization. Schmitt will now fight nihilism's swarming multitudes under the NSDAP's black and red banner. There is a proposed merger of bio-identity state and deity; to be governed by a new *priestly* class. The oracular potentate receives and decides, communicating the sacred and ambiguous glyph. The priests interpret and enact. The enemy is named for a Manichean duel against evil: The forces of sovereign necessity will combat nihilism. The leader's sacred state is the restrainer of evil—κατέχων. Only it can delay the apocalyptic end of history by restraining modernity's *Son(s) of Perdition*; namely, the secular hydra arising from the debris of Christianity's collapse: Communism, liberalism, socialism, and so on.

It is theologically correct of Schmitt to view *to katechon* as "some entity which can be regarded both as a principle and as a person."[15] His theological error is not his assertion that he knows that the restrainer exists; rather, and without the guidance of the Gospels and the Trinity, it is his contention that he knows *who* the present restrainer is. Schmitt's mistake is abysmal, nearly unforgiveable: A lethal ideological mirage. He places the sovereign "miracle" or "exception" that the *deistic* "rationalism of the Enlightenment rejected" on a specific person and political movement: "The transgression of the laws of nature through an exception brought about by direct intervention, as is found in the idea of a miracle, but also the sovereign's direct

---

12. Schmitt, *Necessity of Politics*, 38, 78. On Schmitt's controversial association with Catholicism and his appropriation of Catholic thought, see Fox, "Carl Schmitt and Political Catholicism."

13. Balakrishnan, *Enemy*, 130.

14. Fox, "Carl Schmitt and Political Catholicism," 176.

15. Marshall, *1 and 2 Thessalonians*, 193.

intervention in a valid legal order."[16] Schmitt, infamously, finds his miracle-worker, not in Christ and His Church, certainly not in progressive rebellion led by a vanguard of history for a classless society, or the global commerce of bourgeois individuals, but in a revival of the *Caesar* cult's god-man. This *miracle* that supposedly institutes a new order is found in the *decisive* power of the secular messiah himself: *The will of the Führer* (Führerprinzip). The National Socialist principle of *Führung* grounds modernity's homeless transcendent in a living voice, a living law in a living body. Schmitt wagers on *the word* of the Führer as the source of the new world's perfect order.

Christian political theology has not been replaced at all. It regresses to the barbarism of neo-pagan political religion in the age of hyper technological power, still accepting the logic of Christian historicism. The katechontical *sovereign de-Christens the world. Violence is sacred. The Trinity is not.* Collingwood recognizes the depth of the crisis, but he makes a more traditional decision on the κατέχων. One of Schmitt's central theological errors is to presume the *katechontical* logic of Christian historical process without its ground in the Trinity. He is guilty of the secularization of the most crucial aspect of Christian political theology—the meaning of historical process as love.

Another Time?

Like Schmitt's, Collingwood's ideas are not political relics; rather, according to Sergei Prozorov, the *bio-messianic* turn of recent leftist politics signals "the logic of the katechon only fully comes into its own in the contemporary condition of biopolitical nihilism and any serious attempt to overcome this nihilism will therefore have to confront this logic."[17] Massimo Cacciari also recognizes, "A political theology focused on the katechon only makes sense within a Christian conception of apocalyptic time."[18] *What is striking here is that there is a consensus among conservative, liberal, and materialist thinkers: We are still in this historical worldview; the dispute emerges on what (if anything) we are to do to amend or abolish it.* As we will see, to overcome *biopolitical nihilism*, unfolding as ecological collapse, Collingwood and Cochrane argue for novel variations on sovereignty within the continuous historical structure of the Christian constellation. Other thinkers attempt to summon the event of a new form of life. Giorgio Agamben, for example, proposes to radicalize Schmitt, to fix his mistake—that is, to truly abandon

16. Schmitt, *Political Theology*, 36–37.
17. Prozorov, "Katechon in the Age of Biopolitical Nihilism," 484.
18. Cacciari, *Withholding Power*, 105.

the *katechontical* form of Christian time. The persistence of its temporal pattern prevents disclosure of a new one. The end of the world is where we live.

Despite its professed Godless secularity—neither sacred nor profane—modernity still operates by *katechontical* historicity. *To katechon* is a temporal force that restrains evil, delaying catastrophe, while simultaneously withholding salvation from it. The power to keep it at bay is not enough to purge or defeat it. As Paolo Virno explains, "*Katechon* is characterized by internal antynomy."[19] He describes its internal opposition as "the double bond to which *katechon* is subjected: if it restrains evil, it blocks the final defeat of evil; if it limits aggression, it gets in the way of having this aggression annihilated once and for all."[20] In theological terms, "By impeding the triumph of the Antichrist, *katechon* impedes, at the same time, the redemption to be accomplished by the Messiah"—that is, "the triumph of the Antichrist constitutes the necessary premise for the coming of the Messiah, for the *parousia* who will save forever and put an end to the world."[21] *To katechon*, then, serves as the link between Christian eschatology and genuine historical existence but, in the secular age, it cannot be solace for the oppressed. Without the trinitarian cosmos, *to katechon* reveals a logic of total perdition, where the restraining power of evil is itself evil.

Unlike the medieval cosmos, Agamben claims, modern biopolitical order exposes living things to being "set outside human jurisdiction without being brought into the realm of divine law."[22] Creatures have no ontological standing beyond representation by sovereign power; these are lives "that may be killed by anyone—an object of violence that exceeds the sphere both of law and sacrifice."[23] *Sacer* simply means that which can be killed. Both the oppressed multitude (*homines sacri*) and the sovereign exist in a state of exception. This "structural analogy" demonstrates "the two extreme limits" of biopolitical order.[24] The sovereign can make any living body *homo sacer*. It can also, conversely, deliver any *bare life* to full legal standing and protection. *Homo sacer* is a life of total vulnerability, exposed to the sovereign power of all. Together, the two extremes define the modern *saeculum*: "The sovereign and *homo sacer* are joined in the figure of an action that, excepting itself from human and divine law, from both *nomos* and *physis*, nevertheless delimits what is, in a certain sense, the first properly political space

19. Virno, *Multitude*, 59.
20. Virno, *Multitude*, 59.
21. Virno, *Multitude*, 60, 59.
22. Agamben, *Homo Sacer*, 82.
23. Agamben, *Homo Sacer*, 86.
24. Agamben, *Homo Sacer*, 84.

of the West distinct from both the religious and profane sphere, and both the regular juridical order."²⁵ The state of exception is all there is: Absolute transcendence (sovereignty), absolute immanence (multitude), and their volatile mixture.

Agamben, like Schmitt, sees no theological solution to contemporary nihilism in a revived (and revised) Christian form of life. The only thing that can be mobilized against the reign of *katechontical* historicity is the full negation of its eschatological roots: "2 Thess 2 may not be used to found a 'Christian doctrine' of power in any manner whatsoever."²⁶ Instead of pushing upward for a new (or renewed) sacred transcendence, we push downward for a new immanence: *The multitude's profane Parousia*. "Redemption," Agamben confesses, "is not an event, in which what was profane becomes sacred and what was lost is found again. Redemption is, on the contrary, the irreparable loss of the lost, the definitive profanity of the profane."²⁷ We seek our solace in an unadorned place, without *katechontical* time. The renunciation of grace, paradoxically returns it to us in a visceral form of post-anthropocentric existence; it is a certain kind of surrendering of transcendental historicity to the ecological event of place, whereby, "everything will be as now, just a little different."²⁸ The kingdom has already come. Our very incapacity for God is holy. The subtraction of *to katechon* in the temporal order removes the foundational split in eschatological history. It is the redemption of time by time itself: An apocalypse of place. The historical binary of hastener and restrainer is no longer needed for being. There is finally connection with universal territoriality without sovereign violence. Only then can there be unconditional openness to lives other than our own. We inherit an irreparable world, one that is truly *ours* for the first time. *Hic et Nunc*—the equality of all profane life means *liberation praxis* belongs to all creation. It is time for a new *Adventure*.²⁹

Ekklesia

Collingwood, by contrast, places his bet on the continuity of Christian political theology. The trinitarian way of life found in the Gospels has not ended its repetition. The order of love is still open: Our time and place can gain entry to its symbolic reality. *Katechontic* historicity means we may fail

25. Agamben, *Homo Sacer*, 84.
26. Agamben, *Time That Remains*, 111.
27. Agamben, *Coming Community*, 102.
28. Agamben, *Coming Community*, 57.
29. See Agamben, *Adventure*, 59–96.

to recognize the proper power, principle, or individual that may embody the properties of a hastener of perdition at any given time, but we can be assured that it exists. Since we are fallen creatures, with only partial knowledge, we can, and often are, mistaken. But we are not entirely without criteria. The Trinity is the ecclesiastical principle of the new. In political terms, it provides the criterion for innovative institutions of peace, capable of meeting various social and ecological crises. According to Augustine—*the founder of Christian political theology that overthrows the sacrificial order of political religion*—"The Trinity is the focus of all Christian attention and the goal of all Christian progress," and it is "constantly at work in history to secure our freedom."[30] Collingwood's *Neochristian progressivism* is initiated on the presupposition that, with respect to experiments *to reduce* (not deify) violence in human and ecological affairs, "all things are become new" (2 Cor 5:17 KJV). But Collingwood's position now encounters another set of problems, issuing not from the *new time materialists*—the bio-messianic left—but, this time, from the traditionalist Christian side.

Ekklesia is to katechon, demolishing every possible political theology, all dialectical compromises, i.e., innovations, with the politics of secular order. As Cacciari clarifies, "Whoever projects onto this [secular political] scene the theology of Deus Trinitas is forced to halt before an unbridgeable abyss."[31] Any temporal power designated *to katechon* will become "the inverted image of the *ekklesia*," and it "cannot fail to participate in the most intimate fashion with the principle it strives to withhold and delay, if not bring to a halt. It is impossible not to *retain* what you seek to *contain*."[32] Any secularized *withholding power*, then, "will drive its force to greater violence," and, "For these reasons the Church is the *katechon* of the end-time, praying it might last until its work is concluded."[33] The most significant figure to hold this position is the German theologian, and Catholic convert, Erik Peterson (†1960).

Against Carl Schmitt's political theology, committed to legitimating the *Führerstaat*, Peterson asserts the impossibility of any political theology based on historicized analogy. As it rages all around him in the nineteen-thirties, he boldly campaigns against the transfer of Christian foundations to messianic sovereignty in the secular order. Schmitt introduces a *theological method* of analysis for modern political concepts, deploying it as a diagnosis of the secular condition. *Political theology* means secularized political

---

30. Augustine, *On Free Choice of the Will*, 12.
31. Cacciari, *Withholding Power*, 9.
32. Cacciari, *Withholding Power*, 40, 51.
33. Cacciari, *Withholding Power*, 51, 61.

concepts enter "fundamentally systematic and methodical analogies" with their theological grounds.[34] Political analysis consists of shuttling back and forth between analogically interrelated theological concepts and their secular translations within political structures. The identity of each framework remains independent. Analogical analysis leaves identities intact while still maintaining productive relations of many kinds, e.g., existential, conceptual, and logico-linguistic. Both individuality and commonality are preserved by analogy, undermining the subordinationism found in methods that distinguish between dominant cause and subservient effect. Political theology enables co-development without competitive erasure. This approach also contrasts with the transformation and absorption of identities in a dialectical synthesis of negation and progression and the alienation of absolute difference. The last position denies every common relation between the orders of secularity and theology. Each order is *wholly other*.

In his 1935 essay "Monotheism as a Political Problem," Peterson argues for the latter view. The appropriation of Christian theology by Schmitt's methodology of political theology is not legitimate because "the Monarchy of the triune God" is an idea of unity that has "no correspondence in the created order."[35] "Orthodox Trinitarian doctrine," he claims, "in effect threatened the political theology of the Roman Empire."[36] The political character of Christianity is defined by its discontinuity with secular power—"a fundamental break was made with every 'political theology' that misuses the Christian proclamation for the justification of a political situation"—its refusal of secular appropriation for legitimating sovereign violence is its principal *political* meaning.[37] Violence in any form is incompatible with the Christian faith; the unconditional love of enemies is its test of truth. Jesus is crucified in the name of the most powerful *to katechon* of the ancient world: *Pax Romana*. With this historical experience, "the linkage of the Christian proclamation to the Roman empire was *theologically* dissolved."[38] In taking this position, Peterson cuts many ties to the Western church's historical compromises with the earthly city. Jürgen Moltmann says Peterson's theology is uncompromising. The "Christian proclamation of the gospel can no longer be misused to justify political power" because "the mystery of the Trinity is only in God, not in a creature, and only God can give the peace Christians

---

34. Schmitt, *Political Theology*, 37.
35. Peterson, "Monotheism as a Political Problem," 103.
36. Peterson, "Monotheism as a Political Problem," 103.
37. Peterson, "Monotheism as a Political Problem," 104.
38. Peterson, "Monotheism as a Political Problem," 103.

seek—no Caesar can do this."[39] The Trinity challenges the legitimacy of Greco-Roman order and, it seems, its successor—Christendom—and all other secular, political orders that follow. It simply cannot be incorporated, in any way, by any degree, into temporal regimes of power; the game of the lesser evil, is still radical evil, as the Nazi regime demonstrates most clearly for Peterson.

By revoking the analogical ground for political theology, Peterson now has significant problems all his own. As György Geréby accurately detects, he may have successfully "answered Schmitt" by denying the theological legitimacy of *historicized* analogy, but in doing so he marginalizes the central theological tradition that provides a real relation between God and world: "The Thomistic concept of the *anologia entis*."[40] He seems to advocate the discontinuous elements of Saint Augustine's political thought without "the Augustinian idea of *vestigia trinitatis*" that leaves emblematic traces in the natural and social order of things.[41] Being as the communication of triune relations dissolves. Divine signatures are erased from the cosmos. On Christian *ekklesia* as *to katechon*, therefore, Peterson too, like Schmitt (and Agamben), diminishes its prospects for an effective public-legal role. Augustine's Heavenly City to come prohibits representative connection to earthly power. Worldly interventions for protest or conciliation, *restraining* the forces of perdition, seem rigorously neutralized.

Secular politics is irredeemable; there is no social-critical confrontation with evil that is not evil, certainly no trinitarian basis for innovation of earthly institutions. The revelation of unconditional love is, categorically, refused a natural and political translation. Unlike Augustine, there is no call for novel compromise, no subversive amendment of secular order on behalf of peace. Outside of the interiority of miraculous grace, there is no established relation between us and God, between us and fellow creatures, only Abyss. The rejection of the analogy of being, properly understood, is a denial that creation is an act of grace that really expresses God's love, rather than a moment of absolute alienation. If revelation is to occur, God must take this-worldly entities and bestow on them a capacity which in and of themselves they do not possess. Redemption cannot occur on political terms because God is wholly other than His created order, both natural and social. The creative act of redemption is not simply given, having already taken place in any sense. It must happen to a world, to a human being, assumed to be negated of all prior possibility, all entitlement, for this

---

39. Moltmann, "European Political Theology," 6.
40. Geréby, "Political Theology versus Theological Politics," 30.
41. Geréby, "Political Theology versus Theological Politics," 30.

transformative breakthrough. There is no *analogical* way to God from our side of things. Grace brings both sides of the relation between God and a human soul. Prior to this *sovereign decision on the event of exception*: Nothing. All others are wholly other. The *empathic event* that opens each to each, pure ontological difference, is the holy, and the holy acts of itself, independently of its terms or subjects, demanding action to bring peace and abolish violence. Grace is the militant praxis of Christian *ekklesia*, alone. To Peterson, the highest form of Christian action is martyrdom: The absolute witness to the ecclesiastical truth of agape. The event of unconditional love that surrenders temporal existence demolishes all mere politics, celebrating and demonstrating the heavenly polis beyond all earthly power.

We Are All Thessalonians, Now

To decide on this complex and divisive matter of Christian politics in the earthy city, perhaps, we should begin our (very circuitous) return to Augustine and Scripture. First, in a mostly implicit way, with Collingwood; then, explicitly, in the thought of Cochrane. Within Christian historicity, the modern *saeculum* is a return to sacrificial time; as cyclic, deterministic, and existentially asphyxiating. Violence is holy because it creates and preserves the territoriality necessary for society. This traumatic process repeats without end because it refuses universality; it refuses eschatological time. The basic Christian promise is emancipation *from* and *beyond* the murderous demands of identity formed by differences of spatial location, which is not only geographical, but also inclusive of social distinctions of class, race, gender, and so on. Species is now added to this open list of predicates. Creation itself is revealed as the common subject of liberation. As God creates "with time," not "in time," so we (*imago Dei*)—who are thrown inside the temporal violence of the earthly city—have the freedom to re-*create* a peaceful place *with* and *in* time.[42] Only through love does human construction turn to co-creation.

One helpful way to view Collingwood's (and Cochrane's) political theology is to position it as the idealist complement (historical dialectic)—now taken in an ecological direction—to the Neothomist movement of the twentieth century. The latter tradition gives us such immensely influential figures as Jacques Maritain. In the name of an "analogically applied," "integral or theocentric humanism," Maritain proposes the construction of a "*secular Christian*" political order.[43] His political theology is an unmistakable answer

---

42. Augustine, *City of God* XI.8 (436).
43. Maritain, *True Humanism*, 156.

to the National Socialist Party position of "M. Carl Schmitt," who seeks to *analogically* ground the post-medieval sovereignty "of the State, The Movement and the People" in a "personal union, primarily realised in the man who is at once *Führer and Reich Chancellor*."[44] For Maritain, the Christian constellation still has the capacity to adapt to novel crises, to be *to katechon*, creating effective institutions dedicated to universal peace, i.e., human rights and the United Nations as a response to State genocide. *Secular* Christian institutions, however, do not replace the Christian Church as an idol of political religion. Rather, in Augustine's *earthly city*, the church remains the church, but it remains in a productive relationship (historically analogical and/or historically dialectical) to its novel-secular expression or offspring: *Universalist* political theology dedicated to peace. The difference between Schmitt and Maritain on the employment of analogy is that the former seeks a replacement for Christian political order while still upholding its form of time, the latter seeks the return and variation of Christian political theology to amplify its universal form of time: Messianic violence versus the political rationality of truth, goodness, and beauty.

This approach to *katechontical* history resonates with the long and rich tradition of liberation associated with the Holy Spirit.[45] Theologically considered, *to katechon* (κατέχων) originates from Saint Paul's (†c. 66 CE) Second Epistle to the Thessalonians: "And now ye know what withholdeth that he might be revealed in his time. For the mystery of iniquity doth already work; only he who now letteth *will let*, until he be taken out of the way" (2 Thess 2:6–7 KJV). Before the return of Christ, the final restrainer (*to katechon*) falls to the final *Son of Perdition*, the lawless one of total sin—the Antichrist—that Christ defeats and, in doing so, completes all history. Charles A. Wanamaker makes a frank and accurate assertion, "These two verses are among the most problematic texts in the whole of the Pauline corpus. They presuppose knowledge to which we do not have access."[46] The Thessalonian community supposedly had it at the time, but such knowledge has been lost ever since. Even Augustine readily admits, "the meaning of this completely escapes me. For all that, I shall not refrain from mentioning a few guesses at the meaning which I have been able to hear or read."[47] It may be correct that "no one has put forward a satisfactory background for

---

44. Maritain, *True Humanism*, 163.

45. See Ratzinger, *Theology of History in St. Bonaventure*, 1–55; McGinn, "Significance of Bonaventure's Theology of History," s64–s81; Hayes, *Gift of Being*, 61–85; Vos, *Pauline Eschatology*, 130; Powell, "Identity of the 'Restrainer,'" 320–32.

46. Wanamaker, *Epistles to the Thessalonians*, 249.

47. Augustine, *City of God* XX.19 (933).

the verses," but their continued reception by the Christian community is theologically decisive on many questions.[48]

The Apostle accomplishes at least three things with his notion of *to katechon*: First, it answers the question, "why is there still history?" The Thessalonians, like all Christian communities that follow, need to be reassured that the Day of the Lord had not already come, leaving them still on earth. They are not post-rapture subjects of damnation. Further, and more commonly, *to katechon* explains to expectant, and increasingly impatient, Christian communities the reason for the delay in the Second Advent of Christ: *Parousia*. With a considerable degree of exegetical perfection on the latter point, Geerhardus Vos (†1949) clarifies Paul's subtle achievement, "There is still delay, before the supreme event transpires; a certain process of hidden preparedness must run its course," but the call "to exercise a peculiar kind of eschatological patience" detracts "nothing from the central value and high seriousness attaching to the matter itself."[49] Second, it protects the faithful from the spiritual effects of the apparently meaningless and overwhelming continuance of historic process: Despair, skepticism, atheism, and so on. There is significance to existence in the interim because it is part of the great drama of divine Providence, progressing to its end. Each lifetime will be involved in hastening and restraining events. The concept also suggests a theodicy: There is evil in the world due to the most recent iteration of the Son of Perdition, one that a restrainer must crusade against. Third, it protects Christians from renunciation of this world because the promised final victory does not subtract us from our duty to act in the meantime(s). We must work on behalf of *to katechon* dispensed to our time, but we are immensely fallible due our fallen nature and the subsequent imprecision of our interpretative systems.

Theologians appear to be divided on the nature of *what restrains*. The history of interpretation offers many different views. Some place their bets on an existing power, principle, or individual. Others portray the restraining force—hidden or manifest—as an evil agent, an occupying power hostile to God, or even Satan himself.[50] According to Paul S. Dixon, "The debate over the interpretation of *to katechon* ("what restrains") in 2 Thess 2:6 can be reduced to a single consideration. The moral nature of the *katechon* is either good or evil."[51] Dixon argues for the latter. For reasons other than ex-

---

48. Wanamaker, *Epistles to the Thessalonians*, 249.

49. Vos, *Pauline Eschatology*, 129, 133.

50. For this view, see Wanamaker, *Epistles to the Thessalonians*, 252–64; Best, *Commentary*, 299–302; Frame, *Critical and Exegetical Commentary*, 261–68.

51. Dixon, "Evil Restraint in 2 Thess 2:6," 445.

egetically conclusive evidence, capable of deciding the matter, I find myself agreeing with I. Howard Marshall's (†2015) more traditional "view that the restraining or occupying power is good rather than evil in character seems essential to making sense of the passage. A contest between two opposing evil forces is most improbable, and the idea of an evil force disappearing to make room for another also seems unlikely."[52] Despite the insecurity of knowledge from our side of things, pertaining to its exact identity, *to katechon* must have a positive connotation, "having a divine origin."[53]

Eschatological history is *mysterion*, but we are not without *good criteria* to guide us. To view *to katechon* as evil seems to lead to the complete subtraction of Christians from historical life: Restrainer and hastener are two sides of the same evil coin. In a moral and politically mobilizing sense, no worldly power, principle, or individual is any different from any other. History is an acosmic duel of exclusively evil forces, perdition without end. Hell is already here. This view is untenable because it undermines Paul's triple victory over Gnostic nihilism: Existential, moral, and political. Creation and its Creator are good. Evil cannot be a positive historical agent, somehow driving eschatological history by playing both parts—evil visible versus good (evil invisible). The criterion that provides historical understanding is also not that mysterious: It is the Trinity found in the Gospel, primarily the historical motion of the Holy Spirit. The divine goodness view also seems more in line with one of Augustine's better *guesses* on *to katechon*—namely, "the pilgrimage goes from that time ['the bodily presence of Christ and the time of his apostles'] up to the end of history, with the persecutions of the world on one side, and on the other the consolations of God."[54] *Consolations* of the Trinity as the Holy Spirit=*to katechon*. Affirmation of the universal beloved community to come signifies love of God, neighbor, and creation. We do not reject this world, but we do reject the modern *saeculum*'s version of it.

Verbum divinum est omnis creatura, quia Deum loquitur. The beloved community to be built is social and ecological: The Trinity's order of love (ordo amoris) means "creation itself will be set free" (Rom 8:21), not just some of us.

The *Advent*ure re-begins.

To Michael S. Northcott, the current ecological catastrophe "has its origins precisely in the demise of the political orders of the medieval

---

52. Marshall, *1 and 2 Thessalonians*, 199.
53. Marshall, *1 and 2 Thessalonians*, 199.
54. Augustine, *City of God* XVIII.52 (835).

Church which restrained absolute claims to sovereignty over land."[55] This *katechontical* predicament stems from purely secular politics shorn of God as Trinity and its overarching cosmological framework of institutions dedicated to something other than the imperial game of domination. Without the divine referent of Christian political theology, sovereign legitimation rests on no other ground but superior force—will of the X. As Agamben has already observed, unlike politics informed by the medieval cosmos, modern biopolitical order exposes living things to total violence. Absent the absolute presupposition of a divine ground, creatures have no ontological standing of themselves. Without the communication of the Trinity's symbolic cosmos, modernity degenerates into the barbarism of *Neo-Pagan political religion*. Sacrificial culture becomes unlimited in scope—*globalization*—and exporting this "idea of sovereign rule to the New World presented Europe with a novel set of problems, of which climate change is the most recent."[56] Modern politics has become such an immense challenge because Christendom reveals itself as *to katechon* only by its demise, leaving an eschatological vacuum of sovereignty inside the continuance of Christian historicity.[57] In more straightforward terms, what can replace *res publica Christiana*, abolishing sacrificial culture *for good*?

ECOLOGICAL CIVILIZATION

The New Leviathan (1942) is best viewed as Collingwood's answer to this strange question on sovereignty within *katechontical* history. The Christian constellation is damaged, constantly ridiculed by *the wise*, said to have expired, replaced by secularity, but it is still foundational for our civilization and it is still operational. We must defend it from the immediate threats of barbarism, but we must also *secularly* regenerate its absolute presuppositions for the future: To be made whole, Christian historicity requires Christian sovereignty. Collingwood is quite clear in his thinking. European barbarism, spectacularly on display by Nazism in his time, is for the most part received from "the Arian heresy, not Christianity in its true or Trinitarian form," which alone could appeal to civilized people (42.21).[58] Victory over Nazi barbarism, however, must be followed by something politically

---

55. Northcott, *Political Theology of Climate Change*, 223.

56. Northcott, *Political Theology of Climate Change*, 224. On the colonization side, especially of the New World, see Sloterdijk, *Globes*, 870–78.

57. See Schmitt, *Nomos of the Earth*, 56–66.

58. Collingwood, *New Leviathan*, 352.

innovative in the historical repetition and realignment of Christian absolute presuppositions to *restrain* repeated disasters.

It is because the political theology of trinitarian "Christendom took time seriously that it refuses to join in the Greco-Roman quest for a superman-ruler"—that is, echoing Balthasar, the messianic sovereign conjured by Schmitt violates the immanent gift of time. Instead of constructing some ersatz, Promethean savior, Collingwood writes, "What we demand is the ability to do the work that has now to be done" (26.3).[59] The work of Neochristian civilization that must be achieved "is living dialectically, that is constantly endeavoring to turn occasions of non-agreement into occasions of agreement," which "indicates abstention from the use of force" in social and ecological relations; concerning the "natural world," utility is factored into rational limits, undermining the barbaric "habit of expecting to get more" than can be scientifically sustained or morally justified without violating "the Christian sense of 'love': ἀγαπή" (40.42; 39.11; 8.59).[60]

To Collingwood, "The birth of love is the act of *limiting your demands*," which means giving up the Promethean "demand for omnipotence" (8.58).[61] Unlike barbaric "hunger, which is an appetite for an object it can neither find nor create, an omnipotent self, love is an appetite for a relation with an object it can and does create, a beautiful non-self" (8.44).[62] The *non-self* signifies our real relation with others, constitutive of our identities; it is not a means for an insatiable (perpetually tragic and traumatic) quest to become superhuman, perfect, or complete. The *non-self* is the co-subject of mutually fragile limitation. We are partners in primordial co-creation, "the act (loving) in which the one creates the other and establishes itself" (8.49).[63] We owe each other dialectical peace but, "Peace is a dynamic thing; a strenuous thing" (40.24).[64] Peace is the work of love, the "dialectical labour whereby occasions of non-agreement are converted into occasions of agreement" (40.24).[65] Peacemaking substitutes for "victory over the other," overcoming the "eristic habit in the community" (40.32, 57).[66] Eristic communities can evolve into civilized societies: "Civilization is something which happens

---

59. Collingwood, *New Leviathan*, 194.
60. Collingwood, *New Leviathan*, 336, 327, 60.
61. Collingwood, *New Leviathan*, 60.
62. Collingwood, *New Leviathan*, 58.
63. Collingwood, *New Leviathan*, 59.
64. Collingwood, *New Leviathan*, 334.
65. Collingwood, *New Leviathan*, 334.
66. Collingwood, *New Leviathan*, 335, 337.

to a community" (40.19).[67] Community is the necessary but not sufficient condition for society. "Whatever is a society must be a community," Collingwood explains, "because a society is a kind of community, a society being a community and something more. It must be a community before it is a society, where 'before' carries a logical sense, the sense indicated by the 'pre' in the statement that its being a community is a 'presupposition' of its being a society" (20.3–31).[68] This *something more* is the realization of human action: Freedom. Instead of competitive elimination there is co-elevation: "Social consciousness involves the consciousness of freedom. A society consists of persons who are free and know themselves to be free. Each knows the others to be free as well as himself" (20.23).[69]

To Collingwood, "being civilized is living dialectically" (40.42).[70] *He revises Plato's dialectic for the second time.* Barbarism is the regressive impulse towards an eristical life in community. Instead of being constitutive of civilized identity in society, the non-self is viewed as a threat to communal identity. The non-self is an enemy, a scapegoat, compelling us to hurt and destroy others: The hollow nihilism of Promethean struggle. Given that civilized societies emerge from eristic communities, politics is persistently vulnerable to barbaric regression. "A degree of force is inevitable in human life," Collingwood admits, "but being civilized means cutting it down, and becoming more civilized means cutting it down still further" (39.15).[71] The eristic violence that has been surmounted through the creation of civil society is "only suspended, not abolished. The process of political life is reversible" (32.44).[72] Collingwood claims that social life is, inevitably, a volatile "mixture of civility and barbarity" because both terms describe "ideal states, not actual states. No society is just civil; no society is just barbarous"—that is, each actual instance of one or the other is "an *asymptotic approximation*" of its ideal condition (34.52, 56).[73] Civilization is a fragile achievement of dialectical freedom. After periods of social and ecological progress, "there may equally well be a regress whereby a freedom and sociality once achieved may be lost and a society breaks down into a non-social

---

67. Collingwood, New Leviathan, 334.
68. Collingwood, New Leviathan, 139.
69. Collingwood, New Leviathan, 139.
70. Collingwood, New Leviathan, 336.
71. Collingwood, New Leviathan, 326.
72. Collingwood, New Leviathan, 262.
73. Collingwood, New Leviathan, 283, 284.

community" (32.44).[74] In the work to reduce force in human and ecological relationships, being civilized means constant vigilance.

The meaning of *force* must be carefully defined. Collingwood tells us, "The word 'force' in political contexts" denotes "a relative term" (20.5–51).[75] *Physical force* is only one meaning of force, revealing the outermost breakdown of relationships; associated internally with crime and externally with war between regressed (barbaric) societies and/or un-progressed communities. In *The New Leviathan*, however, Collingwood focuses on force as a moral relationship—in Aristotle's (*Nicomachean Ethics*) sense of the distributional or economic good of justice: The dialectic of wealth versus the eristic of riches. In a preliminary essay to *The New Leviathan*, we read, "There is no such thing as an enrichment that does not involve an impoverished party," "Riches are thus economic force," and "Riches imply poverty, but wealth does not."[76] Moreover, "economic force or domination over an-other" is the root of barbarism because it turns "free action" into "forced action" as the principal relationship in securing the material conditions of life, generating and aggravating an unholy host of other intersectional dominations, not the least of which is the human relationship with the natural world.[77] Collingwood, echoing Aristotle again (*Politics*), goes as far as to claim that the unlimited desire generating good of *chresis*—"the pursuit of riches"—is "incompatible with the very idea of civilization."[78] Collingwood admits his philosophical debt readily: "In our terminology Aristotle's 'good life' is called civilization. This is the only motive for which men accumulate wealth: in order to pursue civilization. To accumulate wealth in order to create by its means a contrast between rich and poor is to use it for the destruction of civilization, or the pursuit of barbarism" (38.81–83).[79] The "civilized pursuit of wealth," conversely, reduces force in "production and exchange."[80] Exchange concerns human to human economic relations, of labor and money, whereas production concerns the "economic activities" of human beings "with the world of nature."[81] A true ecological civilization employs "natural science" to enhance the common *wealth* of society. Science can achieve the sustainable production of the material conditions of

---

74. Collingwood, *New Leviathan*, 283, 284.
75. Collingwood, *New Leviathan*, 142.
76. Collingwood, "What 'Civilization' Means," 503, 504, 505.
77. Collingwood, "What 'Civilization' Means," 504, 505.
78. Collingwood, "What 'Civilization' Means," 506.
79. Collingwood, *New Leviathan*, 325.
80. Collingwood, "What 'Civilization' Means," 507.
81. Collingwood, "What 'Civilization' Means," 508.

life; it does not have to aid the hegemonic power of an eristic community of rich individuals: Ecological barbarism. Without its bondage to riches, the natural sciences can serve free human action "in a scientific, reasonable and rational manner."[82]

David Boucher provides a key summary: "Civilization, for Collingwood, is not a condition, nor an ideal, of society: It is the process of converting the nonsocial into the social community," and, "Similarly, barbarism is the revolt against the conversion process. It is the attempt to retard or reverse the process of civilization and reduce the body politic to a non-social community."[83] The process of civilization promotes dialectical relations among members of a body politic—internally and externally—"a process whereby members of that community become less addicted to force in their dealings with one another" (36.12).[84] Barbarism reverts to eristic relations of domination, both within a community and between communities. There are, then, two basic orientations for political life. The work of civilization proceeds "*dialectically*: that is, by a process leading from non-agreement to agreement," whereas the work of barbarism proceeds "*eristically*, that is, by hardening non-agreement into disagreement and settling the disagreement by a victory of one party over another" (29.61).[85] The trajectory of dialectical relations, of civilization itself, moves from the individual *I not-I* to the *we not-we* of community to the third level of society, leaving eristic relations behind. Each community will have its own unique, *pragmatic* way of accomplishing civilization. But *second-order* plurality in the reduction of the use of force in relations with others also affirms its commensurate universality: *Its self-differentiating unity*. Ecologically speaking, this opens society to creatures and places beyond our own species, fulfilling what he calls the "third-order ideal" of "universal civility," the "source of all other ideals of civilized conduct," which Collingwood says is not "left without a witness" in the historical world: "Christian literature teems with reference to it, from the Sermon on the Mount downwards."[86] To fully grasp this direction of thought, and its Augustinian basis, we need to turn to Charles Norris Cochrane, Collingwood's metaphysical and political ally.

82. Collingwood, "What 'Civilization' Means," 508.
83. Boucher, *Social and Political Thought of R. G. Collingwood*, 195.
84. Collingwood, *New Leviathan*, 299.
85. Collingwood, *New Leviathan*, 229.
86. Collingwood, "What 'Civilization' Means," 494.

REINTRODUCTION

Harold Innis (†1952) credits the work of Charles Norris Cochrane as being nothing less than "the first major Canadian contribution to the intellectual history of the West."[87] Like Collingwood's philosophical reception in his home country, however, recognition of Cochrane's achievements has been slow to appear. At least part of the problem, for a generation or two, is their shared Christian political theology: *Neochristian progressivism*. In post-war politics, this kind of view seems incomprehensible to *secular political science*; good propaganda for the war effort, i.e., *onward Christian soldier* against fascism, but now carrying unneeded and antiquated religiosity, attended by its consequent chauvinistic and irrational overtones. But with the recent revival of serious interest in theologically infused political ideas, their novel convergence has a deepening resonance. The great secular, post-war hope is approaching social and ecological insolvency. Our crisis appears to be orientated to a fundamental reconsideration of political form. At this befogged crossroads, the signs that distinguish the paths to perdition from those of redemption are not clearly marked. Collingwood and Cochrane prove to be valuable companions in our endeavor to decipher the sense of how we arrived at our position; they also put forward a persuasive directive to seek another collective way of life: *An ecological civilization*. In the last sentence of his *An Autobiography* (1939), Collingwood makes an open commitment to its truth, "Henceforth I shall fight in the daylight."[88]

We should, too.

As his forward looking editor clarifies, recovery of Cochrane's ideas should not be misunderstood as "a project for national patriotism, but for a broader audience that must wrestle with Augustine and the political implications of his inquiry into the foundations of Western culture that we take for granted in the modern world."[89] Although Cochrane's work is the exemplar *par excellence* of both Collingwood's method of historical metaphysics and political theology, he is not a disciple in the sense of the mere application of an authority's ideas. The two thinkers appear to overlap and influence each other considerably, forming a unique view on history, logic, and politics. Cochrane publishes *Christianity and Classical Culture* in the same year (nineteen-forty), with the same Oxford publisher, as Collingwood's *Essay*. Collingwood is thanked for his assistance in the Preface. The

---

87. Innis, "Obituaries," 96.
88. Collingwood, *Autobiography*, 167.
89. Beer, "Introduction," 24.

latter philosopher is involved in editing *Christianity and Classical Culture* from at least nineteen thirty-eight onwards.

In a letter dated January 6, 1938, to his co-editor, Ronald Syme (†1989), Collingwood praises the initial draft of *Christianity and Classical Culture*, "This is a very remarkable piece of work. I don't think anyone has tried, previously, to write a history of the change by which the Pagan society of the time of Augustus turned into the Christian society of the time of Augustine, treating that change both as a change in the outward structure of society and as a corresponding change in the philosophical ideas which underlie (as an idealist would say) or reflect (as a Marxist would say) that structure. To my mind it is very important both for political and for philosophical history that they should be thus written simultaneously and by the same hand: and the fact that Cochrane has tried to do it gives him a very strong claim on our services."[90] As with the decisive chapter in Collingwood's own *Essay*—"Quicunque Vult"—Cochrane's *Christianity and Classical Culture* centers itself in "the crucial passage in which the author tries to sum up the philosophical implications of Augustine's notion of the Trinity."[91] Collingwood even says, "more work is certainly needed. I have tried to offer some materials for this in my notes."[92] In a letter dated June 16, 1939, on "Cochrane's proofs," Collingwood worries about the response to *Christianity and Classical Culture* because of its radical nature, cutting across compartmentalized areas of specialty in history (Christian or Classical, but never the blend in motion from one to the other!), theology, philosophy, and politics: "It will not be well received, because it is too good. But I think the office ought to know my opinion that it is, as I say, the most important thing we have done in my time."[93] To accurately understand their common position we must deal with Cochrane's presentation of Augustine's original Christian political theology.

Secular Perversity

"The plain truth," according to Cochrane, "is that Augustine's message was, as it was blindly felt to be, profoundly subversive to established order."[94] It still is. The ancient cosmos has changed its base. Our world must find

---

90. Collingwood, "Correspondence with the Clarendon Press." I am immensely grateful to Professor James Connelly for bringing this letter to my attention.
91. Collingwood, "Correspondence with the Clarendon Press."
92. Collingwood, "Correspondence with the Clarendon Press."
93. Collingwood, "Correspondence with the Clarendon Press."
94. Cochrane, "Augustine and the Problem of Power," 86.

Augustine's new foundation once again. "This is not to suggest (as might be supposed)," he argues, "that what is sometimes called the message of ancient wisdom, whether classical or Christian, may be taken to provide a ready-made solution for historical problems which are more or less specific to the twentieth century."[95] Nevertheless, the uniqueness of time and circumstances does not result in "historical relativism"—*constellational continuity* is upheld for Augustine's "original and distinctively Christian philosophy of power."[96] Cochrane takes over from Collingwood the view that the best way to get "meaning out of history" is to replace "methods of enquiry indigenous to the field of natural philosophy or science" with an analysis of "presuppositions, whether explicit or implicit," which underlie "the positive findings of classical *scientia*."[97] "From this point of view," he summarizes, "the question is not whether we are to approach history without presuppositions or preconceptions, but rather what presuppositions and preconceptions it may be legitimate and profitable to entertain. To recognize the truth of this proposition is to take the first step toward a sympathetic and intelligent appreciation of Augustine."[98] History concerns presuppositions that structure the appearances of things for human action. By "challenging the presuppositions upon which scientific thought proceeded," Augustine, for instance, broke the impasse of Classical science; "thereby giving a wholly new turn to the problem of human freedom."[99] Furthermore, "Augustine in effect declared that the concept of nature was not (as Greek speculative activity appears to have assumed) something to be composed or constructed by any effort of the imagination; but that, on the contrary, it was itself presupposed in any attempt to think positively about nature, i.e., before the scientific intelligence could fruitfully go to work."[100] In other words, the foundations of Greek science are historical not eternal; time-*filled* not timeless.

The Latin Church Father opens "the possibility of a fresh approach in terms of the *arché, principium* or *philosophic starting point*," which "is a radically new and specifically Christian picture of nature, and the status therein of mankind."[101] Moreover, "the doctrine of human freedom (*liberum voluntatis arbitrium*) propounded by Christian realism served as a charter of emancipation from moral and intellectual difficulties inherent

---

95. Cochrane, "Augustine and the Problem of Power," 32.
96. Cochrane, "Augustine and the Problem of Power," 32.
97. Cochrane, "Augustine and the Problem of Power," 34.
98. Cochrane, "Augustine and the Problem of Power," 35.
99. Cochrane, "Augustine and the Problem of Power," 42.
100. Cochrane, "Augustine and the Problem of Power," 59.
101. Cochrane, "Augustine and the Problem of Power," 60, 36.

in the naturalism of classical antiquity—difficulties from which, within the self-imposed limitations of classical ideology, there does not appear to have been the slightest possibility of escape."[102] Cochrane identifies the "characteristic vice of Greek speculation" as "its inability to establish an intelligible relationship between order and process," and he agrees with Collingwood "that the disease of pagan philosophy was metaphysical, and further that this disease of pagan metaphysics meant death to pagan civilization."[103] The radicalness of Classical difficulties engenders "a radical cure"—"'God created the world.'"[104] "Positively," to Cochrane, "the first fruits of Christian doctrine were to be found in a refreshingly novel attitude towards nature."[105] Augustine envisages the cosmos "neither as chaos nor mechanism, but as a specious and hospitable abode provided by God for the human spirit."[106] The Christian sense of nature overcomes paganism's *secular perversity* (perversitas saeculi); a mistaken "relationship between 'nature' and 'art' which as Augustine held, was defective or vicious."[107] It is *vicious* because it rests on the false presupposition "that what 'nature' did was supply to man the raw materials (in Augustinian terminology a pure *possibilitas* or potentiality)" for self-perfection through "means of arts or techniques devised by himself."[108] Nature falls victim to secular pride, used as the mere means for the impossible task of self-sufficiency or autarky—*superbia perverse imitator Deum*.

This insatiable lust for domination (*libido dominandi*), as Augustine calls it, pervades secular society and, as Cochrane rightly claims, this condition has no sense of temporal limits, "From this point of view, secular history emerges as a process (procursus) to which there is no logical end or term."[109] Secularity's profane time, as Balthasar has already presaged, is a *vicious* burden on the human condition but, ecologically considered, it a mortal sin reaching beyond sin itself—that is, nature will be used and abused without impediment until it collapses, as our will to self-transcendence grows more (not less) efficient in power: "We must remember that secular pride rejects the major premise of the faith, viz., that God created the universe and the work of creation is thorough and complete. By rejecting this proposition,

---

102. Cochrane, "Augustine and the Problem of Power," 63.
103. Cochrane, "Augustine and the Problem of Power," 37, 38.
104. Cochrane, "Augustine and the Problem of Power," 39.
105. Cochrane, "Augustine and the Problem of Power," 39.
106. Cochrane, "Augustine and the Problem of Power," 39.
107. Cochrane, "Augustine and the Problem of Power," 70.
108. Cochrane, "Augustine and the Problem of Power," 70.
109. Cochrane, "Augustine and the Problem of Power," 81.

and by claiming the right to perfect what it conceives to be the imperfection of nature's handiwork, pride arrogates to itself the prerogative of a god."[110] Secular logic "is guilty of the presumption of supposing that to 'construct' is to 'create,'" which is "perhaps the most subtle and seductive of all forms of self-idolatry."[111] The drive for self-transcendence follows an iterative logic of domination and failure because it operates on a false presupposition: Construction is creation. Secular existence is tragic and traumatic.

Misreading reality leads to a recurrent mistake on "the root-cause of human imperfection."[112] Political-technical projects of self-creation seek *secular transcendence*. These endeavors will (and must) fail because they reveal themselves as merely flawed constructions; neither creative nor attuned to creation. Tragic failure, however, does not mean this cultural logic is abandoned. Rather, human power is intensified. Each cycle increases the capacity for godlike violence, not salvation. Secularity is, therefore, also increasingly traumatic, bringing living death to all things as their principle of utility, objectification, and commodification: "The corruption of love and reason is the corruption of life itself, or rather of the being which finds expression therein."[113] "In other words," Cochrane summarizes, "it deliberately cuts itself off from the authentic source of being, truth and goodness and condemns itself to a life of subjectivity."[114] *Essential* estrangement from reality means the denial "that all truly significant human situations are relationships of personality," and the consequent fact that "any attempt to escape from or transcend those relationships is self-defeating; it is to mutilate the very texture of human experience."[115] But, given the truth of *Being*, even errant or *fallen* humanity still bears the signature of *vestigia Dei*—"even in the state of intellectual, moral and physical disintegration brought about through secular perversity, man still confesses to the reality of a shattered wholeness original to his nature."[116] *To be made whole*, then, we must be liberated from the secular perversity of self-creation. This conversion dispenses from the ground of reality itself: The Trinity.

Cochrane explains the unusual—secularly counter-intuitive—meaning of Christian freedom. To be "created in the image of the Trinity is to assert that, by the constitution of his nature, man is predestined to freedom

---

110. Cochrane, "Augustine and the Problem of Power," 99.
111. Cochrane, "Augustine and the Problem of Power," 99.
112. Cochrane, "Augustine and the Problem of Power," 98.
113. Cochrane, "Augustine and the Problem of Power," 100.
114. Cochrane, "Augustine and the Problem of Power," 100.
115. Cochrane, "Augustine and the Problem of Power," 91.
116. Cochrane, "Augustine and the Problem of Power," 95.

but in a somewhat peculiar sense, a sense analogous to that whereby freedom and power are ascribed to God Himself as the creative and moving principle."[117] We surrender creation back to divinity. By doing so, we gain the true "freedom and power of voluntary motion" over our political and technical constructions; the drama of this conversion "is peculiar to and distinctive of human experience and human history."[118] Like Collingwood, Cochrane affirms the Christian freedom of human action; it "alone is capable of history."[119] The *will to action* is fundamentally different than the *will to power* because it rests on reality's true *arché*: The Trinity. For Nietzscheans like Arthur Kroker, however, this assertion is incomprehensible; it is a quaint philosophy, belonging to an irretrievable time.

While admiring Cochrane's neglected views, for mostly nationalist reasons, Kroker (like Agamben) claims modernity's *secular perversity* simply has no alternative: Being cannot be *re*-rescued by Christian conversion. In its secular form, Christian temporality has become a central aspect of nihilism's continuance. Consequently, "Cochrane's weakness" is the naïve view that Christian civilization is not exhausted—"that he took refuge in the carceral of the 'trinitarian formula.'"[120] To Kroker, "the decisive intervention by Augustine into western metaphysics" has turned, in an irreparable fashion, into just another minority report; it joins the long list of historical dominations that initially present themselves as liberations.[121] That such a valuation depends on the absolute presupposition of Christian liberation being true cannot be conceived of, let alone admitted, by adherents of this kind of critical historicism. Their oft presented alternative of a revival of *neopagan creativity* in art, science and politics to fulfill Christian liberation goals is the modern disaster. Christian historicism is indeed marred by eras of political religion, barbarism in Collingwood's sense of social backsliding. But, to Cochrane, unlike pagan forms of life, so re-envisioned to replace them, such errancies of creative political religion are self-undermined by Christianity's own historical essence of emancipatory action: "The order of nature revealed by Christ and the Scriptures is, in fact, the true order," and, "To accept that conviction is to recognize that nature" is created (and still being created) by the Trinity, "by the will of the Father, operating by His Word and through His Spirit to create and sustain it."[122] Modern Nietzsche-

---

117. Cochrane, "Augustine and the Problem of Power," 93.
118. Cochrane, "Augustine and the Problem of Power," 93.
119. Cochrane, "Augustine and the Problem of Power," 93.
120. Kroker, "Augustine as the Founder of Modern Experience," 105.
121. Kroker, "Augustine as the Founder of Modern Experience," 105.
122. Cochrane, "Augustine and the Problem of Power," 78.

ans notwithstanding, we must accept as true that what is still needed is "a complete reversal of the attitude characteristic of secularism"—namely, that free human action cannot be dedicated to "'creation,' as secularism in its arrogance has supposed, but rather one of 'construction,'" aligned with the divine will.[123] And even Kroker confesses, "the easy academic" acceptance of modern nihilism—and the consequent denial of "highly original insights" represented by Cochrane, Collingwood, and others in the Christian idealist tradition—is a "repression that wounds" because their ideas "bear no immediate relation to my existence."[124] The *easy* road is no longer an option if a new ecological civilization must be built. Ideas count. In the tally of affliction, some will wound, some will heal.

City of God

In *Christianity and Classical Culture*, Cochrane targets *creative politics*. It is best interpreted as a co-equal pillar that stands alongside Collingwood's philosophy. It offers the political complement to the latter philosopher's critique of *creative science*. Cochrane also accepts historical metaphysics as a methodology; one that detects and traces a civilization's absolute, "necessary presupposition to a wider intelligibility, if not to all intelligibility whatsoever."[125] Descriptive practice strives to liberate human action, presenting "history in this way to serve as a kind of conscience to mankind."[126] Christianity is not only a social and religious movement, it is a constellational revolution of absolute presuppositions. In the twilight of the Classical world, we find the great drama of liberation and imperial domination. Rich contrasts and correspondences appear between (*ad extra*) and within (*ad intra*) salvation projects offered by *Pax Romana* and its seemingly improbable successor: *Pax Christi* or Christendom. Christianity offers a novel message and practice of universal benevolence. It is a comprehensive program of *salus*/σωτηρία—*from, for, in,* and *beyond* the world—that eventually overwhelms and replaces pagan alternatives.[127] Pagan political religion becomes Christian political theology. The climax of this historical process is realised in Saint Augustine's *De civitate Dei* (426 CE). Cochrane's *Christianity and Classical Culture* is the narrative of this constellational change.

123. Cochrane, "Augustine and the Problem of Power," 78.
124. Kroker, "Augustine as the Founder of Modern Experience," 86.
125. Cochrane, *Christianity and Classical Culture*, 401.
126. Cochrane, *Christianity and Classical Culture*, 149.
127. See Simmons, *Universal Salvation in Late Antiquity*, 107–226.

In Augustine's definitive text, we read, "This then is the universal way for the soul's liberation: universal because it is granted to all nations by the divine compassion."[128] Only through Christ is there salvation, "And apart from this way no one has been set free, no one is being set free, no one will be set free."[129] Augustine then goes on to distinguish "the two cities," which are "intermixed with each other in this present world."[130] The way of the secular or *earthly* city is "lust for domination," which is "self-love reaching the point of contempt for God."[131] It is associated with Cain, who founds a city on sacrificial fratricide (XV). Abel "belonged to the City of God" because, "as a pilgrim," he "did not found one. For the City of the saints is up above, although it produces citizens here below, and in their persons the City is on pilgrimage until the time of its kingdom comes."[132] The nomadic path of *the Mediator* is indifferent to territoriality. His crucifixion exposes the lie of violence as a necessary foundation for community. The call for an alternative society *not of this world* means "We are speaking of the City of God which is not on our pilgrimage in this mortal life, but is eternally immortal in heaven."[133] Nevertheless, affirmation of the universal beloved community on this side of the divide (salvation *for* and *in*) signifies love of God, neighbor, and creation. We do not reject this world, but we do reject the earthly city's version of it.

Given the spatial situation that Christians will inevitably find themselves in—i.e., we all live somewhere and embody different bundles of identity predicates—the edges separating Augustine's two cities are more permeable than one might expect. Followers of eschatological time leave traces of universality in their variously dispersed contexts. Christian pilgrims *en route* to the Heavenly City must exist in an "earthly city" of some definite kind, and depend on its "earthly peace."[134] To a certain extent, pilgrims experience lives "of captivity in this earthly city as in a foreign land," but "their establishment of a kind of compromise" does not leave the earthy city unchanged.[135] Eschatological place arises from eschatological time. This novel territoriality "relates the earthly peace to the heavenly peace," "having the attainment of that peace in view in every good action it performs

---

128. Augustine, *City of God* X.32 (422).
129. Augustine, *City of God* X.32 (424).
130. Augustine, *City of God* X.32 (426).
131. Augustine, *City of God* XIV.28 (593).
132. Augustine, *City of God* XV.2 (596).
133. Augustine, *City of God* XI.28 (463).
134. Augustine, *City of God* XIX.17 (877).
135. Augustine, *City of God* XIX.17 (877).

in relation to God, and in relation to neighbour, since the life of a city is inevitably a social life."[136] Cochrane explains further, "To this peace they pledge themselves in a new oath or sacrament (*sacramentum, sacrum signum*)," which is "a covenant of emancipation from temporality, mutually undertaken by men who thus profess themselves aliens from secularism. It is a testament, not of subjection to, but of salvation from, the divinity of Caesar, mystically proclaimed through baptism in the name of the Father, the Son, and the Holy Spirit."[137] The trinitarian form of life reverses the Classical ideology of power: "The tragedy of the Caesars" is, "in a word, the tragedy of men who, being required to play the part of the gods, descended to that of beasts."[138] "The claim to divinity made on behalf of the emperor" is null and void.[139] "The doctrine of the Trinity," Cochrane claims, "provided the basis for a radically new and unclassical account of the structure and content of experience," and "the question of primary importance was not so much their capacity for thinking as the presuppositions which governed their thought."[140] The sacred force of empire's secular political religion gives way to a counter universalism of sacred benevolence. Christian political theology achieves a triumph for persons who, being forced to play the part of subjugated beasts, ascend to that of God as Trinity.

Only through peace is plurality created and only through peace does it persist: Christian society is dedicated to harmonizing the love of peace found in different earthly cities.[141] From Augustine, we hear yet another revolutionary statement of true political theology: "While this Heavenly City, therefore, is on pilgrimage in this world, she calls out citizens from all nations and so collects a society of aliens, speaking all languages. She takes no account of any difference in customs, laws, and institutions, by which the earthly peace is achieved and preserved—not that she annuls or abolishes any of those, rather, she maintains them and follows them (for whatever divergences there are among diverse nations, those institutions have one single aim—earthly peace)."[142] Instead of fleeing from the *reprobate* earthly cities, R. A. Markus claims that Augustine imparts a "vivid sense of appreciating and fostering secular institutions catering for the cohesion of a mixed society," which "is formulated in terms of intermediate goods which

---

136. Augustine, *City of God* XIX.17 (878, 879).
137. Cochrane, *Christianity and Classical Culture*, 565.
138. Cochrane, *Christianity and Classical Culture*, 141.
139. Cochrane, *Christianity and Classical Culture*, 148.
140. Cochrane, *Christianity and Classical Culture*, 261.
141. See Gilson, *Christian Philosophy of Saint Augustine*, 171–84.
142. Augustine, *City of God* XIX.19 (878).

are to be valued by members of both the earthly and heavenly cities."[143] Augustine's political theology is transformative of *civitas terrena* on behalf of *civitas caelestis*.

The Christian sense of nature is essential for true earthly peace: "That is to say, the universe is to be understood as a product of the free, creative activity of God."[144] With the triadic absolute presupposition, "it becomes possible to envisage the divine principle as both transcendent and immanent, 'prior' to nature, the world of time and space in which we live, and yet operative within it."[145] The order of the creative act of the Father is the Word or the Son. The Son is that by and in which all things are made, embodying "the whole substance, life, and power of the Father."[146] But creation is neither mechanical necessity nor arbitrary fiat because the Spirit is the principle of "novelty," the creation "of something which has not existed before."[147] New things happen *because of* "the ordered course of God's providential government of events."[148] Providential freedom is not necessity or chance, and it may not even be exclusive to humanity. *Vestigia trinitatis*: There is a *nisus* for new events and entities in the created (and creating) natural order. The doctrine of creation challenges "those measured and regulated cycles, in which there is no novelty, but the repetition of the same things which have been already."[149] Augustine's revolutionary principle of historicity encompasses humanistic and, conceivably, naturalistic realities of free activity—"novelties are possible, things which have not happened before and yet are not at variance with the ordering of the world."[150] Cochrane describes "the working of the Spirit" as being characterized by "its permeability," its temporal openness to the production of a "new starting point."[151] This kind of history exists "as a record of divine economy," and, what it offers is an unparalleled account of liberation.[152] *The Spirit is free.* We are to experience

---

143. Markus, *Signs and Meanings*, 120. See also his *Saeculum*, 45–71; Hollingworth, *Pilgrim City*, 159–194.

144. Cochrane, *Christianity and Classical Culture*, 406.

145. Cochrane, *Christianity and Classical Culture*, 406.

146. Cochrane, *Christianity and Classical Culture*, 406.

147. Augustine, *City of God* XII.21 (500).

148. Augustine, *City of God* XII.21 (500).

149. Augustine, *City of God* XII.21 (500).

150. Augustine, *City of God* XII.21 (500).

151. Cochrane, *Christianity and Classical Culture*, 407.

152. Cochrane, *Christianity and Classical Culture*, 407.

ourselves and fellow creatures "no longer either as mechanisms or organisms, but as persons."[153]

Nova Concordia

Christian historicity "is not Promethean; it tells no story of 'virtue' in conflict with 'chance' or 'necessity.' For with the disappearance from Christian thought of the classical antithesis between 'man' and the 'environment,' there disappears also the possibility of such a conflict."[154] Human destiny "is, indeed, determined, but neither by a soulless mechanism nor by the fiat of an arbitrary or capricious power external to himself. For the laws which govern physical, like the laws which govern human, nature are equally the laws of God."[155] On this view, human history may be as regarded as the history of action, which is "the life of beings created free and with potential for happiness, this freedom and this happiness depending upon their capacity for deliberate choice."[156] History concerns free human action and, because nature is also imbued with the same historical process that welcomes novelty, our relation to the natural world turns from domination to co-liberation of persons. The more we liberate from oppression, the more we are liberated in return. Through the acceptance of divine economy, there is "the fact of its salutary influence upon the life of individuals and societies, claiming that it embodied the sole hope of creative peace, since it alone imbued human beings with a really pacific disposition and, by transmuting the strife of man with nature and his fellows into a conflict against evil."[157] To Cochrane, "The discovery of personality was, at the same time, the discovery of history."[158] To confess the Trinity as the principle of order and motion opens the way to a *humanistic* philosophy of history, "But, as distinct from its classical prototype, Christian humanism is emphatically neither anthropocentric nor anthropomorphic. On the contrary, it accuses Classicism of that very vice."[159] Our relationship to nature overcomes force and illusion. It is neither tyrannical nor mythological. Christian realism "gives to the 'object' world a wholly fresh complexion, thus 'making all things new'"—it is "the one fundamental principle for individual regeneration and social reformation,

---

153. Cochrane, *Christianity and Classical Culture*, 411.
154. Cochrane, *Christianity and Classical Culture*, 407.
155. Cochrane, *Christianity and Classical Culture*, 407.
156. Cochrane, *Christianity and Classical Culture*, 407.
157. Cochrane, *Christianity and Classical Culture*, 409.
158. Cochrane, *Christianity and Classical Culture*, 503.
159. Cochrane, *Christianity and Classical Culture*, 530.

the point of departure for a fresh experiment in human relationships."[160] The achievement of the *pax caelestis* is a personal struggle for conversion of self and world, "between the love of power and the power of love."[161]

Humanity and all things belong to a dynamic trinitarian cosmos, "exhibiting their dependence upon a principle which being beyond them and in them, cosmic and personal, is put forward as genuinely 'creative.'"[162] *We* are co-subjects of its economic movement. To be subjects of creation means order and process "are not mutually exclusive or antithetic. In other words the opposition between them is purely and simply one of internal, necessary relations."[163] But this kind of necessity serves "to dissipate the nightmare involved in the concept of nature as a closed system, determined by its own exclusive laws and, therewith, of the antithesis between human liberty and natural necessity which rendered mankind a stranger in his own household."[164] If "the Trinity" offers "a fresh foundation for what we have called the values of personality," then "being is not to be resolved into order, nor is order to be resolved into process."[165] To hold this principle as an absolute presupposition is an act of *faith* in "an account of being, of movement, and of the order or relationship between them"—properly understood, it is "not as a substitute for, but as a condition of understanding," and, therefore, "the Trinitarian principle presents itself, not as a refinement of the scientific intelligence, a tissue of metaphysical abstractions having no existence except in the imagination of theologians, but rather as an attempt to formulate what is 'imposed' upon the intelligence as the precondition of science; and its acceptance as such marks a rejection of the claim that the discursive reason can authenticate the presumptions which determine the nature and scope of its activity otherwise than in terms of their 'working and power.'"[166] A subject can, through a special or *faithful* science, understand the creative *principium*—the *arché*—that "is presumed or presupposed in the consciousness of his own existence and activity."[167]

"Accordingly, the choice for man," as Cochrane formulates it, "does not so much lie between science and superstition as between two kinds of

---

160. Cochrane, *Christianity and Classical Culture*, 553.
161. Cochrane, *Christianity and Classical Culture*, 553.
162. Cochrane, *Christianity and Classical Culture*, 443.
163. Cochrane, *Christianity and Classical Culture*, 454.
164. Cochrane, *Christianity and Classical Culture*, 454–55.
165. Cochrane, *Christianity and Classical Culture*, 467, 454.
166. Cochrane, *Christianity and Classical Culture*, 444, 456.
167. Cochrane, *Christianity and Classical Culture*, 451.

faith, the one salutary, the other destructive."[168] The former is the new deliverance of the Trinity's "'wholeness,'" "its fulfillment," which "implies that the life of sense must be brought into intelligible relationship with the life of reason."[169] The organization of sense-perception depends on its faithful presuppositions: "Its working is therefore contingent upon the assumption that the material in question will present itself in 'patterns' capable of apprehension by the mind; and this assumption it can by no means verify."[170] Trinitarian reason, then, underpins reality. To those who accept its truth, goodness, and beauty, it is capable of replacing the *destructive Promethean faith*, which is based "on a distorted or partial apprehension of ultimate reality, its character is necessarily felt as oppressive; and the sense of oppression bears its inevitable fruits in defiance and revolt to be followed by confusion, defeat, and despair."[171]

Two pathways now open for knowledge of the world: *Ratio scientia* and *ratio sapientiae*. The first continues the error of Classicism—that is, it mistakes creation for construction. This kind of science "does not create; it constructs, using for this purpose the material of sense perception."[172] Thus, Promethean science (both natural and political) is equally tragic and traumatic because its drive "'to become like gods'" is an irrational end that cannot be satisfied.[173] It results in an insatiable "'will to power'" that instills a "thirst for domination over one's fellow men," and a consequent desire "to explore the secrets of nature" to fulfill this pernicious goal.[174] *Ratio scientia* turns on its perpetrators, destroying all things in a pointless exercise "to possess itself of an instrument by which to control the environment."[175] Practitioners of this science are *willfully* blind to "its dependence upon the principle of its life and being."[176] As Collingwood has already equipped us to comprehend, *ratio sapientiae* is the sense of metaphysics known as theology, the non-constructive "method of science" that leads to "insight or wisdom" because "what it provides is nothing less than an apprehension of the creative principle upon which the very possibility of reasoning

---

168. Cochrane, *Christianity and Classical Culture*, 456.
169. Cochrane, *Christianity and Classical Culture*, 457.
170. Cochrane, *Christianity and Classical Culture*, 457.
171. Cochrane, *Christianity and Classical Culture*, 456.
172. Cochrane, *Christianity and Classical Culture*, 457.
173. Cochrane, *Christianity and Classical Culture*, 495.
174. Cochrane, *Christianity and Classical Culture*, 495.
175. Cochrane, *Christianity and Classical Culture*, 495.
176. Cochrane, *Christianity and Classical Culture*, 466.

depends."[177] This science requires "the substitution of a new standard of objectivity for that proposed by classical *scientia*; this objectivity was that of history, envisaged as a progressive disclosure of the creative and moving principle."[178] History upholds the continuous tension of being and becoming. *Creative temporality* is capable of "producing novelty without innovation of will, and with potentialities which were simply inexhaustible," and it has a clear, emancipatory meaning: "This it did by emphasizing the fact that the days of the *hostia*, the victim or scapegoat, were thenceforth at an end: hereby proclaiming the salutary truth of the future as against the deadly errors of the past."[179] But historical time, on its own, is not a constitutive relationship or immanent *principium*, "Accordingly, to recognize ourselves as creatures in time is to recognize ourselves as in relation to other creatures. These relationships constitute our 'nature.'"[180] Historicity is the revelation of personality throughout the created order.

Trinitarian Christianity presents itself as a thorough scientific reorientation. Power must serve the wisdom of love. To free creation, "it was necessary to begin with the findings of *sapientia* rather than with those of *scientia*, i.e., with 'creative' rather than 'poetic' or 'scientific' truth."[181] Cochrane concludes, "In the light of *sapientia*, man no longer sees himself over against a 'nature,' conceived anthropomorphically whether as 'thought' or 'mechanism.' On the contrary, he sees himself and his universe together as an expression of beneficent activity, the activity of the creative and moving principle—in the language of religion, as a 'creature,' whose origin, nature, and destiny are determined by the will of God."[182] A person infused with Christian *sapientia* is "transfigured by the fact that he sees it [nature] as the theatre of divine activity."[183] To experience reality this way "is thus to relinquish the aspiration to omniscience, recognizing that his powers of apprehension are determined by the conditions of his existence as a creature in time and space and, as such, irrevocably subject to what Augustine calls the *vicissitudo spatiorum temporalium*."[184] But to become a historical creature is not to be wholly other than the divine nature. There is no alienating gap or caesura. Rather, the motion and pattern of space and time participate

---

177. Cochrane, *Christianity and Classical Culture*, 458.
178. Cochrane, *Christianity and Classical Culture*, 460.
179. Cochrane, *Christianity and Classical Culture*, 461.
180. Cochrane, *Christianity and Classical Culture*, 485.
181. Cochrane, *Christianity and Classical Culture*, 477.
182. Cochrane, *Christianity and Classical Culture*, 481.
183. Cochrane, *Christianity and Classical Culture*, 482.
184. Cochrane, *Christianity and Classical Culture*, 486.

in continuous communication as economic Trinity, "inasmuch as the working of that principle was direct and immediate, 'intrinsic' to the natures in which it operated, there could not possibly arise any antinomy between Creator and Creation."[185] Further, "To say this was to deny the opposition which Classicism had set up between man and nature and, therewith, the heroic ideal, the conquest of chance or necessity by human virtue. It was to see nature as a whole, in which, from the lowest to the highest forms, there was absolutely no *saltus* or break; since all, without exception, were equally dependent upon the creative principle."[186] In other words, "it is precisely the same divine *hormé* which, on the lowest plane of instinctive life, impels the animal to fight for bare existence and which, on the highest, provides the saint with power to triumph over such obstacles as may interfere with a realization of felicity through the knowledge and love of God."[187] Creation is continuous, dynamic inter-relation and inter-communication.

Since the creative principle is also the principle of the new, necessity does not encounter the problem of spontaneous change of order or *miracle* and, equally, chance is not deified, worshipped as "the incalculable" intervention that destroys and creates *the logics of worlds*: The "divine event."[188] Cochrane tells us, "the denial of fate is at the same time a denial of fortune."[189] The "philosophy of history in terms of the *logos* of Christ; i.e., in terms of the Trinity, recognized as the creative and moving principle," is an assurance "that the individual historical event is *ipso facto* unique and unpredictable."[190] Actuality is the historical space and time of human action, experiencing itself as free in newly arising circumstances. "For the Christian," Cochrane claims, "time, space, matter, and form are all alike" in the sense that they "present themselves, not as causes but as opportunity."[191] Order is not at war with the new. But the new is not its own independent principle. The new, simply by being new, is not enough to justify its continuance in existence. Novelty "in terms of the embodied *logos* means history in terms of personality."[192] Consequently, the evolution of personality signifies "Christian humanism is empathically neither

---

185. Cochrane, *Christianity and Classical Culture*, 488.
186. Cochrane, *Christianity and Classical Culture*, 489.
187. Cochrane, *Christianity and Classical Culture*, 492.
188. Cochrane, *Christianity and Classical Culture*, 523.
189. Cochrane, *Christianity and Classical Culture*, 527.
190. Cochrane, *Christianity and Classical Culture*, 529.
191. Cochrane, *Christianity and Classical Culture*, 534.
192. Cochrane, *Christianity and Classical Culture*, 530.

anthropocentric nor anthropomorphic."[193] "The *logos* of Christ thus serves to introduce a new principle of unity and of division into human life and human history," and nature is transfigured by love, becoming creation.[194] Creation communicates personality: "From this standpoint the problem of the Christian is not so much to read into nature the values of truth, beauty, and goodness as to detect these values in it."[195] "As truth," the creative principle "may be described as reason irradiated by love; as morality, love irradiated by reason."[196] To recognize "its existence is to recognize the existence of divine grace. The need for grace is the need of perceiving a relationship, the reality of which is or rather would be self-evident, except for the willful and perverse blindness of mankind."[197] The acceptance of the gift of grace as "an essential part of the constitution of things" is perpetually obstructed by the Classical will to power that filters into the Christian tradition through the figure of Pelagius.[198] The *creative* barbarism of secularity and Christian political religion defines this strain of Christian historical process.

Salvation, for Pelagius, can come through heroic acts of will power; so initiated, the remedy for human evil "lay entirely within the individual so affected."[199] But, to Augustine, salvation cannot come from yet another perfectionist *construction*; the creative principle must self-donate recognition of its reality. Pelagius Christianizes the Classical pride that "arrogates to itself the status and prerogative of a god."[200] In the light of true Christian wisdom, however, we need forgiveness, "a realization of the possibility of a clean sheet or new deal to follow automatically as a consequence of accepting the Christian starting point."[201] Acceptance, forgiveness, and grace are interchangeable terms, signifying *faith* in the personal evolution of creation, "To anticipate such a future is to believe that the values which are metaphysically and physically real are, at the same time, historically real. Inherent in the creative principle, they reveal themselves in history as the values of creative experience, as such to be progressively embodied in the consciousness of the race."[202]

---

193. Cochrane, *Christianity and Classical Culture*, 530.
194. Cochrane, *Christianity and Classical Culture*, 537.
195. Cochrane, *Christianity and Classical Culture*, 530.
196. Cochrane, *Christianity and Classical Culture*, 558.
197. Cochrane, *Christianity and Classical Culture*, 554.
198. Cochrane, *Christianity and Classical Culture*, 556.
199. Cochrane, "Augustine and the Problem of Power," 97.
200. Cochrane, "Augustine and the Problem of Power," 99.
201. Cochrane, *Christianity and Classical Culture*, 557.
202. Cochrane, *Christianity and Classical Culture*, 567.

Nova Concordia: The Trinity communicates solutions for a multitude of human crises. The most important one is surmounting the Promethean conflict between human beings and our environment. The Trinity is the key absolute presupposition for political theology of environment. On behalf of the ecological civilization to come, we are called to conversion.

Bibliography

Abrams, M. H. *Natural Supernaturalism: Tradition and Revolution in Romantic Literature*. New York: Norton, 1971.
Adorno, Theodor W. *Metaphysics: Concept and Problems*. Edited by Ralph Tiedemann. Translated by Edmund Jephcott. Cambridge: Polity, 2000.
Aeschylus. *Oresteia*. Translated by Richard Lattimore. Chicago: University of Chicago Press, 1953.
———. *Prometheus Bound*. Translated by David Grene. Chicago: University of Chicago Press, 1942.
Agamben, Giorgio. *The Adventure*. Translated by Lorenzo Chisea. Cambridge, MA: MIT Press, 2018.
———. *The Coming Community*. Translated by Michael Hardt. Theory Out of Bounds 1. Minneapolis: University of Minnesota Press, 1993.
———. *Homo Sacer: Sovereign Power and Bare Life*. Translated by Daniel Heller-Roazen. Stanford, CA: Stanford University Press, 1998.
———. *The Kingdom and the Glory: For a Theological Genealogy of Economy and Government*. Translated by Lorenzo Chisea and Matteo Mandarini. Homo Sacer 2. Stanford, CA: Stanford University Press, 2011.
———. "On Potentiality." In *Potentialities: Collected Essays in Philosophy*, by Giorgio Agamben, 177–84. Translated by Daniel Heller-Roazen. Stanford, CA: Stanford University Press, 1999.
———. *The Signature of All Things: On Method*. Translated by Luca D'Isanto and Kevin Attell. Brooklyn: Zone, 2009.
———. *The Time That Remains: A Commentary on the Letter to the Romans*. Translated by Patricia Dailey. Stanford, CA: Stanford University Press, 2005.
———. *The Use of Bodies*. Translated by Adam Kotsko. Homo Sacer 4.2. Stanford, CA: Stanford University Press, 2016.
Ahmed, Sara. *Queer Phenomenology: Orientations, Objects, Others*. Durham, NC: Duke University Press, 2006.
Aiken, William. "Ethical Issues in Agriculture." In *Earthbound: New Introductory Essays in Environmental Ethics*, edited by Tom Regan, 247–88. New York: Random, 1984.
Aitkenhead, Decca. "James Lovelock: 'Enjoy Life While You Can: In Twenty Years Global Warming Will Hit The Fan.'" *Guardian*, March 1, 2008. Online. https://www.theguardian.com/theguardian/2008/mar/01/scienceofclimatechange.climatechange.

Alliez, Éric. *Capital Times: Tales from the Conquest of Time*. Translated by Georges Van Den Abbeele. Theory Out of Bounds 6. Minneapolis: University of Minnesota Press, 1996.

Apel, Karl-Otto. "The Ecological Crisis as a Problem for Discourse Ethics." In *Ecology and Ethics*, edited by Audun Ofsti, 219–60. Trondheim: Nordland Academy of Arts and Sciences, 1992.

Aquinas, Thomas. *Summa Theologiae*. Translated by Fathers of the English Dominican Province. New York: Christian Classics, 1981. Online. http://newadvent.org/summa.

Arendt, Hannah. *On Violence*. New York: Harcourt, 1970.

Argyrou, Vassos. *The Logic of Environmentalism: Anthropology, Ecology, and Postcoloniality*. Oxford: Berghahn, 2005.

Aristotle. *The Complete Works of Aristotle*. Edited by Jonathan Barnes. 2 vols. Princeton, NJ: Princeton University Press, 1991, 1995.

———. *Nicomachean Ethics*. Translated by Martin Ostwald. Indianapolis, IN: Bobbs-Merrill, 1962.

———. *Politics*. Translated by Ernest Baker. Oxford: Oxford University Press, 1982.

Armour, Leslie. "Descartes and the Ethics of Generosity." In *The Bases of Ethics*, edited by William Sweet, 79–102. Milwaukee, WI: Marquette University Press, 2001.

———. "Speculative versus Critical Philosophy of History." In *The Philosophy of History: A Re-Examination*, edited by William Sweet, 131–62. Aldershot, UK: Ashgate, 2004.

———. "Values, God, and the Problem about Why There is Anything at All." *The Journal of Speculative Philosophy* 1.2 (1987) 147–62.

Ashworth, William B., Jr. "Natural History and the Emblematic World View." In *Reappraisals of the Scientific Revolution*, edited David C. Lindberg and Robert S. Westman, 303–32. Cambridge: Cambridge University Press, 1990.

Augustine. *City of God (Concerning the City of God Against the Pagans)*. Translated by Henry Bettenson. Introduction by David Knowles. London: Pelican, 1972.

———. *De Doctrina Christiana*. Edited and translated by R. P. H. Green. Oxford: Clarendon, 1995. Online. https://www.augustinus.it/latino/dottrina_cristiana/index2.htm.

———. "Excerpt: *Reconsiderations*." In *On Free Choice of the Will*, by Augustine, 124–29. Translated by Thomas William. Indianapolis, IN: Hackett, 1993.

———. "In What Respects Predestination and Grace Differ." In *Anti-Pelagian Writings*, by Augustine. Online. https://biblehub.com/library/augustine/anti-pelagian_writings/chapter_19_xin_what_respects.htm.

———. *On Free Choice of the Will*. Translated by Thomas Williams. Indianapolis, IN: Hackett, 1993.

———. *The Trinity*. Translated by Stephen Mckenna. Fathers of the Church 45. Washington, DC: Catholic University of America Press, 1963.

———. "What True Grace Is." In *The Essential Augustine*, edited by Vernon J. Bourke, 176–78. Indianapolis, IN: Hackett, 1985.

Aurelius, Marcus. *Meditations*. Translated by George Long. Online. http://classics.mit.edu/Antoninus/meditations.2.two.html.

Axelrod, R., and D. Dion. "The Further Evolution of Cooperation." *Science* 242.4884 (1988) 1385–90.

Ayer, A. J. *Language, Truth, and Logic*. 2nd ed. New York: Dover, 1952.

———. *The Origins of Pragmatism*. San Francisco: Freeman, Cooper, 1968.
Babcock, William S. "*Caritas* and Signification in *De doctrina christiana* 1–3." In *De doctrina christiana: A Classic of Western Culture*, edited by Duane W. H. Arnold and Pamela Bright, 145–63. Christianity and Judaism in Antiquity 9. Notre Dame: University of Norte Dame Press, 1995.
Bacon, Francis. *The New Organon and Related Writings*. Edited by Fulton H. Anderson. Indianapolis, IN: Bobbs-Merrill, 1960.
———. *The Philosophical Works of Francis Bacon*. Edited by John M. Robinson. London: Routledge, 2011.
———. "Thoughts and Conclusions on the Interpretation of Nature or A Science of Productive Works." In *The Philosophy of Francis Bacon: An Essay on its Development from 1603 to 1609 with New Translations of Fundamental Texts*, edited by Benjamin Farrington, 93. Liverpool: Liverpool University Press, 1964.
Balakrishnan, Gopal. *The Enemy: An Intellectual Portrait of Carl Schmitt*. London: Verso, 2000.
Balthasar, Hans Urs von. *Presence and Thought: An Essay on the Religious Philosophy of Gregory of Nyssa*. Translated by Marc Sebanc. Communio. San Francisco: Ignatius, 1995.
———. *A Theology of History*. Communio. San Francisco: Ignatius, 1994.
Barbieri, Marcello. "Biosemiotics: A New Understanding of Life." *Naturwissenschaften* 95 (2008) 577–99.
———. *The Organic Codes: An Introduction to Semantic Biology*. Cambridge: Cambridge University Press, 2003.
Barnouw, Jeffrey. *Propositional Perception: Phantasia, Predication, and Sign in Plato, Aristotle, and the Stoics*. Lanham, MD: University Press of America, 1992.
Basil of Caesarea. *Against Eunomius*. Translated by Mark Delcogliano and Andrew Radde-Gallwitz. Washington, DC: Catholic University of America Press, 2011.
Beaney, Michael. "Collingwood's Conception of Presuppositional Analysis." *Collingwood and British Idealism Studies* 11.2 (2005) 41–114.
Becker, Carl L. *The Heavenly City of the Eighteenth-Century Philosophers*. Foreword by Johnson Kent Wright. 2nd ed. New Haven, CT: Yale University Press, 2003.
Beer, David. "Introduction." In *Augustine and the Problem of Power: The Essays and Lectures of Charles Norris Cochrane*, edited by David Beer, 1–25. Eugene, OR: Cascade, 2017.
Benjamin, Walter. "Critique of Violence." In *Reflections: Essays, Aphorisms, Autobiographical Writings*, by Walter Benjamin, edited by Peter Demetz, 277–300. New York: Harcourt Brace Jovanovich, 1978.
Bentham, Jeremy. *An Introduction to the Principles of Morals and Legislation*. Oxford: Clarendon, 1907. Online. https://www.econlib.org/library/Bentham/bnthPML.html?chapter_num=19#book-reader.
Benzoni, Francisco. "Thomas Aquinas and Environmental Ethics: A Reconsideration of Providence and Salvation." *Journal of Religion* 85.3 (2005) 446–76.
Berdyaev, Nicolas. "Unground and Freedom." In *Six Theosophic Points and Other Writings*, by Jacob Boehme, v–xxxvii. Translated by John Rolleston Earle. Ann Arbor: University of Michigan Press, 1958.
Berger, Peter L., and Thomas Luckmann. *The Social Construction of Reality: A Treatise in the Sociology of Knowledge*. New York: Doubleday, 1966.

Bergmann, Sigurd. *Creation Set Free: The Spirit as Liberator of Nature.* Translated by Douglas Stott. Foreword by Jürgen Moltmann. Grand Rapids; Cambridge: Eerdmans, 2005.

Berlin, Isaiah. "Two Concepts of Liberty." In *Liberty*, by Isaiah Berlin, edited by Henry Hardy, 166–217. Oxford: Oxford University Press, 2002.

Bernard of Clairvaux. *The Letters of St. Bernard of Clairvaux.* Translated by Bruno Scott James. London: Burns and Oates, 1953.

Best, Ernest. *A Commentary on the First and Second Epistles to the Thessalonians.* London: A. & C. Black, 1986.

Bloch, Ernst. *Natural Law and Human Dignity.* Translated by Dennis J. Schmidt. Cambridge, MA: MIT Press, 1987.

Boehme, Jacob. "Appendix: Four Tables of Divine Revelation." In *Jacob Boehme: Essential Readings*, edited by Robin Waterfield, 215–39. Wellingborough, UK: Crucible/Thorsens, 1989.

———. *Aurora.* Translated by John Sparrow. London: James Clarke, 1960.

———. *The Forty Questions of the Soul and The Clavis.* Translated by John Sparrow. London: John M. Watkins, 1911.

———. *Jacob Boehme: Essential Readings.* Edited by Robin Waterfield. Wellingborough, UK: Crucible/Thorsens, 1989.

———. *The Signature of All Things and Other Writings.* Translated by Clifford Bax. Cambridge: James Clark, 1969.

———. *Six Theosophic Points and Other Writings.* Translated by John Rolleston Earle. Introduction by Nicolas Berdyaev. Ann Arbor: University of Michigan Press, 1958.

Boersma, Gerald P. *Augustine's Early Theology of Image: A Study in the Development of Pro-Nicene Theology.* Oxford Studies in Historical Theology. Oxford: Oxford University Press, 2016.

Bonin, Thérèse. *Creation as Emanation: The Origin of Diversity in Albert the Great's On the Causes and the Procession of the Universe.* Medieval Institute 29. Notre Dame: Notre Dame University Press, 2001.

Bono, James J. *Ficino to Descartes.* Vol. 1 of *The Word of God and the Languages of Man: Interpreting Nature in Early Modern Science and Medicine.* Madison: University of Wisconsin Press, 1995.

———. "From Paracelsus to Newton: The Word of God, the Book of Nature, and the Eclipse of the 'Emblematic World View.'" In *Newton and Religion: Context, Nature, and Influence*, edited by James Force and Richard H. Popkin, 45–76. Dordrecht: Kluwer, 1999.

Booth, Edward. *Aristotelian Aporetic Ontology in Islamic and Christian Thinkers.* Cambridge: Cambridge University Press, 1983.

Boucher, David. "Human Conduct, History, and Social Science in the Works of R. G. Collingwood and Michael Oakeshott." *New Literary History* 24.3 (1993) 607–717.

———. *The Social and Political Thought of R. G. Collingwood.* Cambridge: Cambridge University Press, 1989.

Bradley, James. "Philosophy and Trinity." *Symposium* 16.1 (2012) 155–78.

———. "The Speculative Generalization of the Function: A Key to Whitehead." *Tijdschrift voor Filosofie* 64 (2002) 253–71.

Bradshaw, David. *Aristotle East and West: Metaphysics and the Division of Christendom.* Cambridge: Cambridge University Press, 2004.

Braudel, Fernand. "Society: 'A Set of Sets.'" In *The Wheels of Commerce*, by Fernand Braudel, 458–61. Vol. 2 of *Civilization and Capitalism (Fifteenth to Eighteenth Century)*. Translated by Siân Reynolds. New York: Harper & Row, 1982.

Brock, Stephen L. *The Philosophy of Saint Thomas Aquinas: A Sketch*. Eugene, OR: Cascade, 2015.

Brower, Jeffrey E. "Aristotelian versus Contemporary Perspectives on Relations." In *The Metaphysics of Relations*, edited by Anna Marmodoro and David Yates, 36–54. Oxford: Oxford University Press, 2016.

Brown, David. *God and Enchantment of Place: Reclaiming Human Experience*. Oxford: Oxford University Press, 2006.

Brown, Peter. *Augustine of Hippo: A Biography*. Berkeley: University of California Press, 1967.

Brown, Robert F. *The Later Philosophy of Schelling: The Influence of Boehme on the Works of 1809–1815*. Lewisburg, PA: Bucknell University Press, 1977.

Bruns, Gerald L. *Hermeneutics: Ancient and Modern*. New Haven, CT: Yale University Press, 1992.

Budiansky, Stephen. *If a Lion Could Talk: Animal Intelligence and the Evolution of Consciousness*. New York: Free Press, 1998.

Cacciari, Massimo. *The Withholding Power: An Essay on Political Theology*. Translated by Edi Pucci and Harry Marandi. Introduction by Howard Caygill. London: Bloomsbury, 2018.

Callicott, J. Baird. "The Conceptual Foundations of the Land Ethic." In *Companion to a Sand County Almanac*, edited by J. Baird Callicott, 186–217. Madison: University of Wisconsin Press, 1987.

———. "Environmental Ethics: Introduction." In *Environmental Philosophy: From Animal Rights to Radical Ecology*, edited by Michael E. Zimmerman et al., 5–15. 4th ed. Upper Saddle River, NJ: Pearson, 2005.

———. "Holistic Environmental Ethics and the Problem of Ecofascism." In *Environmental Philosophy: From Animal Rights to Radical Ecology*, edited by Michael E. Zimmerman et al., 116–29. 4th ed. Upper Saddle River, NJ: Pearson, 2005.

Cameron, Michael. "Signs." In *Augustine through the Ages: An Encyclopedia*, edited by Alan D. Fitzgerald, 793–98. Grand Rapids: Eerdmans, 1999.

Campbell, Richard. *Truth and Historicity*. Oxford: Clarendon, 1992.

Casiday, A. M. C. *Tradition and Theology in St. John Cassian*. Oxford Early Christian Studies. Oxford: Oxford University Press, 2007.

Cassian, John. *The Conferences*. Translated by Boniface Ramsey. New York; Mahwah, NJ: Paulist, 1997.

———. *The Twelve Books on the Institutes of the Coenobia and the Remedies for the Eight Principal Faults*. Online. http://documentacatholicaomnia.eu/o3d/0360-0435,_Cassianus,_Institutes_Of_The_Coenobia_And_The_Remedies_Vol_3,_EN.pdf.

Cassirer, Ernst. "The Concept of Thing and the Concept of Relation." In *Substance and Function & Einstein's Theory of Relativity*, by Ernst Cassirer, 3–233. Translated by William Curtis Swabey and Marie Collins Swabey. New York: Dover, 1953.

———. *The Individual and the Cosmos in Renaissance Philosophy*. Translated by Mario Domandi. Chicago: University of Chicago Press, 2010.

———. *Mythical Thought*. Vol. 2 of *The Philosophy of Symbolic Forms*. Translated by Ralph Manheim. New Haven, CT: Yale University Press, 1968.

———. *The Philosophy of the Enlightenment*. Translated by Fritz C. A. Koelln and James P. Pettegrove. Boston: Beacon, 1960.

———. *The Platonic Renaissance in England*. Translated by James P. Pettegrove. Austin: University of Texas Press, 1953.

Cavarnos, Constantine. *The Classical Theory of Relations: A Study in the Metaphysics of Plato, Aristotle, and Thomism*. Belmont, MA: Institute for Byzantine and Modern Greek Studies, 1975.

———. *The Hellenic-Christian Philosophical Tradition*. Belmont, MA: Institute for Byzantine and Modern Greek Studies, 1989.

Ceric, Mustafa. "Judaism, Christianity, Islam: Hope or Fear of Our Times." In *Beyond Violence: Religious Sources of Social Transformation in Judaism, Christianity, and Islam*, edited by James L. Heft, 43–56. New York: Fordham University Press, 2004.

Chadwick, Henry. *The Sentences of Sextus: A Contribution to the History of Early Christian Ethics*. Texts and Studies: Contributions to Biblical and Patristic Literature NS 5. Cambridge: Cambridge University Press, 1959.

Chadwick, Owen. *John Cassian*. 2nd ed. Cambridge: Cambridge University Press, 1968.

Charles-Saget, Annick. *L'architecture du divin: Mathématique et philosophie chez Plotin et Proclus*. Paris: Les Belles Lettres, 1982.

Chatterjee, P. *Nationalist Thought and the Colonial World: A Derivative Discourse*. Minneapolis: University of Minnesota Press, 1986.

Chauvet, Louis-Marie. *Symbol and Sacrament: A Sacramental Reinterpretation of Christian Existence*. Translated by Patrick Madigan and Madeline Beaumont. Collegeville, MN: Pueblo/Liturgical, 1995.

Checker, Melissa. "Double Jeopardy: Carbon Offsets and Human Rights Abuses." *Counterpunch*, September 9, 2009. Online. https://www.counterpunch.org/2009/09/09/double-jeopardy-carbon-offsets-and-human-rights-abuses.

Chenu, Marie-Dominique. "The Symbolist Mentality." In *Nature, Man and Society in the Twelfth Century: Essays on New Theological Perspectives in the Latin West*, edited by Jerome Taylor and Lester K. Little, 99–145. Preface by Étienne Gilson. Toronto: University of Toronto Press; Medieval Academy of America, 1997.

Chevalier, Irénée. *S. Augustin et la pensée grecque. Les relations trinitaires*. Fribourg: Collectanea Friburgensia, 1940.

Chlup, Radek. *Proclus: An Introduction*. Cambridge: Cambridge University Press, 2012.

Clark, Mary T. "Introduction." In *Theological Treatises on the Trinity*, by Victorinus, 3–44. Translated by Mary T. Clark. Washington, DC: Catholic University Press of America, 1981.

Cleary, John J. "On the Terminology of 'Abstraction' in Aristotle." *Phronesis* 30.1 (1985) 13–45.

Closmann, Charles. "Nazi Germany's Reich Nature Protection Law of 1935." In *How Green Were the Nazis?*, edited by Franz-Josef Brüggemeier et al., 18–42. Athens: Ohio University Press, 2005.

Coakley, Sara, and Martin A. Nowak. "Introduction: Why Cooperation Makes a Difference." In *Evolution, Games, and God: The Principle of Cooperation*, edited by Sara Coakley and Martin A. Nowak, 1–34. Cambridge, MA: Harvard University Press, 2013.

Cochrane, Charles Norris. "Augustine and the Problem of Power." In *Augustine and the Problem of Power: The Essays and Lectures of Charles Norris Cochrane*, edited by David Beer, 26–102. Eugene, OR: Cascade, 2017.

———. *Christianity and Classical Culture: A Study of Thought and Action from Augustus to Augustine*. Indianapolis, IN: Amagi, 2003.
Colish, Marcia L. *The Stoic Tradition from Antiquity to the Early Middle Ages*. Vol. 1. Leiden: Brill, 1985.
Collingwood, R. G. *An Autobiography and Other Writings*. Edited by David Boucher and Teresa Smith. Oxford: Oxford University Press, 2013.
———. "Correspondence with the Clarendon Press Concerning C. N. Cochrane, *Christianity and Classical Culture*." Received from James Connelly in correspondence with the author and used with his permission. Partially available in *R. G. Collingwood: A Research Companion*, edited by James Connelly et al., 87–90. Clar67–Clar78. London: Bloomsbury, 2015.
———. *An Essay on Metaphysics*. Oxford: Clarendon, 1940.
———. *An Essay on Philosophical Method*. Oxford: Clarendon, 1933.
———. "Fascism and Nazism." *Philosophy* 15.58 (1940) 168–76.
———. *The Idea of History*. Edited by Jan Van Der Dussen. Rev. ed. Oxford: Oxford University Press, 2005.
———. *The New Leviathan or Man, Society, Civilization and Barbarism*. Edited by David Boucher. Rev. ed. Oxford: Clarendon, 1992.
———. "Political Action." *Proceedings of the Aristotelian Society* 29 (1929) 155–76.
———. *The Principles of History and Other Writings in Philosophy of History*. Edited by W. H. Dray and W. J. van der Dussen. Oxford: Oxford University Press, 1999.
———. "What 'Civilization' Means." In *The New Leviathan or Man, Society, Civilization and Barbarism*, by R. G. Collingwood, 480–512. Rev. ed. Oxford: Clarendon, 1992.
Connelly, James. "Collingwood, Gentile, and Italian Neo-Idealism in Britain." *Collingwood and British Idealism Studies* 20.1–2 (2014) 205–34.
———. *Metaphysics, Method, and Politics: The Political Philosophy of R. G. Collingwood*. Exeter, UK: Imprint Academic, 2003.
Connelly, James, et al. *Politics and the Environment: From Theory to Practice*. 3rd ed. New York: Routledge, 2012.
Cooper, John W. *Panentheism—The Other God of the Philosophers: From Plato to the Present*. Grand Rapids: Baker Academic, 2006.
Corbin, Henry. *Avicenna and the Visionary Recital*. Translated by W. R. Trask. Princeton, NJ: Princeton University Press, 1988.
Cornford, F. M. *From Religion to Philosophy: A Study in the Origins of Western Speculation*. New York: Harper & Brothers, 1957.
———. "Mathematics and Dialectic in the *Republic* VI–VII (I)." *Mind* 41.161 (1932) 37–52.
———. "Mathematics and Dialectic in the *Republic* VI–VII (II)." *Mind* 41.162 (1932) 173–90.
Costanza, Robert, et al. "The Value of the World's Ecosystem Services and Natural Capital." *Nature* 387 (1997) 253–60.
Cottingham, John G. *Descartes*. Oxford: Blackwell, 1986.
Courtenay, William J. "Antiqui and Moderni in Late Medieval Thought." *Journal of the History of Ideas* 48.1 (1987) 3–10.
Cox Miller, Patricia. *The Corporeal Imagination: Signifying the Holy in Late Ancient Christianity*. Philadelphia: University of Pennsylvania Press, 2009.
———. "Origen and the Bestial Soul: A Poetics of Nature." *Vigiliae Christianae* 36.2 (1982) 115–40.

———. "The Physiologus: A Poiēsis of Nature." *Church History* 52.4 (1983) 433–43.

———. "Pleasure of the Text, Text of Pleasure: Eros and Language in Origen's Commentary on the Song of Songs." *Journal of the American Academy of Religion* 54.2 (1986) 241–53.

Crane, Stephen. *The Open Boat and Other Stories*. Mineola, NY: Dover, 1993.

Croce, Benedetto. *The Philosophy of Giambattista Vico*. Translated by R. G. Collingwood. New York: Macmillan, 1913.

Crosby, Alfred W. *Ecological Imperialism: The Biological Expansion of Europe, 900–1900*. Cambridge: Cambridge University Press, 1986.

Cross, Richard. *Duns Scotus*. Great Medieval Thinkers. Oxford: Oxford University Press, 1999.

Crouzel, Henri. *Théologie de l'Image de Dieu chez Origène*. Paris: Aubier-Montaigne, 1956.

Cullen, Christopher M. *Bonaventure*. Great Medieval Thinkers. Oxford: Oxford University Press, 2006.

Cunningham, David S. *These Three Are One: The Practice of Trinitarian Theology*. Oxford: Blackwell, 1998.

Davies, Oliver. "The Sign Redeemed: A Study in Christian Fundamental Semiotics." *Modern Theology* 19.2 (2003) 219–41.

Deacon, Terrence. *Incomplete Nature: How Mind Emerged from Matter*. New York: Norton, 2011.

———. "What Is Missing from Theories of Information?" In *Information and the Nature of Reality*, edited by Paul Davies and Niels Henrik Gregersen, 186–216. Cambridge: Cambridge University Press, 2010.

Deason, Gary B. "Reformation Theology and the Mechanistic Conception of Nature." In *God and Nature: Historical Essays on the Encounter between Christianity and Science*, edited by David C. Lindberg and Ronald L. Numbers, 167–91. Berkeley: University of California Press, 1986.

Deely, John. *Four Ages of Understanding: The First Postmodern Survey of Philosophy from Ancient Times to the Turn of the Twenty-First Century*. Toronto Studies in Semiotics and Communication. Toronto: University of Toronto Press, 2001.

———. *Medieval Philosophy Redefined: The Development of Cenoscopic Science, AD 354 to 1644 (From the Birth of Augustine to the Death of Poinsot)*. Scranton, PA: University of Scranton Press, 2010.

———. "Postmodernity as the Unmasking of Objectivity: Identifying the Positive Essence of Postmodernity as a New Era in the History of Philosophy." *Semiotica* 183.1.4 (2011) 31–57.

Deleuze, Gilles. *The Logic of Sense*. Edited by Constantin V. Boundas. Translated by M. Lester and Charles Stivale. New York: Columbia University Press, 1990.

———. *Proust and Signs: The Complete Text*. Translated by Richard Howard. Theory Out of Bounds 17. Minneapolis: University of Minnesota Press, 2000.

Dennett, Daniel C. *Breaking the Spell: Religion as a Natural Phenomenon*. New York: Viking, 2006.

Derrida, Jacques. "The Force of Law: 'The Mystical Foundation of Authority.'" *Cardozo Law Review* 11.5–6 (1990) 919–1046.

Descartes, René. "Discourse on the Method of Rightly Conducting the Reason." In vol. 1 of *The Philosophical Works of Descartes*, edited by Elizabeth S. Haldane and G. R. T. Ross, 79–130. Cambridge: Cambridge University Press, 1968.

———. "Letter to Mersenne: 20 November 1629." In *Descartes: Philosophical Letters*, edited by Anthony Kenny, 5–9. Oxford: Clarendon, 1970.

———. "Meditations on First Philosophy." In *Descartes: Selected Philosophical Writings*, edited by John Cottingham et al., 73–122. Cambridge: Cambridge University Press, 1998.

———. "Objections and Replies." In *Descartes: Selected Philosophical Writings*, edited by John Cottingham et al., 123–59. Cambridge: Cambridge University Press, 1998.

———. "The Principles of Philosophy." In vol. 1 of *The Philosophical Works of Descartes*, edited by Elizabeth S. Haldane and G. R. T. Ross, 201–302. Cambridge: Cambridge University Press, 1968.

———. "The Principles of Philosophy." In *Descartes: Selected Philosophical Writings*, edited by John Cottingham et al., 160–212. Cambridge: Cambridge University Press, 1998.

———. "Rules for the Direction of Our Native Intelligence." In *Descartes: Selected Philosophical Writings*, edited by John Cottingham et al., 1–19. Cambridge: Cambridge University Press, 1998.

———. "The World and Treatise on Man." In vol. 1 of *The Philosophical Writings of Descartes*, edited by John Cottingham et al., 79–108. Cambridge: Cambridge University Press, 1985.

DesJardins, Joseph R. *Environmental Ethics: Case Studies*. Toronto: Wadsworth, 2001.

Devall, Bill, and George Sessions. *Deep Ecology: Living as if Nature Mattered*. Salt Lake City: Peregrine Smith, 1985.

Dewan, Lawrence. "The Importance of Substance." In *Form and Being: Studies in Thomistic Metaphysics*, by Lawrence Dewan, 96–130. Studies in Philosophy and the History of Philosophy 45. Washington, DC: Catholic University Press of America Press, 2006.

———. "St. Thomas and the Distinction between Form and *Esse* in Caused Things." In *Form and Being: Studies in Thomistic Metaphysics*, by Lawrence Dewan, 188–204. Studies in Philosophy and the History of Philosophy 45. Washington, DC: Catholic University Press of America Press, 2006.

———. *St. Thomas and Form as Something Divine in Things*. The Aquinas Lecture 2007. Milwaukee, WI: Marquette University Press, 2007.

———. "St. Thomas, Ideas, and Immediate Knowledge." *Dialogue* 18.3 (1979) 392–404.

Dixon, Paul S. "The Evil Restraint in 2 Thess 2:6." *Journal of the Evangelical Theological Society* 33.4 (1990) 445–49.

Dominick, Raymond H., III. "The Völkisch Temptation." In *The Environmental Movement in Germany: Prophets & Pioneers, 1871–1971*, by Raymond H. Dominick III, 81–115. Bloomington: Indiana University Press, 1992.

Donne, John. *The Sermons of John Donne*. Vol. 3. Edited by George R. Potter and Evelyn M. Simpson. Berkeley: University of California Press, 1953–1962.

D'Oro, Giuseppina. *Collingwood and the Metaphysics of Experience*. London: Routledge, 2002.

———. "Unlikely Bedfellows? Collingwood, Carnap, and the Internal/External Distinction." *British Journal for the History of Philosophy* 23.4 (2015) 802–17.

Dourley, John P. "Jacob Boehme and Paul Tillich on Trinity and God: Similarities and Differences." *Religious Studies* 31.4 (1995) 429–45.

Doyle, John P. "Introduction." In *On Real Relation (Disputatio Metaphyica XLVII)*, by Francisco Suárez, 9–29. Translated by John P. Doyle. Milwaukee, WI: Marquette University Press, 2006.
Drake, H. A. *Constantine and the Bishops: The Politics of Intolerance*. Baltimore, MD: Johns Hopkins University Press, 2000.
Drozdek, Adam. *In the Beginning Was the Apeiron: Infinity in Greek Philosophy*. Stuttgart: Franz Steiner Verlag, 2008.
Drury, Shadia B. *Political Ideas of Leo Strauss*. New York: Palgrave Macmillan, 2005.
Dryzek, John S., and David Schlosberg, eds. *Debating the Earth: The Environmental Politics Reader*. Oxford: Oxford University Press, 2005.
Duchrow, Ulrich, and Franz J. Hinkelammert. *Property for People, Not for Profit: Alternatives to the Global Tyranny of Capital*. Translated by Elaine Griffiths et al. London: CIIR, 2004.
Dummett, Michael. "The Philosophical Significance of Gödel's Theorem." *Ratio* 5 (1963) 140–55.
Dunham, Scott A. "The Ecological Violence of Apocalyptic Eschatology." *Studies in Religion/Sciences Religieuses* 32.1–2 (2003) 101–12.
Eagleton, Terry. *The Ideology of the Aesthetic*. Oxford: Blackwell, 1990.
———. *Reason, Faith, and Revolution: Reflections on the God Debate*. New Haven, CT: Yale University Press, 2009.
Eckersley, Robyn. *The Green State: Rethinking Democracy and Sovereignty*. Cambridge, MA: MIT Press, 2004.
Eco, Umberto. *A Theory of Semiotics*. Bloomington: Indiana University Press, 1976.
Edwards, Denis. *The God of Evolution: A Trinitarian Theology*. Mahwah, NJ: Paulist, 1999.
Emery, Gilles. *The Trinitarian Theology of St. Thomas Aquinas*. Translated by Francesca Aran Murphy. Oxford: Oxford University Press, 2007.
Emmeche, Claus, and Kalevi Kull, eds. *Towards A Semiotic Biology: Life is the Action of Signs*. London: Imperial College Press, 2011.
Escobar, Arturo. *Encountering Development: The Making and Unmaking of the Third World*. Princeton, NJ: Princeton University Press, 1995.
Eunomius. *Eunomius: The Extant Works*. Translated by Richard Paul Vaggione. Oxford Early Christian Texts. Oxford: Clarendon, 1987.
Euripides. *The Bacchae*. Translated by Michael Cacoyannis. New York: Meridian, 1987.
Evans, Robert F. *Pelagius: Inquiries and Reappraisals*. New York: Seabury, 1968.
Fackenheim, Emil L. "Man and His World in the Perspective of Judaism: Reflections on Expo '67." In *New Theology 5*, edited by Martin E. Marty and Dean G. Peerman, 56–71. Toronto: Collier-Macmillan, 1969.
———. "Metaphysics and Historicity." In *The God Within: Kant, Schelling, and Historicity*, by Emil Fackenheim, 122–47. Toronto: University of Toronto Press, 1996.
Farrington, B. *The Philosophy of Francis Bacon: An Essay on Its Development from 1603 to 1609, with New Translations of Fundamental Texts*. Liverpool: Liverpool University Press, 1964.
Favareau, Donald. "Understanding Natural Constructivism." *Semiotica* 172.1/4 (2008) 489–528.
Ferguson, Everett. *Backgrounds of Early Christianity*. 3rd ed. Grand Rapids: Eerdmans, 2003.

Ferré, Frederick. "Persons in Nature: Toward an Applicable and Unified Environmental Ethics." *Ethics and the Environment* 1 (1996) 15–25.

Ferry, Luc. *The New Ecological Order*. Translated by Carol Volk. Chicago: University of Chicago Press, 1995.

Findlen, Paula. "The Janus Faces of Science in the Seventeenth Century: Athanasius Kircher and Isaac Newton." In *Rethinking the Scientific Revolution*, edited by Margaret J. Osler, 221–46. Cambridge: Cambridge University Press, 2000.

Fleet, Barrie. "Introduction." In *On Aristotle's "Categories 7–8,"* by Simplicius, 1–3. Translated by Barrie Fleet. Ithaca, NY: Cornell University Press, 2002.

Flikschuh, Katrin. *Freedom: Contemporary Liberal Perspectives*. Cambridge: Polity, 2007.

Forrester, John. "On Kuhn's Case: Psychoanalysis and Paradigm." *Critical Inquiry* 33.4 (2007) 782–819.

Foster, Jay. "Between Economics and Capital: Some Historical and Historical Considerations for Modelers of Natural Capital." *Environmental Monitoring and Assessment* 86 (2003) 63–74.

Foster, M. B. "Christian Theology and Modern Science of Nature." *Mind* 44 (1935) 439–66.

Foucault, Michel. *The Birth of Biopolitics*. Edited by Arnold I. Davidson. Translated by Graham Burchell. Lectures at the Collège de France 1978–1979. New York: Palgrave Macmillan, 2008.

———. *Discipline and Punish: The Birth of the Prison*. Translated by Alan Sheridan. New York: Vintage, 1979.

———. "The Ethic of Care for the Self as a Practice of Freedom: An Interview with Michel Foucault on January 20, 1984." Translated by J. D. Gauthier. *Philosophy & Social Criticism* 12.2–3 (1987) 112–31.

———. *Lectures on the Will to Know*. Edited by Arnold I. Davidson. Translated by Graham Burchell. Lectures at the Collège de France 1970–1971. New York: Palgrave Macmillan, 2013.

———. *Les Mots et les choses*. Paris: Gallimard, 1966.

———. "Omnes et Singulatim: Towards a Criticism of Political Reason." Lectures delivered at Stanford University, October 10 and 16, 1979. *The Tanner Lectures On Human Values*. Online. https://tannerlectures.utah.edu/_documents/a-to-z/f/foucault81.pdf

———. *On the Government of the Living*. Edited by Arnold I. Davidson. Translated by Graham Burchell. Lectures at the Collège de France 1979–1980. New York: Palgrave Macmillan, 2014.

———. *The Order of Things: An Archaeology of the Human Sciences*. Translated by A. M. S. Smith. London: Routledge, 2002.

———. *Security, Territory, Population*. Edited by Arnold I. Davidson. Translated by Graham Burchell. Lectures at the Collège de France 1977–1978. New York: Palgrave Macmillan, 2007.

Fox, Brian J. "Carl Schmitt and Political Catholicism: Friend or Foe?" PhD diss., City University of New York, 2015.

Frame, James Everett. *A Critical and Exegetical Commentary on the Epistles of St Paul to the Thessalonians*. International Critical Commentary on the Holy Scriptures of the Old and New Testaments 38. Edinburgh: T & T Clark, 1912.

Francis. *Encyclical on Climate Change and Inequality: On Care for Our Common Home.* Brooklyn; London: Melville, 2015.

Fransen, Piet F. "Augustine, Pelagius and the Controversy on the Doctrine of Grace." *Louvain Studies* 12.2 (1987) 172–81.

Frey, R. G. "Utilitarianism and Animals." In *The Oxford Handbook of Animal Ethics*, edited by Tom L. Beauchamp and R. G. Frey, 172–97. Oxford: Oxford University Press, 2011.

Furton, Edward J. "Constitution of the Object in Kant and Poinsot." *The Review of Metaphysics* 51.1 (1997) 55–75.

Gadamer, Hans-Georg. "Dialectic and Sophism in Plato's *Seventh Letter*." In *Dialogue and Dialectic: Eight Hermeneutical Studies on Plato*, by Hans-Georg Gadamer, 93–123. Translated by P. Christopher Smith. New Haven, CT: Yale University Press, 1980.

———. *Plato's Dialectical Ethics: Phenomenological Interpretations Relating to the Philebus.* Translated by Robert M. Wallace. New Haven, CT: Yale University Press, 1991.

———. *Truth and Method.* Translated by Garrett Barden and John Cumming. New York: Crossroad, 1982.

Galen. *Three Treatises on the Natural Sciences.* Translated by R. Walzer and M. Frede. Indianapolis, IN: Hackett, 1985.

Galilei, Galileo. "The Assayer." In *Discoveries and Opinions of Galileo*, edited by Stillman Drake, 229–80. Garden City, NY: Anchor/Doubleday, 1957.

Galtung, Johan. "Cultural Violence." *Journal of Peace Research* 27.3 (1990) 291–305.

Gare, Arran E. *The Philosophical Foundations of Ecological Civilization: A Manifesto for the Future.* Routledge Environmental Humanities. New York: Routledge, 2017.

———. *Postmodernism and the Environmental Crisis.* New York: Routledge, 1995.

Garland, Robert. *The Piraeus: From the Fifth to the First Century BC.* London: Duckworth, 1987.

Gaukroger, Stephen. *Descartes: An Intellectual Biography.* Oxford: Oxford University Press, 1995.

Geréby, György. "Political Theology versus Theological Politics: Erik Peterson and Carl Schmitt." *New German Critique* 35.3 (2008) 7–33.

Gerson, Lloyd P. "Categories and the Tradition." In *Plotinus: Arguments of the Philosophers*, edited by Ted Honderich, 79–103. London: Routledge, 1994.

Geus, Marius de. *Ecological Utopias: Envisioning the Sustainable Society.* Utrecht: International, 1999.

Gilbert, N. W. "Ockham, Wyclif, and the 'Via Moderna.'" *Miscellanea Mediaevalia* 9 (1974) 85–125.

Gillespie, Michael Allen. "Descartes and the Origin of Modernity." Paper presented at the American Political Science Association, Boston Marriott Copley Place, Boston, MA, August 28, 2002. Online. http://citation.allacademic.com/meta/p66660_index.html.

———. "Descartes and the Question of Toleration." In *Early Modern Skepticism and the Origins of Toleration*, edited by Alan Levine, 103–26. Lanham, MD: Lexington, 1999.

———. *Nihilism Before Nietzsche.* Chicago: University of Chicago Press, 1995.

Gilson, Étienne. *The Christian Philosophy of Saint Augustine.* Translated by L. E. M. Lynch. New York: Random House, 1960.

———. *The Elements of Christian Philosophy*. Garden City, NY: Doubleday, 1960.
———. *History of Christian Philosophy in the Middle Ages*. New York: Random, 1955.
———. *The Philosophy of St. Bonaventure*. Translated by Dom Illtyd Trethowan and Frank J. Sheed. Paterson, NJ: St. Anthony Guild, 1965.
———. *The Unity of Philosophical Experience*. New York: Scribner's Sons, 1950.
Girard, René. "Dionysus versus the Crucified." *MLN* 99.4 (1984) 816–35.
———. "Dionysus and the Violent Genesis of the Sacred." Translated by Sandor Goodhart. *boundary 2* 5.2 (1977) 487–506.
———. "Innovation and Repetition." *Substance* 19.2/3 (1990) 7–20.
———. *Things Hidden since the Foundation of the World*. Translated by Stephen Bann and Michael Metteer. Stanford, CA: Stanford University Press, 1987.
———. *Violence and the Sacred*. Translated by Patrick Gregory. Baltimore, MD: Johns Hopkins University Press, 1979.
Gould, Stephen Jay. "The Golden Rule: A Proper Scale for our Environmental Crisis." *Natural History* 99.9 (1990) 24–30.
———. *The Structure of Evolutionary Theory*. Cambridge, MA: Belknap/Harvard University Press, 2002.
Gracia, Jorge J. E., and John Kronen. "John of Saint Thomas." In *Individuation in Scholasticism: The Latter Middle Ages and the Counter-Reformation, 1150–1650*, edited by Jorge J. E. Gracia, 511–34. Albany, NY: State University of New York Press, 1994.
Graham, Daniel W., ed. *The Texts of Early Greek Philosophy: The Complete Fragments and Selected Testimonies of the Major Presocratics—Part I*. Translated by Daniel W. Graham. Cambridge: Cambridge University Press, 2010.
Grajewski, Maurice. "The Formal Distinction of Duns Scotus." PhD diss., Catholic University of America, 1944.
Gray, John. *Berlin*. London: Fontana, 1995.
———. *Black Mass: Apocalyptic Religion and the Death of Utopia*. Toronto: Doubleday, 2007.
———. *The Silence of Animals: On Progress and Other Myths*. New York: Farrar, Straus, and Giroux, 2014.
———. *Straw Dogs: Thoughts on Humans and Other Animals*. New York: Farrar, Straus, and Giroux, 2007.
Grayling, A. C. *Descartes: The Life and Times of a Genius*. New York: Walker, 2005.
Green, T. H. *Prolegomena to Ethics*. Edited by A.C. Bradley. 4th ed. Oxford: Clarendon, 1899.
Grim, P. "Spatialization and Greater Generosity in the Stochastic Prisoner's Dilemma." *BioSystems* 37.1–2 (1996) 3–17.
Gunderson, L. H., and C. S. Holling, eds. *Panarchy: Understanding Transformations in Human and Natural Systems*. Washington, DC: Island, 2001.
Habermas, Jürgen. *The Future of Human Nature*. Translated by Hella Beister et al. Cambridge: Polity, 2003.
Hadot, Ilsetraut. *Simplicius: sa vie, son oeuvre, sa survie*. Berlin: de Gruyter, 1987.
Hadot, Pierre. *The Veil of Isis: An Essay on the History of the Idea of Nature*. Translated by Michael Chase. Cambridge, MA: Belknap/Harvard University Press, 2008.
Hanby, Michael. "Augustine and Descartes: An Overlooked Chapter in the Story of Modern Origins." *Modern Theology* 19.4 (2003) 455–82.
———. *Augustine and Modernity*. London: Routledge, 2003.

———. "Reconsiderations: The Central Arguments of *Augustine and Modernity*." *Ars Disputandi* 7 (2007) 43–53.

Haraway, Donna. *When Species Meet*. Posthumanities 3. Minneapolis: University of Minnesota Press, 2008.

Harris, Errol E. "Collingwood On Eternal Problems." *The Philosophical Quarterly* 1.3 (1951) 228–41.

Harris, H. S. "Introduction." In *Genesis and Structure of Society*, by Giovanni Gentile, 1–20. Translated by H. S. Harris. Urbana: Illinois University Press, 1960.

Harrison, Peter. *The Fall of Man and the Foundations of Science*. Cambridge: Cambridge University Press, 2007.

———. "Original Sin and the Problem of Knowledge in Early Modern Europe." *Journal of the History of Ideas* 63.2 (2002) 239–59.

———. *The Territories of Science and Religion*. Chicago: University of Chicago Press, 2015.

Harrison, Verna. "Perichoresis in the Greek Fathers." *St. Vladimir's Theological Quarterly* 35.1 (1991) 53–65.

Harvey, David. *A Brief History of Neoliberalism*. Oxford: Oxford University Press, 2005.

———. *Justice, Nature, and the Geography of Difference*. Oxford: Blackwell, 1997.

Hawken, Paul, et al. *Natural Capitalism: Creating the Next Industrial Revolution*. New York: Little, Brown, 1999.

Hayek, F. A. *The Fatal Conceit: The Errors of Socialism*. Vol. 1 of *The Collected Works*. Edited by W. W. Bartley III. Chicago: University of Chicago Press, 1991.

———. *The Road to Serfdom*. Chicago: University of Chicago Press, 1991.

Hayes, Zachary. *The Gift of Being: A Theology of Creation*. New Theology Studies 10. Collegeville, MN: Michael Glazier/Liturgical, 2001.

Heft, James L. "Introduction: Religious Sources for Social Transformation in Judaism, Christianity, and Islam." In *Beyond Violence: Religious Sources of Social Transformation in Judaism, Christianity, and Islam*, edited by James L. Heft, 1–14. New York: Fordham University Press, 2004.

Heidegger, Martin. *The Basic Problems of Phenomenology*. Translated by Albert Hofstadter. Bloomington: Indiana University Press, 1988.

———. *Being and Time*. Translated by John Macquarrie and Edward Robinson. New York: Harper & Row, 1962.

———. *Contributions to Philosophy (Of the Event)*. Translated by Richard Rojcewicz and Daniela Vallega-Neu. Bloomington: Indiana University Press, 2012.

———. "The End of Philosophy." In *On Time and Being*, by Martin Heidegger, 55–73. Translated by Joan Stambaugh. New York: Harper & Row, 1972.

———. *The Essence of Reasons*. Translated by Terrence Malick. Evanston, IL: Northwestern University Press, 1969.

———. *The Fundamental Concepts of Metaphysics: World, Finitude, Solitude*. Bloomington: Indiana University Press, 2001.

———. "The Question Concerning Technology." In *The Question Concerning Technology and Other Essays*, by Martin Heidegger, 3–35. Translated by William Lovitt. New York: Harper, 1977.

———. *Schelling's Treatise on the Essence of Human Freedom*. Translated by Joan Stambaugh. Athens: Ohio University Press, 1985.

Henninger, Mark G. *Relations: Medieval Theories (1250–1325)*. Oxford: Clarendon, 1989.

Hintikka, Jaakko. *Lingua Universalis versus Calculus Ratiocinator: An Ultimate Presupposition of Twentieth-Century Philosophy*. Dordrecht: Kluwer, 1997.
Hinz, Michael. *Self-Creation and History: Collingwood and Nietzsche on Conceptual Change*. Lanham, MD: University Press of America, 1993.
Hitchens, Christopher. *God Is Not Great: How Religion Poisons Everything*. New York: Twelve, 2007.
Hobbes, Thomas. *Leviathan*. Edited by C. B. Macpherson. London: Pelican, 1968.
Hollingworth, Miles. *Pilgrim City: St. Augustine of Hippo and His Innovation in Political Thought*. London: T & T Clark, 2010.
Horkheimer, Max, and Theodor W. Adorno. *Dialectic of Enlightenment*. Translated by John Cumming. New York: Herder & Herder, 1972.
Hughes, Christopher. "Matter and Actuality in Aquinas." In *Thomas Aquinas: Contemporary Philosophical Perspectives*, edited by Brian Davies, 61–76. Oxford: Oxford University Press, 2002.
Husserl, Edmund. *The Crisis of European Sciences and Transcendental Phenomenology: An Introduction to Phenomenological Philosophy*. Translated by David Carr. Evanston, IL: Northwestern University Press, 1970.
Ignatieff, Michael. *Isaiah Berlin: A Life*. Toronto: Viking, 1998.
———. *The Lesser Evil: Political Ethics in the Age of Terror*. Toronto: Penguin, 2004.
Immler, Hans. *Natur in der ökonomischen Theorie*. Opladen: Verlag, 1985.
Innis, Harold. "Obituaries: Charles Norris Cochrane, 1889–1945." *The Canadian Journal of Economics and Political Science* 12 (1945) 95–97.
Jaspers, Karl. *Plato And Augustine*. Edited by Hannah Arendt. Translated by Ralph Manheim. New York: Harcourt Brace, 1962.
Jauss, Hans Robert. "Literary History as a Challenge to Literary Theory." *New Literary History* 2.1 (1970) 7–37.
Jenkins, Willis. "Biodiversity and Salvation: Thomistic Roots for Environmental Ethics." *The Journal of Religion* 83.3 (2003) 401–20.
Ji, Sungchul. "Semiotics of Life: A Unified Theory of Molecular Machines, Cells, the Mind, Peircean Signs, and the Universe based on the Principle of Information-Energy Complementarity." Paper presented at the XVII Tarragona Seminar on Formal Syntax and Semantics, Rovira i Virgili University, Tarragona, Spain, April 23–27, 2003. *Cell Language* (blog). Online. http://www.conformon.net/wp-content/uploads/2012/12/SOLManuscriptsubmitted_final_downloaded_from_Taragona_09032011_modified_07282012.pdf.
Jonas, Hans. "Epilogue: Gnosticism, Existentialism, and Nihilism." In *The Gnostic Religion: The Message of the Alien God and the Beginnings of Christianity*, by Hans Jonas, 320–39. Boston: Beacon, 2001.
———. "The Meaning of Cartesianism for the Theory of Life." In *The Phenomenon of Life: Toward a Philosophical Biology*, by Hans Jonas, 58–63. Evanston, IL: Northwestern University Press, 2001.
Judt, Tony. *Postwar: A History of Europe Since 1945*. London: Penguin, 2005.
Judt, Tony, and Timothy Snyder. *Thinking the Twentieth Century*. New York: Penguin, 2012.
Kant, Immanuel. *Groundwork of the Metaphysic of Morals*. Translated by H. J. Paton. New York: Harper & Row, 1964.
———. *Lectures on Ethics*. Translated by Peter Heath. Cambridge: Cambridge University Press, 1997.

———. *The Metaphysical Principles of Virtue: Part II of The Metaphysics of Morals*. Translated by James Ellington. Indianapolis, IN: Bobbs Merrill, 1964.

Karsten, Siegfried G. "Nature in Economic Theories: Hans Immler Traces Recognition of the Environment—and Its Neglect—in Various Classics." *American Journal of Economics and Sociology* 46.1 (1987) 61–70.

Keech, Dominic. *The Anti-Pelagian Christology of Augustine of Hippo, 396–430*. Oxford: Oxford University Press, 2012.

Kenny, Anthony. *The God of the Philosophers*. Oxford: Clarendon, 1979.

———. *The Rise of Modern Philosophy*. Vol. 3 of *A New History of Western Philosophy*. Oxford: Oxford University Press, 2006.

Kirk, G. S., and J. E. Raven. *The Presocratic Philosophers: A Critical History with a Selection of Texts*. Cambridge: Cambridge University Press, 1966.

Klein, Jacob. *Greek Mathematical Thought and the Origin of Algebra*. Translated by Eva Brann. Cambridge, MA: MIT Press, 1968.

Klein, Naomi. *This Changes Everything: Capitalism vs. The Climate*. Toronto: Knopf, 2014.

Koenker, Ernest B. *Great Dialecticians in Modern Christian Thought*. Minneapolis, MN: Augsburg, 1971.

Koninck, Charles de. "Abstraction from Matter." *Laval Théologique et Philosophique* 13 (1957) 133–96; 16 (1960) 53–69, 169–88.

———. *The Hollow Universe*. Laval, Québec: Les Presses de l'Université Laval, 1964.

Kotsko, Adam. *Neoliberalism's Demons: On the Political Theology of Late Capital*. Stanford, CA: Stanford University Press, 2018.

Koyré, Alexandre. *La philosophie de Jacob Boehme*. 1929. Reprint, New York: Burt Franklin, 1968.

Kroker, Arthur. "Augustine as the Founder of Modern Experience: The Legacy of Charles Norris Cochrane." *The Canadian Journal of Political and Social Theory/ Revue canadienne de théorie politique et sociale* 6.3 (1982) 79–119.

Kropotkin, Peter. "Anarchist Morality." In *Kropotkin's Revolutionary Pamphlets: A Collection of Writings by Peter Kropotkin*, edited by Roger N. Baldwin, 79–113. New York: Dover, 1970.

Kuhn, Thomas S. *The Structure of Scientific Revolutions*. Chicago: University of Chicago Press, 1962.

Ladner, Gerhart B. "Medieval and Modern Understanding of Symbolism: A Comparison." *Speculum* 54.2 (1979) 223–56.

Laslett, Peter. "Introduction." In *Two Treatises of Government*, by John Locke, 3–126. Edited by Peter Laslett. Cambridge: Cambridge University Press, 1988.

Latour, Bruno. *Facing Gaia: Eight Lectures on the New Climatic Regime*. Translated by Catherine Porter. Cambridge: Polity, 2017.

———. "It's Development, Stupid! Or: How To Modernize Modernization." Unpublished essay. 2007. *Bruno Latour*. Online. http://www.bruno-latour.fr/sites/default/files/107-NORDHAUS%26SHELLENBERGER.pdf.

———. *Pandora's Hope: Essays on the Reality of Science Studies*. Cambridge, MA: Harvard University Press, 1999.

———. *Politics of Nature: How to Bring the Sciences into Democracy*. Translated by Catherine Porter. Cambridge, MA: Harvard University Press, 2004.

———. *Reassembling the Social: An Introduction to Actor-Network-Theory*. Oxford: Oxford University Press, 2005.

———. "Will Non-Humans Be Saved? An Argument in Ecotheology." *The Journal of the Royal Anthropological Institute* 15.3 (2009) 459–75.
Lawler, Michael G. *Symbol and Sacrament: A Contemporary Sacramental Theology*. Mahwah, NJ: Paulist, 1987.
Leff, Gordon. *Bradwardine and the Pelagians: A Study of His "De causa Dei" and Its Opponents*. Cambridge: Cambridge University Press, 1957.
Legge, Dominic. *The Trinitarian Christology of St. Thomas Aquinas*. Oxford: Oxford University Press, 2018.
Leibniz, Gottfried Wilhelm. *The Monadology and Other Philosophical Writings*. Translated by Robert Latta. Oxford: Oxford University Press, 1965.
Leiss, William. *The Domination of Nature*. Boston: Beacon, 1974.
Leopold, Aldo. *A Sand County Almanac: And Sketches Here And There*. New York: Oxford University Press, 1966.
Leslie, John. *Value and Existence*. Oxford: Blackwell, 1979.
Levering, Matthew. *Predestination: Biblical and Theological Paths*. Oxford: Oxford University Press, 2011.
Levi, Anthony. "Ficino, Augustine and the Pagans." In *Marsilio Ficino: His Theology, His Philosophy, His Legacy*, edited by Michael J. B. Allen et al., 99–113. Leiden: Brill, 2002.
Levinas, Emmanuel. *Totality and Infinity: An Essay on Exteriority*. Translated by Alphonso Lingis. Pittsburgh, PA: Duquesne University Press, 1969.
Lewis, C. S. *The Problem of Pain: How Human Suffering Raises Almost Intolerable Intellectual Problems*. New York: Macmillan, 1962.
Lisska, Anthony J. *Aquinas's Theory of Perception: An Analytic Reconstruction*. Oxford: Oxford University Press, 2016.
Lloyd, G. E. R. *Polarity and Analogy: Two Types of Argumentation in Early Greek Thought*. Cambridge: Cambridge University Press, 1966.
Locke, John. *The Educational Writings of John Locke*. Cambridge: Cambridge University Press, 1968.
———. *An Essay Concerning Human Understanding*. Edited by A. D. Woozley. New York: Meridan, 1974.
———. *Two Treatises of Government*. Edited by Peter Laslett. Cambridge: Cambridge University Press, 1988.
Long, Christopher P. "Between the Universal and the Singular in Aristotle." *Telos* 126 (2003) 25–40.
Losev, Aleksei Fyodorvich. *The Dialectics of Myth*. Translated by Vladimir Marchenkov. London: Routledge, 2003.
Lossky, Vladimir. *The Mystical Theology of the Eastern Church*. Translated by the Fellowship of St. Alban and St. Sergius. London: James Clarke, 1968.
Lovelock, James. "Gaia as Seen through the Atmosphere." *Atmospheric Environment* 6.8 (1972) 579–80.
———. *The Revenge of Gaia: The Earth's Climate Crisis and the Fate of Humanity*. New York: Basic, 2007.
Lowry, S. Todd. *Archaeology of Economic Ideas: The Classical Greek Tradition*. Durham, NC: Duke University Press, 1988.
Luther, Martin. *Luther's Works*. Vol. 46. Edited by Helmut T. Lehmann and Robert C. Schultz. Philadelphia: Fortress, 1967.

Lyons, Nathan. *Signs in the Dust: A Theory of Natural Culture and Cultural Nature*. Oxford: Oxford University Press, 2019.

MacCallum, Gerald C., Jr. "Negative and Positive Freedom." *The Philosophical Review* 76.3 (1967) 312–34.

MacCulloch, Diarmaid. *Reformation: Europe's House Divided (1490–1700)*. London: Allen Lane, 2003.

MacIntyre, Alasdair. *After Virtue: A Study in Moral Theory*. 3rd ed. Notre Dame: University of Notre Dame Press, 2007.

MacIsaac, D. Gregory. "The Soul and Discursive Reason in the Philosophy of Proclus." PhD diss., University of Notre Dame, 2001.

Malebranche, Nicolas. *The Search after Truth: With Elucidations of the Search after Truth*. Translated by Thomas M. Lennon and Paul J. Olscamp. Cambridge: Cambridge University Press, 1997.

Manetti, Giovanni. *Theories of the Sign in Classical Antiquity*. Translated by Christine Richardson. Bloomington: Indiana University Press, 1993.

Margerie, Bertrand de. *The Christian Trinity in History*. Vol. 1 of *Studies in Historical Theology*. Translated by Edmund J. Fortman. Still River, MA: St. Bede's, 1982.

Marion, Jean-Luc. "Descartes and Onto-Theology." In *Post-Secular Philosophy: Between Philosophy and Theology*, edited by Phillip Blond, 67–106. London: Routledge, 1998.

———. *On Descartes's Passive Thought: The Myth of Cartesian Dualism*. Translated by Christina M. Gschwandtner. Chicago: University of Chicago Press, 2018.

Maritain, Jacques. "Appendix I: The Concept." In *Distinguish to Unite or the Degrees of Knowledge*, by Jacques Maritain, 387–417. Translated by Gerald B. Phelan. New York: Scribner's Sons, 1959.

———. "Language and the Theory of the Sign." In *Language: An Enquiry into Its Meaning and Function*, edited by Ruth Nanda Anshen, 86–101. New York: Harper & Brothers, 1957.

———. "Sign and Symbol." In *Redeeming the Time*, by Jacques Maritain, 191–224. Translated by Henry Lorin Bisse. London: Geoffrey Bles/Centenary, 1944.

———. *True Humanism*. Translated by Margot Adamson. 4th ed. London: Geoffrey Bles/Centenary, 1946.

Markus, R. A. *Saeculum: History and Society in the Theology of St. Augustine*. Cambridge: Cambridge University Press, 1970.

———. *Signs and Meanings: World and Text in Ancient Christianity*. Eugene, OR: Wipf and Stock, 2011.

———. "Signs, Communication, and Communities in Augustine's *De doctrina christiana*." In *De doctrina christiana: A Classic of Western Culture*, edited by Duane W. H. Arnold and Pamela Bright, 97–108. Christianity and Judaism in Antiquity 9. Notre Dame: University of Norte Dame Press, 1995.

———. "St. Augustine on Signs." In *Augustine: A Collection of Critical Essays*, edited by R. A. Markus, 61–85. Garden City, NY: Anchor/Doubleday, 1972.

Marshall, I. Howard. *1 and 2 Thessalonians: Based on the Revised Standard Version*. New Century Bible Commentary. Grand Rapids: Eerdmans, 1983.

Martin, Rex. "Collingwood's Doctrine of Absolute Presuppositions and the Possibility of Historical Knowledge." In *Substance and Form in History: A Collection of Essays in Philosophy of History*, edited by L. Pompa and W. H. Dray, 89–106. Edinburgh: University of Edinburgh Press, 1981.

Martos, Joseph. *Doors to the Sacred: A Historical Introduction to Sacraments in the Catholic Church.* Garden City, NY: Doubleday, 1981.

Marx, Karl. *Grundrisse.* Translated by David McLellan. London: Macmillan, 1971.

Maximus Confessor. *Selected Writings.* Translated by George C. Berthold. Classics of Western Spirituality. Mahwah, NJ: Paulist, 1985.

McCullough, Michael E. *Beyond Revenge: The Evolution of the Forgiveness Instinct.* San Francisco: Jossey-Bass/Wiley, 2008.

McGinn, Bernard. "The Significance of Bonaventure's Theology of History." *The Journal of Religion: Supplement* 58 (1978) s64–s81.

McGrath, S. J. *The Dark Ground of Spirit: Schelling and the Unconscious.* New York: Routledge, 2012.

Meikle, Scott. *Aristotle's Economic Thought.* Oxford: Oxford University Press, 1995.

Merchant, Carolyn. *The Death of Nature: Women, Ecology, and the Scientific Revolution.* San Francisco: Harper & Row, 1980.

———. *Reinventing Eden: The Fate of Nature in Western Culture.* New York: Routledge, 2003.

———. "The Scientific Revolution and *The Death of Nature*." *Isis* 97.3 (2006) 513–33.

———. "Secrets of Nature: The Bacon Debates Revisited." *Journal of the History of Ideas* 69.1 (2008) 147–62.

Merton, Thomas. *Cassian and the Fathers: Initiation into The Monastic Tradition.* Edited by Patrick F. O'Connell. Kalamazoo, MI: Cistercian, 2005.

Midgley, Mary. *Science as Salvation: A Modern Myth and Its Meaning.* London: Routledge, 1992.

Milbank, John. "Theology Without Substance: Christianity, Signs, Origins (Part Two)." *Journal of Literature and Theology* 2.2 (1988) 131–52.

Miller, James. *The Passion of Michel Foucault.* New York: Simon & Schuster, 1993.

Miller, Paula Jean. "Cosmic Semiosis: Contuiting the Divine." *Semiotica* 178.1/4 (2010) 303–44.

Millett, Paul. *Lending and Borrowing in Ancient Athens.* Cambridge: Cambridge University Press, 1991.

Mitchell, Andrew J. *The Fourfold: Reading the Late Heidegger.* Evanston, IL: Northwestern University Press, 2015.

Modrak, Deborah K. W. *Aristotle's Theory of Language and Meaning.* Cambridge: Cambridge University Press, 2009.

Moltmann, Jürgen. "European Political Theology." In *The Cambridge Companion to Christian Political Theology*, edited by Craig Hovey and Elizabeth Phillips, 3–22. Cambridge: Cambridge University Press, 2015.

———. *God in Creation: An Ecological Doctrine of Creation.* Translated by Margaret Kohl. London: SCM, 1985.

Monbiot, George. *Heat: How to Stop the Planet from Burning.* Toronto: Doubleday, 2006.

———. "Mocking Our Dreams." *Guardian*, February 15, 2005. Online. https://www.theguardian.com/society/2005/feb/15/environment.comment.

Mondzain, Marie-José. *Image, Icon, Economy: The Byzantine Origins of the Contemporary Imaginary.* Translated by Rico Franses. Cultural Memory in the Present. Stanford, CA: Stanford University Press, 2004.

Montefiore, Hugh. *Can Man Survive?* London: Fontana, 1970.

Moore, A. W. *The Evolution of Modern Metaphysics: Making Sense of Things*. Cambridge: Cambridge University Press, 2012.

Moore, S. D. "Revolting Revelations." In *The Personal Voice In Biblical Interpretation*, edited by I. R. Kitzberger, 183–200. London: Routledge, 1999.

Morgan, Edward. *The Incarnation of the Word: The Theology of Language of Augustine of Hippo*. London: T & T Clark, 2010.

Moyise, Steve. "Does the Lion Lie down with the Lamb?" In *Studies in the Book of Revelation*, edited by Steve Moyise, 181–94. Edinburgh: T & T Clark, 2001.

Mueller, I. "Mathematics and Philosophy in Proclus's *Commentary on Book I of Euclid's Elements*." In *Proclus lecteur et interprète des anciens*, edited by J. Pépin and H. D. Saffrey, 305–18. Paris: Edition du CNRS, 1987.

Murphy, James Bernard. "Nature, Custom, and Stipulation in the Semiotic of John Poinsot." *Semiotica* 83.1.2 (1991) 33–68.

Murphy, Raymond. *Rationality and Nature: A Sociological Inquiry into a Changing Relationship*. Oxford: Westview, 1994.

Murphy, Richard. *Collingwood and the Crisis of Civilisation: Art, Metaphysics, and Dialectic*. Exeter, UK: Imprint Academic, 2008.

Naess, Arne. "A Defense of the Deep, Long-Range Ecology Movement." *Environmental Ethics* 6 (1984) 264–87.

Nano Science and Technology Institute (NSTI). *Clean Technology: Bio Energy, Renewables, Green Building, Smart Grid, Storage, and Water*. Oxford: CRC/Taylor & Francis, 2008–2019.

Naugle, David K. *Worldview: The History of a Concept*. Grand Rapids: Eerdmans, 2002.

Negri, Antonio. *Marx Beyond Marx: Lessons on the Grundrisse*. Translated by Harry Cleaver et al. London: Pluto, 1991.

Neuman, John von. *Theory of Self-Reproducing Automata*. Edited by A. W. Burks. Urbana: University of Illinois Press, 1966.

Newton, Lisa H. *Ethics and Sustainability: Sustainable Development and the Moral Life*. Upper Saddle River, NJ: Prentice-Hall, 2003.

Nietzsche, Friedrich. *Beyond Good and Evil*. Translated by Walter Kaufman. New York: Vintage, 1966.

———. "Ecce Homo." In *A Nietzsche Reader*, edited by R. J. Hollingdale, 260–62. London: Penguin, 1977.

———. "Twilight of the Idols." In *A Nietzsche Reader*, edited by R. J. Hollingdale, 212, 256. London: Penguin, 1977.

———. *The Will to Power*. Translated by Walter Kaufman and R. J. Hollingdale. New York: Random, 1968.

Nikulin, Dmitri. *Matter, Imagination, and Geometry: Ontology, Natural Philosophy, and Mathematics in Plotinus, Proclus, and Descartes*. Aldershot, UK: Ashgate, 2002.

Norris, Frederick W. *Faith Gives Fullness to Reasoning: The Five Theological Orations of Gregory Nazianzen*. Translated by Lionel Wickham and Frederick Williams. Leiden: Brill, 1991.

Northcott, Michael S. *A Political Theology of Climate Change*. London: SPCK, 2014.

Novak, Ralph Martin. *Christianity and the Roman Empire: Background Texts*. Harrisburg, PA: Trinity, 2001.

Nowak, Martin A. "Five Rules for the Evolution of Cooperation." *Science* 314.5805 (2006) 1560–63.

Nowak, Martin A., and Karl Sigmund. "Tit for Tat in Heterogeneous Populations." *Nature* 355.6357 (1992) 250–52.
Nuchelmans, Gabriël. *Theories of the Proposition: Ancient and Medieval Conceptions of the Bearers of Truth and Falsity*. Linguistic Series 8. Amsterdam: North-Holland, 1973.
Nygren, Anders. *Agape and Eros*. Translated by Phillip S. Watson. New York: Harper & Row, 1969.
Oberman, Heiko A. "*Via Antiqua* and *Via Moderna*: Late Medieval Prolegomena to Early Reformation Thought." *Journal of the History of Ideas* 48.1 (1987) 23–40.
Ochs, Peter. "Reparative Reasoning: From Peirce's Pragmatism to Augustine's Scriptural Semiotic." *Modern Theology* 25.2 (2009) 187–215.
O'Regan, Cyril. "The Trinity in Kant, Hegel, and Schelling." In *The Oxford Handbook of the Trinity*, edited by Gilles Emery and Matthew Levering, 254–66. Oxford: Oxford University Press, 2011.
Origen. *On First Principles*. Introduction by Henri de Lubac. Translated by G. W. Butterworth. New York: Harper & Row, 1966.
Ortigues, Edmond. *Le discours et le symbole*. Paris: Aubier-Montaigne, 1962.
Osler, Margaret J. "Canonical Imperative: Rethinking the Scientific Revolution." In *Rethinking the Scientific Revolution*, edited by Margaret J. Osler, 3–24. Cambridge: Cambridge University Press, 2000.
Owens, Joseph. *Aristotle's Gradation of Being in Metaphysics E–Z*. Edited by Lloyd P. Gerson. South Bend, IN: St. Augustine's, 2007.
———. *The Doctrine of Being in Aristotelian Metaphysics: A Study in the Greek Background of Medieval Thought*. 2nd ed. Toronto: Pontifical Institute of Medieval Studies, 1957.
Pabst, Adrian. *Liberal World Order and Its Critics: Civilizational States and Cultural Commonwealths*. London: Routledge, 2018.
———. *Metaphysics: The Creation of Hierarchy*. Interventions. Grand Rapids: Eerdmans, 2012.
Paine, Scott Randall. "The Seven Signa: Implications of a Medieval Notion." *Mediaevalia: Textos e Estudos* 23 (2004) 51–62.
Palmer, Clare. "The Moral Relevance of the Distinction between Domesticated and Wild Animals." In *The Oxford Handbook of Animal Ethics*, edited by Tom L. Beauchamp and R. G. Frey, 701–25. Oxford: Oxford University Press, 2011.
———. "Stewardship: A Case Study in Environmental Ethics." In *Environmental Stewardship: Critical Perspectives—Past and Present*, edited by R. J. Berry, 63–75. London: T & T Clark, 2006.
Pap, Levente. "Stoic Virtues in Tertullian's Works and Their Relation to Cicero." *Acta Universitatis Sapientiae, Philologica* 6.1 (2014) 7–16.
Parente, Pietro, et al. *Dictionary of Dogmatic Theology*. Translated by Emmanuel Doronzo. Milwaukee, WI: Bruce, 1951.
Pasnau, Robert. *Thomas Aquinas on Human Nature: A Philosophical Study of Summa theologiae Ia, 75–89*. Cambridge: Cambridge University Press, 2002.
Passmore, John. *Man's Responsibility for Nature: Ecological Problems and Western Traditions*. 2nd ed. London: Duckworth, 1980.
———. *The Perfectibility of Man*. London: Duckworth, 1970.
Pattee, H. H. "The Physics of Symbols: Bridging the Epistemic Cut." *BioSystems* 60 (2001) 5–21.

Pearce, Fred. *With Speed and Violence: Why Scientists Fear Tipping Points in Climate Change*. Boston: Beacon, 2007.

Pecknold, C. C. *Transforming Postliberal Theology: George Lindbeck, Pragmatism and Scripture*. London: T & T Clark, 2005.

Peifer, John Frederick. *The Concept in Thomism*. New York: Bookman, 1952.

Pelagius. "Letter to Demetrias." In *The Letters of Pelagius and His Followers*, edited by B. R. Rees, 29–70. Woodbridge, UK: Boydell, 1991.

Pelikan, Jaraslov. *Christianity and Classical Culture: The Metamorphosis of Natural Theology in the Christian Encounter with Hellenism*. New Haven, CT: Yale University Press, 1993.

———. *Imago Dei: The Byzantine Apologia for Icons*. Princeton, NJ: Princeton University Press, 1990.

Peters, Rik. *History as Thought and Action: The Philosophies of Croce, Gentile, de Ruggiero, and Collingwood*. British Idealist Studies, Series Two (Collingwood) 6. Exeter, UK: Imprint Academic, 2013.

Peterson, Erik. "Monotheism as a Political Problem: A Contribution to the History of Political Theology in the Roman Empire." In *Theological Tractates*, by Erik Peterson, edited by Michael J. Hollerich, 68–105. Stanford, CA: Stanford University Press, 2011.

Petty, William. *The Economic Writings of Sir William Petty*. London: C. H. Hull, 1899.

Pickstock, Catherine. "The Late Arrival of Language: Word, Nature, and the Divine in Plato's *Cratylus*." *Modern Theology* 27.2 (2011) 238–62.

Piketty, Thomas. *Capital in the Twenty-First Century*. Translated by Arthur Goldhammer. Cambridge, MA: Harvard University Press, 2014.

Plato. "Cratylus." Translated by C. D. C. Reeve. In *Plato: Complete Works*, edited by John M. Cooper, 101–56. Indianapolis, IN: Hackett, 1997.

———. "Letters: VII." Translated by L. A. Post. In *The Collected Dialogues of Plato (Including the Letters)*, edited by Edith Hamilton and Huntington Cairns, 1574–98. Princeton, NJ: Princeton University Press, 1989.

———. *Statesman*. Translated by J. B. Skemp. Edited by Martin Ostwald. New York: Bobbs-Merrill, 1957.

———. "Theaetetus." Translated by F. M. Cornford. In *The Collected Dialogues of Plato (Including the Letters)*, edited by Edith Hamilton and Huntington Cairns, 845–919. Princeton, NJ: Princeton University Press, 1989.

Plaxco, Kellen. "Didymus the Blind, Origen, and the Trinity." PhD diss., Marquette University, 2016.

Plotinus. *Enneads*. Translated by A. H. Armstrong. 7 vols. LCL. Cambridge, MA: Harvard University Press, 1966–1988.

Poinsot, John (John of St. Thomas). *The Gifts of the Holy Spirit*. Translation by Dominic Hughes. Introduction by Cajetan Cuddy. Tacoma, WA: Cluny, 2016.

———. *Tractatus de Signis: The Semiotic of John Poinsot*. Edited by John Deely. Berkeley: University of California Press, 1985.

Polanyi, Karl. *The Great Transformation: The Political and Economic Origins of Our Time*. Boston: Beacon, 2001.

Polanyi, Michael. "Life's Irreducible Structure." *Science* 160 (1968) 1308–12.

———. "The Logic of Tacit Inference." *Philosophy* 41.155 (1966) 1–18.

———. "Sense-Giving and Sense-Reading." *Philosophy* 42.162 (1967) 301–25.

———. *The Tacit Dimension*. New York: Doubleday, 1967.

Powell, Charles E. "The Identity of the 'Restrainer' in 2 Thessalonians 2:6–7." *Bibliotheca Sacra* 154 (1997) 320–32.

Priestly, Joseph. *An Essay on the First Principles of Government; and on the Nature of Political, Civil, and Religious Liberty*. London: J. Dooley, Pall Mall, 1768. Online. https://oll.libertyfund.org/titles/priestley-an-essay-on-the-first-principles-of-government.

Proclus. *A Commentary on the First Book of Euclid's Elements*. Translation Glenn R. Morrow. Princeton, NJ: Princeton University Press, 1992.

———. *Elements of Theology*. Rev. ed. Translated by E. R. Dodds. Oxford: Clarendon, 2004.

———. *The Theology of Plato*. Translated by Thomas Taylor. Frome, Somerset, UK: Prometheus Trust, 1995.

Proctor, Robert N. *The Nazi War on Cancer*. Princeton, NJ: Princeton University Press, 1999.

Prosch, Harry. *Michael Polanyi: A Critical Exposition*. Albany, NY: State University of New York Press, 1986.

Prozorov, Sergei. "The Katechon in the Age of Biopolitical Nihilism." *Continental Philosophy Review* 45.4 (2012) 483–503.

Przywara, Erich, ed. *An Augustine Synthesis*. New York: Harper & Row, 1958.

Rahner, Karl. *The Trinity*. Translated by Joseph Donceel. New York: Herder & Herder, 1970.

Ramsey, Boniface. "John Cassian and Augustine." In *Grace for Grace: The Debates After Augustine and Pelagius*, edited by Alexander Y. Hwang et al., 114–30. Washington, DC: Catholic University Press of America, 2014.

Randall, John Hermann, Jr. *Aristotle*. New York: Columbia University Press, 1960.

Ratzinger, Joseph. *Introduction to Christianity*. San Francisco: Ignatius, 2004.

———. *The Theology of History in Bonaventure*. Translated by Zachary Hayes. Chicago: Franciscan Herald, 1971.

Rawls, John. *A Theory of Justice*. Cambridge, MA: Harvard University Press, 1971.

Rayman, Joshua. "Ockham's Theory of Natural Signification." *Franciscan Studies* 63 (2005) 289–323.

Rees, R. B. *Pelagius: A Reluctant Heretic*. Woodbridge, UK: Boydell, 1988.

Reesor, Margaret. "The Stoic Categories." *The American Journal of Philology* 78.1 (1957) 63–82.

Regan, Tom. "Animal Rights, Human Wrongs." In *Environmental Philosophy from Animal Rights to Radical Ecology*, edited by Michael E. Zimmerman et al., 39–52. 4th ed. Upper Saddle River, NJ: Pearson, 2005.

———. *The Case for Animal Rights*. Berkeley: University of California Press, 1983.

———. "Ethical Considerations Relevant to the Harvesting of Seals: A Brief Prepared for the Royal Commission on Seals and the Sealing Industry in Canada on Behalf of the International Fund for Animal Welfare." Pamphlet at Memorial University Center of Newfoundland and Labrador Studies, St. John's, NL, Canada. Ottawa: Royal Commission on Seals and the Sealing Industry in Canada, 1985.

Rice, E. F. *The Renaissance Idea of Wisdom*. Cambridge, MA: Harvard University Press, 1958.

Richter, Klemens. *The Meaning of the Sacramental Symbols*. Translated by Linda M. Maloney. Collegeville, MN: Liturgical, 1990.

Ricoeur, Paul. *The Reality of the Historical Past*. The Aquinas Lecture 1984. Milwaukee, WI: Marquette University Press, 1984.
———. "Structure and Hermeneutics." Translated by Kathleen Mclaughlin. In *The Conflict of Interpretations: Essays in Hermeneutics*, by Paul Ricoeur, 27–61. Edited Don Ihde. Evanston, IL: Northwestern University Press, 1974.
Rist, John M. "Categories and Their Uses." In *Problems in Stoicism*, edited by A. A. Long, 38–57. London: Athlone, 1971.
Robin, Léon. *Aristote*. Paris: PUF, 1944.
Robinson, Thomas M. *Logos and Cosmos: Studies in Greek Philosophy*. Sankt Augustin: Academic Verlag, 2008.
Rorem, Paul. *Eriugena's Commentary on the Dionysian Celestial Hierarchy*. Studies and Texts 150. Toronto: Pontifical Institute of Medieval Studies, 2005.
Rorty, Richard. "Truth without Correspondence to Reality." In *Philosophy and Social Hope*, by Richard Rorty, 23–46. London: Penguin, 1999.
Rosen, Stanley. "A Central Ambiguity in Descartes." In *Cartesian Essays: A Collection of Critical Studies*, edited by Bernd Magnus and James B. Wilbur, 17–35. The Hague: Martinus Nijhoff, 1969.
Rosenfield, Leonora Cohen. *From Beast-Machine to Man-Machine: Animal Soul in French Letters from Descartes to La Mettrie*. New York: Octagon, 1968.
Rotman, Brian. *Signifying Nothing: The Semiotics of Zero*. London: Macmillan, 1987.
Rousseau, Jean-Jacques. "On the Social Contract." 1762. Online. https://www.marxists.org/reference/subject/economics/rousseau/social-contract/ch01.htm.
Rovelli, C. "Relational Quantum Mechanics." *International Journal of Theoretical Physics* 35 (1996) 1637–78.
Rowland, Tracey. "Globalization, Postmodern Theories of Culture, and the Trinity." In *The Oxford Handbook of the Trinity*, edited by Gilles Emery and Matthew Levering, 586–99. Oxford: Oxford University Press, 2011.
Rudolph, Enno. "Symbol and History: Ernst Cassirer's Critique of the Philosophy of History." In *The Symbolic Construction of Reality: The Legacy of Ernst Cassirer*, edited by Jeffrey Andrew Barash, 3–16. Chicago: University of Chicago Press, 2008.
Russell, Bertrand. *Our Knowledge of the External World*. London: Routledge, 1993.
———. *Power*. London: Routledge, 2004.
———. *The Principles of Mathematics*. New York: Norton, 1966.
———. *The Problems of Philosophy*. London: Oxford University Press, 1978.
———. *Why I Am Not A Christian*. London: Unwin, 1967.
Sagoff, Mark. *The Economy of the Earth*. Cambridge: Cambridge University Press, 1990.
Sandler, Ronald L. *Character and Environment: A Virtue-Oriented Approach to Environmental Ethics*. New York: Columbia University Press, 2007.
Sartre, Jean-Paul. *Being and Nothingness: An Essay on Phenomenological Ontology*. Translated by Hazel E. Barnes. New York: Philosophical Library, 1956.
———. *Theory of Practical Ensembles*. Vol. 1 of *Critique of Dialectical Reason*. Translated by Alan Sheridan-Smith. London: Verso, 1982.
Sasaki, Chikara. *Descartes's Mathematical Thought*. Dordrecht: Kluwer, 2003.
Sax, Boria. *Animals in the Third Reich: Pets, Scapegoats, and the Holocaust*. London: Continuum, 2000.
Sayers, Dorothy L. "Toward a Christian Esthetic." In *The Whimsical Christian: Eighteen Essays*, by Dorothy L. Sayers, 73–91. New York: Macmillan, Collier, 1987.

Scheffler, Samuel. *The Rejection of Consequentialism: A Philosophical Investigation of the Considerations Underlying Rival Moral Conceptions*. Oxford: Clarendon, 1984.
Schelling, F. W. J. *The Philosophy of Art*. Edited by Douglas W. Stott. Foreword by David Simpson. Minneapolis: University of Minnesota Press, 1989.
Schillebeeckx, Edward. *Christ: The Experience of Jesus as Lord*. Translated by John Bowden. New York: Crossroad, 1980.
Schindler, D. C. *The Perfection of Freedom: Schiller, Schelling, and Hegel between the Ancients and the Moderns*. Veritas 8. Eugene, OR: Cascade, 2012.
Schmidt, Alfred. *The Concept of Nature in Marx*. Translated by Ben Fowkes. London: NLB, 1971.
Schmitt, Carl. *The Necessity of Politics: An Essay on the Representative Idea in the Church and Modern Europe*. Translated by E. M. Codd. Introduction by Christopher Dawson. Catholic Book-a-Month Club, Essays in Order 5. London: Sheed & Ward, 1931.
———. *The Nomos of the Earth in the International Law of Jus Publicum Europaeum*. Translated by G. L. Ulmen. New York: Telos, 2003.
———. *Political Romanticism*. Translated by Guy Oakes. Cambridge, MA: MIT Press, 1986.
———. *Political Theology: Four Chapters on the Concept of Sovereignty*. Translated by George Schwab. Foreword by Tracy B. Strong. Chicago: University of Chicago Press, 2005.
———. "Three Possibilities for a Christian Conception of History." *Telos* 147 (2009) 167–70.
Schmitz, Markus. *Euklids Geometrie und ihre mathematiktheoretische Grundlegung in der neuplatonischen Philosophie des Proclos*. Würzburg: Königshausen & Neumann, 1997.
Scott, John A. "The Problem of Demonstration in Aristotle." PhD diss., University of Edinburgh, 1976.
Scully, Matthew. *Dominion: The Power of Man, the Suffering of Animals, and the Call to Mercy*. New York: St. Martin's/Griffin, 2002.
Searle, John R. *The Construction of Social Reality*. New York: Free Press, 1995.
———. "What Is an Institution?" *Journal of Institutional Economics* 1.1 (2005) 1–22.
Seifert, Josef. *Back to "Things in Themselves": A Phenomenological Foundation for Classical Realism*. London: Routledge, 1987.
Sellars, John. *Stoicism*. Berkeley: University of California Press, 2006.
Serres, Michel. *The Natural Contract*. Translated by Elizabeth MacArthur and William Paulson. Ann Arbor: University of Michigan Press, 1995.
Sessions, George. "Deep Ecology as Worldview." In *Worldviews and Ecology*, edited by Mary Evelyn Tucker et al., 207–23. Toronto: Associated University Presses, 1993.
Sextus Empiricus. *Against Logicians*. Translated by R. G. Bury. LCL 291. Cambridge, MA: Harvard University Press, 1935.
Shapin, Steven. *The Scientific Revolution*. Chicago: University of Chicago Press, 1996.
———. *A Social History of Truth: Civility and Science in Seventeenth-Century England*. Chicago: University of Chicago Press, 1994.
Sharma, I. C. *Ethical Philosophies of India*. New York: Harper & Row, 1965.
Shaw, Gregory. "Theurgy: Rituals of Unification in the Neoplatonism of Iamblichus." *Traditio* 41 (1985) 1–28.
Shelley, Percy. *Prometheus Unbound*. London: C. and J. Ollier, 1820.

Siecienski, Edward A. *The Filioque: History of a Doctrinal Controversy*. Oxford Studies in Historical Theology. Oxford University Press, 2010.

Simmons, Michael Bland. *Universal Salvation in Late Antiquity: Porphyry of Tyre and the Pagan-Christian Debate*. Oxford Studies in Late Antiquity. New York: Oxford University Press, 2015.

Simon, Derek J. "*Ad Regnum Caritatis:* The Finality of Biblical Interpretation in Augustine and Ricoeur." *Augustine Studies* 30.1 (1999) 105–27.

Simplicius. *On Aristotle's "Categories 7–8."* Translated by Barrie Fleet. Ithaca, NY: Cornell University Press, 2002.

Singer, Peter. "All Animals Are Equal." In *Environmental Philosophy from Animal Rights to Radical Ecology*, edited by Michael E. Zimmerman et al., 25–38. 4th ed. Upper Saddle River, NJ: Pearson, 2005.

———. *Animal Liberation: A New Ethics for Our Treatment of Animals*. Rev. ed. New York: Avon, 1990.

———. *Practical Ethics*. 2nd ed. Cambridge: Cambridge University Press, 1994.

———. *Marx*. Past Masters. Oxford: Oxford University Press, 1980.

Sloterdijk, Peter. *Bubbles*. Vol. 1 of *Spheres*. Translated by Wieland Hoban. Los Angeles: Semiotext(e), 2011.

———. *Globes*. Vol. 2 of *Spheres*. Translated by Wieland Hoban. Los Angeles: Semiotext(e), 2014.

Sorabji, Richard. "Preface." In *On Aristotle's "Categories 7–8,"* by Simplicius, vii–xiv. Translated by Barrie Fleet. Ithaca, NY: Cornell University Press, 2002.

Spade, Paul Vincent. "Introduction." In *Five Texts on the Medieval Problem of Universals: Porphyry, Boethius, Abelard, Duns Scotus, Ockham*, edited by Paul Vincent Spade, vii–xvii. Indianapolis, IN: Hackett, 1994.

———. "Ockham's Nominalist Metaphysics: Some Main Themes." In *The Cambridge Companion to Ockham*, edited by Paul Vincent Spade, 100–117. Cambridge: Cambridge University Press, 1999.

Squires, Stuart. *The Pelagian Controversy: An Introduction to the Enemies of Grace and the Conspiracy of Lost Souls*. Eugene, OR: Pickwick, 2019.

Stavins, Robert N., ed. *Economics of the Environment: Selected Readings*. New York: Norton, 2005.

Stead, Christopher. *Divine Substance*. Oxford: Clarendon, 1977.

Steel, C. "Breathing Thought: Proclus on the Innate Knowledge of the Soul." In *The Perennial Tradition of Neoplatonism*, edited by J. Cleary, 293–309. Ancient and Medieval Philosophy 1.24. Leuven: Leuven University Press, 1997.

Stirner, Max. *The Ego and His Own: The Case of the Individual Against Authority*. Translated by Steven T. Byington. London: A. C. Fifield, 1913.

Stjernfelt, Frederik. *Natural Propositions: The Actuality of Peirce's Doctrine of Dicisigns*. Boston: Docent, 2014.

Strauss, Leo. "On Collingwood's Philosophy of History." *The Review of Metaphysics* 5.4 (1952) 559–86.

Strawson, P. F. *Individuals: An Essay in Descriptive Metaphysics*. London: Methuen, 1959.

Stroumsa, Guy G. *The End of Sacrifice: Religious Transformations in Late Antiquity*. Translated by Susan Emanuel. Chicago: University of Chicago Press, 2009.

Struck, Peter T. *Birth of the Symbol: Ancient Readers at the Limits of Their Texts*. Princeton, NJ: Princeton University Press, 2004.

Taille, Maurice de la. *The Mystery of Faith and Human Opinion Contrasted and Defined.* London: Sheed & Ward, 1930.
Taubes, Jacob. "Dialectic and Analogy." *The Journal of Religion* 34.2 (1954) 111–19.
Taylor, Alfred Edward. *Platonism and Its Influence.* New York: Cooper Square, 1963.
Taylor, Charles. "Notes on the Sources of Violence: Perennial and Modern." In *Beyond Violence: Religious Sources of Social Transformation in Judaism, Christianity, and Islam*, edited by James L. Heft, 15–42. New York: Fordham University Press, 2004.
———. *A Secular Age.* Cambridge, MA: Belknap/Harvard University Press, 2007.
TeSelle, Eugene. *Augustine The Theologian.* New York: Herder & Herder, 1970.
TeVelde, Rudi A. *Participation and Substantiality in Thomas Aquinas.* Leiden: Brill, 1995.
Ticciati, Susannah. "The Castration of Signs: Conversing with Augustine on Creation, Language and Truth." *Modern Theology* 23.2 (2007) 161–79.
Todorov, Tzvetan. "The Romantic Crisis." In *Theories of the Symbol*, by Tzvetan Todorov, 147–221. Translated by Catherine Porter. Ithaca, NY: Cornell University Press, 1982.
Toole, D. "Divine Ecology and the Apocalypse: A Theological Description of Natural Disasters and the Environmental Crisis." *Theology Today* 55.4 (1999) 547–61.
Torrance, Thomas F. *The Christian Doctrine of God: One Being Three Persons.* Edinburgh: T & T Clark, 1996.
Trinkaus, Charles. *In Our Image and Likeness: Humanity and Divinity in Italian Humanist Thought.* London: Constable, 1970.
Uekoetter, Frank. "The Nazis and the Environment: A Relevant Topic?" In *The Green & The Brown: A History Of Conservation in Nazi Germany*, by Frank Uekoetter, 1–16. Cambridge: Cambridge University Press, 2006.
Uždavinys, Algis. *Philosophy and Theurgy in Late Antiquity.* Tacoma, WA: Angelico, 2014.
Vaggione, Richard Paul. *Eunomius of Cyzicus and the Nicene Revolution.* Oxford Early Christian Studies. Oxford: Oxford University Press, 2002.
VanRuler, J. A. *The Crisis of Causality: Voetius and Descartes on God, Nature, and Change.* Leiden: Brill, 1995.
Vandervelde, George. *Original Sin: Two Major Trends in Contemporary Roman Catholic Reinterpretation.* Lanham, MD: University Press of America, 1981.
Verbeek, Theo. *Descartes and the Dutch: Early Reactions to Cartesian Philosophy, 1637–1650.* Carbondale: Southern Illinois University Press, 1992.
Verene, Donald Phillip. *Metaphysics and the Modern World.* Eugene, OR: Cascade, 2016.
Vickers, Brian. "Francis Bacon, Feminist Historiography, and the Domination of Nature." *Journal of the History of Ideas* 69.1 (2008) 117–41.
Virno, Paolo. *Multitude: Between Innovation and Negation.* Translated by Isabella Bertoletti et al. Los Angeles: Semiotext(e), 2008.
———. *When the Word Becomes Flesh: Language and Human Nature.* Translated by Giuseppina Mecchia. South Pasadena, CA: Semiotext(e), 2015.
Vos, Geerhardus. *The Pauline Eschatology.* Grand Rapids: Baker, 1979.
Waal, Frans B. M. de. *Peacemaking Among Primates.* Cambridge, MA: Harvard University Press, 1989.

Wahle, Hedwig. "Human Responsibility for God's Creation in Jewish Teaching and Practice." *Journal of Dharma (Special Edition: Ecology and World Religions)* 26.1 (2001) 60–86.

Wanamaker, Charles A. *The Epistles to the Thessalonians: A Commentary on the Greek Text*. Grand Rapids: Eerdmans, 1990.

Warfield, Benjamin B. *Calvin and Augustine*. Philadelphia: Presbyterian and Reformed, 1956.

Weeks, Andrew. *Boehme: An Intellectual Biography of the Seventeenth-Century Philosopher and Mystic*. Albany, NY: State University of New York Press, 1991.

———. "Jacob Boehme and the Thirty Years' War." *Central European History* 24.2–3 (1991) 213–21.

Weinberg, Julius R. "Abstraction in the Formation of Concepts." In vol. 1 of *Dictionary of the History of Ideas*, 1–9. New York: Scribner's Sons, 1973.

———. *Abstraction, Relation, and Induction: Three Essays in the History of Thought*. Madison: University of Wisconsin Press, 1965.

Westfall, Richard S. "The Rise of Science and the Decline of Orthodox Christianity: A Study of Kepler, Descartes, and Newton." In *God and Nature: Historical Essays on the Encounter between Christianity and Science*, edited by David C. Lindberg and Ronald L. Numbers, 218–37. Berkeley: University of California Pres, 1986.

Wheeler, Wendy. *The Whole Creature: Complexity, Biosemiotics, and the Evolution of Culture*. London: Lawrence and Wishart, 2006.

White, Lynn, Jr. "Cultural Climates and Technological Advance in the Middle Ages." *Viator* 2 (1971) 171–201.

———. "The Historical Roots of Our Ecologic Crisis." In *Environmental Ethics*, edited by David Schmidtz and Elizabeth Willott, 7–14. Oxford: Oxford University Press, 2002.

Wiley, Tatha. *Original Sin: Origins, Developments, Contemporary Meanings*. New York/Mahwah, NJ: Paulist, 2002.

Williams, Bernard. *Descartes: The Project of Pure Enquiry*. Harmondsworth, UK: Pelican, 1978.

———. "Must a Concern for the Environment Be Centered on Human Beings?" In *Making Sense of Humanity and Other Philosophical Papers 1982–1993*, by Bernard Williams, 233–40. Cambridge: Cambridge University Press, 1995.

Williams, Rowan. *Arius: Heresy and Tradition*. London: Darton Longmann Todd, 1987.

———. "Language, Reality, and Desire in Augustine's *De Doctrina*." *Journal of Literature and Theology* 3.2 (1989) 138–50.

Witzany, Günter. "Review: Marcello Barbieri (Ed.) (2007) *Introduction to Biosemiotics: The New Biological Synthesis*. Dordrecht: Springer." *tripleC* 5.3 (2007) 104–9.

Wolff, Robert Paul. "On Violence." *Journal of Philosophy* 66.19 (1969) 601–16.

Wolfson, Harry Austryn. *Faith, Trinity, Incarnation*. Vol. 1 of *The Philosophy of the Church Fathers*. 2nd ed. Cambridge, MA: Harvard University Press, 1964.

World Commission on Environment and Development (WCED). *Our Common Future*. Oxford: Oxford University Press, 1987.

Worster, Donald. *Nature's Economy: A History of Ecological Ideas*. 2nd ed. Cambridge: Cambridge University Press, 1994.

Index

Abrams, M. H., 340n94
Absolute Presuppositions, xi, 46, 48–63, 67, 69–71, 74, 76–81, 84–90, 93, 94n1, 99, 106n60, 112, 121–23, 146, 149, 167–71, 176, 186, 203, 217, 222, 226, 269, 342–43, 345, 356–57, 366–67, 370, 372, 377
Abstraction, 46, 113, 144–45, 144n82, 149–51, 372
Actuality, xii, 69, 147, 157, 193, 242, 248, 281–83, 285, 288–94, 296–300, 304–6, 308–16, 318, 322, 324, 329, 329n49, 331, 375
Actus Purus, 242, 282, 282n5, 314, 324, 332
Adorno, Theodor W., 164, 316n8, 324
Aeschylus, 125, 205–7
Aetius, 119
Aëtius, 244
Agamben, Giorgio, xv, 32n92, 255, 320–24, 320n20, 320n23, 346–48, 348n29, 351, 356, 366
Agape, xii–xiii, 199, 203, 212–13, 217–18, 223–27, 231, 309, 325, 352, 357
Ahmed, Sara, 165n13
Aiken, William, 37
Alliez, Éric, 31–32
Animal Liberation, 6–8, 10
Anthropocene, xiii, 24, 87, 178, 200
Anthropocentrism, xi, 35, 92–93, 219, 222–23, 226, 280
Apatheia, 97–98, 154, 224, 231
Apel, Karl-Otto, 203n15

Aporetic, 31n90, 247–51, 265n27, 316, 322
Aporia, 105, 107, 109, 115n96, 247–49, 255, 282n5, 299, 310
Aquinas, Thomas, xii, 197, 281–98, 282n5, 297n52, 302–3, 305n76, 309, 312
Arendt, Hannah, 208n31
Argyrou, Vassos, ix
Arianism, 224, 243, 244, 356
Aristo, 250
Aristotelian, 77, 112n84, 144–48, 158–59, 239, 249–51, 266, 272, 281, 289, 292, 295, 300, 304, 323
Aristotle, xii, 25–27, 29–34, 31n90, 36, 45–48, 52, 66, 77–79, 232, 237n24, 239–43, 239n37, 247–52, 265–66, 265n27, 272, 282–84, 282n5, 290–92, 299, 301, 312, 314–24, 316n10, 319n19, 329, 359
Arius, 243
Arminius, Jacob, 158
Armour, Leslie, 5n10, 76–77, 132n26
Ashworth, William B., Jr., 254
Ataraxia, 223
Augustine of Hippo, xii, xv, 82, 94, 94n1, 97–105, 107, 112n81, 115–19, 126, 158, 230, 261, 263–65, 264n16, 267–78, 280–81, 284, 287–88, 298, 309, 331, 349, 351–53, 355, 361–64, 366–70, 374, 376
Augustinian, 99, 115n96, 117, 123, 126, 131, 158, 229, 351, 360, 364

Aurelius, Marcus, 119, 123
Axelrod, R., 211n41
Ayer, A. J., 59–62, 59n48, 79

Babcock, William S., 271
Bacon, Francis, 86, 93, 125–30, 152, 163, 175
Balakrishnan, Gopal, 345
Balthasar, Hans Urs von, 81–84, 86, 357, 364
Barbarism, 218, 346, 356, 358–60, 366, 376
Barbieri, Marcello, 203n10
Barnouw, Jeffrey, 237
Basil of Ancyra, 245n53
Basil of Caesarea, 243n46
Beaney, Michael, 63, 76–77
Becker, Carl L., 119–20
Becoming, xii, 62–63, 76, 78, 157, 213, 232–33, 236–38, 253, 266–67, 274–75, 277, 291, 304, 312–13, 318, 323–25, 327–28, 374, 376
Beer, David, 361
Being, x, 7, 10, 13–14, 24, 26, 32, 41, 44–46, 48, 50–51, 62, 67, 69–71, 73–74, 76–77, 81, 84, 92–93, 98–99, 101–2, 112–13, 130–35, 134n39, 137–52, 154, 156, 162, 166–67, 174, 180, 186, 194–95, 198, 201, 204, 211–13, 217, 223–26, 231–37, 239–54, 257–59, 263, 265n27, 266–67, 272, 274–76, 281–85, 282n5, 287–315, 317, 319, 321–25, 328, 330–39, 348, 351, 365–66, 372–75
Being as Communication, x, 201, 231, 351
Benjamin, Walter, 208n31
Bentham, Jeremy, 6–7, 9
Benzoni, Francisco, 197n152, 210n36
Berdyaev, Nicolas, 327–28
Berger, Peter L., 201–2
Bergmann, Sigurd, 227–31
Berlin, Isaiah, 187–88, 192, 194
Bernard of Clairvaux, 260
Best, Ernest, 354n50
Bloch, Ernst, 190

Boehme, Jacob, xii, 312, 324–40, 326n39, 328n43–44, 329n49, 331n53, 336n73
Boersma, Gerald P., 103
Boethius, 283–84
Bonaventure of Bagnoregio, 254
Bonin, Thérèse, 141n72
Bono, James J., 162, 262n4
Booth, Edward, 31n90, 247–48
Boucher, David, 66n74, 84–85, 85n151, 342, 360
Bovelles, C., 116
Bradley, James, 82n127, 174n47
Bradshaw, David, 239n37
Bradwardine, Thomas, 111–14
Braudel, Fernand, 170n24
Brock, Stephen L., 289, 292
Brower, Jeffrey E., 112n84
Brown, David, 264n20
Brown, Peter, 94, 97, 102
Brown, Robert F., 326n37, 328n45, 335–36
Bruno, G., 116
Bruns, Gerald L., 235n14, 258–59, 262n6
Budiansky, Stephen, 34n105

Cacciari, Massimo, 346, 349
Caecus, Claudius, 155
Callicott, J. Baird, 5n12, 38–40
Cameron, Michael, 269
Campbell, Richard, 58
Caracalla (Roman Emperor), 188
Cartesian(ism), 144, 150, 152–53, 156–58, 161–63, 165, 175, 184, 202–3, 208
Casiday, A. M. C., 106, 106n63, 107n64
Cassian, John, 105–11, 106n60, 106n63, 111–12n81, 115n96, 117, 182
Cassirer, Ernst, 43n146, 115–18, 123–24, 128–29, 266n29
Cavarnos, Constantine, 240n39, 250n79, 251, 295n44, 295n47, 298nn58–59, 301
Ceric, Mustafa, 209n33
Chadwick, Henry, 97n16

Index

Chadwick, Owen, 111
Charles-Saget, Annick, 134n43
Chatterjee, P., 164n7
Chauvet, Louis-Marie, 256
Checker, Melissa, 221n91
Chenu, Marie-Dominique, 261, 262n2
Chevalier, Irénée, 243n46, 245n53
Chlup, Radek, 136–37, 139n63–64, 141n71
Chresis, 31–32, 32n92, 45, 66, 359
Christendom, 116, 249, 328, 345, 351, 356–57, 367
Christian Historicity, 82, 343–44, 352, 356, 371
Christina (Queen of Sweden), 160
Civilization, xii, 1, 2, 33–34, 34n104, 54, 56, 63, 65, 68–69, 71, 80–81, 84–85, 90, 94, 123–24, 163–64, 180, 187, 196, 205–6, 212, 216–19, 223, 225, 342–45, 356–61, 364, 366–67, 377
Clark, Mary T., 243n46
Cleary, John J., 144n82
Closmann, Charles, 35n107
Coakley, Sara, 211n41
Cochrane, Charles Norris, x, xiii, 86, 89, 94n1, 342–43, 346, 352, 360–67, 369–76
Colish, Marcia L., 250n77, 251
Collingwood, R.G., xi, xiii, 46–66, 47n2, 66n72, 66n74, 68–72, 70n86, 74, 76–82, 78n109, 82n127, 84–87, 85–86n151, 89–90, 94n1, 121–22, 141, 167–68, 170–71, 342–44, 346, 348–49, 352, 356–64, 366–67, 373
Commodity (Commodification), x, 7, 9, 18, 23, 30, 31–36, 44–45, 121, 186, 190, 220, 226, 365
Communication, x, xii, xiv–xv, 7, 12, 20n57, 33, 48, 54, 69, 83, 89, 97, 113, 140, 144, 147–48, 151, 154, 161, 166, 172, 187, 200–201, 203, 211, 219, 222, 225–26, 228–35, 237–38, 246–48, 252–57, 264–65, 268, 270–76, 280–83, 287–88, 290, 292–93, 296–300, 302, 304, 305n76, 306–14, 318, 325, 327, 330, 332–37, 339, 343, 351, 356, 375–77
Communication (Triadic Relation), 268, 293
Connelly, James, xn1, 3n8, 28n80, 55–56, 66n72, 362n90
Consequentialism, 5, 6, 34
Constantine, Roman Emperor, 189, 243
Construction, 68, 93, 118, 129, 132, 134, 151, 166, 168, 170, 190, 202, 228, 308, 326n39, 352, 365, 367, 373, 376
Conversion, 30, 71, 139, 152, 211–12, 219, 243, 258, 280, 360, 365–66, 372, 377
Cooper, John W., 239n36
Corbin, Henry, 139
Cornford, F. M., 234, 235n11, 141n81
Costanza, Robert, 220n88
Cottingham, John G., 133n37, 142n75–76, 159n136–37
Courtenay, William J., 112n82
Cox Miller, Patricia, 140, 258–59, 259n132
Crane, Stephen, 294
Cratylus, 233
Creation, xi–xiv, 42–43, 67–69, 78–80, 82–83, 88–91, 93, 95, 99, 101, 112–16, 120, 126–27, 129, 132, 134, 140–41, 151–56, 158–59, 161, 166, 172–76, 179, 190, 192, 196, 199–200, 202–4, 210–12, 222–23, 227–33, 238, 243–44, 247, 253–55, 258–64, 271, 273–78, 280, 282–83, 287–88, 294–96, 301–2, 309, 311–14, 321, 325, 327, 329n49, 330–33, 335–37, 339, 343, 348, 351–52, 355, 357–58, 364–68, 370, 372–76
Creation as Communicative Liberation, 262
Creation as Sign, 231
Critical-Historical Phenomenology, 167
Croce, Benedetto, 66n72,
Crosby, Alfred W., 219n82
Cross, Richard, 197n149
Crouzel, Henri, 259

Cruelty, 16–19, 25, 91, 211, 218
Cullen, Christopher M., 254nn102–3
Cunningham, David S., 253

Darwin, Charles, 174
Davies, Oliver, 263
Deacon, Terrence, xiii, 319n19
Deason, Gary B, 133
Deely, John, 249n75, 297, 309–11
Deep Ecology, 35–36, 40–41
Deleuze, Gilles, 238, 309n82
Dennett, Daniel C., 211n40
Deontology, 5, 12, 22–23, 25, 34
Derrida, Jacques, 208n31
Descartes, René, 93, 125, 130–35, 141–43, 146, 148–66, 171, 184, 318, 326, 326n39
Descriptive Metaphysics, 71, 84
Desire, xv, 21, 30, 101–2, 109, 116, 118, 123, 154–55, 217, 225, 236, 249, 259, 278–80, 314, 317, 319–20, 322, 324–25, 329–30, 333, 335, 338–39, 359, 373
DesJardins, Joseph R., 35n110, 41
Devall, Bill, 41
Dewan, Lawrence, 134n39, 288–89, 288n14–15, 289n16, 291, 291n29–31, 315
Dialectic, 47–48, 51, 80, 108, 137–38, 140–42, 141n70–71, 144–45, 144n81, 167, 187, 189, 196, 202, 235–37, 236n18, 240, 247–49, 255, 316, 329–32, 334–35, 349–50, 352–53, 357–60
Didymus the Blind, 245n53
Difference, xiv, 1, 4–7, 15, 20, 50, 72–75, 79, 81, 85, 109, 120, 148, 163, 170–72, 175–76, 179, 183, 186–87, 195, 198, 205, 205n19, 215, 221, 223, 233, 237, 242, 245–46, 249, 256–57, 272, 275, 277, 290, 296, 298, 300, 320, 326n39, 328, 329n49, 333–34, 350, 352
Dion, D., 211n41
Dionysian, 213–18
Dixon, Paul S., 354

Domination, ix, xi, xiii, 9–10, 17–18, 43–44, 65, 71, 73–74, 81, 83, 86, 91, 93, 118, 126, 129, 132, 152, 161, 163–65, 169, 175–77, 179, 182, 185, 189, 192, 214, 231, 262, 262n4, 278–79, 280, 296, 340, 342–43, 356, 359–60, 364–68, 371, 373
Dominick III, Raymond H., 40n136
Dominion, 32, 35n109, 88, 90–93, 95, 114, 116, 126, 128, 130, 153–54, 175–78, 259, 337–39
Donne, John, 264
D'Oro, Giuseppina, 50–51
Dourley, John P., 328
Doyle, John P., 249n75
Drake, H. A., 189, 189n113, 243
Drozdek, Adam, 323n31, 324n32–33
Drury, Shadia B., 214n58
Dryzek, John S., 3n8
Duchrow, Ulrich, 120, 123
Dummett, Michael, 141n71
Dunham, Scott A., 210n37

Eagleton, Terry, 210n39, 262n3
Eckersley, Robyn, 3n8
Eco, Umberto, xn3
Ecological Civilization, xiii, 342, 356, 359, 361, 367, 377
Ecology, xii, xiv, 29, 35–36, 40–41, 43, 65, 210n37, 287
Economy, xi–xii, xv, 28–29, 31, 33, 35, 81, 84, 89, 109, 111, 128, 156, 175, 179, 185n96, 207, 212, 225, 238, 254–56, 271, 275, 280, 309, 311, 370–71
Ecopolitics, xi, 1–3, 3n8, 210n37
Edwards, Denis, 247
Emanation, 136, 141n72, 149
Emancipation, xii–xiii, xv, 8, 34, 124, 155, 171, 173, 185, 191, 227, 231, 277, 338–40, 342, 352, 363, 369
Emblematic Worldview, 254, 262, 326, 351,
Emery, Gilles, 272n64
Emmeche, Claus, xiii
Environment as Communication, 235

Index

Environmental Cosmology, xi, 1, 40–44, 90, 93
Environmental Ethics, 3, 5, 12, 22, 25, 27, 35, 40
Epictetus, 252
Epiphanius of Salamis, 245n53
Eristic, 76, 167, 171, 249–50, 357–60
Eschaton, 84, 192, 272, 283
Escobar, Arturo, ixn1
Esse, 239n37, 281–84, 288–90, 294–304, 306–7, 309–10, 313
Essence, 6, 44–45, 67, 86, 94, 127, 132–33, 135, 139–40, 157, 183, 187, 206, 212, 216, 244–46, 251, 272–73, 277, 284–85, 287, 294–96, 313, 315, 324, 329n49, 330, 334–36, 338, 366
Ethics, xi, 1, 3–6, 8, 12–13, 16, 22–28, 32–38, 40–41, 52, 56, 73, 115, 123, 131–32, 154, 162, 167–68, 203, 213, 224–26, 228, 230, 241, 243, 249, 266, 359
Eunomius, 244
Euripides, 212
Evans, Robert F., 96n12
Event, ix, 4, 43–45, 49, 57, 63, 66–67, 82–83, 86–87, 93, 97, 99, 101–2, 106, 109, 117, 122–23, 131, 135, 138–40, 145, 150, 168–69, 192, 212, 227, 230, 232–33, 235, 237–38, 246, 257–59, 263, 265–68, 271, 277, 294, 305, 309n82, 311, 314, 319, 326, 338, 343, 346, 348, 352, 354, 370, 375
Evil, 3–4, 8–9, 12–14, 16–19, 22, 26, 44, 65, 71, 94–97, 99–103, 105, 118–20, 123–24, 156, 158, 162, 181–82, 190, 201–2, 204, 207, 209, 211, 215–18, 231, 314, 320–21, 327, 331–32, 336–38, 340, 345, 347, 351, 354–55, 371, 376
Evil Sacred, 215–16, 218
Expressed Species (Concept), 304–8, 310, 317

Fackenheim, Emil L., 51, 155–57, 191–92
Farrington, B., 116n103
Favareau, Donald, 204
Ferguson, Everett, 97n16
Ferré, Frederick, 37
Ferry, Luc, 34n107, 40
Ficino, M., 114–15, 115n96, 116, 309n82
Filioque, 285–87, 285n9
Findlen, Paula, 134
First Intention, 143–44, 147, 299–301, 304, 306–8
Fleet, Barrie, 252
Flikschuh, Katrin, 188n110, 192
Formula, 145, 147
Forrester, John, 86n151
Foster, Jay, 221
Foster, M. B., 88, 91
Foucault, Michel, 9–10, 9n22, 85–86n151, 99–100, 105n57, 106, 106n60, 110n76, 172, 172nn26–27, 179–88, 179n71, 182n82, 183n87, 185nn96–97, 187n100, 187n102, 188n108, 192, 218, 218n78
Fox, Brian J., 345n12
Frame, James Everett, 354n50
Francis, xiv
Fransen, Piet F., 97n16
Frederick Henry (Prince of Orange), 159
Freedom, xii, 8n19, 14–15, 18, 20, 34, 44–45, 47, 56, 66–68, 70n86, 71, 76, 83, 93, 95–97, 98n18, 100, 103, 105, 107–9, 114–16, 115n96, 120, 122–24, 126, 129, 155–58, 162, 171, 183, 186–88, 187n102, 190, 192, 195, 198, 227, 231, 265, 265n23, 266n31, 277–78, 314, 320, 322–25, 326n39, 327–30, 329n49, 332–34, 336–37, 339, 349, 352, 358, 363, 365–66, 370–71
Frey, R. G., 10–11
Function, xiii, 136, 174n47, 196, 240, 256, 266, 276, 325
Furton, Edward J., 299–300

Gadamer, Hans-Georg, 85n151, 141n70, 167, 236n18, 248–49
Gaia, 36–37, 202
Galen, 237
Galilei, Galileo, 262
Galtung, Johan, 199
Gare, Arran E., 43n144, 196
Garland, Robert, 30n84
Gaukroger, Stephen, 159n138
Gentile, G., 66n72
Geréby, György, 351
Gerson, Lloyd P., 250n76
Geus, Marius, de, 43n145
Gilbert, N. W., 112n82
Gillespie, Michael Allen, 132n29, 154, 157, 161–62
Gilson, Étienne, 164, 249n75, 254, 277n83, 296, 369n141
Girard, René, 206–11, 214–18, 238n31, 329n49
Gould, Stephen Jay, 174n47, 178
Governmentality, xv, 100, 181, 185n96, 187, 189n115
Grace, 45, 92–93, 96–99, 96n12, 102–11, 113–15, 115n96, 117, 123, 126, 131, 155–56, 158–59, 207, 210, 210n36, 224, 229–30, 253, 257, 273, 277–78, 331, 348, 351–52, 376
Gracia, Jorge J. E., 298n55–57
Graham, Daniel W., 234–35
Grajewski, Maurice, 197n149
Gray, John, 188, 210n37, 218–22
Grayling, A. C., 326n38
Green, T. H., 198
Gregory of Nyssa, 242
Grim, P., 211n41
Gunderson, L.H., 203

Habermas, Jürgen, 11
Hadot, Ilsetraut, 252n92
Hadot, Pierre, 139, 192
Hanby, Michael, 106n58, 155–57, 264n22
Hansen, James, 3
Haraway, Donna, xiv
Harris, Errol E., 53
Harris, H. S., 66n72

Harrison, Peter, 152–54
Harrison, Verna, 246
Harvey, David, 40, 43, 190
Hawken, Paul, 220n88
Hayek, F. A., 33–34, 185n96, 221
Hayes, Zachary, 353n45
Heft, James L., 210n35
Hegel, G. W. F., 8n19, 328, 328n44
Heidegger, Martin, 44–45, 167, 233–34, 249n75, 265n23
Henninger, Mark G., 112n84, 249n74, 295
Heraclitean, 233, 235, 238, 238n31, 325
Heraclitus, 232–35, 237, 327
Hinkelammert, Franz J., 120, 123
Hintikka, Jaakko, 202n9, 223
Hinz, Michael, 82, 85n150
Historical Metaphysics, xi, 56, 66–67, 69, 77, 85, 85n151, 161, 165, 167–70, 201, 361, 367
Historical Metaphysics of Environment, xi, 85, 161, 165, 167–69
Historicity, 82, 218, 343–44, 347–48, 352, 356, 370–71, 374
Hitchens, Christopher, 210n38
Hobbes, Thomas, 118–20, 122, 152
Holism, 5, 34, 36, 38, 41
Holling, C. S., 203
Hollingworth, Miles, 370n143
Horkheimer, Max, 164
Hughes, Christopher, 289, 289n20, 290n24
Husserl, Edmund, 165

Icon, xii, 138–39, 213, 236, 271
Ideology, ixn1, 8, 33, 43, 165, 168, 192, 316, 323, 328, 343, 364, 369
Idolatry, 14, 18, 86, 138, 140, 152, 166, 261, 273, 278, 353, 365
Ignatieff, Michael, 122n131, 188
Imago Dei, 88, 103, 131–32, 134, 151, 156–57, 175, 232, 253, 287–88, 296, 329n49, 352
Immler, Hans, 220n87
Impressed Species (Sense), 304–6, 308, 310, 317

Infinity, 109, 131–32, 132n27, 134, 142, 154, 157, 195, 211, 220–21, 241, 243–44, 253, 280, 283, 287, 296, 300, 303, 322–24, 326n39, 332–34, 337, 341
Innis, Harold, 361
Interpretation, ix–x, xii–xiii, ix*n*1, 52, 54, 58–59, 62, 64, 69, 79, 86n151, 90–93, 111, 119, 131–32, 153, 164, 166, 171, 173, 175–76, 189, 195, 201, 203, 213, 215–16, 220, 222, 230, 232–34, 254–60, 264–65, 267–71, 273–75, 278, 280–81, 283, 287, 293–94, 297, 301–2, 304, 306, 308–14, 316n10, 318, 322, 329–30, 345, 354, 367

Jaspers, Karl, 264n16
Jauss, Hans Robert, 85n151
Jenkins, Willis, 197, 210n36
Ji, Sungchul, 203n11
John Paul II, xiv, 176
Jonas, Hans, 156, 164–65
Judt, Tony, ix*n*1, 33
Justice, 26–31, 35, 95, 113, 116, 124, 161, 184, 188–89, 197, 200, 205–7, 210, 216, 225, 231, 235, 237, 250, 344, 359

Kairos, 271
Kant, Immanuel, 13–20, 15n40, 22–23, 299n60, 300n61, 318, 329n50
Karsten, Siegfried G., 220n87
Katechon, 190, 345–51, 353–56
Keech, Dominic, 101–2, 102nn41–42
Kenny, Anthony, 133, 133n33, 158n133
Keynes, J. M., 221
King, Martin Luther, Jr., 209
Kirk, G. S., 233n2–3
KJV (King James Version), 124, 192, 205, 209, 254–55, 271, 328, 338, 349, 353
Klein, Jacob, 143, 145–47, 146n86–90, 148n92–94, 149–50, 149n97–98, 150n100–1, 151n104
Klein, Naomi, 29n83

Koenker, Ernest B., 331, 333
Koninck, Charles, de, 144n82, 291, 323
Kotsko, Adam, 98n18
Koyré, Alexandre, 328n43, 330
Kroker, Arthur, 366–67
Kronen, John, 298n55–57
Kropotkin, Peter, 211
Kuhn, Thomas S., 85–86n151
Kull, Kalevi, xiii

Ladner, Gerhart B., 124
Language, x, xiii, xv, 4, 32, 59, 62, 75, 143–46, 172, 177, 185, 201, 205n19, 219–20, 222–23, 225–26, 228–29, 232, 234–35, 237, 237n24, 248, 259, 261–62, 265, 265n27, 269, 276–78, 299–301, 306–8, 311, 318, 325, 331–32, 339, 369, 374
Laslett, Peter, 120–21
Latour, Bruno, x*n*1, xi, xiv, 170n24, 173–75, 173n34, 192, 228
Lawler, Michael G., 257
Leff, Gordon, 113, 114n91
Legge, Dominic, 283n7
Leibniz, Gottfried Wilhelm, 135, 135n49
Leiss, William, 262n4
Leopold, Aldo, 36–39
Leslie, John, 5
Levering, Matthew, 104n49
Levi, Anthony, 115n96
Levinas, Emmanuel, 132n27
Lewis, C. S., 34
Lex Talionis, 205
Liberation, x–xii, xiv, 6–8, 10, 33, 93, 102, 124, 126, 129, 129n15, 132, 154–55, 161, 173, 183, 185–86, 189–91, 196, 200, 218, 222, 226–27, 229–31, 254, 259, 262, 272, 280, 283, 314, 325, 330–31, 339–40, 343, 348, 352–53, 366–68, 370–71
Liberation Semiology, x, xii, 254
Life (*psychē*), 316–20, 324
Lipsius, Justus, 224
Lisska, Anthony J., 282

Lloyd, G. E. R., 235n13
Locke, John, 16, 119–22, 120n120, 124, 152, 318
Logos, 41, 229, 233–37, 238n31, 248–49, 253, 288, 318, 325, 375–76
Logic, ix, ixn1, 8–11, 13, 26, 32, 43, 48, 51, 54, 59, 65, 68, 74, 78, 98n18, 113, 145, 164, 167–69, 183–84, 186, 189, 192–95, 200, 203n10, 205, 208, 210, 237, 247–48, 250, 252–53, 265–69, 272, 277, 303–4, 308, 314, 342, 346–47, 361, 365
Long, Christopher P., 313, 316
Losev, Aleksei Fyodorvich, 262n3
Lossky, Vladimir, 243n46, 260, 285
Love, xii, xv, 16–17, 83–84, 93, 97, 99, 102, 108, 131–32, 155, 183–84, 189, 204, 206–7, 210–12, 218, 224–25, 228–32, 238, 238n31, 246, 251–54, 259–60, 264, 268–71, 273–75, 277–80, 283, 287–88, 296, 301, 305n76, 309–11, 314, 324–25, 327, 329, 332–41, 346, 348, 350–52, 355, 357, 365, 368–69, 372, 374–76
Lovelock, James, 2n4, 36, 36n111, 209n32, 219
Lowry, S. Todd, 32
Luckmann, Thomas, 201–2
Luther, Martin, 117, 189
Lyons, Nathan, 192, 288n12, 297n52, 305n76

MacCallum, Gerald C., Jr., 198, 198n154
MacCulloch, Diarmaid, 117
Machiavelli, N., 116
MacIntyre, Alasdair, 28n78
MacIsaac, D. Gregory, 134n43
Malebranche, Nicolas, 153
Manetti, Giannozzo, 114
Manetti, Giovanni, 252n91, 265, 265n27, 267n34
Margerie, Bertrand de, 309n81
Marion, Jean-Luc, 131n25, 132n28
Maritain, Jacques, 281, 303–4, 304n73, 352–53

Markus, R. A., 252n91, 265, 267–68, 369–70, 370n143
Marshall, I. Howard, 345, 355
Martin, Rex, 53
Martos, Joseph, 255, 257
Marx, Karl, 8n19, 31, 42, 89, 221, 227, 362
Mastery, xi, 44, 46, 65, 89, 93–94, 97, 99, 107, 114, 125–26, 132, 141, 154–55, 157, 161–62, 164–66, 176, 179, 182, 184, 189, 226, 339
Mathesis Universalis, 130, 134–35, 141, 152, 172, 308
Maximus Confessor, 242,
McCullough, Michael E., 211n41
McGinn, Bernard, 353n45
McGrath, S. J., 262n3, 328n47, 332–33
Me on, 157, 291, 319, 321, 332
Meikle, Scott, 29
Meontological Metaphysics, 157
Merchant, Carolyn, 43n144, 129, 129n15, 168
Merton, Thomas, 111–12n81
Metanarrative, 2, 42–43, 45, 73, 202
Midgley, Mary, 129n15
Milbank, John, 262
Miller, James, 182n85, 185n96, 186, 187n102, 188n108
Miller, Paula Jean, 254n100
Millett, Paul, 29
Mirandola, G.P., 114
Mitchell, Andrew J., 45n153–54
Modrak, Deborah K. W., 32, 265n27
Moltmann, Jürgen, 88, 91, 162–63, 189n115, 350–51
Monbiot, George, 2–3, 35, 221
Mondzain, Marie-José, 253, 255–57, 271
Money, 3, 18, 29–33, 120–22, 177, 359
Montefiore, Hugh, 175
Moore, A. W., 51
Moore, S. D., 210n37
Moral Agents, 20–21, 24
Moral Patients, 20–21, 23–24
Morgan, Edward, 238, 263–64, 271, 273, 277
Moyise, Steve, 210n37
Mueller, I., 134n43

Index

Murphy, James Bernard, 313
Murphy, Raymond, 210n39
Murphy, Richard, 344

Naess, Arne, 40
Nature (vs. Creation), xi–xii, 111–13, 173–75, 200–204, 210–211, 223, 262
Naugle, David K., xn3, 75
Nazianzus, Gregory, 229–31, 243, 245–46, 245n53, 253, 267n31, 284, 298
Negri, Antonio, 32
Neochristian Progressivism, 349, 361
Neoliberalism, 33, 98n18, 183, 185n96, 186–87, 190, 227
Neoplatonism, 112, 115n96, 134, 139, 141n72, 142, 147, 192, 243, 245n53, 251
Nero (Roman Emperor), 188
Neuman, John von, 203n10
Newton, Lisa H., 28
Nicaea (Council, 325 CE), 243–44
Nietzsche, Friedrich, 188–89, 212–19, 214n58, 366
Nihilism, 3, 44, 75–76, 85, 134, 157, 166, 190–92, 201–3, 212–13, 217, 332, 344–48, 355, 358, 366–67
Nikulin, Dmitri, 152n106
Nisus, 370
Nominalism, 31n90, 163, 183, 249, 300
Norris, Frederick W., 245n53–57, 246n61
Northcott, Michael S., 355–56
Novak, Ralph Martin, 243
Nowak, Martin A., 211n41
NSTI (Nano Science and Technology Institute), 3
Nuchelmans, Gabriël, 237n25
Nygren, Anders, 210n36

Oberman, Heiko A., 112n82–83
Ochs, Peter, 265
Ockham, William, 111–14, 112n84, 114n91, 161
O'Regan, Cyril, 329
Orexis, 317, 322
Origen, 258–59

Ortigues, Edmond, 256
Osler, Margaret J., 169
Ouk on, 332
Ousia, 237 (syn), 244 (homo), 248–49, 272, 315–16, 318
Owens, Joseph, 247, 290

Pabst, Adrian, xv, 31n90, 34n104, 112–13
Paine, Scott Randall, 305n76
Palmer, Clare, 23, 176–77
Panarchy, 203
Pap, Levente, 98n17
Parente, Pietro, 284n8
Parousia, 347–48, 354
Participation, 88, 227, 241, 273, 282–83, 295–96, 330
Pasnau, Robert, 289–91, 290n25, 291n26, 291n28
Passmore, John, xi, 46, 90–93, 93n194, 96n13, 97, 126, 175–76
Pastoral Power, 179, 181–85, 187, 189, 192
Pattee, H.H., 203n10
Paul (The Apostle), 353–55
Pearce, Fred, 2n3
Pecknold, C. C., 263–64, 270
Peifer, John Frederick, 134n39, 296n50
Peirce, Charles Sanders, 328n44
Pelagianism, xi, 93–94, 106, 111–12, 114–17, 115n96, 126, 155, 158, 182, 223n98
Pelagius, xi, 93–101, 94n1, 103, 105, 113, 115, 119, 126–27, 155, 158, 184, 186, 376
Pelikan, Jaraslov, 242n44–45, 257
Perfection(ism), xiv, 26–27, 92, 96, 98–101, 106–8, 110, 114, 116, 127, 131, 182, 184, 186, 284, 287, 325, 330–31, 336, 364–65, 376
Perichoresis, 246, 313
Peters, Rik, 66n72
Peterson, Erik, 349–52
Petty, William, Sir, 121
Phenomenology, 165–68, 165n13
Philosophy of Environment, ix–xi, 1, 3, 6, 40–41, 46, 167, 200
Pickstock, Catherine, 235–36

Piketty, Thomas, 190n120
Plato, 47–48, 51, 76, 78, 135, 141, 141n70, 144–45, 144n81, 156, 187, 232–33, 235–37, 241, 247, 249, 358
Plaxco, Kellen, 245n53
Plotinus, 140, 250,
Plutarch, 250
Poinsot, John (John of St. Thomas), xii, 281–83, 281n1, 282n3, 297–98, 297n52, 300–304, 302n67, 305n76, 306–13
Polanyi, Karl, 33–34
Polanyi, Michael, 203n10, 292–94
Political Theology, xiii–xiv, 71, 82n127, 84, 89, 189–90, 343–44, 346, 348–53, 356–57, 361–62, 367, 369–70, 377
Potentiality, xii, 120, 151, 157, 193, 198, 231, 242, 253, 283, 287–89, 291–92, 298, 312–24, 327–32, 334, 337–38, 364
Powell, Charles E., 353n45
Pragmatism, 42, 61–64, 66, 69, 71, 74–76, 78, 141, 170, 191, 202, 237, 248, 360
Praxis, 62, 196, 229, 231, 236, 266, 318, 320, 348, 352
Priestly, Joseph, 127
Prime Matter, 290–93, 323
Process Semiotics, 312
Proclus, 134–41, 134n43, 135n47, 136n50, 141n71, 146, 148–49, 152, 231
Proctor, Robert N., 35n108
Projection, 43, 135n47, 136–37, 149, 152, 168, 202
Promethean, 78, 83–86, 93, 126–29, 357–58, 371, 373, 377
Pros ti, 239, 247, 250–53, 265–66, 301, 323
Prosch, Harry, 293
Proust, M., 309n82
Prozorov, Sergei, 346
Przywara, Erich, 268n43, 269n44–45, 269n49, 270n50–52, 270n55, 274n70

Radix, x, xiii, xiv, xv, 44, 62, 78
Radix Naturalis, x, xiii, xiv
Rahner, Karl, 272, 287
Ramsey, Boniface, 111
Randall, John Hermann, Jr., 248–49, 316–18, 316n10, 317n15
Ratzinger, Joseph, 247, 254n99, 262, 353n45
Raven, J.E., 233n2–3
Rawls, John, 11–12, 31, 31n90
Rayman, Joshua, 112n84
Rees, R. B., 96n12
Reesor, Margaret, 250
Reference, 31–32, 74, 76, 81, 112, 150, 165, 170, 173–74, 220, 224, 230, 240, 267, 272, 284, 300, 360
Regan, Tom, 19–25, 20n57, 35, 37
Regius, Henri, 158
Relation, x–xv, 1
  Ethics, 5, 8–11, 13, 16–18, 21, 23, 26–27, 30–32, 36–37
  Enviro-Cosmology, 40–41, 43–45
  Metaphysics, 48, 51–55, 57, 61, 63–68, 73, 75–76, 78, 80–81, 83–84, 86, 88, 91–92, 97
  Pelagianism, 97–99, 106n60
  Ockham, 112–13, 112n84
  Bacon and Descartes, 125, 131–33, 136, 139, 143, 147, 150, 158–59, 162–63
  Historicized Phenomenology, 165–67, 169–71
  Foucault's Science of Order and Latour's Neocreationism, 172–73
  Stewardship, 175–77, 181, 184–86
  Triadic: Russell, Sartre, and MacCallum Jr., 193–98, 197n150
  Stewardship of Sign, 201–2, 219, 222–23, 226
  Nazianzus, 228, 231
  Language of the Real, 232–33, 235–36, 238
  Aristotle's Accidental Category of Pros Ti, 239–41, 239n37, 240n39
  Substantial Relationships of the Trinity, 242–46, 243n46, 245n53
  Ta Pros Ti and Skhesis, 247–53

The Symbolist Worldview, 253–58, 262
Augustine, 263–75, 265n23, 265n27, 266–67n31, 277–80
Aquinas and Poinsot, 281–82, 282n5
Aquinas's Trinity, 283–87
Vestigia, Imago, and Triunity, 288–90
Creator and Creation, 294–96
Poinsot's Relations, 297–303
Signs and Cognition, 303–9, 305n76
Things and Signs, 309–11
Semiosis to Boehme, 312–13, 318, 320–24, 326n39, 327–29, 331–32, 336
Ecological Civilization, 350–53, 357, 359–60, 364–65, 367, 369, 371–76
Relativism, 4, 5, 30, 32, 68, 71–76, 191, 363
Relativum, 272, 274, 277, 284, 298–302, 304, 306–7, 309
Ressentiment, 213, 216–18
Revisionary Metaphysics, 84
Rice, E. F., 116n102
Richter, Klemens, 255, 263
Ricoeur, Paul, 69, 255
Rist, John M., 251n82–83
Robin, Léon, 324
Robinson, Thomas M., 234–35
Rorem, Paul, 230n120
Rorty, Richard, 42
Rosen, Stanley, 152
Rosenfield, Leonora Cohen, 151n105
Rotman, Brian, 134n42
Rousseau, Jean-Jacques, 123–24, 123n137
Rovelli, C., 197n150
Rowland, Tracey, 311
Rudolph, Enno, 72
Ruggiero, G. de, 66n72
Russell, Bertrand, 194–95, 194n137, 197n150, 266, 266–67n31

Sacrament, xii, xiv–xv, 45, 83, 88, 117, 138–40, 154–55, 253, 255–59, 262–64, 269–70, 273, 276, 279–80, 309, 309n82, 369
Sacrifice, 23, 36, 39, 84, 156, 180, 181, 182, 184, 187, 188, 206, 208, 216, 221, 225, 331, 340, 347
Sacrifice as Sign, 305, 309–11
Saeculum, 112, 116, 265, 274, 347, 352, 355, 364, 370n143
Sagoff, Mark, 28
Salvation, xi, 88–89, 91–94, 96–100, 102–11, 112n81, 114–15, 117, 119, 123, 126–27, 139, 152, 154, 158–59, 164, 169, 171, 173–74, 179–83, 189–90, 210n36, 227, 231, 253, 259, 269, 325, 330–31, 335, 339, 347, 365, 367–69, 376
Sandler, Ronald L., 27
Sartre, Jean-Paul, 194–96, 195n38, 195n40, 198, 201
Sasaki, Chikara, 134n43, 141n71, 142
Sax, Boria, 34–35n107
Sayers, Dorothy L., xn3, 238
Scapegoat, 19, 165, 180, 204, 206, 208–10, 218, 358, 374
Scheffler, Samuel, 9
Schelling, F. W. J., 262n3, 328n44
Schillebeeckx, Edward, 227
Schindler, D. C., 8n19, 70n86
Schlosberg, David, 3n8
Schmidt, Alfred, 42n141–42
Schmitt, Carl, 189–92, 190n119, 344–46, 348–51, 353, 356n57, 357
Schmitz, Markus, 134n43
Science of Order, xi, 125, 151, 162, 172–73, 176, 181, 183–84
Scott, John A., 248n69
Scotus, D., 197n149
Scully, Matthew, 35n109
Searle, John R., 201, 201n4, 202n8
Second Intention, 143–45, 147, 299–301, 304, 306–8
Secular, xii, 89, 93, 94n1, 115–18, 124, 163, 177, 189–92, 210, 223, 239, 261, 274, 311, 326, 342–47, 349–53, 356, 361–62, 364–69, 376
Seifert, Josef, 166

Self-differentiating Unity, 76, 78, 171, 360
Sellars, John, 119n116, 120n117
Semiology, x, xii, 254, 279
Semiosis, x, xii–xiii, 283, 294, 297n52, 305n76, 311–13, 327
Semiotic, x, xn3, xii–iv, 203, 223, 229, 231–34, 237–38, 237n24, 249, 252, 254, 259, 261–63, 265, 268–70, 273–75, 279, 281–82, 288, 293, 304, 305n76, 309, 311–14, 324–27, 331, 340
Semiotic Worldview, x, xn3, xii–xiii, 232, 234, 237n24, 238, 252, 262, 326
Seneca, 182
Sentience, 7, 10–12, 14, 23
Serres, Michel, 172, 175–76
Sessions, George, 41, 42n140
Sextus Empiricus, 252, 267
Shapin, Steven, 128n13, 169–70
Sharma, I. C., 210n35
Shaw, Gregory, 138
Shelley, Percy, 340
Siecienski, Edward A., 285n9
Sign, x, xiii, 17, 32, 41, 45, 143, 148, 158, 172, 200–203, 229, 231–33, 236, 238–40, 249, 252–58, 252n91, 262–63, 265–71, 265n27, 274–83, 287, 293, 297, 303–13, 309n82, 318, 325, 327
Sign (Definition), 265 (sēmeîon), 267, 271, 274, 283, 293, 303–5, 305n76, 309–11, 313, 327
Sign (vs. Symbol), 256–58, 265n27
Signature, xii, xiv, 113, 172, 254–57, 259, 324–25, 330–31, 334–35, 337–38, 340, 351, 365
Simmons, Michael Bland, 367n127
Simon, Derek J., 270–71
Simplicius, 250–53, 252n89, 267n31
Sin, 83, 88–89, 97–104, 110, 116, 118, 120, 123, 126–27, 152–54, 158, 178, 274, 353, 364
Singer, Peter, 6–12, 8n19, 10n27, 22–23, 35, 178–79,

Skhesis, 245–47, 250–53, 255–57, 265–67, 267n31, 272, 277, 284, 298, 323
Sloterdijk, Peter, xv, 356n56
Smith, Adam, 184
Socrates, 3
Sorabji, Richard, 251
Soteria, 90, 180, 226, 294, 320
Soteriology, 180, 227, 254
Spade, Paul Vincent, 112n84, 114n91, 249n74
Squires, Stuart, 95
Stavins, Robert N., 3n8
Stead, Christopher, 242n42, 244n50
Steel, C., 135n47
Stevin, Simon, 143, 146–49
Stewardship, xii, 91–92, 161, 175–79, 183, 185, 189–90, 192, 197–200, 204, 210, 231
Stirner, Max, 212
Stjernfelt, Frederik, xiii
Stoicism, 92–93, 97–98, 97n16, 98n17, 100, 116, 119, 123, 154–56, 182–83, 188–89, 223–26, 223n98, 229–30, 232, 237, 243, 250–52, 251n82, 252n91, 265, 267–68, 272, 277, 304
Strawson, P. F., 84
Stroumsa, Guy G., 84
Strauss, Leo, 85–86n151
Struck, Peter T., 258n124
Subject-of-a-life, 20– 21, 23–25
Substance, xii, 63, 95–96, 131–32, 138, 149, 156–57, 239–48, 239n37, 244n50, 250, 252, 258–59, 262, 265–67, 272–73, 275–77, 281–85, 282n5, 288–89, 295, 297–98, 300, 303–4, 314, 318, 322–24, 328, 339, 370
Suffering, 6–8, 18, 26, 33–35, 98, 178, 200, 226, 228, 230–31, 336
Sumbol(a)on, 255, 257
Symbol, x, xii–xiv, 69, 72–74, 76, 88–89, 93, 121, 136–40, 142–54, 157–59, 162, 165–66, 172–73, 192, 198, 201–2, 202n8, 203n10, 230–32, 234, 238–39, 253–65, 258n124, 265n27, 268–75, 277,

Index

279–80, 288, 310, 325–29, 331, 333–37, 348, 356
Symbolist Worldview, 253–62
Symbolon, 140, 258
Syme, Ronald, 362

Tacit Knowledge, 292–93, 305, 314
Taille, Maurice, de la, 238
Taubes, Jacob, 327
Taylor, Alfred Edward, 230–31
Taylor, Charles, 204, 223–26
TeSelle, Eugene, 243n46, 245–46, 272n62, 287
TeVelde, Rudi A., 295
Theurgy, 138–41, 145
Thing (Aristotelian *Res*), 146, 148, 239–42, 244, 246, 251, 253, 258, 262–63, 266n29, 267, 273, 275–80, 282–84, 289, 290, 299, 302, 306–7, 309–10, 312, 315–16, 318–19, 321
Thomistic Sign, 310–11
Ticciati, Susannah, 277–78, 280
Todorov, Tzvetan, 262n3, 267–68, 276–77
Toole, D., 210n37
Torrance, Thomas F., 325
Trace, xii, 69, 77, 88, 96, 108, 112–13, 131, 133, 138, 219, 253, 259, 262, 273, 282–83, 287, 289–90, 294, 302, 305, 334, 351, 367–68
Triadic Relation, 194, 197–98, 265, 268, 278, 305n76, 313
Trieb, 333
Trinitarian, xii, xiv-xv, 81, 103, 156, 192, 232, 243–44, 243n46, 253–55, 259, 263–65, 272n64, 281, 283–84, 287–88, 303, 309, 312, 328–29, 329n49, 336, 347–48, 350–51, 356–57, 366, 369, 372–74
Trinitarian Cosmos, 347, 372
Trinitarian Ichnos, 259
Trinitarian Persons, 283, 336
Trinity, xii, 81–84, 82n127, 85–86n151, 154, 230, 232, 238–39, 242–43, 245–47, 253–55, 260, 262–64, 270–73, 275–77, 279–80, 282–88, 282n5, 296–97, 297n52, 302, 305n76, 308, 309n81, 324, 326–29, 328n43, 329n49, 331, 333, 336–37, 339–40, 343–46, 349–51, 355–56, 362, 365–66, 369, 371–72, 375, 377
Trinity (As Semiotic Substance), 288, 297n52, 305n76
Trinkaus, Charles, 114n92–93, 115n94–95

Uekoetter, Frank, 40n136
Ungrund, 332–34, 336
Uždavinys, Algis, 139–40

Vaggione, Richard Paul, 244
VanRuler, J. A., 159n134
Vandervelde, George, 102n43
Verbeek, Theo, 158n132, 159n135
Verene, Donald Phillip, 66n73, 75–76
Vestigia Trinitatis, xii, 88, 232, 264, 282, 287–88, 325, 351, 370
Vickers, Brian, 168n18
Vico, G., 66, 66n72–73, 71
Victorinus, Gaius Marius, 243n46
Viète, F., 143–46
Violence, xii, 14, 57, 65, 73, 83–84, 116, 118, 128, 132, 159, 191, 199–212, 205n19, 214–18, 221–22, 227–28, 231, 235–37, 238n31, 259, 280, 305n76, 314, 319, 325, 336, 346–50, 352–53, 356, 358, 365, 368
Virno, Paolo, 269, 311, 347
Virtue, 5, 25–31, 28n78, 33–35, 95, 158, 182, 188, 224, 250, 340, 371, 375,
Voetius, G., 158–59
Void, 75, 156, 212, 237, 256, 301, 340
Vos, Geerhardus, 353n45, 354

Waal, Frans B. M., de, 205n19
Wahle, Hedwig, 90–91
Wanamaker, Charles A., 353–54
Warfield, Benjamin B., 117
WCED (World Commission on Environment and Development), ix

Weeks, Andrew, 326n37–38, 329n48, 331n53
Weinberg, Julius R., 144n82, 239, 247, 249n74, 250n76
Westfall, Richard S., 133, 154–55
Wheeler, Wendy, 203n16
White, Lynn, Jr., xi, 46, 86–93, 171n25
Whitehead, A. N., 174, 174n47
Wiley, Tatha, 99n21, 102
Williams, Bernard, 130, 223n94
Williams, Rowan, 243–44, 274–75, 278–79
Wilson, E. O., 222
Wittgenstein, Ludwig, 75, 220
Witzany, Günter, 203n12
Wolff, Robert Paul, 208n31
Wolfson, Harry Austryn, 243n46
Worldview, x, xn3, xii–xiii, 31, 41, 42n140, 70, 72, 76, 156, 161, 232, 234, 237n24, 243, 253, 261–62, 326, 343, 346
Worster, Donald, 179

Zeno of Citium, 92, 250
Zero, 142–43, 146, 148, 156, 172, 290, 326n39

www.ingramcontent.com/pod-product-compliance
Lightning Source LLC
Chambersburg PA
CBHW071226290426
44108CB00013B/1301